ACCA

STUDY TEXT

PAPER P6

ADVANCED TAXATION

FA 2013

BPP Learning Media is the **sole ACCA Platinum Approved Learning Partner – content** for the ACCA qualification. In this, **the only Paper P6 study text to be reviewed by the examiner:**

- We **discuss** the **best strategies** for studying for ACCA exams
- We **highlight** the **most important elements** in the syllabus and the **key skills** you will need
- We **signpost** how each chapter links to the syllabus and the study guide
- We **provide** lots of **exam focus points** demonstrating what the examiner will want you to do
- We **emphasise key points** in regular **fast forward summaries**
- We **test your knowledge** of what you've studied in **quick quizzes**
- We **examine your understanding** in our **exam question bank**
- We **reference all the important topics** in our **full index**

BPP's **Practice & Revision Kit, i-Learn** and **i-Pass** products also support this paper.

FOR EXAMS IN 2014

First edition 2007
Seventh edition November 2013

ISBN 9781 4727 5303 8
(Previous ISBN 9781 4453 9658 3)
eISBN 9781 4453 6745 3

British Library Cataloguing-in-Publication Data
A catalogue record for this book is available from the British Library

Published by

BPP Learning Media Ltd
BPP House, Aldine Place
142-144 Uxbridge Road
London W12 8AA

www.bpp.com/learningmedia

Printed in the United Kingdom by

RICOH
Ricoh House
Ullswater Crescent
Coulsdon
CR5 2HR

Your learning materials, published by BPP Learning Media Ltd, are printed on paper obtained from traceable sustainable sources.

We are grateful to the Association of Chartered Certified Accountants for permission to reproduce past examination questions. The suggested solutions in the exam answer bank have been prepared by BPP Learning Media Ltd, unless otherwise stated.

Contents

A note about copyright

Dear Customer

What does the little © mean and why does it matter?

Your market-leading BPP books, course materials and elearning materials do not write and update themselves. People write them: on their own behalf or as employees of an organisation that invests in this activity. Copyright law protects their livelihoods. It does so by creating rights over the use of the content.

Breach of copyright is a form of theft – as well being a criminal offence in some jurisdictions, it is potentially a serious breach of professional ethics.

With current technology, things might seem a bit hazy but, basically, without the express permission of BPP Learning Media:

- Photocopying our materials is a breach of copyright
- Scanning, ripcasting or conversion of our digital materials into different file formats, uploading them to facebook or emailing them to your friends is a breach of copyright

You can, of course, sell your books, in the form in which you have bought them – once you have finished with them. (Is this fair to your fellow students? We update for a reason.) But the e-products are sold on a single user licence basis: we do not supply 'unlock' codes to people who have bought them second hand.

And what about outside the UK? BPP Learning Media strives to make our materials available at prices students can afford by local printing arrangements, pricing policies and partnerships which are clearly listed on our website. A tiny minority ignore this and indulge in criminal activity by illegally photocopying our material or supporting organisations that do. If they act illegally and unethically in one area, can you really trust them?

Helping you to pass – the ONLY P6 Study Text reviewed by the examiner!

BPP Learning Media – the sole Platinum Approved Learning Partner – content

As ACCA's **sole Platinum Approved Learning Partner – content**, BPP Learning Media gives you the **unique opportunity** to use **examiner-reviewed** study materials for the 2014 exams. By incorporating the examiner's comments and suggestions regarding the depth and breadth of syllabus coverage, the BPP Learning Media Study Text provides excellent, **ACCA-approved** support for your studies.

The PER alert

Before you can qualify as an ACCA member, you do not only have to pass all your exams but also fulfil a three year **practical experience requirement** (PER). To help you to recognise areas of the syllabus that you might be able to apply in the workplace to achieve different performance objectives, we have introduced the '**PER alert**' feature. You will find this feature throughout the Study Text to remind you that what you are **learning to pass** your ACCA exams is **equally useful to the fulfilment of the PER requirement**.

Your achievement of the PER should now be recorded in your on-line *My Experience* record.

Tackling studying

Studying can be a daunting prospect, particularly when you have lots of other commitments. The **different features** of the text, the **purposes** of which are explained fully on the **Chapter features** page, will help you whilst studying and improve your chances of **exam success**.

Developing exam awareness

Our Texts are completely **focused** on helping you pass your exam.

Our advice on **Studying P6** outlines the **content** of the paper and the **necessary skills** the examiner expects you to demonstrate.

Exam focus points are included within the chapters to highlight when and how specific topics were examined, or how they might be examined in the future.

Using the Syllabus and Study Guide

You can find the syllabus and Study Guide on page x of this Study Text.

Testing what you can do

Testing yourself helps you develop the skills you need to pass the exam and also confirms that you can recall what you have learnt.

We include **Questions** – lots of them – both within chapters and in the **Exam Question Bank**, as well as **Quick Quizzes** at the end of each chapter to test your knowledge of the chapter content.

Chapter features

Each chapter contains a number of helpful features to guide you through each topic.

Topic list

Topic list	Syllabus reference

Tells you what you will be studying in this chapter and the relevant section numbers, together the ACCA syllabus references.

Introduction

Puts the chapter content in the context of the syllabus as a whole.

Study Guide

Links the chapter content with ACCA guidance.

Exam Guide

Highlights how examinable the chapter content is likely to be and the ways in which it could be examined.

Knowledge brought forward from earlier studies

What you are assumed to know from previous studies/exams.

FAST FORWARD

Summarises the content of main chapter headings, allowing you to preview and review each section easily.

Examples

Demonstrate how to apply key knowledge and techniques.

Key terms

Definitions of important concepts that can often earn you easy marks in exams.

Exam focus points

Tell you when and how specific topics were examined, or how they may be examined in the future.

This gives you a useful indication of syllabus areas that closely relate to performance objectives in your Practical Experience Requirement (PER).

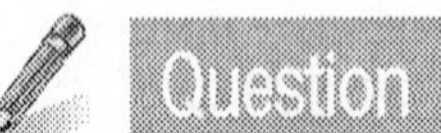

Give you essential practice of techniques covered in the chapter.

Chapter Roundup

A full list of the Fast Forwards included in the chapter, providing an easy source of review.

Quick Quiz

A quick test of your knowledge of the main topics in the chapter.

Exam Question Bank

Found at the back of the Study Text with more comprehensive chapter questions. Cross referenced for easy navigation.

Studying P6

As the name suggests, this paper examines Advanced Taxation. It builds on the foundations of Paper F6 in two ways. First, it introduces more advanced taxation topics in relation to inheritance tax and specialised personal and corporate tax. Second, it requires the ability to communicate clearly with clients, HM Revenue & Customs and other professionals in a clear and professional manner. It is an options paper which will be chosen by those who work in a tax environment.

The P6 examining team

The P6 examining team expect you to demonstrate a highly **professional approach** to all questions – **demonstrating technical knowledge** and also **commercial awareness**. Members of the P6 examining team have written several articles in Student Accountant which are also available on ACCA website. There are four non-technical articles that focus on the structure of the exam and exam technique These are *Stepping up from Paper F6(UK) to Paper P6(UK), Examiner's approach to Paper P6 (UK), Guidance on approach to questions in Section A of Paper P6 (UK) and Improving your technique.* There are also technical articles covering the following topics: *Taxation of the unincorporated business, Capital gains and inheritance tax, Corporation tax and groups – group relief, Corporation tax and groups – capital gains groups, Trusts and tax, Corporation tax, International travellers, and Finance Act 2013.* Make sure you read these articles to gain further insight into what the examining team is looking for.

1 What P6 is about

The P6 syllabus builds on the basic knowledge of core taxes gained from F6 and introduces candidates to additional capital taxes in the form of stamp duty, stamp duty reserve tax and stamp duty land tax. It also extends knowledge of income tax, inheritance tax, corporation tax and capital gains taxes, including overseas aspects, taxation of trusts and additional exemptions and reliefs.

The emphasis of the paper is on the candidate's skills of analysis and interpretation of information provided and communication of recommendations in a manner appropriate to the intended audience eg clients. Computations will normally only be required in support of explanations or advice and not in isolation.

2 What skills are required?

- Be able to **calculate** tax charges in support of explanations or advice.
- Be able to **explain** the tax charges in a particular scenario: what taxes are applicable and why.
- Be able to **analyse** a set of facts to ascertain when tax charges arise and any options that may be available to the taxpayer to mitigate such charges.
- Be able to **evaluate** your results and **recommend** a course of action, justifying your recommendations and setting out any other factors which the taxpayer should take into account when reaching his decision.

3 How to improve your chances of passing

Study the **entire** syllabus – **60 marks** of the marks available to you are contained in the compulsory Section A questions. Section B questions allow you to show more **specialised knowledge** and allow the examiner to test a wide range of topics.

Practise as many questions as you can under **timed conditions** – this is the best way of developing good exam technique. Make use of the **Question Bank** at the back of this Text. **BPP's Practice and Revision Kit** contains numerous exam standard questions (many of them taken from past exam papers) as well as three mock exams for you to try.

Answer selectively – the examiner will expect you to consider carefully what is relevant and significant enough to include in your answer. Don't include unnecessary information.

Present your answers in a **professional** manner – use subheadings and leave spaces between paragraphs, make sure that your numerical workings are clearly set out.

Answer all parts of the question – leaving out a five mark part may be the difference between a pass and a fail.

4 Brought forward knowledge

The P6 syllabus covers almost every topic that was included in F6, with a few minor exceptions. Since tax law changes every year, this text includes all the topics covered at F6 again, updated to the latest Finance Act. At the start of each chapter, we highlight topics which have changed between the latest Finance Act and the previous Finance Act. We also highlight new topics which you have not studied at F6.

The exam paper

The **time allowed** for the paper is 3 hours plus 15 minutes reading and planning time.

The paper consists of two sections:

Section A consists of two compulsory questions. Question 1 will have 35 marks and question 2 will have 25 marks. There are no set topics for Section A questions, but you should expect to see coverage of technical taxation topics new at P6.

Section B consists of three questions, two of which must be answered. Each question will have 20 marks. Again, there are no set topics, but you might expect to find more specialist questions concentrating on such areas as advanced corporation tax, advanced personal tax or capital taxes.

All questions are scenario based and will normally involve consideration of more than one tax, together with some elements of planning and the interaction of taxes.

Syllabus and Study Guide

The P6 syllabus and study guide can be found below.

Advanced Taxation (UK) (P6) June & December 2014

This syllabus and study guide is designed to help with planning study and to provide detailed information on what could be assessed in any examination session.

THE STRUCTURE OF THE SYLLABUS AND STUDY GUIDE

Relational diagram of paper with other papers

This diagram shows direct and indirect links between this paper and other papers preceding or following it. Some papers are directly underpinned by other papers such as Advanced Performance Management by Performance Management. These links are shown as solid line arrows. Other papers only have indirect relationships with each other such as links existing between the accounting and auditing papers. The links between these are shown as dotted line arrows. This diagram indicates where you are expected to have underpinning knowledge and where it would be useful to review previous learning before undertaking study.

Overall aim of the syllabus

This explains briefly the overall objective of the paper and indicates in the broadest sense the capabilities to be developed within the paper.

Main capabilities

This paper's aim is broken down into several main capabilities which divide the syllabus and study guide into discrete sections.

Relational diagram of the main capabilities

This diagram illustrates the flows and links between the main capabilities (sections) of the syllabus and should be used as an aid to planning teaching and learning in a structured way.

Syllabus rationale

This is a narrative explaining how the syllabus is structured and how the main capabilities are linked. The rationale also explains in further detail what the examination intends to assess and why.

Detailed syllabus

This shows the breakdown of the main capabilities (sections) of the syllabus into subject areas. This is the blueprint for the detailed study guide.

Approach to examining the syllabus

This section briefly explains the structure of the examination and how it is assessed.

Study Guide

This is the main document that students, tuition providers and publishers should use as the basis of their studies, instruction and materials. Examinations will be based on the detail of the study guide which comprehensively identifies what could be assessed in any examination session. The study guide is a precise reflection and breakdown of the syllabus. It is divided into sections based on the main capabilities identified in the syllabus. These sections are divided into subject areas which relate to the sub-capabilities included in the detailed syllabus. Subject areas are broken down into sub-headings which describe the detailed outcomes that could be assessed in examinations. These outcomes are described using verbs indicating what exams may require students to demonstrate, and the broad intellectual level at which these may need to be demonstrated (*see intellectual levels below).

Learning Materials

ACCA's Approved Learning Partner - content (ALP-c) is the programme through which ACCA approves learning materials from high quality content providers designed to support study towards ACCA's qualifications.

ACCA has one Platinum Approved Learning Partner content which is BPP Learning Media. In addition, there are a number of Gold Approved Learning

Partners - content.

For information about ACCA's Approved Learning Partners - content, please go to ACCA's Content Provider Directory.

The Directory also lists materials by Subscribers, these materials have not been quality assured by ACCA but may be helpful if used in conjunction with approved learning materials. You will also find details of Examiner suggested Additional Reading which may be a useful supplement to approved learning materials.

ACCA's Content Provider Directory can be found here–
http://www.accaglobal.com/learningproviders/alpc/content_provider_directory/search/.

Relevant articles will also be published in Student Accountant.

INTELLECTUAL LEVELS

The syllabus is designed to progressively broaden and deepen the knowledge, skills and professional values demonstrated by the student on their way through the qualification.

The specific capabilities within the detailed syllabuses and study guides are assessed at one of three intellectual or cognitive levels:

Level 1: Knowledge and comprehension
Level 2: Application and analysis
Level 3: Synthesis and evaluation

Very broadly, these intellectual levels relate to the three cognitive levels at which the Knowledge module, the Skills module and the Professional level are assessed.

Each subject area in the detailed study guide included in this document is given a 1, 2, or 3 superscript, denoting intellectual level, marked at the end of each relevant line. This gives an indication of the intellectual depth at which an area could be assessed within the examination. However, while level 1 broadly equates with the Knowledge module, level 2 equates to the Skills module and level 3 to the Professional level, some lower level skills can continue to be assessed as the student progresses through each module and level. This reflects that at each stage of study there will be a requirement to broaden, as well as deepen capabilities. It is also possible that occasionally some higher level capabilities may be assessed at lower levels.

LEARNING HOURS AND EDUCATION RECOGNITION

The ACCA qualification does not prescribe or recommend any particular number of learning hours for examinations because study and learning patterns and styles vary greatly between people and organisations. This also recognises the wide diversity of personal, professional and educational circumstances in which ACCA students find themselves.

As a member of the International Federation of Accountants, ACCA seeks to enhance the education recognition of its qualification on both national and international education frameworks, and with educational authorities and partners globally. In doing so, ACCA aims to ensure that its qualifications are recognized and valued by governments, regulatory authorities and employers across all sectors. To this end, ACCA qualifications are currently recognized on the education frameworks in several countries. Please refer to your national education framework regulator for further information.

Each syllabus contains between 23 and 35 main subject area headings depending on the nature of the subject and how these areas have been broken down.

GUIDE TO EXAM STRUCTURE

The structure of examinations varies within and between modules and levels.

The Fundamentals level examinations contain 100% compulsory questions to encourage candidates to study across the breadth of each syllabus.

The Knowledge module is assessed by equivalent two-hour paper based and computer based examinations.

The Skills module examinations are all paper based

three-hour papers. The structure of papers varies from ten questions in the *Corporate and Business Law* (F4) paper to four 25 mark questions in *Financial Management* (F9). Individual questions within all Skills module papers will attract between 10 and 30 marks.

The Professional level papers are all three-hour paper based examinations, all containing two sections. Section A is compulsory, but there will be some choice offered in Section B.

For all three hour examination papers, ACCA has introduced 15 minutes reading and planning time.

This additional time is allowed at the beginning of each three-hour examination to allow candidates to read the questions and to begin planning their answers before they start writing in their answer books. This time should be used to ensure that all the information and exam requirements are properly read and understood.

During reading and planning time candidates may only annotate their question paper. They may not write anything in their answer booklets until told to do so by the invigilator.

The Essentials module papers all have a Section A containing a major case study question with all requirements totalling 50 marks relating to this case. Section B gives students a choice of two from three 25 mark questions.

Section A of both the P4 and P5 Options papers contain one 50 mark compulsory question, and Section B will offer a choice of two from three questions each worth 25 marks each.

Section A of each of the P6 and P7 Options papers contains 60 compulsory marks from two questions; question 1 attracting 35 marks, and question 2 attracting 25 marks. Section B of both these Options papers will offer a choice of two from three questions, with each question attracting 20 marks.

All Professional level exams contain four professional marks.

The pass mark for all ACCA Qualification examination papers is 50%.

GUIDE TO EXAMINATION ASSESSMENT

ACCA reserves the right to examine anything contained within the study guide at any examination session. This includes knowledge, techniques, principles, theories, and concepts as specified.

For the tax papers, ACCA will publish *examinable documents,* or tax rates and allowances tables, once a year to indicate exactly what legislation could potentially be assessed within identified examination sessions. These should be read in conjunction with the information below.

For UK tax papers, examinations falling within the financial year 1 April to 31 March will examine the Finance Act which was passed in the previous July. I.e. Exams falling in the period 1 April 2014 to 31 March 2015 will examine the Finance Act 2013.

For SGP tax papers, examinations falling within the year 1 April to 31 March will be based on legislation passed before the previous 30 September. I.e. examinations falling in the year 1 April 2014 to 31 March 2015 will be based on legislation passed by 30 September 2013.

For MYS tax papers, examinations falling within the year 1 October to 30 September will be based on legislation passed before the previous 31 March. I.e. examinations falling in the year 1 October 2014 to 30 September 2015 will be based on legislation passed before the previous 31 March 2014.

For CYP tax papers, June and December examinations will be based on regulation or legislation published in the Official Gazette of the Republic of Cyprus ("the Gazette") on or before 30 September. I.e. June and December 2014 papers will be based on regulation or legislation published in the Official Gazette of the Republic of Cyprus ("the Gazette") on or before 30 September 2013.

For CZE tax papers, December and June examinations will be based on legislation passed before the previous 31 May. I.e. December 2014 and June 15 papers will be based on legislation in force at 31 May 2014.

For VNM tax papers, June and December examinations will be based on legislation passed before the previous 31 December. I.e. June and

December 2014 papers will be based on legislation passed by 31 December 2013.

Tax papers for the following variants:
BWA, CHN, HUN, HKG, IRL, LSO, MWI, MLA, POL, PKN, ROM, RUS, ZAF, ZWE.
The June and December examinations will be based on legislation passed before the previous 30 September. I.e. June and December 2014 papers will be based on legislation passed by 30 September 2013.

Syllabus

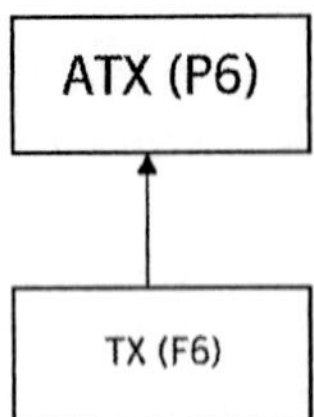

ATX (P6)
TX (F6)

AIM

To apply relevant knowledge and skills and exercise professional judgement in providing relevant information and advice to individuals and businesses on the impact of the major taxes on financial decisions and situations.

MAIN CAPABILITIES

On successful completion of this paper candidates should be able to:

A Apply further knowledge and understanding of the UK tax system through the study of more advanced topics within the taxes studied previously and the study of stamp taxes

B Identify and evaluate the impact of relevant taxes on various situations and courses of action, including the interaction of taxes

C Provide advice on minimising and/or deferring tax liabilities by the use of standard tax planning measures

D Communicate with clients, HM Revenue and Customs and other professionals in an appropriate manner.

RELATIONAL DIAGRAM OF MAIN CAPABILITIES

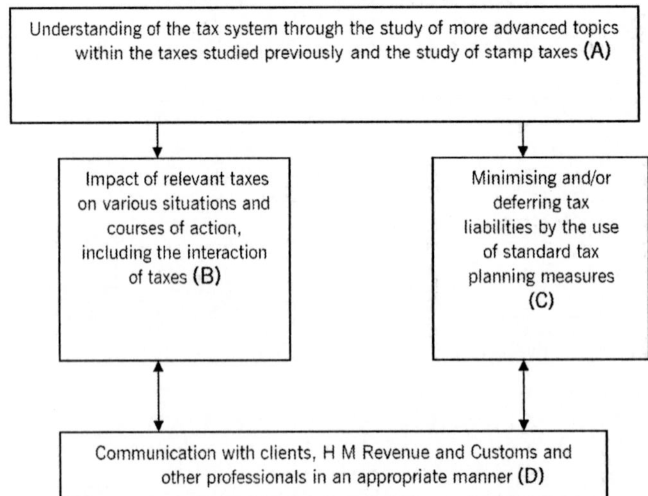

Understanding of the tax system through the study of more advanced topics within the taxes studied previously and the study of stamp taxes (A)
Impact of relevant taxes on various situations and courses of action, including the interaction of taxes (B)
Minimising and/or deferring tax liabilities by the use of standard tax planning measures (C)
Communication with clients, H M Revenue and Customs and other professionals in an appropriate manner (D)

5

RATIONALE

The Advanced Taxation syllabus further develops the key aspects of taxation introduced in the compulsory Taxation syllabus within the Skills module and extends the candidates' knowledge of the tax system, together with their ability to apply that knowledge to the issues commonly encountered by individuals and businesses, such that successful candidates should have the ability to interpret and analyse the information provided and communicate the outcomes in a manner appropriate to the intended audience.

The syllabus builds on the basic knowledge of core taxes from the earlier taxation paper and introduces candidates to stamp taxes. As this is an optional paper, aimed at those requiring/desiring more than basic tax knowledge for their future professional lives, the syllabus also extends the knowledge of income tax, corporation tax, capital gains tax and inheritance tax to encompass, further overseas aspects of taxation, the taxation of trusts and additional exemptions and reliefs.

Computations will normally only be required in support of explanations or advice and not in isolation.
Candidates are not expected to concentrate on the computational aspects of taxation. Instead this paper seeks to develop candidates' skills of analysis, interpretation and communication. Candidates are expected to be able to use established tax planning methods and consider current issues in taxation.

DETAILED SYLLABUS:

A Knowledge and understanding of the UK tax system through the study of more advanced topics within the taxes studied previously and the study of stamp taxes.

1. Income and income tax liabilities in situations involving further overseas aspects and in relation to trusts, and the application of additional exemptions and reliefs.

2. Corporation tax liabilities in situations involving overseas and further group aspects and in relation to special types of company, and the application of additional exemptions and reliefs.

3. Chargeable gains and capital gains tax liabilities in situations involving further overseas aspects and in relation to closely related persons and trusts, and the application of additional exemptions and reliefs.

4. Inheritance tax in situations involving further aspects of the scope of the tax and the calculation of the liabilities arising, the principles of valuation and the reliefs available, transfers of property to and from trusts, overseas aspects and further aspects of administration

5. Stamp taxes

6. National Insurance, value added tax and tax administration

B The impact of relevant taxes on various situations and courses of action, including the interaction of taxes

1. Taxes applicable to a given situation or course of action and their impact.

2. Alternative ways of achieving personal or business outcomes may lead to different tax consequences.

3. Taxation effects of the financial decisions made by businesses (corporate and unincorporated) and by individuals.

4. Tax advantages and/or disadvantages of alternative courses of action.

5. Statutory obligations imposed in a given situation, including any time limits for action and the implications of non-compliance.

C Minimising and/or deferring tax liabilities by the use of standard tax planning measures

1. Types of investment and other expenditure that will result in a reduction in tax liabilities for an individual and/or a business.

2. Legitimate tax planning measures, by which the tax liabilities arising from a particular situation or course of action can be mitigated.

6

3. The appropriateness of such investment, expenditure or measures, given a particular taxpayer's circumstances or stated objectives.

4. The mitigation of tax in the manner recommended, by reference to numerical analysis and/or reasoned argument.

5. Ethical and professional issues arising from the giving of tax planning advice.

6. Current issues in taxation.

D **Communicating with clients, HM Revenue and Customs and other professionals**

1. Communication of advice, recommendations and information in the required format.

2. Presentation of written information, in language appropriate to the purpose of the communication and the intended recipient.

3. Conclusions reached with relevant supporting computations.

4. Assumptions made or limitations in the analysis provided, together with any inadequacies in the information available and/or additional information required to provide a fuller analysis.

5. Other non-tax factors that should be considered.

APPROACH TO EXAMINING THE SYLLABUS

The paper consists of two sections:

Section A consists of two compulsory questions. Question 1 has 35 marks, including 4 professional marks, and question 2 has 25 marks

Section B consists of three 20-mark questions, two of which must be answered.

Questions will be scenario based and will normally involve consideration of more than one tax, together with some elements of planning and the interaction of taxes. Computations will normally only be required in support of explanations or advice and not in isolation.

The examination is a three hour paper, with 15 minutes additional reading and planning time.

Tax rates, allowances and information on certain reliefs will be given in the examination paper.

8

Study Guide

A APPLY FURTHER KNOWLEDGE AND UNDERSTANDING OF THE UK TAX SYSTEM THROUGH THE STUDY OF MORE ADVANCED TOPICS WITHIN THE TAXES STUDIED PREVIOUSLY AND THE STUDY OF STAMP TAXES

1. **Income and income tax liabilities in situations involving further overseas aspects and in relation to trusts, and the application of exemptions and reliefs**

a) The contents of the Paper F6 study guide for income tax, under headings: [2]

- B1 The scope of income tax
- B2 Income from employment
- B3 Income from self employment
- B4 Property and investment income
- B5 The comprehensive computation of taxable income and the income tax liability
- B6 The use of exemptions and reliefs in deferring and minimising income tax liabilities

The following additional material is also examinable:

b) The scope of income tax: [3]
   i) Explain and apply the concepts of residence and domicile and advise on the relevance to income tax
   ii) Advise on the availability of the remittance basis to UK resident individuals [2]
   iii) Advise on the tax position of individuals coming to and leaving the UK
   iv) Determine the income tax treatment of overseas income
   v) Understand the relevance of the OECD model double tax treaty to given situations
   vi) Calculate and advise on the double taxation relief available to individuals

c) Income from employment: [3]
   i) Advise on the tax treatment of share option and share incentive schemes
   ii) Advise on the tax treatment of lump sum receipts
   iii) Advise on the overseas aspects of income from employment, including travelling and subsistence expenses
   iv) Identify personal service companies and advise on the tax consequences of providing services via a personal service company

d) Income from self employment: [3]
   i) Advise on a change of accounting date
   ii) Advise on the relief available for trading losses following the transfer of a business to a company
   iii) Recognise the tax treatment of overseas travelling expenses
   iv) Advise on the allocation of the annual investment allowance between related businesses
   v) Identify the enhanced capital allowances available in respect of expenditure on green technologies[2]
   vi) Recognise the tax treatment of the investment income of a partnership [2]

e) Property and investment income: [3]
   i) Assess the tax implications of pre-owned assets
   ii) Recognise income subject to the accrued income scheme
   iii) Advise on the tax implications of jointly held assets
   iv) Income from trusts and settlements: Understand the income tax position of trust beneficiaries

f) The comprehensive computation of taxable income and the income tax liability:[3]
   i) Advise on the income tax position of the income of minor children

g) The use of exemptions and reliefs in deferring and minimising income tax liabilities:
   i) Understand and apply the rules relating to investments in the seed enterprise investment scheme and the enterprise investment scheme [3]
   ii) Understand and apply the rules relating to investments in venture capital trusts [3]
   iii) Explain the conditions that need to be satisfied for pension schemes to be registered by HM Revenue and Customs [2]

Excluded topics

The scope of income tax:

9

- *Details of specific anti-avoidance provisions, except as stated in the study guide.*

Income from employment:

- *Explanation of the PAYE system.*
- *The calculation of a car benefit where emission figures are not available.*

Income from self employment:

- *The 100% first year allowance for renovating business premises in disadvantaged areas and flats above shops.*
- *Capital allowances for agricultural buildings, patents, scientific research and know how.*
- *Enterprise zones.*
- *The allocation of notional profits and losses for a partnership.*
- *Farmers averaging of profits.*
- *The averaging of profits for authors and creative artists.*
- *Details of specific anti-avoidance provisions, except as stated in the study guide.*

Property and investment income:

- *The deduction for expenditure by landlords on energy-saving items*

Income from trusts and settlements:

- *The computation of income tax payable by trustees.*
- *Overseas aspects.*

The comprehensive computation of taxable income and the income tax liability:

- *The blind person's allowance and the married couple's age allowance.*
- *Tax credits*
- *Maintenance payments*
- *Charitable donations.*
- *Social security benefits apart from the State Retirement Pension.*

2. **Corporation tax liabilities in situations involving further overseas and group aspects and in relation to special types of company, and the application of additional exemptions and reliefs**

a) The contents of the Paper F6 study guide, for corporation tax, under headings:[2]
   - C1 The scope of corporation tax
   - C2 Taxable total profits
   - C3 The comprehensive computation of the corporation tax liability
   - C4 The effect of a group structure for corporation tax purposes
   - C5 The use of exemptions and reliefs in deferring and minimising corporation tax liabilities

   The following additional material is also examinable:

b) The scope of corporation tax: [3]
   i) Identify and calculate corporation tax for companies with investment business.
   ii) Close companies:
      - Apply the definition of a close company to given situations
      - Conclude on the tax implications of a company being a close company or a close investment holding company
   iii) Identify and evaluate the significance of accounting periods on administration or winding up
   iv) Conclude on the tax treatment of returns to shareholders after winding up has commenced
   v) Advise on the tax implications of a purchase by a company of its own shares
   vi) Identify personal service companies and advise on the tax consequences of services being provided via a personal service company

c) Taxable total profits: [3]
   i) Identify qualifying research and development expenditure, both capital and revenue, and determine the reliefs available by reference to the size of the individual company/group
   ii) Recognise the relevance of a company generating profits attributable to patents
   iii) Identify the enhanced capital allowances available in respect of expenditure on green technologies, including the tax credit available in the case of a loss making company
   iv) Determine the tax treatment of non trading deficits on loan relationships

v) Recognise the alternative tax treatments of intangible assets and conclude on the best treatment for a given company
vi) Advise on the impact of the transfer pricing and thin capitalisation rules on companies
vii) Advise on the restriction on the use of losses on a change in ownership of a company

d) The comprehensive calculation of the corporation tax liability: [3]
i) Assess the impact of the OECD model double tax treaty on corporation tax
ii) Evaluate the meaning and implications of a permanent establishment
iii) Identify and advise on the tax implications of controlled foreign companies
iv) Advise on the tax position of overseas companies trading in the UK
v) Calculate double taxation relief

e) The effect of a group structure for corporation tax purposes: [3]
i) Advise on the allocation of the annual investment allowance between group or related companies
ii) Advise on the tax consequences of a transfer of intangible assets
iii) Advise on the tax consequences of a transfer of a trade and assets where there is common control
iv) Understand the meaning of consortium owned company and consortium member [2]
v) Advise on the operation of consortium relief
vi) Determine pre-entry losses and understand their tax treatment
vii) Determine the degrouping charge where a company leaves a group within six years of receiving an asset by way of a no gain/no loss transfer
viii) Determine the effects of the anti-avoidance provisions, where arrangements exist for a company to leave a group
ix) Advise on the tax treatment of an overseas branch
x) Advise on the relief for trading losses incurred by an overseas subsidiary

f) The use of exemptions and reliefs in deferring and minimising corporation tax liabilities: [3]
i) Advise on the availability, and the application of disincorporation relief

Excluded topics

The scope of corporation tax:
- *Details of specific anti-avoidance provisions, except as stated in the Study Guide.*

The comprehensive calculation of the corporation tax liability:
- *Corporation tax rates for companies in the process of winding up.*
- *Relief for overseas tax as an expense.*
- *Detailed knowledge of specific double taxation agreements.*
- *Migration of a UK resident company.*
- *Mixer companies.*
- *Detailed computational questions on the carry back and carry forward of unrelieved foreign tax.*
- *Quarterly accounting for income tax.*

3. Chargeable gains and capital gains tax liabilities in situations involving further overseas aspects and in relation to closely related persons and trusts together with the application of additional exemptions and reliefs

a) The contents of the Paper F6 study guide for chargeable gains under headings: [2]
- D1 The scope of the taxation of capital gains
- D2 The basic principles of computing gains and losses
- D3 Gains and losses on the disposal of movable and immovable property
- D4 Gains and losses on the disposal of shares and securities
- D5 The computation of capital gains tax payable by individuals
- D6 The use of exemptions and reliefs in deferring and minimising tax liabilities arising on the disposal of capital assets

The following additional material is also examinable:

b) The scope of the taxation of capital gains: [3]

i) Determine the tax implications of independent taxation and transfers between spouses
ii) Identify the concepts of residence and domicile and determine their relevance to capital gains tax
iii) Advise on the availability of the remittance basis to non-UK domiciled individuals [2]
iv) Determine the UK taxation of foreign gains, including double taxation relief
v) Conclude on the capital gains tax position of individuals coming to and leaving the UK
vi) Identify the occasions when a capital gain would arise on a partner in a partnership

c) Capital gains tax and trusts:
   i) Advise on the capital gains tax implications of transfers of property into trust. [3]
   ii) Advise on the capital gains tax implications of property passing absolutely from a trust to a beneficiary.[2]

d) The basic principles of computing gains and losses: [3]
   i) Identify connected persons for capital gains tax purposes and advise on the tax implications of transfers between connected persons
   ii) Advise on the impact of dates of disposal and conditional contracts
   iii) Evaluate the use of capital losses in the year of death

e) Gains and losses on the disposal of movable and immovable property: [3]
   i) Advise on the tax implications of a part disposal, including small part disposals of land
   ii) Determine the gain on the disposal of leases and wasting assets
   iii) Establish the tax effect of appropriations to and from trading stock
   iv) Establish the tax effect of capital sums received in respect of the loss, damage or destruction of an asset
   v) Advise on the tax effect of making negligible value claims
   vi) Determine when capital gains tax can be paid by instalments and evaluate when this would be advantageous to taxpayers

f) Gains and losses on the disposal of shares and securities: [3]
   i) Extend the explanation of the treatment of rights issues to include the small part disposal rules applicable to rights issues
   ii) Determine the application of the substantial shareholdings exemption
   iii) Define a qualifying corporate bond (QCB), and understand what makes a corporate bond non-qualifying. Understand the capital gains tax implications of the disposal of QCBs in exchange for cash or shares
   iv) Apply the rules relating to reorganisations, reconstructions and amalgamations and advise on the most tax efficient options available in given circumstances
   v) Establish the relief for capital losses on shares in unquoted trading companies [3]

g) The use of exemptions and reliefs in deferring and minimising tax liabilities arising on the disposal of capital assets: [3]
   i) Understand and apply enterprise investment scheme reinvestment relief
   ii) Advise on the availability of entrepreneurs' relief in relation to associated disposals
   iii) Understand and apply the relief that is available on the transfer of an unincorporated business to a limited company
   iv) Understand the capital gains tax implications of the variation of wills

Excluded topics

The scope of the taxation of capital gains:

- *Detailed knowledge of the statements of practice on partnership capital gains.*

Capital gains tax and trusts:

- *Overseas aspects of capital gains tax and trusts*
- *The computation of capital gains tax payable by trustees*
- *Transfers of property to or from trustees prior to 22 March 2006*
- *Knowledge of situations where property is transferred between trusts or where the terms or nature of the trust is altered.*
- *Knowledge of situations where property within a trust with an immediate post-death interest passes to the spouse or*

civil partner of the settlor on the death of the life tenant.

- *Knowledge of the special rules concerning trusts for the disabled, trusts for bereaved minors, transitional serial interest trusts and age 18 to 25 trusts.*

The basic principles of computing gains and losses:

- *Assets held at 31 March 1982.*
- *Relief for losses on loans made to traders.*

Gains and losses on the disposal of movable and immovable property:

- *Chattels where the cost or proceeds are less than £6,000.*
- *Sets of chattels in relation to the chattels exemption.*
- *The grant of a lease or sub-lease out of either a freehold, long lease or short lease.*

Gains and losses on the disposal of shares and securities:

- *Computation of cost and indexed cost within the s.104 TCGA 1992 share pool*

The use of exemptions and reliefs in deferring and minimising tax liabilities arising on the disposal of capital assets.

- *Seed enterprise investment scheme reinvestment relief.*

4. Inheritance tax in situations involving further aspects of the scope of the tax and the calculation of the liabilities arising, the principles of valuation and the reliefs available, transfers of property to and from trusts, overseas aspects and further aspects of administration

a) The contents of the Paper F6 study guide for chargeable gains under headings:[2]
- E1 The scope of inheritance tax
- E2 The basic principles of computing transfers of value
- E3 The liabilities arising on the chargeable lifetime transfers and on the death of an individual
- E4 The use of exemptions in deferring and minimising inheritance tax liabilities
- E5 Payment of inheritance tax

The following additional material is also examinable:

b) The scope of inheritance tax:
   i) Explain the concepts of domicile and deemed domicile and understand the application of these concepts to inheritance tax [2]
   ii) Identify excluded property [2]
   iii) Identify and advise on the tax implications of the location of assets [3]
   iv) Identify and advise on gifts with reservation of benefit [3]
   v) Identify and advise on the tax implications of associated operations [2]

c) The basic principles of computing transfers of value:
   i) Advise on the principles of valuation[3]
   ii) Advise on the availability of business property relief and agricultural property relief[3]
   iii) Identify exempt transfers [2]

d) The liabilities arising on chargeable lifetime transfers and on the death of an individual: [3]
   i) Advise on the tax implications of chargeable lifetime transfers
   ii) Advise on the tax implications of transfers within seven years of death
   iii) Advise on the tax liability arising on a death estate
   iv) Advise on the relief for the fall in value of lifetime gifts
   v) Advise on the operation of quick succession relief
   vi) Advise on the operation of double tax relief for inheritance tax
   vii) Advise on the inheritance tax effects and advantages of the variation of wills

e) The liabilities arising in respect of transfers to and from trusts and on property within trusts:
   i) Define a trust [2]
   ii) Distinguish between different types of trust [3]

iii) Advise on the inheritance tax implications of transfers of property into trust [3]
iv) Advise on the inheritance tax implications of property passing absolutely from a trust to a beneficiary [2]
v) Identify the occasions on which inheritance tax is payable by trustees [3]

f) The use of exemptions and reliefs in deferring and minimising inheritance tax liabilities: [3]
   i) Advise on the use of reliefs and exemptions to minimise inheritance tax liabilities, as mentioned in the sections above

g) The system by which inheritance tax is administered, including the instalment option for the payment of tax:
   i) Identify who is responsible for the payment of inheritance tax.[2]
   ii) Identify the occasions on which inheritance tax may be paid by instalments.[2]
   iii) Advise on the due dates, interest and penalties for inheritance tax purposes.[3]

Excluded topics

The scope of inheritance tax:
- *Pre 18 March 1986 lifetime transfers*
- *Transfers of value by close companies*

The liabilities arising on chargeable lifetime transfers and on the death of an individual:
- *Double grossing up on death*
- *Post mortem reliefs*
- *Relief on relevant business property and agricultural property given as exempt legacies*
- *Detailed knowledge of the double charges legislation*

Computing transfers of value:
- *Valuation of an annuity or an interest in possession where the trust interest is subject to an annuity*
- *Woodlands relief*
- *Conditional exemption for heritage property*

Inheritance tax and trusts:
- *IHT aspects of discretionary trusts prior to 27 March 1974*
- *Trusts created prior to 22 March 2006*
- *Computation of ten year charges and exit charges*
- *Overseas aspects of inheritance tax and trusts*
- *The conditions that had to be satisfied for a trust to be an accumulation and maintenance trust*
- *Knowledge of situations where property is transferred between trusts or where the terms or nature of the trust is altered.*
- *Knowledge of situations where property within a trust with an immediate post-death interest passes to the spouse or civil partner of the settlor on the death of the life tenant.*
- *Knowledge of the special rules concerning trusts for the disabled, trusts for bereaved minors, transitional serial interest trusts and age 18 to 25 trusts.*

5. Stamp taxes (stamp duty, stamp duty reserve tax, and stamp duty land tax)

a) The scope of stamp taxes: [3]
   i) Identify the property in respect of which stamp taxes are payable.

b) Identify and advise on the liabilities arising on transfers. [3]
   i) Advise on the stamp taxes payable on transfers of shares and securities
   ii) Advise on the stamp taxes payable on transfers of land

c) The use of exemptions and reliefs in deferring and minimising stamp taxes: [3]
   i) Identify transfers involving no consideration
   ii) Advise on group transactions

d) Understand and explain the systems by which stamp taxes are administered.[2]

Excluded topics

The scope of stamp taxes:
- *Leases*

The liabilities arising on transfers:
- *The contingency principle*
- *Residential property held by non-natural persons*

The systems by which stamp taxes are administered:
- *Detailed rules on interest and penalties*

14

6. **National insurance, value added tax, tax administration and the UK tax system:**

a) The contents of the Paper F6 study guide for national insurance under headings:[2]
- F1 The scope of national insurance
- F2 Class 1 and class 1A contributions for employed persons
- F3 Class 2 and class 4 contributions for self-employed persons

No additional material at this level.

b) The contents of the Paper F6 study guide for value added tax (VAT) under headings:
- G1 The scope of value added tax (VAT)
- G2 The VAT registration requirements:
- G3 The computation of VAT liabilities:
- G4 The effect of special schemes

The following additional material is also examinable:

i) Advise on the impact of the disaggregation of business activities for VAT purposes [3]
ii) Advise on the impact of divisional registration [3]
iii) Advise on the VAT implications of the supply of land and buildings in the UK
iv) Advise on the VAT implications of partial exemption
v) Advise on the application of the capital goods scheme

c) The contents of the Paper F6 study guide for the obligations of taxpayers and/or their agents under headings:
- H1 The systems for self assessment and the making of returns
- H2 The time limits for the submission of information, claims and payment of tax, including payments on account
- H3 The procedures relating to compliance checks, appeals and disputes
- H4 Penalties for non-compliance

No additional material at this level

d) The contents of the Paper F6 study guide for the UK tax system under headings:
- A1 The overall function and purpose of taxation in a modern economy
- A2 Different types of taxes
- A3 Principal sources of revenue law and practice
- A4 Tax avoidance and tax evasion

Excluded topics

National insurance:
- *The calculation of directors' national insurance on a month by month basis*
- *Contracted out contributions*
- *The offset of trading losses against non-trading income and capital gains*

Value added tax:
- *The determination of the tax point*
- *The contents of a valid VAT invoice*
- *Do it yourself builders*
- *Second hand goods scheme*
- *Retailers' schemes*
- *Schemes for farmers*

B THE IMPACT OF RELEVANT TAXES ON VARIOUS SITUATIONS AND COURSES OF ACTION, INCLUDING THE INTERACTION OF TAXES

1. **Identify and advise on the taxes applicable to a given course of action and their impact.**[3]

2. **Identify and understand that the alternative ways of achieving personal or business outcomes may lead to different tax consequences**

a) Calculate the receipts from a transaction, net of tax and compare the results of alternative scenarios and advise on the most tax efficient course of action.[3]

3. **Advise how taxation can affect the financial decisions made by businesses (corporate and unincorporated) and by individuals**

a) Understand and compare and contrast the tax treatment of the sources of finance and investment products available to individuals.[3]

b) Understand and explain the tax implications of the raising of equity and loan finance.[3]

c) Explain the tax differences between decisions to lease, use hire purchase or purchase outright.[3]

d) Understand and explain the impact of taxation on the cash flows of a business.[3]

4 Assess the tax advantages and disadvantages of alternative courses of action.[3]

5. Understand the statutory obligations imposed in a given situation, including any time limits for action and advise on the implications of non-compliance.[3]

C MINIMISE AND/OR DEFER TAX LIABILITIES BY THE USE OF STANDARD TAX PLANNING MEASURES

1. Identify and advise on the types of investment and other expenditure that will result in a reduction in tax liabilities for an individual and/or a business.[3]

2. Advise on legitimate tax planning measures, by which the tax liabilities arising from a particular situation or course of action can be mitigated.[3]

3. Advise on the appropriateness of such investment, expenditure or measures given a particular taxpayer's circumstances or stated objectives.[3]

4. Advise on the mitigation of tax in the manner recommended by reference to numerical analysis and/or reasoned argument.[3]

5. Be aware of the ethical and professional issues arising from the giving of tax planning advice.[3]

6. Be aware of and give advice on current issues in taxation.[3]

D COMMUNICATE WITH CLIENTS, HM REVENUE AND CUSTOMS AND OTHER PROFESSIONALS IN AN APPROPRIATE MANNER

1. Communicate advice, recommendations and information in the required format:[3]

For example the use of:

- Reports
- Letters
- Memoranda
- Meeting notes

2. Present written information, in language appropriate to the purpose of the communication and the intended recipient.[3]

3. Communicate conclusions reached, together, where necessary with relevant supporting computations.[3]

4. State and explain assumptions made or limitations in the analysis provided; together with any inadequacies in the information available and/or additional information required to provide a fuller analysis.[3]

5. Identify and explain other, non-tax, factors that should be considered.[3]

16

SUMMARY OF CHANGES TO PAPER P6 (UK)

ACCA periodically reviews its qualification syllabuses so that they fully meet the needs of stakeholders such as employers, students, regulatory and advisory bodies and learning providers.

Amendments to P6 (UK)

Section and subject area	Amendment
Throughout	References to 'stamp duty and stamp duty land tax' changed to 'stamp taxes'
Throughout Areas excluded from Paper F6 that continue to be examinable at Paper P6	A1 d) i) Change of accounting date A1 d) ii) The relief available for trading losses following the transfer of a business to a company A2 d) v) Double taxation relief A2 e) ix) Treatment of overseas branch A3 g) iii) Incorporation relief
Corporation tax	A2 c) ii) Profits attributable to patents A2 e) vi) Pre-entry gains removed from syllabus A2 f) i) Disincorporation relief
Inheritance tax *excluded topics*	Trusts created prior to 22 March 2006
Stamp taxes *excluded topic*	Residential property held by non-natural persons

Analysis of past papers

The table below provides details of when each element of the syllabus has been examined in the nine most recent sittings and the question number and section in which each element was examined.

Covered in Text chapter	TAXATION OF INDIVIDUALS	June 2013	Dec 2012	June 2012	Dec 2011	June 2011	Dec 2010	June 2010	Dec 2009	June 2009
	INCOME TAX									
1	Principles of income tax	3(a)	2(a)	4(c)	2(a)	1(a)		2	1(a)	
2	Pensions and other tax efficient investment products	3(a)		4(c)		4(b)		4(a)		2
3	Property and other investment income									
4	Employment income	3(a), 5(b)	2(a)	3(b), 3(c)	3(b)	1(a), 2(a)	5	2, 5(c)	1(a), 4	
5	Employment income: additional aspects	5(b)	1(a), 2(a)	4(a)	3(a)		5	4(a)	4(a)	
6	Trade profits		2(a)	3(b), 4(b)	2(a)	3(a)				
7	Capital allowances	4(b)	1(a)	5(c)				5(a)		3(a)
8	Trading losses	5(a)	2(a)		2(a)	3(b)		3(a)	3(a)	3(a)
9	Partnerships and limited liability partnerships			4(b)		3(b)				3(a)
10	Overseas aspects of income tax	3(b)			2(b)		2		5(b)	
	CAPITAL GAINS TAX									
11	Chargeable gains: an outline	2(b)	4(a)	1(a)	2(a)	1(a)	4	3(b)	3(a)	1
12	Shares and securities					4(c)			3(a)	4(a)
13	Chargeable gains: reliefs	2(b)	2(b), 4(a)	1(a)	2(a)	1(a)		5(b)		1, 4(b)
14	Chargeable gains: additional aspects	2(a)	4(a)		2(a), (b)		4		5(a)	
	TAX ADMINISTRATION FOR INDIVIDUALS									
15	Self assessment for individuals and partnerships		4(c), 5(a), 5(b)	1(b)			4			
	INHERITANCE TAX									
16	An introduction to inheritance tax	2(b)	2(b), 5(c)	1(a)	4(b)	1(b), 4(a)	2, 4	2, 3(b)		2, 4(b)
17	Inheritance tax: valuation, reliefs and the death estate	2(b)	5(c)	1(a)	4(b)	1(b)	2	2	3(b)	4(a)
18	Inheritance tax: additional aspects		5(c)	1(a)	2(b), 4(b)	1(b)	2		1(b)	
	TRUSTS AND STAMP TAXES									
19	Trusts and stamp taxes	2(b)		1(a)	4(a)	1(a)	1	2	1(b)	

Covered in Text chapter	TAXATION OF COMPANIES	June 2013	Dec 2012	June 2012	Dec 2011	June 2011	Dec 2010	June 2010	Dec 2009	June 2009
	CORPORATION TAX									
20	Computing taxable total profits		1(a)	2(b), 5(c)				1	2	1
21	Chargeable gains for companies	4(a)	1(a)	2(b), 2(c)		2(b), 5(c)	1		2	
22	Computing corporation tax payable	1(a)		2(d), 3(b), 5(a), 5(b)	1(a)	2(a)	1	2	2	1
23	Administration, winding up, purchase of own shares	1(c)	3(a)				3			
24	Losses and deficits on non-trading loan relationships			2(a)	1(a),5(b)			3(a)		5(a)
25	Close companies and investment companies		3(a), 3(b)		1(a)		3			
26	Groups and consortia	1(a)	1(a)	2(a), 5(c)	1(a), 5(a)		1	1		5(a)
27	Overseas aspects of corporate tax		3(b)			5(a), (b)		1		5(b)
	VALUE ADDED TAX									
28	Value added tax (1)	4(c)	4(b)		2(b), 5(c)	2(a), (b)		3(b)		1, 3(b)
29	Value added tax (2)	1(b)	1(a)	2(b), (c)	1(a), 5(c)	2(a), (b)	1, 5	1	1(a), 2	1
	IMPACT OF TAXES AND TAX PLANNING									
30	Impact of taxes and tax planning	1(a), 1(c), 1(d), 3(a)	1(b)	1(b), 3(a)	1(b)	2(b)	1	1	1(b)	2

PART A

Income tax

1

Principles of income tax

Topic list	Syllabus reference
1 The aggregation of income	A1(a)B5
2 Various types of income	A1(a)B5,B6
3 Deductible interest	A1(a)B5
4 Allowances deductible from net income	A1(a)B5
5 Computing tax liability	A1(a)B5, A1(g)(i),(ii)
6 Computing tax payable	A1(a)B5
7 Families	A1(e)(iii),(f)(i)

Introduction

We start our study of taxation with a look at income tax, which is a tax on what individuals make from their jobs, their businesses and their savings. We see how to collect together all of an individual's income in a personal tax computation, and then work out the tax on that income.

We also look at the family aspects of income tax, how joint income of spouses/civil partners is taxed and the anti-avoidance provisions for minor children.

In later chapters, we look at particular types of income in more detail.

Study Guide

		Intellectual level
1	**Income and income tax liabilities in situations involving further overseas aspects and in relation to trusts, and the application of exemptions and reliefs**	
(a)	The contents of the Paper F6 study guide for income tax, under headings:	2
•	B5 The comprehensive computation of taxable income and the income tax liability	
•	B6 The use of exemptions and reliefs in deferring and minimising income tax liabilities	
(e)	Property and investment income:	3
(iii)	Advise on the tax implications of jointly held assets	
(f)	The comprehensive computation of taxable income and the income tax liability:	3
(i)	Advise on the income tax position of the income of minor children	
(g)	The use of exemptions and reliefs in deferring and minimising income tax liabilities:	3
(i)	Understand and apply the rules relating to investments in the seed enterprise investment scheme and the enterprise investment scheme	
(ii)	Understand and apply the rules relating to investments in venture capital trusts	

Exam guide

Although you are unlikely to have to perform a complete income tax computation in the exam, you need to understand how the computation is put together as you may be asked to calculate the after tax income that would be derived from a particular new source. Do not overlook the effect of an increase in income on the personal allowance or higher personal allowance.

The chapter also introduces tax planning concepts. Note the treatment of joint income of spouses/civil partners and the anti-avoidance rules that apply if a parent gives funds to a minor child.

Knowledge brought forward from earlier studies

This chapter revises the basic income tax computation that you will already have met in Paper F6. The examiner has identified essential underpinning knowledge from the F6 syllabus which is particularly important that you revise as part of your P6 studies. In this chapter, the relevant topics are:

		Intellectual level
B5	**The comprehensive computation of taxable income and income tax liability**	
(b)	Calculate the amount of personal allowance available generally, and for people born before 6 April 1948	2
(c)	Compute the amount of income tax payable.	2

The main changes in 2013/14 from 2012/13 in the material you have previously studied at F6 level are the changes in the basic rate limit, the additional rate, and amounts of the personal allowances.

Topics that will be new to you in this chapter are the child benefit tax charge (a new addition to the F6 syllabus for exams in 2014 and therefore also new for P6), tax reducers and the taxation of families.

1 The aggregation of income

In a personal income tax computation, bring together income from all sources, splitting the sources into non-savings, savings and dividend income.

One of the competencies you require to fulfil performance objective 19 of the PER is the ability to evaluate and compute taxes payable. You can apply the knowledge you obtain from this section of the text to help to demonstrate this competence.

As a general rule, income tax is charged on receipts which might be expected to recur (such as weekly wages or profits from running a business). **An individual's income from all sources is brought together (aggregated) in a personal tax computation for the tax year.**

Key terms

The **tax year**, or **fiscal year**, or **year of assessment** runs from 6 April to 5 April. For example, the tax year 2013/14 runs from 6 April 2013 to 5 April 2014.

Here is an example. All items are explained later in this Text.

RICHARD: INCOME TAX COMPUTATION 2013/14

	Non-savings income	*Savings income*	*Dividend income*	*Total*
	£	£	£	£
Income from employment	50,000			
Building society interest		1,000		
National savings & investments account interest		360		
UK dividends			1,000	
Total income	50,000	1,360	1,000	
Less interest paid	(2,000)			
Net income	48,000	1,360	1,000	50,360
Less personal allowance	(9,440)			
Taxable income	38,560	1,360	1,000	40,920

	£	£
Income tax on non savings income		
£32,010 × 20%		6,402
£6,550 × 40%		2,620
Tax on savings income		
£1,360 × 40%		544
Tax on dividend income		
£1,000 × 32.5%		325
		9,891
Less tax reducer		
Investment under the EIS £10,000 × 30%		(3,000)
Tax liability		6,891
Less tax suffered		
PAYE tax on salary (say)	6,400	
Tax on building society interest	200	
Tax credit on dividend income	100	
		(6,700)
Tax payable		191

Key terms

Total income is all income subject to income tax. Each of the amounts which make up total income is called a component. **Net income** is total income less deductible interest and trade losses. The **tax liability** is the amount charged on the individual's income. **Tax payable** is the balance of the liability still to be settled in cash.

Income tax is charged on **'taxable income'**. Non-savings income is dealt with first, then savings income and then dividend income.

For non-savings income, income up to £32,010 (the basic rate limit) is taxed at the basic rate (20%), income between £32,010 and £150,000 (the higher rate limit) at the higher rate (40%) and any remaining income at the additional rate (45%). We will look at the taxation of the other types of income later in this chapter.

The remainder of this chapter gives more details of the income tax computation.

2 Various types of income

FAST FORWARD

Don't forget to gross up dividends by 100/90 and interest by 100/80.

2.1 Classification of income

All income received must be **classified** according to the nature of the income. This is because different computational rules apply to different types of income. The main types of income are:

- Income from employment, pensions and some social security benefits
- Profits of trades, professions and vocations
- Profits of property businesses
- Savings and investment income, including interest and dividends
- Miscellaneous income.

The rules for computing employment income, profits from trades, professions and vocations and property letting income will be covered in later chapters. These types of income are **non-savings income**. Pension income is also non-savings income.

2.2 Savings income

2.2.1 What is savings income?

Savings income is interest. Interest is paid on bank and building society accounts, on Government securities, such as Treasury Stock, and on company loan stock.

Interest may be paid net of 20% tax or it may be paid gross.

2.2.2 Savings income received gross

The following savings income is received gross.

(a) National Savings & Investments interest including interest from Direct Saver Accounts, Investment Accounts and Income Bonds

(b) Interest from company loan stock which is listed on a recognised stock exchange

(c) Interest on government securities (these are also called 'gilts')

2.2.3 Savings income received net of 20% tax

The following savings income is received net of 20% tax. **This is called income taxed at source.**

(a) Bank and building society interest paid to individuals

(b) Interest paid to individuals from company loan stock which is not listed on a recognised stock exchange

(c) Savings income from non discretionary trusts (dealt with later in this Text)

The amount received is grossed up by multiplying by 100/80 and is included gross in the income tax computation. The tax deducted at source is deducted in computing tax payable and may be repaid.

Exam focus point

In examinations you may be given either the net or the gross amount of such income: read the question carefully. If you are given the net amount (the amount received or credited), you should gross up the figure at the rate of 20%. For example, net building society interest of £160 is equivalent to gross income of £160 × 100/80 = £200 on which tax of £40 (20% of £200) has been suffered.

Although bank and building society interest paid to individuals is generally paid net of 20% tax, if a recipient is not liable to tax, they can recover the tax suffered, or they can certify in advance that they are a non-taxpayer and receive the interest gross.

2.3 Dividends on UK shares

Dividends on UK shares are received net of a 10% tax credit. This means a dividend of £90 has a £10 tax credit, giving gross income of £100 to include in the income tax computation. The tax credit can be deducted in computing tax payable but **it cannot be repaid**.

2.4 Exempt income

One of the competencies you require to fulfil performance objective 20 of the PER is the ability to assist with tax planning. You can apply the knowledge you obtain from this section of the text to help to demonstrate this competence.

Some income is exempt from income tax. Several of these exemptions are mentioned at places in this Text where the types of income are described in detail, but you should note the following types of exempt income now.

(a) Scholarships (exempt as income of the scholar. If paid by a parent's employer, a scholarship may be taxable income of the parent)

(b) Betting and gaming winnings, including **premium bond prizes**

(c) Interest or terminal bonus on **National Savings & Investments Certificates**

(d) Certain social security benefits

(e) Income on investments made through **Individual Savings Accounts (ISAs).**

3 Deductible interest

Deductible interest is deducted from total income to compute net income.

3.1 Interest payments

An individual who pays interest on a loan in a tax year is entitled to relief in that tax year if the loan is for one of the following purposes:

(a) **Loan to buy plant or machinery for partnership use**. Interest is allowed for three years from the end of the tax year in which the loan was taken out. If the plant is used partly for private use, the allowable interest is apportioned.

(b) **Loan to buy plant or machinery for employment use.** Interest is allowed for three years from the end of the tax year in which the loan was taken out. If the plant is used partly for private use, the allowable interest is apportioned.

(c) **Loan to acquire any part of the ordinary share capital of a close company (other than a close investment-holding company) or to lend money to such a company which is used wholly and exclusively for the purpose of its business or that of an associated close company.** A close company is a company controlled by its shareholder-directors or by five or fewer shareholders (see later in this Text).

When the interest is paid, the borrower must *either* hold some shares in the close company and work the greater part of their time in the actual management or conduct of the company (or of an associated company) *or* have a material interest in the close company (ie hold more than 5% of the shares). Also, the individual usually must not have recovered any capital from the company.

Relief is not available if Enterprise Investment Scheme (EIS) relief (see later in this Text) is claimed on the shares.

(d) **Loan to buy interest in employee-controlled company.** The company must be an unquoted trading company resident in the UK with at least 50% of the voting shares held by employees.

(e) **Loan to invest in partnership.** The investment may be a share in the partnership or a contribution to the partnership of capital or a loan to the partnership. The individual must be a partner (other than a limited partner) and relief ceases when they cease to be a partner.

(f) **Loan to invest in a co-operative.** The investment may be shares or a loan. The individual must spend the greater part of their time working for the co-operative.

Tax relief is given by deducting the interest from total income to calculate net income for the tax year in which the interest is paid. It is deducted from **non-savings income first, then from savings income and lastly from dividend income.**

There is a **limit on the amount of deductions from total income, including deductible interest,** which an individual taxpayer can make in a tax year. This limit is discussed in the chapter on trading losses later in this Text.

3.2 Example

Frederick has taxable trading income for 2013/14 of £43,000, savings income of £1,320 (gross) and dividend income of £1,000 (gross).

Frederick pays interest of £1,370 in 2013/14 on a loan to invest in a partnership.

Frederick's net income is:

	Non-savings income	*Savings income*	*Dividend income*	*Total*
	£	£	£	£
Total income	43,000	1,320	1,000	
Less: interest paid	(1,370)			
Net income	41,630	1,320	1,000	43,950

4 Allowances deductible from net income

4.1 Personal allowance

FAST FORWARD

All persons are entitled to a personal allowance. It is deducted from net income, first against non savings income, then against savings income and lastly against dividend income. The personal allowance is reduced by £1 for every £2 that adjusted net income exceeds £100,000 and can be reduced to nil.

Once income from all sources has been aggregated and any deductible interest deducted, the remainder is the taxpayer's net income. An allowance, the **personal allowance,** is **deducted from net income**. Like deductible interest, it reduces non **savings income first, then savings income and lastly dividend income**.

All individuals born after 5 April 1948 (including children) **are entitled to the personal allowance of £9,440.** However, if the **individual's adjusted net income exceeds £100,000,** the **personal allowance is reduced by £1 for each £2 by which adjusted net income exceeds £100,000 until the personal allowance is nil (which is when adjusted net income is £118,880 or more).**

Key term

Adjusted net income is net income less the gross amounts of personal pension contributions (and gift aid donations – not in your syllabus).

We will look at personal pension contributions later in this Text and revisit this topic again then. At the moment, we will look at the situation where net income and adjusted net income are the same amounts.

Question — Personal allowance

Clare was born in 1965. In 2013/14, Clare receives employment income of £97,000, bank interest of £6,400 and dividends of £6,750.

Calculate Clare's taxable income for 2013/14.

Answer

	Non-savings income	*Savings income*	*Dividend income*	*Total*
	£	£	£	£
Employment income	97,000			
Bank interest £6,400 × 100/80		8,000		
Dividends £6,750 × 100/90			7,500	
Net income	97,000	8,000	7,500	112,500
Less: personal allowance (W)	(3,190)			
Taxable income	93,810	8,000	7,500	109,310

Working

Net income	112,500
Less income limit	(100,000)
Excess	12,500
Personal allowance	9,440
Less half excess £12,500 × ½	(6,250)
	3,190

Where an individual has an adjusted net income between £100,000 and £118,880, the rate of tax on the income between these two amounts will usually be 60%. This is calculated as 40% (the higher rate on income) plus 40% of half (ie 20%) of the excess adjusted net income over £100,000 used to restrict the personal allowance. The individual should consider **making personal pension contributions to reduce adjusted net income to below £100,000**.

4.2 Higher personal allowance

FAST FORWARD

Taxpayers born between 6 April 1938 and 5 April 1948 are entitled to an higher personal allowance of £10,500 and taxpayers born before 6 April 1938 are entitled to a higher personal allowance of £10,660. The allowance is reduced by £1 for every £2 that adjusted net income exceeds £26,100 but is generally not reduced below the amount of the personal allowance available for taxpayers born after 5 April 1948.

An individual born between 6 April 1938 and 5 April 1948 **receives an higher personal allowance of £10,500** instead of the personal allowance of £9,440.

An individual born before 6 April 1938 **receives a higher higher personal allowance of £10,660** instead of the personal allowance of £9,440.

If the individual's adjusted net income exceeds £26,100 the higher personal allowance is reduced by £1 for each £2 by which adjusted net income exceeds £26,100. The higher personal allowance **cannot usually be reduced below the amount of the personal allowance available for taxpayers born after 5 April 1948 (£9,440).** However, **if the individual has adjusted net income in excess of £100,000**, the **personal allowance will be reduced** as described in Section 4.1 above.

Question — **Higher personal allowance**

Three taxpayers have the following net income for 2013/14.

A £27,450
B £36,000
C £26,610

Calculate their taxable income assuming taxpayers A and B were born between 6 April 1938 and 5 April 1948 and taxpayer C was born before 6 April 1938.

Answer

Taxable income is:	*A*	*B*	*C*
	£	£	£
Net income	27,450	36,000	26,610
Less higher personal allowance (W)	(9,825)	(9,440)	(10,405)
Taxable income	17,625	26,560	16,205

Working

Net income	27,450	36,000	26,610
Less income limit	(26,100)	(26,100)	(26,100)
Excess	1,350	9,900	510
Higher personal allowance	10,500	10,500	10,660
Less half excess £1,350/9,900/510 × 1/2	(675)	(4,950)	(255)
	9,825	5,550	10,405
Minimum		9,440	

5 Computing tax liability

Income tax is worked out on taxable income. First tax non-savings income, then savings income and then dividend income.

One of the competencies you require to fulfil performance objective 19 of the PER is the ability to evaluate and compute taxes payable. You can apply the knowledge you obtain from this section of the text to help to demonstrate this competence.

5.1 Tax rates

Income tax payable is computed on an individual's taxable income, which comprises net income less the personal allowance or higher personal allowance. The tax rates are applied to taxable income which is non-savings income first, then to savings income and finally to dividend income.

5.1.1 Savings income starting rate

There is a **tax rate of 10% for savings income up to £2,790 (the savings income starting rate limit)**. This rate is called the **savings income starting rate**.

The savings income starting rate only applies where the savings income falls wholly or partly below the starting rate limit. Remember that income tax is charged first on non-savings income. So, in most cases, an individual's non-savings income will exceed the starting rate limit and the savings income starting rate will not be available on savings income.

Question — Savings income starting rate

Joe was born in 1958. In 2013, he earns a salary of £10,000 from a part-time job and receives bank interest of £4,000.

Calculate Joe's tax liability for 2013/14.

Answer

	Non-savings income	*Savings income*	*Total*
	£	£	£
Employment income	10,000		
Bank interest £4,000 × 100/80		5,000	
Net income	10,000	5,000	15,000
Less: personal allowance	(9,440)		
Taxable income	560	5,000	5,560

Income tax	
Non-savings income	
	£
£560 × 20%	112
Savings income	
£(2,790 – 560) = 2,230 × 10%	223
£(5,000 – 2,230) = 2,770 × 20%	554
Tax liability	889

5.1.2 Basic rate

The basic rate of tax is 20% for 2013/14 for both non-savings income and savings income.

The basic rate of tax is 10% for 2013/14 for dividend income.

The basic rate limit for 2013/14 is £32,010.

5.1.3 Higher rate

The higher rate of tax is 40% for 2013/14 for non-savings and saving income.

The higher rate of tax is 32.5% for 2013/14 for dividend income.

The higher rate limit for 2013/14 is £150,000.

Question — **Basic and higher rates**

Margery was born in 1978. In 2013/14, she has employment income of £35,475, receives building society interest of £2,000 and dividends of £9,000.

Calculate Margery's tax liability for 2013/14.

Answer

	Non-savings income	*Savings income*	*Dividend income*	*Total*
	£	£	£	£
Employment income	35,475			
BSI £2,000 × 100/80		2,500		
Dividends £9,000 × 100/90			10,000	
Net income	35,475	2,500	10,000	47,975
Less: personal allowance	(9,440)			
Taxable income	26,035	2,500	10,000	38,535

Income tax	
	£
Non-savings income	
£26,035 × 20%	5,207
Savings income	
£2,500 × 20%	500
Dividend income	
£(32,010 – 26,035 – 2,500) = 3,475 × 10%	347
£(10,000 – 3,475) = 6,525 × 32.5%	2,121
Tax liability	8,175

5.1.4 Additional rate

The additional rate of tax is 45% for 2013/14 for non-savings and saving income.

The additional rate of tax is 37.5% for 2013/14 for dividend income.

The additional rate of tax applies to taxable income in excess of £150,000.

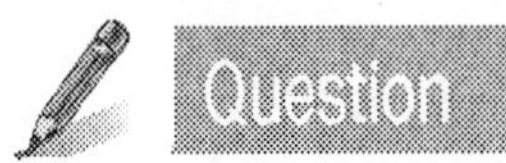

Question

Additional rate

In 2013/14, Julian has employment income of £148,000, receives bank interest of £5,000 and dividends of £18,000.

Calculate Julian's tax liability for 2013/14.

Answer

	Non-savings income	*Savings income*	*Dividend income*	*Total*
	£	£	£	£
Employment income	148,000			
Bank interest £5,000 × 100/80		6,250		
Dividends £18,000 × 100/90			20,000	
Taxable income (no personal allowance available)	148,000	6,250	20,000	174,250

Income tax

	£
Non-savings income	
£32,010 × 20%	6,402
£(148,000 - 32,010) = 115,990 × 40%	46,396
Savings income	
£(150,000 – 148,000) = 2,000 × 40%	800
£(6,250 – 2,000) = 4,250 × 45%	1,912
Dividend income	
£20,000 × 37.5%	7,500
Tax liability	63,010

5.2 Child benefit income tax charge

FAST FORWARD

There is an income tax charge to recover child benefit if the recipient or their partner has adjusted net income over £50,000 in a tax year.

An **income tax charge** applies if a taxpayer receives child benefit (or their partner receives child benefit) and the taxpayer has **adjusted net income over £50,000 in a tax year. Adjusted net income is defined in the same way as for the restriction of the personal allowance** described earlier in this chapter.

A 'partner' is a **spouse**, a **civil partner,** or an **unmarried partner** where the couple are **living together as though they were married or were civil partners**. Civil partners are members of a same sex couple which has registered as a civil partnership under the Civil Partnerships Act 2004.

If the taxpayer has **adjusted net income over £60,000,** the charge is equal to the **full amount of child benefit received.**

If the taxpayer has **adjusted net income between £50,000 and £60,000**, the charge is **1% of the child benefit amount for each £100 of adjusted net income in excess of £50,000**. The calculation, at all stages, is rounded down to the nearest whole number.

If **both partners have adjusted net income in excess of £50,000**, the **partner with the higher adjusted net income** is liable for the charge.

The child benefit income tax charge is collected through the self-assessment system (dealt with later in this Text). This includes the need for **taxpayers to submit tax returns**, which can be time consuming and costly. To avoid this, **taxpayers can opt not to receive child benefit at all** so that the income tax charge does not apply.

Question — Child benefit income tax charge (1)

Robert and Roslyn are not married but live together as though they were married. They have a five year old son.

Robert (born in 1975) has net income of £52,000 (all non-savings income) in 2013/14. His adjusted net income is also £52,000 since he made no personal pension contributions in 2013/14. Roslyn has no income. She receives child benefit of £1,056 in 2013/14.

Calculate Robert's tax liability for 2013/14.

Answer

Robert will be liable to the child benefit income tax charge in 2013/14 since his partner receives child benefit during that year and he has adjusted net income over £50,000.

	£
Net income	52,000
Less: personal allowance	(9,440)
Taxable income	42,560
Income tax	
£32,010 @ 20%	6,402
£10,550 @ 40%	4,220
	10,622
Add: child benefit income tax charge (W)	211
Tax liability	10,833

Working

	£
Adjusted net income	52,000
Less: threshold	(50,000)
Excess	2,000
÷ £100	20
Child benefit income tax charge: 1% × £1,056 × 20	211

Question — Child benefit income tax charge (2)

Samantha (born in 1980) is divorced and has two children aged ten and six. She has net income of £56,000 (all non-savings income) in 2013/14. Samantha made personal pension contributions of £4,500 (gross) during 2013/14. She receives child benefit of £1,752 in 2013/14.

Calculate the Samantha's income tax liability for 2013/14.

Answer

Samantha

	£
Net income	56,000
Less: personal allowance	(9,440)
Taxable income	46,560

	£
Income tax:	
£36,510 @ 20% (W1)	7,302
£10,050 @ 40%	4,020
	11,322
Add: child benefit income tax charge (W2)	262
Tax liability	11,584

Workings

1 Basic rate limit

£32,010 + £4,500 = £36,510

2 Child benefit income tax charge

	£
Net income	56,000
Less: personal pension contributions (gross)	(4,500)
Adjusted net income	51,500
Less: threshold	(50,000)
Excess	1,500
÷ £100	15
Child benefit income tax charge: 1% × £1,752 × 15	262

At all stages of the calculation, round down to the nearest whole number.

Tutorial note

If Samantha had made an extra gross personal pension contribution of £1,500 during 2013/14, her adjusted net income would not have exceeded £50,000 and she would not have been subject to the child benefit income tax charge.

5.3 Tax reducers

FAST FORWARD

Tax reducers reduce tax on income at a set rate of relief.

One of the competencies you require to fulfil performance objective 19 of the PER is the ability to evaluate and compute taxes payable. You can apply the knowledge you obtain from this section of the text to help to demonstrate this competence.

5.3.1 Introduction

Tax reducers do not affect income; they reduce tax on income. The tax reducers are:

(a) Investments in venture capital trusts (VCTs) and
(b) Investments under the enterprise investment scheme (EIS)
(c) Investments under the seed enterprise investment scheme (SEIS).

Investments in the above companies may qualify for a tax reduction of up to the lower of:

(a) A percentage of the amount subscribed for qualifying investments, and
(b) The individual's tax liability.

For investments in VCTs and under the EIS, the percentage is 30%. For investments under the SEIS, the percentage is 50%. Further details are given later in this Text.

5.3.2 Giving tax reductions

Tax reducers are deducted in computing an individual's income tax liability. The tax liability can only be reduced to zero: a tax reducer cannot create a repayment.

If the individual is entitled to more than one tax reducer, the VCT reducer is deducted first, then the EIS reducer and finally the SEIS reducer.

Question — **Tax reducers**

During 2013/14 Peter, who was born in 1942, makes qualifying investments of £5,000 in a venture capital trust and of £2,000 under the seed enterprise investment scheme. Show his tax position for 2013/14 if his income consists of:

(a) trading profits of £45,975
(b) trading profits of £17,045.

Answer

	(a): High income Non-savings	*(b): Low income Non-savings*
	£	£
Trading profits	45,975	17,045
Less personal allowance/higher personal allowance	(9,440)	(10,500)
Taxable income	36,535	6,545
Income tax		
	£	£
Non-savings income		
£32,010/£6,545 × 20%	6,402	1,309
£4,525/nil × 40%	1,810	
	8,212	1,309
Tax reducers		
VCT £5,000 × 30%	(1,500)	(1,309)
	6,712	0
SEIS £2,000 × 50%	(1,000)	–
Tax liability	5,712	0

The tax reducers cannot lead to repayments of tax, so in (b) the SEIS relief and some of the VCT relief is wasted. In (a) Peter is not entitled to the higher personal allowance because his net income is too high.

6 Computing tax payable

FAST FORWARD

From tax liability, first deduct the tax credit on dividend income and any income tax suffered at source to arrive at tax payable. The tax credit on dividend income cannot be repaid if it exceeds the tax liability calculated so far. Other tax suffered at source can be repaid.

One of the competencies you require to fulfil performance objective 19 of the PER is the ability to evaluate and compute taxes payable. You can apply the knowledge you obtain from this section of the text to help to demonstrate this competence.

6.1 Steps in the personal tax computation

Step 1 **The first step in preparing a personal tax computation is to set up three columns**
One column for non-savings income, one for savings income and one for dividend income. Add up income from different sources. The sum of these is known as 'total income'. Deduct deductible interest and trade losses to compute 'net income'. Deduct the personal allowance or higher personal allowance to compute 'taxable income'.

Step 2 **Deal with non-savings income first**
Any non-savings income up to the basic rate limit of £32,010 is taxed at 20%. Non-savings income between the basic rate limit and the higher rate limit of £150,000 is taxed at 40%. Any further non-savings income is taxed at 45%.

Step 3 **Now deal with savings income**
If savings income is below the starting rate limit of £2,790, it is taxed at the savings income starting rate of 10%. Savings income between the starting rate limit and the basic rate limit of £32,010 is taxed at 20%. Savings income between the basic rate limit and the higher rate limit of £150,000 is taxed at 40%. Any further savings income is taxed at 45%. In most cases, non-savings income and savings income can be added together and tax calculated on the total, provided that the savings income starting rate does not apply.

Step 4 **Lastly, tax dividend income**
If dividend income is below the basic rate limit of £32,010, it is taxed at 10%. Dividend income between the basic rate limit and the higher rate limit of £150,000 is taxed at 32.5%. Any further dividend income is taxed at 37.5%.

Step 5 Add the amounts of tax together.

Step 6 Once tax has been computed, **deduct any available tax reducers** (eg EIS).

Step 7 Calculate the amount of any **child benefit income tax charge** and add to the tax remaining after step 6. The resulting figure is the **income tax liability**.

Step 8 Next, **deduct the tax credit on dividends**. Although deductible this tax credit cannot be repaid if it exceeds the tax liability calculated so far.

Step 9 Finally **deduct the tax deducted at source from savings income and any PAYE**. These amounts can be repaid to the extent that they exceed the income tax liability.

Question — Calculation of income tax payable

In 2013/14, Jules (born in 1966) has a business profit of £54,750, net dividends of £6,750 and building society interest of £3,000 net. He pays deductible interest of £3,000. Jules makes an investment of £5,000 under the Enterprise Investment Scheme. How much income tax is payable?

Answer

	Non-savings income	*Savings income*	*Dividend income*	*Total*
	£	£	£	£
Business profits	54,750			
Dividends £6,750 × 100/90			7,500	
Building society interest £3,000 × 100/80		3,750		
Total income	54,750	3,750	7,500	
Less interest paid	(3,000)			
Net income	51,750	3,750	7,500	63,000
Less personal allowance	(9,440)			
Taxable income	42,310	3,750	7,500	53,560

	£
Non-savings income	
£32,010 × 20%	6,402
£10,300 × 40%	4,120
	10,522
Savings income	
£3,750 × 40%	1,500
Dividend income	
£7,500 × 32.5%	2,437
Tax reducer	14,459
EIS £5,000 × 30%	(1,500)
Tax liability	12,959
Less tax credit on dividend income	(750)
Less tax suffered on building society interest	(750)
Tax payable	11,459

Savings income and dividend income fall above the basic rate limit but below the higher rate limit so they are taxed at 40% and 32.5% respectively.

6.2 Calculating additional tax due

Higher rate taxpayers pay an effective rate of 25% on their dividend income. Additional rate taxpayer pay an effective rate of 30.555% on their dividend income.

The above question showed a full income tax computation. **Often a taxpayer is more interested in looking at the after tax return from a particular investment or transaction**. In each of the following examples we will **calculate the additional tax due as a result of acquiring a new investment**. Note how it is **not necessary here to use the full income tax proforma**.

6.3 Examples: additional tax due

(a) Kate (born in 1975) receives an annual salary of £75,000. Her grandfather dies leaving her shares in Axle plc. She receives dividends of £18,000 during 2013/14. The additional tax due as a result of receiving the dividend income can be calculated as follows:

Income tax on dividends of (£18,000 × 100/90) = £20,000 is all at the higher rate as Kate's taxable income is above the basic rate limit but below the higher rate limit:

	£
£20,000 @ 32.5%	6,500
Less tax credit @ 10%	(2,000)
Additional tax due	4,500

This is the same as taking 25% of the net dividend taxable at the higher rate ie £18,000 (20,000 × 90%) @ 25% = £4,500.

(b) Kate (born in 1975) receives an annual salary of £40,475. Her grandfather dies leaving her shares in Axle plc. She receives dividends of £18,000 during 2013/14. The additional tax due as a result of receiving the dividend income can be calculated as follows:

Income tax on dividends of (£18,000 × 100/90) = £20,000

Amount remaining below basic rate limit:
£32,010 – (£40,475 – £9,440) = £975

	£
£975 @ 10%	97
£19,025 @ 32.5%	6,183
	6,280
Less tax credit @ 10%	(2,000)
Additional tax due	4,280

Dividend income below the basic rate limit is taxed at 10% (*not* 20%).

This is the same as taking 25% of the net dividend taxable at the higher rate ie (£19,025 × 90%) @ 25% = £4,280.

(c) Kate (born in 1975) receives an annual salary of £99,000. Her grandfather dies leaving her shares in Axle plc. She receives dividends of £18,000 during 2013/14. The additional tax due as a result of receiving the dividend income can be calculated as follows:

Income tax on dividends of (£18,000 × 100/90) = £20,000 is all at the higher rate as Kate's taxable income is above the higher rate limit. In addition, Kate will no longer be entitled to the personal allowance since her net income is £(99,000 + 20,000) = £119,000. The additional tax due is therefore calculated as follows:

	£
£20,000 @ 32.5%	6,500
Less tax credit @ 10%	(2,000)
Additional tax on dividend income	
Tax on income previously covered by personal allowance £9,440 @ 40%	
Additional tax due	8,276

(d) Kate (born in 1975) receives an annual salary of £175,000. Her grandfather dies leaving her shares in Axle plc. She receives dividends of £18,000 during 2013/14. The additional tax due as a result of receiving the dividend income can be calculated as follows:

Income tax on dividends of (£18,000 × 100/90) = £20,000 is all at the additional rate as Kate's taxable income is above the higher rate limit:

	£
£20,000 @ 37.5%	7,500
Less tax credit @ 10%	(2,000)
Additional tax due	5,500

This is the same as taking 30.555% of the net dividend taxable at the higher rate ie £18,000 (20,000 × 90%) @ 30.555% = £5,500.

6.4 Income taxed as top slice of income

One type of income (covered later in this Text) is taxed after dividend income, so that dividend income is not always the top slice of income. This is the taxable portions of partly exempt payments on the termination of employment.

So someone with wages of £21,450 (using the personal allowance of £9,440 and £12,010 of basic rate band), dividend income of £20,000 and a £50,000 termination payment will have the dividend income taxed at 10%, instead of 32.5% as the dividend income will be within the basic rate band. The termination payment will be wholly taxed at 40% since it is above the basic rate limit of £32,010.

6.5 The complete proforma

Here is a complete proforma computation. You can refer back to it as you work through this Text. You will also see how losses fit into the proforma later in this Text.

	Non-savings income	*Savings income*	*Dividend income*	*Total*
	£	£	£	£
Trading income	X			
Employment income	X			
Property business income	X			
Bank/building society interest (gross)		X		
Other interest (gross)		X		
(as many lines as necessary)				
Dividends (gross)			X	
Total income	X	X	X	
Less interest paid	(X)	(X)	(X)	
Net income	X	X	X	X
Less personal allowance	(X)	(X)	(X)	
Taxable income	X	X	X	X

7 Families

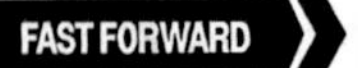

Spouses, civil partners and children are all separate taxpayers. There are special rules to prevent parents from exploiting a child's personal allowance.

One of the competencies you require to fulfil performance objective 20 of the PER is the ability to assist with tax planning. You can apply the knowledge you obtain from this section of the text to help to demonstrate this competence.

7.1 Spouses and civil partners

Spouses and civil partners are taxed as two separate people. Each spouse/civil partner is entitled to a personal allowance or an age related personal allowance depending on his or her own age and income.

7.2 Joint property

When spouses/civil partners jointly own income-generating property, it is assumed that they are entitled to equal shares of the income. This does not apply to income from shares held in close companies (see later in this Text for an explanation of close companies).

If the spouses/civil partners are not entitled to equal shares in the income-generating property (other than shares in close companies), **they may make a joint declaration to HMRC, specifying the proportion to which each is entitled.** These proportions are used to tax each of them separately, in respect of income arising on or after the date of the declaration. For capital gains tax purposes it is always this underlying beneficial ownership that is taken into account.

7.3 Example: income tax planning for spouses/civil partners

Mr Buckle (born in 1965) is a higher rate taxpayer who owns a rental property producing £23,000 of property income on which he pays tax at 40%, giving him a tax liability of £9,200. His spouse has no income.

If he transfers only 5% of the asset to his wife, they will be treated as jointly owning the property and will each be taxed on 50% of the income. Mr Buckle's tax liability will be reduced to £4,600.

His wife's liability is then calculated as follows:

	£
Net income	11,500
Less personal allowance	(9,440)
Taxable income	2,060
Tax on £2,060 @ 20%	412

This gives an overall tax saving of £(4,600 – 412) = £4,188. This could alternatively be calculated as £9,440 @ 40% = £3,776 plus £2,060 @ 20% = £412 giving the total saving of £4,188.

7.4 Minor children

Income which is directly transferred by a parent to their minor child, or is derived from capital so transferred, remains income of the parent for tax purposes. This applies only to parents, however, and not to any other relatives. Even where a parent is involved, the child's income is not treated as the parent's if it does not exceed £100 (gross) a year.

Chapter roundup

- In a personal income tax computation, bring together income from all sources, splitting the sources into non-savings, savings and dividend income.
- Don't forget to gross up dividends by 100/90 and interest by 100/80.
- Deductible interest is deducted from total income to compute net income.
- All persons are entitled to a personal allowance. It is deducted from net income, first against non savings income, then against savings income and lastly against dividend income. The personal allowance is reduced by £1 for every £2 that adjusted net income exceeds £100,000 and can be reduced to nil.
- Taxpayers born between 6 April 1938 and 5 April 1948 are entitled to an higher personal allowance of £10,500 and taxpayers born before 6 April 1938 are entitled to a higher personal allowance of £10,660. The allowance is reduced by £1 for every £2 that adjusted net income exceeds £26,100 but is generally not reduced below the amount of the personal allowance available for taxpayers born after 5 April 1948.
- Income tax is worked out on taxable income. First tax non-savings income, then savings income and then dividend income.
- There is an income tax charge to recover child benefit if the recipient or their partner has adjusted net income over £50,000 in a tax year.
- Tax reducers reduce tax on income at a set rate of relief.
- From tax liability, first deduct the tax credit on dividend income and any income tax suffered at source to arrive at tax payable. The tax credit on dividend income cannot be repaid if it exceeds the tax liability calculated so far. Other tax suffered at source can be repaid.
- Higher rate taxpayers pay an effective rate of 25% on their dividend income. Additional rate taxpayer pay an effective rate of 30.555% on their dividend income.
- Spouses, civil partners and children are all separate taxpayers. There are special rules to prevent parents from exploiting a child's personal allowance.

Quick quiz

1. At what rates is income tax charged on non-savings income?
2. Is UK rental income savings income?
3. List three types of savings income that are received by individuals net of 20% tax.
4. How is tax relief given on interest payable on a loan to invest in a partnership?
5. How is dividend income taxed?
6. What is the amount below which a child's income deriving from a parental disposition (ie gift) is not taxed as the parents' income?

Answers to quick quiz

1 Income tax on non-savings income is charged at 20% below the basic rate limit, at 40% between the basic rate limit and the higher rate limit and at 45% above the higher rate limit.

2 No. It is non-savings income.

3 Bank and building society interest, interest paid on loan stock which is not listed on a recognised stock exchange, savings income from non discretionary trusts.

4 Interest payable on a loan to invest in a partnership is deductible from total income to compute net income.

5 Dividend income below the basic rate limit is taxed at 10%. Dividend income between the basic rate limit and the higher rate limit is taxed at 32.5% and at 37.5% above the higher rate limit. A tax credit of 10% is available.

6 £100

Now try the question below from the Exam Question Bank

Number	Level	Marks	Time
Q1	Introductory	20	36 mins

Pensions and other tax efficient investment products

Topic list	Syllabus reference
1 Types of pension scheme and membership	A1(a)B6
2 Contributing to a pension scheme	A1(a)B6
3 Receiving benefits from pension arrangements	A1(a)B6
4 Registration of pension schemes	A1(g)(iii)
5 The enterprise investment scheme (EIS)	A1(g)(i)
6 The seed enterprise investment scheme (SEIS)	A1(g)(i)
7 Venture capital trusts (VCTs)	A1(g)(ii)

Introduction

In the previous chapter we looked at the basic income tax computation. We now look at some of the tax reliefs given to encourage individuals to invest in certain types of savings.

The most important type of saving is through pensions. Tax relief is given on contributions to pension schemes, and the schemes themselves can grow tax free. There are limits on the amounts that can be invested, and breach of these limits will incur tax charges. Failure to comply with the rules will also result in tax charges.

Investment in smaller companies is encouraged through the enterprise investment scheme, the seed enterprise investment scheme and venture capital trusts. We saw how relief is given as a tax reducer in the previous chapter, and here we will examine the conditions which must be satisfied before relief is available.

In the next chapter we will look at income from UK property and other investments.

Study guide

		Intellectual level
1	**Income and income tax liabilities in situations involving further overseas aspects and in relation to trusts, and the application of exemptions and reliefs**	
(a)	The contents of the Paper F6 study guide for income tax, under heading:	2
•	B6 The use of exemptions and reliefs in deferring and minimising income tax liabilities	
(g)	The use of exemptions and reliefs in deferring and minimising income tax liabilities:	
(i)	Understand and apply the rules relating to investments in the seed enterprise investment scheme and the enterprise investment scheme	3
(ii)	Understand and apply the rules relating to investments in venture capital trusts	3
(iii)	Explain the conditions that need to be satisfied for pension schemes to be registered by HM Revenue and Customs	2

Exam guide

You may well come across pension contributions or investments under the EIS, under the SEIS, or in VCTs as part of a question. These investments all give tax relief for the amount invested, although the reliefs vary in amount. They are commonly used to mitigate tax liabilities, but you should note that they should be used for in-year tax planning, although there is limited carry back for EIS relief.

Knowledge brought forward from earlier studies

This chapter builds upon the basic knowledge of tax relief for pension contributions necessary in Paper F6. The examiner has identified essential underpinning knowledge from the F6 syllabus which is particularly important that you revise as part of your P6 studies. In this chapter, the relevant topic is:

		Intellectual level
B6	**The use of exemptions and reliefs in deferring and minimising income tax liabilities**	
(a)	Explain and compute the relief given for contributions to personal pension schemes, using the rules applicable from 6 April 2011.	2

There are no changes for 2013/14 from the material you studied at F6 for 2012/13.

EIS, SEIS and VCTs are new topics.

One of the competencies you require to fulfil performance objective 20 of the PER is the ability to assist with tax planning. You can apply the knowledge you obtain from this chapter of the text to help to demonstrate this competence.

1 Types of pension scheme and membership

FAST FORWARD

An employee may be entitled to join their employer's occupational pension scheme. Both employees and the self employed can take out a 'personal pension' with a financial institution such as a bank or building society.

1.1 Types of pension provision

An individual is encouraged by the Government to make financial provision to cover their needs when they reach a certain age. There are state pension arrangements which provide some financial support, but the Government would like an individual not to rely on state provision but to make their own pension provision.

Therefore tax relief is given for such pension provision. This includes relief for contributions to a pension and an exemption from tax on income and gains arising in a pension fund.

1.2 Pension arrangements

An individual may make pension provision in a number of ways.

Key terms

Occupational pension schemes are run by employers for their employees. **Personal pension schemes** are run by financial institutions: anyone may contribute to a personal pension.

Personal pension schemes and the majority of occupational pension schemes are **money purchase schemes**. These are also known as **defined contributions schemes**. The level of pension that the member can draw from such schemes will depend on the investment performance of the money invested.

Some occupational schemes are **final salary schemes**, where the pension depends on the period for which the individual has been a member of the scheme and their salary at the time of retirement. These are also known as **defined benefits schemes**, and are becoming less common due to the high level of contributions required.

An individual may make a number of different pension arrangements depending on their circumstances. For example, they may be a member of an occupational pension scheme and also make pension arrangements independently with a financial provider. If the individual has more than one pension arrangement, the rules we will be looking at in detail later apply to all the pension arrangements they make. For example, **there is a limit on the amount of contributions that the individual can make in a tax year. This limit applies to all the pension arrangements that they make, not *each* of them.**

2 Contributing to a pension scheme

FAST FORWARD

An individual can make tax relievable contributions to their pension arrangements up to the higher of their earnings and £3,600. Contributions to personal pensions are paid net of basic rate tax. Employers normally operate 'net pay' arrangements in respect of contributions to occupational schemes.

2.1 Contributions by a scheme member attracting tax relief

An individual who is **under the age of 75 is entitled to tax relief on their contributions** to a registered pension scheme in a tax year.

The maximum contributions made by an individual in a tax year attracting tax relief is the higher of:

(a) **the individual's UK relevant earnings chargeable to income tax in the year; and**
(b) **the basic amount (set at £3,600 for 2013/14).**

Relevant UK earnings include employment income, trading income, and income from furnished holiday lettings (see later in this Text). If the individual does not have any UK earnings in a tax year, the maximum contribution they can obtain tax relief on is £3,600.

Where an individual contributes to more than one pension scheme, the aggregate of their contributions will be used to give the total amount of tax relief.

There is an interaction between this provision and the annual allowance, which will be discussed later.

2.2 Methods of giving tax relief

2.2.1 Relief given at source

This method will be used where an individual makes a contribution to a pension scheme run by a personal pension provider such as an insurance company.

Relief is given at source by the contributions being deemed to be made net of basic rate tax. This applies whether the individual is an employee, self-employed or not employed at all and whether or not they have taxable income. HMRC then pay the basic rate tax to the pension provider.

Further tax relief is given if the individual is a higher rate or additional rate taxpayer. The relief is given by increasing the basic rate limit and the higher rate limit for the year by the gross amount of contributions for which the taxpayer is entitled to relief.

Question — **Higher rate relief**

Joe was born in 1980. He has earnings of £60,000 in 2013/14. He pays a personal pension contribution of £7,200 (net). He has no other taxable income.

Show Joe's tax liability for 2013/14.

Answer

	Non savings Income
	£
Earnings/Net income	60,000
Less personal allowance	(9,440)
Taxable income	50,560

Tax

	£
£41,010 (W) × 20%	8,202
£9,550 × 40%	3,820
50,560	12,022

Working

Basic rate limit £32,010 + (£7,200 × 100/80) = £41,010

In this question, higher rate relief of 20% has been obtained as non savings income, ordinarily taxed at 40%, has instead been taxed at 20%. Added to the basic rate relief of 20% given at source due to the pension payment being made net, this gives 40% relief.

The effective rate of relief can be higher where dividend income is also received in the year, as the higher rate relief on dividends shifted from higher rate to the basic rate is 22½% (32½% –10%).

2.2.2 Example: rate of tax relief

Adam was born in 1972. He has earnings of £44,750 in 2013/14. He also receives net dividends of £9,000. He is thinking of making a contribution of £7,200 (equivalent of £9,000 gross) to his personal pension. Adam's effective rate of tax saved by making the pension contribution can be found as follows:

	Non savings income	*Dividend income*
	£	£
Earnings	44,750	
Dividends × 100/90		10,000
Net income	44,750	10,000
Less personal allowance	(9,440)	
Taxable income	35,310	10,000

Tax (before contribution)

	£
£32,010 × 20%	6,402
£3,300 × 40%	1,320
£35,310	
£10,000 × 32½%	3,250
45,310	10,972

Tax (after contribution)

	£
£35,310 × 20%	7,062
£5,700 × 10%	570
£41,010 (W)	
£4,300 × 32½%	1,397
45,310	9,029

Basic rate limit £32,010 + (£7,200 × 100/80) = £41,010

The tax saved by increasing the basic rate limit is £1,943 (£10,972 – £9,029). If we add to this the basic rate tax saved by making the contribution net (ie £9,000 – £7,200 = £1,800) the total tax saved is £3,743.

The effective rate of tax relief on the pension contribution is $\frac{£3,743}{£9,000} \times 100$, which is 41.59%.

2.2.3 Adjusted net income

Adjusted net income is net income less the gross amounts of personal pension contributions (and gift aid donations – these are not in your syllabus). **The restrictions on the personal allowance and higher personal allowance are calculated in relation to adjusted net income.**

Question — **Adjusted net income**

Maria was born in 1965. She earns a salary of £116,000 in 2013/14. In January 2014, she made a net personal pension contribution of £5,000.

Compute Maria's income tax liability for 2013/14.

Answer

	Non savings income
	£
Salary/Net income	116,000
Less: personal allowance (W)	(4,565)
Taxable income	111,435

Income tax	£	£
Basic rate £32,010 + (£5,000 × 100/80)	38,260 × 20%	7,652
Higher rate	73,175 × 40%	29,270
	111,435	36,922

Working	£
Net income	116,000
Less: personal pension £5,000 × 100/80	(6,250)
Adjusted net income	109,750
Less: income limit	(100,000)
Excess	9,750
Personal allowance	9,440
Less: half excess £9,750 × ½	(4,875)
	4,565

Where an individual has an adjusted net income between £100,000 and £118,880, the rate of tax on the income between these two amounts will usually be 60%. This is calculated as 40% (the higher rate on income) plus 40% of half (ie 20%) of the excess adjusted net income over £100,000 used to restrict the personal allowance. The individual should consider **making personal pension to reduce adjusted net income to below £100,000.**

2.2.4 Net pay arrangements

An occupational scheme will normally operate net pay arrangements.

In this case, the employer will deduct gross pension contributions from the individual's earnings before operating PAYE. The individual therefore obtains tax relief at their marginal rate of tax without having to make any claim.

Question — **Net pay arrangements**

Maxine was born in 1980. She has taxable earnings of £60,000 in 2013/14. Her employer deducts a pension contribution of £9,000 from these earnings before operating PAYE. She has no other taxable income.

Show Maxine's tax liability for 2013/14.

Answer

	£
Earnings	60,000
Less: pension contribution	(9,000)
Net income	51,000
Less: personal allowance	(9,440)
Taxable income	41,560

Tax

	£
£32,010 × 20%	6,402
£9,550 × 40%	3,820
41,560	10,222

This is the same result as Joe in the question earlier in this Chapter. Joe had received basic rate tax relief of £(9,000 – 7,200) = £1,800 at source, so his overall tax position was £(12,022 – 1,800) = £10,222.

2.3 Contributions not attracting tax relief

An individual can also make contributions to their pension arrangements which do not attract tax relief, for example out of capital. The member must notify the scheme administrator if they make contributions in excess of the higher of their UK relevant earnings and the basic amount.

Such contributions do not count towards the annual allowance limit (discussed below) but will affect the value of the pension fund for the lifetime allowance.

2.4 Employer pension contributions

FAST FORWARD

Employers may make contributions to pension schemes. In certain circumstances employers contributions are spread over a number of years.

Where the active scheme member is an employee, their **employer will often make contributions to their pension scheme**. Such contributions are **exempt benefits** for the employee.

There is **no limit** on the amount of the contributions that may be made by an employer but **they always count towards the annual allowance and will also affect the value of the pension fund for the lifetime allowance** (see further below).

All contributions made by an employer are made gross and the employer will usually obtain tax relief for the contribution by deducting it as an expense in calculating trading profits for the period of account in which the payment is made.

However, HMRC may seek to disallow a contribution which it considers is not a revenue expense or is not made wholly and exclusively for the purposes of the trade.

There are 'spreading provisions' for large contributions, so that part of the contribution is treated as paid in a later period of account.

2.5 Annual allowance

FAST FORWARD

The annual allowance is the limit on the amount that can be paid into a pension scheme each year. If this limit is exceeded there is an income tax charge on the excess contributions. Unused annual allowance can be carried forward for up to three years.

2.5.1 Introduction

The **annual allowance** effectively restricts the amount of tax relievable contributions that can be paid into an individual's pension scheme each year. The amount of the annual allowance for 2013/14 is **£50,000**.

2.5.2 Carry forward of unused annual allowance

Where **an individual is a member of a registered pension scheme** but **does not make contributions of at least the annual allowance in a tax year**, the individual can **carry forward the unused amount of the annual allowance for up to three years.**

The annual allowance in the current tax year is treated as being used first, then any unused annual allowance from earlier years, using the earliest tax year first. In 2011/12, when these carry forward rules were introduced, the annual allowance was also £50,000 and for tax years before 2011/12, a notional £50,000 annual allowance applies to calculate the unused annual allowance in those years.

Ted is a sole trader. His gross contributions to his personal pension scheme have been as follows:

2009/10	£21,000
2010/11	£26,000
2011/12	£46,000
2012/13	£35,000

In 2013/14 Ted has a good trading year and wishes to make a large pension contribution.

(a) What is the maximum gross pension contribution Ted can make in 2013/14 without incurring an annual allowance charge, taking into account any brought forward annual allowance?

(b) If Ted makes a gross personal pension contribution of £53,000 in 2013/14, what are the unused annual allowances he can carry forward to 2014/15?

Answer

(a)

	£
Annual allowance 2013/14	50,000
Annual allowance unused in 2010/11 £(50,000 – 26,000)	24,000
Annual allowance unused in 2011/12 £(50,000 – 46,000)	4,000
Annual allowance unused in 2012/13 £(50,000 – 35,000)	15,000
Maximum gross pension contribution in 2013/14	93,000

Note

The unused allowance from 2009/10 cannot be used in 2013/14 as this is more than three years after 2009/10.

(b)

	£
Annual allowance 2013/14 used in 2013/14	50,000
Annual allowance unused in 2010/11 used in 2013/14	3,000
Contribution in 2013/14	53,000

The remaining £(24,000 – 3,000) = £21,000 of the 2010/11 annual allowance cannot be carried forward to 2014/15 since this is more than three years after 2010/11. The unused annual allowances are therefore £4,000 from 2011/12 and £15,000 from 2012/13 and these are carried forward to 2014/15.

2.5.3 Contributions in excess of annual allowance

FAST FORWARD

An annual allowance charge arises if tax-relievable contributions exceed the available annual allowance.

If tax-relievable pension contributions exceed the annual allowance, there is a charge to income tax based on the individual's taxable income. This will occur if the taxpayer has relevant earnings in excess of the available annual allowance and makes a contribution in excess of the available annual allowance (including any brought forward annual allowance).

The taxpayer is primarily liable for the tax on the excess contribution but in certain circumstances can give notice to the pension scheme for the charge to be payable from the taxpayer's pension benefits fund.

The annual allowance charge is calculated by taxing the excess contribution as an extra amount of income received by the taxpayer. The calculation therefore claws back the tax relief given on the pension contribution.

Annual allowance charge

Jaida was born in 1963. She had employment income of £240,000 in 2013/14. She made a gross personal pension contribution of £80,000 in 2013/14. She does not have any unused annual allowance brought forward. What is Jaida's income tax liability for 2013/14?

Answer

	Non-savings income £
Taxable income (no personal allowance available)	240,000
Tax	
£112,010 (W1) × 20%	22,402
£117,990 × 40%	47,196
£230,000 (W2)	
£10,000 × 45%	4,500
£240,000 (W2)	
£30,000 (W3) × 45%	13,500
	87,598

Workings

1 Basic rate limit £32,010 + £80,000 (gross contribution) = £112,010

2 Higher rate limit £150,000 + £80,000 (gross contribution) = £230,000

3 Excess pension contribution £(80,000 – 50,000) = £30,000

Exam focus point

The examiner has said that questions involving the annual allowance charge will be kept straightforward. For example, no question will be set where there is a partial restriction of the personal allowance or where the annual allowance charge arises in a different tax year to that in which the related tax relief on the pension contributions was given.

3 Receiving benefits from pension arrangements

FAST FORWARD The maximum value that can be built up in a pension fund is known as the lifetime allowance.

3.1 The lifetime allowance

An individual is not allowed to build up an indefinitely large pension fund. **There is a maximum value for a pension fund (for money purchase arrangements) or for the value of benefits (for defined benefits arrangements). This is called the lifetime allowance.**

The amount of the lifetime allowance in 2013/14 is £1,500,000.

The individual does not have to keep a running total of the value of their pension scheme. Instead, **the lifetime allowance limit is tested only when a benefit crystallisation event occurs**, for example when a member becomes **entitled to a scheme pension** or **a lump sum.**

3.2 Pension benefits

No pension payment can be made before the member reaches normal minimum pension age of 55, unless the member is incapacitated by ill health. **At this age the member may take an income pension** (often called an annuity) **and a lump sum from the pension scheme.**

Pension benefits do not all have to be taken or provided for at one time. After reaching the minimum pension age, an individual may 'vest' the benefits, ie set aside all or part of the pension fund to provide pension benefits. An individual under the age of 75 can usually both make contributions and receive pension benefits.

Up to 25% of the pension fund (for money purchase schemes, or 25% of the value of the benefits for defined benefit schemes) **can be taken as a tax free lump sum**, subject to the lifetime allowance limit (see below). **The remainder is usually used to buy an annuity to provide a pension income.** Pension income is taxable as non savings income.

An alternative to buying an annuity is for the individual to drawdown income from the pension fund, usually subject to an annual maximum amount. This income again is taxable as pension income.

The maximum withdrawal of income that an individual is able to make is capped at 120% of the equivalent annuity that could have been bought with the pension fund value. An individual able to demonstrate that they have a secure pension income for life of at least £20,000 a year can drawdown any amount of income without any annual cap.

3.3 Lifetime allowance charge

3.3.1 Occasions of charge

When a member takes a benefit from a pension scheme, there is usually a benefit crystallisation event so that the value of the pension fund has to be tested against the lifetime allowance for the year in which the event occurs.

In many cases, the lifetime limit will not have been exceeded and there will be no income tax charge. **In some cases, the pension fund will exceed the lifetime allowance and this will give rise to an income tax charge on the excess value of the fund which has been vested to provide either a lump sum or a pension income.** The rate of the charge depends on the type of benefit that will be taken from the excess funds.

3.3.2 Calculation and payment of the lifetime allowance charge

Where funds are vested to provide a lump sum, there will be a **charge to tax at 55% on the value of the lump sum.**

Where the excess funds are vested to provide a pension income, the rate is 25%. In this case, it is necessary to look at the value of the vested funds to work out the tax charge, not the annual value of the pension income that will be provided.

3.3.3 Example: lifetime allowance exceeded

Amy attained the age of 60 on 1 July 2013 and decided to vest her pension benefits on that date. She has a money purchase fund which was valued at £2,300,000 on 1 July 2013. Amy took the maximum tax-free lump sum of £1,500,000 × 25% = £375,000. The balance of the lifetime allowance is £(1,500,000 – 375,000) = £1,125,000 and this is vested to provide pension income benefits from an annuity.

Amy also took the excess of the fund over the lifetime allowance as a lump sum ie £(2,300,000 – 1,500,000) = £800,000.

The tax charge is therefore £800,000 × 55% = £440,000.

4 Registration of pension schemes

In order for the tax advantages described above to apply to a pension scheme, the scheme must be registered with HMRC.

A pension scheme may only be registered if it is an occupational pension scheme or if it is established by certain financial institutions such as insurance companies and banks.

HMRC must register the scheme unless it believes that the information in the application is incorrect or that any accompanying declaration is false.

5 The enterprise investment scheme (EIS)

FAST FORWARD

The enterprise investment scheme, seed enterprise investment scheme and venture capital trusts are designed to help unquoted trading companies raise finance.

Key term

The **enterprise investment scheme (EIS)** is a scheme designed to promote enterprise and investment by helping high-risk, unlisted trading companies raise finance by the issue of shares to individual investors who are unconnected with that company.

5.1 Conditions for relief

Individuals who subscribe for EIS shares are entitled to both income tax and capital gains tax reliefs where certain conditions are satisfied.

5.1.1 The investor

The investor must **subscribe for shares wholly in cash in the company and must not be connected with it. Connection can broadly occur through employment or owning more than 30%** (including holdings of associates ie spouse/civil partner or child, but not a brother or sister) **of the issued ordinary share capital, issued share capital or voting power of the company or a subsidiary.**

The investor must also qualify for the two years prior to and three years after the share issue date or if later, three years from the date trading commences.

5.1.2 The company

The company must have a permanent establishment in the UK throughout the qualifying period for income tax relief. A permanent establishment is either a fixed place of business through which the business of the company is wholly or partly carried on or an agent acting on behalf of the company who has and habitually exercises authority to enter into contracts on behalf of the company.

The company must be unquoted (eg not listed on a recognised stock exchange) and **the funds raised must be used by that company or by a 90% subsidiary in carrying out a qualifying trade.** Qualifying trades broadly include all trades except for certain prohibited trades, including dealing in land, financial activities, legal/accountancy services and property backed activities. Research and development prior to starting a trade also qualifies.

The money raised by the EIS share issue must be used for this purpose within two years of the issue of the shares (or within two years of the commencement of the trade).

The company must have fewer than 250 full-time employees (or their equivalents) on the date of the share issue.

The gross assets of the company must not exceed £15m prior to nor £16m after the investment. The company must not have raised more than £5m in venture capital schemes (EIS, VCT and SEIS) **in the 12 months ending on the date of the investment.**

The company must meet the financial health requirement when the shares are issued. This requirement is that the company is not 'in difficulty' as defined in the Community Guidelines on State Aid for Rescuing and Restructuring Firms in Difficulty (2004/C 244/02).

5.1.3 The shares

Eligible shares are usually any new ordinary shares issued for bona fide commercial reasons which, throughout the period of three years beginning with the date on which they are issued, carry no preferential rights to assets on liquidation of the company. The shares may carry certain preferential rights to dividends but these are limited, for example, the rights to dividends cannot be cumulative.

The shares must be fully paid up at the time of issue and they cannot be redeemable.

5.2 Income tax relief

5.2.1 Tax reducer

Individuals can claim a **tax reducer** (see earlier in this Text) **of the lower of**:

(a) **30% of the amount subscribed for qualifying investments** and
(b) **The individual's tax liability for the year.**

A claim for EIS relief in respect of shares issued by a company in a tax year may by the fifth anniversary of the normal self-assessment filing date for the tax year (ie by 31 January 2020 for an investment made in 2013/14).

5.2.2 Limit for relief

The annual maximum for EIS investments qualifying for income tax relief is £1,000,000, but individuals can invest in excess of this amount if they wish.

The investor may claim to have the shares treated as issued in the previous tax year. When carrying back relief, relief given in the previous year must not exceed overall EIS limit for that year.

5.2.3 Withdrawal of relief

Shares must be held by an investor for at least three years if the income tax relief is not to be withdrawn or reduced if the company was carrying on a qualifying trade at the time of issue. For companies which were preparing to trade at the time of issue, the minimum holding period ends when the company has been carrying on a qualifying trade for three years.

The main reason for the withdrawal of relief will be the sale of the shares by the investor within the three year period mentioned above. The consequences depend on whether the disposal is at arm's length or not:

(a) If the disposal is not a bargain at arm's length the full amount of relief originally obtained is withdrawn.
(b) If the disposal is a bargain at arm's length there is a withdrawal of relief on the consideration received. As the relief was originally given as a tax reduction, the withdrawal of relief must be made at the same rate of tax.

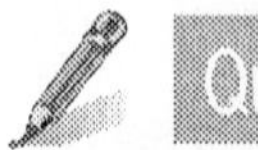

Question — **Withdrawal of EIS relief**

Ted Edwards was born in 1967. He makes a £60,000 EIS investment in 2013/14. His income (all non-savings) for the year is £50,000. In 2014/15, Ted sells the shares (an arm's length bargain) for £50,000. How much EIS relief is withdrawn as a result of the sale of the shares?

Answer

	£
2013/14	
Net income	50,000
Less: personal allowance	(9,440)
Taxable income	40,560
	£
£32,010 × 20%	6,402
£8,550 × 40%	3,420
	9,822
Less: EIS relief: £60,000 × 30% = £18,000, restricted to	(9,822)
Income tax liability	Nil

The effective rate of EIS relief is $\frac{9,822}{60,000} \times 100 = 16.37\%$

2014/15

The sale of the shares for £50,000 as a bargain at arm's length results in the withdrawal of income tax relief in 2013/14 of £8,185 (ie £50,000 × 16.37%).

Although the company must be unlisted when the EIS shares are issued, there is no withdrawal of relief if the company becomes listed, unless there were arrangements in place for the company to cease to be unlisted at the time of issue.

There are anti-avoidance rules to prevent an individual extracting money from the company without disposing of their shares. However, the rules do not apply where the amount is of an insignificant value (eg any amount of £1,000 or under) or if the receipt is returned without unreasonable delay.

5.3 CGT reliefs

Where shares qualify for income tax relief under the EIS there are also special rules that apply to those shares for capital gains purposes:

(a) Where shares are disposed of after the three year period any gain is exempt from CGT. If the shares are disposed of within three years any gain is computed in the normal way.

(b) If EIS shares are disposed of at a loss at any time, the loss is allowable but the acquisition cost of the shares is reduced by the amount of EIS relief attributable to the shares. The loss is eligible for relief against general income (see later in this Text).

Question

Allowable losses

During 2012/13 Martin invested £35,000 in EIS shares and received relief against income tax of £35,000 × 30% = £10,500.

The shares are sold in February 2014 for £15,000. This will lead to a withdrawal of EIS relief of £15,000 × 30% = £4,500. What is the allowable loss for CGT purposes?

Answer

	£	£
Disposal proceeds		15,000
Less: cost	35,000	
EIS relief (10,500 – 4,500)	(6,000)	(29,000)
Allowable loss		(14,000)

If the shares had instead been sold outside the three year relevant period (ie so that there was no withdrawal of income tax relief), the allowable loss would instead be:

	£	£
Disposal proceeds		15,000
Less: cost	35,000	
EIS relief	(10,500)	(24,500)
Allowable loss		(9,500)

EIS reinvestment relief may be available to defer chargeable gains if an individual invests in EIS shares in the period commencing one year before and ending three years after the disposal of the asset (see later in this Text).

6 The seed enterprise investment scheme (SEIS)

Key term

The **seed enterprise investment scheme (SEIS)** is a scheme similar to the EIS scheme but rewards investment in small, start-up unquoted trading companies with a more generous tax reducer.

6.1 Conditions for relief

Individuals who subscribe for SEIS shares are entitled to similar income tax relief (although at a more generous rate) **as subscribers for EIS shares** but the conditions that the company and investor must satisfy are slightly different.

6.1.1 The investor

The investor must not be an employee of the company, but can be a director. This condition must be satisfied during the period starting with the issue of the shares and the third anniversary of the date on which the shares are issued.

The investor must not be connected with the company. Connection can broadly occur through employment or owning more than 30% (including holdings of associates ie spouse/civil partner or child, but not a brother or sister) **of the issued ordinary share capital, issued share capital or voting power of the company or a subsidiary**. This condition must be satisfied during the period starting with the incorporation of the company and the third anniversary of the date on which the shares are issued.

6.1.2 The company

To obtain the relief, the following conditions must be satisfied in respect of the company:

(a) **The company must be unquoted** (eg not listed on a recognised stock exchange), **have a permanent establishment in the UK, and meet the financial health requirement of not being in difficulty.**

(b) **The total value of the company's gross assets must not exceed £200,000 immediately before the issue of the shares.**

(c) **The company must have fewer than 25 full-time employees on the date of the share issue.**

(d) **The company must not have raised more than £150,000 from SEIS investments in a three-year period.**

(e) **The funds raised must be used by the company, or a 90% subsidiary, to carry out a new qualifying trade.** The meaning of qualifying trade is the same as that for the EIS and excludes dealing in land and property backed activities, financial activities, and providing legal or accountancy services. A new qualifying trade is one which has been carried on for less than two years at the date of issue of the shares. The company must not have carried on any other trade before this new trade.

(f) **The funds must be used within three years of the issue of the shares.**

6.1.3 The shares

The share requirements are the same as for EIS investments, ie the investor must subscribe in cash for new ordinary shares for genuine commercial reasons, although shares with limited preferential rights to dividends can still be qualifying shares.

6.2 Income tax relief

6.2.1 Tax reducer

Individuals can claim a **tax reducer** (see earlier in this Text) **of the lower of**:

(a) **50% of the amount subscribed for qualifying investments** and
(b) **The individual's tax liability for the year**.

A claim for SEIS relief in respect of shares issued by a company in a tax year may by the fifth anniversary of the normal self-assessment filing date for the tax year (ie by 31 January 2020 for an investment made in 2013/14).

6.2.2 Limit for relief

The annual maximum SEIS investments qualifying for income tax relief is £100,000 (ie the maximum tax reducer is £50,000).

The investor may claim to have the shares treated as issued in the previous tax year. When carrying back relief, relief given in the previous year must not exceed overall SEIS limit for that year.

Question EIS and SEIS

In 2013/14 Arthur invested £40,000 in a qualifying EIS company, and £20,000 in a qualifying SEIS company. He had pension income of £120,000 in 2013/14. Calculate Arthur's income tax liability for 2013/14. He does not wish to treat any shares as issued in 2012/13.

Answer

	£
2013/14	
Taxable income(no personal allowance)	120,000
£32,010 × 20%	6,402
£87,990 × 40%	35,196
	41,598
Less: EIS relief: £40,000 × 30%	(12,000)
Less: SEIS relief: £20,000 × 50%	(10,000)
Income tax liability	19,598

Remember that if the individual is entitled to more than one tax reducer, the VCT reducer is deducted first, then the EIS reducer and finally the SEIS reducer (see earlier in this Text).

6.2.3 Withdrawal of relief

As for EIS, **shares must be held by an investor for at least three years** if the income tax relief is not to be withdrawn. Where the disposal is a bargain at arm's length, the amount withdrawn will usually be 50% of the amount received for the shares (as for EIS relief it will be less if full relief was not given because the taxpayer's tax liability was less than the amount subscribed for). Where the disposal is not at arm's length, the whole of the relief given is withdrawn.

Exam focus point

Although EIS and SEIS investments carry attractive tax reliefs remember that they are high risk investments.

6.3 CGT reliefs

Where shares qualify for income tax relief under the SEIS there are also special rules that apply to those shares for capital gains purposes in the same way as for EIS shares (see section 5.3 above).

Exam focus point

Individuals are able to claim an exemption from capital gains tax on gains made in 2013/14 if a subscription is made in SEIS shares in that year. This exemption is excluded from the P6 syllabus.

7 Venture capital trusts (VCTs)

Key term

Venture capital trusts (VCTs) are listed companies which invest in unquoted trading companies and meet certain conditions.

7.1 Conditions for relief

Individuals who subscribe for VCT shares are entitled to both income tax and capital gains tax reliefs where certain conditions are satisfied.

7.1.1 The investor

The VCT scheme differs from EIS as the individual investor invests directly in a quoted VCT company that itself invests in higher risk unquoted companies. The investor therefore spreads their risk.

7.1.2 The company

A Venture Capital Trust is a company, whose shares are admitted to trading on a regulated European market, **that invests in small unquoted EIS-type companies.**

To be HMRC approved, a VCT must satisfy (and continue to satisfy) the following conditions:

(a) Its income comes wholly or mainly from shares or securities

(b) At least 70% of its investments are in shares in qualifying holdings. Qualifying holdings are broadly holdings in unquoted companies carrying on qualifying trades in the UK.

(c) At least 70% of its holdings must be in ordinary shares and no one holding can amount to more than 15% of its total investments

(d) It has not kept more than 15% of its income from shares and securities ie it must distribute 85% of its income from shares and securities

The companies invested in must have fewer than 250 full-time employees (or their equivalents) on the date of the share issue.

The money invested in a company by the VCT must be used wholly for the purposes of the company's qualifying trade within two years.

The gross assets of the company invested in must not exceed £15m prior to nor £16m after the investment. The company must not have raised more than £5m in venture capital schemes in the 12 months ending on the date of the investment.

The companies invested in must have a permanent establishment in the UK at all times from the issue of the VCT shares to the time in question.

The companies invested in must meet the financial health requirement when the VCT shares are issued.

7.2 Tax reliefs

An individual investing in a VCT obtains the following tax benefits on a maximum qualifying investment of £200,000:

- **A tax reducer** (see earlier in this Text) **of the lower of 30% of the amount invested and the individual's income tax liability for the year.**
- **Dividends received are tax-free income.**
- **Capital gains on the sale of shares in the VCT are exempt from CGT (and losses are not allowable).**

7.3 Withdrawal of relief

If the shares in the VCT are disposed of within five years of issue the following consequences ensue:

- **If the shares are not disposed of under a bargain made at arm's length, the tax reduction is withdrawn.**
- **If the shares are disposed of under a bargain made at arm's length, the tax reduction is withdrawn, up to the disposal proceeds × 30%.**

If a VCT's approval is withdrawn within five years of the issue, any tax reduction given is withdrawn.

Note that there is no minimum holding period requirement for the benefits of tax-free dividends and CGT exemption.

Chapter roundup

- An employee may be entitled to join their employer's occupational pension scheme. Both employees and the self employed can take out a 'personal pension' with a financial institution such as a bank or building society.
- An individual can make tax relievable contributions to their pension arrangements up to the higher of their earnings and £3,600. Contributions to personal pensions are paid net of basic rate tax. Employers normally operate 'net pay' arrangements in respect of contributions to occupational schemes.
- Employers may make contributions to pension schemes. In certain circumstances employers contributions are spread over a number of years.
- The annual allowance is the limit on the amount that can be paid into a pension scheme each year. If this limit is exceeded there is an income tax charge on the excess contributions. Unused annual allowance can be carried forward for up to three years.
- An annual allowance charge arises if tax-relievable contributions exceed the available annual allowance.
- The maximum value that can be built up in a pension fund is known as the lifetime allowance.
- The enterprise investment scheme, seed enterprise investment scheme and venture capital trusts are designed to help unquoted trading companies raise finance.

Quick quiz

1. What are the two types of occupational pension scheme?
2. What is the maximum lump sum that can be taken on retirement (lifetime allowance not exceeded)?
3. What is the limit on contributions to an registered pension scheme?
4. What are the consequences of the total of employee and employer contributions exceeding the annual allowance?
5. What are the consequences of exceeding the lifetime allowance?
6. What income tax relief is available in respect of investments under the enterprise investment scheme for investments in 2013/14?
7. What is the maximum tax reducer available for investment by an individual under the seed enterprise investment scheme in 2013/14?

Answers to quick quiz

1. Occupational pension schemes may be final salary schemes or money purchase schemes.
2. 25% of the fund.
3. Higher of relevant earnings and the basic amount (£3,600).
4. The excess is subject to the annual allowance charge on the employee. (Any contributions by the employee which were not eligible for tax relief are ignored.)
5. The excess is charged at 55% (if taken as a lump sum) or 25% (if taken as a pension).
6. EIS income tax relief is tax reducer up to 30% of amount subscribed up to £1,000,000.
7. £50,000

Now try the question below from the Exam Question Bank

Number	Level	Marks	Time
Q2	Introductory	16	29 mins

Property and other investment income

Topic list	Syllabus reference
1 UK property business	A1(a)B4
2 Furnished holiday lettings	A1(a)B4
3 Rent a room relief	A1(a)B4
4 Accrued income scheme	A1(e)(ii)
5 Pre-owned assets	A1(e)(i)
6 Trust income	A1(e)(iv)

Introduction

In the previous chapters we have covered the income tax computation, including tax reliefs on certain investments.

This chapter starts with the taxation of income arising from the letting of property in the UK. It looks at the basis of assessment of such income and at the computation of assessable profits and losses, and then covers the special rules for furnished holiday lettings and the rent a room relief.

The chapter then covers the accrued income scheme and pre-owned assets.

Finally, it deals with the taxation of trust income received by beneficiaries.

The following chapters will deal with income from employment and self-employment.

Study guide

		Intellectual level
1	**Income and income tax liabilities in situations involving further overseas aspects and in relation to trusts, and the application of exemptions and reliefs**	
(a)	The contents of the Paper F6 study guide for income tax, under headings:	2
•	B4 Property and investment income	
(e)	Property and investment income:	3
(i)	Assess the tax implications of pre-owned assets	
(ii)	Recognise income subject to the accrued income scheme	
(iv)	Income from trusts and settlements: Understand the income tax position of trust beneficiaries	

Exam guide

The computation of income from a UK property business is a generally straight forward matter, but you need to look out for the special areas of lease premiums, furnished holiday lettings and rent a room relief.

You need to watch out for the accrued income scheme if fixed interest securities are bought and sold.

The rules for pre-owned assets effectively stop inheritance tax mitigation schemes where the donor managed to give away property but still retain a benefit.

Although you are not required to know how to calculate the income tax liability of trustees, you need to know how the trust income is taxed in a beneficiary's hands.

Knowledge brought forward from earlier studies

Property income was dealt with at the F6 level. The rest of the material in this chapter will be new to you at the P6 level.

There are no changes in 2013/14 from 2012/13 in the material you have studied in F6.

1 UK property business

1.1 Profits of a UK property business

FAST FORWARD

Income from a UK property business is computed for tax years on an accruals basis.

One of the competencies you require to fulfil performance objective 19 of the PER is the ability to evaluate and compute taxes payable. You can apply the knowledge you obtain from this section of the text to help to demonstrate this competence.

Income from land and buildings in the UK, including caravans and houseboats which are not moved, is taxed as non-savings income.

(a) **A taxpayer (or a partnership) with UK rental income is treated as running a business, their 'UK property business'. All the rents and expenses for all properties are pooled, to give a single profit or loss. Profits and losses are computed in the same way as trading profits are computed for tax purposes**, on an accruals basis.

Expenses will often include rent payable where a landlord is himself renting the land which he, in turn, lets to sub tenants. For individuals, interest on loans to buy or improve properties is treated as an expense (on an accruals basis). The rules on post-cessation receipts and expenses apply to UK property businesses in the same way that they apply to trades (see later in this Text). Relief is available for irrecoverable rent as an impairment loss.

(b) **Capital allowances are given on plant and machinery used in the UK property business in the same way as they are given for a trading business** with an accounting date of 5 April. Capital allowances are not normally available on plant or machinery used in a dwelling. As a taxpayer who lets property furnished cannot claim capital allowances on the furniture, he can instead claim a **wear and tear allowance**.

Under such a claim, the actual cost of furniture is ignored and instead, **an annual deduction is given of 10% of rents**. The rents are first reduced by amounts which are paid by the landlord but are normally a tenant's burden. These amounts include any **water rates** and **council tax** paid by the landlord.

If plant and machinery is used partly in a dwelling house and partly for other purposes a just and reasonable apportionment of the expenditure can be made to determine the capital allowances that are available.

1.2 Losses of UK property business

FAST FORWARD

A loss on a UK property business is carried forward to set against future profits from the UK property business.

A loss from a UK property business is carried forward to set against the first future profits from the UK property business. It may be carried forward until the UK property business ends, but it must be used as soon as possible.

Question — UK property income

Over the last few years, Peter has purchased several properties in Manchester as 'buy to let' investments.

5 Whitby Ave is let out furnished at £500 per month. A tenant moved in on 1 March 2013 but left unexpectedly on 1 May 2014 having paid rent only up to 31 December 2013. The tenant left no forwarding address.

17 Bolton Rd has been let furnished to the same tenant for a number of years at £800 per month.

A recent purchase, 27 Turner Close has been let unfurnished since 1 August 2013 at £750 per month. Before then it was empty whilst Peter redecorated it after its purchase in March 2013.

Peter's expenses during 2013/14 are:

	No 5	*No 17*	*No 27*
	£	£	£
Insurance	250	250	200
Letting agency fees	–	–	100
Repairs	300	40	–
Redecoration	–	–	500

No 27 was in a fit state to let when Peter bought it but he wanted to redecorate the property as he felt this would allow him to achieve a better rental income.

Water rates and council tax are paid by the tenants. Peter made a UK property business loss in 2012/13 of £300.

Peter claims the wear and tear allowance where relevant.

What is Peter's taxable property income for 2013/14?

Answer

2013/14	No 5 £	No 17 £	No 27 £
Accrued income			
12 × £500	6,000		
12 × £800		9,600	
8 × £750			6,000
Less:			
Insurance	(250)	(250)	(200)
Letting agency fees			(100)
Impairment loss (irrecoverable rent)			
3 × £500	(1,500)		
Repairs	(300)	(40)	
Redecoration (N)			(500)
Wear and tear allowance			
£(6,000 – 1,500) × 10%	(450)		
£9,600 × 10%		(960)	
Property Income	3,500	8,350	5,200

	£
Total property income	17,050
Less: loss b/fwd	(300)
Taxable property income for 2013/14	16,750

Note: The redecoration of No.27 is an allowable expense. This is an example of the application of the case of *Odeon Associated Theatres Ltd v Jones 1971* (covered in more detail later in this Text) which showed that the cost of initial repairs to remedy normal wear and tear of a recently acquired asset was an allowable expense. This contrasts with the case of *Law Shipping v. CIR 1921* where the cost of initial repairs to improve an asset recently acquired to make it fit to earn profits was disallowable capital expenditure. The key point in relation to No. 27 is that it was fit state to let when acquired.

1.3 Premiums on leases

FAST FORWARD

Part of the premium received on the grant of a short lease is taxed as rent.

When a premium or similar consideration is received on the grant (that is, by a landlord to a tenant) **of a short lease (50 years or less), part of the premium is treated as rent received in the year of grant.** A lease is considered to end on the date when it is most likely to terminate.

The premium taxed as rental income is the whole premium, less 2% of the premium for each complete year of the lease, except the first year. This is shown in the following formula:

Formula to learn

Premium	P
Less: 2% × (n–1) × P	(a)
Taxable as income	X

This rule does not apply on the **assignment** of a lease (ie one tenant selling their entire interest in the property to another).

1.4 Premiums paid by traders

Where a trader pays a premium for a lease, he may deduct an amount from his taxable trading profits in each year of the lease. The amount deductible is the figure treated as rent received by the landlord divided by the number of years of the lease.

1.5 Example: deduction for premium paid by trader

On 1 July 2013 Bryony, a trader, pays Scott, the landlord, a premium of £30,000 for a ten year lease on a shop. Bryony makes up accounts to 31 December each year.

Scott is taxable on property income in 2013/14 of £30,000 – (£30,000 × (10 – 1) × 2%) = £24,600.

Bryony can therefore deduct £24,600/10 = £2,460 in each of the ten years of the lease. She starts with the accounts year in which the lease starts (year ended 31 December 2013) and apportions the relief to the nearest month. Her deduction for the year ended 31 December 2013 (basis period for 2013/14) is therefore:

1 July 2013 to 31 December 2013: 6/12 × £2,460	£1,230

1.6 Real Estate Investment Trusts (REITs)

Property companies may operate as **Real Estate Investment Trusts** (REITs).

REITs can elect for their property income (and gains) to be exempt from corporation tax and must withhold basic rate (20%) tax from distributions paid to shareholders (who cannot own more than 10% of a REIT's shares) out of these profits. These distributions are taxed as property income, not as dividends.

Distributions by REITs out of other income (ie not property income or gains) are taxed as dividends in the normal way.

2 Furnished holiday lettings

FAST FORWARD

Special rules apply to income from furnished holiday lettings. Whilst the income is taxed as normal as property business income, the letting is treated as if it were a trade. Capital allowances are available on the furniture and the income is relevant earnings for pension purposes. However, only carry forward trade loss relief is available.

One of the competencies you require to fulfil performance objective 20 of the PER is the ability to assist with tax planning. You can apply the knowledge you obtain from this section of the text to help to demonstrate this competence.

There are special rules for furnished holiday lettings (FHLs). The letting is treated as if it were a trade. This means that, although the income is taxed as income from a property business, the provisions which apply to actual trades also apply to furnished holiday lettings.

(a) Capital allowances are available on furniture instead of the 10% wear and tear allowance.

(b) The income from a UK furnished holiday lettings business qualifies as relevant earnings for pension relief (see earlier in this Text).

(c) Capital gains tax rollover relief, entrepreneurs' relief and relief for gifts of business assets are available (see later in this Text).

However, losses from FHLs are not treated as trade losses for relief against general income, early years loss relief and terminal loss relief. If a loss arises on a FHL, the only trade loss relief available is carry forward loss relief by deduction from the first available future profits of the FHL. Trading loss reliefs are dealt with later in this Text.

Note, however, that the basis period rules for trades do not apply, and the profits or losses must be computed for tax years.

A FHL must be situated in the UK or in another state within the European Economic Area. Separate computations must be made for a UK furnished holiday lettings business and a EEA furnished holiday lettings business (which consists of lettings in one or more EEA countries other than the UK).

Exam focus point

The examiner has stated that any question in the exam would make it clear whether or not a property was situated in the EEA.

The letting must be of furnished accommodation made on a **commercial basis with a view to the realisation of profit**. The property must also satisfy the following three conditions.

(a) **The availability condition** – during the **relevant period**, the accommodation is available for **commercial let** as **holiday accommodation** to the **public** generally, for **at least 210 days**.

(b) **The letting condition** – during the **relevant period**, the accommodation is **commercially let** as holiday accommodation to members of the public **for at least 105 days** (the days let exclude any days that are longer term occupation as defined in condition (c) below).

If the **landlord has more than one FHL**, at least one of which satisfies the 105 day rule ('qualifying holiday accommodation') and at least one of which does not, ('the underused accommodation'), they may elect to **average the occupation of the qualifying holiday accommodation and any or all of the underused accommodation**. If the average of occupation is at least 105 days, the underused accommodation will be treated as qualifying holiday accommodation.

Exam focus point

It is possible to make an election so that a rental property continues to qualify as a furnished holiday letting for up to two years after the 105 day test ceases to be met. This election is not examinable.

(c) **The pattern of occupation condition** – during the **relevant period**, **not more that 155 days fall during periods of longer term occupation**. Longer term occupation is defined as a continuous period of more than 31 days during which the accommodation is in the same occupation unless there are abnormal circumstances.

If someone has a UK furnished holiday lettings business and other UK lettings, **draw up two income statements as if they had two separate property businesses**. This is so that the profits and losses can be identified for the special rules which apply to FHLs. The same rule also applies where someone has an EEA furnished holiday lettings business and other overseas lettings.

3 Rent a room relief

FAST FORWARD

The first £4,250 of rent received from letting a room or rooms in a main residence is tax free.

One of the competencies you require to fulfil performance objective 20 of the PER is the ability to assist with tax planning. You can apply the knowledge you obtain from this section of the text to help to demonstrate this competence.

If an individual lets a room or rooms, furnished, in his or her main residence as living accommodation, a special exemption may apply.

The limit on the exemption is gross rents (before any expenses or capital allowances) of £4,250 a year. This limit is halved if any other person (including the first person's spouse/civil partner) also received income from renting accommodation in the property while the property was the first person's main residence.

If gross rents (plus balancing charges arising because of capital allowances in earlier years) **are not more than the limit, the rents** (and balancing charges) **are wholly exempt from income tax** and expenses and capital allowances are ignored. However, the taxpayer may claim to ignore the exemption, for example to generate a loss by taking into account both rent and expenses.

If gross rents exceed the limit, the taxpayer will be taxed in the ordinary way, ignoring the rent a room scheme, unless he elects for the 'alternative basis'. If he so elects, he will be taxable on gross receipts plus balancing charges less £4,250 (or £2,125 if the limit is halved), with no deductions for expenses or capital allowances.

An election to ignore the exemption or an election for the alternative basis must be made by the 31 January which is 22 months from the end of the tax year concerned.

An election to ignore the exemption applies only for the tax year for which it is made, but an election for the alternative basis remains in force until it is withdrawn or until a year in which gross rents do not exceed the limit.

Exam focus point

Note the different elections carefully and the relevant time limits.

Question

Rent a room relief

Sylvia owns a house near the sea in Norfolk. She has a spare bedroom and during 2013/14 this was let to a chef working at a nearby restaurant for £85 per week which includes the cost of heating, lighting etc.

Sylvia estimates that each year her lodger costs her an extra £50 on gas, £25 on electricity and £50 on buildings insurance. The wear and tear allowance applicable under the normal method would be £435.

How much property income must Sylvia pay tax on?

Answer

Sylvia's gross rents are above the rent a room limit. Therefore she has the following choices:

(1) Under the normal method (no election needed), she can be taxed on her actual profit:

	£
Rental income	4,420
Less expenses (50 + 25 + 50 + 435)	(560)
	3,860

(2) Under the 'alternative basis' (elect for rent a room relief):

Total rental income of £85 × 52 = £4,420 exceeds £4,250 limit so taxable income is £170 (ie 4,420 – 4,250) if rent a room relief claimed.

Sylvia would be advised to claim the 'alternative basis'.

4 Accrued income scheme

FAST FORWARD

The accrued income scheme taxes interest that arose up to the date that a security was sold cum interest and gives relief for interest arising between the sale and next interest payment date for sales ex interest.

If the owner of securities sells them before a certain date, he will not be entitled to the next interest payment on them. The new owner will receive it. This is called selling **cum interest.** However, the sale proceeds will include interest accrued to the date of sale.

If securities are sold after a certain date, they are sold **ex interest** and the original owner is entitled to the whole of the next interest payment despite the fact that they have sold the securities to a new owner. This time, the sale proceeds will exclude interest accruing after the date of sale.

Under the **accrued income scheme**, where **securities are transferred cum interest, the accrued interest reflected in the value of securities is taxed separately as savings income. The seller is treated as entitled to the proportion of interest which has accrued since the last interest payment. The buyer is entitled to relief against the interest they receive.** This relief is equal to the amount assessable on the seller.

Conversely, **where the transfer is ex interest, the seller will receive the whole of the next interest payment. He will be entitled to relief for the amount of interest assessed on the purchaser. The purchaser is treated as entitled to the proportion of the interest accrued between the sale and the next payment date and it is taxed as savings income.**

The accrued income scheme does not apply where the seller:

- carries on a trade and the sale is taken into account in computing trading profits
- did not hold securities with a nominal value exceeding £5,000 during the tax year in which the interest period ends
- was not resident in the UK during any part of the period in question (see later in this Text)
- is taxed on the interest under the manufactured payment rules (not examinable).

Question — **Accrued income scheme**

Nigel bought £10,000 5% Loan Stock many years ago. Interest is payable on 30 June and 31 December each year. Nigel sells the loan stock to Evie on 30 November 2013 cum interest.

What are the amounts assessable for Nigel and Evie in respect of the loan stock for 2013/14?

Answer

Nigel

	£
Interest paid 30.6.13	
£10,000 × 5% × 6/12	250
Accrued interest deemed received 31.12.13	
£10,000 × 5% × 5/12	208
Total assessable	458

Evie

	£
Interest paid 31.12.13	
£10,000 × 5% × 6/12	250
Less relief for accrued interest	
£10,000 × 5% × 5/12	(208)
Total assessable (ie 1 month's interest)	42

5 Pre-owned assets

FAST FORWARD There is an income tax charge on the use of pre-owned assets such as land and chattels.

There is an income tax charge on the annual benefit of using or enjoying certain assets that were once owned by the user. The charge does not apply if the asset was sold to an unconnected person, or if the proceeds were not money or readily convertible assets.

The charge applies to:

- **Land**: the taxable amount is **the annual rental value of the land less any amount paid by the individual for the use of the land**
- **Chattels**, such as works of art: the taxable amount is **the value of the chattel multiplied by the official rate of interest less any amount paid by the individual for the use of the chattel, and**
- **Intangible property**, such as cash and insurance policies, held in a trust where the settlor can benefit: the taxable amount is **the value of the property multiplied by the official rate of interest, less any income or capital gains tax paid by the settlor in respect of that property**

The property is valued at the date the asset falls within the scope of the legislation. Land and chattels are valued every 5 years, at the start of the tax year in which the relevant anniversary falls. So if a chattel first comes within the charge on 17 May 2013 it must be valued at that date and then on 6 April 2018.

There is no charge if the taxable amount is £5,000 or less. If this de minimis limit is exceeded the full amount is taxable.

There is no charge if the disposition falls within the 'gifts with reservation' rules so that the asset is treated as part of the taxpayer's estate for IHT purposes (see later in this Text). **A taxpayer can choose to disapply the income tax charge by electing that the disposition should be treated as a gift with reservation**. The election must usually be made by 31 January following the first year in which the charge arises, by 31 January 2015 for the charge first arising in 2013/14.

There are various other exemptions including:

(a) transactions at arms length
(b) gifts between spouses
(c) deeds of variation.

6 Trust income

FAST FORWARD

Income from trusts must be grossed up by either 100/55 (discretionary trusts) or by 100/80 or 100/90 (interest in possession trusts).

A trust is a vehicle in which assets are legally owned by the trustees for the benefit of the beneficiaries.

There are **two types of trust for income tax purposes**:

(a) An **interest in possession trust** (a 'life interest' trust) where the income must be paid out to the beneficiary (often called the life tenant).

(b) A **discretionary trust** where the income is distributed at the trustees' discretion.

Income from discretionary trusts is received net of 45% tax. Gross it up in the income tax computation by multiplying by 100/55 and give credit for the tax already suffered when working out the final amount of tax payable. Such income is always treated as non-savings income.

If income from an interest in possession trust is paid out of the trust's non-savings income or savings income, it will be received by the beneficiary net of 20% tax and must be grossed up by multiplying by 100/80. If it is paid out of dividend income it must be grossed up by multiplying by 100/90. This tax credit cannot be repaid. Each type of income is then taxed on the beneficiary under the normal rules.

If a **minor beneficiary** receives income from a **trust set up by a parent**, then under the anti-avoidance rules the income is **taxed as the parent's income**. As we saw earlier, there is a £100 de minimis limit.

Question — Income from trusts

Victoria was born in 1970. She received the following income in 2013/14.

	£
Building society interest (received net)	6,200
Dividends	2,250
Income from discretionary trust	6,875
Income from life interest trust	800

The income from the life interest trust was paid out of the trust's property business income.

What income tax is payable by/repayable to Victoria?

Answer

	Non-savings income	Savings income	Dividend income	Total
	£	£	£	£
Building society interest (× 100/80)		7,750		
Dividends (× 100/90)			2,500	
Income from discretionary trust (× 100/55)	12,500			
Income from life interest trust (× 100/80)	1,000			
Net income	13,500	7,750	2,500	23,750
Less: PA	(9,440)			
Taxable income	4,060	7,750	2,500	14,310

		£
Tax on non savings income	£4,060 × 20%	812
Tax on savings income	£7,750 × 20%	1,550
Tax on dividend income	£2,500 × 10%	250
		2,612
Less: Dividend tax credits		(250)
Tax on building society interest		(1,550)
Discretionary trust		(5,625)
Life interest trust		(200)
Income tax repayable		(5,013)

Exam focus point

Although you need to know the rate of tax deducted from income distributions from trusts, you do not need to know how to calculate the trustees' income tax liability.

Chapter roundup

- Income from a UK property business is computed for tax years on an accruals basis.
- A loss on a UK property business is carried forward to set against future profits from the UK property business.
- Part of the premium received on the grant of a short lease is taxed as rent.
- Special rules apply to income from furnished holiday lettings. Whilst the income is taxed as normal as property business income, the letting is treated as if it were a trade. Capital allowances are available on the furniture and UK income is relevant earnings for pension purposes. However, only carry forward trade loss relief is available.
- The first £4,250 of rent received from letting a room or rooms in a main residence is tax free.
- The accrued income scheme taxes interest that arose up to the date that a security was sold cum interest and gives relief for interest arising between the sale and next interest payment date for sales ex interest.
- There is an income tax charge on the use of pre-owned assets such as land and chattels.
- Income from trusts must be grossed up by either 100/55 (discretionary trusts) or by 100/80 or 100/90 (interest in possession trusts).

Quick quiz

1 Describe the 10% wear and tear allowance.

2 What are the conditions for a letting to be a furnished holiday letting?

3 What are the tax consequences of selling fixed interest stock cum interest one month after the normal interest payment date?

4 Michela is a beneficiary of a discretionary trust. In 2013/14, she receives £495 income from a trust.

How much does she enter as the gross amount in her tax return? Is it savings or non-savings income?

Answers to quick quiz

1 10% wear and tear – cost of furniture ignored
– annual deduction of 10% of rents (less water rates and council tax)

2 FHL is – available for letting at least 210 days per tax year
– actually let at least 105 days per tax year
– not more than 155 days fall during periods of longer occupation (continuous period of more than 31 days).

3 The sale price of the stock will reflect the fact that one month's worth of interest is included in the price. This amount is excluded from the proceeds but is taxed as interest (ie savings income).

4 $£495 \times \frac{100}{55}$ = £900 gross. Non-savings income.

Now try the question below from the Exam Question Bank

Number	Level	Marks	Time
Q3	Introductory	25	45 mins

Employment income

4

Topic list	Syllabus reference
1 Employment income	A1(a)B2
2 Taxable benefits	A1(a)B2
3 Exempt benefits	A1(a)B2
4 Allowable deductions	A1(a)B2
5 Personal service companies	A1(c)(iv), A2(b)(vi)
6 National insurance for employers and employees	A6(a)F1,F2

Introduction

In the previous chapters we have looked at the basic income tax computation and the taxation of investments.

Most people have jobs, which pay them wages or salaries. They may also get other benefits from their employers and/or they may pay expenses connected with their employment. In this chapter, we see how to work out the basic employment income they must pay tax on.

We also look at the rules for personal service companies, where the taxpayer is deemed to receive employment income even if he has routed his services through a company.

We conclude with a study of the national insurance contributions payable in respect of employees.

In the next chapter we will look at share options and share incentives, and at lump sum receipts.

Study guide

		Intellectual level
1	**Income and income tax liabilities in situations involving further overseas aspects and in relation to trusts, and the application of exemptions and reliefs**	
(a)	The contents of the Paper F6 study guide for income tax, under headings:	2
•	B2 Income from employment	
(c)	Income from employment:	3
(iv)	Identify personal service companies and advise on the tax consequences of providing services via a personal service company	
2	**Corporation tax liabilities in situations involving further overseas and group aspects and in relation to special types of company, and the application of additional exemptions and reliefs**	
(b)	The scope of corporation tax	3
(vi)	Identify personal service companies and advise on the tax consequences of services being provided via a personal service company	
6	**National insurance, value added tax, tax administration and the UK tax system**	
(a)	The contents of the Paper F6 study guide for national insurance under headings:	2
•	F1 The scope of national insurance	
•	F2 Class 1 and Class 1A contributions for employed persons	

Exam guide

In the exam you may get a question which asks you to compare the after tax income from one benefit package with another, or the salary foregone in a salary sacrifice scheme. As well as calculating the marginal tax on the benefit provided or foregone, remember to take into account other costs. For example, an employee who chooses to receive a higher salary and use his own car for business will have to bear the running costs of the car as well as the capital depreciation. Don't forget national insurance!

Knowledge brought forward from earlier studies

With the exception of the rules for personal service companies, this chapter is revision of your Paper F6 studies. The examiner has identified essential underpinning knowledge from the F6 syllabus which is particularly important that you revise as part of your P6 studies. In this chapter, the relevant topic is:

		Intellectual level
B2	**Income from employment**	
(h)	Compute the amount of benefits assessable.	2

There are some changes in 2013/14 from the material covered in F6 in 2012/13. The first 15p of meals vouchers and refreshments for cyclists are no longer exempt benefits. The CO_2 emissions for car benefit has been reduced from 100g/km to 95g/km for the 11% rate. The 10% rate now applies to cars with CO_2 emissions between 76g/km and 94g/km. The fuel benefit base figure has been increased to £21,100. The fuel benefit for private use of vans has increased to £564. The exempt limit for childcare vouchers received by additional rate taxpayers has increased, because of the decrease in the additional rate of income tax.

For Class 1 NICs the thresholds for primary (employee) contributions and secondary (employer) contributions have increased, and the upper earnings limit has decreased.

1 Employment income

1.1 Outline of the charge

One of the competencies you require to fulfil performance objective 19 of the PER is the ability to evaluate and compute taxes payable. You can apply the knowledge you obtain from this section of the text to help to demonstrate this competence.

Employment income includes income arising from an employment under a contract of service (see below) and the income of office holders, such as directors. The term 'employee' is used in this text to mean anyone who receives employment income (ie both employees and directors).

There are two types of employment income:

- **General earnings**, and
- **Specific employment income.**

General earnings are an employee's earnings (see key term below) plus the 'cash equivalent' of any taxable non-monetary benefits.

Key term

'Earnings' means any salary, wage or fee, any gratuity or other profit or incidental benefit obtained by the employee if it is money or money's worth (something of direct monetary value or convertible into direct monetary value) or anything else which constitutes an emolument of the employment.

'Specific employment income' includes payments on termination of employment and share related income. This type of income is covered in the next chapter of this Text.

The residence and domicile status of an employee determines whether earnings are taxable. If an employee is resident and domiciled in the UK, **taxable earnings from an employment in a tax year are the general earnings received in that tax year**. The rules relating to other employees are dealt with later in this Text.

1.2 When are earnings received?

FAST FORWARD

General earnings are taxed in the year of receipt. Money earnings are generally received on the earlier of the time payment is made and the time entitlement to payment arises. Non-money earnings are generally received when provided.

General earnings consisting of money are treated as received at the earlier of:

- **The time when payment is made**
- **The time when a person becomes entitled to payment of the earnings**.

If the employee is a director of a company, earnings from the company are received on the earliest of:

- The earlier of the two alternatives given in the general rule (above)
- The time when the amount is credited in the company's accounting records
- The end of the company's period of account (if the amount was determined by then)
- The time the amount is determined (if after the end of the company's period of account).

Taxable benefits are generally treated as received when they are provided to the employee.

The receipts basis does not apply to pension income or taxable social security benefits. These sources of income are taxed on the amount accruing in the tax year, whether or not it is received in that year.

When are earnings received?

John is a director of X Corp Ltd. His earnings for 2013/14 are:

Salary	£60,000
Taxable benefits	£5,000

For the year ended 31 December 2013 the Board of Directors decide to pay John a bonus of £40,000. This is decided on 1 March 2014 at a board meeting and credited in the company accounts 7 days later. However John only received the bonus in his April pay on 30 April 2014.

What is John's taxable income from employment for 2013/14?

Answer

	£
Salary	60,000
Taxable benefits	5,000
Bonus (1.3.14)	40,000
Taxable employment Income	105,000

The salary and benefits were paid/made available during 2013/14 and hence taxed in 2013/14. The bonus was paid/made available on 30 April 2014 (2014/15) *but* was determined after the company's year end (31.12.13) by the board meeting on 1 March 2014 (2013/14) – hence taxed in 2013/14.

1.3 Net taxable earnings

Total taxable earnings less total allowable deductions (see below) **are net taxable earnings of a tax year. Deductions cannot usually create a loss: they can only reduce the net taxable earnings to nil.**

1.4 Person liable for tax on employment income

The person liable to tax on employment income is generally the **person to whose employment the earnings relate**. However, if the tax relates to general earnings received after the death of the person to whose employment the earnings relate, the person's personal representatives are liable for the tax. The tax is a liability of the estate.

1.5 Employment and self employment

Employment involves a contract of service whereas self employment involves a contract for services.

1.5.1 Introduction

The distinction between employment (receipts taxable as earnings) and self employment (receipts taxable as trading income) is a fine one. Employment involves a contract of service, whereas self employment involves a contract for services. Taxpayers tend to prefer self employment, because the rules on deductions for expenses are more generous. A worker's status also affects **national insurance**: the self-employed generally pay less than employees.

1.5.2 Factors indicating employment

- The **degree of control** exercised over the person doing the work (a high level of control indicates employment)
- Whether the worker must **accept further work if offered** (if yes, indicates employment)

- Whether the person who has offered work **must provide further work** (if yes, indicates employment)
- Whether the worker is entitled to **employment benefits** such as sick pay, holiday pay and pension facilities (entitlement indicates employment)
- Whether the worker works for **just one person or organisation** (such working indicates employment)

1.5.3 Factors indicating self-employment

- Whether the worker **provides his own equipment** (if yes, indicates self-employment)
- Whether the worker **hires his own helpers** (if yes, indicates self-employment)
- What degree of **financial risk** the worker takes (if high risk, indicates self-employment)
- What degree of **responsibility for investment and management** the worker has (if most of responsibility is the worker's, indicates self-employment)
- Whether the worker can profit from **sound management** (if can do so, indicates self-employment)
- Whether the worker can **work when he chooses** (if can do so, indicates self-employment)
- Whether the worker works for **a number of different persons or organisations** (such working indicates self-employment)

1.5.4 Wording of agreement

The **wording used in any agreement between the worker and the person for whom he performs work may also be taken into account**. For example, if the contract is described as a contract for services, this would suggest that the worker is self employed. However, **such wording is not conclusive** about the actual legal relationship and other factors may show that the contract is, in fact, a contract of service.

1.5.5 Case law

Relevant cases on the distinction between employment and self-employment include:

(a) *Edwards v Clinch 1981*

A civil engineer acted occasionally as an inspector on temporary ad hoc appointments.

Held: there was no ongoing office which could be vacated by one person and held by another so the fees received were from self employment not employment.

(b) *Hall v Lorimer 1994*

A vision mixer was engaged under a series of short-term contracts.

Held: the vision mixer was self employed, not because of any one detail of the case but because the overall picture was one of self-employment.

(c) *Carmichael and Anor v National Power plc 1999*

Individuals engaged as visitor guides on a casual 'as required' basis were not employees. An exchange of correspondence between the company and the individuals was not a contract of employment as there was no provision as to the frequency of work and there was flexibility to accept work or turn it down as it arose. Sickness, holiday and pension arrangements did not apply and neither did grievance and disciplinary procedures.

2 Taxable benefits

2.1 Introduction

FAST FORWARD

Most employees are taxed on benefits under the benefits code. 'Excluded employees' (lower paid/non-directors) are only subject to part of the provisions of the code.

The Income Tax (Earnings and Pensions) Act 2003 (ITEPA 2003) provides comprehensive legislation covering the taxation of benefits. **The legislation generally applies to all employees. However, only certain parts of it apply to 'excluded employees'**

Key term

An excluded employee is an employee in lower paid employment who is either not a director of a company or is a director but has no material interest in the company ('material' means control of more than 5% of the ordinary share capital) and either:

(i) **He is full time working director**, or
(ii) **The company is non-profit-making or is established for charitable purposes only.**

The term 'director' refers to any person who acts as a director or any person in accordance with whose instructions the directors are accustomed to act (other than a professional advisor).

Lower paid employment is one where earnings for the tax year are less than £8,500. To decide whether this applies, add together the **total earnings and benefits that would be taxable if the employee were *not* an excluded employee.**

A number of **specific deductions** must be taken into account to determine lower paid employment. These include **contributions to registered pension schemes and payroll giving**. However, general deductions from employment income (see later in this chapter) are not taken into account. Where a car is provided but the employee could have chosen a cash alternative, then the higher of the cash alternative and the car benefit should be used in the computation of earnings to determine whether or not the employee is an excluded employee.

Question — **Excluded employee?**

Tim earns £6,500 per annum working full time as a sales representative at Chap Co Ltd. The company provides the following staff benefits to Tim:

Private health insurance	£300
Company car	£1,500
Expense allowance	£2,000

Tim used £1,900 of the expense allowance on business mileage petrol. Is Tim an excluded employee?

Answer

No. Although Tim's taxable income is less than £8,500 this is only after his expense claim. The figure to consider and compare to £8,500 is the £10,300 as shown below:

		£
Salary		6,500
Benefits:	health insurance	300
	car	1,500
	expense allowance	2,000
Earnings to consider if Tim is lower paid		10,300
Less: claim for expenses paid out		(1,900)
Taxable income		8,400

Employees, including directors, who are not excluded employees may be referred to as '**P11D employees**'. The P11D is the form that the employer completes for each such employee with details of expenses and benefits.

2.2 General business expenses

If business expenses on such items as travel or hotel stays, are reimbursed by an employer, the reimbursed amount is a taxable benefit for employees other than excluded employees. To avoid being taxed on this amount, **an employee must then make a claim to deduct it as an expense** under the rules set out below. **In practice**, however, **many such expense payments are not reported to HMRC and can be ignored because it is agreed in advance that a claim to deduct them would be possible (a P11D dispensation**).

When an individual has to spend one or more nights away from home, their employer may reimburse expenses on items incidental to their absence (for example meals and private telephone calls). **Such incidental expenses are exempt** if:

(a) The expenses of travelling to each place where the individual stays overnight, throughout the trip, are incurred necessarily in the performance of the duties of the employment (or would have been, if there had been any expenses).

(b) The total (for the whole trip) of incidental expenses not deductible under the usual rules is no more than £5 for each night spent wholly in the UK and £10 for each other night. If this limit is exceeded, all of the expenses are taxable, not just the excess. The expenses include any VAT.

This incidental expenses exemption applies to expenses reimbursed, and to benefits obtained using credit tokens and non-cash vouchers.

2.3 Vouchers

If any employee (including an excluded employee):

(a) receives cash vouchers (vouchers exchangeable for cash)
(b) uses a credit token (such as a credit card) to obtain money, goods or services, or
(c) receives exchangeable vouchers (such as book tokens), also called non-cash vouchers

they are taxed on the cost of providing the benefit, less any amount made good.

Where a voucher is provided for a benefit which is exempt from income tax, the provision of the voucher itself is also exempt.

2.4 Accommodation

FAST FORWARD

The benefit in respect of accommodation is its annual value. There is an additional benefit if the property cost the employer over £75,000.

The taxable value of accommodation provided to an employee (including an excluded employee) is the rent that would have been payable if the premises had been let at an amount equal to their annual value (taken to be their **rateable value**). **If the premises are rented** rather than owned by the employer, then **the taxable benefit is the higher of the rent actually paid and the annual value.** If property does not have a rateable value, HMRC estimate a value.

If a property cost the employer more than £75,000, an additional amount is chargeable:

Formula to learn

(Cost of providing the accommodation – £75,000) × the official rate of interest at the start of the tax year.

Thus with an official rate of say 4%, the total benefit for accommodation costing £95,000 and with an annual value of £2,000 would be £2,000 + £(95,000 – 75,000) × 4% = £2,800.

The 'cost of providing' the living accommodation is the aggregate of the cost of purchase and the cost of any improvements made before the start of the tax year for which the benefit is being computed. It is therefore not possible to avoid the charge by buying an inexpensive property requiring substantial repairs and improving it.

If a property was acquired more than six years before first being provided to the employee, the market value when first provided plus the cost of subsequent improvements is used as the cost of providing the accommodation. However, unless the actual cost plus improvements to the start of the tax year in question exceeds £75,000, the additional charge cannot be imposed, however high the market value. In addition, the additional charge can only be imposed if the employer owns (rather than rents) the property concerned.

Exam focus point

The 'official rate' of interest will be given to you in the exam.

There is no taxable benefit in respect of job related accommodation.

Key term

A person lives in **job-related accommodation** if:

(a) It **is necessary for the proper performance of the employee's duties** (as with a caretaker), or
(b) It is provided **for the better performance of the employee's duties** and the employment is of a kind in which it is **customary for accommodation to be provided** (as with a policeman), or
(c) There is a **special threat to the employee's security**, and use of the accommodation is part of security arrangements

Directors can only claim exemptions (a) or (b) if:

(i) They have no **material interest** ('material' means over 5%) in the company, and
(ii) Either they are **full time working directors** or the company is **non-profit making or is a charity**.

Any contribution paid by the employee is deducted from the annual value of the property and then from the additional benefit.

If the employee is given a cash alternative to living accommodation, the benefits code still applies in priority to treating the cash alternative as earnings. If the cash alternative is greater than the taxable benefit, the excess is treated as earnings.

2.5 Expenses connected with living accommodation

In addition to the benefit of living accommodation itself, **employees, other than excluded employees, are taxed on related expenses paid by the employer**, such as:

(a) **Heating, lighting or cleaning the premises**
(b) **Repairing, maintaining or decorating the premises**
(c) **The provision of furniture (the annual value is 20% of the cost)**

Unless the accommodation qualifies as 'job related' (as defined above) **the full cost of ancillary services** (excluding structural repairs) **is taxable. If the accommodation is 'job related'**, however, **taxable ancillary services are restricted to a maximum of 10% of the employee's 'net earnings'**.

For this purpose, net earnings are all earnings from the employment (excluding the ancillary benefits (a)-(c) above) less any allowable expenses, statutory mileage allowances, contributions to registered occupational pension schemes (but not personal pension plans), and capital allowances.

If there are ancillary benefits other than those falling within (a)-(c) above (such as a telephone) they are taxable in full.

Question — **Expenses connected with living accommodation**

Mr Quinton has a gross salary in 2013/14 of £28,850. He works as head of security for a company with a large office in London. He is required to live in a company house adjoining his employer's office, so that he can carry out his duties. The house cost £70,000 three years ago and its annual value is £650. In 2013/14 the company pays an electricity bill of £550, a gas bill of £400, a gardener's bill of £750 and redecoration costs of £1,800. Mr Quinton makes a monthly contribution of £50 for his accommodation. He also pays £1,450 occupational pension contributions each year.

Calculate Mr Quinton's taxable employment income for 2013/14.

Answer

	£	£
Salary		28,850
Less occupational pension scheme contributions		(1,450)
Net earnings		27,400
Accommodation benefits		
Annual value: exempt (job related)		
Ancillary services		
Electricity	550	
Gas	400	
Gardener	750	
Redecorations	1,800	
	3,500	
Restricted to 10% of £27,400	2,740	
Less employee's contribution	(600)	
		2,140
Employment income		29,540

2.6 Cars

FAST FORWARD

Employees who have a company car are taxed on a % of the car's list price which depends on the level of the car's CO_2 emissions. The same % multiplied by £21,100 determines the benefit where private fuel is also provided. Authorised mileage allowances can be paid tax free to employees who use their own vehicle for business journeys.

A car provided by reason of the employment to an employee, or member of his family or household, for private use gives rise to a taxable benefit. This does not apply to excluded employees. **'Private use' includes home to work travel.**

(a) A tax charge arises whether the car is provided by the employer or by some other person. The benefit is computed as shown below, even if the car is taken as an alternative to another benefit of a different value.

(b) The starting point for calculating a car benefit is the list price of the car (plus accessories). **The percentage of the list price that is taxable depends on the car's CO_2 emissions.**

(c) The price of the car is the sum of the following items.

   (i) The list price of the car for a single retail sale at the time of first registration, including charges for delivery and standard accessories. The manufacturer's, importer's or distributor's list price must be used, even if the retailer offered a discount. A notional list price is estimated if no list price was published.

   (ii) The price (including fitting) of all optional accessories provided when the car was first provided to the employee, excluding mobile telephones and equipment needed by a disabled employee. The extra cost of adapting or manufacturing a car to run on road fuel gases is not included.

   (iii) The price (including fitting) of all optional accessories fitted later and costing at least £100 each, excluding mobile telephones and equipment needed by a disabled employee. Such accessories affect the taxable benefit from and including the tax year in which they are fitted. However, accessories which are merely replacing existing accessories and are not superior to the ones replaced are ignored. Replacement accessories which *are* superior are taken into account, but the cost of the old accessory is then deducted.

(d) There is a special rule for classic cars. If the car is at least 15 years old (from the time of first registration) at the end of the tax year, and its market value at the end of the year (or, if earlier, when it ceased to be available to the employee) is over £15,000 and greater than the price found under (c), that market value is used instead of the price. The market value takes account of all accessories (except mobile telephones and equipment needed by a disabled employee).

(e) Capital contributions are payments by the employee in respect of the price of the car or accessories. In any tax year, we take account of capital contributions made in that year and previous years (for the same car). The maximum deductible capital contributions is £5,000; contributions beyond that total are ignored.

(f) For cars that emit **CO_2 of 95 g/km (2013/14), the taxable benefit is 11% of the car's list price. This percentage increases by 1% for every 5g/km (rounded down to the nearest multiple of 5) by which CO_2 emissions exceed 95g/km up to a maximum of 35%.** Therefore the 11% rate also applies to cars with emissions between 96g/km and 99g/km as these are rounded down to 95g/km. Then, for cars with emissions between 100g/km and 104g/km, the relevant percentage will be 11 + ((100 – 95)/5) = 12% etc.

Exam focus point

The CO_2 baseline figure of 95g/km will be given to you in the tax rates and allowances section of the exam paper.

(g) **For cars that emit CO_2 between 76g/km and 94g/km, the taxable benefit is 10% of the car's list price. For cars that emit 75g/km or less, the taxable benefit is 5% of the car's list price.**

Exam focus point

The examiner has stated that zero emission company cars are not examinable.

(h) **Diesel cars have a supplement of 3% of the car's list price added to the taxable benefit.** The maximum percentage, however, remains 35% of the list price.

(i) **The benefit is reduced on a time basis where a car is first made available or ceases to be made available during the tax year** or is incapable of being used for a continuous period of not less than 30 days (for example because it is being repaired).

(j) **The benefit is reduced by any payment the user must make for the private use of the car** (as distinct from a capital contribution to the cost of the car). Payments for insuring the car do not count. The benefit cannot become negative to create a deduction from the employee's income.

(k) Pool cars are exempt. A car is a pool car if **all** the following conditions are satisfied.

   (i) It is used by more than one employee and is not ordinarily used by any one of them to the exclusion of the others

   (ii) Any private use is merely incidental to business use

   (iii) It is not normally kept overnight at or near the residence of an employee

There are many ancillary benefits associated with the provision of cars, such as insurance, repairs, vehicle licences and a parking space at or near work. No extra taxable benefit arises as a result of these, with the exception of the cost of providing a driver.

2.7 Fuel for cars

Where fuel is provided there is a further benefit in addition to the car benefit.

No taxable benefit arises where either

(a) **All the fuel provided was made available only for business travel, or**

(b) **The employee is required to make good, and has made good, the whole of the cost of any fuel provided for his private use.**

Unlike most benefits, a reimbursement of only part of the cost of the fuel available for private use does not reduce the benefit.

The taxable benefit is a percentage of a base figure. The base figure for 2013/14 is £21,100. The percentage is the same percentage as is used to calculate the car benefit (see above).

Exam focus point

> The fuel base figure will be given to you in the tax rates and allowances section of the exam paper.

The fuel benefit is reduced in the same way as the car benefit **if the car is not available for 30 days or more**.

The fuel benefit is also reduced if private fuel is not available for part of a tax year. However, if private fuel later becomes available in the same tax year, the reduction is not made. If, for example, fuel is provided from 6 April 2013 to 30 June 2013, then the fuel benefit for 2013/14 will be restricted to just three months. This is because the provision of fuel has permanently ceased. However, if fuel is provided from 6 April 2013 to 30 June 2013, and then again from 1 September 2013 to 5 April 2014, then the fuel benefit will not be reduced since the cessation was only temporary.

Question

Car and fuel benefit

An employee was provided with a new car costing £15,000 for the whole of 2013/14. The car emits 166g/km of CO_2. During the year, the employer spent £900 on insurance, repairs and a vehicle licence. The firm paid for all petrol, costing £1,500, without reimbursement. The employee paid the firm £270 for the private use of the car. Calculate the taxable benefit.

Answer

Round CO_2 emissions figure down to the nearest 5, ie 165 g/km.

Amount by which CO_2 emissions exceed the baseline:

(165 – 95) = 70 g/km

Divide by 5 = 14

Taxable percentage = 11% + 14% = 25%

	£
Car benefit £15,000 × 25%	3,750
Fuel benefit £21,100 × 25%	5,275
	9,025
Less contribution towards use of car	(270)
	8,755

If the contribution of £270 had been towards the petrol the benefit would have been £9,025.

2.8 Vans and heavier commercial vehicles

If a van (of normal maximum laden weight up to 3,500 kg) **is made available for an employee's private use, there is an annual scale charge of £3,000**. The scale charge covers ancillary benefits such as insurance and servicing. Paragraphs 2.6 (i) and (j) above apply to vans as they do to cars.

There is, however, **no taxable benefit where an employee takes a van home** (ie uses the van for home to work travel) but is not allowed any other private use.

If the employer provides **fuel for unrestricted private use**, an additional **fuel charge of £564** applies).

If a commercial vehicle of normal maximum laden weight over 3,500 kg is made available for an employee's private use, but the employee's use of the vehicle is not wholly or mainly private, no taxable benefit arises except in respect of the provision of a driver.

2.9 Statutory approved mileage allowances

A single approved mileage allowance for business journeys in an employee's own vehicle applies to all cars and vans. There is no income tax on payments up to this allowance and employers do not have

to report mileage allowances up to this amount. The allowance for 2013/14 is 45p per mile on the first 10,000 miles in the tax year with each additional mile over 10,000 miles at 25p per mile. The approved mileage allowance for employees using their own motor cycle is 24p per mile. For employees using their own pedal cycle it is 20p per mile.

If employers pay less than the statutory allowance, employees can claim tax relief up to that level.

The statutory allowance does not prevent employers from paying higher rates, but any excess will be subject to income tax. There is a similar (but slightly different) system for NICs, covered later in this chapter.

Employers can make income tax and NIC free payments of up to 5p per mile for each fellow employee making the same business trip who is carried as a passenger. If the employer does not pay the employee for carrying business passengers, the employee cannot claim any tax relief.

Question — Mileage allowance

Sophie uses her own car for business travel. During 2013/14, Sophie drove 15,400 miles in the performance of her duties. Sophie's employer paid her a mileage allowance. How is the mileage allowance treated for tax purposes assuming that the rate paid is:

(a) 40p a mile, or
(b) 25p a mile?

Answer

(a)

	£
Mileage allowance received (15,400 × 40p)	6,160
Less: tax free [(10,000 × 45p) + (5,400 × 25p)]	(5,850)
Taxable benefit	310

£5,850 is tax free and the excess amount received of £310 is a taxable benefit.

(b)

	£
Mileage allowance received (15,400 × 25p)	3,850
Less: tax free amount [(10,000 × 45p) + (5,400 × 25p)]	(5,850)
Allowable deduction	(2,000)

There is no taxable benefit and Sophie can claim a deduction from her employment income of £2,000.

2.10 Beneficial loans

FAST FORWARD

Taxable cheap loans are charged to tax on the difference between the official rate of interest and any interest paid by the employee.

2.10.1 Introduction

Employment related loans to employees (other than excluded employees) and their relatives give rise to a benefit equal to:

(a) **Any amounts written off** (unless the employee has died), and

(b) **The excess of the interest based on an official rate prescribed by the Treasury, over any interest actually charged ('taxable cheap loan').** Interest payable during the tax year but paid after the end of the tax year is taken into account, but if the benefit is determined before such interest is paid a claim must be made to take it into account.

The following loans are normally not treated as taxable cheap loans for calculation of the interest benefits (but are taxable for the purposes of the charge on loans written off).

(a) A loan on normal commercial terms made in the ordinary course of the employer's money-lending business.

(b) A loan made by an individual in the ordinary course of the lender's domestic, family or personal arrangements.

2.10.2 Calculating the interest benefit

There are two alternative methods of calculating the taxable benefit. The simpler **'average' method** automatically applies unless the taxpayer or HMRC elect for the alternative **'strict' method**. (HMRC normally only make the election where it appears that the 'average' method is being deliberately exploited.) In both methods, the benefit is the interest at the official rate minus the interest payable.

The 'average' method averages the balances at the beginning and end of the tax year (or the dates on which the loan was made and discharged if it was not in existence throughout the tax year) and applies the official rate of interest to this average. If the loan was not in existence throughout the tax year only the number of complete tax months (from the 6th of the month) for which it existed are taken into account.

The 'strict' method is to compute interest at the official rate on the actual amount outstanding on a daily basis. However, for exam purposes, it is acceptable to work on a monthly basis.

Question — **Loan benefit**

At 6 April 2013 a taxable cheap loan of £30,000 was outstanding to an employee earning £12,000 a year, who repaid £20,000 on 6 December 2013. The remaining balance of £10,000 was outstanding at 5 April 2014. Interest paid during the year was £250. What was the benefit under both methods for 2013/14?

Answer

Average method

	£
$4\% \times \frac{30{,}000 + 10{,}000}{2}$	800
Less interest paid	(250)
Benefit	550

Alternative method (strict method)

	£
£30,000 × $\frac{8}{12}$ (6 April - 5 December) × 4%	800
£10,000 × $\frac{4}{12}$ (6 December - 5 April) × 4%	133
	933
Less interest paid	(250)
Benefit	683

HMRC might opt for the alternative method.

2.10.3 The de minimis test

The benefit is not taxable if:

(a) The **total of all taxable cheap loans to the employee did not exceed £5,000** at any time in the tax year, or

(b) **The loan is not a qualifying loan and the total of all non-qualifying loans to the employee did not exceed £5,000** at any time in the tax year.

A qualifying loan is one on which all or part of any interest paid would qualify as deductible interest.

When the £5,000 threshold is exceeded, a benefit arises on interest on the whole loan, not just on the excess of the loan over £5,000.

When a loan is written off and a benefit arises, there is no £5,000 threshold: writing off a loan of £1 gives rise to a £1 benefit.

2.10.4 Qualifying loans

If the whole of the interest payable on a qualifying loan is eligible for tax relief as deductible interest, then no taxable benefit arises. If the interest is only partly eligible for tax relief, then the employee is treated as receiving earnings because the actual rate of interest is below the official rate. He is also treated as paying interest equal to those earnings. This **deemed interest paid may qualify as a business expense or as deductible interest in addition to any interest actually paid.**

Question — **Beneficial loans**

Anna has an annual salary of £30,000, and two loans from her employer.

(a) A season ticket loan of £2,300 at no interest

(b) A loan, 90% of which was used to buy shares in her employee-controlled company, of £71,000 at 1.5% interest

What is Anna's tax liability for 2013/14?

Answer

	£
Salary	30,000
Season ticket loan: not over £5,000	0
Loan to buy shares £71,000 × (4 – 1.5 = 2.5%)	1,775
Earnings	31,775
Less deductible interest paid (£71,000 × 4% × 90%)	(2,556)
	29,219
Less personal allowance	(9,440)
Taxable income	19,779
Income tax	
£19,779 × 20%	3,956

2.11 Other assets made available for private use

FAST FORWARD

20% of the value of assets made available for private use is taxable.

When assets are made available to employees or members of their family or household, the taxable benefit is the higher of 20% of the market value when first provided as a benefit to any employee, or on the rent paid by the employer if higher. The 20% charge is time-apportioned when the asset is provided for only part of the year. The charge after any time apportionment is reduced by any contribution made by the employee.

Certain assets, such as bicycles provided for journeys to work, are exempt. These are described later in this chapter.

If an asset made available is subsequently acquired by the employee, **the taxable benefit on the acquisition is the *greater* of:**

- The **current market value minus the price paid by the employee.**

- The **market value when first provided minus any amounts already taxed (ignoring contributions by the employee) minus the price paid by the employee.**

This rule prevents tax free benefits arising on rapidly depreciating items through the employee purchasing them at their low second-hand value.

There is an exception to this rule for bicycles which have previously been provided as exempt benefits. The taxable benefit on acquisition is restricted to current market value, minus the price paid by the employee.

2.12 Example: assets made available for private use

A suit costing £400 is purchased by an employer for use by an employee on 6 April 2012. On 6 April 2013 the suit is purchased by the employee for £30, its market value then being £50.

The benefit in 2012/13 is £400 × 20%		£80
The benefit in 2013/14 is £290, being the **greater** of:		
		£
(a)	Market value at acquisition by employee	50
	Less price paid	(30)
		20
(b)	Original market value	400
	Less taxed in respect of use	(80)
		320
	Less price paid	(30)
		290

Question — **Bicycles**

Rupert is provided with a new bicycle by his employer on 6 April 2013. The bicycle is available for private use as well as commuting to work. It cost the employer £1,500 when new. On 6 October 2013 the employer transfers ownership of the bicycle to Rupert when it is worth £800. Rupert does not pay anything for the bicycle.

What is the total taxable benefit on Rupert for 2013/14 in respect of the bicycle?

Answer

Use benefit	Exempt
Transfer benefit (use MV at acquisition by employee only)	
MV at transfer	£800

2.13 Scholarships

If scholarships are given to members an employee's family, the **employee is taxable on the cost** unless the scholarship fund's or scheme's payments by reason of people's employments are not more than 25% of its total payments.

2.14 Childcare

FAST FORWARD

Workplace childcare is an exempt benefit. Employer-supported childcare and childcare vouchers are exempt up to £55 per week. Maximum tax relief is limited to £11 per week (the equivalent of £55 × 20%).

The cost of running a **workplace nursery or playscheme is an exempt benefit (without limit).**

Otherwise a certain amount of childcare is tax free if the employer contracts with an approved childcarer or provides childcare vouchers to pay an approved childcarer. The childcare must usually be available to all employees and the childcare must either be registered or approved home-childcare.

A **£55 per week limit applies to basic rate employees** who use employer-supported childcare schemes or receive childcare vouchers. The amount of tax relief for a basic rate taxpayer is therefore £55 x 20% = £11 per week.

Higher rate and additional rate employees who use employer-supported childcare schemes or receive childcare vouchers have their tax relief restricted so that it is the equivalent of that received by a basic rate taxpayer. Higher and additional rate employees can therefore receive vouchers tax-free up to £28 per week and £25 per week respectively, each giving £11 of tax relief which is the same amount a basic rate taxpayer would receive.

Exam focus point

Whether an employee is considered basic rate, higher rate or additional rate for these purposes, is determined by the level of his earnings only (and not other income). However, the examiner has stated that in an exam question involving childcare, it will be quite clear at what rate a taxpayer is paying tax.

Question — **Childcare**

Archie is employed by M plc and is paid a salary of £80,000 in 2013/14. He starts receiving childcare vouchers from M plc worth £50 per week for his daughter in June 2013 and receives them for 26 weeks during 2013/14.

What is Archie's employment income for 2013/14?

Answer

	£
Salary (higher rate employee)	80,000
Childcare vouchers £(50 – 28) x 26 weeks	572
Employment income 2013/14	80,572

2.15 Residual charge

FAST FORWARD

There is a residual charge for other benefits, usually equal to the cost of the benefits.

We have seen above how certain specific benefits are taxed. **A 'residual charge' is made on the taxable value of other benefits. In general, the taxable value of a benefit is the cost of the benefit less any part of that cost made good by the employee to the persons providing the benefit.**

The residual charge applies to any benefit provided for an employee or a member of their family or household, by reason of the employment. There is an exception where the employer is an individual and the provision of the benefit is made in the normal course of the employer's domestic, family or personal relationships.

This rule does not apply to taxable benefits provided to excluded employees. **These employees are taxed only on the second hand value of any benefit that could be converted into money**.

3 Exempt benefits

FAST FORWARD

Some benefits are exempt from tax such as removal expenses and the provision of sporting facilities (subject to certain limits).

Various benefits are exempt from tax. These include:

(a) **Entertainment provided to employees by genuine third parties** (eg seats at sporting/cultural events), even if it is provided by giving the employee a voucher.

(b) **Gifts of goods** (or vouchers exchangeable for goods) from third parties (ie not provided by the employer or a person connected to the employer) if the total cost (incl. VAT) of all gifts by the same donor to the same employee in the tax year is £250 or less. If the £250 limit is exceeded, the full amount is taxable, not just the excess.

(c) **Non-cash awards for long service** if the period of service was at least 20 years, no similar award was made to the employee in the past 10 years and the cost is not more than £50 per year of service.

(d) **Awards under staff suggestion schemes if**:

  (i) There is a formal scheme, open to all employees on equal terms.

  (ii) The suggestion is outside the scope of the employee's normal duties.

  (iii) Either the award is not more than £25, or the award is only made after a decision is taken to implement the suggestion.

  (iv) Awards over £25 reflect the financial importance of the suggestion to the business, and either do not exceed 50% of the expected net financial benefit during the first year of implementation or do not exceed 10% of the expected net financial benefit over a period of up to five years.

  (v) Awards of over £25 are shared on a reasonable basis between two or more employees putting forward the same suggestion.

  If an award exceeds £5,000, the excess is always taxable.

(e) **The first £8,000 of removal expenses if:**

  (i) The employee does not already live within a reasonable daily travelling distance of their new place of employment, but will do so after moving.

  (ii) The expenses are incurred or the benefits provided by the end of the tax year following the tax year of the start of employment at the new location.

(f) **Some childcare** (see earlier in this chapter)

(g) **Sporting or recreational facilities available to employees generally and not to the general public**, unless they are provided on domestic premises, or they consist in an interest in or the use of any mechanically propelled vehicle or any overnight accommodation. Vouchers only exchangeable for such facilities are also exempt, but membership fees for sports clubs are taxable.

(h) **Assets or services used in performing the duties of employment** provided any private use of the item concerned is insignificant. This exempts, for example, the benefit arising on the private use of employer-provided tools.

(i) **Welfare counselling** and similar minor benefits if the benefit concerned is available to employees generally.

(j) **Bicycles or cycling safety equipment provided to enable employees to get to and from work or to travel between one workplace and another**. The equipment must be available to the employer's employees generally. Also, it must be used mainly for the aforementioned journeys.

(k) **Workplace parking**

(l) **Up to £15,480 a year paid to an employee who is on a full-time course lasting at least a year,** with average full-time attendance of at least 20 weeks a year. If the £15,480 limit is exceeded, the whole amount is taxable.

(m) **Work related training and related costs. This includes the costs of** training material and assets either made during training or incorporated into something so made.

(n) **Air miles or car fuel coupons** obtained as a result of business expenditure but used for private purposes.

(o) **The cost of work buses and minibuses or subsidies to public bus services.**

A works bus must have a seating capacity of 12 or more and a works minibus a seating capacity of 9 or more but not more than 12 and be available generally to employees of the employer concerned. The bus or minibus must mainly be used by employees for journeys to and from work and for journeys between workplaces.

(p) Transport/overnight costs where public transport is disrupted by industrial action, late night taxis and travel costs incurred where car sharing arrangements unavoidably breakdown.

(q) The private use of one **mobile phone (which can be a smartphone)**. Top up vouchers for exempt mobile phones are also tax free. If more than one mobile phone is provided to an employee for private use only the second or subsequent phone is a taxable benefit.

(r) **Employer provided uniforms** which employees must wear as part of their duties.

(s) The cost of **staff parties** which are open to staff generally provided that the **cost per head per year (including VAT) is £150 or less**. The £150 limit may be split between several parties.

(t) **Private medical insurance premiums paid to cover treatment when the employee is outside the UK in the performance of their duties**. Other medical insurance premiums are taxable as is the cost of medical diagnosis and treatment except for routine check ups. Eye tests and glasses for employees using VDUs are exempt.

(u) Cheap loans **that do not exceed £5,000** at any time in the tax year (see above).

(v) **Job related accommodation** (see above).

(w) **Employer contributions towards additional household costs incurred by an employee who works wholly or partly at home**. Payments up to £4 per week (or £18 per month for monthly paid employees) may be made without supporting evidence. Payments in excess of that amount require supporting evidence that the payment is wholly in respect of additional household expenses.

Where a voucher is provided for a benefit which is exempt from income tax the provision of the voucher itself is also exempt.

4 Allowable deductions

FAST FORWARD

To be deductible, expenses must be for qualifying travel or wholly, exclusively and necessarily incurred.

4.1 General principles

Certain expenditure is specifically deductible in computing net taxable earnings:

(a) **Contributions** (within certain limits) **to registered occupational pension schemes** (see earlier in this Text).

(b) **Subscriptions to professional bodies** on the list of bodies issued by HMRC (which includes most UK professional bodies), if relevant to the duties of the employment

(c) Payments for certain **liabilities relating to the employment** and for insurance against them (see below)

(d) **Payments to charity made under the payroll deduction scheme** operated by an employer

(e) **Mileage allowance** relief (see above)

Otherwise, **allowable deductions are notoriously hard to obtain. They are limited to**:

- **Qualifying travel expenses** (see below)
- **Other expenses the employee is obliged to incur and pay as holder of the employment which are incurred wholly, exclusively and necessarily in the performance of the duties of the employment**
- **Capital allowances on plant and machinery (other than cars or other vehicles) necessarily provided for use in the performance of those duties.**

4.2 Liabilities and insurance

If a director or employee incurs a liability related to their employment or pays for insurance against such a liability, the cost is a deductible expense. If the employer pays such amounts, there is no taxable benefit.

A liability relating to employment is one which is imposed in respect of the employee's acts or omissions as employee. Thus, for example, liability for negligence would be covered. Related costs, for example the costs of legal proceedings, are included.

For insurance premiums to qualify, the insurance policy must:

(a) Cover only liabilities relating to employment, vicarious liability in respect of liabilities of another person's employment, related costs and payments to the employee's own employees in respect of their employment liabilities relating to employment and related costs, and

(b) It must not last for more than two years (although it may be renewed for up to two years at a time), and the insured person must not be not required to renew it.

4.3 Travel expenses

Tax relief is not available for an employee's normal commuting costs. This means relief is not available for any costs an employee incurs in getting from home to their normal place of work. However **employees are entitled to relief for travel expenses which basically are the full costs that they are obliged to incur and pay as holder of the employment in travelling in the performance of their duties or travelling to or from a place which they have to attend in the performance of their duties (other than a permanent workplace).**

4.4 Example: travel in the performance of duties

Judi is an accountant. She often travels to meetings at the firm's offices in the North of England returning to her office in Leeds after the meetings. Relief is available for the full cost of these journeys as the travel is undertaken in the performance of her duties.

Question — **Relief for travelling costs**

Zoe lives in Wycombe and normally works in Chiswick. Occasionally she visits a client in Wimbledon and travels direct from home. Distances are shown in the diagram below:

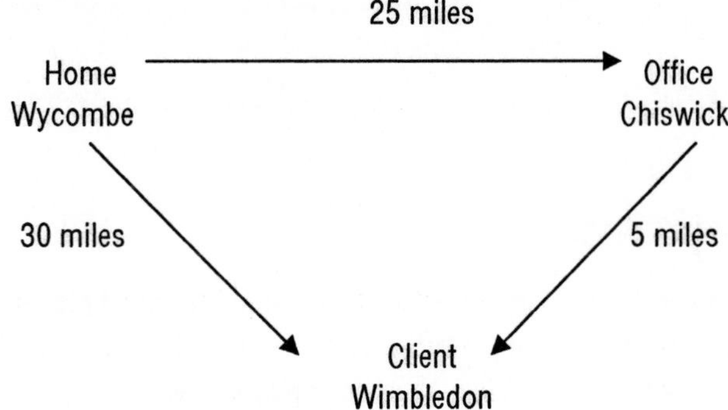

What tax relief is available for Zoe's travel costs?

Answer

Zoe is not entitled to tax relief for the costs incurred in travelling between Wycombe and Chiswick since these are normal commuting costs. However, relief is available for all costs that Zoe incurs when she travels from Wycombe to Wimbledon to visit her client.

To prevent manipulation of the basic rule normal commuting will not become a business journey just because the employee stops en-route to perform a business task (eg make a 'phone call'). Nor will relief be available if the journey is essentially the same as the employee's normal journey to work.

4.5 Example: normal commuting

Judi is based at her office in Leeds City Centre. One day she is required to attend a 9.00 am meeting with a client whose premises are around the corner from her Leeds office. Judi travels from home directly to the meeting. As the journey is substantially the same as her ordinary journey to work relief is not available.

Site based employees (eg construction workers, management consultants etc) who do not have a permanent workplace, are entitled to relief for the costs of all journeys made from home to wherever they are working. This is because these employees do not have an ordinary commuting journey or any normal commuting costs. However there is a caveat that the employee does not spend more than 24 months of continuous work at any one site.

Tax relief is available for travel, accommodation and subsistence expenses incurred by an employee who is working at a temporary workplace on a secondment expected to last up to 24 months. If a secondment is initially expected not to exceed 24 months, but it is extended, relief ceases to be due from the date the employee becomes aware of the change. When looking at how long a secondment is expected to last, HMRC will consider not only the terms of the written contract but also any verbal agreement by the employer and other factors such as whether the employee buys a house etc.

Question — **Temporary workplace**

Philip works for Vastbank at its Newcastle City Centre branch. Philip is sent to work full-time at another branch in Morpeth for 20 months at the end of which he will return to the Newcastle branch. Morpeth is about 20 miles north of Newcastle.

What travel costs is Philip entitled to claim as a deduction?

Answer

Although Philip is spending all of his time at the Morpeth branch it will not be treated as his normal work place because his period of attendance will be less than 24 months. Thus Philip can claim relief in full for the costs of travel from his home to the Morpeth branch.

There is also tax relief for certain travel expenses relating to overseas employment. These are dealt with later in this Text.

4.6 Other expenses

The word 'exclusively' strictly implies that the expenditure must give no private benefit at all. If it does, none of it is deductible. In practice inspectors may ignore a small element of private benefit or make an apportionment between business and private use.

Whether an expense is 'necessary' is not determined by what the employer requires. The test is whether the duties of the employment could not be performed without the outlay.

- *Sanderson v Durbridge 1955*

  The cost of evening meals taken when attending late meetings was not deductible because it was not incurred in the performance of the duties.

- *Blackwell v Mills 1945*

  As a condition of their employment, an employee was required to attend evening classes. The cost of their textbooks and travel was not deductible because it was not incurred in the performance of the duties.

- *Lupton v Potts 1969*

  Examination fees incurred by a solicitor's articled clerk were not deductible because they were incurred neither wholly nor exclusively in the performance of the duties, but in furthering the clerk's ambition to become a solicitor.

- *Brown v Bullock 1961*

  The expense of joining a club that was virtually a requisite of an employment was not deductible because it would have been possible to carry on the employment without the club membership, so the expense was not necessary.

- *Elwood v Utitz 1965*

  A managing director's subscriptions to two residential London clubs were claimed by him as an expense on the grounds that they were cheaper than hotels.

  The expenditure was deductible as it was necessary in that it would be impossible for the employee to carry out his London duties without being provided with first class accommodation. The residential facilities (which were cheaper than hotel accommodation) were given to club members only.

- *Lucas v Cattell 1972*

  The cost of business telephone calls on a private telephone is deductible, but no part of the line or telephone rental charges is deductible.

- *Fitzpatrick v IRC 1994; Smith v Abbott 1994*

  Journalists cannot claim a deduction for the cost of buying newspapers which they read to keep themselves informed, since they are merely preparing themselves to perform their duties.

The cost of clothes for work is not deductible, except that for certain trades requiring protective clothing there are annual deductions on a set scale.

An employee required to work at home may be able to claim a deduction for an appropriate proportion of his or her expenditure on lighting, heating and (if a room is used exclusively for work purposes) **the council tax.** Employers can pay up to £4 per week (or £18 per month to monthly paid employees) without the need for supporting evidence of the costs incurred by the employee (see above). Payments above the limit require evidence of the employee's actual costs.

5 Personal service companies

FAST FORWARD The IR35 provisions prevent avoidance of tax by providing services through a company.

5.1 Application and outline of computation

We looked at the distinction between employment and self employment earlier in this chapter. **Workers normally prefer to avoid being classified as employees as the tax and national insurance burden on the self-employed is lower**. However, there is a risk that workers claiming to be self employed will be classified by HMRC as employees, leading to increased taxation and liability to penalties, both for the workers and those who use their services.

One way to avoid this potential pitfall was for the **worker to set up a company (known as a personal service company or PSC) to provide services to a client**. The worker was **both the owner of the PSC** (usually as its sole shareholder) and **an employee of the PSC**. An employment relationship could not arise between the client and the worker because of the existence of the intermediary PSC and so payments by the client were not subject to PAYE and no NICs were payable.

In addition, it was **possible for the worker to arrange the affairs of the personal service company to obtain tax advantages in extracting profits from the PSC** as compared with the situation where the worker was self-employed. Thus the arrangement had advantages for both the client and the worker.

A typical arrangement is shown in the following diagram where a taxpayer called Ada used a PSC called Quality Ltd to provide computer services to a business client, Mr Evans:

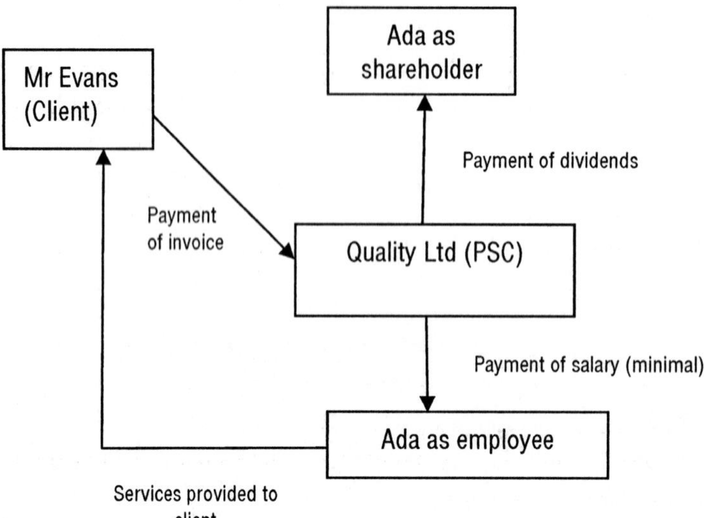

Quality Ltd invoiced Mr Evans for the services provided. This **payment was made gross by Mr Evans, rather than under PAYE** and there were **no national insurance contributions payable**.

Quality Ltd might then have paid Ada a salary (usually only a minimal amount to ensure that a small amount of national insurance contributions were payable which gave entitlement to state benefits such as Jobseeker's Allowance). **Quality Ltd paid corporation tax on its net income** after deduction of expenses wholly and exclusively incurred for the purposes of the trade (a more generous basis than the test for employment expenses), including Ada's salary and any employer national insurance contributions. The tax charge was **likely to be at the small profits rate**, substantially lower than the higher and additional rates of income tax.

Quality Ltd could then have distributed post-tax profits as dividends. Dividends are not subject to PAYE or national insurance contributions. There was also scope for paying dividends to Ada in a tax efficient manner, for example limiting them to the basic rate band so that her tax liability was covered by the dividend tax credit. Ada could also spread the payment of dividends over a number of tax years to take advantage of the basic rate band each year - compare this with the situation where Ada was self-employed and thus taxable on the whole of her taxable trading profit on the current year basis, possibly at the higher or additional rates in a year when profits were high.

Such PSCs were so popular that the loss of tax and national insurance contributions as a result of their use caused serious concerns to HMRC. Consequently, there are now anti-avoidance rules which restrict the avoidance of tax and national Insurance contributions by workers offering their services through an intermediary, such as a PSC. **These provisions are commonly known as the IR35 provisions.**

Broadly, the **IR35 provisions apply** where:

(a) **an individual ('the worker') performs, or has an obligation to perform, services for 'a client'**, and

(b) the **performance of those services is referable to arrangements involving a third party** (eg the personal service company), rather than referable to a contract between the client and the worker, and

(c) **if the services were to be performed by the worker under a contract between himself and the client, they would be regarded as employed by the client.**

In relation to the last condition, **the usual tests of whether an individual is employed or self-employed**, considered earlier in this chapter, **are used**.

5.2 Computation of deemed salary payment

If the IR35 rules apply, then **a salary payment may be deemed to have been made to the worker at the end of the tax year**. The deemed payment is **subject to PAYE and NICs**.

The following steps should be followed to compute the amount of the deemed payment:

Step 1 **Take 95% of all payments and benefits received in respect of the relevant engagements by the third party.**

Step 2 **Add amounts received in respect of the relevant engagements by the worker otherwise than from the third party**, if they are not chargeable as employment income, but would have been so chargeable if the worker had been employed by the client.

Step 3 **Deduct expenses met by the third party** if those expenses would have been deductible had they been paid out of the taxable earnings of the employment by the worker. This also includes expenses paid by the worker and reimbursed by the third party. Mileage allowances up to the statutory amounts are also deductible where a vehicle is provided by the third party.

Step 4 **Deduct capital allowances on expenditure incurred by the third party** if the worker would have been able to deduct them had they incurred the expenditure and had they been employed by the client.

Step 5 **Deduct any registered pension contributions and employer's NICs paid by the third party** in respect of the worker.

Step 6 **Deduct amounts received by the worker from the third party** that are chargeable as employment income but were not deducted under Step 3.

Step 7 Find the amount that together with employer's NIC (see below) on it, is equal to the amount resulting from Step 6 above. This means that you should multiply the amount in Step 6 by 13.8/113.8 and deduct this amount from the amount in Step 6.

Step 8 The result is the amount of the deemed employment income.

5.3 Effect on company

The deemed employment income is an allowable trading expense for the personal service company and is treated as made on the last day of the tax year. If dividends are paid out of this income, they are treated as exempt in order to avoid a double charge to tax on the same income.

The personal service company should consider having an accounting date of 5 April, or shortly thereafter.

For example, if accounts are prepared to 5 April the deemed employment income for 2013/14 is deductible in the company in the year to 5 April 2014, whereas with a 31 March year end the deemed payment would be deductible in the year to 31 March 2015.

5.4 Example: personal service company

Alison offers technical writing services through a company. During 2013/14 the company received income of £40,000 in respect of relevant engagements performed by Alison. The company paid Alison a salary of £20,000 plus employer's NIC of £1,698. The company also pays £3,000 into an occupational pension scheme in respect of Alison. Alison incurred travelling expenses of £400 in respect of the relevant engagements.

The deemed employment income taxed on Alison is

		£
Income (£40,000 × 95%)		38,000
Less:	travel	(400)
	pension	(3,000)
	salary	(20,000)
	employer's NIC on actual salary	(1,698)
		12,902
Less: employer's NIC on deemed payment		
$\frac{13.8}{113.8} \times$ £12,902		(1,565)
Deemed employment income		11,337

6 National insurance for employers and employees

6.1 Classes of National Insurance contributions

FAST FORWARD

National insurance contributions are divided into four classes.

Four classes of national insurance contribution (NIC) exist, as set out below.

(a) **Class 1**. This is divided into:
   (i) **Primary**, paid by employees
   (ii) **Secondary**, **Class 1A and Class 1B** paid by employers

(b) **Class 2**. Paid by the self-employed

(c) **Class 3**. Voluntary contributions (paid to maintain rights to certain state benefits)

(d) **Class 4**. Paid by the self-employed

Exam focus point

Class 1B and Class 3 contributions are outside the scope of your syllabus.

In this section we focus on NIC for employees and their employers.

6.2 General principles

FAST FORWARD

Employees pay primary Class 1 NICs. Employees pay the main primary rate between the primary earnings threshold and upper earnings limit and the additional rate on earnings above the upper earnings limit. Employers pay secondary Class 1 NICs above the secondary earnings threshold. For employers, there is no upper earnings limit.

6.2.1 Introduction

The National Insurance Contributions Office (NICO), which is part of HMRC, examines employers' records and procedures to ensure that the correct amounts of NICs are collected.

Both employees and employers pay Class 1 NICs related to the employee's earnings. NICs are not deductible from an employee's gross salary for income tax purposes. However, employers' contributions are deductible trade expenses.

6.2.2 What is 'earnings'?

'Earnings' broadly comprise gross pay, excluding benefits which cannot be turned into cash by surrender (eg holidays, cars, accommodation, use of employer's assets – these are subject to Class 1A contributions, see 6.3 below). It also includes mileage payments over the approved amount (see below) and readily convertible assets given to employees. No deduction is made for employee pension contributions.

An employer's contribution to a registered personal pension or a registered occupational pension is not 'earnings'. However, NICs are due on employer contributions to non-registered schemes.

In general income tax and NIC exemptions mirror one another. For example, payment of personal incidental expenses covered by the £5/£10 a night income tax de minimis exemption are excluded from NIC earnings. Relocation expenses of a type exempt from income tax are also excluded from NIC earnings but without the income tax £8,000 upper limit (although expenses exceeding £8,000 are subject to Class 1A NICs as described below). Similarly, the income tax rules for travel expenses are exactly mirrored for NIC treatment.

An expense with a business purpose is not treated as earnings. For example, if an employee is reimbursed for business travel or for staying in a hotel on the employer's business this is not normally 'earnings'. However, if an employee is reimbursed for their own home telephone charges the reimbursed cost of private calls (and all reimbursed rental) is earnings.

Where an employer reimburses an employee using their own car for business mileage, the earnings element is the excess of the mileage rate paid over HMRC's 'up to 10,000 business miles' 'approved mileage allowance payments' (AMAPs). This applies even where business mileage exceeds 10,000 pa.

In general, non cash vouchers are subject to NICs. However, the following are exempt:

- Childcare vouchers up to the amount exempt for income tax
- Vouchers for the use of sports and recreational facilities (where tax exempt)
- Vouchers for meals on the employer's premises
- Transport vouchers where the employee earns less than £8,500 a year
- Top up vouchers for pay as you go mobile phones where the provision of the phone itself is exempt from income tax
- Vouchers for eye tests and glasses for employees using VDUs
- Any other voucher which is exempt from income tax.

6.2.3 Rates

The rates of contribution for 2013/14, and the earnings bands to which they apply, are set out in the Rates and Allowances Tables in this text.

Non-contracted out **employees pay main primary contributions of 12% of earnings between the primary earnings threshold of £7,755 and the upper earnings limit of £41,450** or the equivalent monthly or weekly limit (see below). They also pay additional primary contributions of 2% on earnings above the upper earnings limit.

Employers pay secondary contributions of 13.8% on earnings above the secondary earnings threshold of £7,696 or the equivalent monthly or weekly limit. There is no upper limit. If an employee is in a contracted out occupational pension scheme, reduced contributions are payable.

Exam focus point

Calculation of reduced contributions payable by contracted-out employees are outside the scope of your syllabus.

6.2.4 Earnings period

FAST FORWARD

NICs are based on earnings periods.

NICs are calculated in relation to an earnings period. This is the period to which earnings paid to an employee are deemed to relate. Where earnings are paid at regular intervals, the earnings period will generally be equated with the payment interval, for example a week or a month. **Company directors have an annual earnings period, regardless of how they are paid.**

Exam focus point

The examiner has stated that calculations of weekly or monthly contributions will not be examined. All calculations will be on an annualised basis.

Question — **Primary and secondary contributions**

Sally works for Red plc. She is paid £48,000 in 2013/14.

Show Sally's primary contributions for 2013/14, assuming she is not contracted out, and the secondary contributions paid by Red plc.

Answer

Sally

Primary contributions	£
£(41,450 – 7,755) = £33,695 × 12% (main)	4,043
£(48,000 – 41,450) = £6,550 × 2% (additional)	131
Total primary contributions	4,174

Red plc

Secondary contributions	£
£(48,000 – 7,696) = £40,304 × 13.8%	5,562

6.3 Class 1A NIC

FAST FORWARD

Employers pay Class 1A NIC on most taxable benefits.

Employers must pay Class 1A NIC at 13.8% on most taxable benefits. However, benefits are exempt if they are:

- Within Class 1, or
- Covered by a PAYE dispensation, or
- Provided for employees earning less than £8,500 a year, or
- Included in a PAYE settlement agreement, or
- Otherwise not required to be reported on P11Ds

Childcare provision in an **employer provided nursery or playscheme is wholly exempt** from Class 1A NICs. Provision of **other childcare**, for example where an employer contracts directly for places in a commercial nursery, **is exempt up to the limit allowable for income tax.**

Class 1A contributions are collected annually in arrears. If the payment is made electronically, payment must reach HMRC's bank account no later than 22 July following the end of the tax year. Payment by cheque must reach HMRC no later than 19 July following the end of the tax year.

6.3.1 Example: Class 1A NICs

An employee is provided with benefits totaling £2,755 during 2013/14. The Class 1A contributions due from the employer are £2,755 @ 13.8% = £380.

Chapter roundup

- General earnings are taxed in the year of receipt. Money earnings are generally received on the earlier of the time payment is made and the time entitlement to payment arises. Non-money earnings are generally received when provided.
- Employment involves a contract of service whereas self employment involves a contract for services.
- Most employees are taxed on benefits under the benefits code. 'Excluded employees' (lower paid/non-directors) are only subject to part of the provisions of the code.
- The benefit in respect of accommodation is its annual value. There is an additional benefit if the property cost the employer over £75,000.
- Employees who have a company car are taxed on a % of the car's list price which depends on the level of the car's CO_2 emissions. The same % multiplied by £21,100 determines the benefit where private fuel is also provided. Authorised mileage allowances can be paid tax free to employees who use their own vehicle for business journeys.
- Taxable cheap loans are charged to tax on the difference between the official rate of interest and any interest paid by the employee.
- 20% of the value of assets made available for private use is taxable.
- Workplace childcare is an exempt benefit. Employer-supported childcare and childcare vouchers are exempt up to £55 per week. Maximum tax relief is limited to £11 per week (the equivalent of £55 x 20%).
- There is a residual charge for other benefits, usually equal to the cost of the benefits.
- Some benefits are exempt from tax such as removal expenses and the provision of sporting facilities (subject to certain limits).
- To be deductible, expenses must be for qualifying travel or wholly, exclusively and necessarily incurred.
- The IR35 provisions prevent avoidance of tax by providing services through a company.
- National Insurance contributions are divided into four classes.
- Employees pay primary Class 1 NICs. Employees pay the main primary rate between the primary earnings threshold and upper earnings limit and the additional rate on earnings above the upper earnings limit. Employers pay secondary Class 1 NICs above the secondary earnings threshold. For employers, there is no upper earnings limit.
- NICs are based on earnings periods.
- Employers pay Class 1A NIC on most taxable benefits.

Quick quiz

1. Ben is employed by C Ltd and paid £14,000 per annum. For the year ended 31 December 2013 he is paid a £5,000 bonus on 1 May 2014. He was paid a similar bonus of £3,000 on 1 May 2013 based on the year ended 31 December 2012 results. Ben is not a director of C Ltd. How much is Ben's taxable income for 2013/14?
2. What accommodation does not give rise to a taxable benefit?
3. Josh was provided with a company car on 1 August 2013. It cost £25,000 and has a CO_2 emission of 135g/km. Josh uses the car 60% for business use as a sales representative. The company pays for Josh's private diesel for use in the car. What is Josh's benefit(s) in respect of the car?
4. When may an employee who is provided with a fuel by their employer avoid a fuel benefit?
5. To what extent are removal expenses paid for by an employer taxable?
6. When may travel expenses be deducted from the taxable earnings of an employee?
7. Lucy is provided with a mobile phone by her employer costing £350 per annum. What is taxable on Lucy?
8. What are the IR35 provisions designed to prevent?
9. On what and by whom are Class 1A NICs paid?

Answers to quick quiz

1 £17,000 (£14,000 + £3,000 bonus paid in 2013/14)

2 Job related accommodation

3 £6,762 (3,667 + 3,095)

Car: $£25,000 \times (\left[\frac{135-95}{5}\right] +11\% + 3\%)$ (diesel car)

$£25,000 \times 22\%$

£5,500 for 12m

$£5,500 \times 8/12$

Car: £3,667

Fuel: $£21,100 \times 22\% \times 8/12 = £3,095$

4 There is no fuel benefit if:

(a) All the fuel provided was made available only for business travel, or
(b) the full cost of any fuel provided for private use was completely reimbursed by the employee

5 The first £8,000 of removal expenses are exempt. Any excess is taxable.

6 An employee can deduct travel costs incurred in travelling in the performance of their duties or in travelling to a place which they have to attend in the performance of their duties (other than the normal place of work).

7 Nothing. The provision of one mobile phone for private use is an exempt benefit.

8 The provisions are designed to prevent workers avoiding tax and NIC by offering their services through an intermediary, such as a company.

9 Class 1A NICs are paid by employers on taxable benefits.

Now try the questions below from the Exam Question Bank

Number	Level	Marks	Time
Q4	Introductory	15	27 mins
Q5	Introductory	10	18 mins

Employment income: additional aspects

Topic list	Syllabus reference
1 Shares and share options	A1(c)(i)
2 Tax efficient share schemes	A1(c)(i)
3 Lump sum payments	A1(c)(ii)

Introduction

In the last chapter we covered the general rules for employment income, including taxable and exempt benefits.

In this chapter we look at the rules for share incentives and share options. Not only are these tax efficient means by which employees can be remunerated but they also provide a link between remuneration and the company's performance.

Finally, we look at the rules for lump sums paid to employees, usually on the termination of the employment.

In the next chapter we will turn our attention to the self-employed.

Study guide

		Intellectual level
1	**Income and income tax liabilities in situations involving further overseas aspects and in relation to trusts, and the application of exemptions and reliefs**	
(c)	Income from employment:	3
(i)	Advise on the tax treatment of share option and share incentive schemes	
(ii)	Advise on the tax treatment of lump sum receipts	

Exam guide

Share incentives and share options may well feature in a question about employees. You may be required to advise the employer as to which incentive scheme would meet their needs. You need to know the different conditions for each scheme – you will not get any marks for recommending an enterprise management incentive scheme to a company whose gross assets exceed £30 million.

Lump sums are commonly paid on the termination of an employment. You may be required to discuss which elements of a termination package are tax free, and the consequences of the ongoing provision of a benefit.

Knowledge brought forward from earlier studies

None of the topics in this chapter were examinable in Paper F6.

1 Shares and share options

FAST FORWARD

Where shares or share options are provided to an employee outside the approved schemes, a tax charge may arise.

One of the competencies you require to fulfil performance objective 20 of the PER is the ability to assist with tax planning. You can apply the knowledge you obtain from this section of the text to help to demonstrate this competence.

1.1 Introduction

An employer may include shares and share options as part of an incentive package offered to employees. Unless they fall within the special schemes which provide tax reliefs (see below) a tax charge may arise as described below.

1.2 Shares

The ownership of shares in an employing company may lead to a tax charge:

(a) **If a director or an employee is given shares, or is sold shares for less than their market value, there is a charge on the difference between the market value and the amount (if any) which the director or employee pays for the shares.**

(b) If, while the director or employee still has a beneficial interest in the shares, a 'chargeable event' occurs, there is a charge on the increase in the value of the interest caused by the chargeable event as specific employment income.

A chargeable event is a change of rights or restrictions attaching to either the shares in question or to other shares which leads to the value of the shares in question increasing, and which takes place while the person concerned is a director or employee (of the company or of an associated company) or within seven years of their ceasing to be one. However, where the change applies to all shares of the same class there is not in general a chargeable event.

(c) If an employee, having obtained shares by reason of their being a director or employee, receives any special benefit because of their owning the shares, they are taxable under on the benefit as specific employment income unless:

   (i) The benefit is available to at least 90% of persons holding shares of the same class, and

   (ii) – The majority of the shares of the same class are not held by directors or employees, or

   – The company is employee-controlled by virtue of holdings of the same class of shares.

(d) If an employee or director receives shares which may later be forfeited, there is no income tax charge when the shares are acquired. There is an income tax charge when the risk of forfeiture is lifted or when the shares are sold, if sooner. The amount of specific employment income will be the difference between the market value of the shares less the cost of the shares.

(e) If shares received as a result of employment are subsequently converted to shares of another class, there is an income tax charge on conversion on the difference between the market value and cost of the shares.

In the above situations when the base cost of the shares is being calculated for capital gains tax purposes (see later in this Text) any amount charged to income tax is added to the acquisition cost of the shares.

1.3 Share options

(a) **If a director or an employee is granted an option to acquire shares (ie is given the right to buy shares at a future date at a price set now), then, in general, there is no income tax charge on the grant of the option.**

(b) On the exercise of the option **there is a charge as specific employment income on the market value of the shares after date of exercise minus the sum of what (if anything) was paid for the option and what was paid for the shares.** If they assign or releases the option for money, or agrees (for money) not to exercise it or to grant someone else a right to acquire the shares, they are likewise taxable on the amount they get minus the amount they paid for the option.

Question — **Exercise of option**

Mr Wilkes was granted an option to buy 10,000 shares in his employer company in September 2010. The cost of the option was £1 per share. The price at which the option could be exercised was £5.

Mr Wilkes exercised his option in August 2013, when the shares had a market value of £8.

What is the amount of specific employment income taxable in 2013/14?

Answer

	£
Market value at exercise 10,000 × £8	80,000
Less price paid for option 10,000 × £1	(10,000)
price paid for shares 10,000 × £5	(50,000)
Chargeable on exercise	20,000

2 Tax efficient share schemes

2.1 Introduction

FAST FORWARD

There are a range of tax efficient HMRC approved share schemes under which an employer may be able to give employees a stake in the business.

One of the competencies you require to fulfil performance objective 20 of the PER is the ability to assist with tax planning. You can apply the knowledge you obtain from this section of the text to help to demonstrate this competence.

Successive governments have recognised the need to encourage schemes that broaden share ownership among employees or reward personnel. **A number of tax efficient schemes exist.** These are detailed in the following sections.

Exam focus point

If you are asked to recommend an incentive scheme ensure that you select one which fits the employer's requirements.

There are four types of approved share scheme:

- **SAYE share option schemes**
- **Company share option plans (CSOP)**
- **Enterprise Management Incentives (EMI)**
- **Share Incentive Plans (SIPs)**

The first three listed above involve share options, whereas SIPs involve employees being given shares.

There are many detailed rules governing these schemes, but in this chapter, the following aspects are considered for each scheme:

- **How the scheme operates.**
- **Taxation implications of grant and exercise of options** (where appropriate). Approved schemes generally allow options to be granted and exercised without income tax and national insurance charges.
- **Taxation implications of sale of shares.** Generally, the only tax charge is when the shares are sold at a gain and the charge is to capital gains tax (rather than income tax and national insurance).
- **Conditions for the scheme.** The conditions required by each scheme vary but may relate to the **company operating the scheme**, the **employees participating in the scheme**, the **shares being issued**, and the **price at which options can be exercised**. In some cases, certain **time limits** must be met eg shares/options must be held for a certain period.
- **Costs of setting up the scheme.** Deductions available for the operating company are considered.

Exam focus point

In the examination, you may be required to advise on any, or all, of these aspects, for a particular scheme or schemes. For example, in the December 2011 exam, candidates were required to assess whether a scheme described in the question met the conditions to be an approved SAYE scheme. They then had to explain and calculate the tax and national insurance implications of grant, exercise, sale etc.

2.2 SAYE share option schemes

FAST FORWARD

A Save As You Earn (SAYE) share option scheme allows employees to save regular monthly amounts for a fixed period and use the funds to take up options to buy shares free of income tax and NIC. Alternatively they can simply take the cash saved.

2.2.1 How the scheme operates

An employer can set up a scheme, which must be open to all employees and full-time directors, under which employees can choose to make regular monthly investments in special bank or building society accounts called sharesave accounts. Employees can save a fixed monthly amount of between £5 and £250.

The investments are made for three or five years, and a tax-free bonus is then added to the account by way of interest.

At the withdrawal date, the employee may take the money in cash. Alternatively, they may leave the money in the scheme for another two years in which case another tax-free bonus is added.

The employee **may alternatively use the money to buy ordinary shares in their employer company, or its holding company, under options granted when the employee started to save in the account.**

The price of these shares is fixed by the option and must be at least 80% of the market value at the date the option was granted.

2.2.2 Tax implications of grant and exercise of options

There is no income tax or national insurance charge:

(a) **when the options are granted** (ie when the employee starts saving in the scheme),

(b) while the employee saves money in the scheme, in particular the bonus given by way of interest is tax-free,

(c) **when the options are exercised,**

(d) if the employee decides not to buy shares, but to withdraw the money instead.

2.2.3 Tax implications of sale of shares

There is no income tax or national insurance contributions payable on the sale of shares acquired under an SAYE scheme.

When the shares are sold, any gain is subject to CGT. The cost in the gain calculation is the price the employee paid for the shares.

2.2.4 Conditions for SAYE schemes

To obtain HMRC approval, a scheme must be open to all employees and full-time directors, and on similar terms. Part-time directors may be included, but can be excluded. However, a minimum qualifying period of employment (of up to five years) may be imposed, and there may be differences based on remuneration or length of service.

2.2.5 Costs of setting up SAYE schemes

The costs of setting up an SAYE scheme incurred by a company are deductible in the accounting period in which they are incurred provided the scheme is approved within nine months of the end of that accounting period.

2.3 Company share option plans (CSOP)

FAST FORWARD

There is no income tax or NIC on the grant of a Company Share Option Plan (CSOP) option. There is also no income tax or NIC on an exercise taking place between three and ten years after the grant. Only CGT will apply to the profit on disposal of the shares.

2.3.1 How the scheme operates

Under a CSOP scheme, which can be restricted to selected employees and full-time directors, an employee is granted options to buy shares. Options must be exercised between three and ten years from grant to achieve the beneficial tax treatment (see below). An employee can be granted options over shares up to the value of £30,000 (at the date of grant).

2.3.2 Tax implications of grant and exercise of options

There is **no income tax** or national insurance on:

(a) **the grant of an option** under a CSOP, nor

(b) **on the profit arising from the exercise of an option under a CSOP between three and ten years after the grant.**

The tax exemption is lost in respect of an option if it is exercised earlier than three years or later than ten years after grant.

The three year waiting period does not apply when personal representatives exercise the options of a deceased employee within twelve months of death (but the ten year rule still applies).

If the options are exercised before three years after the grant, they will remain tax exempt if the exercise (and exit from the scheme) arises due to certain circumstances which include:

(a) cessation of employment due to the injury, disability, redundancy or retirement of the employee,
(b) a cash takeover of the company which results in a forced exercise of the options.

2.3.3 Tax implications of sale of shares

There are no income tax or national insurance consequences of the sale of shares acquired under a CSOP.

When the shares are sold, any gain is subject to CGT. The cost in the gain calculation is the option price paid by the employee to acquire the shares.

2.3.4 Conditions for CSOPs

To obtain HMRC approval, CSOPs must satisfy the following **conditions:**

(a) The shares must be **fully paid ordinary shares.**

(b) The **price of the shares must not be less than their market value at the time of the grant of the option.**

(c) **Participation in the scheme must be limited to employees and full-time directors**, but the scheme need not be open to all employees and full-time directors.

(d) **No options may be granted which take the total market value of shares for which an employee holds options above £30,000.** Shares are valued as at the times when the options on them are granted. Options must not be transferable.

(e) If the issuing company has more than one class of shares, the **majority of shares in the class for which the scheme operates must be held other than by:**

  (i) **Persons acquiring them through their positions as directors or employees (unless the company is an employee controlled company)**

  (ii) **A holding company (unless the scheme shares are quoted)**

(f) **Anyone who has within the preceding 12 months held over 30% of the shares of a close company which is the company whose shares may be acquired under the scheme, or which controls that company either alone or as part of a consortium, must be excluded from the scheme.**

2.3.5 Costs of setting up CSOPs

The costs of setting up a CSOP incurred by a company are deductible in the accounting period in which they are incurred provided the scheme is approved within nine months of the end of that accounting period.

2.4 Enterprise Management Incentives (EMI)

FAST FORWARD

No income tax or NIC is chargeable on either the grant or exercise of options under the enterprise management incentive (EMI) scheme provided the exercise takes place within 10 years of the grant and the exercise price is at least equal to the market value of the shares at the date of the grant.

2.4.1 How the scheme operates

The EMI scheme is intended to help smaller, higher risk companies recruit and retain employees who have the skills to help them grow and succeed. They are also a way of rewarding employees for taking a risk by investing their time and skills to help small companies achieve their potential. **Employees must spend a certain amount of time working for the company each week (see below) to be eligible to be given EMI options, but the company can choose to which of the eligible employees it grants such options. Therefore the EMI scheme is particularly useful if a company wishes to reward its key employees.**

EMIs are similar to CSOPs, as an employee is granted options to buy shares. Specific features of the EMI scheme include the following:

(a) **a qualifying company can grant each of its employees options over shares worth up to £250,000 at the time of grant, subject to a maximum of £3m in total.**

(b) **the company may set a target** to be achieved before an option can be exercised. The target must clearly be defined at the time the option is granted.

(c) **options can be granted at a discount below the market value at the date of grant**, although there are tax consequences of this (see below).

Some of these features make the EMI a more attractive scheme than a CSOP, but there are restrictions, in particular regarding which companies can operate EMI schemes.

2.4.2 Tax implications of grant and exercise of options

No income tax or national insurance is chargeable on either the grant or exercise of the options provided the exercise takes place within 10 years of the grant and the exercise price is at least equal to the market value of the shares at the date of the grant.

If **the options were granted at a discount to the market value at the date of grant, there is an income tax charge** (and possibly a national insurance contributions charge) **when the options are exercised** (not when they are granted) **on the lower of:**

(a) **The discount** (ie the difference between the market value of the shares at the date of grant and the price paid for the shares (the 'exercise' price)), and

(b) **The difference between the market value of the shares at the date of exercise and the exercise price.**

2.4.3 Tax implications of sale of shares

No income tax or national insurance is chargeable on the disposal of shares acquired under an EMI scheme.

When the shares are sold, any gain is subject to CGT. The cost in the gain calculation is the amount paid for the shares *plus* any discount taxed as earnings as described above.

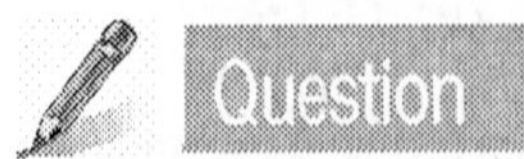

Question

EMI shares

Melody is employed by J plc. In October 2013, J plc granted Melody options to purchase 25,000 shares at a price of £4.50 per share under the EMI scheme. The market value of the shares at the date of the grant was £4.75 per share. Melody intends to exercise her options in June 2015 (when the market value is estimated to be £5.50 per share) and sell the shares in December 2016, when she thinks they will be worth £6.50 per share.

What are the tax implications for Melody when she exercises her EMI share options and when she sell the shares? Assume that the tax rules in 2013/14 continue to apply for the foreseeable future.

Answer

In 2015/16, when Melody exercises the options and purchases shares in J plc, she will be liable to income tax and national insurance on the amount by which the value of the shares at the time the options were granted exceeded the price she pays for the shares, ie £6,250 (25,000 × (£4.75 – £4.50)). This is the amount taxed as it is lower than the difference between the market value at the time of exercise and the exercise price (ie 25,000 × (£5.50 – £4.50) = £25,000).

In 2016/17, when she sells the shares, she will have the following gain on sale:

	£	£
Sale proceeds 25,000 × £6.50		162,500
Less price paid for shares 25,000 × £4.50	112,500	
discount taxed as earnings on exercise	6,250	
		(118,750)
Gain		43,750

Where an individual **acquires shares on the exercise of an EMI option** and disposes of them on or after 6 April 2013, the gain is eligible for **entrepreneurs' relief where the option was granted at least one year before the date of disposal** (ie **the period of ownership of the option counts towards the one year ownership condition** for entrepreneurs' relief to apply). The individual must have been an **employee or officer for at least one year** ending with the disposal date, but **does not need to own at least 5% of the company's shares**, which is one of the usual conditions for entrepreneurs' relief to apply. We look at entrepreneurs' relief in detail later in this Text.

2.4.4 Conditions for EMI schemes: qualifying company

The company, which **can be listed on a stock exchange**, must meet certain conditions when the options are granted. In particular, **the company's gross assets must not exceed £30m. The company must not be under the control of any other company.**

The company must carry on one of a number of qualifying trades.

The company must have less than 250 full-time equivalent employees at the time the options are granted.

2.4.5 Conditions for EMI schemes: eligible employees

Employees must be employed by the company or group for at least 25 hours a week, or, if less, for at least 75% of their working time (including self-employment). **Employees who own 30% or more of the ordinary shares in the company** (disregarding unexercised options shares) **are excluded.**

2.4.6 Conditions for EMI schemes: qualifying shares

The share must be **fully paid up irredeemable ordinary shares**. The rules permit restrictions on sale, forfeiture conditions and performance conditions.

2.4.7 Conditions for EMI schemes: limit

At any one time, an employee may hold EMI options over shares with a value of up to £250,000 at the date of grant. Restrictions and conditions attaching to the shares may not be taken into account when valuing shares.

Where options are granted above the £250,000 limit, relief is given on options up to the limit. Once the employee has reached the limit, no more EMI options may be granted for 3 years ie the employee may not immediately top up with new options following the exercise of old options.

Any options granted under a CSOP reduce the £250,000 limit, but SAYE share options can be ignored.

2.4.8 Conditions for EMI schemes: disqualifying events

There are a number of disqualifying events including an employee ceasing to spend at least 75% of their working time with the company. EMI relief is available up to the date of the event.

2.4.9 Costs of EMI schemes

The costs of setting up a scheme and on-going administration are deductible in computing profits.

2.4.10 Notification of grant of options in EMI schemes

It is not necessary to submit schemes to HMRC for approval. Instead, **HMRC must be notified of the grant of options within 92 days**. HMRC then has 12 months to check whether the grants satisfy the EMI rules.

A company may submit details in writing to the Small Company Enterprise Centre before the options are granted. The Officer of Revenue and Customs will then confirm in writing whether they are satisfied that the company will be a qualifying company on the basis of information supplied.

The details to be submitted include:

(a) a copy of the latest accounts for the company and its subsidiaries

(b) a company of the memorandum and articles of association and details of any proposed changes, and

(c) details of trading and other activities carried on, or to be carried on, by the company or its subsidiaries.

Advance approval is not possible in respect of any other aspect of EMI such as whether an employee is an eligible employee.

2.5 Share Incentive Plans (SIPs)

FAST FORWARD

Employees may be given £3,000 of 'free' shares a year under a share incentive plan (SIP). In addition, they can purchase up to £1,500 worth of 'partnership' shares a year and employers can provide up to £3,000 worth of matching shares. Once the shares have been held for five years there is no income tax or NIC when shares are taken out of the plan.

2.5.1 How the scheme operates

SIPs differ from the other approved schemes, in that options are not granted to employees, but, instead, they are given shares which are held in the plan. All full and part-time employee of the company (subject to a minimum period of employment) must be eligible to participate in the plan.

Employers can give up to £3,000 of 'free shares' a year to employees. Employers offering free shares must offer a minimum amount to each employee on 'similar terms'. Between the minimum and the maximum of £3,000, the employer can offer shares in different amounts and on different bases to different employees. This means that employers can reward either individual or team performance. Employers can set performance targets subject to the overriding requirement that a plan must not contain any features that concentrate rewards on directors and more highly paid employees.

Employees can also purchase '**partnership shares**' at any time in the year. These shares are funded through deductions of **up to £1,500 in any tax year**.

Employers can also award **'matching shares'** free to employees who purchase partnership shares at a maximum ratio of 2:1.

A plan may provide for free and matching shares to be forfeited if the employee leaves within three years, unless the employee leaves for specified reasons such as retirement or redundancy.

The plan must be operated through a UK resident trust. The trustees acquire the shares from the company or – if the plan incorporates partnership shares – from the employees. The existence of arrangements to enable employees to sell shares held in a new plan trust will not of itself make those shares readily convertible into cash and require employers, for example, to operate national insurance.

Stamp duty is not payable when an employee purchases shares from a SIP trust. The trust must pay stamp duty when it acquires the shares. No taxable benefit arises on an employee as a result of a SIP trust or an employer paying either stamp duty or the incidental costs of operating the plan.

2.5.2 Tax implications on giving shares and on withdrawal of shares from plan

There is no income tax or national insurance when shares are given to employees (and put in the plan) as described above.

Free and matching shares must normally be held in a plan for at least three years. If **shares are withdrawn within three years** (because the employee leaves) there is a **charge to income tax** (as specific employment income) **and NIC on the market value of the shares at the time of withdrawal. If shares are taken out of the plan after three years but before five years, there is charge to income tax and NIC based on the lower of the initial value of the shares and their value at the date of withdrawal**, so any increase in value is free of income tax and NIC. If one of the specified reasons applies, eg redundancy or retirement, there is no tax or NIC charge. **Once the shares have been held for five years, there is no income tax or national insurance when shares are taken out of the plan.**

Partnership shares can be taken out at any time. If the shares are **held for less than three years**, there is a **charge to income tax and NIC on the market value at the time the shares are removed.** If the shares are removed **after three years but before five years**, the **charge to income tax and NIC is based on the lower of salary used to buy the shares and the market value at the date of removal. Once the shares have been held for five years, there is no income tax or national insurance when shares are taken out of the plan.**

2.5.3 Tax exemption for dividends used to acquire dividend shares

Dividends on shares in the plan are tax-free provided the dividends are used to acquire additional shares in the company, which are then held in the plan for three years. These 'dividend' shares do not affect entitlement to partnership or matching shares.

The company may specify a percentage (which may be 100%) of dividends that may be used to acquire dividend shares and modify that percentage from time to time.

2.5.4 Tax implications of sale of shares

There is no charge to CGT on shares taken out of a plan and sold immediately. A charge to CGT will arise on sale to the extent that the shares increase in value after they are withdrawn from the plan.

2.5.5 Conditions for SIPs

Shares in the plan must be fully paid irredeemable ordinary shares in a company either:

(a) **Listed on a recognised stock exchange** (or in its subsidiary), or
(b) **Not controlled by another company.**

A plan established by a company that controls other companies, may be extended to any or all of these other companies. Such a plan is called a group plan.

A plan need not include all the components – it is possible to have a plan with only free shares.

Companies must offer all full and part-time employees the opportunity to participate in the plan. A minimum qualifying period of employment of up to 18 months may be specified. Any minimum period specified can be satisfied by working for any company within a group.

2.5.6 Costs of SIPs

A **deduction in computing profits** for the company is given for:

(a) The costs of setting up and administering the plan.

(b) The gross salary allocated by employees to buy partnership shares.

(c) The costs of providing shares to the extent that the costs exceed the employees contributions.

(d) The market value of free and matching shares when they are acquired by the trustees.

(e) Interest paid by the trustees on borrowing to acquire shares where the company meets the trustees' costs.

2.6 Approved schemes summary

Scheme name	Gift/purchase/option scheme	Tax advantages	Employees
SAYE	Option scheme	• Tax free savings bonus • No income tax/NIC on exercise • CGT on sale of shares	All employees
CSOP	Option scheme	• No income tax/NIC on exercise • CGT on sale of shares	Selected employees
EMI	Option scheme	• No income/NIC tax on exercise (unless granted at a discount) • CGT on sale of shares	Key employees
SIP	Gift from employer and/or purchase by employee	• Favourable income tax charge if shares held ≥ 3yrs • No income tax/NIC if held ≥ 5 yrs • CGT on sale of shares	All employees

3 Lump sum payments

FAST FORWARD

Payments made on the termination of employment may be fully taxable, partially exempt or exempt. The first £30,000 of a genuinely *ex gratia* termination payment is normally exempt.

3.1 Payments on the termination of employment

Termination payments may be entirely exempt, partly exempt or entirely chargeable.

3.1.1 Exempt termination payments

The following payments on the termination of employment are exempt.

- Payments on account of injury, disability or accidental death
- Lump sum payments from registered pension schemes
- Legal costs recovered by the employee from the employer following legal action to recover compensation for loss of employment, where the costs are ordered by the court or (for out-of-court settlements) are paid directly to the employee's solicitor as part of the settlement.

3.1.2 Fully taxable termination payments

Payments to which the employee is contractually entitled are, in general, taxable in full as general earnings. Payments for work done (terminal bonuses), for doing extra work during a period of notice, payments in lieu of notice where stated in the original contract, or for extending a period of notice are therefore taxable in full. A payment by one employer to induce an employee to take up employment with another employer is also taxable in full.

An employee may, either on leaving an employment or at some other time, accept a limitation on their future conduct or activities in return for a payment. This is known as a restrictive covenant. **Such payments are taxable as general earnings.** However, a payment accepted in full and final settlement of any claims the employee may have against the employer is not automatically taxable under this rule.

3.1.3 Partly taxable termination payments

Other payments on termination (such as compensation for loss of office and statutory redundancy pay), which are not taxable under the general earnings rules because they are not in return for services, are nevertheless brought in as amounts which count as employment income. These are often called *ex gratia* payments. Such payments **are partly exempt: the first £30,000 is exempt; any excess is taxable as specific employment income.**

3.1.4 Benefits provided on termination

Payments and other benefits provided in connection with termination of employment (or a change in terms of employment) **are taxable in the year in which they are received.** 'Received' in this case means when it is paid or the recipient becomes entitled to it (for cash payments) or when it is used or enjoyed (non-cash benefits).

All payments to an employee on termination, both cash and non-cash, should be considered. Non-cash benefits are taxed by reference to their cash equivalent (using the normal benefits rules). Thus if a company car continues to be made available to an ex-employee say for a further year after redundancy they will be taxed on the same benefit value as if they had remained in employment. The normal exemptions apply, so that the continued use of one mobile telephone and work related training would be exempt.

3.1.5 Special situations

HMRC regard payments notionally made as compensation for loss of office but which are made on retirement or death (other than accidental death) as **lump sum payments under non registered pension schemes, and therefore taxable in full**. Also, payments in circumstances which amount to unfair dismissal are treated as eligible for the £30,000 exemption.

3.1.6 Practical issues

If the termination package is a partially exempt one and exceeds £30,000 then the £30,000 exempt limit is allocated to earlier benefits and payments. In any particular year the exemption is allocated to cash payments before non-cash benefits.

Employers have an obligation to report termination settlements which include benefits to HMRC by 6 July following the tax year end. No report is required if the package consists wholly of cash. Employers must also notify HMRC by this date of settlements which (over their lifetime) may exceed £30,000.

3.2 Example: redundancy package

Jonah is made redundant on 31 December 2013. He receives (not under a contractual obligation) the following redundancy package:

- total cash of £40,000 payable £20,000 in January 2014 and £20,000 in January 2015
- use of company car for period to 5 April 2015 (benefit value per annum £5,000)

In 2013/14 Jonah receives as redundancy:

	£
Cash	20,000
Car (£5,000 × $^3/_{12}$)	1,250
	21,250

wholly exempt (allocate £21,250 of £30,000 exemption to cash first then benefit).

In 2014/15 Jonah receives:

	£
Cash	20,000
Car	5,000
	25,000
Exemption (remaining)	(8,750)
Taxable	16,250

£11,250 (£20,000 less £8,750) of the cash payment is taxable.

3.3 Other lump sum payments

Where lump sums are received otherwise than in connection with the termination of employment they will be taxable if they derive from the employment. Examples are:

(a) A golden hello, which is a one-off payment made to encourage someone to join a new employer. As it is effectively a reward for future services it is subject to both tax and NIC.

(b) A payment for a change in the terms of employment is also taxable.

Chapter roundup

- Where shares or share options are provided to an employee outside the approved schemes, a tax charge may arise.
- There are a range of tax efficient HMRC approved share schemes under which an employer may be able to give employees a stake in the business.
- A Save As You Earn (SAYE) share option scheme allows employees to save regular monthly amounts for a fixed period and use the funds to take up options to buy shares free of income tax and NIC. Alternatively they can simply take the cash saved.
- There is no income tax or NIC on the grant of a Company Share Option Plan (CSOP) option. There is also no income tax or NIC on an exercise taking place between three and ten years after the grant. Only CGT will apply to the profit on disposal of the shares.
- No income tax or NIC is chargeable on either the grant or exercise of options under the enterprise management incentive (EMI) scheme provided the exercise takes place within 10 years of the grant and the exercise price is at least equal to the market value of the shares at the date of the grant.
- Employees may be given £3,000 of 'free' shares a year under a share incentive plan (SIP). In addition, they can purchase up to £1,500 worth of 'partnership' shares a year and employers can provide up to £3,000 worth of matching shares. Once the shares have been held for five years there is no income tax or NIC when shares are taken out of the plan.
- Payments made on the termination of employment may be fully taxable, partially exempt or exempt. The first £30,000 of a genuinely *ex gratia* termination payment is normally exempt.

Quick quiz

1. Which approved share option scheme allows employees to take a cash amount instead of exercising their options?
2. What is the maximum amount of enterprise management incentive scheme options that an employee can hold?
3. How may 'free shares' can an employee receive under a share incentive plan?
4. How many matching shares can be given in respect of each partnership share purchased?
5. On what value is income tax charged if shares held within a share incentive plan are disposed of within three years?
6. Which termination payments are partly exempt?
7. Thomas was made redundant on 4 January 2014. His severance package was:

Statutory redundancy pay	£12,000
Golden Goodbye	£40,000

The 'Golden Goodbye' was a payment made by the company to 'soften the blow' of redundancy to Thomas. It was not paid as part of his contract of employment.

How much of the above is taxable?

Answers to quick quiz

1. SAYE share option scheme.
2. At any one time an employee may hold options over shares worth up to £250,000 at the date of grant.
3. Up to £3,000 worth of free shares.
4. Up to two.
5. Income tax is charged on the market value of the shares on the date of withdrawal.
6. The first £30,000 of genuinely *ex gratia* termination payments ie not in return for services.
7. £22,000.

Golden Goodbye	£40,000
Partial exemption £(30,000 – 12,000)	£(18,000)
	£22,000

Statutory redundancy of £12,000 is exempt and the £30,000 exemption for *ex gratia* amounts is reduced by this amount.

Now try the question below from the Exam Question Bank

Number	Level	Marks	Time
Q6	Introductory	20	36 mins

Trade profits

Topic list	Syllabus reference
1 The badges of trade	A1(a)B3
2 The computation of trade profits	A1(a)B3
3 Basis periods	A1(a)B3
4 Change of accounting date	A1(d)(i)
5 National insurance	A6(a)F3

Introduction

In previous chapters we have looked at the income tax computation, property and investment income and employment income. We are now going to look at the taxation of unincorporated businesses. We work out a business's profit as if it were a separate entity (the separate entity concept familiar to you from basic bookkeeping) but as an unincorporated business has no legal existence apart from its proprietor, we cannot tax it separately. We have to feed its profit into the proprietor's personal tax computation.

In this chapter, we look at the computation and taxation of profits. Standard rules on the computation of profits are used instead of individual traders' accounting policies, so as to ensure fairness. We also need special rules, the basis period rules, to link the profits of periods of account to the personal computations of tax years.

Finally, we see how national insurance contributions apply to the self-employed.

In the next chapters we study the allowances available for capital expenditure and then we look at losses and partnerships.

Study guide

		Intellectual level
1	**Income and income tax liabilities in situations involving further overseas aspects and in relation to trusts, and the application of exemptions and reliefs**	
(a)	The contents of the Paper F6 study guide for income tax, under heading:	2
•	B3 Income from self employment	
(d)	Income from self employment	3
(i)	Advise on a change of accounting date	
6	**National insurance, value added tax, tax administration and the UK tax system:**	
(a)	The contents of the Paper F6 study guide for national insurance under heading:	2
•	F3 Class 2 and Class 4 contributions for self-employed persons	

Exam guide

Rather than being asked to calculate taxable trade profits you are more likely to be asked about the effect on after tax income of taking on an additional contract. This will involve calculating the incremental profits, deducting tax payable, and taking any other costs into account. This will normally include VAT considerations. To be able to do this you need a full understanding of the rules for calculating taxable trade profits and allocating them to tax years.

Knowledge brought forward from earlier studies

Most of this chapter is revision from Paper F6. The examiner has identified essential underpinning knowledge from the F6 syllabus which is particularly important that you revise as part of your P6 studies. In this chapter, the relevant topic is:

		Intellectual level
B3	**Income from self-employment**	
(f)	Compute the assessable profits on commencement and on cessation.	2

You are already familiar with change of accounting date which was in the F6 syllabus in previous years.

Unincorporated businesses can make fixed rate deductions for some expenses from 2013/14. The cash basis of accounting can be used by small unincorporated businesses from 2013/14.

There is also one minor change in 2013/14 from 2012/13 in the material you have already studied, which is that the CO_2 limit for the restriction for car leasing costs has been reduced to 130 g/km for leases starting on or after 6 April 2013 (1 April 2013 for companies).

1 The badges of trade

FAST FORWARD

The badges of trade can be used to decide whether or not a trade exists.

1.1 Introduction

Before a tax charge can be imposed it is necessary to establish the existence of a trade.

Key terms

A **trade** is defined in the legislation only in an unhelpful manner as including any venture in the nature of trade. It has therefore been left to the courts to provide guidance. This guidance is often summarised in a collection of principles known as the **'badges of trade'**. These are set out below. **Profits from professions and vocations are taxed in the same way as profits from a trade.**

1.2 The subject matter

Whether a person is trading or not may sometimes be decided by examining the subject matter of the transaction. Some assets are commonly held as investments for their intrinsic value: an individual buying some shares or a painting may do so in order to enjoy the income from the shares or to enjoy the work of art. A subsequent disposal may produce a gain of a capital nature rather than a trade profit. But **where the subject matter of a transaction is such as would not be held as an investment** (for example, 34,000,000 yards of aircraft linen (*Martin v Lowry 1927*) or 1,000,000 rolls of toilet paper (*Rutledge v CIR 1929*)), **it is presumed that any profit on resale is a trade profit.**

1.3 The frequency of transactions

Transactions which may, in isolation, be of a capital nature will be interpreted as trading transactions where their **frequency indicates the carrying on of a trade**. It was decided that whereas normally the purchase of a mill-owning company and the subsequent stripping of its assets might be a capital transaction, where the taxpayer was embarking on the same exercise for the fourth time they must be carrying on a trade *(Pickford v Quirke 1927).*

1.4 Existence of similar trading transactions or interests

If there is an **existing trade**, then a **similarity to the transaction which is being considered** may point to that transaction having a trading character. For example, a builder who builds and sells a number of houses may be held to be trading even if they retain one or more houses for longer than usual and claims that they were held as an investment (*Harvey v Caulcott 1952).*

1.5 The length of ownership

The courts may infer adventures in the nature of trade where items purchased are sold soon afterwards.

1.6 The organisation of the activity as a trade

The courts may infer that a trade is being carried on if the transactions are **carried out in the same manner as someone who is unquestionably trading**. For example, an individual who bought a consignment of whiskey and then sold it through an agent, in the same way as others who were carrying on a trade, was also held to be trading (*CIR v Fraser 1942*). On the other hand, if an asset has to be sold in order to raise funds in an emergency, this is less likely to be treated as trading.

1.7 Supplementary work and marketing

When work is done to make an asset more marketable, or steps are taken to find purchasers, the courts will be more ready to ascribe a trading motive. When a group of accountants bought, blended and recasked a quantity of brandy they were held to be taxable on a trade profit when the brandy was later sold *(Cape Brandy Syndicate v CIR 1921)*.

1.8 A profit motive

The absence of a profit motive will not necessarily preclude a tax charge as trading income, but its presence is a strong indication that a person is trading. The purchase and resale of £20,000 worth of silver bullion by the comedian Norman Wisdom, as a hedge against devaluation, was held to be a trading transaction *(Wisdom v Chamberlain 1969)*.

1.9 The way in which the asset sold was acquired

If goods are acquired deliberately, trading may be indicated. If goods are acquired unintentionally, for example by gift or inheritance, their later sale is unlikely to be trading.

1.10 Method of finance

If the **purchaser has to borrow money to buy an asset such that they have to sell that asset quickly to repay the loan**, it may be inferred that trading was taking place. This was a factor in the *Wisdom v Chamberlain* case as Mr Wisdom financed his purchases by loans at a high rate of interest. It was clear that he had to sell the silver bullion quickly in order to repay the loan and prevent the interest charges becoming too onerous. On the other hand, taking out a long term loan to buy an asset (such as a mortgage on a house) would not usually indicate that trading is being carried on.

1.11 The taxpayer's intentions

Where a transaction is clearly trading on objective criteria, **the taxpayer's intentions are irrelevant**. If, however, a transaction has (objectively) a dual purpose, the taxpayer's intentions may be taken into account. An example of a transaction with a dual purpose is the acquisition of a site partly as premises from which to conduct another trade, and partly with a view to the possible development and resale of the site. This test is not one of the traditional badges of trade, but it may be just as important.

Exam focus point

If on applying the badges of trade HMRC do not conclude that income is 'trade income' then they can potentially treat it as other income or a capital gain. Remember that capital gains are taxable at a maximum rate of 28% whereas income is taxed at a maximum rate of 45%. HMRC will therefore be looking very carefully to see if a transaction really results in a capital gain or whether it is really a trade receipt.

2 The computation of trade profits

FAST FORWARD

The accounts profits need to be adjusted in order to establish the taxable trade profits.

One of the competencies you require to fulfil performance objective 19 of the PER is the ability to evaluate and compute taxes payable. You can apply the knowledge you obtain from this section of the text to help to demonstrate this competence.

2.1 The adjustment of profits

The net profit shown in the statement of profit or loss is the starting point in computing the taxable trade profits. Many adjustments may be required to calculate the taxable amount.

Exam focus point

> Only International Accounting Standard terminology is used when presenting accounting information contained within an examination question. This applies for companies, sole traders and partnerships.

Here is an illustrative adjustment of a statement of profit or loss:

	£	£
Net profit		140,000
Add: expenditure charged in the accounts which is not deductible from trading profits	50,000	
income taxable as trading profits which has not been included in the accounts	30,000	
		80,000
		220,000
Less: profits included in the accounts but which are not taxable trading profits	40,000	
expenditure which is deductible from trading profits but has not been charged in the accounts	20,000	
		(60,000)
Adjusted taxable trading profit		160,000

You may refer to deductible and non-deductible expenditure as allowable and disallowable expenditure respectively. The two sets of terms are interchangeable.

2.2 Accounting policies

The fundamental concept is that the profits of the business must be calculated in accordance with generally accepted accounting practice. These profits are subject to any adjustment specifically required for income tax purposes.

2.3 Capital allowances

Under the Capital Allowances Act 2001 (CAA 2001) **capital allowances are treated as trade expenses and balancing charges are treated as trade receipts** (see later in this Text).

2.4 Non-deductible expenditure

Certain expenses are specifically disallowed by the legislation. These are covered in paragraphs 2.4.1-2.4.10. If however a deduction is specifically permitted this overrides the disallowance.

2.4.1 Capital expenditure

Income tax is a tax solely on income so capital expenditure is not deductible. This denies a deduction for depreciation or amortisation (although there are special rules for companies in relation to intangible assets – see later in this Text). **The most contentious items of expenditure will often be repairs** (revenue expenditure) **and improvements** (capital expenditure).

- The cost of restoration of an asset by, for instance, replacing a subsidiary part of the asset is revenue expenditure. Expenditure on a new factory chimney replacement was allowable since the chimney was a subsidiary part of the factory (*Samuel Jones & Co (Devondale) Ltd v CIR 1951*). However, in another case a football club demolished a spectators' stand and replaced it with a modern equivalent. This was held not to be repair, since repair is the restoration by renewal or replacement of subsidiary parts of a larger entity, and the stand formed a distinct and *separate* part of the club (*Brown v Burnley Football and Athletic Co Ltd 1980).*
- The cost of initial repairs to improve an asset recently acquired to make it fit to earn profits is disallowable capital expenditure. In *Law Shipping Co Ltd v CIR 1923* the taxpayer failed to obtain relief for expenditure on making a newly bought ship seaworthy prior to using it.
- The cost of initial repairs to remedy normal wear and tear of recently acquired assets is allowable. *Odeon Associated Theatres Ltd v Jones 1971* can be contrasted with the *Law Shipping* judgement. Odeon were allowed to charge expenditure incurred on improving the state of recently acquired cinemas.

Other examples to note include:

- A one-off payment made by a hotel owner to terminate an agreement for the management of a hotel was held to be revenue rather than capital expenditure in *Croydon Hotel & Leisure Co v Bowen 1996.* The payment did not affect the whole structure of the taxpayer's business; it merely enabled it to be run more efficiently.
- A one-off payment to remove a threat to the taxpayer's business was also held to be revenue rather than capital expenditure in *Lawson v Johnson Matthey plc 1992.*
- An initial payment for a franchise (as opposed to regular fees) is capital and not deductible.

2.4.2 Expenditure not wholly and exclusively for the purposes of the trade

Expenditure is not deductible if it is not for trade purposes (the remoteness test), or if it reflects more than one purpose (the duality test). The private proportion of payments for motoring expenses, rent, heat and light and telephone expenses of a proprietor is not deductible. If an exact apportionment is possible relief is given on the business element. Where the payments are to or on behalf of employees, the full amounts are deductible but the employees are taxed under the benefits code (see earlier in this Text).

The remoteness test is illustrated by the following cases:

- *Strong & Co of Romsey Ltd v Woodifield 1906*

  A customer injured by a falling chimney when sleeping in an inn owned by a brewery claimed compensation from the company. The compensation was not deductible: 'the loss sustained by the appellant was not really incidental to their trade as innkeepers and fell upon them in their character not of innkeepers but of householders'.

- *Bamford v ATA Advertising Ltd 1972*

  A director misappropriated £15,000. The loss was not allowable: 'the loss is not, as in the case of a dishonest shop assistant, an incident of the company's trading activities. It arises altogether outside such activities'.

- Expenditure which is wholly and exclusively to benefit the trades of several companies (for example, in a group) but is not wholly and exclusively to benefit the trade of one specific company is not deductible (*Vodafone Cellular Ltd and others v Shaw 1995*).

- *McKnight (HMIT) v Sheppard (1999)* concerned expenses incurred by a stockbroker in defending allegations of infringements of Stock Exchange regulations. It was found that the expenditure was incurred to prevent the destruction of the taxpayer's business and that as the expenditure was incurred for business purposes it was deductible. It was also found that although the expenditure had the effect of preserving the taxpayer's reputation, that was not its purpose, so there was no duality of purpose.

The **duality test** is illustrated by the following cases:

- *Caillebotte v Quinn 1975*

  A self-employed carpenter spent an average of 40p per day when obliged to buy lunch away from home but just 10p when he lunched at home. He claimed the excess 30p. It was decided that the payment had a dual purpose and was not deductible: a taxpayer 'must eat to live not eat to work'.

- *Mallalieu v Drummond 1983*

  Expenditure by a lady barrister on black clothing to be worn in court (and on its cleaning and repair) was not deductible. The expenditure was for the dual purpose of enabling the barrister to be warmly and properly clad as well as meeting her professional requirements.

- *McLaren v Mumford 1996*

  A publican traded from a public house which had residential accommodation above it. He was obliged to live at the public house but he also had another house which he visited regularly. It was held that the private element of the expenditure incurred at the public house on electricity, rent, gas, etc was not incurred for the purpose of earning profits, but for serving the non-business purpose of satisfying the publican's ordinary human needs. The expenditure, therefore had a dual purpose and was disallowed.

However, the cost of overnight accommodation when on a business trip may be deductible and reasonable expenditure on an evening meal and breakfast in conjunction with such accommodation is then also deductible.

2.4.3 Impairment losses (bad debts)

Only impairment losses where the liability was incurred wholly and exclusively for the purposes of the trade are deductible for taxation purposes. For example, **loans to employees written off are not deductible** unless the business is that of making loans, or it can be shown that the writing-off of the loan was earnings paid out for the benefit of the trade.

Under FRS 26 *Financial instruments: measurement*, a review of all trade receivables should be carried out to assess their fair value at the balance sheet date and any impairment losses written off. **The tax treatment follows the accounting treatment so no adjustment is required for tax purposes.** As a result of FRS 26, it is less likely that any general provisions will now be seen. In the event that they do arise, increases or decreases in a general provision are not allowable /taxable and an adjustment will need to be made.

If an impairment loss which has been deducted for tax purposes is later recovered, the recovery is taxable so no adjustment is required to the amount of the recovery shown in the statement of profit or loss.

2.4.4 Unpaid remuneration

If earnings for employees are charged in the accounts but are not paid within nine months of the end of the period of account, the cost is only deductible for the period of account in which the earnings are paid. When a tax computation is made within the nine month period, it is initially assumed that unpaid earnings will not be paid within that period. The computation is adjusted if they are so paid.

Earnings are treated as paid at the same time as they are treated as received for employment income purposes.

2.4.5 Entertaining and gifts

The general rule is that expenditure on entertaining and gifts is non-deductible. This applies to amounts reimbursed to employees for specific entertaining expenses and gifts, and to round sum allowances which are exclusively for meeting such expenses. There is no distinction between UK and overseas customer entertaining for income tax and corporation tax purposes (a different rule applies for value added tax).

There are specific exceptions to the general rule:

- **Entertaining for and gifts to employees are normally deductible** although where gifts are made, or the entertainment is excessive, a charge to tax may arise on the employee under the benefits legislation.
- **Gifts to customers not costing more than £50 per donee per year are allowed if they carry a conspicuous advertisement for the business and are not food, drink, tobacco or vouchers exchangeable for goods.**

- Gifts to charities may also be allowed although many will fall foul of the 'wholly and exclusively' rule above. If a gift aid declaration is made by an individual in respect of a gift, tax relief will be given under the gift aid scheme, not as a trading expense. If a qualifying charitable donation is made by a company, it will be given tax relief by deduction from total profits (see later in this Text).

2.4.6 Lease charges for cars with CO_2 emissions exceeding 130g/km

For leases starting on or after 6 April 2013 (1 April 2013 for companies), there is a restriction on the leasing costs of a car with CO_2 emissions exceeding 130 g/km. 15% of the leasing costs will be disallowed in the calculation of taxable profits.

2.4.7 Interest payments

Interest which is allowed as deductible interest (see earlier in this Text) is not also allowed as a trading expense.

2.4.8 National Insurance contributions

No deduction is allowed for any National Insurance contributions **except for employer's contributions.** For the purpose of your exam, these are Class 1 secondary contributions and Class 1A contributions (Class 1B contributions are not examinable). National Insurance contributions for self employed individuals are dealt with later in this chapter.

2.4.9 Penalties and interest on tax

Penalties and interest on late paid tax are not allowed as a trading expense. Tax includes income tax, capital gains tax, VAT and stamp duty land tax.

2.4.10 Crime related payments

A payment is not deductible if making it constitutes an offence by the payer. This covers protection money paid to terrorists, bribes and similar payments made overseas which would be criminal payments if they were made in the UK. Statute also prevents any deduction for payments made in response to blackmail or extortion.

2.5 Deductible expenditure

Most expenses will be deductible under the general rule that expenses incurred wholly and exclusively for the purpose of the trade are not disallowed. Some expenses which might otherwise be disallowed under the 'wholly or exclusively' rule, or under one or other of the specific rules discussed above are, however, specifically allowed by the legislation. These are covered in paragraphs 2.5.1 to 2.5.12.

2.5.1 Pre-trading expenditure

Expenditure incurred before the commencement of trade is deductible, if it is incurred within seven years of the start of trade and it is of a type that would have been deductible had the trade already started. **It is treated as a trading expense incurred on the first day of trading.**

2.5.2 Incidental costs of obtaining finance

Incidental costs of obtaining loan finance, or of attempting to obtain or redeeming it, are deductible other than a discount on issue or a premium on redemption (which are really alternatives to paying interest). This deduction for incidental costs does not apply to companies because they obtain a deduction for the costs of borrowing in a different way. We will look at companies later in this Text.

2.5.3 Short leases

A trader may deduct an annual sum in respect of the amount liable to income tax on a lease premium which they paid to their landlord (see earlier in this Text). Normally, the amortisation of the lease will have been deducted in the accounts (and must be added back as capital expenditure).

2.5.4 Renewals

Where a tool is replaced or altered then the cost of the renewal or alteration may be deducted as an expense in certain instances. These are that:

- A deduction would only be prohibited because the expenditure is capital expenditure, and
- No deduction can be given under any other provisions, such as under the capital allowances legislation.

2.5.5 Restrictive covenants

When an employee leaves their employment they may accept a limitation on their future activities in return for a payment. **Provided the employee is taxed on the payment as employment income** (see earlier in this Text) **the payment is a deductible trading expense.**

2.5.6 Secondments

The **costs of seconding employees to charities or educational establishments are deductible.**

2.5.7 Contributions to agent's expenses

Many employers run payroll giving schemes for their employees. **Any payments made to the agent who administers the scheme towards running expenses are deductible.**

2.5.8 Counselling and retraining expenses

Expenditure on providing counselling and retraining for leaving employees is allowable.

2.5.9 Redundancy

Redundancy payments made when a trade ends are deductible on the earlier of the day of payment and the last day of trading. If the trade does not end, they can be deducted as soon as they are provided for, so long as the redundancy was decided on within the period of account, the provision is accurately calculated and the payments are made within nine months of the end of the period of account. **The deduction extends to additional payments of up to three times the amount of the redundancy pay on cessation of trade.**

2.5.10 Personal security expenses

If there is a particular security threat to the trader because of the nature of the trade, **expenditure on their personal security is allowable.**

2.5.11 Contributions to local enterprise organisations/urban regeneration companies

This allows a deduction for donations made to a local enterprise agency, a training and enterprise council, a Scottish local enterprise company, a business link organisation or an urban regeneration company. If any benefit is received by the trade from the donation, this must be deducted from the allowable amount.

2.5.12 Patents, trade marks and copyrights

The costs of **registering patents and trade marks** are deductible for trades only (not professions or vocations). Copyright arises automatically and so does not have to be registered. **Patent royalties and copyright royalties paid in connection with a trade are deductible as trading expenses.**

2.6 Trade income

There are also statutory rules governing whether certain receipts are taxable or not. These are discussed in 2.6.1 to 2.6.5.

2.6.1 Capital receipts

As may be expected, capital receipts are not included in trade income. They may, of course, be taken into account in the capital allowances computation, or as a capital gain.

However, compensation received in one lump sum for the loss of income is likely to be treated as income (*Donald Fisher (Ealing) Ltd v Spencer 1989*).

In some trades, (eg petrol stations and public houses), a wholesaler may pay a lump sum to a retailer in return for the retailer only supplying that wholesaler's products for several years (an **exclusivity agreement**). If the payment must be used for a specific capital purpose, it is a capital receipt. If that is not the case, it is an income receipt. If the sum is repayable to the wholesaler but the requirement to repay is waived in tranches over the term of the agreement, each tranche is a separate income receipt when the requirement is waived.

2.6.2 Debts released

If the trader incurs a deductible expense but does not settle the amount due to the supplier, then if the creditor releases the debt other than under a statutory arrangement, the amount released must be brought into account as trade income.

2.6.3 Takeover of trade

If a trader takes over a trade from a previous owner, then if they receive any amounts from that trade which related to a period before the takeover they must be brought into account unless the previous owner has already done so.

2.6.4 Insurance receipts

Insurance receipts which are revenue in nature, such as for loss of profits, are trading receipts. Otherwise the receipt must be brought in as trade income if, and to the extent that, any deduction has been claimed for the expense that the receipt is intended to cover.

2.6.5 Gifts of trading stock to educational establishments or schools

When a business makes a gift of equipment manufactured, sold or used in the course of its trade to an educational establishment or for a charitable purpose, nothing need be brought into account as a trading receipt or (if capital allowances had been obtained on the asset) as disposal proceeds, so full relief is obtained for the cost.

2.7 Excluded income

Although the accounts may include other income, such as interest, such income is not trade income. It will instead be taxed under the specific rules for that type of income, such as the rules for savings income. It is therefore excluded from trade profits.

Certain types of income are specifically exempt from tax, and should be excluded from trade profits.

2.8 Application of general rules

These general rules can be applied to particular types of expenditure and income that you are likely to come across.

2.8.1 Appropriations

Salary or interest on capital paid to the trader are not deductible.

2.8.2 Subscriptions and donations

The general 'wholly and exclusively' rule determines the deductibility of expenses. Subscriptions and donations are not deductible unless the expenditure is for the benefit of the trade. The following are the main types of subscriptions and donations you may meet and their correct treatments:

(a) Trade subscriptions (such as to a professional or trade association) are generally deductible.

(b) Charitable donations are deductible only if they are small and to local charities. Tax relief may be available for donations under the gift aid scheme. In the latter case they are not a deductible trading expense.

(c) Political subscriptions and donations are generally not deductible.

(d) Where a donation represents the most effective commercial way of disposing of stock (for example, where it would not be commercially effective to sell surplus perishable food), the donation can be treated as for the benefit of the trade and the disposal proceeds taken as £Nil. In other cases, the amount credited to the accounts in respect of a donation of stock should be its market value.

2.8.3 Legal and professional charges

Legal and professional charges relating to capital or non-trade items are not deductible. These include charges incurred in acquiring new capital assets or legal rights, issuing shares, drawing up partnership agreements and litigating disputes over the terms of a partnership agreement.

Charges are deductible if they relate directly to trading. Deductible items include:

- Legal and professional charges incurred defending the taxpayer's title to fixed assets
- Charges connected with an action for breach of contract
- Expenses of the **renewal** (not the original grant) of a lease for less than 50 years
- Charges for trade debt collection
- Normal charges for preparing accounts/assisting with the self assessment of tax liabilities

Accountancy expenses arising out of an enquiry into the accounts information in a particular year's return are not allowed where the enquiry reveals discrepancies and additional liabilities for the year of enquiry, or any earlier year, which arise as a result of negligent or fraudulent conduct.

Where, however, the enquiry results in no addition to profits, or an adjustment to the profits for the year of enquiry only and that assessment does not arise as a result of negligent or fraudulent conduct, the additional accountancy expenses are allowable.

2.8.4 Goods for own use

The usual example is when a trader takes goods for their own use. In such circumstances the selling price of the goods if sold in open market is added to the accounting profit. If the trader pays anything for the goods, this is left out of account. In other words, the trader is treated for tax purposes as having made a sale to themselves. This rule does not apply to supplies of services, which are treated as sold for the amount (if any) actually paid (but the cost of services to the trader or their household is not deductible).

2.8.5 Other items

Here is a list of various other items that you may meet.

Item	Treatment	Comment
Educational courses for staff	Allow	
Educational courses for trader	Allow	If to update existing knowledge or skills, not if to acquire new knowledge or skills
Removal expenses (to new business premises)	Allow	Only if not an expansionary move
Travelling expenses to the trader's place of business	Disallow	*Ricketts v Colquhoun 1925*: unless an itinerant trader (*Horton v Young 1971*)
Compensation for loss of office and ex gratia payments	Allow	If for benefit of trade: *Mitchell v B W Noble Ltd 1927*
Pension contributions (to schemes for employees and company directors)	Allow	Special contributions may be spread over the year of payment and future years
Parking fines	Allow Disallow	For employees using their employer's cars on business. For proprietors/directors
Damages paid	Allow	If not too remote from trade: *Strong and Co v Woodifield 1906*
Preparation and restoration of waste disposal sites	Allow	Spread preparation expenditure over period of use of site. Pre-trading expenditure is treated as incurred on the first day of trading. Allow restoration expenditure in period of expenditure
Dividends on trade investments	Deduct	Taxed as savings income
Rental income from letting part of premises	Deduct	Taxed as income of a UK property business unless it is the letting of surplus business accommodation

2.9 Rounding

Where an individual, a partnership or a single company (not a group of companies) has an annual turnover of at least £5,000,000, and prepares its accounts with figures rounded to at least the nearest £1,000, figures in computations of adjusted profits (including, for companies, non-trade profits but excluding capital gains) may generally be rounded to the nearest £1,000.

2.10 Cash basis of accounting for small businesses

2.10.1 Introduction

FAST FORWARD

An individual who is carrying on a trade may elect for the profits of the trade to be calculated on the cash basis (instead of in accordance with generally accepted accounting practice) in certain circumstances.

Usually, **businesses prepare accounts using generally accepted accounting practice for tax purposes.** In particular, this means that **income and expenses are dealt with on an accruals basis**. This is referred to as **'accruals accounting'** in this section.

Certain small unincorporated businesses may elect to use cash accounting (known as 'the cash basis') rather than accruals accounting for the purposes of calculating their taxable trading income.

Exam focus point

The detailed cash basis rules are quite complex. These **more complex aspects are not examinable at Paper P6(UK).** In any examination question involving an unincorporated business, **it should be assumed that the cash basis is not relevant unless it is specifically mentioned.**

2.10.2 Which businesses can use the cash basis?

The cash basis can only be used by unincorporated businesses (sole traders and partnerships) **whose receipts for the tax year do not exceed the value added tax (VAT) registration threshold (currently £79,000 – this figure is given in the Tax rates and Allowances available in the exam).**

An election must be made for the cash basis to apply. The election is generally effective for the tax year for which it is made and all subsequent tax years.

However **a business must cease to use the cash basis** if:

(a) (i) **Receipts in the previous tax year exceeded twice the VAT registration threshold for that year,** and

(ii) **Receipts for the current year exceed the VAT registration for that year**; or

(b) Its 'commercial circumstances' change such that the cash basis is no longer appropriate and an election is made to use accruals accounting.

2.10.3 Calculation of taxable profits under the cash basis

The taxable trading profits under the cash basis are calculated as:

(a) **Cash receipts; less**
(b) **Deductible business expenses actually paid in the period.**

Cash receipts include all amounts received relating to the business including cash and card receipts. They include **amounts received from the sale of plant and machinery, other than on the sale of motor cars.** We look at the definition of plant and machinery when we look at capital allowances later in this Text.

Receipts from the sale of motor cars and capital assets which are not classed as plant and machinery (eg land) are not taxable receipts.

Under the cash basis, business expenses are deductible when they are paid. Business expenses for the cash basis of accounting include capital expenditure on plant and machinery (except motor cars). Other capital expenses are not business expenses eg purchase of land, motor cars, and legal fees on such purchases.

The majority of the specific tax rules covered earlier in this chapter concerning the deductibility of business expenses also apply when the cash basis is used. It should be remembered, in particular, that only business expenses are tax deductible so that any private element must be disallowed. **Fixed rate expenses** for private use of motor cars and business premises used for private purposes may be used instead (see further below).

2.10.4 Basis of assessment

A trader using the cash basis can, like any other trader, prepare his accounts to any date in the year. The basis of assessment rules which determine in which tax year the profits of an accounting period are taxed apply in the same way for accruals accounting and cash basis traders (see later in this chapter).

2.10.5 Losses

A net cash deficit (ie a loss) can normally only be relieved against future cash surpluses (ie future trading profits). Cash basis traders cannot offset a loss against other income or gains. Trading losses for the accruals accounting traders are dealt with in detail later in this Text.

2.10.6 Fixed rate expenses

FAST FORWARD

Fixed rate expenses can be used in relation to expenditure on motor cars and business premises partly used as the trader's home.

Exam focus point

Although the **use of fixed rate expenses is optional**, in **any examination question involving the cash basis**, it should be assumed that, where relevant, **expenses are claimed on this basis.**

The option of claiming expenses on a flat rate basis is also available to unincorporated businesses generally, but it will **only be examined in P6(UK) within the context of the cash basis.**

Where a business elects to use the cash basis, for Paper P6(UK) purposes, it will be assumed to use fixed rate expenses rather than make deductions on the usual basis of actual expenditure incurred.

For Paper P6(UK) purposes, fixed rate expenses relate to:

(a) **Expenditure on motor cars**; and
(b) **Business premises partly used as the trader's home.**

The **fixed rate mileage (FRM) expense** can be claimed in respect of **motor cars which are owned or leased by the business** and **which are used for business purposes by the sole trader/partner or an employee of the business.**

The FRM expense is calculated as the business mileage times the appropriate rate per mile. The appropriate mileage rates for motor cars are 45p per mile for the first 10,000 miles, then 25p per mile thereafter.

Exam focus point

These rates will be given in the examination question, if relevant.

A fixed rate monthly adjustment can be made where a sole trader/partner uses part of the business premises as his home eg where a sole trader runs a small hotel or guesthouse and also lives in it. The adjustment is deducted from the actual allowable business premises costs to reflect the private portion of household costs, including food, and utilities (eg heat and light). It does not include mortgage interest, rent, council tax or rates: apportionment of these expenses must be made based on the extent of the private occupation of the premises.

The deductible fixed rate amount depends on **how many people use the business premises each month as a private home**:

Number relevant occupants	Non-business use amount
1	£350
2	£500
3 or more	£650

Exam focus point

These rates will be **given in the examination question**, if relevant.

Be careful when using these amounts – they are **not the deductible expense but the disallowable amount.**

2.11 Example

Larry started trading as an interior designer on 6 April 2013. The following information is relevant for the year to 5 April 2014.

- Revenue was £65,000 of which £8,000 was owed as receivables at 5 April 2014.
- A motor car was acquired on 6 April 2013 for £15,000. Larry drove 10,000 miles in the car during the year to 5 April 2014 of which 3,000 miles were for private journeys. The car qualifies for a capital allowance of £1,890, after taking account of private use. The motoring costs were £2,000. The fixed rate mileage expense for motoring is 45p per mile for the first 10,000 miles, then 25p per mile after that.
- Machinery was acquired on 1 May 2013 for £4,000. The machinery qualifies for a capital allowance of £4,000.
- Other allowable expenses were £12,000 of which £1,000 was owed as payables at 5 April 2014.

If Larry uses the accruals accounting basis and does not use fixed rate expenses, his trading profit will be calculated as follows:

	£	£
Revenue (accruals)		65,000
Less: capital allowance on motor car	1,890	
business motoring expenses £2,000 × 7/10	1,400	
capital allowance on machinery	4,000	
other allowable expenses (accruals)	12,000	
		(19,290)
Taxable trading profit		45,710

If Larry uses the cash basis of accounting and fixed rate expenses, his trading profit will be calculated as follows:

	£	£
Revenue (cash received £65,000 – £8,000)		58,000
Less: FRM on car 7,000 × 45p	3,150	
cost of machinery	4,000	
other allowable expenses (cash paid £12,000 – £1,000)	11,000	
		(18,150)
Taxable trading profit		38,850

2.12 The cessation of trades

2.12.1 Post cessation receipts and expenses

Post-cessation receipts (including any releases of debts incurred by the trader) **are chargeable to income tax as miscellaneous income.**

If they are received in the tax year of cessation or the next six tax years, the trader can elect that they be treated as received on the day of cessation. The time limit for electing is the 31 January which is 22 months after the end of the tax year of receipt.

Certain post cessation expenses paid within seven years of discontinuance may be relieved against other income. The expenses must relate to costs of remedying defective work or goods, or legal expenses of or insurance against defective work claims. Relief is also available for trade receivable that subsequently prove to be impaired.

2.12.2 Valuing trading stock on cessation

When a trade ceases, the closing stock must be valued. The higher the value, the higher the profit for the final period of trading.

If the stock is sold to a UK trader who will deduct its cost in computing their taxable profits, it is valued under the following rules.

(a) If the seller and the buyer are unconnected, take the actual price.

(b) If the seller and the buyer are connected (see below), take what would have been the price in an arm's length sale.

(c) However, if the seller and the buyer are connected, the arm's length price exceeds both the original cost of the stock and the actual transfer price, and both the seller and the buyer make an election, then take the greater of the original cost of the stock and the transfer price. The time limit for election for unincorporated business is the 31 January which is 22 months after the end of the tax year of cessation (for companies, it is two years after the end of the accounting period of cessation).

In all cases covered above, the value used for the seller's computation of profit is also used as the buyer's cost.

Key term

An individual is **connected** (connected person) with their spouse (or civil partner), with the relatives (brothers, sisters, ancestors and lineal descendants) of themselves and their spouse (or civil partner), and with the spouses (or civil partners) of those relatives. In-laws and step family are included; uncles, aunts, nephews, nieces and cousins are not. He is also connected with their business partners (except in relation to bona fide commercial arrangements for the disposal of partnership assets), and with their spouses (or civil partners) and relatives (see diagram below). An individual is also connected with a company if he has control of that company (or if he and persons connected with him together have control of it). An individual is also connected with the trustees of a trust of which that individual is the settlor.

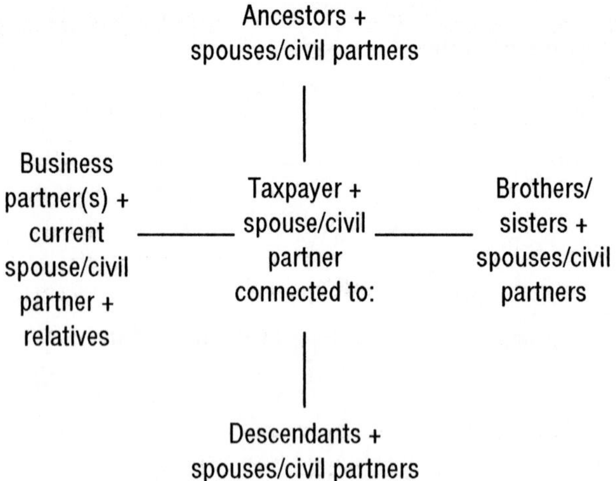

If the stock is not transferred to a UK trader who will be able to deduct its cost in computing their profits, then it is valued at its open market value as at the cessation of trade.

3 Basis periods

FAST FORWARD

Basis periods are used to link periods of account to tax years.

3.1 Introduction

A tax year runs from 6 April to 5 April, but most businesses do not have periods of account ending on 5 April. **Thus there must be a link between a period of account of a business and a tax year.** The procedure is to **find a period to act as the basis period for a tax year. The profits for a basis period are taxed in the corresponding tax year**. If a basis period is not identical to a period of account, the profits of periods of account are time-apportioned as required on the assumption that profits accrue evenly over a period of account. We will apportion to the nearest month for exam purposes.

We will now look at the basis period rules that apply in the opening, continuing and closing years of a business when there is no change of accounting date. Special rules are needed when the trader changes their accounting date. We will look at these rules in the next section.

The first tax year is the year during which the trade commences. For example, if a trade commences on 1 June 2013 the first tax year is 2013/14.

3.2 The first tax year

FAST FORWARD

In opening and closing years, special rules are applied so that a new trader can start to be taxed quickly, and a retiring trader need not be taxed long after their retirement.

The **basis period for the first tax year runs from the date the trade starts to the next 5 April** (or to the date of cessation if the trade does not last until the end of the tax year).

So continuing the above example a trader commencing in business on 1 June 2013 will be taxed on profits arising from 1 June 2013 to 5 April 2014 in 2013/14, the first tax year.

3.3 The second tax year

(a) **If the accounting date falling in the second tax year is at least 12 months after the start of trading, the basis period is the 12 months to that accounting date.**

(b) **If the accounting date falling in the second tax year is less than 12 months after the start of trading, the basis period is the first 12 months of trading.**

(c) **If there is no accounting date falling in the second tax year**, because the first period of account is a very long one which does not end until a date in the third tax year, **the basis period for the second tax year is the year itself (from 6 April to 5 April).**

The following flowchart may help you determine the basis period for the second tax year.

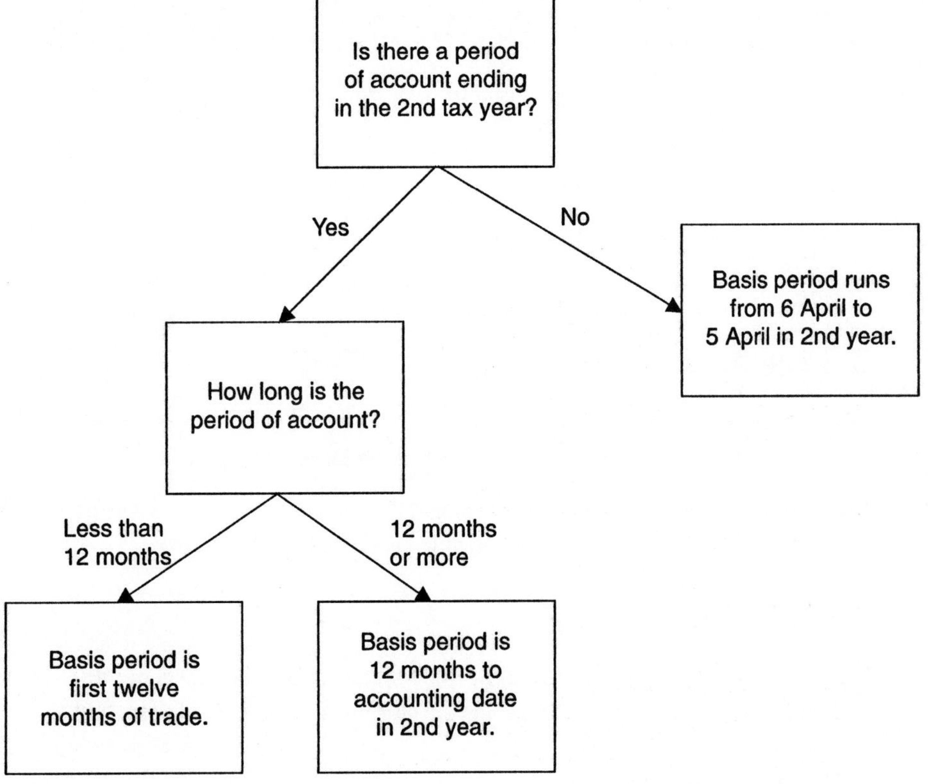

3.4 Examples: the first and second tax year

(a) John starts to trade on 1 January 2014 making up accounts to 31 December 2014.

1st tax year: 2013/14 – tax profits 1.1.14 – 5.4.14

2nd tax year: 2014/15

- Is there a period of account ending in 2014/15?
- How long is the period of account?

  12 months or more ie 12 months (exactly) to 31.12.14.
- So in 2014/15 tax profits of 12 months to 31.12.14.

(b) Janet starts to trade on 1 January 2014 making up accounts as follows:

6 months to 30 June 2014

12 months to 30 June 2015

1st tax year: 2013/14 – tax profits 1.1.14 – 5.4.14

2nd tax year: 2014/15

- Is there a period of account ending in 2014/15?
- How long is the period of account?

  Less than 12 months ie 6 months long.
- So in 2014/15 tax profits of first 12 months of trade ie 1.1.14 – 31.12.14, ie

  p.e. 30.6.14 profits

  plus

  6/12 of y.e 30.6.15 profits

(c) Jodie starts to trade on 1 March 2014 making up a 14 month set of accounts to 30 April 2015.

1st tax year: 2013/14 – tax profits 1.3.14 – 5.4.14

2nd tax year: 2014/15

- Is there a period of account ending in 2014/15?

  No (p.e. 30.4.15 ends in 2015/16)
- So in 2014/15 tax profits of 6.4.14 – 5.4.15.

3.5 The third tax year

(a) **If there is an accounting date falling in the second tax year, the basis period for the third tax year is the period of account ending in the third tax year.**

(b) If there is no accounting date falling in the second tax year, the basis period for the third tax year is the 12 months to the accounting date falling in the third tax year.

3.6 Later tax years

For later tax years, except the year in which the trade ceases, **the basis period is the period of account ending in the tax year**. This is known as the **current year basis of assessment**.

3.7 The final year

(a) If a trade starts and ceases in the same tax year, the basis period for that year is the whole lifespan of the trade.

(b) If the final year is the second year, the basis period runs from 6 April at the start of the second year to the date of cessation. This rule overrides the rules that normally apply for the second year.

(c) If the final year is the third year or a later year, **the basis period runs from the end of the basis period for the previous year to the date of cessation**. This rule overrides the rules that normally apply in the third and later years.

3.8 Overlap profits

Key term

Profits which have been taxed more than once are called **overlap profits.**

When a business starts, some profits may be taxed twice because the basis period for the second year includes some or all of the period of trading in the first year or because the basis period for the third year overlaps with that for the second year.

Overlap profits may be deducted on a change of accounting date (see below). Any overlap profits unrelieved when the trade ceases are deducted from the final year's taxable profits. Any deduction of overlap profits may create or increase a loss. The usual loss reliefs (covered later in this Text) are then available.

3.9 Example: accounting date in 2nd year at least 12 months

Jenny trades from 1 July 2008 to 31 December 2013, with the following results.

Period	*Profit*
	£
1.7.08 – 31.8.09	7,000
1.9.09 – 31.8.10	12,000
1.9.10 – 31.8.11	15,000
1.9.11 – 31.8.12	21,000
1.9.12 – 31.8.13	18,000
1.9.13 – 31.12.13	5,600
	78,600

The profits to be taxed in each tax year from 2008/09 to 2013/14, and the total of these taxable profits are calculated as follows.

Year	*Basis period*	*Working*	*Taxable profit*
			£
2008/09	1.7.08 – 5.4.09	£7,000 × 9/14	4,500
2009/10	1.9.08 – 31.8.09	£7,000 × 12/14	6,000
2010/11	1.9.09 – 31.8.10		12,000
2011/12	1.9.10 – 31.8.11		15,000
2012/13	1.9.11 – 31.8.12		21,000
2013/14	1.9.12 – 31.12.13	£(18,000 + 5,600 – 3,500)	20,100
			78,600

The overlap profits are those in the period 1 September 2008 to 5 April 2009, a period of seven months. They are £7,000 × 7/14 = £3,500. Overlap profits are either relieved on a change of accounting date (see below) or are deducted from the final year's taxable profit when the business ceases. In this case the overlap profits are deducted when the business ceases. Over the life of the business, the total taxable profits equal the total actual profits.

Peter trades from 1 September 2008 to 30 June 2013, with the following results.

Period	*Profit*
	£
1.9.08 – 30.4.09	8,000
1.5.09 – 30.4.10	15,000
1.5.10 – 30.4.11	9,000
1.5.11 – 30.4.12	10,500
1.5.12 – 30.4.13	16,000
1.5.13 – 30.6.13	950
	59,450

Show the profits to be taxed in each year from 2008/09 to 2013/14, the total of these taxable profits and the overlap profits.

Answer

Year	*Basis period*	*Working*	*Taxable profits*
			£
2008/09	1.9.08 – 5.4.09	£8,000 × 7/8	7,000
2009/10	1.9.08 – 31.8.09	£8,000 + (£15,000 × 4/12)	13,000
2010/11	1.5.09 – 30.4.10		15,000
2011/12	1.5.10 – 30.4.11		9,000
2012/13	1.5.11 – 30.4.12		10,500
2013/14	1.5.12 – 30.6.13	£(16,000 + 950 – 12,000)	4,950
			59,450

The overlap profits are the profits from 1 September 2008 to 5 April 2009 (taxed in 2008/09 and in 2009/10) and those from 1 May 2009 to 31 August 2009 (taxed in 2009/10 and 2010/11).

	£
1.9.08 – 5.4.09 £8,000 × 7/8	7,000
1.5.09 – 31.8.09 £15,000 × 4/12	5,000
Total overlap profits	12,000

3.10 Example: no accounting date in the second year

Thelma starts to trade on 1 March 2012. Her first accounts, covering the 16 months to 30 June 2013, show a profit of £36,000. The taxable profits for the first three tax years and the overlap profits are as follows.

Year	*Basis period*	*Working*	*Taxable profits*
			£
2011/12	1.3.12 – 5.4.12	£36,000 × 1/16	2,250
2012/13	6.4.12 – 5.4.13	£36,000 × 12/16	27,000
2013/14	1.7.12 – 30.6.13	£36,000 × 12/16	27,000

The overlap profits are the profits from 1 July 2012 to 5 April 2013: £36,000 × 9/16 = £20,250.

3.11 The choice of an accounting date

A new trader should consider which accounting date would be best. There are **a number of factors to consider** from the point of view of taxation.

- **If profits are expected to rise, a date early in the tax year** (such as 30 April) will delay the time when rising accounts profits feed through into rising taxable profits, whereas a date late in the tax year (such as 31 March) will accelerate the taxation of rising profits. This is because with an accounting date of 30 April, the taxable profits for each tax year are mainly the profits earned in the previous tax year. With an accounting date of 31 March the taxable profits are almost entirely profits earned in the current year.
- If the accounting date in the second tax year is less than 12 months after the start of trading, the taxable profits for that year will be the profits earned in the first 12 months. If the accounting date is at least 12 months from the start of trading, they will be the profits earned in the 12 months to that date. **Different profits may thus be taxed twice**, and if profits are fluctuating this can make a considerable difference to the taxable profits in the first few years.
- **The choice of an accounting date affects the profits shown in each set of accounts**, and this may affect the taxable profits.
- **An accounting date of 30 April gives the maximum interval between earning profits and paying the related tax liability.** For example if a trader makes up accounts to 30 April 2014, this falls into the tax year 2014/15 with payments on account being due on 31 January 2015 and 31 July 2015, and a balancing payment due on 31 January 2016 (details of payment of income tax are dealt with later in this Text). If the trader makes up accounts to 31 March 2014, this falls in the tax year 2013/14 and the payments will be due one year earlier (ie on 31 January 2014, 31 July 2014 and 31 January 2015).
- **Knowing profits well in advance of the end of the tax year makes tax planning much easier.** For example, if a trader wants to make personal pension contributions and makes up accounts to 30 April 2014 (2014/15), he can make contributions up to 5 April 2015 based on those relevant earnings. If he makes up accounts to 31 March 2014, he will probably not know the amount of his relevant earnings until after the end of the tax year 2013/14, too late to adjust his pension contributions for 2013/14.
- **However, a 31 March or 5 April accounting date means that the application of the basis period rules is more straightforward and there will be no overlap profits.** This may be appropriate for small traders.
- **With an accounting date of 30 April, the assessment for the year of cessation could be based on up to 23 months of profits.** For example, if a trader who has made up accounts to 30 April ceases trading on 31 March 2014 (2013/14), the basis period for 2013/14 will run from 1 May 2012 to 31 March 2014. This could lead to larger than normal trading profits being assessable in the year of cessation.

  However, this could be avoided by carrying on the trade for another month so that a cessation arises on 30 April 2014 so that the profits from 1 May 2012 to 30 April 2013 are taxable in 2013/14 and those from 1 May 2013 to 30 April 2014 are taxable in 2014/15. Each case must be looked at in relation to all relevant factors, such as other income which the taxpayer may have and loss relief – there is no one rule which applies in all cases.

Question — The choice of an accounting date

Christine starts to trade on 1 December 2011. Her monthly profits are £1,000 for the first seven months, and £2,000 thereafter. Show the taxable profits for the first three tax years with each of the following accounting dates (in all cases starting with a period of account of less than 12 months).

(a) 31 March
(b) 30 April
(c) 31 December

Answer

(a) *31 March*

Period of account	*Working*	*Profits*
		£
1.12.11 – 31.3.12	£1,000 × 4	4,000
1.4.12 – 31.3.13	£1,000 × 3 + £2,000 × 9	21,000
1.4.13 – 31.3.14	£2,000 × 12	24,000

Year	*Basis period*	*Taxable profits*
		£
2011/12	1.12.11 – 5.4.12	4,000
2012/13	1.4.12 – 31.3.13	21,000
2013/14	1.4.13 – 31.3.14	24,000

(b) *30 April*

Period of account	*Working*	*Profits*
		£
1.12.11 – 30.4.12	£1,000 × 5	5,000
1.5.12 – 30.4.13	£1,000 × 2 + £2,000 × 10	22,000

Year	*Basis period*	*Working*	*Taxable profits*
			£
2011/12	1.12.11 – 5.4.12	£5,000 × 4/5	4,000
2012/13	1.12.11 – 30.11.12	£5,000 + £22,000 × 7/12	17,833
2013/14	1.5.12 – 30.4.13		22,000

(c) *31 December*

Period of account	*Working*	*Profits*
		£
1.12.11 – 31.12.11	£1,000 × 1	1,000
1.1.12 – 31.12.12	£1,000 × 6 + £2,000 × 6	18,000
1.1.13 – 31.12.13	£2,000 × 12	24,000

Year	*Basis period*	*Working*	*Taxable profits*
			£
2011/12	1.12.11 – 5.4.12	£1,000 + £18,000 × 3/12	5,500
2012/13	1.1.12 – 31.12.12		18,000
2013/14	1.1.13 – 31.12.13		24,000

4 Change of accounting date

FAST FORWARD

On a change of accounting date, special rules apply for fixing basis periods.

4.1 Introduction

A trader may change the date to which they prepare their annual accounts for a variety of reasons. For example, they may wish to move to a calendar year end or to fit in with seasonal variations of their trade. Special rules normally apply for fixing basis periods when a trader changes their accounting date.

On a change of accounting date there may be

- One set of accounts covering a period of less than twelve months, or
- One set of accounts covering a period of more than twelve months, or

- No accounts, or
- Two sets of accounts

ending in a tax year. In each case, the basis period for the year relates to the new accounting date. We will look at each of the cases in turn.

4.2 One short period of account

When a change of accounting date results in one short period of account ending in a tax year, the basis period for that year is always the 12 months to the new accounting date.

4.3 Example: change of accounting date (1)

Sue prepares accounts to 31 December each year until she changes her accounting date to 30 June by preparing accounts for the six months to 30 June 2013.

There is one short period of account ending during 2013/14. This means the basis period for 2013/14 is the twelve months to 30 June 2013.

Sue's basis period for 2012/13 was the twelve months to 31 December 2012. This means the profits of the six months to 31 December 2012 are overlap profits that have been taxed twice. These overlap profits must be added to any overlap profits that arose when the business began. The total is either relieved when the business ceases or it is relieved on a subsequent change of accounting date.

4.4 One long period of account

When a change of accounting date results in one long period of account ending in a tax year, the basis period for that year ends on the new accounting date. It begins immediately after the basis period for the previous year ends. This means the basis period will exceed 12 months.

No overlap profits arise in this situation. However, more than twelve months worth of profits are taxed in one income tax year and to compensate for this, relief is available for brought forward overlap profits. The overlap relief must reduce the number of months' worth of profits taxed in the year to no more than twelve. So, if you have a fourteen month basis period you can give relief for up to two months worth of overlap profits.

4.5 Example: change of accounting date (2)

Zoe started trading on 1 October 2010 and prepared accounts to 30 September until she changed her accounting date by preparing accounts for the fifteen months to 31 December 2013. Her results were as follows.

Year to 30 September 2011	£24,000
Year to 30 September 2012	£48,000
Fifteen months to 31 December 2013	£75,000

Profits for the first three tax years of the business are:

2010/11 (1.10.10 – 5.4.11)	
6/12 × £24,000	£12,000
2011/12 (1.10.10 – 30.9.11)	£24,000
2012/13 (1.10.11 – 30.9.12)	£48,000

Overlap profits are £12,000. These arose in the six months to 5.4.11.

The change in accounting date results in one long period of account ending during 2013/14 which means the basis period for 2013/14 is the fifteen months to 31 December 2013. Three months' worth of the brought forward overlap profits can be relieved.

	£
2013/14 (1.10.12 – 31.12.13)	75,000
Less overlap profits 3/6 × £12,000	(6,000)
	69,000

The unrelieved overlap profits of £6,000 (£12,000 – £6,000) are carried forward for relief either when the business ceases or on a further change of accounting date.

4.6 No accounting date ending in the year

If a change of accounting date results in there being no period of account ending in a tax year there is a potential problem because basis periods usually end on an accounting date. To get round this problem **you must manufacture a basis period by taking the new accounting date and deducting one year. The basis period is then the twelve months to this date.**

4.7 Example: change of accounting date (3)

Anne had always prepared accounts to 31 March. She then changed her accounting date by preparing accounts for the thirteen months to 30 April 2014.

There is no period of account ending during 2013/14 so the basis period for this year is the manufactured basis period of the twelve months to 30 April 2013.

You've probably spotted that this produces an overlap with the previous basis period. The overlap period is the eleven months from 1 May 2012 to 31 March 2013. The overlap profits arising in this period are added to any other unrelieved overlap profits and are carried forward for future relief.

4.8 Two accounting dates ending in the year

When two periods of account end in a tax year, the basis period for the year ends on the new accounting date. It begins immediately following the previous basis period. This means that the basis period will exceed 12 months and overlap relief can be allowed to ensure that only twelve months worth of profits are assessed in the tax year.

4.9 Example: change of accounting date (4)

Elizabeth prepared accounts to 30 September until 2014 when she changed her accounting date by preparing accounts for the six months to 31 March 2014.

The new accounting date is 31 March 2014. This is the end of the basis period for 2013/14. The basis period for 2012/13 ended on 30 September 2012. The 2013/14 basis period is therefore the eighteen month period 1 October 2012 to 31 March 2014. Six months' worth of overlap profits can be relieved in this year.

4.10 Conditions

The above changes in basis period automatically occur if the trader changes their accounting date during the first three tax years of their business.

In other cases **the following conditions must be met before a change in basis periods can occur**:

- The trader must notify HMRC of the change by the 31 January, following the tax year in which the change is made (by 31 January 2015 for a change made during 2013/14).
- The period of account resulting from the change must not exceed 18 months.
- In general, there must have been no previous change of accounting date in the last 5 tax years. However, a second change can be made within this period if the later change is for genuine commercial reasons. If HMRC do not respond to a notification of a change of accounting date within 60 days of receiving it, the trader can assume that they are satisfied that the reasons for making the change are genuine commercial ones.

If the above conditions are not satisfied because the first period of account ending on the new date exceeds 18 months or the change of accounting date was not notified in time, but the 'five year gap or commercial reasons' condition is satisfied, then the basis period for the year of change is the 12 months to the *old* accounting date in the year of change. The basis period for the next year is then found using rules above as if it were the year of change.

If the 'five year gap or commercial reasons' test is not satisfied, the old accounting date remains in force for tax purposes (with the profits of accounts made up to the new date being time-apportioned as necessary) until there have been five consecutive tax years which were not years of change. The sixth tax year is then treated as the year of change to the new accounting date, and the rules above apply.

5 National insurance

5.1 National insurance contributions (NICs) for the self employed

FAST FORWARD

The self employed pay Class 2 and Class 4 NICs. Class 4 NICs are based on the level of the individual's taxable profits. Class 2 NICs are paid at a weekly flat rate.

The self employed (sole traders and partners) **pay NICs in two ways. Class 2 contributions are payable at a flat rate.** It is possible, however, to be excepted from payment of Class 2 contributions (or to obtain a repayment of contributions already paid) if annual accounts profits are less than £5,725 (2013/14). **The Class 2 rate for 2013/14 is £2.70 a week.**

HMRC recommend that Class 2 contributions be paid monthly or six monthly by direct debit. Alternatively payments can be made in response to notices issued by HMRC twice yearly. Whichever method is used, payment for the first six months of Class 2 NICs for the tax year must be received by HMRC no later than 31 January in the tax year, and payment for the remaining six months must be received by HMRC no later than 31 July following the end of the tax year. Payment by direct debit will guarantee that these deadlines are met.

Self employed people must register with HMRC for Class 2 contributions by 31 January following the tax year in which they start self employment. People who fail to register may incur a late notification penalty.

Additionally, **the self employed pay Class 4 NICs, based on the level of the individual's trade profits.**

Main rate Class 4 NICs are calculated by applying a fixed percentage (9% for 2013/14) to the individual's profits between the lower limit (£7,755 for 2013/14) and the upper limit (£41,450 for 2013/14). Additional rate contributions are 2% (for 2013/14) on profits above that limit.

5.2 Example: Class 4 contributions

If a sole trader had profits of £16,420 for 2013/14 their Class 4 NIC liability would be as follows.

	£
Profits	16,420
Less lower limit	(7,755)
	8,665

Class 4 NICs = 9% × £8,665 = £780 (main only)

5.3 Example: additional Class 4 contributions

If an individual's profits were £50,000, additional Class 4 NICs are due on the excess over the upper limit. Thus the amount payable in 2013/14 is as follows.

	£
Profits (upper limit)	41,450
Less lower limit	(7,755)
	33,695
Main rate Class 4 NICs 9% × £33,695	3,033
Additional rate class 4 NICs £(50,000 – 41,450) = £8,550 × 2%	171
	3,204

For Class 4 NIC purposes, profits are the trade profits for income tax purposes less trade losses (see later in this Text).

Class 4 NICs are collected by HMRC. They are paid **at the same time as the associated income tax liability**. Interest is charged on overdue contributions.

5.4 Comparison of NICs for the employees and the self employed

The NIC burden on the self employed tends to be lower than that on employees, although the relative burdens vary with the level of income. The following example shows how a comparison may be made.

5.5 Example: employed and self employed NICs

Two single people, one employed (not in a contracted out pension scheme) and one self employed, each have annual gross income of £25,000. Show their national insurance contributions for 2013/14.

Solution

	Employed	*Self-employed*
	£	£
NICs		
Class 1: £(25,000 – 7,755) × 12% (main only)	2,069	
Class 2: £2.70 × 52		140
Class 4: £(25,000 – 7,755) × 9%		1,552
	2,069	1,692

The self-employed person is better off by £(2,069 – 1,692) = £377 a year.

Chapter roundup

- The badges of trade can be used to decide whether or not a trade exists.
- The accounts profits need to be adjusted in order to establish the taxable trade profits.
- An individual who is carrying on a trade may elect for the profits of the trade to be calculated on the cash basis (instead of in accordance with generally accepted accounting practice) in certain circumstances.
- Fixed rate expenses can be used in relation to expenditure on motor cars and business premises partly used as the trader's home.
- Basis periods are used to link periods of account to tax years.
- In opening and closing years, special rules are applied so that a new trader can start to be taxed quickly, and a retiring trader need not be taxed long after their retirement.
- On a change of accounting date, special rules apply for fixing basis periods.
- The self employed pay Class 2 and Class 4 NICs. Class 4 NICs are based on the level of the individual's taxable profits. Class 2 NICs are paid at a weekly flat rate.

Quick quiz

1. List the six traditional badges of trade.
2. What are the remoteness test and the duality test?
3. What pre-trading expenditure is deductible?
4. In which period of account are earnings paid 12 months after the end of the period for which they are charged deductible?
5. What is the maximum allowable amount of redundancy pay on the cessation of a trade?
6. Which businesses can use the cash basis of accounting?
7. What is the basis period for the tax year in which a trade commenced?
8. On what two occasions may overlap profits potentially be relieved?
9. How are Class 4 NICs calculated?

Answers to quick quiz

1 The subject matter
The frequency of transactions
The length of ownership
Supplementary work and marketing
A profit motive
The way in which goods were acquired

2 Expenditure is not deductible if it is not for trade purposes (the remoteness test), or if it reflects more than one purpose (the duality test).

3 Pre-trading expenditure is deductible if it is incurred within seven years of the start of the trade and is of a type that would have been deductible if the trade had already started.

4 In the period in which they are paid.

5 3 × statutory amount

6 Unincorporated businesses (sole traders and partnerships) whose receipts for the tax year do not exceed the value added tax (VAT) registration threshold can use the cash basis of accounting.

7 Date of commencement to 5 April in that year.

8 On a change of accounting date where a basis period resulting from the change exceeds 12 months or on the cessation of a business.

9 The main rate is a fixed percentage of an individual's profits between the upper limit and lower limit. The additional rate applies above the upper limit.

Now try the question below from the Exam Question Bank

Number	Level	Marks	Time
Q7	Introductory	17	31 mins

7

Capital allowances

Topic list	Syllabus reference
1 Capital allowances in general	A1(a)B3
2 Plant and machinery – qualifying expenditure	A1(a)B3
3 The main pool	A1(a)B3, A1(d)(iv), (v)
4 Special rate pool	A1(a)B3
5 Private use assets	A1(a)B3
6 Motor cars	A1(a)B3
7 Short-life assets	A1(a)B3
8 Hire purchase and leasing	A1(a)B3
9 Successions	A1(a)B3

Introduction

In the previous chapter we saw how to adjust the accounting profit to find taxable trade profits and how to allocate those profits to tax years. The adjustments included adding back depreciation as a disallowable expenses and deducting capital allowances instead. In this chapter, we look at capital allowances on plant and machinery.

Our study of plant and machinery falls into three parts. First, we look at what qualifies for allowances: many business assets get no allowances at all. Second, we see how to compute the allowances and lastly, we look at special rules for assets with short lives, for private use assets, for assets which the taxpayer does not buy outright, and for transfers of whole businesses.

Study guide

		Intellectual level
1	**Income and income tax liabilities in situations involving further overseas aspects and in relation to trusts, and the application of exemptions and reliefs**	
(a)	The contents of the Paper F6 study guide for income tax, under headings:	2
•	B3 Income from self employment	
(d)	Income from self employment:	
(iv)	Advise on the allocation of the annual investment allowance between related businesses	3
(v)	Identify the enhanced capital allowances in respect of expenditure on green technologies	2

Exam guide

If you are asked to consider the tax costs of business strategies, whether for a sole trader or a company, you should always take capital allowances into account. This could apply when considering a particular contract, or when comparing the costs of different assets, or it could be in a buy or lease context.

Knowledge brought forward from earlier studies

This chapter is mainly revision from Paper F6. The allocation of the annual investment allowance between related business and enhanced capital allowances are new.

The major changes for 2013/14 from 2012/13 in the material you have studied at F6 are to the amount of the annual investment allowance and to the CO_2 thresholds for low and high emission cars.

1 Capital allowances in general

FAST FORWARD

Capital allowances are available on plant and machinery.

One of the competencies you require to fulfil performance objective 19 of the PER is the ability to evaluate and compute taxes payable. You can apply the knowledge you obtain from this section of the text to help to demonstrate this competence.

Capital expenditure cannot be deducted in computing taxable trade profits, but it *may* attract capital allowances. Capital allowances are treated as a trading expense and are deducted in arriving at taxable trade profits. Balancing charges, effectively negative allowances, are added in arriving at those profits.

Capital expenditure on plant and machinery qualifies for capital allowances.

Both unincorporated businesses and companies are entitled to capital allowances. For completeness, in this chapter we will look at the rules for companies alongside those for unincorporated businesses. We will look at companies in more detail later in this Text.

For unincorporated businesses, capital allowances are calculated for periods of account. These are simply the periods for which the trader chooses to make up accounts. For companies, capital allowances are calculated for accounting periods (see later in this Text).

For capital allowances purposes, expenditure is generally deemed to be incurred when the obligation to pay becomes unconditional. This will often be the date of a contract, but if for example payment is due a month after delivery of a machine, it would be the date of delivery. However, amounts due more than four months after the obligation becomes unconditional are deemed to be incurred when they fall due.

2 Plant and machinery – qualifying expenditure

2.1 Introduction

Capital expenditure on plant and machinery qualifies for capital allowances if the plant or machinery is used for a qualifying activity, such as a trade. 'Plant' is not defined by the legislation, although some specific exclusions and inclusions are given. The word 'machinery' may be taken to have its normal everyday meaning.

2.2 The statutory exclusions

FAST FORWARD

Statutory rules generally exclude specified items from treatment as plant, rather than include specified items as plant.

2.2.1 Buildings

Expenditure on a building and on any asset which is incorporated in a building or is of a kind normally incorporated into buildings does not qualify as expenditure on plant, but see below for exceptions.

In addition to complete buildings, **the following assets count as 'buildings', and are therefore not plant.**

- Walls, floors, ceilings, doors, gates, shutters, windows and stairs
- Mains services, and systems, of water, electricity and gas
- Waste disposal, sewerage and drainage systems
- Shafts or other structures for lifts etc.

2.2.2 Structures

Expenditure on structures and on works involving the alteration of land **does not qualify as expenditure on plant**, but see below for exceptions.

A 'structure' is a fixed structure of any kind, other than a building.

2.2.3 Exceptions

Over the years a large body of case law has been built up under which plant and machinery allowances have been given on certain types of expenditure which might be thought to be expenditure on a building or structure. Statute therefore gives a list of various assets which *may* still be plant. These are:

- Any machinery not within any other item in this list
- Electrical (including lighting), cold water, gas and sewerage systems:
  - Provided mainly to meet the particular requirements of the trade, or
  - Provided mainly to serve particular machinery or plant used for the purposes of the trade
- Space or water heating systems and powered systems of ventilation
- Manufacturing and display equipment
- Cookers, washing machines, refrigeration or cooling equipment, sanitary ware and furniture and furnishings
- Lifts etc
- Sound insulation provided mainly to meet the particular requirements of the trade

- Computer, telecommunication and surveillance systems
- Sprinkler equipment, fire alarm and burglar alarm systems
- Strong rooms in bank or building society premises, safes
- Partition walls, where movable and intended to be moved
- Decorative assets provided for the enjoyment of the public in the hotel, restaurant or similar trades, advertising hoardings
- Glasshouses which have, as an integral part of their structure, devices which control the plant growing environment automatically
- Swimming pools (including diving boards, slides) and structures for rides at amusement parks
- Caravans provided mainly for holiday lettings
- Movable buildings intended to be moved in the course of the trade
- Expenditure on altering land for the purpose only of installing machinery or plant
- Dry docks and jetties
- Pipelines, and also underground ducts or tunnels with a primary purpose of carrying utility conduits
- Silos provided for temporary storage and storage tanks, slurry pits and silage clamps
- Fish tanks, fish ponds and fixed zoo cages
- A railway or tramway

Items falling within the above list of exclusions will only qualify as plant if they fall within the meaning of plant as established by case law. This is discussed below.

2.2.4 Land

Land or an interest in land does not qualify as plant and machinery. For this purpose 'land' excludes buildings, structures and assets which are installed or fixed to land in such a way as to become part of the land for general legal purposes.

2.3 The statutory inclusions

Certain expenditure is specifically deemed to be expenditure on plant and machinery.

The following are deemed to be on plant and machinery.

- Expenditure incurred by a trader in complying with fire regulations for a building which they occupy
- Expenditure by a trader on thermal insulation of a building used for the trade
- Expenditure by a trader in meeting statutory safety requirements for sports ground
- Expenditure (by an individual or a partnership, not by a company) on *security assets* provided to meet a special threat to an individual's security that arises wholly or mainly due to the particular trade concerned. Cars, ships, aircraft and dwellings are specifically excluded from the definition of a security asset

On disposal, the sale proceeds for the above are deemed to be zero, so no balancing charge (see below) can arise.

Capital expenditure on computer software (both programs and data) **qualifies as expenditure on plant and machinery**:

(a) Regardless of whether the software is supplied in a tangible form (such as a disk) or transmitted electronically, and

(b) Regardless of whether the purchaser acquires the software or only a licence to use it.

Disposal proceeds are brought into account in the normal way, except that if the fee for the grant of a licence is taxed as income of the licensor, no disposal proceeds are taken into account in computing the licensee's capital allowances.

Where someone has incurred expenditure qualifying for capital allowances on computer software (or the right to use software), and receives a capital sum in exchange for allowing someone else to use the software, that sum is brought into account as disposal proceeds. However, the cumulative total of disposal proceeds is not allowed to exceed the original cost of the software, and any proceeds above this limit are ignored for capital allowances purposes (although they may lead to chargeable gains).

If software is expected to have a useful economic life of less than two years, its cost may be treated as revenue expenditure.

For companies the rules for computer software are overridden by the rules for intangible fixed assets unless the company elects otherwise.

2.4 Case law

FAST FORWARD

There are several cases on the definition of plant. To help you to absorb them, try to see the function/setting theme running through them.

The original case law **definition of plant** (applied in this case to a horse) is **'whatever apparatus is used by a businessman for carrying on his business: not his stock in trade which he buys or makes for sale; but all goods and chattels, fixed or movable, live or dead, which he keeps for permanent employment in the business'** *(Yarmouth v France 1887)*.

Subsequent cases have refined the original definition and have largely been concerned with the **distinction between plant actively used in the business (qualifying) and the setting in which the business is carried on (non-qualifying). This is the 'functional' test**. Some of the decisions have now been enacted as part of statute law, but they are still relevant as examples of the principles involved.

The whole cost of excavating and installing a swimming pool was allowed to the owners of a caravan park. *CIR v Barclay Curle & Co 1969* was followed: the pool performed **the function** of giving 'buoyancy and enjoyment' to the persons using the pool *(Cooke v Beach Station Caravans Ltd 1974)* (actual item now covered by statute).

A barrister succeeded in his claim for his law library: 'Plant includes a man's tools of his trade. It extends to what he uses day by day in the course of his profession. It is not confined to physical things like the dentist's chair or the architect's table' *(Munby v Furlong 1977)*.

Office partitioning was allowed. Because it was movable it was not regarded as part of the setting in which the business was carried on *(Jarrold v John Good and Sons Ltd 1963)* (actual item now covered by statute).

A ship used as a floating restaurant was regarded as a 'structure in which the business was carried on rather than apparatus employed ... ' (Buckley LJ). No capital allowances could be obtained *(Benson v Yard Arm Club 1978)*. The same decision was made in relation to a football club's spectator stand. The stand performed no function in the actual carrying out of the club's trade *(Brown v Burnley Football and Athletic Co Ltd 1980)*.

At a motorway service station, false ceilings contained conduits, ducts and lighting apparatus. **They did not qualify because they did not perform a function in the business. They were merely part of the setting in which the business was conducted** *(Hampton v Fortes Autogrill Ltd 1979)*.

Light fittings, decor and murals can be plant. A company carried on business as hoteliers and operators of licensed premises. The function of the items was the creation of an atmosphere conducive to the comfort and well being of its customers *(CIR v Scottish and Newcastle Breweries Ltd 1982)* (decorative assets used in hotels etc, now covered by statute).

On the other hand, it has been held that when an attractive floor is provided in a restaurant, the fact that the floor performs the function of making the restaurant attractive to customers is not enough to make it plant. It functions as premises, and the cost therefore does not qualify for capital allowances *(Wimpy International Ltd v Warland 1988)*.

General lighting in a department store is not plant, as it is merely setting. Special display lighting, however, can be plant *(Cole Brothers Ltd v Phillips 1982)*.

Free-standing decorative screens installed in the windows of a branch of a building society qualified as plant. Their function was not to act a part of the setting in which the society's business was carried on; it was to attract local custom, and accordingly the screens formed part of the apparatus with which the society carried on its business *(Leeds Permanent Building Society v Proctor 1982)*.

In *Bradley v London Electricity plc 1996* an electricity substation was held not to be plant because it functioned as premises in which London Electricity carried on a trading activity rather than apparatus with which the activity was carried out.

3 The main pool

With capital allowances computations, the main thing is to get the layout right. Having done that, you will find that the figures tend to drop into place.

3.1 Main pool expenditure

Most expenditure on plant and machinery, including cars with CO_2 emissions of 130g/km or less acquired on or after 6 April 2013 (1 April 2013 for companies), is put into a pool of expenditure (the main pool) on which capital allowances may be claimed. An addition increases the pool whilst a disposal decreases it.

Exceptionally the following items are not put into the main pool:

(a) assets dealt with in the special rate pool
(b) assets with private use by the trader
(c) short life assets where an election has been made.

These exceptions are dealt with later in this chapter.

Expenditure on plant and machinery by a person about to begin a trade is treated as incurred on the first day of trading. Assets previously owned by a trader and then brought into the trade (at the start of trading or later) are treated as bought for their market values at the times when they are brought in.

3.2 Annual investment allowance

Businesses are entitled to an annual investment allowance (AIA) of £250,000 for a 12 month period of account. Related businesses share one allowance between them.

3.2.1 Amount of annual investment allowance

Businesses can claim an **annual investment allowance (AIA) on the first £250,000 spent each year on plant or machinery**, including assets in the main pool, but not including motor cars. Expenditure on motorcycles does qualify for the AIA.

Where the period of account is more or less than a year, the maximum allowance is proportionately increased or reduced.

After claiming the AIA, the balance of expenditure on main pool assets after the AIA is transferred to the main pool immediately and is eligible for writing down allowances in the same period.

Exam focus point

The amount of the annual investment allowance changed on 1 January 2013. The apportionment in order to determine the amount of the annual investment allowance where a period of account spans the date of change is not examinable.

3.2.2 Allocation of annual investment allowance between related businesses

Related business are entitled to a single annual investment allowance between the businesses. The businesses may **allocate the allowance between them as they think fit.**

Business are related if **they are carried on or controlled by the same individual or partnership and either:**

- the businesses are **engaged in the same activity**; or
- the businesses **share the same premises.**

A business is **controlled by a person in a tax year** if it is controlled by the person **at the end of the chargeable period for that business ending in that tax year.**

The **nature of expenditure** by one business may be relevant when deciding how to allocate the allowance between the businesses. For example, it is **more tax efficient to set the annual investment allowance against special rate pool expenditure** because of the lower rate of subsequent writing down allowances on the special rate pool (8% pa) as opposed to the main pool (18% pa).

There are similar (but separate) rules relating to companies under common control and companies in a group. We will deal with these rules when we look at companies later in this Text.

3.3 First year allowances and enhanced capital allowances

FAST FORWARD

A first year allowance (FYA) at the rate of 100% is available on new low emission cars. Enhanced capital allowances (ECAs) are available on green technologies. FYAs and ECAs are never pro-rated in short periods of account.

3.3.1 FYA on low emission cars

Key term

A **low emission car** is one which has **CO_2 emissions of 95g/km or less.**

A 100% first year allowance (FYA) is available for expenditure incurred on new low emission motor cars.

If the FYA is not claimed in full, the balance of expenditure is transferred to the main pool after any writing down allowance has been calculated on the main pool.

Exam focus point

In the exam you will be given a car's CO_2 emissions. You will not be told whether it is low emission.

3.3.2 Enhanced capital allowances

Capital expenditure on new (ie not second hand) energy and water saving plant and machinery ("green technologies") qualifies for 100% enhanced capital allowances (ECAs) .

Companies can surrender ECAs for a tax credit of 19%. This is dealt with in more detail when we look at companies later in this Text.

3.3.3 Short periods of account

FYAs and ECAs are not reduced pro-rata in a short period of account, unlike the AIA and writing down allowances.

3.4 Writing down allowances

Most expenditure on plant and machinery qualifies for a WDA at 18% every 12 months.

Key term

A **writing down allowance (WDA)** is given on main pool expenditure **at the rate of 18% a year** (on a reducing balance basis). The WDA is calculated on the tax written down value (TWDV) of pooled plant, after adding the current period's additions and taking out the current period's disposals.

When plant is sold, proceeds, **limited to a maximum of the original cost,** are taken out of the pool. Provided that the trade is still being carried on, the pool balance remaining is written down in the future by WDAs, even if there are no assets left.

3.5 Example: writing down allowances

Elizabeth has a tax written down value on her main pool of plant and machinery of £16,000 on 6 April 2013. In the year to 5 April 2014 she bought a car with CO_2 emissions of 110g/km for £8,000 (no non-business use) and she disposed of plant (which originally cost £4,000) for £6,000.

Calculate the maximum capital allowances claim for the year.

	Main pool	*Allowances*
	£	£
Twdv b/f	16,000	
Addition (not qualifying for AIA or FYA)	8,000	
Less disposal (proceeds limited to cost)	(4,000)	
	20,000	
WDA @ 18%	(3,600)	3,600
TWDV c/f	16,400	
Maximum capital allowances claim		3,600

Question — **Capital allowances**

Julia is a sole trader making up accounts to 5 April each year. At 5 April 2013, the tax written down value on her main pool is £12,500.

In the year to 5 April 2014, Julia bought the following assets:

1 June 2013	Machine	£240,000
12 November 2013	Van	£17,500
10 February 2014	Car for salesman (CO_2 emissions 120g/km)	£9,000

She disposed of plant on 15 December 2013 for £12,000 (original cost £16,000).

Calculate the maximum capital allowances claim that Julia can make for the year ended 5 April 2014.

Answer

	AIA	*Main pool*	*Allowances*
	£	£	£
y/e 5 April 2014			
TWDV b/f		12,500	
Additions qualifying for AIA			
1.6.13 Machine	240,000		
12.11.13 Van	17,500		
	257,500		
AIA	(250,000)		250,000
	7,500		
Transfer balance to pool	(7,500)	7,500	
Additions not qualifying for AIA			
10.2.14 Car		9,000	
Disposal			
15.12.13 Plant		(12,000)	
		17,000	
WDA @ 18%		(3,060)	3,060
TWDV c/f		13,940	
Maximum capital allowances			253,060

3.6 Short and long periods of account

WDAs are 18% × number of months/12:

(a) For unincorporated businesses where the period of account is longer or shorter than 12 months

(b) For companies where the accounting period is shorter than 12 months (a company's accounting period for tax purposes is never longer than 12 months), or where the trade concerned started in the accounting period and was therefore carried on for fewer than 12 months. Remember that we will be studying companies in detail later in this Text.

Question

Short period of account

Venus is a sole trader and has made up accounts to 30 April each year. At 30 April 2013, the tax written down value of her main pool was £66,667. She decides to make up her next set of accounts to 31 December 2013.

In the period to 31 December 2013, the following acquisitions were made:

1 May 2013	Plant	£180,000
10 July 2013	Car (CO_2 emissions 110 g/km)	£9,000
3 August 2013	Car (CO_2 emissions 85 g/km)	£11,000

Venus disposed of plant on 1 November 2013 for £20,000 (original cost £28,000).

Calculate the maximum capital allowances that Venus can claim for the period ending 31 December 2013.

Answer

	AIA	*FYA*	*Main pool*	*Allowances*
	£	£	£	£
p/e 31 December 2013				
TWDV b/f			66,667	
Additions qualifying for AIA				
1.5.13 Plant	180,000			
AIA £250,000 × 8/12	(166,667)			166,667
	13,333			
Transfer balance to pool	(13,333)		13,333	
Additions qualifying for FYA				
3.8.13 Car (low emission)		11,000		
Less: 100% FYA		(11,000)		11,000
Additions not qualifying for AIA nor FYA				
10.7.13 Car			9,000	
Disposals				
1.11.13 Plant			(20,000)	
			69,000	
WDA @ 18% × 8/12			(8,280)	8,280
TWDVs c/f			60,720	
Maximum allowances claim				185,947

Note that the annual investment allowance and the writing down allowance are reduced for the short period of account, but the first year allowance is given in full.

Question — Long period of account

Oscar started trading on 1 July 2013 and made up his first set of accounts to 31 December 2014. He bought the following assets:

1 July 2013	Plant	£325,000
10 October 2013	Car for business use only (CO_2 emissions 110g/km)	£11,000
12 February 2014	Plant	£115,000

Calculate the maximum capital allowances claim that Oscar can make for the period ended 31 December 2014. Assume the capital allowances rules in 2013/14 also apply in 2014/15.

Answer

	AIA	Main pool	Allowances
	£	£	£
p/e 31 December 2014			
Additions qualifying for AIA			
10.7.13 Plant	325,000		
12.2.14 Plant	115,000		
	440,000		
AIA £250,000 × 18/12	(375,000)		375,000
	65,000		
Transfer balance to main pool	(65,000)	65,000	
Additions not qualifying for AIA			
1.10.13 Car		11,000	
		76,000	
WDA @ 18% × 18/12		(20,520)	20,520
TWDV c/f		55,480	
Maximum capital allowances			395,520

Note that the AIA and the WDA are increased pro rata for the long period of account.

3.7 Small balance on main pool

A writing down allowance equal to unrelieved expenditure in the main pool can be claimed where this is **£1,000 or less**. If the maximum WDA is claimed, the main pool will then have a nil balance carried forward.

Question

Small balance on main pool

Alan has traded for many years, making up accounts to 30 April each year. At 1 May 2013, the tax written down value of his main pool was £15,000.

On 1 October 2013, he sold some plant and machinery for £14,200 (original cost £16,000).

Calculate the maximum capital allowances claim that Alan can make for the period ending 30 April 2014. Assume the capital allowances rules in 2013/14 also apply in 2014/15.

Answer

	Main pool	Allowances
	£	£
y/e 30 April 2014		
TWDV b/f	15,000	
Disposal	(14,200)	
	800	
WDA (small pool)	(800)	800
TWDV c/f	nil	
Maximum capital allowances		800

Exam focus point

Note the tax planning opportunities available. It may be important to buy plant just before an accounting date, so that allowances become available as soon as possible. Alternatively, it may be desirable to claim less than the maximum allowances to even out annual taxable profits and avoid a higher rate of tax in later years.

3.8 Balancing charges and allowances

Balancing charges occur when the disposal value deducted exceeds the balance remaining in the pool. The charge equals the excess and is effectively a negative capital allowance, increasing profits. Most commonly this happens when the trade ceases and the remaining assets are sold. It may also occur, however, whilst the trade is still in progress.

Balancing allowances on the main and special pools of expenditure arise only when the trade ceases. The balancing allowance is equal to the remaining unrelieved expenditure after deducting the disposal value of all the assets. Balancing allowances may also arise on single pool items (see below) whenever those items are disposed of.

4 Special rate pool

FAST FORWARD

The special rate pool contains expenditure on thermal insulation, long life assets, features integral to a building, solar panels, and cars with CO_2 emissions over 130g/km. The AIA can be used against such expenditure except cars. The WDA is 8%.

4.1 Operation of the special rate pool

Expenditure on thermal insulation, long life assets, features integral to a building, solar panels, and cars with CO_2 emissions over 130g/km acquired on or after 6 April 2013 (1 April 2013 for companies), is not dealt with in the main pool but in a special rate pool.

The Annual Investment Allowance can apply to expenditure on such assets except on cars. The taxpayer can decide how to allocate the AIA. It will be more tax efficient to set the allowance against special rate pool expenditure in priority to main pool expenditure where there is expenditure on assets in both pools in the period.

The writing down allowance for the special rate pool is 8% for a twelve month period. As with the writing down allowance on the main pool, this is adjusted for short and long periods of account. Where the tax written down balance of the special rate pool is £1,000 or less, a writing down allowance can be claimed of up to £1,000. This is in addition to any similar claim in relation to the main pool.

4.2 Long life assets

Key term

Long life assets are assets with an expected working life of 25 years or more.

The **long life asset rules only apply to businesses whose total expenditure on assets with an expected working life of 25 years or more in a chargeable period is more than £100,000**. If the expenditure exceeds £100,000, the whole of the expenditure enters the special rate pool. For this purpose all expenditure incurred under a contract is treated as incurred in the first chargeable period to which that contract relates.

The £100,000 limit is reduced or increased proportionately in the case of a chargeable period of less or more than 12 months.

The following are **not** treated as long life assets:

(a) **Plant and machinery in dwelling houses, retail shops, showrooms, hotels and offices**
(b) **Cars**

4.3 Integral features

Features which are integral to a building include the following:

- **electrical and lighting systems**
- **cold water systems**
- **space or water heating systems**
- **powered systems of ventilation, cooling or air conditioning**
- **lifts and escalators**

When a building is sold, the vendor and purchaser can make a joint election to determine how the sale proceeds are apportioned between the building and its integral features.

4.4 Example: integral features

Lucy has been trading for many years, making up accounts to 5 April each year. The tax written down value of her main pool at 5 April 2013 was £110,000. In the year to 5 April 2014, Lucy had the following expenditure:

10 June 2013	General plant costing £45,000
12 December 2013	Lighting system in shop £120,000
15 January 2014	Car for business use only (CO_2 emissions 175 g/km) £25,000
26 January 2014	Delivery van £15,000
4 March 2014	Lifts £132,500

The maximum capital allowances claim that Lucy can make for the year to 5 April 2014 is:

		AIA	*Main pool*	*Special rate pool*	*Allowances*
		£	£	£	£
y/e 5 April 2014					
TWDV b/f			110,000		
Additions for AIA (best use)					
12.12.13	Lighting	120,000			
4.3.14	Lifts	132,500			
		252,500			
AIA		(250,000)			250,000
		2,500			
Transfer balance to special rate pool		(2,500)		2,500	
Additions not given AIA					
10.6.13	Plant		45,000		
26.1.14	Van		15,000		
Additions not qualifying for AIA					
15.1.14	Car			25,000	
			170,000	27,500	
WDA @ 18%			(30,600)		30,600
WDA @ 8%				(2,200)	2,200
TWDVs c/f			139,400	25,300	
Allowances					282,800

5 Private use assets

FAST FORWARD

An asset which is used privately by a trader is dealt with in a single asset pool and the capital allowances are restricted.

An asset (for example, a car) which is used partly for private purposes by a sole trader or a partner is put into its own pool (single asset pool).

Capital allowances are calculated on the full cost. However, only the business use proportion of the allowances is allowed as a deduction from trading profits. This restriction applies to the AIA, FYAs, WDAs, balancing allowances and balancing charges.

An asset with some private use by an employee (not the owner of the business) suffers no such restriction. The employee may be taxed on an employment benefit (see earlier in this Text) so the business receives capital allowances on the full cost of the asset.

Exam focus point

Capital allowances on assets with some private use is a common exam topic. Check carefully whether the private use is by the owner of the business or by an employee.

Question — Capital allowances on private use asset

Jacinth has been in business as a sole trader for many years, making up accounts to 31 March. On 1 November 2013 she bought computer equipment for £2,700 which she uses 75% in her business and 25% privately. She has already used the AIA against other expenditure in the year to 31 March 2014.

Calculate the maximum capital allowance that Jacinth can claim in respect to the computer equipment in the year to 31 March 2014.

Answer

	Computer equipment	*Allowances @ 75%*
	£	£
y/e 31 March 2014		
Acquisition	2,700	
WDA @ 18%	(486)	365
TWDV c/f	2,214	
Maximum capital allowance on computer equipment		365

6 Motor cars

FAST FORWARD

Motor cars are generally dealt with in the special rate pool (cars emitting over 130g/km) or the main pool, unless there is private use by the trader.

As we have already seen, motor cars are categorised in accordance with their CO_2 emissions:

(a) **Cars emitting over 130g/km**: expenditure is added to the special rate pool,

(b) **Cars emitting between 96 and 130 g/km**: expenditure is added to the main pool,

(c) **Cars emitting 95 g/km or less**: expenditure eligible for 100% first year allowance, if allowance not claimed in full, excess added to main pool.

Exam focus point

Different rules applied to cars acquired prior to 6 April 2013 (1 April 2013 for companies) but the examiner has stated that questions will not be set involving such cars.

Cars with an element of private use are kept separate from the main and special pools and are dealt with in single asset pools. They are entitled to a WDA of 18% (car with CO_2 emissions between 96 and 130 g/km) or 8% (car with CO_2 emissions over 130 g/km).

Question — Capital allowances on private use car

Quodos started to trade on 1 July 2013, making up accounts to 31 December 2013 and each 31 December thereafter. On 1 August 2013 he bought a car for £17,000 with CO_2 emissions of 110 g/km. The private use proportion is 10%. The car was sold in July 2016 for £4,000.

Calculate the capital allowances, assuming:

(a) The car was used by an employee, or
(b) The car was used by Quodos

and that the capital allowances rates in 2013/14 apply throughout.

Answer

(a)

	Main pool	*Allowances*
	£	£
1.7.13 – 31.12.13		
Purchase price	17,000	
WDA 18% × 6/12 × £17,000	(1,530)	1,530
	15,470	
1.1.14 – 31.12.14		
WDA 18% × £15,470	(2,785)	
	12,685	
1.1.15 – 31.12.15		
WDA 18% × £12,685	(2,283)	2,283
	10,402	
1.1.16 – 31.12.16		
Proceeds	(4,000)	
	6,402	
WDA 18% × £6,402	(1,152)	1,152
TWDV c/f	5,250	

The private use of the car by the employee has no effect on the capital allowances due to Quodos. The car will be placed in the main pool. No balancing allowance is available on the main pool until trade ceases even though the car has been sold.

(b)

	Car	*Allowances*
		90%
	£	£
1.7.13 – 31.12.13		
Purchase price	17,000	
WDA 18% × 6/12 × £17,000	(1,530)	1,377
	15,470	
1.1.14 – 31.12.14		
WDA 18% × £15,470	(2,785)	2,507
	12,685	
1.1.15 – 31.12.15		
WDA 18% × £12,685	(2,283)	2,055
	10,402	
1.1.16 – 31.12.16		
Proceeds	(4,000)	
Balancing allowance	6,402	5,762

As the private use is by the proprietor, Quodos, only 90% of the WDAs and balancing allowance are available.

7 Short-life assets

FAST FORWARD

Short life asset elections can bring forward the allowances due on an asset.

A trader can elect that specific items of plant, which are expected to have a short working life, be kept separately from the main pool.

Key term

Any asset subject to this election is known as a 'short life asset', and the election is known as a 'de-pooling election'.

The election is irrevocable. For an unincorporated business, the time limit for electing is the 31 January which is 22 months after the end of the tax year in which the period of account of the expenditure ends. (For a company, it is two years after the end of the accounting period of the expenditure). **Short life asset treatment cannot be claimed for any motor cars, or plant used partly for non-trade purposes.**

The short life asset is kept in a single asset pool. Provided that the short life asset is disposed of **within eight years of the end of the accounting period** in which it was bought, a balancing charge or allowance arises on its disposal.

If the asset is not disposed of within this time period, its tax written down value is added to the main pool at the beginning of the next period of account (accounting period for companies). This will be after allowances have been claimed nine times on the asset; once in the period of acquisition and then each year for the following eight years. The election should therefore be made for assets likely to be sold for less than their tax written down values within eight years. It should not usually be made for assets likely to be sold within eight years for more than their tax written down values. There is no requirement to show from the outset that the asset will actually have a 'short life', so it is a matter of judgment whether the election should be made.

The Annual Investment Allowance can be set against short-life assets. The taxpayer can decide how to allocate the AIA. It will be more tax efficient to set the allowance against main pool expenditure in priority to short-life asset expenditure.

Question | **Short life assets**

Caithlin bought a machine for business use on 1 May 2013 for £9,000 and elected for de-pooling. She did not claim the AIA in respect of this asset. Her accounting year end is 30 April.

Calculate the capital allowances due if:

(a) The asset is scrapped for £300 in August 2021
(b) The asset is scrapped for £200 in August 2022

and assuming that the capital allowances rates in 2013/14 apply throughout.

Answer

(a)

	£
Year to 30.4.14	
Cost	9,000
WDA 18%	(1,620)
	7,380
Year to 30.4.15	
WDA 18%	(1,328)
	6,052
Year to 30.4.16	
WDA 18%	(1,089)
	4,963
Year to 30.4.17	
WDA 18%	(893)
	4,070
Year to 30.4.18	
WDA 18%	(733)
	3,337
Year to 30.4.19	
WDA 18%	(601)
	2,736
Year to 30.4.20	
WDA 18%	(492)
	2,244
Year to 30.4.21	
WDA 18%	(404)
	1,840
Year to 30.4.22	
Disposal proceeds	(300)
Balancing allowance	1,540

(b) If the asset is still in use at 30 April 2022, WDAs up to 30.4.21 will be as above. In the year to 30.4.22, a WDA can be claimed of 18% × £1,840 = £331. The tax written down value of £1,840 – £331 = £1,509 will be added to the main pool at the beginning of the next period of account. The disposal proceeds of £200 will be deducted from the main pool in that period's capital allowances computation. No balancing allowance will arise and the main pool will continue.

Short-life asset treatment cannot be claimed for motor cars or plant used partly for non-trade purposes.

8 Hire purchase and leasing

FAST FORWARD

Capital allowances are available on assets acquired by hire purchase or lease.

8.1 Assets on hire purchase or long term leases

Any asset (including a car) bought on hire purchase (HP) is treated as if purchased outright for the cash price. Therefore:

(a) The buyer normally obtains **capital allowances on the cash price** when the agreement begins.

(b) He may write off the **finance charge as a trade expense** over the term of the HP contract.

Long term leases, (those with a term of 5 or more years), are treated in the same way as HP transactions.

8.2 Assets on long term leases

Under a long term lease, the lessee merely hires the asset over a period. The hire charge can normally be deducted in computing trade profits. If a car with emissions over 130g/km is leased, the maximum allowable deduction from trading profits for lease rentals is limited by 15% as described earlier in this Text.

A long term lessor of plant normally obtains the benefit of capital allowances although there are anti-avoidance provisions which deny or restrict capital allowances on certain finance leases. Leasing is thus an activity which attracts tax allowances and which can be used to defer tax liabilities where the capital allowances given exceed the rental income. For individuals, any losses arising from leasing are available for offset against other income only if the individual devotes substantially all of their time to the conduct of a leasing business.

9 Successions

FAST FORWARD

Balancing adjustments are calculated when a business ceases. If the business is transferred to a connected person, the written down value can be transferred instead.

Balancing adjustments arise on the cessation of a business. No writing down allowances are given, but the final proceeds (limited to cost) on sales of plant are compared with the tax WDV to calculate balancing allowances or charges.

Balancing charges may be avoided where the trade passes from one connected person to another. If a succession occurs both parties must elect if the avoidance of the balancing adjustments is required. **An election will result in the plant being transferred at its tax written down value for capital allowances purposes.** Even where a succession election is made, there is a cessation of trade so no allowances are available to the transferor in the final period in which the transfer of trade occurs.

If no election is made on a transfer of business to a connected person, assets are deemed to be sold at their market values.

As we saw earlier, an individual is connected with their spouse, their, or their spouse's brothers, sisters, ancestors and lineal descendants, with their spouses, with business partners and their spouses and relatives, and with a company they control (either alone or in conjunction with persons connected with them). **'Spouses' includes civil partners.**

Where a person succeeds to a business under a will or on intestacy, then even if they were not connected with the deceased they may elect to take over the assets at the lower of their market value and their tax written down value.

For both connected persons transfers and transfers on death, where the elections are made, the limit on proceeds to be brought into account on a later sale of an asset is the original cost of the asset, not the deemed transfer price.

Chapter roundup

- Capital allowances are available on plant and machinery.
- Statutory rules generally exclude specified items from treatment as plant, rather than include specified items as plant.
- There are several cases on the definition of plant. To help you to absorb them, try to see the function/setting theme running through them.
- With capital allowances computations, the main thing is to get the layout right. Having done that, you will find that the figures tend to drop into place.
- Businesses are entitled to an annual investment allowance (AIA) of £250,000 for a 12 month period of account. Related businesses share one allowance between them.
- A first year allowance (FYA) at the rate of 100% is available on new low emission cars. Enhanced capital allowances (ECAs) are available on green technologies. FYAs and ECAs are never pro-rated in short periods of account.
- Most expenditure on plant and machinery qualifies for a WDA at 18% every 12 months.
- The special rate pool contains expenditure on thermal insulation, long life assets, features integral to a building, solar panels, and cars with CO_2 emissions over 130g/km. The AIA can be used against such expenditure. The WDA is 8%.
- An asset which is used privately by a trader is dealt with in a single asset pool and the capital allowances are restricted.
- Motor cars are generally dealt with in the special rate pool (cars emitting over 130g/km) or the main pool, unless there is private use by the trader.
- Short life asset elections can bring forward the allowances due on an asset.
- Capital allowances are available on assets acquired by hire purchase or lease.
- Balancing adjustments are calculated when a business ceases. If the business is transferred to a connected person, the written down value can be transferred instead.

Quick quiz

1. For what periods are capital allowances for unincorporated businesses calculated?
2. Are writing down allowances pro-rated in a six month period of account?
3. Are first year allowances pro-rated in a six month period of account?
4. When may balancing allowances arise?
5. Within what period must an asset be disposed of if it is beneficial for it to be treated as a short life asset?

Answers to quick quiz

1 Periods of account

2 Yes. In a six month period, writing down allowance are pro-rated by multiplying by 6/12.

3 No. First year allowances are given in full in a short period of account.

4 Balancing allowances may arise in respect of pooled expenditure only when the trade ceases. Balancing allowances may arise on non-pooled items whenever those items are disposed of.

5 Within eight years of the end of the period of account (or accounting period) in which it was bought.

Now try the question below from the Exam Question Bank

Number	Level	Marks	Time
Q8	Introductory	10	18 mins

Trading losses

Topic list	Syllabus reference
1 Losses – an overview	A1(a)B3
2 Carry forward trade loss relief	A1(a)B3
3 Trading loss relief against general income	A1(a)B3
4 Trade transferred to company	A1(d)(ii)
5 Early trading losses relief	A1(a)B3
6 Terminal trading loss relief	A1(a)B3
7 Share loss relief against general income	A3(f)(v)

Introduction

In earlier chapters we have seen how to compute taxable trading profits, after capital allowances, and allocate them to tax years.

Traders sometimes make losses rather than profits. In this chapter we consider the reliefs available for losses. A loss does not in itself lead to receiving tax back from HMRC. Relief is obtained by setting a loss against trading profits, against other income or against capital gains, so that tax need not be paid on them. There are restrictions on how much loss relief can be claimed in a tax year.

An important consideration is the choice between different reliefs. The aim is to use a loss to save as much tax as possible, as quickly as possible.

Finally we consider how a loss on the disposal of shares in an unquoted trading company can be relieved against income in a similar fashion.

In the next chapter we will see how individuals trading in partnership are taxed.

Study guide

		Intellectual level
1	**Income and income tax liabilities in situations involving further overseas aspects and in relation to trusts, and the application of exemptions and reliefs**	
(a)	The contents of the Paper F6 study guide for income tax, under heading:	2
•	B3 Income from self employment	
(d)	Income from self employment	3
(ii)	Advise on the relief available for trading losses following the transfer of a business to a company	
3	**Chargeable gains and capital gains tax liabilities in situations involving further overseas aspects and in relation to closely related persons and trusts together with the application of additional exemptions and reliefs**	
(f)	Gains and losses on the disposal of shares and securities:	
(v)	Establish the relief for capital losses on shares in unquoted trading companies	3

Exam focus

There are various ways in which a trader can obtain relief for trading losses. You are likely to have to advise the most beneficial way of obtaining relief. This will involve considering the rate of tax relief, the potential waste of personal allowances, and how soon relief can be obtained. Read the question carefully to establish if the taxpayer has any particular requirements such as to obtain relief as soon as possible.

Knowledge brought forward from earlier studies

Trading losses have been covered in Paper F6. The examiner has identified essential underpinning knowledge from the F6 syllabus which is particularly important that you revise as part of your P6 studies. In this chapter, the relevant topics are:

		Intellectual level
B3	**Income from self-employment**	
(i)	Relief for trading losses	
i (i)	Understand how trading losses can be carried forward.	2
i (ii)	Understand how trading losses can be claimed against total income and chargeable gains, and the restriction that can apply.	2
i (iii)	Explain and compute the relief for trading losses in the early years of a trade.	1
i (iv)	Explain and compute terminal loss relief.	1

You will be familiar with loss relief on the transfer of a business to a company as this was in the F6 syllabus in previous years.

There is one change for 2013/14 for the rules relating to losses which you studied for F6 in 2012/13. This is the introduction of a limit on the amount of loss relief which can be claimed in a tax year.

Share loss relief against general income is new at P6 level.

1 Losses – an overview

FAST FORWARD

Trading losses may be relieved against future profits of the same trade, against general income and against capital gains.

1.1 Trading losses in general

This chapter considers how losses are calculated and how a loss-suffering taxpayer can use a loss to reduce their tax liability. Most of the chapter concerns losses in respect of trades, professions and vocations.

The rules in this chapter apply only to individuals, trading alone or in partnership. Loss reliefs for companies are completely different and are covered later in this Text.

When computing taxable trading profits, profits may turn out to be negative, meaning a loss has been made in the basis period. **A loss is computed in exactly the same way as a profit**, making the same adjustments to the accounts profit or loss.

If there is a loss in a basis period, the taxable trading profits for the tax year based on that basis period are nil.

1.2 The computation of the loss

The trading loss for a tax year is the trading loss in the basis period for that tax year. However, **if basis periods overlap then a loss in the overlap period is a trading loss for the earlier tax year only.**

1.3 Example: computing the trading loss

Here is an example of a trader who starts to trade on 1 July 2013 and makes losses in opening years.

Period of account	*Loss*
	£
1.7.13 – 31.12.13	9,000
1.1.14 – 31.12.14	24,000

Tax year	*Basis period*	*Working*	*Trading loss for the tax year*
			£
2013/14	1.7.13 – 5.4.14	£9,000 + (£24,000 × 3/12)	15,000
2014/15	1.1.14 – 31.12.14	£24,000 – (£24,000 × 3/12)	18,000

1.4 Example: losses and profits

The same rule against using losses twice applies when losses are netted off against profits in the same basis period. Here is an example, again with a commencement on 1 July 2013 but with a different accounting date.

Period of account	*(Loss)/profit*
	£
1.7.13 – 30.4.14	(10,000)
1.5.14 – 30.4.15	24,000

Tax year	*Basis period*	*Working*	*Trading (Loss)/Profit*
			£
2013/14	1.7.13 – 5.4.14	£(10,000) × 9/10	(9,000)
2014/15	1.7.13 – 30.6.14	£(10,000) × 1/10 + £24,000 × 2/12	3,000

1.5 Other losses

Losses incurred in foreign trades are computed and relieved in a similar manner to those of UK trades and are discussed later in this Text.

Losses from a UK property business have been discussed earlier, and losses on an overseas property business are relieved similarly. Losses on furnished holiday lettings can only be relieved using carry forward loss relief against future income from furnished holiday lettings. Losses on UK furnished holiday lettings and EEA furnished holiday lettings must be dealt with separately.

If a loss arises on a transaction which, if profitable, would give rise to taxable miscellaneous income (see earlier in this Text), it can be set against any other similar income in the same year, and any excess carried forward for relief against miscellaneous income in future years.

2 Carry forward trading loss relief

FAST FORWARD

A trading loss carried forward must be set against the first available profits of the same trade.

A trading loss not relieved in any other way must be **carried forward to set against the first available profits of the same trade** in the calculation of net trading income. Losses may be carried forward for any number of years.

2.1 Example: carrying forward losses

B has the following results.

Year ending	£
31 December 2011	(6,000)
31 December 2012	5,000
31 December 2013	11,000

B's net trading income, after carry forward loss relief, is:

	2011/12		*2012/13*		*2013/14*
	£		£		£
Trading profits	0		5,000		11,000
Less carry forward loss relief	(0)	(i)	(5,000)	(ii)	(1,000)
Profits	0		0		10,000

Loss memorandum		
Trading loss, y/e 31.12.11		6,000
Less: claim in y/e 31.12.12	(i)	(5,000)
claim in y/e 31.12.13 (balance of loss)	(ii)	(1,000)
		0

3 Trading loss relief against general income

FAST FORWARD

Where a loss relief claim is made, trading losses can be set against general income (and also gains if a further claim is made) in the current tax year and/or general income (and also gains if a further claim is made) in the preceding tax year.

3.1 Introduction

Instead of carrying a trading loss forward against future trading profits, it may be relieved against general income.

3.2 Relieving the loss

Relief is against the income of the tax year in which the loss arose. In addition or instead, relief may be claimed **against the income of the preceding year.**

If there are losses in two successive years, and relief is claimed against the first year's income both for the first year's loss and for the second year's loss, relief is given for the first year's loss before the second year's loss.

A claim for a loss must be made by the 31 January which is 22 months after the end of the tax year of the loss: so by 31 January 2016 for a loss in 2013/14.

The taxpayer cannot choose the amount of loss to relieve: so the loss may have to be set against income part of which would have been covered by the personal allowance. However, the taxpayer can choose whether to claim full relief in the current year and then relief in the preceding year for any remaining loss, or the other way round.

When calculating the income tax liability, the loss is set against non-savings income, then against savings income and finally against dividend income.

Relief is available by carry forward for any loss not relieved against general income.

Question — **Loss relief against general income**

Janet was born in 1970. She has a loss in her period of account ending 31 December 2013 of £26,500. Her other income is £19,500 rental income a year, and she wishes to claim loss relief for the year of loss and then for the preceding year. Her trading income in the previous year was £nil. Show her taxable income for each year, and comment on the effectiveness of the loss relief. Assume that tax rates and allowances for 2013/14 have always applied.

Answer

The loss-making period ends in 2013/14, so the year of the loss is 2013/14.

	2012/13	*2013/14*
	£	£
Income	19,500	19,500
Less loss relief against general income	(7,000)	(19,500)
Net income	12,500	0
Less personal allowance	(9,440)	(9,440)
Taxable income	3,060	0

In 2013/14, £9,440 of the loss has been wasted because that amount of income would have been covered by the personal allowance. If Janet claims loss relief against general income, there is nothing she can do about this waste of loss relief or the personal allowance.

3.3 Capital allowances

One of the competencies you require to fulfil performance objective 20 of the PER is the ability to assist with tax planning. You can apply the knowledge you obtain from this section of the text to help to demonstrate this competence.

The trader may adjust the size of the total loss relief claim by not claiming all the capital allowances they are entitled to: a reduced claim will increase the balance carried forward to the next year's capital allowances computation. This may be a useful **tax planning point where the effective rate of relief for capital allowances in future periods will be greater than the rate of tax relief for the loss relief.**

3.4 Trading losses relieved against capital gains

Where relief is claimed against general income of a given year, the taxpayer may include **a further claim to set the loss against their chargeable gains for the year** less any allowable capital losses for the same year or for previous years. This amount of net gains is computed ignoring the annual exempt amount (see later in this Text).

The trading loss is first set against general income of the year of the claim, and only any excess of loss is set against capital gains. The taxpayer cannot specify the amount to be set against capital gains, so the annual exempt amount may be wasted. We include an example here for completeness. You will study chargeable gains later in this Text and we suggest that you come back to this example at that point.

Question — Loss relief against income and gains

Sibyl had the following results for 2013/14.

	£
Loss available for loss relief against general income	27,000
Income	19,500
Capital gains less current year capital losses	11,000
Annual exempt amount for capital gains tax purposes	10,900
Capital losses brought forward	5,000

Show how the loss would be relieved against income and gains.

Answer

	£
Income	19,500
Less loss relief against general income	(19,500)
Net income	0
Capital gains	11,000
Less loss relief: lower of £(27,000 – 19,500) = £7,500 (note 1) and £(11,000 – 5,000) = £6,000 (note 2)	(6,000)
	5,000
Less annual exempt amount (restricted)	(5,000)
	0

Note 1 This equals the loss left after the loss relief against general income claim
Note 2 This equals the gains left after losses b/fwd but ignoring the annual exempt amount

A trading loss of £(7,500 – 6,000) = £1,500 is carried forward. Sibyl's personal allowance and £(10,900 – 5,000) = £5,900 of her capital gains tax annual exempt amount are wasted. Her capital losses brought forward of £5,000 are carried forward to 2014/15. Although we deducted this £5,000 in working out how much trading loss we were allowed to use in the claim, we do not actually use any of the £5,000 unless there are gains remaining in excess of the annual exempt amount.

3.5 Restrictions on trading loss relief against general income

3.5.1 Commercial basis

FAST FORWARD

Loss relief cannot be claimed against general income unless the loss-making business is conducted on a commercial basis.

Relief cannot be claimed against general income unless the loss-making business is conducted on a commercial basis with a view to the realisation of profits throughout the basis period for the tax year.

3.5.2 Relief cap

FAST FORWARD

An individual taxpayer can only deduct the greater of £50,000 and 25% of adjusted total income when making a claim for loss relief against general income.

There is a **restriction on certain deductions which may be made by an individual from total income for a tax year**. For P6(UK) purposes, the restricted deductions concern **trade loss relief against general income (whether claimed for the tax year of the loss or the previous year), early trading losses relief, share loss relief against general income** (these latter two reliefs are both dealt with later in this chapter), and **deduction of interest for qualifying purposes** (see earlier in this Text).

The total deductions in a tax year cannot exceed the greater of:

(a) **£50,000**; and
(b) **25% of the taxpayer's adjusted total income for the tax year.**

Key term

Adjusted total income is total income plus payroll giving less the gross amounts of personal pension contributions.

If a claim is made for relief against general income in the previous year, there is no restriction on the amount of loss that can be used against trading income (of the same trade). The restriction only applies to the other income in that year. Any loss which exceeds the maximum deduction can still be carried forward against future profits from the same trade.

The limits apply in each year for which relief is claimed. If a current year and a prior year claim are made, the relief in the current year is restricted to the greater of £50,000 and 25% of the adjusted total income in the current year. The relief in the prior year is restricted to the greater of £50,000 and 25% of the adjusted total income in the prior year.

The restriction only applies to relief against income, not if a claim is extended to capital gains.

Question — **Restriction on loss relief**

Grace was born in 1966. She has been trading for many years, preparing accounts to 5 April each year. Her recent results have been as follows:

	Profit/(loss)
	£
Year to 5 April 2013	20,000
Year to 5 April 2014	(210,000)

Grace also owns a number of investment properties and her property business income is £130,000 in 2012/13 and £220,000 in 2013/14.

Show Grace's taxable income for the tax years 2012/13 and 2013/14 assuming that she claims relief for her trading loss against general income in both of those years.

Answer

	2012/13	*2013/14*
	£	£
Trading income	20,000	0
Property business income	130,000	220,000
Total income	150,000	220,000
Less loss relief against general income	(70,000)	(55,000)
Net income	80,000	165,000
Less personal allowance	(9,440)	(0)
Taxable income	70,560	165,000

Loss relief for 2013/14 is capped at £(220,000 × 25%) = £55,000 since this is greater than £50,000. The personal allowance is not available as adjusted net income exceeds £118,880.

In 2012/13, the loss relief claim is not capped against the trading profit of £20,000. Relief against other income is capped at £50,000 since this is greater than £(150,000 × 25%) = £37,500. The total loss relief claim is therefore £(20,000 + 50,000) = £70,000. The balance of the loss is £(210,000 – 55,000 – 70,000) = £85,000 is carried forward against future profits of the same trade.

Note that the restriction on loss relief means that the loss has been relieved at the additional rate in 2013/14 and at the higher rate in 2012/13. The personal allowance has also been restored for 2012/13.

3.6 The choice between loss reliefs

FAST FORWARD

It is important for a trader to choose the right loss relief, so as to save tax at the highest possible rate and so as to obtain relief reasonably quickly.

When a trader has a choice between loss reliefs, they should aim to obtain relief both quickly and at the highest possible tax rate. However, do consider that losses relieved against income which would otherwise be covered by the personal allowance are wasted.

Question — The choice between loss reliefs

Felicity's trading results are as follows.

Year ended 30 September	*Trading profit/(loss)*
	£
2011	1,900
2012	(21,000)
2013	14,000

Her other income (all non-savings income) is as follows.

	£
2011/12	4,500
2012/13	30,900
2013/14	16,000

Show the most efficient use of Felicity's trading loss. Assume that her personal allowance has been £9,440 throughout.

Answer

Relief could be claimed against general income for 2011/12 and/or 2012/13, with any unused loss being carried forward. Relief in 2011/12 would be against general income of £(1,900 + 4,500) = £6,400, all of which would be covered by the personal allowance anyway, so this claim should not be made. A loss relief claim against general income should be made for 2012/13 as this saves tax more quickly than a carry forward loss relief claim in 2013/14 would. The final results will be as follows:

	2011/12	*2012/13*	*2013/14*
	£	£	£
Trading income	1,900	0	14,000
Less carry forward loss relief	(0)	(0)	(0)
	1,900	0	14,000
Other income	4,500	30,900	16,000
	6,400	30,900	30,000
Less loss relief against general income	(0)	(21,000)	(0)
Net income	6,400	9,900	30,000
Less personal allowance	(9,440)	(9,440)	(9,440)
Taxable income	0	460	20,560

Exam focus point

> Before recommending loss relief against general income consider whether it will result in the waste of the personal allowance and any tax reducers. Such waste is to be avoided if at all possible.

Another consideration is that a trading loss cannot be set against the capital gains of a year unless relief is first claimed against general income of the same year. It may be worth making the claim against income and wasting the personal allowance in order to avoid a CGT liability. However, remember that using a loss against capital gains will only result in a maximum 28% tax saving, whereas setting losses against income can give a maximum 45% tax saving.

Finally, it is important to consider how offsetting a loss against income will impact the taxation of any income which remains taxable. For example, setting a loss against non-savings income might mean that savings income becomes taxable at the starting rate, rather than the basic rate, or higher rate income becomes taxable at the basic rate. Remember that the tax on dividend income in the basic rate band will be covered by the 10% tax credit.

3.7 Example

Luke was born in 1980. He has been in business as a sole trader for many years, preparing accounts to 31 December each year. In the year ended 31 December 2013, Luke made a profit of £21,440. He anticipates that he will make a loss of £(12,000) in the year ending 31 December 2014. In 2013/14, Luke received gross interest of £4,000. He will have no other income in 2014/15, so no claim can be made to set off the loss in that tax year. Before the loss relief claim, Luke's income tax liability in 2013/14 is as follows:

	Non-savings income	*Savings income*	*Total*
	£	£	£
Trading income	21,440		
Interest		4,000	
Total/net income	21,440	4,000	25,440
Less: personal allowance	(9,440)		
Taxable income	12,000	4,000	16,000

Tax	
Non-savings income	
£12,000 × 20%	2,400
Savings income	
£4,000 × 20%	800
Income tax liability	3,200

If loss relief is claimed against general income for 2013/14, Luke's income tax liability will be:

	Non-savings income	*Savings Income*	*Total*
Total income	21,440	4,000	25,440
Less: carry back loss	(12,000)		
Net income	9,440	4,000	13,440
Less: personal allowance	(9,440)		
Taxable income	0	4,000	4,000

Tax	
Savings income	
£2,790 × 10%	279
£(4,000 – 2,790) = £1,210 × 20%	242
Income tax liability	521

The tax saved by making the loss relief claim is therefore £(3,200 – 521) = £2,679, which is 22.325% of the loss.

4 Trade transferred to company

FAST FORWARD

If a business is transferred to a company, a loss of the unincorporated business can be set against income received from the company.

Although carry forward loss relief is restricted to future profits of the same business, this is extended to cover income received from a company to which the business is sold.

The amount carried forward is the total unrelieved trading losses of the business. The set-off must be made against the first available income from the company, including dividends, interest and salary.

Set-off the loss against non-savings income or savings income and then against dividend income.

The consideration for the transfer of the business must be wholly or mainly in the form of shares (at least 80%) which must be retained by the vendor throughout any tax year in which the loss is relieved.

5 Early trading losses relief

FAST FORWARD

In opening years, a special relief involving the carry back of losses against general income is available. Losses arising in the first four tax years of a trade may be set against general income in the three years preceding the loss making year, taking the earliest year first.

Early trading losses relief is available for **trading losses incurred in the first four tax years of a trade.**

Relief is obtained by **setting the allowable loss against general income in the three years preceding the year of loss**, applying the loss to the earliest year first. Thus a loss arising in 2013/14 may be set off against income in 2010/11, 2011/12 and 2012/13 in that order.

A claim for early trading losses relief applies to all three years automatically, provided that the loss is large enough. The taxpayer cannot choose to relieve the loss against just one or two of the years, or choose to relieve only part of the loss. However, the relief cap which was discussed earlier in this chapter, restricting loss relief against other income, also applies here. This means that losses may be restricted by the cap in earlier years (leaving some income left in charge) with the result that the remaining losses will be available for use in later years, again subject to the cap. Also, the taxpayer has some control as they could reduce the size of the loss by not claiming the full capital allowances available to them. This will result in higher capital allowances in future years.

Do not double count a loss. If basis periods overlap, a loss in the overlap period is treated as a loss for the earlier tax year only.

Claims for the relief must be made by the 31 January which is 22 months after the end of the tax year in which the loss is incurred.

The 'commercial basis' test is stricter for this loss relief. The trade must be carried on in such a way that profits could reasonably have been expected to be realised in the period of the loss or within a reasonable time thereafter.

Question — Early trade losses relief

Mr A is employed as a dustman until 1 January 2012. On that date he starts up his own business as a scrap metal merchant, making up his accounts to 30 June each year. His earnings as a dustman are:

	£
2008/09	5,000
2009/10	6,000
2010/11	7,000
2011/12 (nine months)	6,000

His trading results as a scrap metal merchant are:

	Profit/(Loss)
	£
Six months to 30 June 2012	(3,000)
Year to 30 June 2013	(1,500)
Year to 30 June 2014	(1,200)

Assuming that loss relief is claimed as early as possible, show the final net income for each of the years 2008/09 to 2014/15 inclusive.

Answer

Since reliefs are to be claimed as early as possible, early trading losses relief is applied. The losses available for relief are as follows.

			Years against which relief is available
	£	£	
2011/12 (basis period 1.1.12 – 5.4.12)			
3 months to 5.4.12 £(3,000) × 3/6		(1,500)	2008/09 to 2010/11
2012/13 (basis period 1.1.12 – 31.12.12)			
6 months to 30.6.12			
(omit 1.1.12 – 5.4.12: overlap) £(3,000) × 3/6	(1,500)		
6 months to 31.12.12 £(1,500) × 6/12	(750)		
		(2,250)	2009/10 to 2011/12
2013/14 (basis period 1.7.12 – 30.6.13)			
12 months to 30.6.13			
(omit 1.7.12 – 31.12.12: overlap) £(1,500) × 6/12		(750)	2010/11 to 2012/13
2014/15 (basis period 1.7.13 – 30.6.14)			
12 months to 30.6.14		(1,200)	2011/12 to 2013/14

The net income is as follows.

	£	£
2008/09		
Original	5,000	
Less 2011/12 loss	(1,500)	
		3,500
2009/10		
Original	6,000	
Less 2012/13 loss	(2,250)	
		3,750
2010/11		
Original	7,000	
Less 2013/14 loss	(750)	
		6,250
2011/12		
Original	6,000	
Less 2014/15 loss	(1,200)	
		4,800

The taxable trading profits for 2011/12 to 2014/15 are zero. There were losses in the basis periods.

6 Terminal trading loss relief

FAST FORWARD

On the cessation of trade, a loss arising in the last 12 months of trading may be set against trading profits of the tax year of cessation and the previous 3 years, taking the last year first.

Loss relief against general income will often be insufficient on its own to deal with a loss incurred in the last months of trading. For this reason there is a special relief, **terminal trading loss relief, which allows a loss on cessation to be carried back for relief against taxable trading profits in previous years.**

6.1 Computing the terminal loss

A terminal loss is **the loss of the last 12 months of trading**.

It is built up as follows.

		£
(a)	The actual trading loss for the tax year of cessation (calculated from 6 April to the date of cessation)	X
(b)	The actual trading loss for the period from 12 months before cessation until the end of the penultimate tax year	X
Total terminal loss		X

If either (a) or (b) above yields a profit rather than a loss, the profit is treated as zero.

Any unrelieved overlap profits are included within (a) above.

If any loss cannot be included in the terminal loss (eg because it is matched with a profit) it can be relieved instead by the loss relief against general income.

6.2 Relieving the terminal loss

Relief is given in the tax year of cessation and the three preceding years, later years first.

Question — **Terminal loss relief**

Set out below are the results of a business up to its cessation on 30 September 2013.

	Profit/(loss)
	£
Year to 31 December 2010	2,000
Year to 31 December 2011	400
Year to 31 December 2012	300
Nine months to 30 September 2013	(1,950)

Overlap profits on commencement were £450. These were all unrelieved on cessation.

Show the available terminal loss relief, and suggest an alternative claim if the trader had had other non-savings income of £11,000 in each of 2012/13 and 2013/14. Assume that 2013/14 tax rates and allowances apply to all years.

Answer

The terminal loss comes in the last 12 months, the period 1 October 2012 to 30 September 2013. This period is split as follows.

2012/13	Six months to 5 April 2013
2013/14	Six months to 30 September 2013

The terminal loss is made up as follows.

		£	£
Unrelieved trading losses			
2013/14			
6 months to 30.9.13	£(1,950) × 6/9		(1,300)
Overlap relief			(450)
2012/13			
3 months to 31.12.12	£300 × 3/12	75	
3 months to 5.4.13	£(1,950) × 3/9	(650)	
			(575)
			(2,325)

Taxable trading profits will be as follows.

Year	*Basis period*	*Profits*	*Terminal loss relief*	*Final taxable profits*
		£	£	£
2010/11	Y/e 31.12.10	2,000	1,625	375
2011/12	Y/e 31.12.11	400	400	0
2012/13	Y/e 31.12.12	300	300	0
2013/14	1.1.13 – 30.9.13	0	0	0
			2,325	

If the trader had had £11,000 of other income in 2012/13 and 2013/14 we could consider loss relief claims against general income for these two years, using the loss of £(1,950 + 450) = £2,400 for 2013/14.

The final results would be as follows (we could alternatively claim loss relief in 2012/13).

	2010/11	*2011/12*	*2012/13*	*2013/14*
	£	£	£	£
Trading profits	2,000	400	300	0
Other income	0	0	11,000	11,000
	2,000	400	11,300	11,000
Less loss relief against general income	0	0	0	(2,400)
Net income	2,000	400	11,300	8,600

Another option would be to make a loss relief claim against general income for the balance of the loss not relieved as a terminal loss. £(2,400 – 2,325) = £75 in either 2012/13 or 2013/14.

However, once the personal allowance has been deducted there is only taxable income in 2012/13 and 2013/14 so the full claim against general income is more tax efficient.

7 Share loss relief against general income

FAST FORWARD

Capital losses arising on certain unquoted shares can be set against general income of the year of the loss and/or against general income of the preceding year.

Relief is available for capital losses on shares in unquoted trading companies (originally **subscribed for**) against general income of the taxpayer for the year **in which the loss arose and/or the preceding year.**

In summary, the relief is only available if the shares satisfy the conditions of the Enterprise Investment Scheme or the Seed Enterprise Investment Scheme (see earlier in this Text). It is not, however, necessary for income tax relief to have been claimed on the shares.

A claim must be made by 31 January 22 months after the end of the year of the loss.

The relief cap, discussed earlier in this chapter, applies to this loss relief.

Chapter roundup

- Trading losses may be relieved against future profits of the same trade, against general income and against capital gains.
- A trading loss carried forward must be set against the first available profits of the same trade.
- Where a loss relief claim is made, trading losses can be set against general income (and also gains if a further claim is made) in the current tax year and/or general income (and also gains if a further claim is made) in the preceding tax year.
- Loss relief cannot be claimed against general income unless the loss-making business is conducted on a commercial basis.
- An individual taxpayer can only deduct the greater of £50,000 and 25% of adjusted total income when making a claim for loss relief against general income.
- It is important for a trader to choose the right loss relief, so as to save tax at the highest possible rate and so as to obtain relief reasonably quickly.
- If a business is transferred to a company, a loss of the unincorporated business can be set against income received from the company.
- In opening years, a special relief involving the carry back of losses against general income is available. Losses arising in the first four tax years of a trade may be set against general income in the three years preceding the loss making year, taking the earliest year first.
- On the cessation of trade, a loss arising in the last 12 months of trading may be set against trading profits of the tax year of cessation and the previous 3 years, taking the last year first.
- Capital losses arising on certain unquoted shares can be set against general income of the year of the loss and/or against general income of the preceding year.

Quick quiz

1. Against what income can trading losses carried forward be set off?
2. When a loss is to be relieved against total income, how are losses linked to particular tax years?
3. Against which years' total income may a loss be relieved against general income for a continuing business which has traded for many years?
4. Maggie has been trading as a decorator for many years. In 2012/13 she made a trading profit of £10,000. She has savings income of £6,000 each year. She makes no capital gains.

   Maggie makes a loss of £(28,000) in 2013/14 and expects to make either a loss or smaller profits in the foreseeable future. How can Maggie obtain loss relief?
5. For which losses is early years trading loss relief available?
6. In which years may relief for a terminal loss be given?

Answers to quick quiz

1 Against profits from the same trade.

2 The loss for a tax year is the loss in the basis period for that tax year. However, if basis periods overlap, a loss in the overlap period is a loss of the earlier tax year only.

3 The year in which the loss arose and/or the preceding year.

4 Maggie could make a claim to set the loss against general income of £6,000 in 2013/14, but should not do so, as this amount will be covered by the personal allowance. She can claim loss relief against general income of £(10,000 + 6,000) = £16,000 in 2012/13. The remaining £(28,000 – 16,000) = £12,000 will be carried forward and set against the first available trading profits of her decorating trade.

5 Losses incurred in the first four tax years of a trade.

6 In the year of cessation and then in the three preceding years, later years first.

Now try the question below from the Exam Question Bank

Number	Level	Marks	Time
Q9	Introductory	25	45 mins

Partnerships and limited liability partnerships

Topic list	Syllabus reference
1 Partnerships	A1(a)B3,(d)(vi)
2 Limited liability partnerships	A1(a)B3

Introduction

In the previous chapters we have dealt with the income tax rules for sole traders. We now see how those rules are adapted to deal with business partnerships.

On the one hand, a partnership is a single trading entity, making profits as a whole. On the other hand, each partner has a personal tax computation, so the profits must be apportioned to the partners. The general approach is to work out the profits of the partnership, then tax each partner as if they were a sole trader running a business equal to their slice of the partnership (for example 25% of the partnership).

This concludes our study of the different types of UK income to be included in an income tax computation. In the following chapter we will turn our attention to the overseas aspects of income tax.

Study guide

		Intellectual level
1	**Income and income tax liabilities in situations involving further overseas aspects and in relation to trusts, and the application of exemptions and reliefs**	
(a)	The contents of the Paper F6 study guide for income tax, under heading:	2
•	B3 Income from self employment	
(d)	Income from self employment:	
(vi)	Recognise the tax treatment of the investment income of a partnership	2

Exam guide

A question involving any aspect of unincorporated businesses may deal with a partnership rather than a sole trader. The principles are exactly the same, whether you are considering incremental income, possible claims for capital allowances or loss reliefs. Just remember that profits are apportioned to partners in the profit sharing ratio for the period of account after allocating interest on capital and/or salaries.

Knowledge brought forward from earlier studies

This chapter is mainly revision of the partnership rules covered in Paper F6. Partnership investment income is a new area.

There are no changes in 2013/14 from 2012/13 in the material you have already studied.

1 Partnerships

A partnership is simply treated as a source of profits and losses for trades being carried on by the individual partners. Divide profits or losses between the partners according to the profit sharing ratio in the period of account concerned. If any of the partners are entitled to a salary or interest on capital, apportion this first, not forgetting to pro-rate in periods of less than 12 months.

1.1 Introduction

PER alert

One of the competencies you require to fulfil performance objective 19 of the PER is the ability to evaluate and compute taxes payable. You can apply the knowledge you obtain from this section of the text to help to demonstrate this competence.

A partnership is treated like a sole trader when computing its profits. Partners' salaries and interest on capital are not deductible expenses and must be added back in computing profits, because they are a form of drawings.

Once the partnership's profits for a period of account have been computed, they are shared between the partners according to the profit sharing arrangements for that period of account.

Question — **Allocating profits**

Steve and Tanya have been in partnership for many years. For the year ended 31 October 2013, taxable trading profits were £70,000. Steve is allocated an annual salary of £12,000 and Tanya's salary is £28,000. The profit sharing ratio is 2:1.

Allocate the trade profit to each partner for the year ended 31 October 2013.

Answer

Allocate the profits for the year ended 31 October 2013.

	Total	*Steve*	*Tanya*
	£	£	£
Profit	70,000		
Salaries	40,000	12,000	28,000
Balance (2:1)	30,000	20,000	10,000
Total	70,000	32,000	38,000

1.2 The tax positions of individual partners

Each partner is taxed like a sole trader who runs a business which:

- Starts when they join the partnership
- Finishes when they leave the partnership
- Has the same periods of account as the partnership (except that a partner who joins or leaves during a period will have a period which starts or ends part way through the partnership's period)
- Makes profits or losses equal to the partner's share of the partnership's profits or losses.

1.3 Changes in profit sharing ratios

The profits for a period of account are allocated between the partners according to the profit sharing agreement. If the salaries, interest on capital and profit sharing ratio change during the period of account the profits are time apportioned to the periods before and after the change and allocated accordingly. The constituent elements are then added together to give each partner's share of profits for the period of account.

Question

Change in profit sharing arrangements

Sue and Tim have been in partnership for many years. For the year ended 31 December 2013, taxable trading profits were £50,000. Sue is allocated an annual salary of £10,000 and Tim's salary is £15,000.

The profit sharing ratio was 1:1 until 31 August 2013 when it changed to 1:2 with no provision for salaries.

Allocate the trade profit to each partner for the year ended 31 December 2013.

Answer

Allocate the profits for the year ended 31 December 2013.

	Total	*Sue*	*Tim*
	£	£	£
Profit	50,000		
1 January – 31 August (8 months)	33,333		
Salaries (8/12 × £10,000/£15,000)	16,667	6,667	10,000
Balance (1:1)	16,666	8,333	8,333
	33,333		
1 September – 31 December (4 months)	16,667		
Salaries	Nil	–	–
Balance (1:2)	16,667	5,556	11,111
	16,667		
Total	50,000	20,556	29,444

Note. Since the profit sharing arrangements changed part way through the period of account, the profits and salaries for the period of account must be pro-rated accordingly.

1.4 Changes in membership

FAST FORWARD

The commencement and cessation rules apply to partners individually when they join or leave.

When a trade continues but partners join or leave (including cases when a sole trader takes in partners or a partnership breaks up leaving only one partner as a sole trader), **the special rules for basis periods in opening and closing years do not apply to the people who were carrying on the trade both before and after the change. They carry on using the period of account ending in each tax year as the basis period for the tax year ie the current year basis. The commencement rules only affect joiners, and the cessation rules only affect leavers.**

However, when no one same individual carries on the trade both before and after the change, as when a partnership transfers its trade to a completely new owner or set of owners, the cessation rules apply to the old owners and the commencement rules apply to the new owners.

Question — Partner joining partnership

Daniel and Ashley have been in partnership for many years preparing accounts to 31 December each year and sharing profits in the ratio 2:1.

On 1 June 2013, Kate joined the partnership. From that date, profits were shared Daniel 50% and Ashley and Kate 25% each.

The partnership profits for the year ended 31 December 2013 were £72,000 and for the year ended 31 December 2014 were £90,000.

Compute the partnership profits taxable on Daniel, Ashley and Kate for 2013/14 and 2014/15 and the overlap profits for Kate on commencement.

Answer

Allocation of partnership profits

	Total	*Daniel*	*Ashley*	*Kate*
y/e 31.12.13	£	£	£	£
1.1.13 – 31.5.13				
Profits (5/12) 2:1	30,000	20,000	10,000	n/a
1.6.13 – 31.2.13				
Profits (7/12) 50:25:25	42,000	21,000	10,500	10,500
Profit allocation	72,000	41,000	20,500	10,500
y/e 31.12.14				
Profits 50:25:25	90,000	45,000	22,500	22,500

Taxable partnership profits for 2013/14 and 2014/15

	Daniel	*Ashley*	*Kate*
	£	£	£
2013/14			
CYB y/e 31.12.13	41,000	20,500	
First year – actual basis			
1.6.13 – 31.12.13			10,500
1.1.14 – 5.4.14			
3/12 × £22,500			5,625
			16,125

	Daniel	Ashley	Kate
	£	£	£
2014/15			
CYB y/e 31.12.14	45,000	22,500	
Second year – 12 months to 31.12.14			22,500

Overlap profits

Kate has overlap profits for the period 1.1.14 to 5.4.14 of £5,625.

Question — Partner leaving partnership

Maxwell, Laura and Wesley traded in partnership for many years, preparing accounts to 30 September.

Each partner was entitled to 5% interest per annum on capital introduced into the partnership. Each partner had introduced £60,000 of capital on the commencement of the partnership. From that date, profits were shared in the ratio 50% to Maxwell, 30% to Laura and 20% to Wesley.

On 1 May 2013, Wesley left the partnership. From that date profits were shared equally between the two remaining partners and no interest was paid on capital. The partnership taxable trading income for the year to 30 September 2013 was £120,000. Wesley had overlap profits on commencement of £5,000.

Compute the partnership profits taxable on Maxwell, Laura and Wesley for 2013/14.

Answer

Allocation of partnership profits

	Total	Maxwell	Laura	Wesley
	£	£	£	£
1.10.12 – 30.4.13				
Interest 7/12 × £60,000 × 5% each	5,250	1,750	1,750	1,750
Profits (7/12) 50:30:20	64,750	32,375	19,425	12,950
	70,000	34,125	21,175	14,700
1.5.13 – 30.9.13				
Profits (5/12) 1:1	50,000	25,000	25,000	n/a
Profits allocated for year	120,000	59,125	46,175	14,700

Taxable partnership profits for 2013/14

	Maxwell	Laura	Wesley
	£	£	£
2013/14			
CYB y/e 30.9.13	59,125	46,175	
Final year			
1.10.12 – 30.4.13			14,700
Less: overlap relief			(5,000)
			9,700

1.5 Loss reliefs

FAST FORWARD: There are restrictions on loss reliefs for non-active partners in the first four years of trading.

Partners are entitled to the same loss reliefs as sole traders. A partner is entitled to early trade losses relief for losses in the four tax years starting with the year in which they are treated as starting to trade and they are entitled to terminal loss relief when they are treated as ceasing to trade. This is so even if the partnership trades for many years before the partner joins or after they leave. Loss relief against general income and carry forward loss relief is also available to partners. Different partners may claim loss reliefs in different ways.

When a partnership business is transferred to a company, each partner can carry forward their share of any unrelieved losses against income from the company.

Question — Partnership losses

Mary and Natalie have been trading for many years sharing profits equally. On 1 January 2014 Mary retired and Oliver joined the partnership. Natalie and Oliver share profits in the ratio of 2:1. Although the partnership had previously been profitable it made a loss of £24,000 for the year to 31 March 2014. The partnership is expected to be profitable in the future.

Calculate the loss accruing to each partner for 2013/14 and explain what reliefs are available.

Answer

We must first share the loss for the period of account between the partners.

	Total	*Mary*	*Natalie*	*Oliver*
	£	£	£	£
y/e 31.3.14				
1.4.13 – 31.12.13				
Total £24,000 × 9/12	(18,000)	(9,000)	(9,000)	
1.1.14 – 31.3.14				
Total £24,000 × 3/12	(6,000)		(4,000)	(2,000)
Total for y/e 31.03.14	(24,000)	(9,000)	(13,000)	(2,000)

Mary

For 2013/14, Mary has a loss of £9,000. She may claim relief against general income of 2013/14 and/or 2012/13 and may extend the claim to capital gains.

Mary has ceased trading and may instead claim terminal loss relief. The terminal loss will be £9,000 (a profit arose in the period 1.1.13 – 31.3.13 which would be treated as zero) and this may be set against her taxable trade profits for 2013/14 (£nil), 2012/13, 2011/12 and 2010/11.

Natalie

For 2013/14, Natalie has a loss of £13,000. She may claim relief against general income of 2013/14 and/or 2012/13 and may extend the claim to capital gains. Any loss remaining unrelieved may be carried forward against future income from the same trade.

Oliver

Oliver's loss for 2013/14 is £2,000. He may claim relief for the loss against general income (and gains) of 2013/14 and/or 2012/13. As he has just started to trade he may claim relief for the loss against general income of 2010/11, 2011/12 and 2012/13. Any loss remaining unrelieved may be carried forward against future income from the same trade.

In addition to the cap on loss reliefs discussed earlier in this Text, **there is a further restriction for loss relief for a partner who does not spend a significant amount of time (less than 10 hours a week) in running the trade of the partnership.** Such a partner can only use loss relief against general income or against capital gains and early trade losses relief **up to an amount equal to the amount that they contribute to the partnership** and there is an overall cap on relief of £25,000. These rules apply in any of the first four years in which the partner carries on a trade.

1.6 Example: loss relief restriction

Laura, Mark and Norman form a partnership and each contribute £10,000. Laura and Mark run the trade full time. Norman is employed elsewhere and plays little part in running the trade. Profits and losses are to be shared 45:35:20 to L:M:N. The partnership makes a loss of £60,000 of which £12,000 is allocated to Norman.

Norman may only use £10,000 of loss against general income (plus against capital gains) or early trade loss relief. £2,000 is carried forward, for example to be relieved against future profits.

1.7 Assets owned individually

Where the partners own assets (such as their cars) individually, a capital allowances computation must be prepared in respect of the assets the partners own (not forgetting any adjustment for private use). **The capital allowances must go into the partnership's tax computation.**

Exam focus point

> Partners are effectively taxed in the same way as sole traders with just one difference. Before you tax the partner you need to take each set of accounts (as adjusted for tax purposes) and divide the trade profit (or loss) between each partner.
>
> Then carry on as normal for a sole trader – each partner is treated as a sole trader in respect of their trade profits for each period of account.

1.8 Partnership investment income

A partnership may have non-trading income, such as interest on the partnership's bank deposit account or dividends on shares, or non-trading losses. **Such items are kept separate from trading income, but they** (and any associated tax credits) **are shared between the partners in a similar way to trading income.** That is, the following steps are applied.

Step 1 Find out in which period of account the income arose.

Step 2 Share the income between the partners using the profit sharing arrangements for that period. If partners have already been given their salaries and interest on capital in sharing out trading income, do not give them those items again in sharing out non-trading income.

Step 3 For income not taxed at source attribute each partner's share of the income to tax years using the same basis periods as are used to attribute their share of trading profits to tax years. When working out the basis periods for untaxed income (which excludes income taxed at source and dividends) or for non-trading losses, we always have a commencement when the partner joins the partnership and a cessation when they leave, even if they carried on the trade as a sole trader before joining or after leaving. If the relief for overlap untaxed income on leaving the firm exceeds the partner's share of untaxed income for the tax year of leaving, the excess is deducted from their total income for that year.

Step 4 For income taxed at source assume that income accrued evenly over the accounting period and time apportion on an actual basis into tax years (6 April to 5 April).

2 Limited liability partnerships

FAST FORWARD

Limited liability partnerships are taxed on virtually the same basis as normal partnerships but loss relief is restricted for all partners.

It is possible to form a limited liability partnership. The difference between a limited liability partnership (LLP) and a normal partnership is that **in a LLP the liability of the partners is limited to the capital they contributed.**

The partners of a LLP are taxed on virtually the same basis as the partners of a normal partnership (see above). However, the amount of loss relief that a partner can claim against general income or by early years trade loss relief when the claim is against non-partnership income is restricted to the capital they contributed and is subject to an overall cap of £25,000. This rule is not restricted to the first four years of trading and the rules apply to all partners whether or not involved in the running of the trade.

Chapter roundup

- A partnership is simply treated as a source of profits and losses for trades being carried on by the individual partners. Divide profits or losses between the partners according to the profit sharing ratio in the period of account concerned. If any of the partners are entitled to a salary or interest on capital, apportion this first, not forgetting to pro-rate in periods of less than 12 months.
- The commencement and cessation rules apply to partners individually when they join or leave.
- There are restrictions on loss reliefs for non-active partners in the first four years of trading.
- Limited liability partnerships are taxed on virtually the same basis as normal partnerships but loss relief is restricted for all partners.

Quick quiz

1. How are partnership trading profits divided between the individual partners?
2. What loss reliefs are partners entitled to?
3. Janet and John are partners sharing profits 60:40. For the years ended 30 June 2013 and 2014 the partnership made profits of £100,000 and £150,000 respectively. What are John's taxable trading profits in 2013/14?
4. Pete and Doug have been joint partners for many years. On 1 January 2013 Dave joins the partnership and it is agreed to share profits 40:40:20. For the year ended 30 June 2013 profits are £100,000. What is Doug's share of these profits?

Answers to quick quiz

1 Profits are divided in accordance with the profit sharing ratio that existed during the period of account in which the profits arose.

2 Partners are entitled to the same loss reliefs as sole traders. These are loss relief against general income, early years trade loss relief, carry forward loss relief, terminal loss relief, and loss relief on transfer of a trade to a company.

3 £40,000.

2013/14: y/e 30 June 2013

£100,000 × 40% = £40,000.

4 £45,000

	Pete	*Doug*	*Dave*
Ye 30 June 2013	£	£	£
1.7.12 – 31.12.12			
6m × 100,000			
£50,000 50:50	25,000	25,000	
1.1.13 – 30.6.13			
6m × £100,000			
£50,000 40:40:20	20,000	20,000	10,000
	45,000	45,000	10,000

Now try the question below from the Exam Question Bank

Number	Level	Marks	Time
Q10	Introductory	25	45 mins

10

Overseas aspects of income tax

Topic list	Syllabus reference
1 Residence and domicile	A1(a)B1,(b)(i),(iii)
2 Liability to UK income tax: basic principles	A1(b)(i),(ii),(iv)
3 Employment overseas and non-residents employed in the UK	A1(b)(iii), A1(c)(iii)
4 Overseas trades	A1(d)(iii)
5 Double taxation relief (DTR)	A1(b)(v),(vi)

Introduction

In the previous chapters we have studied most aspects of income tax. In this chapter we will look at the overseas aspects of income tax.

We start this chapter by considering where taxpayers are resident and domiciled and at how this affects their tax position. We then consider the special rules which apply to people working away from their home countries. We briefly consider the tax implications of trading overseas. Finally, we look at the tax relief which can be available when income is taxed both overseas and in the UK.

In the next chapter will we turn our attention to CGT. We will consider the administration of income tax when we have finished studying CGT as the personal tax return deals with both income and capital gains.

Study guide

		Intellectual level
1	**Income and income tax liabilities in situations involving further overseas aspects and in relation to trusts, and the application of exemptions and reliefs**	
(a)	The contents of the Paper F6 study guide for income tax, under headings:	2
•	B1 The scope of income tax	
(b)	The scope of income tax:	3
(i)	Explain and apply the concepts of residence and domicile and advise on the relevance to income tax	
(ii)	Advise on the availability of the remittance basis to UK resident individuals	2
(iii)	Advise on the tax position of individuals coming to and leaving the UK	
(iv)	Determine the income tax treatment of overseas income	
(v)	Understand the relevance of the OECD model double tax treaty to given situations	
(vi)	Calculate and advise on the double taxation relief available to individuals	
(c)	Income from employment	3
(iii)	Advise on the overseas aspects of income from employment, including travelling and subsistence expenses	
(d)	Income from self employment:	
(iii)	Recognise the tax treatment of overseas travelling expenses	3

Exam guide

In an exam question you may have to advise an individual how they will be taxed on their income from overseas. You may also need to advise an individual who has gone overseas how they will be taxed on their UK income, or how a taxpayer who is not domiciled in the UK is taxed on their non-UK income whilst they are resident in the UK. You must be sure that you can correctly determine an individual's residence status.

Knowledge brought forward from earlier studies

The topics covered in this chapter are mostly new at P6 level. There is a new test of statutory residence applicable from 2013/14 and the category of ordinary residence has been abolished.

1 Residence and domicile

FAST FORWARD

An individual may be both or either of resident and domiciled in the UK.

One of the competencies you require to fulfil performance objective 19 of the PER is the ability to evaluate and compute taxes payable. You can apply the knowledge you obtain from this section of the text to help to demonstrate this competence.

1.1 Residence

1.1.1 Statutory residence test

FAST FORWARD

An individual will automatically not be UK resident if he meets any of the automatic overseas tests. An individual, who does not meet any of the automatic overseas tests, will automatically be UK resident if he meets any of the automatic UK tests. An individual who has not met any of the automatic overseas tests nor any of the automatic UK tests will be UK resident if he meets the sufficient ties test.

Statute sets out a test to determine whether or not an individual is UK resident in a tax year.

The **operation of the test** can be summarised as follows.

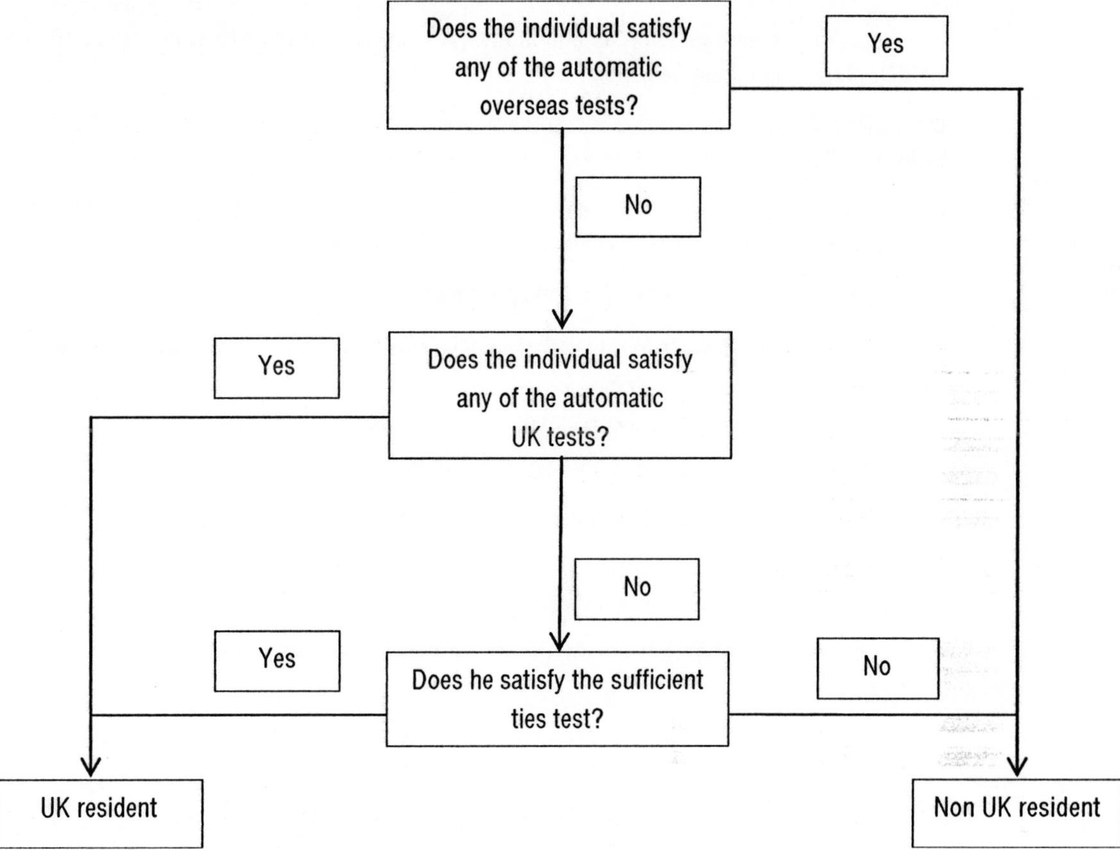

1.1.2 Automatic overseas tests

The automatic overseas tests must be considered first.

The automatic overseas tests treat an individual as not resident in the UK in a tax year if that individual:

- **Spends less than 16 days in the UK in that tax year and was resident in the UK for one or more of the three previous tax years** (typically someone who is leaving the UK); or
- **Spends less than 46 days in the UK in that tax year and was not resident in the UK for any of the previous three tax years** (typically someone who is arriving in the UK); or
- **Works full-time overseas in that tax year and does not spend more than 90 days in the UK during that tax year.**

1.1.3 Automatic UK tests

If none of the automatic overseas tests are met, then the automatic UK tests are considered.

The **automatic UK tests treat an individual as UK resident in a tax year** if that individual:

- **Spends 183 days or more in the UK** during that tax year; or
- **Spends 30 days or more in the UK** during the tax year and has a **home in the UK** and **no home overseas**; or
- **Works full-time in the UK during a 365-day period**, some of which falls within that tax year.

1.1.4 Sufficient UK ties tests

If the **individual meets none of the automatic overseas tests and none of the automatic UK tests**, the **'sufficient ties' test** must be considered.

The **sufficient ties test** compares the **number of days spent in the UK** and the **number of connection factors or 'ties' to the UK.**

An **individual who was not UK resident in any of the previous three tax years** (typically someone who is arriving in the UK) must determine whether any of the following ties apply:

- **UK resident close family** (eg spouse/civil partner, child under the age of 18);
- **Substantive UK work** (employment or self-employment) where **40 days or more is regarded as substantive**;
- **UK accommodation** which is **available for at least 91 days in the tax year** and in which the individual **spends at least one night during the tax year;**
- **More than 90 days spent in the UK in either or both of the previous two tax years.**

An **individual who was UK resident in any of the previous three tax years** (typically someone who is leaving the UK) must also determine whether an additional tie applies:

- **Present in the UK at midnight for the same or more days** in that tax year than in any other country.

The following table shows **how an individual's UK residence status is found** by comparing **the number of days in the UK** during a tax year and the **number of UK ties**:

Days in UK	Previously resident	Not previously resident
Less than 16	Automatically not UK resident	Automatically not UK resident
Between 16 and 45	Resident if 4 UK ties (or more)	Automatically not UK resident
Between 46 and 90	Resident if 3 UK ties (or more)	Resident if 4 UK ties
Between 91 and 120	Resident if 2 UK ties (or more)	Resident if 3 UK ties (or more)
Between 121 and 182	Resident if 1 UK ties (or more)	Resident if 2 UK ties (or more)
183 or more	Automatically UK resident	Automatically UK resident

Exam focus point

This table will be given in the tax rates and allowances section of the examination paper.

1.1.5 Days spent in UK

Generally, **if a taxpayer is present in the UK at the end of a day (ie midnight)**, that **day counts as a day spent by the taxpayer in the UK**. However he **does not need to count the first 60 days in a tax year that he spends in the UK due to circumstances beyond his control**, such as serious illness.

1.1.6 Examples

(a) James had not previously been resident in the UK before he arrived on 6 April 2013. He spent 40 days in the UK during the tax year 2013/14. James did not work during 2013/14.

James is arriving in the UK. He satisfies one of the automatic overseas tests since he spent less than 46 days in the UK in 2013/14 and was not resident in the UK for any of the previous three tax years. James is therefore not UK resident for the tax year 2013/14.

(b) Caroline had not previously been resident in the UK before she arrived on 6 April 2013. She spent 60 days in the UK during the tax year 2013/14. She did not work during 2013/14. Her only home during 2013/14 is in the UK.

Caroline is arriving in the UK. She does not satisfy any of the automatic overseas tests since she spends 46 days or more in the UK and does not work overseas. She satisfies one of the automatic UK tests since she spends 30 days or more in the UK in 2013/14 and her only home is in the UK. Caroline is therefore UK resident for the tax year 2013/14.

(c) Miranda had always been resident in the UK before the tax year 2013/14 and has spent more than 90 days in the UK in every tax year. Miranda does not work during 2013/14. Miranda is married to Walter who is UK resident in 2013/14. They own a house in the UK which is available to them for the whole of 2013/14. On 6 April 2013, Miranda bought an overseas apartment where she spent 285 days during 2013/14. The remaining 80 days were spent in her UK house.

Miranda is leaving the UK. She does not satisfy any of the automatic overseas tests since she spends 16 days or more in the UK and does not work overseas. She does not satisfy any of the automatic UK tests since she spends less than 183 days in the UK, has an overseas home and does not work in the UK. The 'sufficient ties' test is therefore relevant. Miranda has three UK ties:

(i) Close family in the UK (spouse);
(ii) Available accommodation in the UK in which she spent at least one night in the tax year;
(iii) More than 90 days spent in the UK in both of the previous two tax years.

Miranda spends between 46 and 90 days in the UK in 2013/14. These three ties are therefore sufficient to make her UK resident in 2013/14.

(d) Norman has not been resident in the UK in any tax year before 2013/14. He has not spent more than 90 days in the UK prior to 2013/14. On 6 April 2013, he arrived in the UK and bought a house in the UK in which he spent 160 days during the tax year 2013/14. Norman also has an overseas house in which he spent the remainder of the tax year 2013/14. Norman did not work in 2013/14 and his close family are not UK resident in 2013/14.

Norman is arriving in the UK. He does not satisfy any of the automatic overseas tests since he spends 46 days or more in the UK and does not work overseas. He does not satisfy any of the automatic UK tests as he spent less than 183 days in the UK, has an overseas home and does not work in the UK. The 'sufficient ties' test is therefore relevant. Norman spends between 121 and 182 days in the UK during 2013/14 and so he would need two UK ties to be UK resident for that tax year. Since Norman has only one tie with the UK in 2013/14 (available accommodation), he is therefore not UK resident for the tax year 2013/14.

1.1.7 Splitting the tax year

In general, an individual is either resident or non-resident for the whole of a tax year. However, in certain circumstances, the tax year may be split into UK and overseas parts.

Strictly, each tax year must be looked at as a whole. The general principle is that an individual is UK resident or non-UK resident either for a whole tax year or not at all.

However an individual may be able to **split a tax year into UK and overseas parts** in some circumstances. The split year treatment **can only apply for a year in which an individual is UK resident under the usual rules.** Where the tax year is split, the individual is **taxed as a UK resident for the UK part** and as a **non-UK resident for the overseas part**.

The **split year treatment** can be used by **an individual arriving in the UK** if that **individual is non-UK resident in the year prior to the split year** and if **one of the following circumstances applies**:

- The individual **comes to the UK, acquires a home in the UK,** and **does not have sufficient ties to the UK in order to be UK resident prior to acquiring the UK home** (the UK part starts when the individual acquires the UK home), or
- The individual **comes to the UK** to **work full-time** for a **period of at least a year** and **does not have sufficient ties to the UK in order to be UK resident prior to starting that work** (the UK part starts when the individual starts the UK work), or
- The individual **returns to the UK** following a **period where the individual has worked full-time overseas** (the UK part starts when the individual ceases working overseas), or
- The individual **returns to the UK** following a **period where the individual's partner** (spouse, civil partner or someone with whom the individual lives) **has worked full-time overseas** (the UK part starts on the later of the individual's partner ceasing working overseas and the individual joining the partner in the UK).

The **split year treatment** can be used by **an individual leaving the UK** if that **individual is UK resident in the tax year prior to the spilt year** and **non-UK resident in tax year following the split year** and if **one of the following circumstances applies**:

- The individual **leaves the UK to begin full-time work overseas** (the overseas part starts when the individual starts the overseas work); or
- The **individual's partner leaves the UK to begin full-time work overseas** and **the individual leaves the UK in order to continue living together with that partner (**the overseas part starts on the later of when the partner starts the overseas work and the individual joining the partner overseas); or
- The individual **leaves the UK in order to live overseas, ceases to have any UK home, spends a minimal amount of time in the UK,** and **establishes ties with the overseas country** by, for example, becoming resident there (the overseas part starts when the individual ceases to have a home in the UK).

1.1.8 Examples

(a) Wolfgang has never been resident in the UK and has no UK ties before 1 July 2013 when he arrives in the UK from Germany. He rents out his flat in Germany on a two year lease from that date. He enters into a 12 month lease on a flat in London from 1 July 2013 when he starts living there. Wolfgang does not work.

Wolfgang is entitled to use split year treatment for 2013/14 since he is UK resident in 2013/14 (under the automatic UK tests as he spends more than 183 days in the UK), he was non-UK resident for 2012/13, he acquires a home in the UK during 2013/14, and spent no time in the UK between 6 April and 1 July2013 so could not have been UK resident prior to acquiring the home (ie ties test irrelevant).

Wolfgang's overseas part of the tax year 2013/14 starts on 6 April 2013 and ends on 30 June 2013,. The UK part of the tax year 2013/14 starts on 1 July 2013 (the day he acquires his home in the UK) and ends on 5 April 2014.

(b) Bruce has always been UK resident. He leaves the UK and begin a three year full-time contract overseas on 15 October 2013. He will not visit the UK during the period of the contract.

Bruce can split the tax year 2013/14 because he is UK resident in 2013/14 (spends more than 183 days in the UK), he was UK resident in 2012/13, he will be non-UK resident in 2014/15 (automatically because he works full-time overseas in that tax year and does not spend more than 90 days in the UK during that tax year), and he is leaving the UK to begin full-time work overseas.

The UK part of the tax year 2013/14 starts on 6 April 2013 and ends 14 October 2013. The overseas part of the tax year 2013/14 starts on 15 October 2013 and ends on 5 April 2014.

Exam focus point

The detailed rules in the statutory residence test are quite complex, especially those in regard to what constitutes work and having a home in the UK. **These more complex aspects are not examinable at Paper P6(UK).**

1.2 Domicile

FAST FORWARD

An individual is domiciled in the country which is the individual's permanent home.

An individual is domiciled in the country which is the individual's permanent home. Domicile is distinct from nationality or residence. An individual may be resident in more than one country, but can be domiciled in only one country at a time.

Individuals acquire a domicile of origin at birth; this is normally the domicile of their father (or that of their mother if their father died before they were born or their parents were unmarried at their birth) and therefore not necessarily the country where they were born. **Individuals retain this domicile until they acquire a different domicile of dependency (if, while they are under 16, their father's domicile changes) or domicile of choice. A domicile of choice can be acquired only by individuals aged 16 or over.**

To acquire a domicile of choice individuals must sever their ties with the country of their former domicile and settle in another country with the clear intention of making their permanent home there. Long residence in another country is not in itself enough to prove that individuals have acquired a domicile of choice: there has to be evidence that they firmly intend to live there permanently.

2 Liability to UK income tax: basic principles

2.1 Overview

FAST FORWARD

Generally, a UK resident is liable to UK income tax on UK and overseas income as it arises. An individual who is UK resident but not UK domiciled is liable to UK income tax on income arising in the UK and may be entitled to be taxed on overseas income on the remittance basis. A non-UK resident is liable to UK income tax only on income arising in the UK.

Generally, a **UK resident individual is liable to UK income tax on UK and overseas income as it arises (the arising basis).**

Under the remittance basis, an individual who is UK resident but not UK domiciled is liable to UK income tax on overseas income only to the extent that it is brought (remitted) to the UK. The individual may be subject to the remittance basis charge (see later in this chapter). If the remittance basis does not apply (for example, if it is not claimed – see later in this chapter), overseas income is taxed on an arising basis. **An individual who is UK resident but not UK domiciled is liable to UK income tax on UK income on an arising basis.**

A non-UK resident is liable to UK income tax only on income arising in the UK.

The diagram below provides a broad **summary** of how an individual is taxed, based on the individual's residence and domicile status.

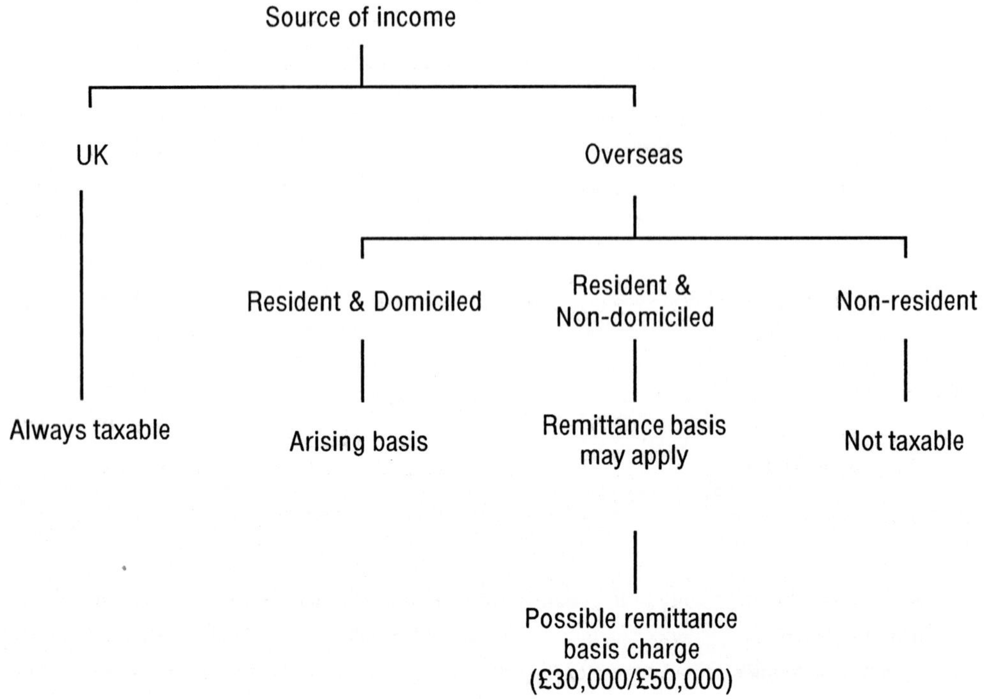

2.2 Individuals resident and domiciled in the UK

2.2.1 Overseas income: general principles

Individuals who are resident and domiciled in the UK are taxable on their overseas income on an arising basis (ie it is irrelevant whether or not the income is remitted to the UK). Double taxation relief may be available if the income is also taxed in the country in which it arises (see later in this chapter).

Overseas income is identified and taxed in broadly the same way as UK income, but the points set out below should be noted. We consider the rules relating to employment income later in this chapter.

2.2.2 Overseas property business

An individual who receives rents and other income from property overseas is treated as carrying on an overseas property business. The income from the overseas property business is liable to income tax in the same way as income from a UK property business, and is calculated in the same way. If an individual has both a UK and an overseas property business, the profits must be calculated separately.

If a loss arises in an overseas property business, it may be carried forward and set against future income from the overseas property business, as soon as it arises.

The special treatment of furnished holiday lettings does not apply to overseas properties other than those in the European Economic Area.

2.2.3 Overseas dividends

Overseas dividends are dividends from non-UK companies. The income is taxable in the year it arises as it is taxed in the same way as UK dividend income, ie at 10% if it falls below the basic rate limit, at 32.5% if it falls between the basic rate limit and the higher rate limit and at 37.5% thereafter.

A dividend from an overseas company is received with a 10% non-refundable tax credit, where the taxpayer holds less than 10% of the shares in that company. If the taxpayer owns 10% or more of the shares in the overseas company, the non-refundable tax credit will also be applicable, provided the company is resident in country which has a double-taxation treaty with the UK which contains a non-discrimination provision which provides that that the country does not tax foreigners more heavily than its own nationals.

2.3 Individuals resident but not domiciled in the UK

2.3.1 Remittance basis

An individual who is UK resident but not UK domiciled may be taxed on overseas income on the remittance basis.

If the remittance basis does not apply, the individual is taxable in the same way as an individual who is UK resident and domiciled (ie on an arising basis on both UK and overseas income).

Where the remittance basis applies, all income from the relevant source is treated as non-savings income. It is taxed in the same way as other non-savings income ie at 20% in the basic rate band, 40% in the higher rate band and thereafter at 45%.

We consider the rules relating to the remittance of employment income later in this chapter.

2.3.2 What is a remittance?

An individual makes a remittance of non-UK income where they have use or enjoyment of that income in the UK.

Clearly, this definition includes remittances in the form of cash. However, it also covers:

- using **non-UK income to settle a non-UK debt** where the money was borrowed in the UK or was borrowed overseas and brought into the UK
- **money, property and services acquired with non-UK income and brought into the UK**. There are exemptions for:
  - personal effects such as clothes, shoes, jewellery and watches
  - assets costing less than £1,000
  - assets brought into the UK for repair and restoration
  - assets in the UK for less than a total period of 275 days.

Remittance of non-UK income is also exempt from UK income tax if it is brought into the UK in order to:

- **acquire shares in or make a loan** to a trading company or a member of a trading group, or
- **pay the remittance basis charge** (see later in this chapter).

2.3.3 Automatic application of remittance basis

If an individual, who is entitled to be taxed on the remittance basis on overseas income, has unremitted non-UK income and gains of less than £2,000 arising in a tax year, the remittance basis will apply to that individual automatically without the need for a claim to be made.

The individual can disapply the remittance basis for a tax year if they wish by giving HMRC notice in their self assessment tax return for that year. They will then be taxed on an arising basis on overseas income arising in that tax year.

The **remittance basis will also apply automatically** in a tax year if an individual:

- is **UK resident but is not UK domiciled** in that year
- **has no UK income or gains other than taxed investment income not exceeding £100**
- **does not remit income or gains to the UK** in the year
- has been **UK resident in not more than six out of the nine tax years** immediately preceding that year or is **under the age of 18 throughout the year**

2.3.4 Claiming the remittance basis

In a particular tax year, **any other individual who is entitled to be taxed on the remittance basis must make a claim if they wish for that basis to apply to their overseas income**. The claim is made on the individual's self assessment tax return. If a claim is not made, the individual is taxed on their overseas income on an arising basis.

An individual who makes a claim for the remittance basis is not entitled to the personal allowance. This does not apply to an individual who is entitled to the remittance basis without a claim (see above).

An individual who makes a claim for the remittance basis is also not entitled to the annual exempt amount against chargeable gains. We deal with overseas aspects of Capital Gains Tax later in this Text.

2.3.5 Example: remittance basis

Claudia has been UK resident for five years, but is not domiciled in the UK. In 2013/14, she has UK source income of £30,000 and overseas income of £5,000, of which she has remitted £1,000 to the UK. Claudia is not entitled to the remittance basis automatically because she has unremitted overseas income of £(5,000 – 1,000) = £4,000.

Claudia should not make a claim for the remittance basis to apply to her overseas income in 2013/14. This is because she would lose her entitlement to the personal allowance of £9,440. Since this exceeds the amount of unremitted overseas income, she would pay less UK tax by having her overseas income taxed on the arising basis.

2.3.6 The remittance basis charge

FAST FORWARD

An individual who claims the remittance basis and is a long term UK resident is required to pay the Remittance Basis Charge of either £30,000 or £50,000 on unremitted income and gains.

An individual is liable to the Remittance Basis Charge if they:

- **claim the remittance basis for the tax year;** and
- **are aged 18 or over in the tax year;** and
- **have been UK resident for at least seven of the nine tax years preceding that tax year.**

The **Remittance Basis Charge is a charge on non-UK income and gains not remitted to the UK**. The individual remains liable to UK tax on their UK source income and non-UK income remitted to the UK in the usual way. We deal with chargeable gains later in this Text.

The amount of the **Remittance Basis Charge** in a tax year depends on the length of time the individual has been resident in the UK.

- An individual who has been resident for **twelve of the fourteen tax years** preceding that tax year has a **Remittance Basis Charge of £50,000**.
- An individual who has been resident for **seven of the nine tax years** preceding that tax year (but not yet twelve of the last fourteen tax years) has a **Remittance Basis Charge of £30,000.**

The Remittance Basis Charge is treated as UK income tax or CGT paid on an arising basis and so should be available for double taxation relief, for example in the country in which the non-UK income or gains arises.

The individual is required to nominate unremitted non-UK income and gains on which the Remittance Basis Charge applies. If the unremitted income or gains are later remitted to the UK, that income or gains will not be taxed again. However, there are ordering rules which treat other untaxed income and gains as being remitted before nominated income and gains.

If the individual does not nominate sufficient non-UK income or gains to cover the £30,000 or £50,000 Remittance Basis Charge, there is an additional element added to the Remittance Basis Charge to ensure that the full £30,000 or £50,000 tax charge is imposed.

2.3.7 Choosing whether or not to use the remittance basis

In each tax year, the individual can chose whether or not to claim the remittance basis. This will be an important decision if the individual would be liable to the remittance basis charge and will depend on:

- the extent of their unremitted non-UK income and gains;
- the effect of the loss of the personal allowance and the annual exempt amount against chargeable gains.

Question — **Choosing the remittance basis**

Nathan has been resident in the UK for tax purposes since 2004/05 but is not UK domiciled.

In 2013/14, he has the following income:

UK trading income	£10,000
Non-UK trading income	£90,000

He remits £10,000 of his non-UK trading income into the UK.

You are required to advise Nathan whether or not he should claim the remittance basis in 2013/14.

Answer

Remittance basis

Nathan has been resident in the UK for nine tax years before 2013/14, so the Remittance Basis Charge is £30,000, if the remittance basis is claimed.

	Non-savings Income
	£
UK trading income	10,000
Non-UK trading income remitted	10,000
Taxable income (no personal allowance)	20,000

His income tax liability will therefore be:

£20,000 × 20%	4,000
Remittance Basis Charge	30,000
	34,000

Worldwide income

	Non-savings Income
	£
UK trading income	10,000
Non-UK trading income	90,000
Net income	100,000
Less: personal allowance	(9,440)
Taxable income	90,560

His income tax liability will therefore be:

£32,010 × 20%	6,402
£58,550 × 40%	23,420
	29,822

Therefore Nathan should not claim the remittance basis for 2013/14.

2.4 Individuals not resident in the UK

2.4.1 Personal allowances for non-UK residents

In general, **non-UK residents are not entitled to personal allowances**. However, some individuals are entitled to allowances despite being non-UK resident including:

- Citizens of the European Economic Area
- Individuals resident in the Isle of Man and the Channel Islands

2.4.2 Limit on income tax liability for non-UK residents

There is a **limit on the income tax liability of an individual who is** not resident in the UK (but not where the tax year is split as described above). The **tax cannot exceed the sum of**:

- The tax liability if the individual was taxed on all income, apart from disregarded income, without a personal allowance; and
- The tax deducted at source from disregarded income (including tax credits on dividends).

Disregarded income includes **UK savings and dividend income**, but does not include non-savings income such as trading, employment or property income.

2.4.3 Savings income and non-UK residents

Interest that arises on UK government 'Free of Tax to Residents Abroad' (FOTRA) securities (broadly UK Treasury Stock) **is not taxable** if received by **an individual who is not resident in the UK**.

Bank and building society interest can be received gross (and so there will be no UK tax liability on this income) if the recipient is not resident in the UK and makes a declaration on Form R105.

3 Employment overseas and non-residents employed in the UK

3.1 Chargeability of employment income

FAST FORWARD

The residence and domicile status of an employee (and, in some cases, whether they carry out their duties in the UK or outside it) determine the tax treatment of their earnings.

3.1.1 Individual resident and domiciled in the UK

A resident and domiciled individual is taxed on their general earnings on a receipts basis (see Chapter 4) whether the duties of the employment are carried out in the UK or outside it.

However, if the individual can **split the tax year as described earlier in this chapter**, any **earnings relating to the overseas part of that year,** as determined on a 'just and reasonable' basis, are **not taxable unless they relate to duties performed in the UK**.

3.1.2 Individual resident but not domiciled in the UK

The general rules is that a UK resident, but not UK domiciled individual, is usually taxed on all general earnings on the receipts basis, wherever the duties of their employment are carried out.

There are two special rules where the individual's income from non-UK duties may be taxable on the remittance basis. These are where either:

- The individual has been **non-UK resident for any three consecutive years out of the previous five tax years**; or

- The earnings are **'chargeable overseas earnings'** which are those where:
  - The **duties** of the employment are performed **wholly outside of the UK**; and
  - The **employer is based outside the UK.**

If **split year treatment** applies, the amount of earnings relating to non-UK duties taxable on the remittance basis is the amount **attributable to the UK part of the year**, as determined on a 'just and reasonable' basis; the amount attributable to the overseas part of the year is not taxable in the UK.

If the remittance basis is claimed or is automatic, only those earnings relating to non-UK duties remitted to the UK are chargeable in the UK. The usual receipts basis applies to earnings relating to UK duties.

3.1.3 Individual not resident in the UK

A non resident is taxed on their general earnings in respect of UK duties on the receipts basis. There is no UK income tax on earnings in respect of non-UK duties.

3.1.4 Taxation of employment income – summary

Residence status of employee	Duties performed wholly or partly in the UK		Duties performed wholly outside the UK
	in the UK	outside the UK	
Resident and domiciled in the UK	Taxable on receipts basis	Taxable on receipts basis	Taxable on receipts basis
Resident in the UK but not UK domiciled	Taxable on receipts basis	Taxable on receipts basis EXCEPT non-UK resident for three consecutive years out of the previous five tax years, when taxable on remittance basis if claimed/ automatic	Taxable on receipts basis EXCEPT non-UK resident for three consecutive years out of the previous five tax years OR employer based outside UK, when taxable on remittance basis if claimed/ automatic
Not resident in the UK	Taxable on receipts basis	Not taxable in the UK	Not taxable in the UK

3.2 Travel and subsistence expenses for employment overseas

FAST FORWARD

Individuals working overseas may claim certain deductions for travel and subsistence expenses.

3.2.1 Travel expenses incurred by the employee

Travel expenses relating to employment duties overseas (whether or not reimbursed by the employer) may be deducted from earnings in certain circumstances.

- **A deduction is allowed for starting and finishing travel expenses**. Starting travel expenses are those incurred by the employee in travelling from the UK to take up employment overseas and finishing travel expenses are those incurred by the employee in travelling to the UK on the termination of the employment. **Three conditions need to be met:**
  - **The duties of the employment are performed wholly outside the UK (incidental UK duties are ignored)**
  - **The employee is resident in the UK**
  - **If the employer is based outside the UK, the employee is domiciled in the UK**

If the travel is only partly attributable to the taking up or termination of the employment, the deduction applies only to that part of the expenses.

- **There is also a deduction from earnings from an employment for travel expenses where an employee has two or more employments and the duties of at least one of them are performed overseas.** The following conditions must be met:
  - **The travel is for the purpose of performing duties of the employment at the destination**
  - **The employee has performed duties of another employment at the place of departure**
  - **The place of departure or the destination or both are outside the UK**
  - **The duties of one or both of the employments are performed wholly or partly outside the UK**
  - **The employee is resident in the UK**
  - **If the employer is based outside the UK, the employee is domiciled in the UK**

3.2.2 Travel expenses borne by employer

There are a number of deductions which may be made from a individual's earnings where an amount has been included in those earnings **in respect of provision of (or reimbursement of expenses relating to) travel overseas. The allowable deduction is generally equal to the amount included in the earnings. Note that these deductions do not apply where the employee incurs such costs but does not receive reimbursement.**

- **The first deduction relates to the provision of travel facilities for a journey made by the employee.** This deduction applies in two circumstances:
  - **The employee is absent from the UK wholly and exclusively for the purpose of performing the duties of one or more employments, the duties can only be performed outside the UK and the journey is from a place outside the UK to the UK or a return journey following such a journey**
  - **The duties of the employment are performed partly outside the UK, the journey is between the UK and the place the non-UK duties are performed, the non-UK duties can only be performed there and the journey is made wholly and exclusively for the purpose of performing the duties or returning after performing them**

  The deduction only applies from earnings which are chargeable because the individual is UK resident but not from 'chargeable overseas earnings' (employer based outside UK/non-domiciled employee/non-UK duties). This is because the overseas earnings are taxed on the remittance basis.

- **There is also a deduction for the provision of travel facilities for a journey made by the employee's spouse/civil partner or child** (aged under 18 at the beginning of the outward journey) **or the reimbursement of expenses incurred by the employee on such a journey**. The following conditions need to be met:
  - **The employee is absent from the UK for a continuous period of at least 60 days for the purpose of performing the duties of the employment**
  - **The journey is between the UK and the place outside the UK that the duties are performed**
  - **The employee's spouse/civil partner/child is either accompanying the employee at the beginning of the period of absence or visiting the employee during that period or is returning to the UK after accompanying or visiting the employee**

  A deduction is not allowed for more than two outward and two return journeys by the same individual in a tax year.

  Again, the deduction only applies from earnings which are chargeable because the individual is UK resident, but not from 'chargeable overseas earnings' taxed on the remittance basis.

- **There are also rules which apply to non-domiciled employee's travel costs and expenses where duties are performed in the UK. The deduction is only from earnings for duties performed in the UK.**

  The first deduction applies to the provision of travel facilities for a journey made by the employee or the reimbursement of expenses incurred by the employee for such a journey. The conditions that must be met are:

  - **The journey ends on or during the period of 5 years beginning with a qualifying arrival date** (see below)
  - **The journey is made from the country outside the UK where the employee normally lives to the UK in order to perform the duties of the employment or to that country from the UK after performing such duties**

  If the journey is only partly for such a purpose, the deduction is equal to so much of the included journey as is properly attributable to that purpose.

- A 'qualifying arrival date' is a date on which the individual arrives in the UK to perform UK duties where either:

  - The individual has not been in the UK for any purpose during the two tax years before the tax year in which the date falls, or
  - The individual was not UK resident in either of the two tax years before the tax year in which the date falls.

Exam focus point

Note carefully the rules under which relief is given. In particular, the costs must be borne by the employer. Note also the limits on journeys for spouses/civil partners/children.

3.2.3 Overseas accommodation and subsistence costs and expenses

A deduction from earnings from an employment is allowed if:

- **The duties of the employment are performed wholly outside the UK (incidental UK duties ignored)**
- **The employee is resident in the UK**
- **If the employer is based outside the UK, the employee is domiciled in the UK**
- **The earnings include an amount in respect of the provision of accommodation or subsistence outside the UK to enable the employee to perform the duties of the employment or the reimbursement of such expenses incurred by the employee.**

The deduction is equal to the amount included in the earnings.

3.3 Overseas pensions

For persons taxed on the arising basis (but not those on the remittance basis), only 90% of the amount of a overseas pension is taxed.

3.4 Tax planning when employed overseas

One of the competencies you require to fulfil performance objective 20 of the PER is the ability to assist with tax planning. You can apply the knowledge you obtain from this section of the text to help to demonstrate this competence.

3.4.1 General considerations

The following points highlight the pitfalls and planning possibilities to be considered when going to work overseas.

- Insurance policies are available to cover the risk of extra tax liabilities should an early return to the UK be necessary.
- If the employer bears the cost of board and lodging overseas this will represent a tax-free benefit. The employee may visit home as many times as they like without the costs being taxed as benefits. Likewise, for absences of 60 days or more, travelling expenses for a spouse/civil partner and minor children are also tax-free if paid or reimbursed by the employer. Up to two return visits per individual per tax year are allowed.
- Where the remittance basis applies it may be advisable to keep funds overseas separate so that it can be proved that sums remitted to the UK are capital (not subject to income tax) or income from a specific source.
- Having established non-residence in the UK, any UK investments should be reviewed to ensure they are still tax effective. Bank and building society interest, otherwise paid net, may be paid gross where the deposit-taker is given a written declaration that the recipient is not resident in the UK.
- Consider carefully the tax system in the overseas country concerned and the terms of any double taxation agreement. The UK has such agreements with most countries: they contain rules on where income and gains are to be taxed, and on other matters (see below).

3.4.2 The OECD Model Agreement

Most double taxation agreements follow fairly closely the Organisation for Economic Co-operation and Development (OECD) Model Double Taxation Agreement. Under that Model, someone who is resident in country R but is employed in country E will normally be taxed on the earnings in country E. They may only be taxed on the earnings in country R if:

- They are in country E for less than 184 days in total in any 12 month period starting or ending in the year,
- The employer is not resident in country E, and
- The earnings are not borne by a permanent establishment or fixed base which the employer has in country E.

If an individual resident in country R is a director of a company resident in country D, their director's fees may be taxed in country D.

4 Overseas trades

FAST FORWARD

Profits of an overseas trade are computed as for UK trades. However, the remittance basis may apply for non-UK domiciled individuals.

4.1 General principles

If a UK resident trader has a business which is conducted wholly or mainly overseas, the trade profits are chargeable to income tax. The trade profits are calculated in the same way as are UK trade profits, and the basis periods are determined in the same way also.

If the trader is not domiciled in the UK then the trader may claim the remittance basis or it may apply automatically under the usual rules.

A trader who is not UK resident is only taxable in the UK on UK income. The profits of trades carried on overseas by non-residents are therefore not liable to UK income tax. Where an individual who carries on a trade wholly or partly overseas becomes or ceases to be UK resident, the profits of the trade carried on overseas will become or cease to be liable to UK income tax respectively. To ensure that only the overseas profits which arise whilst the trader is UK resident are taxed there is a deemed cessation and recommencement of the trade. This rule also applies to a partner who changes residence if the partnership is carrying on a trade wholly or partly overseas.

This deemed cessation and recommencement does not prevent any losses that were being carried forward from before the change from being set off against profits arising after the change.

Under the OECD Model Agreement, a resident of country R trading in country T is taxable in country T on their profits only if they have a permanent establishment there (see later in this text). A resident of country R carrying on a profession in country P is taxable in country P on their profits only if they have a fixed base regularly available to them in country P.

The general rule for overseas traders doing business with UK customers is that they are trading in the UK (and therefore liable to UK tax on their profits) if contracts are concluded in the UK.

4.2 Travel expenses

A deduction is available against trade profits income for travel expenses incurred by UK domiciled individuals who carry on a trade wholly outside the UK and who travel to and from the UK. So long as the taxpayer's absence overseas is wholly and exclusively for the purposes of their trade then any travel expenses to and from the UK together with the cost of board and lodging at the overseas location are deductible. If the taxpayer's absence is for a continuous period of 60 days or more, the cost of up to two visits in any tax year by their spouse/civil partner and/or children under 18 is also deductible.

No deduction is however given for these travel expenses where the trade profits are taxed on a remittance basis. Instead the trader should arrange and pay for the travel whilst overseas, thus avoiding the need to remit that amount to the UK.

4.3 Overseas losses

A loss sustained in a trade (or profession or vocation) carried on overseas can be relieved in the same manner as UK trade losses against general income or under early trade losses relief.

However, if relief is sought for a loss in a trade which is wholly carried on overseas, the income which the loss can be set against is restricted to:

- Overseas trade profits
- Overseas pensions
- Overseas earnings

5 Double taxation relief (DTR)

FAST FORWARD

Double taxation relief may be available to reduce the burden of taxation. It is generally given by reducing the UK tax charged by the overseas tax suffered.

5.1 Introduction

As we have seen, **UK tax applies to the worldwide income of UK residents and the UK income of non-residents.**

When other countries adopt the same approach it is clear that some income may be taxed twice:

- Firstly in the country where it arises
- Secondly in the country where the taxpayer resides

Double taxation relief (DTR) as a result of international agreements may avoid the problem, or at least diminish its impact.

5.2 Double taxation agreements

Typical provisions of double taxation agreements based on the OECD Model are:

- Total exemption from tax is given in the country where income arises in the hands of, for example visiting diplomats and teachers on exchange programmes
- Preferential rates of withholding tax are applied to, for example, payments of rent, interest and dividends. The usual rate is frequently replaced by 15% or less
- DTR is given to taxpayers in their country of residence by way of a credit for tax suffered in the country where income arises. This may be in the form of relief for withholding tax only or, given a holding of specified size in a overseas company, for the underlying tax on the profits out of which dividends are paid
- There are exchanges of information clauses so that tax evaders can be chased internationally
- There are rules to determine a person's residence and to prevent dual residence (tie-breaker clauses)
- There are clauses which render certain profits taxable in only one rather than both of the contracting states
- There is a non-discrimination clause so that a country does not tax foreigners more heavily than its own nationals

5.3 Unilateral relief

If no relief is available under a double taxation agreement, UK legislation provides for unilateral relief. However, unilateral relief is not available if relief is specifically excluded under the terms of a double tax agreement.

Overseas income must be included gross (ie including overseas tax) in the UK tax computation. The overseas tax is deducted from the UK tax liability (this is credit relief) but the relief cannot exceed the UK tax on the overseas income so the taxpayer bears the higher of:

- The UK tax
- The overseas tax

The UK tax on the overseas income is the difference between:

- The UK tax before DTR on all income including the overseas income
- The UK tax on all income except the overseas income

In both cases, we take account of tax reducers.

Question — Double tax relief

A UK resident and domiciled individual has the following income for 2013/14.

	£
UK salary	35,680
Interest on overseas loan stock (net of overseas tax at 5%)	4,750
Overseas rents (net of overseas tax at 60%)	1,500

Assuming that maximum DTR is claimed, show the UK tax liability.

Answer

	Non-savings income	Savings income	Total
	£	£	£
Salary	35,680		
Overseas interest £4,750 × 100/95		5,000	
Overseas property business £1,500 × 100/40	3,750		
Net income	39,430	5,000	44,430
Less personal allowance	(9,440)		
Taxable income	29,990	5,000	34,990

		£
Non-savings income		
£29,990 × 20%		5,998
Savings income		
£2,020 × 20%		404
£2,980 × 40%		1,192
		7,594
Less double taxation relief		
Interest	250	
Rents (see below)	1,346	
		(1,596)
UK tax liability		5,998

Since the rents are taxed more highly overseas, these should be regarded as the top slice of UK taxable income. Taxable income excluding the rents is £31,240 and the UK tax on this is:

	£
Non-savings income	
£26,240 × 20%	5,248
Savings income	
£5,000 × 20%	1,000
	6,248

The UK tax on the rents is £1,346 (£7,594 – 6,248). Since overseas tax of £2,250 (60% of £3,750) is greater, the DTR is the smaller figure of £1,346. Overseas interest was taxed overseas at the rate of 5% (£250). Since the UK rate (20%) is clearly higher, the DTR given is £250.

Where there is no point in claiming this credit relief, perhaps because loss relief has eliminated any liability to UK tax, the taxpayer may elect for expense relief instead. No credit is given for overseas tax suffered, but only the income after overseas taxes is brought into the tax computation.

If overseas taxes are not relieved in the year in which the income is taxable in the UK, no relief can be obtained in any earlier or later year.

Taxpayers who have claimed relief against their UK tax bill for taxes paid overseas must notify HMRC in writing of any changes to the overseas liabilities if these changes result in the DTR claimed becoming excessive. This rule applies to all taxes not just income tax.

Chapter roundup

- An individual may be both or either resident and domiciled in the UK.
- An individual will automatically not be UK resident if he meets any of the automatic overseas tests. An individual, who does not meet any of the automatic overseas tests, will automatically be UK resident if he meets any of the automatic UK tests. An individual who has not met any of the automatic overseas tests nor any of the automatic UK tests will be UK resident if he meets the sufficient ties test.
- In general, an individual is either resident or non-resident for the whole of a tax year. However, in certain circumstances, the tax year may be split into UK and overseas parts.
- An individual is domiciled in the country which is the individual's permanent home.
- Generally, a UK resident is liable to UK income tax on UK and overseas income as it arises. An individual who is UK resident but not UK domiciled is liable to UK income tax on income arising in the UK and may be entitled to be taxed on overseas income on the remittance basis. A non-UK resident is liable to UK income tax only on income arising in the UK.
- An individual who claims the remittance basis and is a long term UK resident is required to pay the Remittance Basis Charge of either £30,000 or £50,000 on unremitted income and gains.
- The residence and domicile status of an employee (and, in some cases, whether they carry out their duties in the UK or outside it) determine the tax treatment of their earnings.
- Individuals working overseas may claim certain deductions for travel and subsistence expenses.
- Profits of an overseas trade are computed as for UK trades. However, the remittance basis may apply for non-UK domiciled individuals.
- Double taxation relief may be available to reduce the burden of taxation. It is generally given by reducing the UK tax charged by the overseas tax suffered.

Quick quiz

1. What are the three automatic UK tests?
2. On what basis is a UK resident who is not domiciled in the UK taxed on overseas income?
3. How will a overseas dividend be taxed on a higher rate UK resident taxpayer if that taxpayer is:

   (a) domiciled in the UK
   (b) not domiciled in the UK and makes a remittance basis claim?
4. How much is the Remittance Basis Charge?
5. What earnings for duties outside the UK are taxed on a remittance basis?
6. How many return journeys by John's family can an employer pay for tax free for John if he is working overseas for 100 days?
7. What is the maximum amount of credit relief that can be given for overseas tax on overseas income?

Answers to quick quiz

1 (a) The individual spends 183 days or more in the UK during a tax year.

(b) The individual spends 30 days or more in the UK during the tax year and has a home in the UK and no home overseas.

(c) The individual works full-time in the UK during a 365-day period, some of which falls within the tax year.

2 On the remittance basis if a claim is made or the individual has unremitted income/gains not exceeding £2,000 in the tax year. Otherwise on the arising basis.

3 (a) On an arising basis as dividend income liable to tax at 32.5%.
(b) On a remittance basis as non-savings income liable to tax at 40%.

4 £30,000 if the individual has been resident in the UK for seven of the previous nine tax years or £50,000 if the individual has been resident in the UK for twelve of the last fourteen tax years

5 Individual resident but not domiciled in the UK and either:

(a) Non-resident for any three consecutive years out of the previous five tax years; or
(b) Chargeable overseas earnings (duties of the employment are performed wholly outside of the UK, and employer is based outside the UK)

6 Two

7 The lower of:

(a) UK tax on the overseas income, and
(b) The overseas tax on the overseas income

Now try the question below from the Exam Question Bank

Number	Level	Marks	Time
Q11	Introductory	20	36 mins

PART B

Capital gains tax

11

Chargeable gains: an outline

Topic list	Syllabus reference
1 Chargeable and exempt persons, disposals and assets	A3(a)D1,D2,(d)(ii),(iii),(e)(iii)
2 Computing a gain or loss	A3(a)D2
3 CGT payable by individuals	A3(a)D5
4 Valuing assets	A3(a)D2
5 Connected persons	A3(d)(i)
6 Married couples and civil partners	A3(b)(i)
7 Business partnerships	A3(b)(vi)
8 Part disposals	A3(e)(i)

Introduction

Now that we have concluded our study of the income tax computation we can consider the capital gains tax computation. The two must be kept separate.

Capital gains arise when taxpayers dispose of assets, such as investments or capital assets used in the business. If, for example, you buy a picture for £10,000, hang it on your wall for 20 years and then sell it for £200,000, you will have a capital gain.

In this chapter we see when a capital gain will be liable to tax and how to work out gains and losses.

We also look at some special cases where the rules are modified because of the relationship between the disposer and the acquirer of an asset; without such rules, people could do deals with their relatives to avoid tax.

We also look at how chargeable gains on partnership assets are dealt with.

In the following chapters we will look at the special rules for certain types of assets and at what reliefs are available.

Study guide

		Intellectual level
3	**Chargeable gains and capital gains tax liabilities in situations involving further overseas aspects and in relation to closely related persons and trusts together with the application of additional exemptions and reliefs**	
(a)	The contents of the Paper F6 study guide for chargeable gains under headings:	2
•	D1 The scope of the taxation of capital gains	
•	D2 The basic principles of computing gains and losses	
•	D5 The computation of capital gains tax payable by individuals	
(b)	The scope of the taxation of capital gains:	3
(i)	Determine the tax implications of independent taxation and transfers between spouses	
(vi)	Identify the occasions when a capital gain would arise on a partner in a partnership	
(d)	The basic principles of computing gains and losses:	3
(i)	Identify connected persons for capital gains tax purposes and advise on the tax implications of transfers between connected persons	
(ii)	Advise on the impact of dates of disposal and conditional contracts	
(iii)	Evaluate the use of capital losses in the year of death	
(e)	Gains and losses on the disposal of movable and immovable property:	3
(i)	Advise on the tax implications of a part disposal, including small part disposals of land	
(iii)	Establish the tax effect of appropriations to and from trading stock	

Exam guide

Taxpayers normally plan major disposals of capital assets so you may get a question asking when would be the best time to make a disposal. You need to know the rules about the date of disposal, and then you need to be able to quantify any tax savings that might result from delaying or advancing a sale.

Knowledge brought forward from earlier studies

This chapter mainly revises topics covered in Paper F6. The examiner has identified essential underpinning knowledge from the F6 syllabus which is particularly important that you revise as part of your P6 studies. In this chapter, the relevant topics are:

		Intellectual level
D2	**The basic principles of computing gains and losses**	
(a)	Compute capital gains for both individuals and companies.	2

		Intellectual level
D5	**The computation of capital gains tax payable by individuals**	
(a)	Compute the amount of capital gains tax payable.	2

The new topics in this chapter include transfers to and from trading stock, carry back losses in the year of death, business partnerships, and small disposals of land.

There are no changes in 2013/14 from the material studied at F6 level in 2012/13 other than the increase in the annual exempt amount from £10,600 to £10,900.

1 Chargeable and exempt persons, disposals and assets

FAST FORWARD

For CGT to apply, there needs to be a chargeable person, a chargeable disposal and a chargeable asset.

Exam focus point

For a chargeable gain to arise there must be:

- A chargeable person; and
- A chargeable disposal; and
- A chargeable asset

otherwise no charge to tax occurs.

1.1 Chargeable persons

The following are chargeable persons:

- Individuals
- Partnerships
- Companies
- Trustees

We will look at the taxation of chargeable gains on companies later in this Text.

Persons who are not resident in the UK are exempt persons. We deal with overseas aspects of CGT later in this Text.

1.2 Chargeable disposals

FAST FORWARD

A chargeable disposal occurs on the date of the contract or when a conditional contract becomes unconditional.

The following are chargeable disposals:

- Sales of assets or parts of assets
- Gifts of assets or parts of assets
- Receipts of capital sums following the surrender of rights to assets
- The loss or destruction of assets
- The appropriation of assets as trading stock

A chargeable disposal occurs on the date of the contract (where there is one, whether written or oral), or the date of a conditional contract becoming unconditional. This may differ from the date of transfer of the asset. However, when a capital sum is received on a surrender of rights or the loss or destruction of an asset, the disposal takes place on the day the sum is received.

The timing of a disposal should be carefully considered bearing in mind these rules. For example, an individual may wish to accelerate a gain into an earlier tax year to obtain earlier loss relief or to delay a gain until a later tax year when an unused annual exempt amount may be available.

Where a disposal involves an acquisition by someone else, their date of acquisition is the same as the date of disposal.

Transfers of assets on death are exempt disposals. The heirs inherit assets as if they bought them at death for their then market values, but there is no capital gain or allowable loss on death. It is possible to vary or disclaim inherited assets. The CGT effect of such a variation or disclaimer is dealt with later in this Text.

1.3 Transfers to and from trading stock

When a taxpayer acquires an asset other than as trading stock and then uses it as trading stock, **the appropriation to trading stock normally leads to an immediate chargeable gain or allowable loss,** based on the asset's market value at the date of appropriation. The asset's cost for income tax purposes is that market value.

Alternatively, the trader can elect to have no chargeable gain or allowable loss: if they do so, the cost for income tax purposes is reduced by the gain or increased by the loss.

When an asset which is trading stock is appropriated to other purposes, the trade profits are calculated as if the trader had sold it for its market value, and for capital gains tax purposes as if they had bought it at the time of the appropriation for the same value.

1.4 Chargeable assets

All forms of property, wherever in the world they are situated, are chargeable assets unless they are specifically designated as exempt.

The following are exempt assets (gains not taxable, losses not usually allowable losses, the few exceptions are explained in this Text).

- **Motor vehicles** suitable for private use
- **National Savings & Investments certificates and premium bonds**
- Foreign currency bank accounts held by individuals, trustees and personal representatives
- Decorations awarded for bravery (unless purchased)
- Damages for personal or professional injury
- **Gilt-edged securities** (eg Treasury Stock)
- **Qualifying corporate bonds (QCBs)**
- **Certain chattels**
- Debts (except debts on a security)
- Investments held in individual savings accounts

There are also exemptions for enterprise investment scheme (EIS) shares, the seed enterprise investment scheme (SEIS), and venture capital trust (VCT) shares (see earlier in this Text).

2 Computing a gain or loss

FAST FORWARD

A gain or loss is computed by taking the proceeds and deducting the cost. Incidental costs of acquisition and disposal are deducted together with any enhancement expenditure reflected in the state and nature of the asset at the date of disposal.

One of the competencies you require to fulfil performance objective 19 of the PER is the ability to evaluate and compute taxes payable. You can apply the knowledge you obtain from this section of the text to help to demonstrate this competence.

2.1 Basic calculation

A gain (or an allowable loss) is generally calculated as follows.

	£
Disposal consideration	45,000
Less incidental costs of disposal	(400)
Net proceeds	44,600
Less allowable costs	(21,000)
Gain	23,600

Usually the disposal consideration is the proceeds of sale of the asset, but a disposal is deemed to take place at market value:

- Where the disposal is **not a bargain at arm's length**
- Where the disposal is made for a **consideration which cannot be valued**
- Where the disposal is by way of a **gift**.

Special valuation rules apply for shares (see later in this Text).

Incidental costs of disposal may include:

- Valuation fees
- Estate agency fees
- Advertising costs
- Legal costs.

Allowable costs include:

- The original cost of acquisition
- Incidental costs of acquisition
- Capital expenditure incurred in enhancing the asset.

Enhancement expenditure is capital expenditure which enhances the value of the asset and is reflected in the state or nature of the asset at the time of disposal, or expenditure incurred in establishing, preserving or defending title to, or a right over, the asset. Excluded from this category are:

- Costs of repairs and maintenance
- Costs of insurance
- Any expenditure deductible from trading profits
- Any expenditure met by public funds (for example council grants).

Question — Calculating the gain

Joanne bought a piece of land as an investment for £20,000. The legal costs of purchase were £250.

Joanne sold the land in December 2013 for £35,000. She incurred estate agency fees of £700 and legal costs of £500 on the sale.

Calculate Joanne's gain on sale.

Answer

	£
Proceeds of sale	35,000
Less costs of disposal £(700 + 500)	(1,200)
Net proceeds of sale	33,800
Less costs of acquisition £(20,000 + 250)	(20,250)
Gain	13,550

3 CGT payable by individuals

FAST FORWARD

CGT is usually payable at the rate of 18% or 28% depending on the individual's taxable income. Individuals are entitled to an annual exempt amount.

One of the competencies you require to fulfil performance objective 19 of the PER is the ability to evaluate and compute taxes payable. You can apply the knowledge you obtain from this section of the text to help to demonstrate this competence.

3.1 Introduction

In general, individuals are liable to CGT on the disposal of assets situated anywhere in the world if, for any part of the tax year of disposal, they are resident in the UK. 'Residence' has the same meaning as for income tax purposes (see earlier in this Text). Trustees also pay CGT on their gains.

An individual pays CGT on any taxable gains arising in the tax year. **Taxable gains are the net chargeable gains (gains minus losses) of the tax year reduced by unrelieved losses brought forward from previous years and the annual exempt amount.**

The annual exempt amount applies each tax year. For 2013/14 it is £10,900. It is the **last deduction** to be made in the calculation of taxable gains. **An individual who has gains taxable at more than one rate of tax may deduct any allowable losses and the annual exempt amount for that year in the way that produces the lowest possible tax charge**. We will look at this topic in detail later in this Text when we consider entrepreneurs' relief.

3.2 Calculating CGT

Taxable gains (other than those qualifying for entrepreneurs' relief) are chargeable to capital gains tax at the rate of 18% or 28% depending on the individual's taxable income for the tax year.

To work out which rate applies, follow these rules:

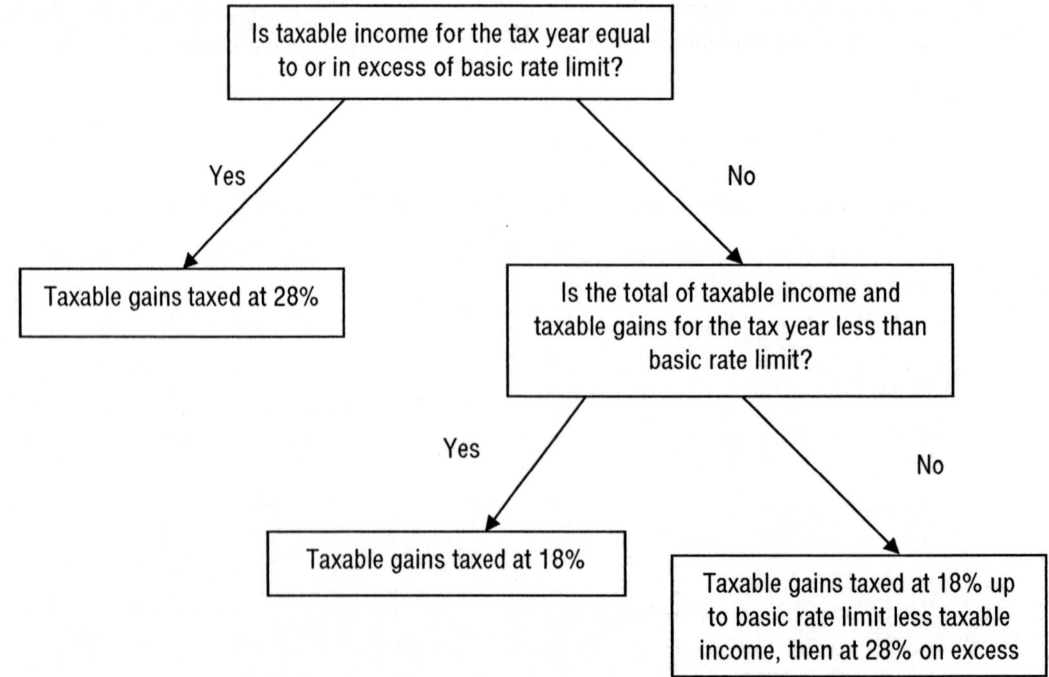

Remember that the basic rate band limit will usually be £32,010 for 2013/14 but the limit will be increased by the gross amount of personal pension contributions.

Question

Rates of CGT

Mo has taxable income of £25,000 in 2013/14. He made personal pension contributions of £200 (net) per month during 2013/14. In December 2013, he makes a chargeable gain of £28,000.

Calculate the CGT payable by Mo for 2013/14.

Answer

	£
Chargeable gain	28,000
Less: annual exempt amount	(10,900)
Taxable gain	17,100
Basic rate band limit	32,010
Add: personal pension contributions £(200 × 12) = £2,400 × 100/80	3,000
Increased basic rate limit	35,010
CGT	
£(35,010 – 25,000) = £10,010 (unused basic rate band) @ 18%	1,802
£(17,100 – 10,010) = £7,090 @ 28%	1,985
Total CGT payable	3,787

There is also a special 10% rate of tax for gains for which the taxpayer claims entrepreneurs' relief. We will look at this situation later in this Text.

3.3 Allowable losses

Deduct allowable capital losses from chargeable gains in the tax year in which they arise. Any loss which cannot be set off is carried forward to set against future chargeable gains. Losses must be used as soon as possible (subject to the following paragraph). Losses may not normally be set against income (unless they arise on the disposal of certain unquoted trading company shares – see earlier in this Text).

Allowable losses brought forward are only set off to reduce current year chargeable gains less current year allowable losses to the annual exempt amount. No set-off is made if net chargeable gains for the current year do not exceed the annual exempt amount.

3.4 Example: the use of losses

(a) George has chargeable gains for 2013/14 of £10,000 and allowable losses of £6,000. As the losses are **current year losses** they must be fully relieved against the £10,000 of gains to produce net gains of £4,000, despite the fact that net gains are below the annual exempt amount.

(b) Bob has gains of £14,800 for 2013/14 and allowable losses brought forward of £6,000. Bob restricts his loss relief to £3,900 so as to leave net gains of £(14,800 – 3,900) = £10,900, which will be exactly covered by his annual exempt amount for 2013/14. The remaining £2,100 of losses will be carried forward to 2014/15.

(c) Tom has chargeable gains of £10,500 for 2013/14 and losses brought forward from 2012/13 of £4,000. He will not use the losses in 2013/14 and will carry forward all of his losses to 2014/15. His gains of £10,500 are covered by his annual exempt amount for 2013/14.

3.5 Losses in the year of death

Losses arising in the tax year in which an individual dies can be carried back to the previous three tax years, later years first, and used so as to reduce gains for each of the years to an amount covered by the appropriate annual exempt amount. Only losses in excess of gains in the year of death can be carried back.

Question — **Loss in year of death**

Joe dies on 1 January 2014. His chargeable gains and allowable loss have been as follows.

	Gain/(loss)	*Annual exempt amount*
	£	£
2013/14	2,000	10,900
	(12,000)	
2012/13	10,800	10,600
2011/12	9,000	10,600
2010/11	28,000	10,100

How will the loss be set off?

Answer

The £10,000 net loss which arises in 2013/14 will be carried back. We must set off the loss against the 2013/14 gains first even though the gains are covered by the 2013/14 annual exempt amount.

£200 of the loss will be used in 2012/13. None of the loss will be used in 2011/12 (because the gains for that year are covered by the annual exempt amount), and so the remaining £9,800 will be used in 2010/11. Repayments of CGT will follow.

4 Valuing assets

FAST FORWARD

Market value must be used in certain capital gains computations. There are special rules for shares and securities.

4.1 General rules

Where market value is used in a chargeable gains computation (see Section 2 above)**, the value to be used is the price which the assets in question might reasonably be expected to fetch on a sale in the open market.**

4.2 Shares and securities

Quoted shares and securities are valued using prices in The Stock Exchange Daily Official List, taking the lower of:

(a) Lower quoted price + ¼ × (higher quoted price – lower quoted price) ('quarter up' rule).

(b) The average of the highest and lowest marked bargains (ignoring bargains marked at special prices).

Question

Calculation of CGT value

Shares in A plc are quoted at 100-110p. The highest and lowest marked bargains were 99p and 110p. What would be the market value for CGT purposes?

Answer

The value will be the lower of:

(a) $100 + \frac{1}{4} \times (110 - 100) = 102.5$

(b) $\frac{110+99}{2} = 104.5$

The market value for CGT purposes will therefore be 102.5p per share.

Unquoted shares are harder to value than quoted shares. HMRC have a special office, Shares and Assets Valuation, to deal with the valuation of unquoted shares.

5 Connected persons

FAST FORWARD

Disposals between connected persons are always deemed to take place for a consideration equal to market value. Any loss arising on a disposal to a connected person can be set only against a gain arising on a disposal to the same connected person.

5.1 Definition and effect

A transaction between 'connected persons' is treated as one between parties to a transaction otherwise than by way of a bargain made at arm's length. This means that the acquisition and disposal are deemed to take place for a consideration equal to the market value of the asset, rather than the actual price paid. In addition, if a loss results, it can be set only against gains arising in the same or future years from disposals to the same connected person and the loss can only be set off if he or she is still connected with the person sustaining the loss.

Key term

Connected person. An individual is connected with:

- Their spouse/civil partner
- Their relatives (brothers, sisters, ancestors and lineal descendants)
- The relatives of their spouse/civil partner
- The spouses/civil partners of their and their spouse/civil partner's relatives
- Their business partners, partners' spouses/civil partners and partners' relatives
- The trustees of a trust of which the individual is the settlor

5.2 Assets disposed of in a series of transactions

A taxpayer might attempt to avoid tax by disposing of their property piecemeal to persons connected with them. For example, a majority holding of shares might be broken up into several minority holdings, each with a much lower value per share, and each of the shareholder's children could be given a minority holding.

To prevent the avoidance of tax in this way, **where a person disposes of assets to one or more persons, with whom they are connected, in a series of linked transactions, the disposal proceeds for each disposal will be a proportion of the value of the assets taken together**. Thus in the example of the shareholding, the value of the majority holding would be apportioned between the minority holdings. Transactions are linked if they occur within six years of each other.

6 Married couples and civil partners

FAST FORWARD

Spouses/civil partners are treated as separate people. Transfers of assets between spouses/civil partners give rise to neither a gain nor a loss.

Spouses/civil partners are taxed as two separate people. Each has an annual exempt amount, and losses of one spouse/civil partner cannot be set against gains of the other.

Disposals between spouses/civil partners who are living together give rise to no gain and no loss, whatever actual price (if any) **was charged by the person transferring the asset** to their spouse/civil partner. This means that there is no chargeable gain or allowance loss and the transferee takes over the transferor's cost.

Since transfers between spouses/civil partners are on a no gain no loss basis, it may be beneficial to transfer the whole or part of an asset to the spouse/civil partner with an unused annual exempt amount or with taxable income below the basic rate limit. The transferee spouse then makes a disposal to a third party, either alone (if the whole asset is transferred) or jointly with the transferor spouse (if only part of the asset is transferred). It is very important that the transferee spouse/civil partner does not have any arrangement to pay back their net proceeds of sale to the transferor spouse/civil partner. If such an arrangement is in place, HM Revenue and Customs may contend that the no gain no loss disposal was not valid and treat the transferor spouse as making the entire disposal.

Question — Inter spouse transfer

Harry has taxable income of £60,000 in 2013/14 and makes chargeable gains of £20,000 in 2013/14 on share disposals. His wife, Margaret, has taxable income of £4,500 in 2013/14 and has no chargeable assets. Harry bought a plot of land for £150,000 in 2011. He gave it to Margaret when it was worth £180,000 on 10 May 2013. Margaret sold it on 27 August 2013 for £188,000. The land does not qualify for entrepreneurs' relief.

Calculate any chargeable gains arising to Harry and Margaret in respect of the land and show the tax saving arising from the transfer between Harry and Margaret, followed by the disposal by Margaret, compared with Harry directly disposing of the land in August 2013.

Answer

The disposal from Harry to Margaret is a no gain no loss disposal. Harry has no chargeable gain, and the cost for Margaret is Harry's original cost.

The gain on the sale by Margaret is:

	£
Proceeds of sale	188,000
Less cost	(150,000)
Gain	38,000

Margaret's gain will be reduced by her annual exempt amount to £27,100 (£38,000 – £10,900). Margaret also has £(32,010 – 4,500) = £27,510 of her basic rate band remaining. She will therefore pay CGT at 18% on the taxable gain. In contrast, Harry would have paid CGT on £38,000 at 28%.

The tax saving is therefore:

	£
Tax saved on annual exempt amount £10,900 @ 28%	3,052
Tax saved at basic rate £27,100 @ (28 – 18)%	2,710
Tax saving on disposal by Margaret instead of Harry	5,762

This tax saving will only be obtained if Margaret does not have an agreement to pay back the net proceeds of sale to Harry.

7 Business partnerships

FAST FORWARD

The CGT position of partnerships recognises the fact that individual partners have (potentially variable) stakes in partnership assets.

7.1 Actual disposals

When a business partnership disposes of an asset, any chargeable gain or allowable loss is apportioned to the partners in their capital profit sharing ratio.

7.2 Change in PSR

Partners may decide to change their profit shares in the firm, for example when a new partner joins the firm or a partner retires. Each partner is treated as acquiring or disposing of an appropriate share in the partnership assets. Thus a partner whose share rises from 20% to 50% acquires a 30% share.

On these deemed disposals, the assets of the firm are treated as sold for their current balance sheet values which would apply on an actual disposal. If assets have not been revalued in the balance sheet, the consequence is that the partners reducing their shares have chargeable gains of zero. If assets have been revalued, each such partner will have gains equal to the revaluations × the percentage fall in their share. A corresponding allowable loss arises if assets have been revalued downwards.

When one partner pays another and the payment does not go through the accounts, each partner receiving money has a chargeable gain equal to the amount they receive, in addition to any gain outlined above. A partner whose share is increased (including a new partner) has a deemed acquisition cost equal to the deemed disposal proceeds of the share they are acquiring from the other partners. If they make a payment outside the accounts, it is generally treated as being for goodwill.

7.3 Revaluations with no change in PSR

When assets are revalued with no changes in shares in the partnership, there is no chargeable gain or allowable loss at that time.

8 Part disposals

FAST FORWARD

On a part disposal, the cost must usually be apportioned between the part disposed of and the part retained. On a small part disposal of land, there is no chargeable gain and the net proceeds of disposal are deducted from the cost of the land retained.

8.1 Basic rule

The disposal of part of a chargeable asset is a chargeable event. The chargeable gain (or allowable loss) is computed by deducting from the disposal value a fraction of the original cost of the whole asset.

Formula to learn

The fraction is:

$$\frac{A}{A+B} = \frac{\text{value of the part disposed of}}{\text{value of the part disposed of} + \text{market value of the remainder}}$$

In this fraction, A is the proceeds (for arm's length disposals) *before* deducting incidental costs of disposal.

The part disposal fraction should not be applied indiscriminately. Any expenditure incurred wholly in respect of a particular part of an asset should be treated as an allowable deduction in full for that part and not apportioned, such as incidental selling expenses, which are wholly attributable to the part disposed of.

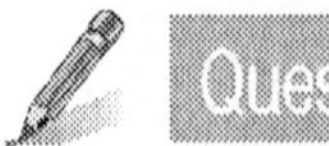

Question

Part disposal

Mr Heal owns a 4 hectare plot of land which originally cost him £150,000. He sold one hectare in July 2013 for £60,000. The incidental costs of sale were £3,000. The market value of the 3 hectares remaining is estimated to be £180,000. What is the gain on the sale of the one hectare?

Answer

The amount of the cost attributable to the part sold is $\frac{60,000}{60,000+180,000} \times £150,000 = £37,500$

	£
Proceeds	60,000
Less: disposal costs	(3,000)
Net proceed of sale	57,000
Less cost (see above)	(37,500)
Gain	19,500

8.2 Land: small part disposal proceeds

Where the **consideration** for a part disposal of land **does not exceed 20% of the market value of the entire holding** of land prior to the part disposal, a chargeable disposal does not take place. The taxpayer must make a **claim** by the first anniversary of 31 January following the end of the tax year. The net disposal proceeds are deducted from allowable expenditure when computing a gain on a later disposal of the remaining land.

Question

Small part disposals of land

Bertha buys 10 acres of land for £20,000. She sells 1½ acres for £5,000 in July 2013 and disposal costs amount to £50. Market value of the land immediately prior to the disposal is £30,000. You are required to show Bertha's CGT position.

Answer

The consideration (£5,000) is less than 20% of market value (20% of £30,000 = £6,000). Bertha may therefore claim for the relief to apply. As a result, no chargeable disposal takes place in July 2013.

Allowable cost of the land retained is:

	£
Cost of 10 acres	20,000
Deduct: net proceeds of part disposal (£5,000 – £50)	(4,950)
Allowable expenditure of land retained	15,050

There are two further conditions to meet before this relief can apply:

- proceeds from the part disposal do not exceed £20,000; and
- aggregate proceeds from the part disposal and any other disposals of land (including buildings) in the same tax year do not exceed £20,000.

8.3 Example: proceeds exceeding £20,000

If, in the previous example, Bertha had made another disposal of land for £15,750 in 2013/14, the relief could not apply since proceeds for the tax year (ie £15,750 + £5,000 = £20,750) would exceed £20,000. The normal part disposal rules would apply.

Chapter roundup

- For CGT to apply, there needs to be a chargeable person, a chargeable disposal and a chargeable asset.
- A chargeable disposal occurs on the date of the contract or when a conditional contract becomes unconditional.
- A gain or loss is computed by taking the proceeds and deducting the cost. Incidental costs of acquisition and disposal are deducted together with any enhancement expenditure reflected in the state and nature of the asset at the date of disposal.
- CGT is usually payable at the rate of 18% or 28% depending on the individual's taxable income. Individuals are entitled to an annual exempt amount.
- Market value must be used in certain capital gains computations. There are special rules for shares and securities.
- Disposals between connected persons are always deemed to take place for a consideration equal to market value. Any loss arising on a disposal to a connected person can be set only against a gain arising on a disposal to the same connected person.
- Spouses/civil partners are treated as separate people. Transfers of assets between spouses/civil partners give rise to neither a gain nor a loss.
- The CGT position of partnerships recognises the fact that individual partners have (potentially variable) stakes in partnership assets.
- On a part disposal, the cost must usually be apportioned between the part disposed of and the part retained. On a small part disposal of land, there is no chargeable gain and the net proceeds of disposal are deducted from the cost of the land retained.

Quick quiz

1 Give some examples of chargeable disposals.

2 Are the following assets chargeable to CGT or exempt?

   (a) Shares (not held in ISA)
   (b) Car
   (c) Land
   (d) Victoria Cross awarded to owner
   (e) National Savings & Investments Certificates

3 Jed buys a house. He repairs the roof, installs central heating and builds an extension. The extension is blown down in a storm and not replaced. Which of these improvements is allowable as enhancement expenditure on a subsequent sale?

4 At what rates do individuals pay CGT on gains not qualifying for entrepreneurs' relief?

5 To what extent must allowable losses be set against chargeable gains?

6 Shares in A plc are quoted at 410 – 414, with bargains at 408, 410 and 416. What is the value for CGT?

7 With whom is an individual connected?

8 What is the CGT effect of a change in partnership profit sharing ratios without any revaluation of assets or payment between business partners?

9 10 acres of land are sold for £15,000, out of a plot of 25 acres. The original cost of the whole plot was £9,000 and costs of sale are £2,000. The rest of the land is valued at £30,000. What is the allowable expenditure?

Answers to quick quiz

1. Sales of assets or parts of assets
   Gifts of assets or parts of assets
   Receipts of capital sums following the surrender of rights to assets
   Loss or destruction of assets
   Appropriation of assets as trading stock

2. (a) Shares – Chargeable
   (b) Car – Exempt as motor vehicle suitable for private use
   (c) Land – Chargeable
   (d) Victoria Cross – Exempt as medal for bravery not acquired by purchase
   (e) National Savings & Investments Certificates – Exempt

3. Repairs to roof – not allowable as enhancement expenditure because not capital in nature
   Central heating – allowable as enhancement expenditure
   Extension – not allowable as not reflected in state of asset at time of disposal.

4. 18% and 28%

5. Current year losses must be set off against gains in full, even if this reduces gains below the annual exempt amount. Losses brought forward or carried back from year of death, are set off to bring down gains to the level of the annual exempt amount.

6. Lower of:

   $410 + \frac{1}{4}(414 - 410) = 411$

   $\frac{416+408}{2} = 412$

   ie 411

7. An individual is connected with:

   (a) their spouse ('spouse' includes civil partners)
   (b) their relatives (brothers, sisters, ancestors and lineal descendants)
   (c) the relatives of their spouse
   (d) the spouses of their and their spouse's relatives
   (e) their business partners, partners' spouses/civil partners and partners' relatives
   (f) trustees of a trust of which they are the settlor

8. The assets of the firm are treated as sold at current balance sheet values. Where there has been no revaluation, the disposing partner will have a nil gain. The acquiring partner will have a base cost equal to the deemed sale proceeds.

9. $\frac{15,000}{15,000+30,000} \times £9,000 = £3,000 + £2,000$ (costs of disposal) $= £5,000$

Now try the question below from the Exam Question Bank

Number	Level	Marks	Time
Q12	Introductory	19	34 mins

12

Shares and securities

Topic list	Syllabus reference
1 The matching rules for individuals	A3(a)D4
2 The share pool	A3(a)D4
3 Alterations of share capital	A3(f)(i),(iv)
4 Gilts and qualifying corporate bonds	A3(f)(iii)

Introduction

In the previous chapter we have revised the basic computation of chargeable gains and how to calculate the CGT payable. In this chapter, we look at shares and securities held by individuals.

Shares and securities need special treatment because an investor may hold several shares or securities in the same company, bought at different times for different prices but otherwise identical.

The rules for shares and securities held by companies are different and are dealt with later in this Text.

In the next chapter we will consider CGT deferral reliefs and the CGT implications of varying a will.

Study guide

		Intellectual level
3	**Chargeable gains and capital gains tax liabilities in situations involving further overseas aspects and in relation to closely related persons and trusts together with the application of additional exemptions and reliefs**	
(a)	The contents of the Paper F6 study guide for chargeable gains under heading:	2
•	D4 Gains and losses on the disposal of shares and securities	
(f)	Gains and losses on the disposal of shares and securities:	3
(i)	Extend the explanation of the treatment of rights issues to include the small part disposal rules applicable to rights issues	
(iii)	Define a qualifying corporate bond (QCB), and understand what makes a corporate bond non-qualifying. Understand the capital gains tax implications of the disposal of QCBs in exchange for cash or shares	
(iv)	Apply the rules relating to reorganisations, reconstructions and amalgamations and advise on the most tax efficient options available in given circumstances	

Exam guide

Shares and securities are some of the more common assets held by individuals, and knowing how to compute the gain on their disposal is fundamental to an understanding of capital gains.

Knowledge brought forward from earlier studies

This chapter revises the identification rules for individuals and the computation of gains on disposals that were covered in Paper F6. It expands on the rules for rights issues, takeovers and reorganisations. There have been no changes to the rules in 2013/14 from 2012/13.

1 The matching rules for individuals

FAST FORWARD

There are special rules for matching shares sold with shares purchased. Disposals are matched first with shares acquired on the same day, then within the following 30 days and finally with the share pool.

Quoted and unquoted shares and securities present special problems when attempting to compute gains or losses on disposal. For instance, suppose that an individual buys some quoted shares in X plc as follows.

Date	*Number of shares*	*Cost*
		£
5 May 2003	100	150
17 August 2013	100	375

On 15 August 2013, he sells 120 of the shares for £1,450. To determine the chargeable gain, we need to be able to work out which shares out of the two original holdings were actually sold.

We therefore need **matching rules**. These **allow us to decide which shares have been sold and so work out what the allowable cost on disposal should be.**

At any one time, we will only be concerned with shares or securities of the same class in the same company. If an individual owns both ordinary shares and preference shares in X plc, we will deal with the two classes of share entirely separately, because they are distinguishable.

Below 'shares' refers to both shares and securities.

For individuals, share disposals are matched with acquisitions in the following order.

(a) **Same day acquisitions.**

(b) **Acquisitions within the following 30 days** (known as the 'bed and breakfast rule') if more than one acquisition on a "first in, first out" (FIFO) basis.

(c) **Any shares in the share pool** (see below).

The 'bed and breakfast' rule stops shares being sold to crystallise a capital gain or loss, usually to use the annual exempt amount and then being repurchased a day or so later. Without the rule a gain or loss would arise on the sale since it would be 'matched' to the original acquisition.

Exam focus point

Learn the 'matching rules' because a crucial first step to getting a shares question right is to correctly match the shares sold to the original shares purchased.

2 The share pool

One of the competencies you require to fulfil performance objective 19 of the PER is the ability to evaluate and compute taxes payable. You can apply the knowledge you obtain from this section of the text to help to demonstrate this competence.

2.1 Composition of pool

We treat any other shares acquired as a 'pool' which grows as new shares are acquired and shrinks as they are disposed.

In making computations which use the share pool, we must keep track of:

(a) The **number** of shares
(b) The **cost** of the shares

2.2 Disposals from the share pool

In the case of a disposal the cost attributable to the shares disposed of is deducted from the amounts within the share pool. The proportion of the cost to take out of the pool should be computed using the A/(A + B) fraction that is used for any other part disposal. However, we are not usually given the value of the remaining shares (B in the fraction). We just use numbers of shares.

Question — **The share pool**

In August 2006 Oliver acquired 4,000 shares in Twist plc at a cost of £10,000. Oliver sold 3,000 shares on 10 July 2013 for £17,000. Compute the gain and the value of the share pool following the disposal.

Answer

The gain is computed as follows:

	£
Proceeds	17,000
Less cost (working)	(7,500)
Gain	9,500

Working – share pool

	No of shares	Cost
		£
Acquisition – August 2006	4,000	10,000
Disposal – July 2013	(3,000)	
Cost $\frac{3,000}{4,000} \times £10,000$	–––	(7,500)
	1,000	2,500

Question

Matching rules

Anita acquired shares in Kent Ltd as follows:

1 July 2000	1,000 shares for	£2,000
11 April 2005	2,500 shares for	£7,500
17 July 2013	400 shares for	£1,680
10 August 2013	500 shares for	£2,000

Anita sold 4,000 shares for £16,400 on 17 July 2013.

Calculate Anita's net gain on sale.

Answer

First match the disposal with the acquisition on the same day:

	£
Proceeds $\frac{400}{4,000} \times £16,400$	1,640
Less: cost	(1,680)
Loss	(40)

Next match the disposal with the acquisition in the next thirty days:

	£
Proceeds $\frac{500}{4,000} \times £16,400$	2,050
Less: cost	(2,000)
Gain	50

Finally, match the disposal with the shares in the share pool:

	£
Proceeds $\frac{3,100}{4,000} \times £16,400$	12,710
Less: cost (working)	(8,414)
Gain	4,296
Net gain £(50 + 4,296 – 40)	4,306

Working

	No. of shares	Cost
		£
1.7.00 Acquisition	1,000	2,000
11.4.05 Acquisition	2,500	7,500
	3,500	9,500
17.7.13 Disposal	(3,100)	(8,414)
c/f	400	1,086

3 Alterations of share capital

On an alteration of share capital, the general principle is only to tax gains immediately if cash is paid to the investors.

3.1 General principle

On a reorganisation we must apportion the original base cost of whatever the shareholder had beforehand between the elements of whatever the shareholder has afterwards.

3.2 Capital distributions

Normally a capital distribution is treated as a part disposal of an asset. If, however, the distribution is small (normally taken to mean not more than the higher of 5% of the value of the shares and £3,000) **then any gain can be deferred by treating the distribution as a deduction from the cost of the shares for the purposes of calculating any gains or losses on future disposals.**

If the taxpayer wants a part disposal (for example to use his annual exempt amount) HMRC will allow this even if the proceeds are small.

Question — **Capital distributions**

S Barr holds 1,000 shares in Woodleigh plc which cost £4,000 in August 2003. The company is now in liquidation and in June 2012 the liquidator made a distribution of 35p per share. The market value of the shares after the distribution was £7,000. In November 2013 S Barr received a final distribution of £7,200.

Show any chargeable gains arising, assuming that there is no part disposal in June 2012.

Answer

No gain arises in June 2012 as the distribution in June 2012 is not more than the higher of £3,000 and 5% of the value of the shares: £(350 + 7,000) × 5% = £368. The November 2013 distribution is treated as follows.

	Cost
	£
Proceeds	7,200
Less cost £(4,000 – 350)	(3,650)
Gain	3,550

3.3 Bonus issues (scrip issues)

When a company issues bonus shares all that happens is that the size of the original holding is increased. Since bonus shares are free shares, issued at no cost, there is no need to adjust the original cost. Instead the numbers purchased at particular times are increased by the bonus. The normal matching rules will then be applied.

3.4 Rights issues

The difference between a bonus issue and a rights issue is that in a rights issue the new shares are paid for and this results in an adjustment to the original cost.

In an **open offer**, shareholders have a right to subscribe for a minimum number of shares based on their existing holdings and may buy additional shares. Subscriptions up to the minimum entitlement are treated as a rights issue. Additional subscriptions are treated as new purchases of shares.

Question

Rights issue

Simon had the following transactions in S Ltd.

1.10.06	Bought 10,000 shares for £15,000
1.2.12	Took up rights issue 1 for 2 at £2.75 per share
14.10.13	Sold 2,000 shares for £6,000

Compute the gain arising in October 2013.

Answer

Share pool

	No. of shares	*Cost*
		£
1.10.06 Acquisition	10,000	15,000
1.2.12 Rights issue	5,000	13,750
	15,000	28,750
14.10.13 Sale	(2,000)	(3,833)
c/f	13,000	24,917

Gain

	£
Proceeds	6,000
Less cost	(3,833)
Gain	2,167

3.5 Sales of rights nil paid

Where the shareholder does not take up his rights but sells them to a third party without paying the company for the rights shares, the proceeds are treated as a capital distribution (see above) **and will be dealt with either under the part disposal rules or, if not more than the higher of £3,000 and 5% of the value of the shareholding giving rise to the disposal, as a reduction of original cost** (unless the taxpayer chooses to use the part disposal treatment, for example if the gain would be covered by the annual exempt amount).

3.6 Reorganisations

A reorganisation takes place where new shares or a mixture of new shares and debentures are issued in exchange for the original shareholdings. The new shares take the place of the old shares. The problem is how to apportion the original cost between the different types of capital issued on the reorganisation.

If the new shares and securities are quoted, then the cost is apportioned by reference to the market values of the new types of capital on the first day of quotation after the reorganisation.

Question

Reorganisations

An original quoted shareholding of 3,000 shares is held in a share pool with a cost of £13,250.

In 2013 there is a reorganisation whereby each ordinary share is exchanged for two 'A' ordinary shares (quoted at £2 each) and one preference share (quoted at £1 each). Show how the original cost will be apportioned.

Answer

Share pool

	New holding	*MV*	*Cost*
		£	£
Ords 2 new shares	6,000	12,000	10,600
Prefs 1 new shares	3,000	3,000	2,650
Total		15,000	13,250

Working

$^{12}/_{15} \times$ £13,250 = cost of ordinary shares

$^{3}/_{15} \times$ £13,250 = cost of preference shares

Where a reorganisation takes place and the new shares and securities are unquoted, the cost of the original holding is apportioned using the values of the new shares and securities when they come to be disposed of.

For both quoted and unquoted shares and securities, any incidental costs (such as professional fees) are treated as additional consideration for the new shares and securities.

3.7 Takeovers

FAST FORWARD

The special rules on takeovers only apply if the exchange is for bona fide commercial reasons and not for the avoidance of tax.

A chargeable gain does not arise on a 'paper for paper' takeover. The cost of the original holding is passed on to the new holding which takes the place of the original holding. **If part of the takeover consideration is cash then a gain must be computed**: the normal part disposal rules will apply.

If the cash received is not more than the higher of 5% of the total value on the takeover, **and £3,000,** then the small distribution rules apply and **the cash received will be deducted from cost** for the purpose of further disposals, unless the taxpayer chooses the part disposal treatment.

The takeover rules apply where the company issuing the new shares ends up with more than 25% of the ordinary share capital of the old company or the majority of the voting power in the old company, or the company issuing the new shares makes a general offer to shareholders in the other company which is initially made subject to a condition which, if satisfied, would give the first company control of the second company.

The exchange must take place for bona fide commercial reasons and must not have as its main purpose, or one of its main purposes, the avoidance of CGT or corporation tax.

Question

Takeover

Mr Le Bon held 20,000 £1 shares in Duran plc out of a total number of issued shares of one million. They were bought in 2002 for £2 each. In 2013 the board of Duran plc agreed to a takeover bid by Spandau plc under which shareholders in Duran plc received three ordinary Spandau plc shares plus one preference share for every four shares held in Duran plc. Immediately following the takeover, the ordinary shares in Spandau plc were quoted at £5 each and the preferences shares at 90p. Show the base costs of the ordinary shares and the preference shares.

Answer

The total value due to Mr Le Bon on the takeover is as follows.

		£
Ordinary	20,000 × 3/4 × £5	75,000
Preference	20,000 × 1/4 × 90p	4,500
		79,500

Original cost of shares = 20,000 × £2 = £40,000

The base costs of the new holdings are therefore:

	£
Ordinary shares: 75,000/79,500 × £40,000	37,736
Preference shares: 4,500/79,500 × £40,000	2,264
	40,000

Part of the takeover consideration may include the right to receive deferred consideration in the form of shares or debentures in the new company. The amount of the deferred consideration may be unascertainable at the date of the takeover, perhaps because it is dependent on the future profits of the company whose shares are acquired. The right is valued and treated as a security. This means the takeover rules apply and there is no need to calculate a gain in respect of the right. The issue of shares or debentures as a result of the right is treated as a conversion of the right and, again, no gain arises.

3.8 Interaction with entrepreneurs' relief

Exam focus point

Entrepreneurs' relief is discussed in Section 1 of Chapter 13. You may wish to read that first before studying this section.

There may be a problem if the rules on reorganisations and takeovers described above apply and the new shares do not qualify for entrepreneurs' relief when they are eventually disposed of (for example because the shareholder no longer works for the company or the level of shareholding is too low). In this case, without special rules, any entrepreneurs' relief accrued on the old shares will be lost.

In this case, **the legislation provides that the shareholder can elect to disapply the usual reorganisation or takeover treatment and can claim entrepreneurs' relief in the year of the reorganisation or takeover.** The shareholder will then make a chargeable disposal with proceeds of the shares acquired and costs apportioned as already described.

The election must be made by the same date as the claim for entrepreneurs' relief. So if the takeover occurs in 2013/14, the claim must be made by 31 January 2016.

4 Gilts and qualifying corporate bonds

FAST FORWARD Gilts and QCBs held by individuals are exempt from CGT.

4.1 Definitions and treatment

Key term

Gilts are British Government and Government guaranteed securities as shown on the Treasury list. Gilt strips (capital or interest entitlements sold separately) are also gilts. You may assume that the list of gilts includes all issues of Treasury Loan, Treasury Stock, Exchequer Loan, Exchequer Stock and War Loan.

Disposals of gilt edged securities (gilts) and qualifying corporate bonds by individuals and trusts are exempt from CGT. The rules for companies are different, and are explained later in this Text.

Key term

A **qualifying corporate bond (QCB)** is a security (whether or not secured on assets) which:

(a) Represents a **'normal commercial loan'**. This excludes any bonds which are convertible into shares (although bonds convertible into other bonds which would be QCBs are not excluded), or which carry the right to excessive interest or interest which depends on the results of the issuer's business

(b) Is **expressed in sterling** and for which no provision is made for conversion into or redemption in another currency

(c) Was **acquired** by the person now disposing of it **after 13 March 1984**, and

(d) Does not have a redemption value which depends on a published index of share prices on a stock exchange.

Permanent interest bearing shares issued by building societies which meet condition (b) above are also QCBs.

4.2 Reorganisations involving QCBs

FAST FORWARD

If a reorganisation involves the acquisition of QCBs, a gain to the date of the takeover is computed but is 'frozen' until the disposal of the QCB.

Special rules apply when a reorganisation involves qualifying corporate bonds, either as the security in issue before the reorganisation (the 'old asset') or as a security issued on the reorganisation (a 'new asset').

Where QCBs are the old asset, the newly issued shares are treated as acquired at the time of the reorganisation, for the then market value of the old asset. This market value is reduced by any money paid to the security-holders, or increased by any money paid by them. If a company holds the QCBs, then the QCBs are treated as sold at the same time for their market value, so as to find the company's profit or loss.

Where QCBs are the new asset, the chargeable gain which would have accrued if the old asset had been sold at its market value at the time of the reorganisation must be computed and apportioned between the new assets issued. When the QCBs are disposed of, the part of that gain apportioned to them becomes chargeable. However, if that disposal is a no gain/no loss disposal to a spouse/civil partner, the gain does not become chargeable until a disposal outside the marriage. Furthermore, if the reorganisation is followed by the owner's death while he still owns the QCBs, the gain never becomes chargeable.

QCBs are often used in takeover situations instead of cash where for most shareholders the cash would not be a small capital distribution. This enables the shareholder to defer the gain until the QCBs are disposed of. This is often done over a period of time so as to use the annual exempt amount and any other reliefs available.

Question — Takeovers including QCBs

Zelda owned 10,000 shares in Red Ltd which she had acquired for £20,000. In July 2012, Red Ltd was taken over by Rainbow plc and Zelda received:

6,000 ordinary shares in Rainbow plc worth £2 per share; and

£9,000 loan stock (which were qualifying corporate bonds) in Rainbow plc worth £4 for each £1 nominal value,

In August 2013 Zelda sold 2,000 shares in Rainbow plc for £2.40 per share, and £3,375 of the loan stock in Rainbow plc for £4.50 for each £1 nominal value.

Show the capital gains implications of the takeover and the subsequent sales.

Answer

July 2012

The total value due to Zelda on the takeover is as follows.

	£
Ordinary shares 6,000 × £2	12,000
Loan stock £9,000 × £4	36,000
Gain	48,000

The base costs of the new holdings are therefore:

	£
Ordinary shares: 12,000/48,000 × £20,000	5,000
Loan stock: 36,000/48,000 × £20,000	15,000
	20,000

On the takeover, there is no disposal for CGT on the exchange of Red Ltd shares for the Rainbow plc shares and the loan stock. However, the gain up to the date of the takeover on the loan stock is calculated as follows:

	£
Market value of loan stock received on takeover	36,000
Less cost	(15,000)
Gain	21,000

This gain is 'frozen'.

August 2013

On the disposal of the shares, a gain arises in the normal way:

	£
Proceeds 2,000 × £2.40	4,800
Less cost £5,000 × 2,000/6,000	(1,667)
Gain	3,133

Note that this gain includes the gain up to the date of the takeover and the gain from the date of the takeover.

On the disposal of the loan stock, part of the frozen gain becomes chargeable:

£21,000 × 3,375/9,000	£7,875

The gain on the loan stock sold is exempt from CGT because the loan stock itself are qualifying corporate bonds.

4.3 Interaction with entrepreneurs' relief

The situation in respect of entrepreneurs' relief available on the frozen gain on QCBs is similar to that involving shares. An election can be made for the gain not to be deferred but instead brought into charge at the time of the takeover, accompanied by a claim for entrepreneurs' relief. If no election is made and the gain is then deferred under the normal gains rules, the frozen gain will usually not qualify for entrepreneurs' relief when it comes back into charge on disposal.

Chapter roundup

- There are special rules for matching shares sold with shares purchased. Disposals are matched first with shares acquired on the same day, then within the following 30 days and finally with the share pool.
- On an alteration of share capital, the general principle is only to tax gains immediately if cash is paid to the investors.
- The special rules on takeovers only apply if the exchange is for bona fide commercial reasons and not for the avoidance of tax.
- Gilts and QCBs held by individuals are exempt from CGT.
- If a reorganisation involves the acquisition of QCBs, a gain to the date of the takeover is computed but is 'frozen' until the disposal of the QCB.

Quick quiz

1 In what order are acquisitions of shares matched with disposals for individuals?

2 In July 2006 an individual acquired 1,000 shares. He acquired 1,000 more shares on each of 15 January 2008 and 15 January 2014 in X plc. He sells 2,500 shares on 10 January 2014. How are the shares matched on sale?

3 Sharon acquired 10,000 share in Z plc in 2006. She takes up a 1 for 2 rights offer in July 2013. How many shares does Sharon have in her share pool after the rights issue?

4 What is a qualifying corporate bond?

Answers to quick quiz

1 The matching of shares sold is in the following order.

(a) Same day acquisitions.

(b) Acquisitions within the following 30 days.

(c) Shares in the shares pool.

2 15 January 2014 1,000 shares (following 30 days)
Share pool 1,500 shares

3 10,000 + 5,000 = 15,000 shares

4 A qualifying corporate bond is a security which:

- represents a normal commercial loan
- is expressed in sterling
- was acquired after 13 March 1984
- is not redeemable in relation to share prices on a stock exchange

Now try the question below from the Exam Question Bank

Number	Level	Marks	Time
Q13	Introductory	15	27 mins

13

Chargeable gains: reliefs

Topic list	Syllabus reference
1 Entrepreneurs' relief	A3(a)D6, A3(g)(ii)
2 Gift relief (holdover relief)	A3(a)D6
3 The replacement of business assets (rollover relief)	A3(a)D6
4 The transfer of a business to a company (incorporation relief)	A3(g)(iii)
5 EIS deferral relief	A3(g)(i)
6 Altering dispositions made on death	A3(g)(iv)

Introduction

In the previous chapters we have seen how to calculate chargeable gains. We now look at various reliefs relating to gains.

Entrepreneurs' relief is a very important relief. It applies on the disposal of a business and on the disposal of certain trading company shares. It reduces the rate of tax payable from 18% or 28% to 10% on all or part of the chargeable gains arising on such disposals.

In certain circumstances it may be possible to defer a gain – that is to remove it from an immediate charge to CGT. However, it is important to realise the gain has not been exempted and it may become charged in the future.

Deferral reliefs operate in two ways. First, the gain may be deducted from the base cost of an asset (for example, rollover relief for replacement with non-depreciating business assets, incorporation relief, gift relief). Second, the gain may be 'frozen' until a certain event occurs (deferral relief for replacement with depreciating business assets, EIS deferral relief).

Finally we consider the CGT implications of varying a will.

In the next chapter we will look some further rules for gains and losses.

Study guide

		Intellectual level
3	**Chargeable gains and capital gains tax liabilities in situations involving further overseas aspects and in relation to closely related persons and trusts together with the application of additional exemptions and reliefs**	
(a)	The contents of the Paper F6 study guide for chargeable gains under headings:	2
•	D6 The use of exemptions and reliefs in deferring and minimising tax liabilities arising on the disposal of capital assets	
(g)	The use of exemptions and reliefs in deferring and minimising tax liabilities arising on the disposal of capital assets:	3
(i)	Understand and apply enterprise investment scheme reinvestment relief	
(ii)	Advise on the availability of entrepreneurs' relief in relation to associated disposals	
(iii)	Understand and apply the relief that is available on the transfer of an unincorporated business to a limited company.	
(iv)	Understand the capital gains tax implications of the variation of wills	

Exam guide

Deferring and minimising tax liabilities is likely to feature at some point in your exam. The methods of deferring capital gains should be very familiar to you.

Knowledge brought forward from earlier studies

This chapter revises entrepreneurs' relief, gift relief, rollover relief for the replacement of business assets and incorporation relief which you will have studied in Paper F6. The examiner has identified essential underpinning knowledge from the F6 syllabus which is particularly important that you revise as part of your P6 studies. In this chapter, the relevant topics are:

		Intellectual level
D6	**The use of exemptions and reliefs in deferring and minimising tax liabilities arising on the disposal of capital assets**	
(a)	Explain and apply entrepreneurs' relief as it applies to individuals.	2
(b)	Explain and apply rollover relief as it applies to individuals and companies.	2
(c)	Explain and apply holdover relief for the gift of business assets.	2

You will be familiar with incorporation relief as this was in the F6 syllabus in previous years.

The chapter extends your studies on entrepreneurs' relief. Gift relief for gifts to trusts, EIS deferral relief, and the CGT consequences of varying a will are new.

There are no changes in 2013/14 from the material studied at F6 level in 2012/13.

1 Entrepreneurs' relief

Entrepreneurs' relief applies on the disposal of a business and certain trading company shares. The rate of tax on gains qualifying for entrepreneurs' relief is 10%.

One of the competencies you require to fulfil performance objective 20 of the PER is the ability to assist with tax planning. You can apply the knowledge you obtain from this section of the text to help to demonstrate this competence.

1.1 Conditions for entrepreneurs' relief

Entrepreneurs' relief is available where there is a **material disposal of business assets. There are three categories of disposal, as explained below.**

1.1.1 Disposal of the whole or part of a business

The first category is a disposal of the **whole or part of a business. The business must have been owned by the individual** throughout the period of **one year** ending with the date of the disposal. It is important to note that there has to be a **disposal of the whole or part of the business as a going concern**, not just a disposal of individual assets in a continuing business.

The business must be a **trade, profession or vocation** conducted on a **commercial basis with a view to the realisation of profits**. It can be a sole trader business or one carried on as a partnership of which the individual is a partner.

Relief is only available on **relevant business assets.** These are assets **used for the purposes of the business** and **cannot include shares and securities** nor **assets held as investments.**

1.1.2 Disposal of assets used in a business which has ceased

The second category is a disposal of **one or more assets in use for the purposes of a business** at the time when the business **ceases to be carried on**. The following conditions must be satisfied:

(a) The business has been owned by the individual throughout **the period of one year** ending with the date on which the business ceases to be carried on; and

(b) The date of cessation is within **three years** before the date of the disposal.

As **for the first category**, relief is only available on **relevant business assets, not shares and securities** nor **assets held as investments.**

1.1.3 Disposal of shares or securities

The third category is a **disposal by an individual of shares or securities in a company**. The following conditions must be usually be satisfied:

(a) The company is **the individual's personal company (see further below)**; and
(b) The company is either a **trading company** or **holding company of a trading group**; and
(c) The individual is an **officer or employee** of the company (or a group company).

These conditions must be satisfied either:

(a) Throughout the period of **one year** ending with the date of the disposal; or

(b) Throughout the period of **one year** ending with the date on which the company (or group) **ceases to be a trading company (or trading group)** and that date is within the period of **three years** ending with the date of the disposal.

A **personal company** in relation to an individual is one where:

(a) The individual holds **at least 5% of the ordinary share capital**; and

(b) The individual can exercise **at least 5% of the voting rights in the company** by virtue of that holding of shares.

If the **shares are qualifying EMI (Enterprise Management Incentive) shares**, the conditions are slightly different. The shares must have been **acquired under an option was had been granted at least one year prior to the date of disposal of the shares** and the **individual must have been an officer or an employee of the trading company (or one of the companies in the trading group) throughout that one year period**. There is no minimum ownership period for the shares themselves nor a minimum percentage shareholding.

1.2 The operation of the relief

Where there is a material disposal of business assets which results in both gains and losses, losses are netted off against gains to give a single chargeable gain on the disposal of the business assets.

The rate of tax on this chargeable gain is 10%.

An individual may use losses on assets not qualifying for entrepreneurs' relief and the annual exempt amount in the most beneficial way. This means that these amounts should **first be set against gains which do not qualify for entrepreneurs' relief** in order to save tax at either 18% or 28% rather than at 10%.

The chargeable gain qualifying for entrepreneurs' relief is treated as the lowest part of the amount on which an individual is chargeable to capital gains tax. Although this does not affect the tax on the gain qualifying for entrepreneurs' relief (which is always at 10%), it may have an effect on the rate of tax on other taxable gains.

1.3 Example: entrepreneurs' relief

Simon sells his business, all the assets of which qualify for entrepreneurs' relief, in September 2013. The chargeable gain arising is £10,000.

Simon also made a chargeable gain of £24,000 in December 2013 on an asset which did not qualify for entrepreneurs' relief.

Simon has taxable income of £18,000 in 2013/14.

The CGT payable for 2013/14 is calculated as follows:

	Gains	*CGT*
	£	£
Gains qualifying for entrepreneurs' relief		
Taxable gain	10,000	
CGT @ 10%		1,000
Gains not qualifying for entrepreneurs' relief		
Gain	24,000	
Less: annual exempt amount (best use)	(10,900)	
Taxable gain	13,100	
CGT on £(32,010 – 18,000 – £10,000)		
= 4,010 @ 18%		722
CGT on £(13,100 – 4,010) = 9,090 @ 28%		2,545
CGT 2013/14		4,267

Note that the £10,000 gain qualifying for entrepreneurs' relief is deducted from the basic rate limit for the purposes of computing the rate of tax on the gain not qualifying for entrepreneurs' relief.

1.4 Lifetime limit

There is a lifetime limit of £10 million of gains on which entrepreneurs' relief can be claimed.

Limit on entrepreneurs' relief

Maureen sells a shareholding, which qualifies for entrepreneurs' relief, in January 2014, realising a gain of £9,300,000. Maureen had already made a claim for entrepreneurs' relief in 2012/13 in respect of gains totalling £900,000. Maureen also makes an allowable loss of £(20,000) in 2013/14 on an asset not qualifying for entrepreneurs' relief. Her taxable income for 2013/14 is £200,000.

Calculate the CGT payable by Maureen for 2013/14.

Answer

	Gains	*CGT*
	£	£
Gain qualifying for entrepreneurs' relief		
£(10,000,000 – 900,000)	9,100,000	
CGT @ 10% on £9,100,000		910,000
Gains not qualifying for entrepreneurs' relief		
£(9,300,000 – 9,100,000)	200,000	
Less: allowable loss (best use)	(20,000)	
Net gain	180,000	
Less: annual exempt amount (best use)	(10,900)	
Taxable gain	169,100	
CGT @ 28% on £169,100		47,348
Total CGT due		957,348

1.5 Associated disposals

Entrepreneurs' relief is also available on associated disposals.

An associated disposal asset is **an asset which is owned by an individual** and **used for at least one year for business purposes by a partnership of which he is a partner or by his personal trading company.**

An associated disposal is one which is associated with a main disposal of all or part of the individual's partnership interest or a disposal of shares in the company, as relevant, **such that there is a single withdrawal from participation in the partnership or the company by the individual.** Because of the requirement for there to be single withdrawal, there should normally not be a significant time interval between the main disposal and the associated disposal.

If the individual charged rent to the partnership or company, entrepreneurs' relief will be restricted. If a full market rent was charged, there will be no entrepreneurs' relief. If less than a full market rent was charged, a just and reasonable proportion of gain will be eligible for entrepreneurs' relief. For example if the rental charged was 75% of the full market rent (100 – 75) = 25% of the gain will be eligible for entrepreneurs' relief.

1.6 Interaction with share reorganisations and takeovers

This topic was dealt in Chapter 12 Section 3.8 and you may wish to re-read this section now.

1.7 Claim

An individual must claim entrepreneurs' relief: it is not automatic.

The claim deadline is the first anniversary of 31 January following the end of the tax year of disposal. For a 2013/14 disposal, the taxpayer must claim by 31 January 2016.

2 Gift relief (holdover relief)

2.1 The relief

Gift relief is available on both outright gifts and sales at an undervalue of business assets. Gift relief is also available on gifts which are immediately chargeable to inheritance tax.

One of the competencies you require to fulfil performance objective 20 of the PER is the ability to assist with tax planning. You can apply the knowledge you obtain from this section of the text to help to demonstrate this competence.

If an individual gives away a qualifying asset, the transferor and the transferee can jointly elect, or where a trust is the transferee, the transferor alone can elect, within four years after the end of the tax year of the transfer (by 5 April 2018 for a disposal in 2013/14), **that the transferor's gain be reduced, possibly to nil. The transferee is then deemed to acquire the asset for market value at the date of transfer less the transferor's deferred gain.**

If a disposal involves actual consideration rather than being an outright gift but is still not a bargain made at arm's length, the proceeds are deemed to be the market value of the asset **and any excess of actual consideration over allowable cost is chargeable immediately and only the balance of the gain is deferred**. The amount chargeable immediately is limited to the full gain.

Question — Gift relief

On 6 December 2013 Angelo sold to his son Michael a freehold shop valued at £200,000 for £50,000, and claimed gift relief. Angelo had originally purchased the shop from which he had run his business in July 2006 for £30,000. He continued to run his business from another shop. Michael decided to sell the shop in May 2014 for £195,000. Compute any chargeable gains arising. Assume the rules of CGT in 2013/14 continue to apply in May 2014.

Answer

(a) *Angelo's CGT position (2013/14)*

	£
Proceeds (market value)	200,000
Less cost	(30,000)
Gain	170,000
Less gain deferred	(150,000)
Chargeable gain £(50,000 – 30,000)	20,000

(b) *Michael's CGT position (2014/15)*

	£
Proceeds	195,000
Less cost £(200,000 – 150,000)	(50,000)
Gain	145,000

You may need to consider whether it would be more beneficial for an individual to claim entrepreneurs' relief or gift relief or both reliefs. Remember that entrepreneurs' relief is only available on the disposal of the whole or part of a business and not on individual business assets, so it is possible that only gift relief will apply to the disposal anyway.

An individual might wish to claim entrepreneurs' relief instead of gift relief if only a very small amount of gains are left in charge and are taxable at the advantageous rate of 10%.

If both reliefs are claimed, gift relief will apply first and then entrepreneurs' relief will apply to the remaining gain. This may be relevant if there is actual consideration paid so that gift relief covers only part of the gain.

Question — Interaction of reliefs

On 10 January 2014, Zack sold his business to his son, Darren. The only chargeable assets were goodwill which Zack had built up from the start of his business and a freehold shop which Zack had bought in September 2003 for £35,000. The goodwill was valued at £25,000 and the shop at £80,000. Darren paid Zack £10,000 for the goodwill and £60,000 for the shop.

Zack made a claim for entrepreneurs' relief and Zack and Darren made a claim for gift relief. Zack has no other chargeable assets.

Show the CGT positions of Zack and Darren.

Answer

(a) Zack's CGT position

	£	£
Goodwill		
Market value	25,000	
Less cost	(nil)	
Gain	25,000	
Less gain deferred	(15,000)	
Chargeable gain £(10,000 – nil)		10,000
Shop		
Market value	80,000	
Less cost	(35,000)	
Gain	45,000	
Less gain deferred	(20,000)	
Chargeable gain £(60,000 – 35,000)		25,000
Gains left in charge after gift relief		35,000
Less annual exempt amount		(10,900)
Taxable gains		24,100
CGT @ 10%		2,410

(b) Darren's CGT position

	£
Goodwill	
Market value	25,000
Less gain deferred	(15,000)
Cost for future disposal	10,000
Shop	£
Market value	80,000
Less gain deferred	(20,000)
Cost for future disposal	60,000

2.2 Qualifying assets

Gift relief can be claimed on gifts or sales at undervalue as follows.

(a) Transfers of **business assets**

  (i) Trade assets
  (ii) Agricultural property (whether farmed by the owner or tenant - see further below)
  (iii) Shares and securities (except where the transferee is a company)

(b) Transfers of **any assets** subject to an immediate inheritance tax (IHT) charge. IHT is covered later in this Text.

Transfers of business assets are transfers of assets

(a) **Used in a trade, profession or vocation** carried on:

  (1) By the donor

  (2) If the donor is an individual, by a trading company which is his 'personal company' or a member of a trading group of which the holding company is his 'personal company' (a personal company is one in which the individual can exercise at least 5% of the voting rights).

  (3) If the donor is a trustee, by the trustee or by a beneficiary who has an interest in possession in the settled property (see later in this Text).

  If the asset was used for the purposes of the trade, profession or vocation for only part of its period of ownership, the gain to be held over is the gain otherwise eligible × period of such use/total period of ownership.

  If the asset was a building or structure only partly used for trade, professional or vocational purposes, only the **part of the gain attributable to the part so used is eligible for gift relief**

(b) **Agricultural property** which would attract inheritance tax agricultural property relief (see later in this Text). The restrictions for periods of non-trade use and for partial trade use mentioned above do not apply.

(c) **Shares and securities in trading companies**, or holding companies of trading groups, where:

  (1) The shares or securities are **not listed on a recognised stock exchange**, or

  (2) If the donor is an individual, the company concerned is his **personal company** (defined as above), or

  (3) If the donor is a trustee, the trustee can exercise 25% or more of the voting rights.

  If the company has chargeable non-business assets (ie investments) at the time of the gift, and either (2) or (3) applied at any time in the last 12 months, **the gain to be held over is the gain otherwise chargeable × the value of the chargeable business assets/the value of the chargeable assets.**

Question — **Gift of shares – CBA/CA restriction**

Morris gifts shares in his personal company to his son Minor realising a gain of £100,000. The company' statement of financial position at the date of the gift shows:

	£
Freehold factory and offices	150,000
Leasehold warehouse	80,000
Investments	120,000
Current assets	200,000
	550,000

You are required to show the gain qualifying for hold-over relief and the chargeable gain.

Answer

Gain qualifying for hold-over relief:

$$£100,000 \times \frac{\text{Chargeable business assets (CBA)}}{\text{Chargeable assets (CA)}} = £100,000 \times \frac{150+80}{150+80+120}$$

$$= £100,000 \times \frac{230}{350}$$

$$= \underline{\underline{£65,714}}$$

The gain which is not held-over (ie chargeable in current year) is £100,000 – £65,714 = $\underline{\underline{£34,286}}$

If relief is claimed on a transfer of business assets, and that transfer is (or later becomes) chargeable to inheritance tax, then when the transferee disposes of the assets his gain is reduced by the IHT finally payable (but not so as to create a loss).

Transfers subject to an immediate IHT charge include most gifts to trusts. A transfer will be regarded as chargeable to IHT even if it falls within the nil rate band of that tax or is covered by the IHT annual exemption. Gifts to settlor interested trusts, however, do not qualify for gift relief.

If a transfer of business assets could also be subject to an immediate charge to inheritance tax, the rules relating to the latter category apply and the restrictions related to period of use and to chargeable business assets therefore do not apply.

Remember that IHT is covered in detail later in this Text. You should return to this section once you have studied the relevant chapters.

2.3 Anti-avoidance rules

Gift relief is not available if the transferee is not resident in the UK at the time of the gift. If the transferee is an individual who becomes not resident in the UK in any of the six tax years following the year of the transfer and before disposing of the asset transferred, then the gain held over is chargeable on him as if it arose immediately before he becomes not resident in the UK.

It is not possible to claim gift relief on transfers to a settlor-interested trust (see later in this Text).

Exam focus point

Gift relief is normally used whenever a business or business asset is gifted, but you should look out for the restriction for a non-resident donee.

You should also consider whether retaining the asset until death so as to obtain the tax free uplift to probate value would be advantageous.

3 The replacement of business assets (rollover relief)

3.1 Conditions

FAST FORWARD

When assets falling within certain classes are sold and other such assets are bought, it is possible to defer gains on the assets sold by claiming rollover relief.

One of the competencies you require to fulfil performance objective 20 of the PER is the ability to assist with tax planning. You can apply the knowledge you obtain from this section of the text to help to demonstrate this competence.

A gain may be 'rolled over' (deferred) where it arises on the disposal of a business asset which is replaced. This is **rollover relief**. A claim cannot specify that only part of a gain is to be rolled over. A claim for the relief must be made by the later of four years from the end of the tax year in which the disposal of the old asset takes place and four years from the end of the tax year in which the new asset is acquired. For example, if the old asset is disposed of in 2012/13 and the new asset is acquired in 2013/14, the time limit for a claim to roll-over relief is 5 April 2018 (four years from the end of the tax year in which the new asset is acquired).

All the following conditions must be met.

(a) **The old asset sold and the new asset bought are both used only in the trade** or trades carried on **by the person claiming rollover relief**. Where part of a building is in non-trade use for all or a substantial part of the period of ownership, the building (and the land on which it stands) can be treated as two separate assets, the trade part (qualifying) and the non-trade part (non-qualifying). This split cannot be made for other assets.

(b) **The old asset and the new asset both fall within one** (but not necessarily the same one) **of the following classes.**

   (i) Land and buildings (including parts of buildings) occupied, as well as used, only for the purpose of the trade

   (ii) Fixed (that is, immovable) plant and machinery

   (iii) Goodwill (not for companies)

(c) **Reinvestment of the proceeds of the old asset takes place in a period beginning one year before and ending three years after the date of the disposal.**

(d) **The new asset is brought into use in the trade on its acquisition** (not necessarily immediately, but not after any significant and unnecessary delay).

The new asset can be for use in a different trade from the old asset.

A rollover claim is not allowed when a taxpayer buys premises, sells part of the premises at a profit and then claims to roll over the gain into the part retained. However, a rollover claim is allowed (by concession) when the proceeds of the old asset are spent on improving a qualifying asset which the taxpayer already owns. The improved asset must already be in use for a trade, or be brought into trade use immediately the improvement work is finished.

3.2 Operation of relief

FAST FORWARD

If an amount less than the proceeds of the old asset is invested in the new assets, a gain equal to the difference will be chargeable up to a maximum of the actual gain.

Deferral is obtained by deducting the chargeable gain from the cost of the new asset. For full relief, the whole of the consideration for the disposal must be reinvested. Where only part is reinvested, a part of the gain equal to the lower of the full gain and the amount not reinvested will be liable to tax immediately.

The new asset will have a base cost for chargeable gains purposes, of its purchase price less the gain rolled over into its acquisition.

Question — **Rollover relief**

A freehold factory was purchased by Zoë for business use in August 2004. It was sold in December 2013 for £70,000, giving rise to a gain of £17,950. A replacement factory was purchased in June 2014 for £60,000. Compute the base cost of the replacement factory, taking into account any possible rollover of the gain from the disposal in December 2013.

Answer

	£
Total gain	17,950
Less gain rolled over	(7,950)
Chargeable immediately (ie amount not reinvested: £(70,000 – 60,000))	10,000
Cost of new factory	60,000
Less rolled over gain	(7,950)
Base cost of new factory	52,050

You may need to consider whether an individual should claim rollover relief or entrepreneurs' relief or both reliefs. It will be relatively unusual for both reliefs to be available. This is because entrepreneurs' relief only applies on the disposal of a business or part of a business and rollover relief is typically relevant where there is the sale of an individual business asset and the individual continues to carry on the business.

However, if both reliefs can be claimed, consider whether it would better for the individual to claim entrepreneurs' relief instead of rollover relief if only a very small amount of gains are left in charge and are taxable at the advantageous rate of 10%.

If both reliefs are claimed, entrepreneurs' relief will apply to the gain left in charge after rollover relief has been applied. This will be relevant when there is an amount not reinvested so that rollover relief does not cover the whole of the gain.

3.3 Non-business use

Where the old asset has not been used in the trade for a fraction of its period of ownership, the amount of the gain that can be rolled over is reduced by the same fraction. If the proceeds are not fully reinvested the restriction on rollover by the amount not reinvested is also calculated by considering only the proportion of proceeds relating to the part of the asset used in the trade or the proportion relating to the period of trade use.

Question

Assets with non-business use

John bought a factory for £150,000 on 11 January 2009, for use in his business. From 11 January 2010, he let the factory out for a period of two years. He then used the factory for his own business again, until he sold it on 10 July 2013 for £225,000. On 13 January 2014, he purchased another factory for use in his business. This second factory cost £100,000.

Calculate the chargeable gain on the sale of the first factory and the base cost of the second factory.

Answer

Gain on first factory

	Non-business	*Business*
	£	£
Proceeds of sale (24:30) (W1)	100,000	125,000
Less cost (24:30)	(66,667)	(83,333)
Gain before rollover relief	33,333	41,667
Less rollover relief		(16,667)
Gain (W2)	33,333	25,000

Base cost of second factory

	£
Cost	100,000
Less gain rolled over	(16,667)
Base cost c/f	83,333

Workings

1 *Use of factory*

Total ownership period:

11.1.09 – 10.07.13 = 54 months

Attributable to non business use:

11.1.10 – 10.1.12 = 24 months

Attributable to business use (remainder: 54m – 24m) = 30 months

2 *Proceeds not reinvested*

	£
Proceeds of business element	125,000
Less: cost of new factory	(100,000)
Not reinvested	25,000

3.4 Depreciating assets

Where the replacement asset is a depreciating asset, the gain is not rolled over by reducing the cost of the replacement asset. Rather it is 'frozen', ie deferred, until it crystallises (ie becomes chargeable) on the earliest of:

(a) The disposal of the replacement asset

(b) The date the replacement asset ceases to be used in the trade (but the gain does not crystallise on the taxpayer's death)

(c) Ten years after the acquisition of the replacement asset

Key term

An asset is a **depreciating asset** if it is, or within the next ten years will become, a wasting asset. So, any asset with an expected life of 60 years or less is covered by this definition. Plant and machinery is always treated as depreciating.

Question — **Deferred gain on investment into depreciating asset**

Norma bought a freehold shop for use in her business in June 2011 for £125,000. She sold it for £140,000 on 1 August 2012. On 10 July 2012, Norma bought some fixed plant and machinery to use in her business, costing £150,000. Norma makes a claim to defer the gain on the shop in relation to the acquisition of the plant and machinery. She then sells the plant and machinery for £167,000 on 19 November 2013. Show Norma's CGT position.

Answer

Gain deferred

	£
Proceeds of shop	140,000
Less cost	(125,000)
Gain	15,000

Sale of plant and machinery

	£
Proceeds	167,000
Less cost	(150,000)
Gain	17,000

Total gain chargeable on sale (gain on plant and machinery plus crystallised gain)

£(15,000 + 17,000) £32,000

Where a gain on disposal is deferred on the purchase of a replacement depreciating asset it is possible to transfer the deferred, or 'frozen', gain to a non-depreciating asset provided the non-depreciating asset is bought before the deferred gain has crystallised.

3.5 Identifying availability of reliefs

It can be confusing to identify the availability of replacement of business assets (rollover) relief and/or gift relief and/or entrepreneurs' relief on a disposal because the conditions are similar. The following examples show whether these reliefs are available in a variety of circumstances. Remember that **all of these reliefs require a claim** so it is possible to choose which relief to claim and that **it may be possible to claim more than one relief** on a disposal.

3.6 Example: rollover relief, gift relief and entrepreneurs' relief

(a) Gary sold 10,000 ordinary shares in N Ltd for their market value of £20,000. Gary had acquired the shares four years previously when he also became an employee of N Ltd, but the shares are not EMI shares. N Ltd has always been a trading company. The shares represent 10% of the ordinary shares in N Ltd and carry the same percentage of voting rights in the company. Two months later, Gary acquired a 5% shareholding in Q plc, another unquoted trading company, for £20,000.

Relief	Available	Comments
Rollover relief	No	Shares are not qualifying assets for replacement of business assets relief (neither as the old assets nor the new asset).
Gift relief	No	Sale at market value does not have an element of gift (must be either outright gift or sale at less than market value).
Entrepreneurs' relief	Yes	(a) N Ltd is Gary's personal company (at least 5% ordinary share capital and voting rights); and (b) N Ltd is a trading company; and (c) Gary is an employee of N Ltd and these conditions are satisfied throughout the period of one year ending with the date of the disposal.

(b) Morton sold a freehold warehouse for £150,000 (market value) which he had occupied and used for five years in his sole trader business. The gain arising was £45,000. He had bought a freehold shop which he immediately occupied and started using in his trade for £130,000 eight months previously.

Relief	Available	Comments
Rollover relief	Yes - partially	(a) The old asset sold and the new asset bought are both used only in the trade or trades carried on by the person claiming rollover relief. (b) The old asset and the new asset both fall within one of the classes of assets (here both are land and buildings). (c) Reinvestment of the proceeds of the old asset takes place in a period beginning one year before and ending three years after the date of the disposal. (d) The new asset is brought into use in the trade on its acquisition. The excess proceeds not reinvested £(150,000 – 130,000) = £20,000 are chargeable immediately. The remainder of the gain £(45,000 – 20,000) = £25,000 is rolled over into the base cost of the new asset.
Gift relief	No	Sale at market value does not have an element of gift (must be either outright gift or sale at less than market value).
Entrepreneurs' relief	No	The disposal of individual assets in a continuing business does not qualify for entrepreneurs' relief.

(c) Lynne had been in business as a sole trader for five years. She closed her business which had two assets, a freehold shop she had owned for three years and a freehold warehouse she had owned for six months. Immediately after cessation, she sold the warehouse to her son Steven at less than market value. The price paid by Steven was £9,000 more than Lynne had paid for the warehouse. Four months after cessation, she sold the shop to Joss at market value. The gain on the warehouse based on market value is £15,000.

Relief	Available	Comments
Rollover relief	No	There is no acquisition of replacement assets.
Gift relief	No – on shop Yes – partial on warehouse	Sale at market value. Sale at undervalue of asset used in business by donor (there is no qualifying period). £9,000 of the gain is chargeable immediately. The remaining £(15,000 – 9,000) = £6,000 is available for gift relief.
Entrepreneurs' relief	Yes on both shop and warehouse	Disposal of one or more assets in use for the purposes of a business at the time at which the business ceases to be carried on since: (a) The business was owned by Lynne throughout the period of one year ending with the date on which the business ceased to be carried on; and (b) The date of cessation is within three years before the date of the disposal. The qualifying period applies to the **business**, not to individual assets and so entrepreneurs' relief is still available on the warehouse.

3.7 Example: gift relief and entrepreneurs' relief

Here we consider the availability of gift relief and entrepreneurs' relief on the gift of shares in a company. When considering reliefs in relation to shares, it is particularly important to look at the percentage shareholding represented by the shares, whether the company is quoted or not, and whether the individual is an employee or officer of the company.

These conditions are illustrated in the examples below where we have assumed that the shares have been owned for two years prior to the disposal (and are not EMI shares) and other circumstances relevant for entrepreneurs' relief (eg whether the company is a trading company, whether the shareholder is an officer or employee of the company) have existed throughout the period of ownership.

Trading company or holding company of trading group	Unquoted company	Percentage shareholding and voting rights	Officer or employee of company or group company	Gift relief available?	Entrepreneurs' relief available?
Yes	Yes	3%	No	Yes – any % of unquoted trading co. shares, no employment condition.	No – must be officer or employee
No	Yes	8%	Yes	No – must be trading company	No – must be trading company
Yes	Yes	4%	Yes	Yes - any % of unquoted trading co. shares	No – must be personal company (at least 5% ordinary share capital and voting rights)
Yes	No	8%	No	Yes – quoted company but personal company (at least 5% of the voting rights), no employment condition.	No – must be officer or employee
Yes	No	15%	Yes	Yes - personal company (at least 5% of the voting rights).	Yes – personal company (at least 5% ordinary share capital and voting rights) and officer or employee.

4 The transfer of a business to a company (incorporation relief)

4.1 The relief

FAST FORWARD

When an individual transfers his unincorporated business to a company, the gain arising will be deducted from the cost of the shares received, unless the individual elects otherwise.

One of the competencies you require to fulfil performance objective 20 of the PER is the ability to assist with tax planning. You can apply the knowledge you obtain from this section of the text to help to demonstrate this competence.

If an individual transfers his business to a company, he makes a disposal of the business assets for CGT purposes and realises net chargeable gains (chargeable gains less allowable losses) on those assets. It is, however, clearly undesirable to discourage traders from incorporating their businesses and so a relief is available.

The relief can also apply where an individual sells his unincorporated business to a company where the vendor and the company were not connected prior to the sale.

The relief (called incorporation relief) is automatic (so no claim need be made). **All or some of the gains are held over if all the following conditions are met.**

(a) The **business is transferred as a going concern**
(b) **All its assets** (or all its assets other than cash) **are transferred**
(c) **The consideration is wholly or partly in shares**

Formula to learn

The amount deferred is found by applying the fraction:

$$\frac{\textbf{Value of shares received from the company}}{\textbf{Total value of consideration from the company}} \times \textbf{gain before relief}$$

This amount is then deducted from the base cost of the shares received. The company is deemed to acquire the assets transferred at their market values.

Question — **Incorporation relief**

Mr P transferred his business to a company in July 2013, realising a gain of £240,000 on its only business asset (a factory). The consideration comprised cash of £150,000 and shares at a market value of £750,000.

(a) What is the gain on the transfer after incorporation relief but before any other reliefs?
(b) What is the base cost of the shares for any future disposal?

Answer

(a)

	£
Gain before incorporation relief	240,000
Less incorporation relief: $\frac{750,000}{150,000 + 750,000} \times £240,000$	(200,000)
Gain after incorporation relief	40,000

(b)

	£
Market value	750,000
Less gain deferred	(200,000)
Base cost of shares	550,000

4.2 Election to disapply incorporation relief

An individual can elect not to receive incorporation relief. The election must usually be made by 31 January, 34 months after the end of the tax year of disposal. An election might be made if the taxpayer can set losses and/or the annual exempt amount against the gains which would otherwise be deferred under incorporation relief. The election therefore results in a higher base cost of the shares received on incorporation and so a lower gain on a future disposal of the shares.

Since incorporation usually involves the disposal of the whole or part of a business, entrepreneurs' relief can usually also be claimed on incorporation. If the election is made to disapply incorporation relief, entrepreneurs' relief can then be claimed. This may be beneficial if only a very small amount of gains are left in charge and are taxable at the advantageous rate of 10%.

Question — **Disclaiming incorporation relief (1)**

Willow transferred her business to B Ltd on 1 December 2013, comprising the following assets:

Asset	*Market value*	*Gain on disposal*
	£	£
Freehold shop	150,000	8,000
Goodwill	20,000	20,000
Inventory	25,000	n/a
Cash	5,000	n/a

The consideration for the transfer was 200,000 £1 B Ltd ordinary shares.

Willow had losses brought forward from 2012/13 of £(15,000). She made no other disposals in 2013/14 and does not intend to make any disposals in the foreseeable future.

Explain the capital gains tax implications if *either*:

(a) incorporation relief applies on the transfer; *or*

(b) Willow makes an election to disapply incorporation relief and claims entrepreneurs' relief.

On the basis of these computations, what advice should be given to Willow?

Answer

(a) If incorporation relief applies on the transfer, the gains of £(8,000 + 20,000) = £28,000 are deferred (ie will not be chargeable in 2013/14). The gains are deducted from the base cost of the shares received. The base cost of the shares is £(200,000 – 28,000) = £172,000.

(b) If Willow makes an election to disapply incorporation relief, the gains of £28,000 will be chargeable in 2013/14. If she makes a claim for entrepreneurs' relief, her capital gains tax payable in 2013/14 will be as follows:

	£
Gains	28,000
Less: loss b/f	(15,000)
Net gains	13,000
Less annual exempt amount	(10,900)
Taxable gains	2,100
CGT on £2,100 @ 10% (entrepreneurs' relief rate)	210

The base cost of the shares will be £200,000.

On the basis of these computations, Willow should be advised to make an election to disapply incorporation relief but to claim entrepreneurs' relief. This will use her brought forward loss (which is unlikely to be utilised in the foreseeable future) and annual exempt amount for 2013/14 and results in only a small amount of capital gains tax being payable. The base cost of the shares in B Ltd is increased by £28,000 which will result in a smaller gain on their eventual disposal.

Another situation where it may be beneficial to disapply incorporation relief and claim entrepreneurs' relief is where the shares received on incorporation will not qualify for entrepreneurs' relief and there are plans to dispose of them. It may be better to pay some capital gains tax on incorporation at 10% and have a higher base cost for the shares received, rather than deferring the gains on incorporation into the base cost of the shares and paying capital gains tax at 18% or 28% on their sale.

Question

Disclaiming incorporation relief (2)

Briony is a dentist who has run her dental practice as a sole trade since 2004. On 1 December 2013, Briony accepted an offer from a company, Brighter Smiles Ltd, to transfer her business to the company in exchange for 25,000 ordinary shares valued at £10 each. These shares represent a 2.5% shareholding in Brighter Smiles Ltd, which is an unquoted trading company. The gains on disposal of the assets of the sole trade on the transfer amounted to £120,000.

Briony also became an employee of Brighter Smiles Ltd at the time of the transfer of her business on fixed term contract until 30 November 2015. On that date she intends to sell her shareholding in Brighter Smiles Ltd. The value of shares in Brighter Smiles Ltd on 30 November 2015 can be taken to be £15 per share and the rates of capital gains tax in 2015/16 can be assumed to be the same as in 2013/14.

Briony makes disposals of quoted shares each year to exactly utilise her annual exempt amount. She is a higher rate taxpayer.

Compute the total capital gains tax payable on the transfer of the business and the disposal of the shares in Brighter Smiles Ltd if *either*:

(a) incorporation relief applies on the transfer; *or*
(b) Briony makes an election to disapply incorporation relief and claims entrepreneurs' relief on the transfer.

On the basis of these computations, what advice should be given to Briony?

Answer

(a) If incorporation relief applies on the transfer, the gains of £120,000 will not be chargeable in 2013/14. The base cost of the shares in Brighter Smiles Ltd will therefore be £([25,000 × £10] – 120,000) = £130,000.

On the disposal of the Brighter Smiles Ltd shares in 2015/16, CGT will be payable as follows:

	£
Proceeds 25,000 × £15	375,000
Less: cost	(130,000)
Taxable gains	245,000
Capital gains tax on £245,000 @ 28%	68,600

The conditions for entrepreneurs' relief are not satisfied on this disposal as Brighter Smiles Ltd is not Briony's personal company since she only owns a 2.5% shareholding (less than the 5% required).

The total capital gains tax payable is therefore £68,600.

(b) If Briony makes an election to disapply incorporation relief and claims entrepreneurs' relief, capital gains tax will be payable as follows:

	£
Taxable gains	120,000
Capital gains tax on £120,000 @ 10%	12,000

On the disposal of the Brighter Smiles Ltd shares in 2015/16, CGT will be payable as follows:

	£
Proceeds 25,000 × £15	375,000
Less: cost 25,000 × £10	(250,000)
Taxable gains	125,000
Capital gains tax on £125,000 @ 28%	35,000

Again, conditions for entrepreneurs' relief are not satisfied on this disposal as Brighter Smiles Ltd is not Briony's personal company since she only owns a 2.5% shareholding.

The total capital gains tax payable is therefore £(12,000 + 35,000) = £47,000.

On the basis of these computations, Briony should be advised to make an election to disapply incorporation relief and claim entrepreneurs' relief as this will save capital gains tax of £(68,600 – 47,000) = £21,600. However, she must be made aware that £12,000 of the capital gains tax will be payable by 31 January 2015, with the balance of £35,000 payable by 31 January 2017, rather than the whole amount being payable by 31 January 2017 if incorporation relief applies.

4.3 Optimising the use of incorporation relief

Although the relief cannot be restricted to utilise losses brought forward, and the annual exempt amount, **it is possible to manipulate the amount of non-share consideration received** (whether in cash, loan stock, or left on loan account) **so that the gain remaining chargeable is equal to losses plus the annual exempt amount.**

A claim for entrepreneurs' relief may usually be made where not all of the consideration is received in the form of shares. In this case, entrepreneurs' relief will apply to the gain left in charge after incorporation relief has been applied.

Question — **Optimising incorporation relief**

Antonio transferred his business (market value £120,000) to a company on 16 August 2013, realising a gain of £90,000. He had capital losses brought forward of £7,100.

Advise Antonio how much of the consideration he should take as shares and how much he should leave on loan account.

Answer

Antonio should take shares worth £96,000 and leave the balance of £24,000 (£120,000 - £96,000) on loan account. These figures are found as follows:

	£
Gain before incorporation relief	90,000
Less incorporation relief (W)	(72,000)
Gain after incorporation relief	18,000
Less losses brought forward	(7,100)
	10,900
Less annual exempt amount	(10,900)
Taxable gain	nil

Working

Work backwards to calculate the incorporation relief required to defer sufficient gains to utilise annual exempt amount and losses:

	£
Annual exempt amount	10,900
Add losses	7,100
Gain covered by annual exempt amount/losses	18,000
Less total gain	(90,000)
Incorporation relief required	72,000

Once the incorporation relief figure is obtained, we can calculate the share consideration required:

$$\text{Total consideration} \times \frac{\text{Deferred gain}}{\text{Gain}}$$

$$£120,000 \times \frac{72,000}{90,000} \qquad £96,000$$

Exam focus point

When advising on the amount of share consideration to take on an incorporation, taking into account losses and the annual exempt amount, you may find it easier to work backwards from the annual exempt amount.

5 EIS deferral relief

FAST FORWARD

Gains can be deferred if an individual invests in shares in an EIS company.

5.1 Introduction

One of the competencies you require to fulfil performance objective 20 of the PER is the ability to assist with tax planning. You can apply the knowledge you obtain from this section of the text to help to demonstrate this competence.

An individual may defer a gain arising on the disposal of any type of asset if he invests in qualifying Enterprise Investment Scheme (EIS) shares (see earlier in this Text). The 'frozen', or deferred, gain will usually become chargeable when the shares are disposed of (subject to a further claim for the relief being made).

It is not necessary for the shares acquired to qualify for the EIS income tax relief.

Where both EIS deferral relief and entrepreneurs' relief can be claimed on the gain, the individual must choose which relief to claim, ie either to claim entrepreneurs' relief and pay tax at 10% on the gain or to defer the gain under the EIS rules and then pay at 18% or 28% when the gain comes back into charge. However, where a gain exceeds the £10 million lifetime limit for entrepreneurs' relief an individual can claim entrepreneurs' relief on the gain up to that limit and then defer the gain above the limit under the EIS rules.

Exam focus point

For 2013/14 individuals are able to claim a partial exemption from capital gains tax on gains made in 2013/14 if a subscription is made in SEIS shares in that year. This exemption is excluded from the P6 syllabus

5.2 Calculation of relief

The amount of the gain that can be deferred is the **lower of:**

(a) **The amount subscribed by the investor for his shares**, which has not previously been matched under this relief, and

(b) **The amount specified by the investor in the claim. This can take into account the annual exempt amount.**

Question — EIS deferral

Robert made a gain of £196,000 on the disposal of a property in 2013/14. He subscribed for some shares in a company which qualified under the EIS rules. What will the gain to defer be if:

(a) The shares cost £200,000 and Robert wants to take the maximum deferral relief possible.

(b) The shares cost £170,000 and Robert wants to take the maximum deferral relief possible.

(c) The shares cost £200,000 and Robert, who has no other chargeable assets, wishes to utilise his annual exempt amount.

Answer

(a) £196,000. The qualifying expenditure on the shares exceeds the gain, so the whole gain can be deferred.

(b) £170,000. The gain deferred is restricted to the qualifying expenditure. The remainder of the gain of £26,000 will remain in charge (subject to relief for any further investment).

(c) A claim can be made to defer £185,100. This is calculated as follows:

	£
Gain before relief	196,000
Less EIS reinvestment relief (balancing figure)	(185,100)
Gain	10,900
Less annual exempt amount	(10,900)
Taxable gain	Nil

5.3 Conditions for the relief

The gain must either arise due to the disposal of an asset or on a gain coming back into charge under this relief.

The investor must be an individual who is UK resident at the time the gain to be deferred was made and at the time the investment was made in the shares.

The company must be a qualifying company under the EIS rules (see earlier in this Text).

The shares must be qualifying shares under the EIS rules (see earlier in this Text).

The shares must be issued to the investor within the period of one year before and three years after the gain to be deferred accrues (or such longer period as HMRC may allow). If the gain accrues after the issue of the shares, the shares must still be held by the investor at the time that the gain arises.

A claim for relief must be made by within four years after the end of the tax year in which the gain to be deferred arose ie by 5 April 2018 for a disposal in 2013/14.

5.4 Gain coming back into charge

The deferred gain will crystallise, ie come back into charge, on the following events:

(a) **The investor disposing of the shares except by an inter-spouse disposal.**

(b) The spouse/civil partner of an investor disposing of the shares, if the spouse/civil partner acquired the shares from the investor.

(c) **The investor becoming non resident, broadly within three years of the issue of the shares** (except if employed full time abroad for up to three years and retaining the shares until his return to the UK).

(d) The spouse/civil partner of an investor becoming non resident, broadly within three years of the issue of the shares (except if employed full time abroad for up to three years and retaining the shares until his return to the UK), if the spouse/civil partner acquired the shares from the investor.

(e) **The shares ceasing to be eligible shares**, eg the company ceases to be a qualifying company, the money subscribed not being used for a qualifying business activity. However, relief is not withdrawn if the company becomes a quoted company. This is provided that there were no arrangements in existence at the time of the issue of the shares for the company to cease to be unquoted.

Note that the gain becomes chargeable in the year of the event, not the year when the original gain was made (if different). It will be charged on the holder of the shares at the date of the event, eg on the investor if he/she still holds the shares or the spouse/civil partner if the shares have been passed to her/him.

5.5 Anti-avoidance

The same provisions that apply for EIS income tax relief apply here (see earlier in this Text).

Exam focus point

Never overlook investment considerations; shares in an unquoted company are a high risk investment.

6 Altering dispositions made on death

FAST FORWARD

A variation or disclaimer can be used to vary a will after death. This can have IHT and CGT consequences.

6.1 Variations and disclaimers

A **variation** or **disclaimer** can be used **to secure a fairer distribution of a deceased person's estate. They can also be used for tax planning.**

A variation of a will is usually made by rewriting the terms of the will so that the assets will pass in accordance with the variation, rather than the original will. For example, if Julius dies leaving an asset to his sister, Kathleen, Kathleen can make a variation which rewrites the will to pass the asset to someone else, such as her son, Luke.

If a beneficiary under a will makes a disclaimer, the disclaimed assets pass under the terms of the will to the beneficiary next entitled. Consider the situation where Petra dies and her will passes her house to her brother, Quayle and the residue of her estate to her sister, Ruby. If Quayle disclaims his entitlement under the will, the house will pass to Ruby as part of the residue of the estate. If this is not what Quayle wants to happen to the house, for example, if he wants it to pass to his daughter, Samantha, he should make a variation, rather than a disclaimer.

6.2 CGT implications of altering dispositions made on death

If, within two years of a death the terms of a will are changed, in writing, either by a variation of the terms of the will made by the persons who benefit or would benefit under the dispositions, or by a disclaimer, the change will not be a disposal for CGT purposes. The assets disposed of are taken by the new beneficiaries at their probate value (ie market value at death), rather than at the value at the date of the disclaimer or variation, as if the assets had been left directly to those persons by the deceased.

If the beneficiaries making a variation wish the relevant terms of the will to be treated as replaced by the terms of the variation for CGT purposes, it is necessary to state this in the variation. Where a disclaimer is made, the relevant terms in the will are *automatically* treated as replaced by the terms of the disclaimer for CGT purposes, regardless of whether this is stated in the disclaimer or not.

6.3 Example: passing on assets received on death

Trevor bought a 4% shareholding in an unquoted trading company in August 2006 for £10,000. He died in May 2013. In his will he left the shares, then worth £15,000 to Clive. You will remember from earlier in this Text that transfers of assets on death are exempt disposals. Clive inherits the shares as if he had bought them at Trevor's death for their then market value of £15,000. There is no capital gain or allowable loss on Trevor's death.

In February 2014, Clive wishes to pass on the shares, now worth £28,000, to his daughter, Imogen. He can do this in either of two ways:

(a) Give the shares to Imogen. If Clive and Imogen make a joint gift relief claim (any shareholding in an unquoted trading company is a business asset for the purposes of gift relief), the gain between Trevor's death and the date of the gift of £(28,000 – 15,000) = £13,000 will be deducted from the Imogen's base cost, giving her a revised base cost of £(28,000 - 13,000) = £15,000. Clive has no CGT liability on the gift.

(b) Vary Trevor's will and include a statement for CGT that the shares are to be treated as passing in Trevor's will to Imogen. She takes them at the value at Trevor's death which is £15,000. The variation is not a CGT disposal by Clive.

The practical effect is the same for both methods – Imogen receives the shares with a base cost of £15,000 and Clive has no CGT liability when he passes the shares to Imogen.

Note that if the shares had been a 4% shareholding in a quoted trading company, gift relief would not be available since the company would not be Clive's personal company (requires at least 5% of the voting rights). In this case, only method (b) would pass the shares to Imogen at their value at Trevor's death.

6.4 IHT implications of altering dispositions made on death

Similar provisions apply for IHT purposes (see later in this Text).

Chapter roundup

- Entrepreneurs' relief applies on the disposal of a business and certain trading company shares. The rate of tax on gains qualifying for entrepreneurs' relief is 10%.
- Gift relief is available on both outright gifts and sales at an undervalue of business assets. Gift relief is also available on gifts which are immediately chargeable to inheritance tax.
- When assets falling within certain classes are sold and other such assets are bought, it is possible to defer gains on the assets sold by claiming rollover relief.
- If an amount less than the proceeds of the old asset is invested in the new assets, a gain equal to the difference will be chargeable up to a maximum of the actual gain.
- When an individual transfers his unincorporated business to a company, the gain arising will be deducted from the cost of the shares received, unless the individual elects otherwise.
- Gains can be deferred if an individual invests in shares in an EIS company.
- A variation or disclaimer can be used to vary a will after death. This can have IHT and CGT consequences.

Quick quiz

1 Peter sells his business as a going concern in August 2013, realising gains of £500,000. He has not made any previous disposals. Calculate Peter's CGT on the disposal.

2 Which disposals of shares qualify for gift relief?

3 What assets are eligible for rollover relief on the replacement of business assets by an individual?

4 What deferral of a gain is available when a business asset is replaced with a depreciating business asset?

5 What are the conditions for deferring gains on the incorporation of a business?

6 When is EIS deferral relief available?

7 When will a gain deferred using EIS deferral relief come back into charge?

Answers to quick quiz

1

	£
Gains	500,000
Less: annual exempt amount	(10,900)
Taxable gain	489,100
CGT @ 10%	48,910

2 Shares which qualify for gift relief are those in trading companies which

- are not listed on a recognised stock exchange, or
- where the donor is an individual, which are in that individual's personal company, or
- where the donor is a trustee, where the trustee can exercise 25% or more of the voting rights in the company

3 Assets eligible for rollover relief by an individual are:

- land and buildings
- fixed plant and machinery
- goodwill

4 Where a depreciating asset is acquired, the gain is 'frozen', or deferred until it crystallises on the earliest of the disposal of the replacement asset, the date the replacement asset ceases to be used in the trade and ten years after the acquisition of the replacement asset.

5 The conditions for incorporation relief are:

- the business is transferred as a going concern,
- all of its assets (or all assets other than cash) are transferred,
- the consideration is wholly or partly in shares

6 EIS deferral relief is available where an individual makes a gain (on any type of asset) and invests in EIS shares within a certain time period.

7 A deferred gain will come back into charge where:

- investor disposes of the shares (except inter-spouse/civil partner)
- investor's civil partner/spouse disposes of shares (if acquired from investor)
- investor (or investor's spouse/civil partner who acquires shares from investor) becomes non-resident within 3 years of issue of shares, unless employed full-time abroad for up to 3 years
- shares cease to be eligible shares (does not generally include becoming quoted)

Now try the question below from the Exam Question Bank

Number	Level	Marks	Time
Q14	Examination	12	22 mins

Chargeable gains: additional aspects

14

Topic list	Syllabus reference
1 Chattels and wasting assets	A3(a)D3,(e)(ii)
2 Wasting assets	A3(e)(ii)
3 Leases	A3(e)(ii)
4 Private residences	A3(a)D6
5 Loss, damage or destruction of an asset	A3(e)(iv),(v)
6 CGT and trusts	A3(c)(i), (ii)
7 Overseas aspects of CGT	A3(a)D1,(b)(ii)-(v)

Introduction

In the previous chapters we have learnt how to calculate capital gains and we have looked at some of the reliefs available. We now look at some more of the rules for particular assets and particular situations.

First we look at wasting assets. Unless capital allowances have been claimed there are special rules to ensure that the cost of the asset is restricted to reflect the fall in value of the asset over time.

Leases of land also fall in value over their lives: a lease with ten years left to run is worth less than one with thirty years left to run. The rules for wasting assets are modified to reflect the fact that the value of a lease falls more steeply the shorter it becomes.

We then look at the gains people make on their homes which are usually exempt. This means there is no capital gains tax charge when people move home, but also means that there is no relief if their house is sold at a loss.

We next look at the rules which apply when an asset is damaged or destroyed and the reliefs available where insurance proceeds are applied to restore or replace the asset.

Next we consider how CGT applies when assets are transferred into trusts and finally we look at the overseas aspects of capital gains tax.

In the next chapter we will study the administration of income tax and capital gains tax.

Study guide

		Intellectual level
3	**Chargeable gains and capital gains tax liabilities in situations involving further overseas aspects and in relation to closely related persons and trusts together with the application of additional exemptions and reliefs**	
(a)	The contents of the Paper F6 study guide for chargeable gains under headings:	2
•	D1 The scope of the taxation of capital gains	
•	D3 Gains and losses on the disposal of movable and immovable property	
•	D6 The use of exemptions and reliefs in deferring and minimising tax liabilities arising on the disposal of capital assets.	
(b)	The scope of the taxation of capital gains:	3
(ii)	Identify the concepts of residence and domicile and determine their relevance to capital gains tax	
(iii)	Advise on the availability of the remittance basis to non-UK domiciled individuals	2
(iv)	Determine the UK taxation of foreign gains, including double taxation relief	
(v)	Conclude on the capital gains tax position of individuals coming to and leaving the UK	
(c)	Capital gains tax and trusts:	
(i)	Advise on the capital gains tax implications of transfers of property into trust	3
(ii)	Advise on the capital gains tax implications of transfers of property passing absolutely from a trust to a beneficiary	2
(e)	Gains and losses on the disposal of movable and immovable property:	3
(ii)	Determine the gain on the disposal of leases and wasting assets	
(iv)	Establish the tax effect of capital sums received in respect of the loss, damage or destruction of an asset	
(v)	Advise on the tax effect of making negligible value claims	

Exam guide

The rules for the damage or destruction of an asset are further rollover reliefs which can be used to defer capital gains. A negligible value claim can be used to crystallise a loss, and you must consider the time of the claim carefully to ensure the best possible use of the loss.

The exemption for the principal private residence and the rules for transfers into trust may be examined in a question about families; watch out for where the PPR relief is restricted.

Do not be caught out by the overseas aspects. For CGT purposes the most useful exclusion is the fact that individuals who are not resident in the UK are not taxable on their UK gains, even on assets situated in the UK.

Knowledge brought forward from earlier studies

The examiner has identified essential underpinning knowledge from the F6 syllabus which is particularly important that you revise as part of your P6 studies. In this chapter, the relevant topic is:

		Intellectual level
D3	**Gains and losses on the disposal of movable and immovable property**	
(d)	Compute the exemption where a principal private residence is disposed of.	2

The other topics in this chapter are new.

1 Chattels and wasting assets

FAST FORWARD

Gains on most wasting chattels are exempt, and losses on them are not allowable. The CGT rules are modified for assets eligible for capital allowances.

1.1 Introduction

Key terms

A **chattel** is tangible movable property.

A **wasting asset** is an asset with an estimated remaining useful life of 50 years or less.

Special rules apply for wasting assets to prevent taxpayers from realising a capital loss simply due to the fall in value of a wasting asset over time. The rules are modified where capital allowances are available.

1.2 Chattels

Plant and machinery, whose predictable useful life is always deemed to be less than 50 years, is an example of a wasting chattel (unless it is immovable, in which case it will be wasting but not a chattel). Machinery includes, in addition to its ordinary meaning, motor vehicles (unless exempt as cars), railway and traction engines, engine-powered boats and clocks.

Wasting chattels are exempt (so that there are no chargeable gains and no allowable losses). There is one **exception** to this: assets used for the purpose of a trade, profession or vocation in respect of which **capital allowances** have been or could have been claimed. This means that items of plant and machinery used in a trade are not exempt merely on the ground that they are wasting. However, cars are always exempt.

Exam focus point

The special rules for non-wasting chattels where the cost and/or sale proceeds are less than £6,000 are excluded from the syllabus. Any disposal of a non-wasting chattel in the exam will therefore give rise to a gain or loss calculated under the normal rules

1.3 Chargeable gains and capital allowances

The wasting chattels exemption does not apply to chattels on which capital allowances have been claimed or could have been claimed.

Where capital allowances have been obtained on any asset, and a loss would arise, the allowable cost for chargeable gains purposes must be reduced by the lower of the loss and the net amount of allowances (taking into account any balancing allowances or charges). The result is no gain and no loss.

If there is a gain, the cost is not adjusted for capital allowances.

2 Wasting assets

Other wasting assets generally have their cost written down over time.

2.1 Introduction

A wasting asset is one which has an estimated remaining useful life of 50 years or less and whose original value will depreciate over time. **Freehold land is never a wasting asset**, and there are special rules for leases of land (see below).

Wasting chattels are exempt except for those on which capital allowances have been (or could have been) **claimed**.

2.2 Options

An option (for example an option to buy shares) is a right to buy or sell something at a specified price within a specified time. **An option is usually a wasting asset** because after a certain time it can no longer be exercised.

2.2.1 The grant of an option

The grant of an option is the disposal of an asset, namely the option itself, rather than a part disposal of the asset over which the option has been granted. The only allowable expenditure will be the incidental costs of the grant, such as legal fees. If the option is exercised the CGT treatment changes.

2.2.2 The exercise of an option

Where an option is exercised, the granting of the option and the subsequent disposal of the asset under the option are treated as a single transaction taking place when the option is exercised. Proceeds from the grant of the option plus the disposal of the asset are combined and become the disposal proceeds of the grantor and the allowable base cost of the grantee.

Where tax was paid on the original grant of the option it will usually be treated as a payment on account of the tax on the exercise.

2.2.3 Example: exercise of an option

Tom owns a plot of investment land which he bought for £10,000 in May 2005. He grants an option to Penelope for £1,000 in July 2007 whereby he will sell the land for £25,000 at any time nominated by Penelope before 30 June 2014. Penelope exercises her option in July 2013.

Tom's gain in 2013/14 will be:

	£
Proceeds (£1,000 + £25,000)	26,000
Less cost	(10,000)
Gain	16,000
Penelope's base cost will be: £1,000 + £25,000 =	26,000

The date of disposal is July 2013 (ie when the option is exercised).

2.2.4 Abandoned options

Where an option is abandoned, the position of the grantor and grantee are different. The grantor makes a chargeable disposal at the time when the option is granted. The grantee acquires a chargeable asset at the same time, but the abandonment of the option amounts to a disposal only where the option is:

(a) a quoted option to subscribe for shares in a company
(b) a traded option or financial option
(c) an option to acquire assets for the purposes of a trade

2.2.5 Disposal of an option

The disposal (eg by sale to a third party) of an option (other than a quoted, traded or financial option) to buy or sell quoted shares or securities gives rise to a chargeable gain or allowable loss computed in accordance with the normal rules for wasting assets (see below). These options are assets which waste on a straight line basis.

2.3 Other wasting assets

The cost is written down on a straight line basis. So, if a taxpayer acquires such an asset with a remaining life of 40 years and disposes of it after 15 years (with 25 years remaining) only 25/40 of the cost is deducted from the disposal consideration.

Examples of such assets are **copyrights** (with 50 years or less to run) and **registered designs**.

Where the asset has an estimated residual value at the end of its predictable life, it is the cost less residual value which is written off on a straight line basis over the asset's life. Where additional expenditure is incurred on a wasting asset the additional cost is written off over the life remaining when it was incurred.

Assets eligible for capital allowances and used throughout the period of ownership in a trade, profession or vocation do not have their allowable expenditure written down.

3 Leases

FAST FORWARD

An ordinary disposal computation is made on the disposal of a lease with 50 years or more to run. For leases of land with less than 50 years to run, a special table of percentages is used.

3.1 Types of disposal

The gain that arises on the disposal of a lease will be chargeable according to the terms of the lease disposed of. We must consider:

(a) The assignment of a lease or sub-lease with 50 years or more to run.
(b) The assignment of a lease or sub-lease with less than 50 years to run.

There is an assignment when a lessee sells the whole of his interest. There is a grant when a new lease or sub-lease is created out of a freehold or existing leasehold, the grantor retaining an interest.

Exam focus point

The CGT rules for the **grant** of leases will not be examined.

The duration of the lease will normally be determined by the contract terms. The expiry date, however, will be taken as the first date on which the landlord has an option to terminate the lease or the date beyond which the lease is unlikely to continue because of, for example, the likelihood that the rent will be substantially increased at that date.

3.2 The assignment of a lease with 50 years or more to run

An **ordinary disposal computation** is made and the whole of any gain on disposal will be chargeable to CGT (subject to any private residence exemption, see below).

3.3 The assignment of a lease with less than 50 years less to run

In calculating the gain on the disposal of a lease with less than 50 years to run only a certain proportion of the original expenditure counts as an allowable deduction. This is because a lease is losing value anyway as its life runs out: only the cost related to the tail end of the lease being sold is deductible. The proportion is determined by a table of percentages.

Exam focus point

The appropriate lease percentages will be given by the examiner.

Formula to learn

The allowable cost is given by:

$$\text{Original cost} \times \frac{X}{Y}$$

where X is the percentage for the number of years left for the lease to run at the date of the assignment, and Y is the percentage for the number of years the lease had to run when first acquired by the seller.

The table only provides percentages for exact numbers of years. Where the duration is not an exact number of years the relevant percentage should be found by adding 1/12 of the difference between the two years on either side of the actual duration for each extra month. Fourteen or more odd days count as a month.

Question — **The assignment of a short lease**

Mr A acquired a 20 year lease on a block of flats on 1 August 2007 for £15,000. He assigned it on 2 August 2013 for £19,000. Compute the gain arising.

The percentage form the lease percentage table for 20 years is 72.770, for 14 years is 58.971 and for 6 years is 39.195.

Answer

	£
Proceeds	19,000
Less cost £15,000 × $\frac{\%14 \text{ years}: 58.971}{\%20 \text{ years}: 72.770}$	(12,156)
Gain	6,844

4 Private residences

4.1 General principles

FAST FORWARD

There is an exemption for gains on principal private residences, but the exemption may be restricted because of periods of non-occupation or because of business use.

A gain arising on the sale of an individual's only or main private residence (his principal private residence or PPR) is exempt from CGT. The exemption covers total grounds, including the house, of up to half a hectare. The total grounds can exceed half a hectare if the house is large enough to warrant it, but if not, the gain on the excess grounds is taxable. If the grounds do not adjoin the house (for example when a road separates the two), they **may** still qualify but they may not; each case must be argued on its merits.

For the exemption to be available the taxpayer must have occupied the property as a residence rather than just as temporary accommodation.

4.2 Occupation

The gain is wholly exempt where the owner has occupied the whole of the residence throughout his period of ownership. Where occupation has been for only part of the period, a proportion of the gain is exempted.

Formula to learn

The exempt proportion is:

$$\text{Gain before relief} \times \frac{\text{Period of occupation}}{\text{Total period of ownership}}$$

The **last 36 months of ownership are always** treated as **a period of occupation**, if at some time the residence has been the taxpayer's main residence, even if within those last 36 months the taxpayer also has another house which is his principal private residence.

4.3 Deemed occupation

The **period of occupation is also deemed to include certain periods of absence, provided the individual had no other exempt residence at the time and the period of absence was at some time both preceded by and followed by a period of actual occupation.** Deemed but non-actual occupation during the last 36 months of ownership does not count for this purpose.

These periods of **deemed occupation** are:

(a) Any period (or periods taken together) of absence, for any reason, **up to three years,** and

(b) **Any periods** during which the owner was **required by his employment (ie employed taxpayer) to live abroad**, and

(c) Any period (or periods taken together) **up to four years** during which the owner was **required to live elsewhere due to his work** (ie both employed and self employed taxpayer) so that he could not occupy his private residence.

It does not matter if the residence is let during the absence.

Exempt periods of absence must normally be preceded and followed by periods of **actual occupation**. An extra-statutory concession relaxes this where an individual who has been required to work abroad or elsewhere (ie the latter two categories mentioned above) is unable to resume residence in his home because the terms of his employment require him to work elsewhere.

Question — **Principal private residence relief**

Mr A purchased a house on 1 April 1988 for £88,200. He lived in the house until 30 June 1988. He then worked abroad for two years before returning to the UK to live in the house again on 1 July 1990. He stayed in the house until 31 December 2006 before retiring and moving out to live with friends in Spain until the house was sold on 31 December 2013 for £150,000.

Calculate the gain arising.

Answer

	£
Proceeds	150,000
Less cost	(88,200)
Gain before PPR exemption	61,800
Less PPR exemption (working)	
$\frac{261}{309} \times £61,800$	(52,200)
Gain	9,600

Working

Exempt and chargeable periods

Period		*Total months*	*Exempt months*	*Chargeable Months*
(i)	April 1988 – June 1988 (occupied)	3	3	0
(ii)	July 1988 – June 1990 (working abroad)	24	24	0
(iii)	July 1990 – December 2006 (occupied)	198	198	0
(iv)	January 2007 – December 2010 (see below)	48	0	48
(v)	January 2011 – December 2013 (last 36 months)	36	36	0
		309	261	48

No part of the period from January 2007 to December 2010 can be covered by the exemption for three years of absence for any reason because it is not followed at any time by actual occupation.

Exam focus point

To help you to answer questions such as that above it is useful to draw up a table showing period of ownership, exempt months (real/deemed occupation) and chargeable months (non-occupation). You should also provide an explanation for any periods of deemed occupation.

4.4 Business use

Where part of a residence is used exclusively for business purposes throughout the period of ownership, the gain attributable to use of that part is taxable.

The 'last 36 months always exempt' rule does not apply to that part.

Question

Business use of PPR

Mr Smail purchased a property for £35,000 on 31 May 2008 and began operating a dental practice from that date in one quarter of the house. He closed the dental practice on 31 December 2013, selling the house on that date for £130,000.

Compute the gain, if any, arising.

Answer

	£
Proceeds	130,000
Less: cost	(35,000)
Gain before PPR exemption	95,000
Less PPR exemption 0.75 × £95,000	(71,250)
Gain	23,750

Exemption is lost on one quarter throughout the period of ownership (including the last 36 months) because of the use of that fraction for business purposes.

If part of a house was used for business purposes for part of the period of ownership, the gain is apportioned between chargeable and exempt parts in a just and reasonable manner. If the business part was **at some time** used as part of the only or main residence, the gain apportioned to that part **will** qualify for the last 36 months exemption.

4.5 More than one residence

4.5.1 The election for a residence to be treated as the main residence

Where a person has more than one residence (owned or rented), he may elect for one to be regarded as his main residence by notice to HMRC within two years of commencing occupation of the second residence. An election can have effect for any period beginning not more than two years prior to the date of election until it is varied by giving further notice. (The further notice may itself be backdated by up to two years.)

In order for the election to be made, the individual must actually reside in both residences.

Any period of ownership of a residence not nominated as the main residence will be a chargeable period for that residence.

Where there are two residences and the second one is being treated as a residence under the 'delay in moving in' rule (see above), the election is not needed and both may count as principal private residences simultaneously.

4.5.2 Job-related accommodation

The rule limiting people to only one main residence is relaxed for individuals living in job-related accommodation.

Such individuals will be treated as occupying any second dwelling house which they own if they intend in due course to occupy the dwelling house as their only or main residence. Thus it is not necessary to establish any actual residence in such cases. This rule extends to self-employed persons required to live in job-related accommodation (for example tenants of public houses).

Key term

A person lives in **job-related accommodation** where:

(a) It is necessary for the **proper performance of his duties**, or

(b) It is provided for the **better performance of his duties** and his is one of the kinds of employment in which it is **customary** for employers to provide accommodation, or

(c) There is a **special threat to the employee's security** and use of the accommodation is part of security arrangements.

4.6 Spouses/civil partners

Where a married couple/civil partners live together only one residence may qualify as the main residence for relief. If each owned one property before marriage/registration of the civil partnership, a new two year period for electing for which is to be treated as the main residence starts on marriage/registration.

Where a marriage/civil partnership has broken down and one spouse/civil partner owning or having an interest in the matrimonial home has ceased to occupy the house, by concession the departing spouse/civil partner will continue to be treated as resident for capital gains tax purposes provided that the other has continued to reside in the home and the departing spouse/civil partner has not elected that some other house should be treated as his or her main residence for this period. This only applies where one spouse disposes of his interest to the other spouse.

Where a house passes from one spouse/civil partner to the other (for example on death), the new owner also inherits the old owner's periods of ownership and occupation for PPR relief purposes.

4.7 Letting relief

FAST FORWARD

There is also a relief for letting out a principal private residence if the gain arising during the letting would not be covered by the main relief.

The principal private residence exemption is extended to any gain accruing while the property is let, up to a certain limit. The two main circumstances in which the letting exemption applies are:

(a) When the owner is absent and lets the property, where the absence is not a deemed period of occupation.

(b) When the owner lets part of the property while still occupying the rest of it. The absence from the let part cannot be a deemed period of occupation, because the owner has another residence (the rest of the property). However, the let part will qualify for the last 36 months exemption **if** the let part has **at some time** been part of the only or main residence.

In both cases the letting must be for residential use. **The extra exemption is restricted to the lowest of:**

(a) The amount of the total **gain** which is already **exempt under the PPR provisions** (including the last 36 months exemption)

(b) The gain accruing during the letting period (the **letting part of the gain**)

(c) **£40,000**

The letting exemption cannot convert a gain into an allowable loss.

If a lodger lives as a member of the owner's family, sharing their living accommodation and eating with them, the whole property is regarded as the owner's main residence.

Question

Letting relief

Miss Coe purchased a house on 31 March 1999 for £90,000. She sold it on 31 August 2013 for £340,000. In 2002 the house was redecorated and Miss Coe began to live on the top floor renting out the balance of the house (constituting 60% of the total house) to tenants between 1 January 2003 and 31 December 2012. On 2 January 2013 Miss Coe put the whole house on the market but continued to live only on the top floor until the house was sold. What is the chargeable gain?

Answer

	£
Proceeds	340,000
Less: cost	(90,000)
Gain before PPR exemption	250,000
Less PPR exemption (working)	
$£250,000 \times \frac{117.8}{173}$	(170,231)
	79,769
Less letting exemption: Lowest of:	
(a) gain exempt under PPR rules: £170,231	
(b) gain attributable to letting: $£250,000 \times \frac{55.2}{173} = £79,769$	
(c) £40,000 (maximum)	(40,000)
Gain	39,769

Working

Period	*Notes*	*Total ownership months*	*Exempt months*	*Chargeable Months*
1.4.99 – 31.12.02	100% of house occupied	45	45	0
1.1.03 – 31.8.10	40% of house occupied	92	36.8	
	60% of house let			55.2
1.9.10 – 31.8.13	Last 36 months treated as 100% of house occupied	36	36	0
		173	117.8	55.2

Note. The gain on the 40% of the house always occupied by Miss Coe is fully covered by PPR relief. The other 60% of the house has not always been occupied by Miss Coe and thus any gain on this part of the house is taxable where it relates to periods of time when Miss Coe was not actually (or deemed to be) living in it. Miss Coe cannot claim exemption for the part of the period of letting under the 3 year absence rule since during this time she has a main residence which qualifies for relief (ie. the rest of the house). However, she can claim exemption for the whole of the house for the last 36 months since the let part was part of her only residence prior to the letting.

5 Loss, damage or destruction of an asset

FAST FORWARD

The gain which would otherwise arise on the receipt of insurance proceeds may, subject to certain conditions, be deferred.

5.1 Destroyed assets

If an asset is destroyed (compared to merely being damaged – see below) any compensation or insurance monies received will normally be brought into an ordinary CGT disposal computation as proceeds. The date of disposal is the date the insurance proceeds are received and not the date the asset is destroyed. If all the insurance proceeds from a non-wasting asset are applied for the replacement of the asset within 12 months, any gain can be deducted from the cost of the replacement asset. If only part of the proceeds are used, the gain immediately chargeable can be limited to the amount not used. The rest of the gain is then deducted from the cost of the replacement. This is similar to rollover relief for replacement of business assets (see earlier in this Text).

Question — **Destroyed assets**

Fiona bought a non-business asset for £25,000 in June 2009. It was destroyed in March 2013. Insurance proceeds of £34,000 were received in September 2013, and Fiona spent £35,500 on a replacement asset. Compute the chargeable gain and the base cost of the new asset.

Answer

2013/14	£
Proceeds	34,000
Less cost	(25,000)
Gain (can be fully deferred as all insurance monies are spent on replacement)	9,000

The base cost of the new asset is £(35,500 – 9,000) = £26,500.

5.2 Damaged assets

If an asset is damaged and compensation or insurance money is received as a result, then **this will normally be treated as a part disposal.**

By election, however, the taxpayer can avoid a part disposal computation. **A capital sum received can be deducted from the cost of the asset rather than being treated as a part disposal if:**

(a) **Any amount not spent in restoring the asset is small** (taken as the higher of 5% of the capital sum and £3,000), or

(b) **The capital sum itself is small** (taken as the higher of 5% of the value of the asset and £3,000).

There are special restrictions if the asset is wasting (that is, it has a remaining useful life of 50 years or less).

(a) The **whole** capital sum must be spent on restoration.

(b) The capital sum can only be deducted from what would have been the allowable expenditure on a sale immediately after its application. If the asset is a wasting asset this will be less than the full cost of the asset, because the cost of a wasting asset is written down over its life.

If the amount not used in restoring the asset is not small, then the taxpayer can elect for the amount used in restoration to be deducted from the cost; the balance will continue to be treated as a part disposal.

Question — **Asset damaged**

Frank bought an investment property for £100,000 in May 2013. It was damaged two and a half months later. Insurance proceeds of £20,000 were received in November 2013, and Frank spent a total of £25,000 on restoring the property. Prior to restoration the property was worth £120,000. Compute the chargeable gain immediately chargeable, if any, and the base cost of the restored property assuming Frank elects for there to be no part disposal.

How would your answer differ if no election were made?

Answer

As all the proceeds have been applied in restoring the property Frank has elected to disregard the part disposal.

The base cost of the restored property is £(100,000 – 20,000 + 25,000) = £105,000.

If no election were made, the receipt of the proceeds would be a part disposal in November 2013. The gain would be:

	£
Proceeds	20,000
Less cost £100,000 × 20,000/(20,000 + 120,000)	(14,286)
Gain	5,714

The base cost of the restored asset is £(100,000 – 14,286 + 25,000) = £110,714.

Assuming this is Frank's only disposal in the tax year, the gain is covered by the annual exempt amount. It may therefore be preferable not to make the election.

5.3 Negligible value claims

If a chargeable asset's value becomes negligible a claim may be made to treat the asset as though it were sold, and then immediately reacquired at the value stated in the claim. This will usually give rise to an allowable loss.

The sale and reacquisition are treated as taking place when the claim is made, or at a specified earlier time. The earlier time can be any time up to two years before the start of the tax year in which the claim is made. (For companies, it can be as far back as the start of the earliest accounting period which ends within two years of the date of claim.) The asset must have been of negligible value at the specified earlier time.

On a subsequent actual disposal, any gain is computed using the negligible value as the acquisition cost.

Exam focus point

Since a negligible value claim can be backdated it can be used to generate an allowable loss to set against a gain that has already been realised.

6 CGT and trusts

FAST FORWARD

CGT may arise when assets are transferred into and out of trusts.

6.1 Assets being put into trusts

If a settlor puts an asset into any type of trust during his lifetime, he makes a disposal for CGT purposes. It will be deemed to take place at market value and gift relief will be available (unless the trust is a settlor-interested trust – see below). This is because there is also an inheritance tax charge (see later in this Text) when the assets enter the trust.

As there is no CGT on death, where a trust is created on death there is no deemed disposal. The trustees of a trust created under a will or on intestacy acquire the trust assets at their market value at death (ie probate value).

Exam focus point

> Inheritance tax for trusts is covered later in this Text. You should return to this section once you have completed your study of the relevant chapters.

6.2 Settlor-interested trusts

It is not possible to claim gift relief on transfers to a settlor-interested trust. This is a trust from which the settlor, or his spouse/civil partner or minor child (who is neither married nor in a civil partnership) can benefit.

6.3 Assets leaving trusts

When an asset leaves a trust, for example, when a beneficiary becomes entitled to trust property, the trustees make a disposal of the asset at market value. This may lead to a gain or loss.

If there is a gain, usually gift relief will be available because there will also be a charge to inheritance tax when property leaves a trust.

7 Overseas aspects of CGT

FAST FORWARD

> CGT applies primarily to individuals resident in the UK. Individuals who are not UK domiciled may be entitled to use the remittance basis.

7.1 Liability to CGT

7.1.1 UK resident and domiciled individuals

In general, individuals are subject to CGT on the disposal of assets situated anywhere in the world if they are resident and domiciled in the UK in the tax year of the disposal.

7.1.2 Non-UK resident individuals

In general, an individual who is not UK resident in a tax year is not subject to CGT on the disposal of any assets, wherever situated, in that tax year. There is an exception where the individual is operating a business through a UK branch or agency: this exception is discussed later in this section.

Exam focus point

> It is important to note that a non-UK resident is not liable to CGT on investment assets, even if those assets are situated in the UK.

7.1.3 UK resident but not UK domiciled individuals

If an individual is resident in the UK but not domiciled in the UK, gains on the disposal of assets situated overseas are taxable only to the extent that the proceeds of the disposal are remitted to the UK if the individual has made a claim for the remittance basis or it applies automatically because his unremitted income and gains are less than £2,000 in the tax year.

As with non-UK income, there is no charge on remittance if the money is brought into the UK in order to pay the Remittance Basis Charge, to acquire shares in or make a loan to a trading company or member of a trading group.

An individual who claims the remittance basis is not entitled to an annual exempt amount against chargeable gains.

Some of the rules about where assets are situated are contained in legislation. Some of them are a matter of general law. Most of the rules are obvious, for example, land is situated where it actually is, chattels are situated where they are physically present. There are special rules relating to intangible assets, the most important of which are shares and securities in a company. **All shares and securities of a UK incorporated company are treated as situated in the UK, regardless of where the share certificate is kept.**

7.1.4 Split year treatment

If an individual is UK resident in a tax year, that individual may be entitled to split year treatment so that the tax year is split into a UK part and an overseas part. The availability of split year treatment is determined in the same way as for income tax (see earlier in this Text).

If an individual makes **a disposal in the UK part of the tax year,** the individual will **be subject to CGT** on that disposal **as a UK resident.**

Conversely, if the individual makes a disposal in the overseas part of the tax year, the individual **will treated as non-UK resident and so will not be subject to CGT** on that disposal.

7.2 Losses on non-UK situated assets

7.2.1 UK resident and domiciled individuals

Losses are allowable losses if the individual is UK resident and domiciled.

7.2.2 UK resident but not UK domiciled individuals

An individual who is non-UK domiciled but has not claimed the remittance basis, for example because his income and gains are less than £2,000 in the tax year, is also automatically given relief for losses on assets situated outside the UK.

An individual who has claimed the remittance basis must make an irrevocable election to treat losses on assets situated outside the UK as allowable losses. The election must be made in relation to the first occasion when a non-UK individual claims remittance basis for a tax year.

If the individual does not make an election on that occasion, overseas losses of that tax year and all future years will not be allowable losses.

If the individual does make the election, there are special rules relating to the deduction to allowable losses where there are foreign chargeable gains. Broadly, losses cannot be set against non-UK gains arising in previous years and where losses are available for deduction, they are set first against non-UK gains arising and remitted in that year, then against other non-UK gains and lastly from UK gains arising in that year.

7.3 Non-UK residents operating through a UK branch or agency

The general rule is that an non-UK resident individual who makes a disposal of an asset situated in the UK is not liable to CGT on that disposal.

However, **there will be a liability to CGT where:**

- the individual is **carrying on a trade, profession or vocation in the UK** through **a branch or agency**, and
- there is a disposal of **an asset**, which has been:
  - used in or for the **purposes of the trade, profession or vocation**, or
  - used or held or acquired **for the purpose of the branch or agency.**

There will also be a deemed disposal at market value where an asset ceases to be a chargeable asset either by being removed from the UK or because the UK trade, profession or vocation ceases.

7.4 Temporary non-residence

FAST FORWARD

Individuals who are temporarily non-UK resident are subject to CGT if they make disposals, during the non-UK resident period, of assets acquired before the individual became non-UK resident.

An individual who wishes to dispose of assets might decide **to become non-UK resident for a short period of time, make disposals during that non-UK resident period**, and then **become UK resident again**. There are **anti-avoidance rules** relating to **temporary non-UK residence.**

Temporary non-UK residents are subject to CGT whilst they are non-UK resident if:

(a) They were **UK resident in a tax year** (either a full tax year or a UK part of a split tax year) – this is referred to as Period A, and

(b) Immediately following that Period A, **one or more residence periods occur for which they are not UK resident,** and

(c) They were **UK resident for at least four out of the seven tax years immediately preceding the tax year of departure** (the tax year consisting of or including period A), and

(d) The **temporary period of non-residence is five years or less.**

Net gains realised in the tax year of departure are subject to CGT under general principles.

Gains/ losses made by temporary non-UK residents in the non-UK resident period are chargeable/allowable in period of return. This is the first residence period after period A for which the individual is UK resident (either for a full tax year or a UK part of a split tax year).

Gains on assets acquired in the non-UK resident period are not included in the above charge nor are gains which are already chargeable because they arise on branch or agency assets (see earlier in this section).

Question **Temporary non residence**

Sue had always been resident in the UK until (and including) the tax year 2013/14. She left the UK on 1 February 2014 to begin full-time work overseas.

Sue was then not resident in the UK for the tax years 2014/2015, 2015/16, 2016/17 and 2017/18. Sue returned to the UK on 1 July 2018 when she ceased full-time work overseas. She was thereafter present in the UK so as to be UK resident.

Sue made the following disposals :

Date of disposal	*Proceeds*	*Date of acquisition*	*Proceeds*
	£		£
9 December 2013	15,000	11 June 2008	18,000
10 March 2014	150,000	15 May 2012	87,000
19 June 2016	80,000	10 August 2009	100,000
25 November 2017	60,000	11 June 2015	55,000

Explain how these disposals will be treated for CGT purposes and compute the amount of taxable gains. Assume 2013/14 tax rates and allowances continue to apply.

Answer

Sue was UK resident in the tax year 2013/14. She can split this tax year into UK and overseas parts since she left the UK to begin full time work overseas. Period A therefore ended on 31 January 2014 and the year of departure is 2013/14. Sue can also split the tax year 2018/19 into overseas and UK parts as she is returning to the UK following a period of full time work overseas.

The disposal in December 2013 is in the UK part of the split tax year 2013/14 and is therefore subject to CGT.

December 2013 disposal

	£
Proceeds	28,000
Less cost	(15,000)
Gain	13,000
Less annual exempt amount	(10,900)
Taxable gain 2013/14	2,100

Sue is then non-UK resident from 1 February 2014 until 30 June 2018. Since this period of temporary non-UK residence is five years or less, she will be subject to CGT on the disposal of assets acquired before she became non-UK resident. The net gains will be chargeable in the period of return which starts on 1 July 2018.

March 2014 disposal

	£
Proceeds	150,000
Less cost	(87,000)
Gain	63,000

June 2016 disposal

	£
Proceeds	80,000
Cost	(100,000)
Loss	(20,000)

The disposal in November 2017 is not subject to CGT because the asset was acquired in the non-UK resident period.

Taxable gains 2018/19

	£
Gain	63,000
Less: loss	(20,000)
	43,000
Less annual exempt amount	(10,900)
Taxable gains 2018/19	32,100

7.5 Double taxation relief

If a gain made on the disposal of an overseas asset suffers overseas taxation, relief will be available in the UK against any CGT on the same disposal.

7.6 Calculation of non-UK gains

If an asset is bought and/or sold for amounts in a foreign currency, each such amount is first translated into sterling (using the rate at the time of purchase or sale), and the gain or loss is computed using these sterling amounts.

7.7 Non-remittable proceeds

Tax on gains accruing on assets situated outside the UK may be deferred if:

- The taxpayer makes a claim;
- The gain could not be remitted to the UK because of the laws of the country where it arose, because of executive action of its government or because it was impossible to obtain foreign currency, and
- This was not because of any lack of reasonable endeavours on the taxpayer's part.

The gain is deferred until the gain becomes remittable.

Chapter roundup

- Gains on most wasting chattels are exempt, and losses on them are not allowable. The CGT rules are modified for assets eligible for capital allowances.
- Other wasting assets generally have their cost written down over time.
- An ordinary disposal computation is made on the disposal of a lease with 50 years or more to run. For leases of land with less than 50 years to run, a special table of percentages is used.
- There is an exemption for gains on principal private residences, but the exemption may be restricted because of periods of non-occupation or because of business use.
- There is also a relief for letting out a principal private residence if the gain arising during the letting would not be covered by the main relief.
- The gain which would otherwise arise on the receipt of insurance proceeds may, subject to certain conditions, be deferred.
- CGT may arise when assets are transferred into and out of trusts.
- CGT applies primarily to individuals resident in the UK. Individuals who are not UK domiciled may be entitled to use the remittance basis.
- Individuals who are temporarily non-UK resident are subject to CGT if they make disposals, during the non-UK resident period, of assets acquired before the individual became non-UK resident.

Quick quiz

1. What is the general treatment of intangible wasting assets (eg a copyright)?
2. When a lease with less than 50 years to run is assigned, what proportion of the cost is allowable?
3. For what periods may an individual be deemed to occupy his principal private residence?
4. What is the maximum letting exemption?
5. Emma drops and destroys a vase. She receives compensation of £2,000 from her insurance company. How can she avoid a charge to CGT arising?
6. Clive has always been UK resident. He acquires an asset in 2010. Clive becomes non-UK resident for the tax year 2013/14. He disposes of the asset in 2015, realising a gain of £50,000. Clive becomes UK-resident again in the tax year 2016/17. Clive is not entitled to split year treatment in any relevant year. How will the gain on the disposal in 2015 be taxed (if at all)?

Answers to quick quiz

1 The cost is written down on a straight line basis

2 Allowable cost is original cost × X/Y where X is the % for the years left of the lease to run at assignment and Y is the % for the years the lease had to run when first acquired by the seller.

3 Periods of deemed occupation are:

- last 36 months of ownership, and
- any period of absence up to three years, and
- any period during which the owner was required by his employment to work abroad, and
- any period up to four years during which the owner was required to live elsewhere due to his work (employed or self-employed) so that he could not occupy his private residence.

4 £40,000

5 Emma can avoid a charge to CGT on receipt of the compensation by investing at least £2,000 in a replacement asset within 12 months.

6 Clive is temporarily non-UK resident for five years or less (non-residence period from 6 April 2013 to 5 April 2016) . He will be taxed on the gain made in 2015 in the period of return to UK residence which is the tax year 2016/17.

Now try the question below from the Exam Question Bank

Number	Level	Marks	Time
Q15	Introductory	25	45 mins

PART C

Tax administration for individuals

Self assessment for individuals and partnerships

Topic list	Syllabus reference
1 The administration of taxation	A6(d)H1
2 Notification of liability to income tax and CGT	A6(c)H1
3 Tax returns and keeping records	A6(c)H1
4 Self-assessment and claims	A6(c)H2
5 Payment of income tax and capital gains tax	A3(e)(vi),A6(c)H2
6 HMRC powers	A6(c)H3
7 Penalties	A6(c)H4
8 Appeals	A6(c)H3
9 Tax offenders	A6(c)H4

Introduction

In the previous chapters we have studied the comprehensive computation of income tax and capital gains tax liabilities.

In this chapter we look at the overall system for the administration of tax. We then see how individuals and partnerships must 'self assess' their liability to income tax and capital gains tax. We deal with self assessment for companies later in this Text.

In the next chapter we will commence our study of inheritance tax.

Study guide

		Intellectual level
3	**Chargeable gains and capital gains tax liabilities in situations involving further overseas aspects and in relation to closely related persons and trusts together with the application of additional exemptions and reliefs**	
(e)	Gains and losses on the disposal of movable and immovable property:	3
(vi)	Determine when capital gains tax can be paid by instalments and evaluate when this would be advantageous to taxpayers	
6	**National insurance, value added tax and tax administration:**	
(c)	The contents of the Paper F6 study guide for the obligations of taxpayers and/or their agents under headings:	2
•	H1 The systems for self assessment and the making of returns	
•	H2 The time limits for the submission of information, claims and payment of tax, including payments on account	
•	H3 The procedures relating to compliance checks, appeals and disputes	
•	H4 Penalties for non-compliance	

Exam guide

In any tax advice question you must consider the administrative requirements and time limits. You must know the taxpayer's responsibilities for making returns and paying tax, and the rules that HMRC can use to enforce compliance.

Knowledge brought forward from earlier studies

This chapter is mainly a revision of material studied in Paper F6. The only new topics are payment of capital gains tax by instalments and tax offenders.

There are no changes for 2013/14 in the rules which you studied at F6 in 2012/13. However, some topics are no longer examinable, for example information powers, pre-return compliance checks and detailed procedures on the carrying out and completion of a compliance check.

1 The administration of taxation

FAST FORWARD

Taxes are administered by Her Majesty's Revenue and Customs.

The **Treasury** formally imposes and collects taxation. The management of the Treasury is the responsibility of the Chancellor of the Exchequer. **The administrative function for the collection of tax is undertaken by Her Majesty's Revenue and Customs (HMRC).** Rules on these administrative matters are contained in the **Taxes Management Act 1970 (TMA 1970)**.

HMRC consists of the Commissioners for Her Majesty's Revenue and Customs and staff known **as Officers of Revenue and Customs** who are responsible for supervising the self-assessment system and agreeing tax liabilities.

Tax appeals are heard by the **Tax Tribunal** which is made up of **two tiers:**

(a) First Tier Tribunal, and
(b) Upper Tribunal

The **First Tier Tribunal deals with most cases** other than complex cases. The **Upper Tribunal deals with complex cases** which either involve an important issue of tax law or a large financial sum. The Upper Tribunal **also hears appeals** against decisions of the First Tier Tribunal. We look at the appeals system in more detail later in this chapter.

Many taxpayers arrange for their accountants to prepare and submit their tax returns. The taxpayer remains responsible for submitting the return and for paying the tax; the accountant acts as the taxpayer's agent.

2 Notification of liability to income tax and CGT

FAST FORWARD

Individuals who do not receive a tax return or who have a new source of income or gains must notify their chargeability to income tax or CGT.

Individuals who have not received a notice to file a return, or who have a new source of income or gains in the tax year, are required to give notice of chargeability to HMRC within six months from the end of the year ie by 5 October 2014 for 2013/14.

A person who has no chargeable gains and who is not liable to higher rate tax does not have to give notice of chargeability if all his income:

(a) Is taken into account under PAYE
(b) Is from a source of income not subject to tax under a self-assessment
(c) Has had (or is treated as having had) income tax deducted at source, or
(d) Is a UK dividend

A penalty is charged for late notification (see later in this Chapter).

3 Tax returns and keeping records

FAST FORWARD

Tax returns must usually be filed by 31 October (paper) or 31 January (electronic) following the end of the tax year.

3.1 Tax returns

The tax return comprises a basic six page return form, together with supplementary pages for particular sources of income. Taxpayers are sent a return and a number of supplementary pages depending on their known sources of income, together with a Tax Return Guide and various notes relating to the supplementary pages. Taxpayers with simple tax returns may be asked to complete a short four page tax return. If a return for the previous year was filed electronically the taxpayer may be sent a notice to file a return, rather than the official HMRC form.

Partnerships must file a separate return which includes a 'Partnership Statement' showing the firm's profits, losses, proceeds from the sale of assets, tax suffered, tax credits and the division of all these amounts between partners. A partnership return must include a declaration of the name and tax reference of each partner, as well as the usual declaration that the return is correct and complete to the best of the signatory's knowledge. Each partner must then include his share of partnership profits on his personal tax return.

3.2 Time limit for submission of tax returns

Key term

The latest **filing date for a personal tax return** for a tax year (Year 1) is:

- 31 October in the next tax year (Year 2), for a non-electronic return (eg a paper return).
- 31 January in Year 2, for an electronic return (eg made via the Internet).

There are **two exceptions to this general rule.**

The **first exception applies if the notice to file a tax return is issued by HMRC to the taxpayer after 31 July in Year 2, but on or before 31 October in Year 2.** In this case, the **latest filing date is:**

- **the end of 3 months following the notice, for a paper return**
- **31 January in Year 2, for an electronic return.**

The second exception applies **if the notice to file the tax return is issued to the taxpayer after 31 October in Year 2.** In this case, **the latest filing date is the end of 3 months following the notice.**

Question — **Submission of tax returns**

Advise each of the following clients of the latest filing date for her personal tax return for 2013/14 if the return is:

(a) paper; or
(b) electronic.

Norma	Notice to file tax return issued by HMRC on 6 April 2014
Melanie	Notice to file tax return issued by HMRC on 10 August 2014
Olga	Notice to file tax return issued by HMRC on 12 December 2014

Answer

	Paper	*Electronic*
Norma	31 October 2014	31 January 2015
Melanie	9 November 2014	31 January 2015
Olga	11 March 2015	11 March 2015

A partnership return may be filed as a paper return or an electronic return. **The general rule and the exceptions to the general rule for personal returns apply also to partnership returns.**

3.3 Standard accounting information

The tax return requires trading results to be presented in a standard format. Although there is no requirement to submit accounts with the return, accounts may be filed. If accounts accompany the return, HMRC's power to raise a discovery assessment (see below) is restricted.

Only 'three line' accounts (ie income less expenses equals profit) need be included on the tax return of businesses with a turnover (or gross rents from property) of less than the threshold for VAT registration (£79,000). This is not as helpful as it might appear, as underlying records must still be kept for tax purposes (disallowable items etc) when producing three line accounts.

Large businesses with a turnover of at least £5 million which have used figures rounded to the nearest £1,000 in producing their published accounts can compute their profits to the nearest £1,000 for tax purposes.

3.4 Keeping of records

All taxpayers must retain all records required to enable them to make and deliver a correct tax return.

Records must be retained until the later of:

(a) (i) 5 years after the 31 January following the tax year where the taxpayer is in business (as a sole trader or partner or letting property). Note that this applies to all of the records, not only the business records, or

(ii) **1 year after the 31 January following the tax year otherwise, or**

(b) Provided notice to deliver a return is given before the date in (a):

(i) **The time after which a compliance check enquiry by HMRC into the return can no longer be commenced, or**

(ii) **The date any such a compliance check enquiry has been completed.**

HMRC can specify a shorter time limit for keeping records where the records are bulky and the information they contain can be provided in another way.

Where a person receives a notice to deliver a tax return after the normal record keeping period has expired, he must keep all records in his possession at that time until no compliance check enquiry can be started in respect of the return or until such a compliance check enquiry has been completed.

Taxpayers can keep 'information', rather than 'records', but must show that they have prepared a complete and correct tax return. The information must also be able to be provided in a legible form on request. Records can be kept in electronic format.

HMRC can inspect 'in-year' records, ie *before* a return is submitted, if they believe it is reasonably required to check a tax position.

4 Self-assessment and claims

FAST FORWARD

If a paper return is filed the taxpayer can ask HMRC to compute the tax due. Electronic returns have tax calculated automatically.

4.1 Self-assessment

Key term

A **self-assessment** is a calculation of the amount of taxable income and gains after deducting reliefs and allowances, and a calculation of income tax and CGT payable after taking into account tax deducted at source and tax credits on dividends.

If the taxpayer is filing a **paper return (other than a Short Tax Return), he may make the tax calculation on his return or ask HMRC to do so on his behalf.**

If the taxpayer wishes HMRC to make the calculation for Year 1, a paper return must be filed:

- **on or before 31 October in Year 2 or,**
- **if the notice to file the tax return is issued after 31 August in Year 2, within 2 months of the notice.**

If the taxpayer is filing an **electronic return, the calculation of tax liability is made automatically when the return is made online.**

4.2 Amending the self-assessment

The taxpayer may amend his return (including the tax calculation) for Year 1 within twelve months after the filing date. For this purpose the filing date means:

- **31 January of Year 2;** or
- **where the notice to file a return was issued after 31 October in Year 2, the last day of the three month period starting with the issue.**

A return may be amended by the taxpayer at a time when a compliance check enquiry is in progress into the return. The amendment does not restrict the scope of a compliance check enquiry into the return but may be taken into account in that enquiry. If the amendment made during a compliance check enquiry is the amount of tax payable, the amendment does not take effect while the compliance check enquiry is in progress.

A return may be amended by HMRC to correct any obvious error or omission in the return (such as errors of principle and arithmetical mistakes) or anything else that an officer has reason to believe is incorrect in the light of information available. The correction must usually be made within nine months after the day on which the return was actually filed. The taxpayer can object to the correction but must do so within 30 days of receiving notice of it.

Similar rules apply to the amendment and correction of partnership returns.

4.3 Claims

All claims and elections which can be made in a tax return must be made in this manner if a return has been issued. A claim for any relief, allowance or repayment of tax must be quantified at the time it is made.

In general, the time limit for making a claim is 4 years from the end of tax year. Where different time limits apply these have been mentioned throughout this Text.

4.4 Recovery of overpaid tax

If a taxpayer discovers that he has overpaid tax, for example because he has made an error in his tax return, he can make a claim to have the overpaid tax repaid to him. The claim must be made within four years of the end of the tax year to which the overpayment relates.

5 Payment of income tax and capital gains tax

FAST FORWARD

Two payments on account and a final balancing payment of income tax and Class 4 NICs are due.

One of the competencies you require to fulfil performance objective 19 of the PER is the ability to evaluate and compute taxes payable. You can apply the knowledge you obtain from this section of the text to help to demonstrate this competence.

5.1 Payments on account and final payment

5.1.1 Introduction

The self-assessment system may result in the taxpayer making three payments of income tax and Class 4 NICs.

Date	Payment
31 January in the tax year	1st payment on account
31 July after the tax year	2nd payment on account
31 January after the tax year	Final payment to settle the remaining liability

HMRC issues 'Statements of Account' which include payslips, but there is no statutory obligation for it to do so and **the onus is on the taxpayer to pay the correct amount of tax by the due date.**

5.1.2 Payments on account

Key term

Payments on account are usually required where the income tax and Class 4 NICs due in the previous year exceeded the amount of income tax deducted at source; this excess is known as **'the relevant amount'**. Income tax deducted at source includes tax suffered, PAYE deductions and tax credits on dividends.

The payments on account are each equal to 50% of the relevant amount for the previous year.

Exam focus point

Payments on account of CGT are never required.

Question — Payments on account

Sue is a self employed writer who paid tax for 2013/14 as follows:

		£
Total amount of income tax charged		9,200
This included:	Tax deducted on savings income	3,200
She also paid:	Class 4 NIC	1,900

How much are the payments on account for 2014/15 and by what dates are they due?

Answer

		£
Income tax:		
Total income tax charged for 2013/14		9,200
Less tax deducted for 2013/14		(3,200)
		6,000
Class 4 NIC		1,900
'Relevant amount'		7,900
Payments on account for 2014/15:		
31 January 2015	£7,900 × 50%	
31 July 2015	£7,900 × 50%	3,950

Payments on account are not required if the relevant amount falls below a de minimis limit of £1,000. Also, payments on account are not required from taxpayers who paid 80% or more of their tax liability for the previous year through PAYE or other deduction at source arrangements.

If the previous year's liability increases following an amendment to a self-assessment, or the raising of a discovery assessment, an adjustment is made to the payments on account due.

5.1.3 Reducing payments on account

Payments on account are normally fixed by reference to the previous year's tax liability but if a taxpayer expects his liability to be lower than this **he may claim to reduce his payments on account to:**

(a) A stated amount, or
(b) Nil.

The claim must state the reason why he believes his tax liability will be lower, or nil.

If the taxpayer's eventual liability is higher than he estimated he will have reduced the payments on account too far. Although the payments on account will not be adjusted, the taxpayer will suffer an interest charge on late payment.

A penalty of the difference between the reduced payment on account and the correct payment on account may be levied if the reduction was claimed fraudulently or negligently.

5.1.4 Balancing payment

The balance of any income tax and Class 4 NICs together with all CGT due for a year, is normally payable on or before the 31 January following the year.

Question — **Payment of tax**

Giles made payments on account for 2013/14 of £6,500 each on 31 January 2014 and 31 July 2014, based on his 2012/13 liability. He then calculates his total income tax and Class 4 NIC liability for 2013/14 at £18,000 of which £2,750 was deducted at source. In addition he calculated that his CGT liability for disposals in 2013/14 is £5,120.

What is the final payment due for 2013/14?

Answer

Income tax and Class 4 NIC: £18,000 – £2,750 – £6,500 – £6,500 = £2,250. CGT = £5,120.

Final payment due on 31 January 2015 for 2013/14 £2,250 + £5,120 = £7,370

In one case the due date for the final payment is later than 31 January following the end of the year. **If a taxpayer has notified chargeability by 5 October but the notice to file a tax return is not issued before 31 October, then the due date for the payment is three months after the issue of the notice.**

Tax charged in an amended self-assessment is usually payable on the later of:

(a) The normal due date, generally 31 January following the end of the tax year, and
(b) The day following 30 days after the making of the revised self-assessment.

Tax charged on a discovery assessment (see below) is due thirty days after the issue of the assessment.

5.2 Penalty for late payment of tax

FAST FORWARD

A penalty is chargeable where tax is paid after the due date based on the amount of unpaid tax. Up to 15% of that amount is payable where the tax is more than 12 months late.

A penalty is chargeable where tax is paid after the penalty date. The penalty date is 30 days after the due date for the tax. Therefore no penalty arises if the tax is paid within 30 days of the due date.

The penalty chargeable is:

Date of payment	Penalty
Not more than 5 months after the penalty date	5% of tax which is unpaid at the penalty date.
More than 5 months after the penalty date but not more than 11 months after the penalty date	5% of tax which is unpaid at the end of the 5 month period. This is in addition to the 5% penalty above.
More than 11 months after the penalty date	5% of tax which is unpaid at the end of the 11 month period. This is in addition to the two 5% penalties above.

Penalties for late payment of tax apply to:

(a) **Balancing payments of income tax and Class 4 NICs and any CGT** under self-assessment or a determination

(b) Tax due on the amendment of a self-assessment

(c) Tax due on a discovery assessment

Penalties for late payment do not apply to late payments on account.

5.3 Interest on late paid tax

Interest is chargeable on late payment of both payments on account and balancing payments. Late payment interest is charged from the due date for payment until the date payment is made.

Exam focus point

You will be given the rate of interest to use in the exam. You should work to the nearest month.

Interest is charged from 31 January following the tax year (or the normal due date for the balancing payment, in the rare event that this is later), even if this is before the due date for payment on:

(a) Tax payable following an amendment to a self-assessment
(b) Tax payable in a discovery assessment, and
(c) Tax postponed under an appeal which becomes payable.

Since a determination (see below) is treated as if it were a self-assessment, interest runs from 31 January following the tax year.

If a taxpayer claims to reduce his payments on account and there is still a final payment to be made, interest is normally charged on the payments on account as if each of those payments had been the lower of:

(a) the reduced amount, plus 50% of the final income tax liability; and
(b) the amount which would have been payable had no claim for reduction been made.

Question — **Interest**

Herbert's payments on account for 2013/14 based on his income tax liability for 2012/13 were £4,500 each. However when he submitted his 2012/13 income tax return in January 2014 he made a claim to reduce the payments on account for 2013/14 to £3,500 each. The first payment on account was made on 1 February 2014, and the second on 1 November 2014.

Herbert filed his 2013/14 tax return in December 2014. The return showed that his tax liabilities for 2013/14 (before deducting payments on account) were income tax and Class 4 NIC: £10,000, capital gains tax: £2,500. Herbert paid the balance of tax due of £5,500 on 1 April 2015.

For what periods (to the nearest month) and in respect of what amounts will Herbert be charged interest?

Answer

Herbert made an excessive claim to reduce his payments on account, and will therefore be charged interest on the reduction. The payments on account should have been £4,500 each based on the original 2012/13 liability (not £5,000 each based on the 2013/14 liability). Interest will be charged as follows:

(a) First payment on account

(i) On £3,500 – nil – paid on time
(ii) On £1,000 from due date of 31 January 2014 to payment date, 1 April 2015 (14 months)

(b) Second payment on account

(i) On £3,500 from due date of 31 July 2014 to payment date, 1 November 2014 (3 months)
(ii) On £1,000 from due date of 31 July 2014 to payment date, 1 April 2015 (8 months)

(c) Balancing payment

(i) On £3,500 from due date of 31 January 2015 to payment date, 1 April 2015 (2 months)

Where interest has been charged on late payments on account but the final balancing settlement for the year produces a repayment, all or part of the original interest is repaid.

5.4 Repayment of tax and repayment supplement

Tax is repaid when claimed unless a greater payment of tax is due in the following 30 days, in which case it is set-off against that payment.

Interest is paid on overpayments of:

(a) Payments on account

(b) Final payments of income tax and Class 4 NICs and CGT, including tax deducted at source or tax credits on dividends, and

(c) Penalties.

Repayment supplement runs from the original date of payment (even if this was prior to the due date), until the day before the date the repayment is made. Income tax deducted at source and tax credits are treated as if they were paid on the 31 January following the tax year concerned.

Repayment supplement paid to individuals is tax free.

5.5 Payment of CGT

FAST FORWARD

Capital gains tax is usually due on 31 January following the end of the tax year. However, CGT may be paid in instalments where consideration is received over a period in excess of 18 months or in certain circumstances where the disposal is a gift.

5.5.1 General rule

Capital gains tax is usually payable in one payment on 31 January following the end of the tax year.

Exam focus point

Payments on account of CGT are never required.

5.5.2 Payment by instalments: extended receipt of consideration

CGT may be paid in instalments where there is a disposal resulting in a gain but the consideration for the disposal is received over a period in excess of 18 months.

To avoid hardship to the taxpayer, the CGT due may be paid by instalments **over the period that consideration is received** up to a **maximum of eight years.** The **amount of the instalments must be agreed with HMRC**. For example, the instalments may be related to the amount of consideration received at various times during the period.

Interest is only paid on late paid instalments, not on the outstanding balance. **This instalment option is therefore very attractive to the taxpayer** who can agree with HMRC to **pay the outstanding CGT when the consideration is received without increasing the overall liability.**

5.5.3 Payment by instalments: gifts of land and shares not attracting gift relief

CGT may also be paid by instalments where the disposal is a gift but gift relief is not wholly available (or, in some circumstances, has been clawed back). It is not possible to pay CGT by instalments under these rules if gift relief was available but was not claimed nor if there is a disposal at an undervalue.

The **gifted asset must be one of the following**:

(a) **land or an interest in land;**

(b) **any shares or securities which gave the donor control of the company** (quoted or unquoted) **immediately before the gift**

(c) **shares in an unquoted company**

An **election for instalments must be made by the taxpayer** to HMRC before the CGT becomes payable. The instalments will be paid as **ten equal annual instalments** starting on the normal due date. The **outstanding balance will attract interest**. Interest will also be due on late paid instalments.

The **outstanding balance of CGT (plus interest to the date of payment) may be paid at any time**. The **outstanding CGT becomes immediately payable** if the disposal was to a **connected person** and the **gifted asset is sold** (whether or not by the original donee).

Generally, **this instalment option is not particularly advantageous for taxpayers** because **interest runs on the unpaid balance.**

6 HMRC powers

6.1 Compliance check enquiries

FAST FORWARD

A compliance check enquiry into a return, claim or election can be started by an officer of HMRC within a limited period.

6.1.1 Starting a compliance check enquiry

HM Revenue and Customs has powers to make compliance check enquiries into returns, claims or elections which have already been submitted.

Some returns, claims or elections are **selected for a compliance check enquiry at random, others for a particular reason**, for example, if HM Revenue and Customs believes that there has been an **underpayment of tax** due to the taxpayer's failure to comply with tax legislation.

An officer of HM Revenue and Customs has a limited period within which to commence a compliance check enquiry on a return or amendment. **The officer must give written notice of his intention by:**

(a) **The first anniversary of the actual filing date, if the return was delivered on or before the due filing date,** or

(b) **The quarter day following the first anniversary of the actual filing date, if the return is filed after the due filing date. The quarter days are 31 January, 30 April, 31 July and 31 October.**

If the taxpayer amends the return after the due filing date, the compliance check enquiry 'window' extends to the quarter day following the first anniversary of the date the amendment was filed. Where the compliance check enquiry was not started within the limit which would have applied had no amendment been filed, the enquiry is restricted to matters contained in the amendment.

The officer does not have to have, or give, any reason for starting a compliance check enquiry. In particular, the taxpayer will not be advised whether he has been selected at random for an audit. Compliance check enquiries may be full enquires, or may be limited to 'aspect' enquiries.

6.1.2 During the compliance check enquiry

In the course of the compliance check enquiry **the officer may require the taxpayer to produce documents, accounts or any other information required. The taxpayer can appeal to the Tax Tribunal against such a requirement.**

6.1.3 Completion of a compliance check enquiry

An officer must issue a notice that the compliance check enquiry is complete, state his conclusions and amend the individual's self-assessment, partnership statement, or claim accordingly.

The officer cannot then make a further compliance check enquiry into that return. HMRC may, in limited circumstances, raise a discovery assessment if they believe that there has been a loss of tax.

6.2 Determinations

If notice has been served on a taxpayer to submit a return but the return is not submitted by the due filing date, an officer of HMRC may make a determination of the amounts liable to income tax and CGT and of the tax due. Such a determination must be made to the best of the officer's information and belief, and is then treated as if it were a self-assessment. This enables the officer to seek payment of tax, including payments on account for the following year and to charge interest.

A determination must be made within four years following the end of the relevant tax year.

6.3 Discovery assessments

If an officer of HMRC discovers that profits have been omitted from assessment, that any assessment has become insufficient, or that any relief given is, or has become excessive, an assessment may be raised to recover the tax lost.

If the tax lost results from an error in the taxpayer's return but the return was made in accordance with prevailing practice at the time, no discovery assessment may be made.

A discovery assessment may only be raised where a return has been made if:

(a) There has been **careless or deliberate understatement** by the taxpayer or his agent, or

(b) At the time that compliance check enquiries on the return were completed, or could no longer be made, the officer **did not have information** to make him aware of the loss of tax.

Information is treated as available to an officer if it is contained in the taxpayer's return or claim for the year or either of the two preceding years, or it has been provided as a result of a compliance check enquiry covering those years, or it has been specifically provided.

The time limit for raising a discovery assessment is 4 years from the end of the tax year but this is extended to 6 years if there has been careless understatement and 20 years if there has been deliberate understatement. The taxpayer may appeal against a discovery assessment within 30 days of issue.

6.4 Dishonest conduct of tax agents

FAST FORWARD

HMRC can investigate dishonest conduct by a tax agent and issue a civil penalty of up to £50,000 where there has been dishonest conduct.

HMRC can investigate whether there has been dishonest conduct by a tax agent (ie an individual who, in the course of business, assists clients with their tax affairs). Dishonest conduct occurs when a tax agent does something dishonest with a view to bringing about a loss of tax.

HMRC can issue a civil penalty of up to £50,000 where there has been **dishonest conduct and the tax agent fails to supply the information or documents that HMRC has requested.**

7 Penalties

7.1 Penalties for errors

FAST FORWARD

There is a common penalty regime for errors in tax returns, including income tax, NICs, corporation tax and VAT. Penalties range from 30% to 100% of the Potential Lost Revenue. Penalties may be reduced.

A common penalty regime for errors in tax returns for income tax, national insurance contributions, corporation tax and value added tax.

A penalty may be imposed where **a taxpayer makes an inaccurate return** if he has:

- been **careless** because he has not taken reasonable care in making the return or discovers the error later but does not take reasonable steps to inform HMRC; or
- made a **deliberate error** but **does not make arrangements to conceal it**; or
- made a **deliberate error** and **has attempted to conceal it** eg by submitting false evidence in support of an inaccurate figure.

Note that **an error which is made where the taxpayer has taken reasonable care** in making the return and which he **does not discover later, does not result in a penalty.**

In order for a penalty to be charged, the **inaccurate return must result in**:

- **an understatement of the taxpayer's tax liability**; or
- **a false or increased loss for the taxpayer**; or
- **a false or increased repayment of tax to the taxpayer**.

If a return contains more than one error, a penalty can be charged for each error.

The rules also extend to **errors in claims for allowances and reliefs** and in **accounts submitted in relation to a tax liability**.

Penalties for error also apply where **HMRC has issued an assessment estimating a person's liability** where:

- a **return has been issued to that person and has not been returned**, or
- the taxpayer was **required to deliver a return to HMRC but has not delivered it**.

The taxpayer will be charged a penalty where

- the **assessment understates the taxpayer's liability** to income tax, capital gains tax, corporation tax or VAT, and
- **the taxpayer fails to take reasonable steps within 30 days of the date of the assessment** to tell HMRC that there is an under-assessment.

The amount of **the penalty for error is based on the Potential Lost Revenue (PLR)** to HMRC as a result of the error. For example, if there is an understatement of tax, this understatement will be the PLR.

The maximum amount of the penalty for error depends on the type of error:

Type of error	Maximum penalty payable
Careless	30% of PLR
Deliberate not concealed	70% of PLR
Deliberate and concealed	100% of PLR

Question — Penalty for error

Alex is a sole trader. He files his tax return for 2013/14 on 10 January 2015. The return shows his trading income to be £60,000. In fact, due to carelessness, his trading income should have been stated to be £68,000.

State the maximum penalty that could be charged by HMRC on Alex for his error.

Answer

The Potential Lost Revenue as a result of Alex's error is:

£(68,000 – 60,000) = £8,000 × [40% (income tax) + 2% (NICs)] £3,360

Alex's error is careless so the maximum penalty for error is:

£3,360 × 30% £1,008

A penalty for error may be reduced if the taxpayer tells HMRC about the error – this is called a disclosure. The reduction depends on the **circumstances of** the disclosure and the **help that the taxpayer gives to HMRC in relation to the disclosure.**

An **unprompted disclosure is one made at a time when the taxpayer has no reason to believe HMRC has discovered, or is about to discover, the error**. Otherwise, the disclosure will be a **prompted disclosure.**

The **minimum penalties** that can be imposed are as follows:

Type of error	Unprompted	Prompted
Careless	0% of PLR	15% of PLR
Deliberate not concealed	20% of PLR	35% of PLR
Deliberate and concealed	30% of PLR	50% of PLR

Question — Reduction of penalty

Sue is a sole trader. She files her tax return for 2013/14 on 31 January 2015. The return shows a trading loss for the year of £(80,000). In fact, Sue has deliberately increased this loss by £(12,000) and has submitted false figures in support of her claim. HMRC initiate a review into Sue's return and in reply Sue then makes a disclosure of the error. Sue is a higher rate taxpayer due to her substantial investment income and she has made a claim to set the loss against general income in 2013/14.

State the maximum and minimum penalties that could be charged by HMRC on Sue for her error.

Answer

The potential lost revenue as a result of Sue's error is:

£12,000 × 40% £4,800

Sue's error is deliberate and concealed so the maximum penalty for error is:

£4,800 × 100% £4,800

Sue has made a prompted disclosure so the minimum penalty for error is:

£4,800 × 50% £2,400

The help that the taxpayer gives to HMRC relates to when, how and to what extent the taxpayer:

- **tells HMRC about the error,** making full disclosure and explaining how the error was made;
- **gives reasonable help** to HMRC to enable it **to quantify the error**; and
- **allows access to business and other records** and other relevant documents.

A taxpayer can appeal to the First Tier Tribunal against:

- the **penalty being charged**;
- the **amount of the penalty**.

7.2 Penalties for late notification of chargeability

FAST FORWARD

A common penalty regime also applies to late notification of chargeability.

A common penalty regime also applies to certain taxes for failures to notify chargeability to, or liability to register for, tax that result in a loss of tax. The taxes affected include income tax, NICs, PAYE, CGT, corporation tax and VAT. Penalties are behaviour related, increasing for more serious failures, and are based on the 'potential lost revenue'.

The minimum and maximum penalties as percentages of PLR are as follows:

Behaviour	Maximum penalty	Minimum penalty with unprompted disclosure		Minimum penalty with prompted disclosure	
Deliberate and concealed	100%	30%		50%	
Deliberate but not concealed	70%	20%		35%	
		>12m	<12m	>12m	<12m
Careless	30%	10%	0%	20%	10%

Note that there is no zero penalty for reasonable care (as there is for penalties for errors on returns – see above), although the penalty may be reduced to 0% if the failure is rectified within 12 months through unprompted disclosure. The penalties may also be reduced at HMRC's discretion in 'special circumstances'. However, inability to pay the penalty is not a 'special circumstance'.

The same penalties apply for failure to notify HMRC of a new taxable activity.

Where the taxpayer's failure is not classed as deliberate, there is no penalty if he can show he has a 'reasonable excuse'. Reasonable excuse does not include having insufficient money to pay the penalty. Taxpayers have a right of appeal against penalty decisions to the First Tier Tribunal, which may confirm, substitute or cancel the penalty.

7.3 Penalties for late filing of tax return

FAST FORWARD

A penalty can be charged for late filing of a tax return based on how late the return is and how much tax is payable.

An individual is liable to a penalty where a tax return is filed after the due filing date. The penalty date is the date on which the return will be overdue (ie the date after the due filing date).

The initial penalty for late filing of the return is £100.

If the failure continues after the end of the period of 3 months starting with the penalty date, HMRC may give the individual notice specifying that a daily penalty of £10 is payable for a maximum of 90 days. The daily penalty runs from a date specified in the notice which may be earlier than the date of the notice but cannot be earlier than the end of the 3-month period.

If the failure continues after the end of the period of 6 months starting with the penalty date, a further penalty is payable. This penalty is the greater of:

- **5% of the tax liability** which would have been shown in the return; and
- **£300.**

If the failure continues after the end of the period of 12 months starting with the penalty date, a further penalty is payable. This penalty is determined in accordance with the taxpayer's conduct in withholding information which would enable or assist HMRC in assessing the taxpayer's liability to tax. **The penalty is computed as follows:**

Type of conduct	Penalty
Deliberate and concealed	Greater of: • 100% of tax liability which would have been shown on return; and • £300
Deliberate not concealed	Greater of: • 70% of tax liability which would have been shown on return; and • £300
Type of conduct	**Penalty**
Any other case (eg careless)	Greater of: • 5% of tax liability which would have been shown on return; and • £300

7.4 Penalty for late payment of tax

This penalty was dealt with in Section 5.2 earlier in this chapter.

7.5 Penalties for failure to keep records

The maximum (mitigable) penalty for each failure to keep and retain records is £3,000 per tax year/accounting period.

8 Appeals

FAST FORWARD

Disputes between taxpayers and HMRC can be dealt with by an HMRC internal review or by a Tribunal hearing.

8.1 Internal reviews

For direct taxes, appeals must first be made to HMRC, which will assign a 'caseworker'.

For indirect taxes, appeals must be sent directly to the Tribunal, although the taxpayer can continue to correspond with his caseworker where, for example, there is new information.

At this stage the taxpayer may be offered, or may ask for, an **'internal review'**, which will be made by an objective HMRC review officer not previously connected with the case. This is a less costly and more effective way to resolve disputes informally, without the need for a Tribunal hearing. An appeal to Tribunal cannot be made until any review has ended.

The taxpayer must either accept the review offer, or notify an appeal to the Tribunal within 30 days of being offered the review, otherwise the appeal will be treated as settled.

HMRC must usually carry out the review within 45 days, or any longer time as agreed with the taxpayer. The review officer may decide to uphold, vary or withdraw decisions.

After the review conclusion is notified, **the taxpayer has 30 days to appeal to the Tribunal.**

8.2 Tribunal hearings

If there is no internal review, or the taxpayer is unhappy with the result of an internal review, the case may be heard by the Tribunal. The person wishing to make an appeal (the appellant) must send a notice of appeal to the Tribunal. The Tribunal must then give notice of the appeal to the respondent (normally HMRC).

The Tribunal is made up of two 'tiers':

(a) **A First Tier Tribunal and**
(b) **An Upper Tribunal.**

The case will be allocated to one of four **case 'tracks'**:

(a) **Complex cases**, which the Tribunal considers will require lengthy or complex evidence or a lengthy hearing, or involve a complex or important principle or issue, or involves a large amount of money. Such cases will usually be heard by the Upper Tribunal,

(b) **Standard cases, heard by the First Tier Tribunal**, which have detailed case management and are subject to a more formal procedure than basic cases,

(c) **Basic cases, also heard by the First Tier Tribunal**, which will usually be disposed of after a hearing, with minimal exchange of documents before the hearing, and

(d) **Paper cases, dealt with by the First Tier Tribunal**, which applies to straightforward matters such as fixed filing penalties and will usually be dealt with in writing, without a hearing.

A decision of the First Tier Tribunal may be appealed to the Upper Tribunal.

Decisions of the Upper Tribunal are binding on the Tribunals and any affected public authorities. A decision of the Upper Tribunal may be appealed to the Court of Appeal.

9 Tax offenders

FAST FORWARD

Deliberate tax defaulters whose actions result in a tax loss in excess of £25,000 may have their details published by HMRC on the Internet.

9.1 'Naming and shaming' tax offenders

All deliberate tax defaulters (individuals and companies) whose actions result in a tax loss to HMRC in excess of £25,000 will have their names and details (such as address and profession) published on the Internet by HMRC.

Names will not be published of those who make a full unprompted disclosure or a full prompted disclosure within the required time. Details will be published quarterly within one year of the penalty becoming final and will be removed from publication one year later.

9.2 Monitoring of serious tax offenders

Taxpayers who incur a penalty for deliberate evasion in respect of tax of £5,000 or more are required to submit returns for up to the following five years showing more detailed business accounts information and detailing the nature and value of any balancing adjustments within the accounts.

Chapter roundup

- Taxes are administered by Her Majesty's Revenue and Customs.
- Individuals who do not receive a tax return or who have a new source of income or gains must notify their chargeability to income tax or CGT.
- Tax returns must usually be filed by 31 October (paper) or 31 January (electronic) following the end of the tax year.
- If a paper return is filed the taxpayer can ask HMRC to compute the tax due. Electronic returns have tax calculated automatically.
- Two payments on account and a final balancing payment of income tax and Class 4 NICs are due.
- A penalty is chargeable where tax is paid after the due date based on the amount of unpaid tax. Up to 15% of that amount is payable where the tax is more than 12 months late.
- Capital gains tax is usually due on 31 January following the end of the tax year. However, CGT may be paid in instalments where consideration is received over a period in excess of 18 months or in certain circumstances where the disposal is a gift.
- A compliance check enquiry into a return, claim or election can be started by an officer of HMRC within a limited period.
- HMRC can investigate dishonest conduct by a tax agent and issue a civil penalty of up to £50,000 where there has been dishonest conduct.
- There is a common penalty regime for errors in tax returns, including income tax, NICs, corporation tax and VAT. Penalties range from 30% to 100% of the Potential Lost Revenue. Penalties may be reduced.
- A common penalty regime also applies to late notification of chargeability.
- A penalty can be charged for late filing of a tax return based on how late the return is and how much tax is payable.
- Disputes between taxpayers and HMRC can be dealt with by an HMRC internal review or by a Tribunal hearing.
- Deliberate tax defaulters whose actions result in a tax loss in excess of £25,000 may have their details published by HMRC on the Internet.

Quick quiz

1. By when must a taxpayer who has a new source of income give notice of his chargeability to capital gains tax due in 2013/14?
2. By when must a taxpayer file a paper tax return for 2013/14?
3. What are the normal payment dates for income tax?
4. What penalties are due in respect of income tax payments on account that are paid two months late?
5. When may CGT be paid by ten annual instalments?
6. Which body hears tax appeals?

Answers to quick quiz

1 Within six months of the end of the year, ie by 5 October 2014.

2 By 31 October 2014 or, if the return is issued after 31 July 2014, by the end of 3 months following the issue of the notice to file the return.

3 Two payments on account of income tax are due on 31 January in the tax year and on the 31 July following. A final balancing payment is due on 31 January following the tax year.

4 None. Penalties do not apply to late payment of payment on account.

5 Provided the disposal is not eligible for gift relief, the ten annual instalment option is available on transfers of:

- land or an interest in land, or
- controlling holdings of share or securities in a company (quoted or unquoted), or
- any shares or securities in an unquoted company

6 The Tax Tribunal which consists of the First Tier Tribunal and the Upper Tribunal.

Now try the question below from the Exam Question Bank

Number	Level	Marks	Time
Q16	Introductory	17	31 mins

PART D

Inheritance tax

An introduction to inheritance tax

Topic list	Syllabus reference
1 Basic principles	A4(a)E1
2 Computing transfers of value	A4(a)E2,(b)(ii)
3 Exemptions	A4(a)E4,(c)(iii), f(i)
4 Excluded property	A4(b)(ii)
5 Calculation of tax on lifetime transfers	A4(a)E3,(d)(i),(ii)
6 Relief for the fall in value of lifetime gifts	A4(d)(iv)

Introduction

In this chapter we move on to inheritance tax (IHT). IHT is primarily a tax on wealth left on death. It also applies to gifts within seven years of death and to certain lifetime transfers of wealth.

The tax is different from income tax and CGT, where the basic question is: how much has the taxpayer made? With IHT, the basic question is, how much has he given away? We tax the amount which the taxpayer has transferred - the amount by which he is worse off. If the taxpayer pays IHT on a lifetime gift, he is worse off by the amount of the gift plus the tax due, and we have to take that into account. Some transfers are, however, exempt from IHT.

We will see that the first £325,000 of transfers is taxed at 0% (the 'nil rate band'), and is therefore effectively tax-free. To stop people from avoiding IHT by, for example, giving away £1,625,000 in five lots of £325,000, we need to look back seven years every time a transfer is made to decide how much of the nil rate band is available to set against the current transfer.

In the next chapter we will look at transfers on death.

Study guide

		Intellectual level
4	**Inheritance tax in situations involving further aspects of the scope of the tax and the calculation of the liabilities arising, the principles of valuation and the reliefs available, transfers of property to and from trusts, overseas aspects and further aspects of administration**	
(a)	The contents of the Paper F6 study guide for inheritance tax under headings:	2
•	E1 The scope of inheritance tax	
•	E2 The basic principles of computing transfers of value	
•	E3 The liabilities arising on chargeable lifetime transfers and on the death of an individual	
•	E4 The use of exemptions in deferring and minimising inheritance tax liabilities	
(b)	The scope of inheritance tax:	
(ii)	Identify excluded property	2
(c)	The basic principles of computing transfers of value:	
(iii)	Identify exempt transfers	2
(d)	The liabilities arising on chargeable lifetime transfers and the death of an individual:	3
(i)	Advise on the tax implications of chargeable lifetime transfers	
(ii)	Advise on the tax implications of transfers within seven years of death	
(iv)	Advise on the relief for the fall in value of lifetime gifts	
(f)	The use of exemptions and reliefs in deferring and minimising inheritance tax liabilities:	3
(i)	Advise on the use of reliefs and exemptions to minimise inheritance tax liabilities, as mentioned in the sections above	

Exam guide

In the P6 exam, you will be expected to deal with basic inheritance tax transfers and the more technical rules covered in this chapter such as fall in value relief for lifetime gifts, excluded property, and further exemptions. You will also be expected to use your knowledge of inheritance tax to advise clients about minimising inheritance tax liabilities.

Knowledge brought forward from earlier studies

This chapter revises the basic principles of inheritance tax covered in Paper F6. The examiner has identified essential underpinning knowledge from the F6 syllabus which is particularly important that you revise as part of your P6 studies. In this chapter, the relevant topics are:

		Intellectual level
E2	**The basic principles of computing transfers of value**	
(a)	State, explain and apply the meaning of transfer of value, chargeable transfer and potentially exempt transfer.	2
(b)	Demonstrate the diminution in value principle.	2
(c)	Demonstrate the seven year accumulation principles taking into account changes in the level of the nil rate band.	2
E3	**The liabilities arising on chargeable lifetime transfers and on the death of an individual**	
(a)	Understand the tax implications of chargeable lifetime transfers and compute the relevant liabilities.	2
(b)	Understand the tax implications of transfers within seven years of death and compute the relevant liabilities.	2

There are no changes in 2013/14 from 2012/13 in the material covered at F6 level. In particular, note that the nil rate band has remained at £325,000.

1 Basic principles

One of the competencies you require to fulfil performance objective 19 of the PER is the ability to evaluate and compute taxes payable. You can apply the knowledge you obtain from this section of the text to help to demonstrate this competence.

IHT is a tax on gifts or '**transfers of value'** made by **chargeable persons**. This generally involves a transaction as a result of which wealth is transferred by one person to another, either directly or via a trust.

1.1 Chargeable persons

Chargeable persons for IHT purposes are:

(a) Individuals, and
(b) Trustees of settled property.

Companies are not chargeable persons although if companies are used to transfer wealth an IHT liability can be charged on the shareholders (the details are outside the scope of your syllabus).

Spouses and civil partners are taxed separately although there is an exemption for transfers between the couple. There are also special valuation rules which are dealt with later.

1.2 The scope of the charge

All transfers of assets (worldwide) made by persons domiciled, or deemed domiciled, in the UK (see later in this Text) **whether during lifetime or on death are within the charge to IHT.**

For individuals not domiciled in the UK, only transfers of UK assets are within the charge to IHT.

2 Computing transfers of value

2.1 Introduction

There are two main chargeable occasions for individuals:

(a) gifts made in the lifetime of the donor (**lifetime transfers**), and
(b) gifts made on death, for example when property is left in a will (**death estate**).

We will look in detail at lifetime transfers later in this chapter and at the death estate in the next chapter.

First, however, we start our study of IHT by looking at some general principles which apply to both chargeable occasions.

2.2 Transfers of value and chargeable transfers

FAST FORWARD

IHT applies to transfers to trusts, transfers on death and to transfers within the seven years before death.

IHT cannot arise unless there is a transfer of value. This is any gratuitous disposition (eg gift) made by a person which results in his being worse off, that is, he suffers a diminution (ie reduction) in the value of his estate.

The measure of a gift is always the loss to the transferor (the diminution in value of his estate), not the amount gained by the transferee.

2.3 Chargeable transfers

Inheritance tax arises on any **chargeable transfer. This is any transfer of value not covered by an exemption.**

Chargeable transfers made during the individual's lifetime are called **chargeable lifetime transfers (CLTs)**.

On death, an individual is treated as if he had made a transfer of value of the property comprised in his estate. This, then, will be a chargeable transfer to the extent that it is not exempt.

2.4 Potentially exempt transfers

Key term

A **PET** is a **lifetime transfer made by an individual to another individual**. Any other lifetime transfer by an individual (eg gift to a trust) not covered by an exemption is a CLT.

A PET is exempt from IHT when made and will remain so if the transferor survives for at least seven years from making the gift. If the transferor dies within seven years of making the gift, it will become chargeable to IHT.

2.5 Diminution in value

In many cases the diminution in value of the transferor's estate will be the same as the increase in the value of the transferee's estate. However, sometimes the two will not be the same.

2.6 Example: diminution in value

Audrey holds 5,100 of the shares in an unquoted company which has an issued share capital of 10,000 shares. Currently Audrey's majority holding is valued at £15 per share.

Audrey wishes to give 200 shares to her son, Brian. However, to Brian the shares are worth only £2.50 each, since he will have only a small minority holding in the company. After the gift Audrey will hold 4,900 shares and these will be worth £10 each. The value per share to Audrey will fall from £15 to £10 per share since she will lose control of the company.

The diminution in value of Audrey's estate is £27,500, as follows.

	£
Before the gift: 5,100 shares × £15	76,500
After the gift: 4,900 shares × £10	(49,000)
Diminution in value	27,500

Brian has only been given shares with a market value of 200 × £2.50 = £500. Remember, a gift is also a deemed disposal at market value for CGT purposes, and it is this value that will be used in any CGT computation. IHT, however, uses the principle of diminution in value which can, as in this case, give a much greater value than the value of the asset transferred.

2.7 Exceptions to the IHT charge

The following are not chargeable to IHT:

(a) **Transfers where there is no gratuitous intent**: for example selling a painting for £1,000 which later turns out to be worth £100,000. The transaction must have been made at arm's length between unconnected persons

(b) **Transfers made in the course of a trade**: for example Christmas gifts to employees

(c) **Expenditure on family maintenance**: for example school fees paid for a child

(d) Waivers of remuneration

(e) Waivers of dividends provided the waiver is made within the 12 months before the dividend is declared

(f) Any transfer covered by a specific exemption (see further below)

(g) **Transfers of excluded property** (see below)

3 Exemptions

FAST FORWARD

Exemptions may apply to make transfers or parts of transfers non chargeable. Some exemptions only apply on lifetime transfers (annual, normal expenditure out of income, marriage/civil partnership), whilst some apply on both life and death transfers (eg spouses, charities, political parties).

3.1 Introduction

There are various exemptions available to eliminate or reduce the chargeable amount of a lifetime transfer or property passing on an individual's death. Some exemptions apply to both lifetime transfers and property passing on death, whilst others apply only to lifetime transfers.

The lifetime exemptions apply to PETs as well as to CLTs. Only the balance of such gifts after the lifetime exemptions have been taken into account is then potentially exempt.

Exam focus point

Where CLTs and PETS are made in the same year the CLTs should be made first to use any available exemptions. If used up against the PETs an exemption will be wasted if the PET never becomes chargeable.

3.2 Exemptions applying to lifetime transfers only

3.2.1 The small gifts exemptions

Outright gifts to individuals totalling £250 or less per donee in any one tax year are exempt. If gifts total more than £250 the whole amount is chargeable. A donor can give up to £250 each year to each of as many donees as he wishes. The small gifts exemption cannot apply to gifts into trusts.

3.2.2 The annual exemption (AE)

The first £3,000 of value transferred in a tax year is exempt from IHT. The annual exemption is used only after all other exemptions (such as for transfers to spouses/civil partners or charities (see below)). If several gifts are made in a year, the £3,000 exemption is applied to earlier gifts before later gifts. The annual exemption is used up by PETs as well as CLTs, even though the PETs might never become chargeable.

Any unused portion of the annual exemption is carried forward for one year only. Only use it the following year *after* that year's own annual exemption has been used.

Question — **Annual exemptions**

Frank has no unused annual exemption brought forward at 6 April 2012.

On 1 August 2012 he makes a transfer of £600 to Peter.
On 1 September 2012 he makes a transfer of £2,000 to Quentin.
On 1 July 2013 he makes a transfer of £3,300 to a trust for his grandchildren.
On 1 June 2014 he makes a transfer of £5,000 to Rowan.

Show the application of the annual exemptions.

Answer

2012/13	£
1.8.12 Gift to Peter	600
Less AE 2012/13	(600)
	0

	£
1.9.12 Gift to Quentin	2,000
Less AE 2012/13	(2,000)
	0

The unused annual exemption carried forward is £3,000 – £600 – £2,000 = £400.

2013/14	£	£
1.7.13 Gift to trust		3,300
Less: AE 2013/14	3,000	
AE 2012/13 b/f	300	
		(3,300)
		0

The unused annual exemption carried forward is zero because the 2013/14 exemption must be used before the 2012/13 exemption brought forward. The balance of £100 of the 2012/13 exemption is lost, because it cannot be carried forward for more than one year.

2014/15	£
1.6.14 Gift to Rowan	5,000
Less AE 2014/15	(3,000)
	2,000

3.2.3 Normal expenditure out of income

Inheritance tax is a tax on transfers of capital, not income. A transfer of value is exempt if:

(a) It is made as part of the normal expenditure of the transferor
(b) Taking one year with another, it was made out of income, and
(c) It leaves the transferor with sufficient income to maintain his usual standard of living.

As well as covering such things as regular presents **this exemption can cover regular payments out of income such as a grandchild's school fees or the payment of life assurance premiums on a policy for someone else.**

3.2.4 Gifts in consideration of marriage/civil partnership

Gifts in consideration of marriage/civil partnership are exempt up to:

(a) **£5,000 if from a parent of a party to the marriage/civil partnership**
(b) **£2,500 if from a remoter ancestor or from one of the parties to the marriage/civil partnership**
(c) **£1,000 if from any other person.**

The limits apply to gifts from any one donor for any one marriage/civil partnership. The exemption is available only if the marriage/civil partnership actually takes place.

3.3 Exemptions applying to both lifetime transfers and transfers on death

3.3.1 Gifts between spouses/civil partners

Any transfers of value between spouses/civil partners are exempt provided the transferee is domiciled or deemed domiciled (see later in this Text) in the UK at the time of transfer. The exemption covers lifetime gifts between them and property passing under a will or on intestacy.

If the transferor spouse/civil partner is domiciled or deemed domiciled in the UK but the transferee spouse/civil partner is not domiciled nor deemed domiciled in the UK, the exemption is limited to a cumulative total equal to the amount of the nil rate band at the date of the transfer ie £325,000 for 2013/14. If neither spouse/civil partner is domiciled nor deemed domiciled in the UK there is no limit on the exemption. An election may be made for a non-UK domiciled individual who is, or was, the spouse or civil partner of a UK domiciled individual, to be treated as UK domiciled for IHT purposes. We look at this election later in this text when we deal with overseas aspects of IHT.

A simple planning point follows from this exemption. Spouses/civil partners may avoid IHT, at least in the short term, if each makes a will leaving his property to the other.

A claim can also be made to transfer any unused nil rate band from one spouse/civil partner to the surviving spouse/civil partner (see later in this Text).

Question — **Exemptions**

Dale made a gift of £153,000 to her son on 17 October 2013 on the son's marriage. Dale gave £400,000 to her spouse on 1 January 2016. Dale gave £70,000 to her daughter on 11 May 2016. The only other gifts Dale made were birthday and Christmas presents of £100 each to her grandchildren.

Show what exemptions are available assuming:

(a) Dale's spouse is domiciled in the UK; or
(b) Dale's spouse is not domiciled in the UK.

Answer

(a) *17 October 2013*

	£
Gift to Dale's son	153,000
Less: ME	(5,000)
AE 2013/14	(3,000)
AE 2012/13 b/f	(3,000)
PET	142,000

1 January 2016

	£
Gift to Dale's spouse	400,000
Less spouse exemption	(400,000)
	0

11 May 2016

	£
Gift to Dale's daughter	70,000
Less: AE 2016/17	(3,000)
AE 2015/16 b/f	(3,000)
PET	64,000

The gifts to the grandchildren are covered by the small gifts exemption.

(b) *17 October 2013*

As in part (a)

1 January 2016

	£
Gift to Dale's spouse	400,000
Less spouse exemption (restricted)	(325,000)
Less: AE 2015/16	(3,000)
AE 2014/15 b/f	(3,000)
PET	69,000

Note that the annual exemption is available to set against the gift remaining after deducting the spouse exemption.

11 May 2016

	£
Gift to D's daughter	70,000
Less AE 2016/17	(3,000)
PET	67,000

3.3.2 Other exempt transfers

Transfers (whether outright or by settlement) **to UK charities are exempt** from inheritance tax.

Gifts to a qualifying political party are exempt. A political party qualifies if, at the general election preceding the transfer of value, either:

(a) At least two members were elected to the House of Commons, or
(b) One member was elected and the party polled at least 150,000 votes.

Gifts for national purposes are exempt. Eligible recipients include museums and art galleries.

4 Excluded property

FAST FORWARD

If excluded property is given away, there are no IHT consequences.

4.1 Types of excluded property

The following are examples of excluded property.

(a) A reversionary interest in settled property. A reversionary interest is a future interest in trust property. An example is when an income beneficiary (with the present interest) dies and the capital passes to the remainderman. A reversionary interest will not, however, be treated as excluded property if:

(i) it has been acquired at any time for consideration in money or money's worth, or
(ii) either the settlor or his spouse is or has been beneficially entitled to the interest at any time

(b) Foreign assets owned by non-UK domiciled individuals (see later in this Text).

5 Calculation of tax on lifetime transfers

5.1 Basic principles

FAST FORWARD

Transfers are cumulated for seven years so that the nil rate band is not available in full on each of a series of transfers in rapid succession.

There are two aspects of the calculation of tax on lifetime transfers:

(a) lifetime tax on CLTs, and
(b) additional death tax on CLTs and on PETs where the transferor dies within seven years of making the transfer.

Exam focus point

You should always calculate the lifetime tax on any CLTs first, then move on to calculate the death tax on all CLTs and PETs made within seven years of death.

5.2 Lifetime tax

FAST FORWARD

IHT is charged on what a donor loses. If the donor pays the IHT on a lifetime gift he loses both the asset given away and the money with which he paid the tax due on it. Grossing up is required.

5.2.1 Transferee pays tax

When a CLT is made and the transferee (ie the trustees) pays the lifetime tax, follow these steps to work out the lifetime IHT on it:

Step 1 Look back seven years from the date of the transfer to see if any other CLTs have been made. If so, these transfers use up the nil rate band available for the current transfer. Work out the value of any nil rate band still available.

Step 2 Compute the gross value of the CLT. You may be given this in the question or you may have to work out the diminution of value, deduct reliefs (such as business property relief as described later in the Text) or exemptions (such as the annual exemption described earlier in this chapter).

Step 3 Any part of the CLT covered by the nil rate band is taxed at 0%. Any part of the CLT not covered by the nil rate band is charged at 20%.

Exam focus point

The life rate of 20%, the current nil rate band and those for previous years are given in the rates and allowances section of the exam paper.

Question — Transferee pays the lifetime tax

Eric makes a gift of £336,000 to a trust on 10 July 2013. He has not used his annual exemption in 2013/14 nor in 2012/13. The trustees agree to pay the tax due.

Calculate the lifetime tax payable by the trustees if Eric has made:

(a) a lifetime chargeable transfer of value of £100,000 in August 2005
(b) a lifetime chargeable transfer of value of £100,000 in August 2006
(c) a lifetime chargeable transfer of value of £350,000 in August 2006.

Answer

(a) **Step 1** No lifetime transfers in seven years before 10 July 2013. Nil rate band of £325,000 available.

Step 2

	£
Gift	336,000
Less: AE 2013/14	(3,000)
AE 2012/13 b/f	(3,000)
Chargeable lifetime transfer	330,000

Step 3

	IHT £
£325,000 × 0%	0
£5,000 × 20%	1,000
£330,000	1,000

(b) **Step 1** Lifetime transfer of value of £100,000 in seven years before 10 July 2013 (transfers after 10 July 2006). Nil rate band of £(325,000 – 100,000) = £225,000 available.

Step 2 Value of CLT is £330,000 (as before).

Step 3

	IHT £
£225,000 × 0%	0
£105,000 × 20%	21,000
£330,000	21,000

(c) **Step 1** Lifetime transfer of value of £350,000 in seven years before 10 July 2013 (transfers after 10 July 2006). No nil rate band available as all covered by previous transfer.

Step 2 Value of CLT is £330,000 (as before)

Step 3

	IHT £
£330,000 @ 20%	66,000

5.2.2 Transferor pays tax

Where IHT is payable on a CLT, the **primary liability to pay tax is on the transferor,** although the transferor may agree with the transferee (as in the above example) that the transferee is to pay the tax instead.

If the transferor pays the lifetime IHT due on a CLT, the total reduction in value of his estate is the transfer of value plus the IHT due on it. The transfer is therefore a net transfer and must be grossed up in order to find the gross value of the transfer. **We do this by working out the tax as follows.**

Formula to learn

$$\textbf{Chargeable amount (ie not covered by nil band)} \times \frac{\textbf{20 (rate of tax)}}{\textbf{80 (100 minus the rate of tax)}}$$

When a CLT is made and the transferor pays the lifetime tax, follow these steps to work out the lifetime IHT on it:

Step 1 Look back seven years from the date of the transfer to see if any other CLTs have been made. If so, these transfers use up the nil rate band available for the current transfer. Work out the value of any nil rate band still available.

Step 2 Compute the net value of the CLT. You may be given this in the question or may have to work out the diminution of value, deduct reliefs (such as business property relief as described later in the Text) or exemptions (such as the annual exemption discussed earlier in this chapter).

Step 3 Any part of the CLT covered by the nil rate band is taxed at 0%. Any part of the CLT not covered by the nil rate band is taxed at 20/80.

Step 4 Work out the gross transfer by adding the net transfer and the tax together. You can check your figure by working out the tax on the gross transfer.

Question

Transferor pays the lifetime tax

James makes a gift of £336,000 to a trust on 10 July 2013. He has not used his annual exemption in 2013/14 nor in 2012/13. James will pay the tax due.

Calculate the lifetime tax payable, if James has made:

(a) a lifetime chargeable transfer of value of £100,000 in August 2005
(b) a lifetime chargeable transfer of value of £100,000 in August 2006
(c) a lifetime chargeable transfer of value of £350,000 in August 2006.

Answer

(a) **Step 1** No lifetime transfers in seven years before 10 July 2013. Nil rate band of £325,000 available.

Step 2

	£
Gift	336,000
Less: AE 2013/14	(3,000)
AE 2012/13 b/f	(3,000)
Net CLT	330,000

Step 3

	IHT £
£325,000 × 0%	0
£5,000 × 20/80	1,250
£330,000	1,250

Step 4 Gross transfer is £(330,000 + 1,250) = £331,250. *Check:* Tax on the gross transfer would be:

	IHT £
£325,000 × 0%	0
£6,250 × 20%	1,250
£331,250	1,250

(b) **Step 1** Lifetime transfer of value of £100,000 in seven years before 10 July 2013 (transfers after 10 July 2006). Nil rate band of £(325,000 – 100,000) = £225,000 available.

Step 2 Net value of CLT is £325,000 (as before).

Step 3

	IHT £
£225,000 × 0%	0
£105,000 × 20/80	26,250
£330,000	26,250

Step 4 Gross transfer is £(330,000 + 26,250) = £356,250. *Check:* Tax on the gross transfer would be:

	IHT
	£
£225,000 × 0%	0
£131,250 × 20%	26,250
£356,250	26,250

(c) **Step 1** Lifetime transfer of value of £350,000 in seven years before 10 July 2013 (transfers after 10 July 2006). No nil rate band available as all covered by previous transfer.

Step 2 Net value of CLT is £330,000 (as before).

Step 3

	IHT
	£
£330,000 × 20/80	82,500

Step 4 Gross transfer is £(330,000 + 82,500) = £412,500. *Check:* Tax on the gross transfer would be:

	IHT
	£
£412,500 × 20%	82,500

5.3 Death tax

The longer the transferor survives after making a gift, the lower the death tax. This is because taper relief applies to lower the amount of death tax payable as follows:

Years between transfer and death	% reduction in death tax
3 years or less	0
More than 3 but less than 4	20
More than 4 but less than 5	40
More than 5 but less than 6	60
More than 6 but less than 7	80

Exam focus point

The rates of taper relief will be given in the rates and allowances section of the exam paper.

Death tax on a lifetime transfer is **always** payable by the transferee, so grossing up is not relevant.

Follow these steps to work out the death tax on a CLT:

Step 1 Look back seven years from the **date of the transfer** to see if any other chargeable transfers were made. If so, these transfers use up the nil rate band available for the current transfer. Work out the value of any nil rate band remaining.

Step 2 Compute the value of the CLT. This is the gross value of the transfer that you worked out for computing lifetime tax.

Step 3 Any part of the CLT covered by the nil rate band is taxed at 0%. Any part of the CLT not covered by the nil rate band is charged at 40%.

Step 4 Reduce the death tax by taper relief (if applicable).

Step 5 Deduct any lifetime tax paid. The death tax may be reduced to nil, but there is no repayment of lifetime tax.

Exam focus point

> The death rate of 40%, the current nil rate band and those for previous years are given in the rates and allowances section of the exam paper.

Question — Lifetime tax and death tax on CLTs

Trevor makes a gross chargeable transfer of value of £207,000 in December 2002. He then makes a gift to a trust of shares worth £206,000 on 15 November 2008. The trustees pay the lifetime tax due.

Trevor dies in August 2013.

Compute:

(a) the lifetime tax payable by the trustees on the lifetime transfer in November 2008, and
(b) the death tax (if any) payable on the lifetime transfer in November 2008.

Answer

Lifetime tax

Step 1 Lifetime transfer of value of £207,000 in 7 years before 15 November 2008 (transfers after 15 November 2001). Nil rate band of £(312,000 – 207,000) = £105,000 available.

Step 2

		£
Gift		206,000
Less	AE 2008/09	(3,000)
	AE 2007/08 b/f	(3,000)
		200,000

Step 3

	IHT
	£
£105,000 × 0%	0
£95,000 × 20%	19,000
£200,000	19,000

Death tax

Step 1 Lifetime transfer of value of £207,000 in seven years before 15 November 2008 (transfers after 15 November 2001). Nil rate band of £(325,000 – 207,000) = £118,000 available.

Step 2 Value of CLT is £200,000.

Step 3

	IHT
	£
£118,000 × 0%	0
£82,000 × 40%	32,800
£200,000	32,800

Step 4 Death more than 4 years but less than 5 years after transfer

	£
Death tax	32,800
Less: taper relief @ 40%	(13,120)
Death tax left in charge	19,680

Step 5 Tax due £(19,680 – 19,000) 680

5.4 Death tax on potentially exempt transfers

If the transferor dies within seven years of making a PET it will become chargeable to death tax in the same way as a CLT. There will be no lifetime tax paid, so Step 5 above will not apply.

Remember that the exemptions which apply to lifetime transfers only, such as the annual exemption and the marriage/civil partner exemption, are available to set against PETs. **You must apply them in chronological order**, so that if a PET is made before a CLT in the same tax year, the exemption is set against the PET. This may waste the exemption (unless the donor dies within seven years), and is disadvantageous in cash flow terms since lifetime tax is paid on CLTs but not on PETs.

We will now work through an example where there is both a PET and a CLT.

Exam focus point

Calculate lifetime tax on CLTs first. Then move on to death tax, working through all CLTs and PETs in chronological order. Remember: on death PETs become chargeable so must be taken into account when calculating the death tax on later CLTs.

Question — **Lifetime tax and death tax on CLTs and PETs**

Louise gave £346,000 to her son on 1 February 2010. This was the first transfer that Louise had made.

On 10 October 2013, Louise gave £376,000 to a trust. The trustees paid the lifetime IHT due.

On 11 January 2014, Louise died.

Compute:

(a) the lifetime tax payable by the trustees on the lifetime transfer made in 2013,
(b) the death tax payable on the lifetime transfer made in 2010, and
(c) the death tax payable on the lifetime transfer made in 2013.

Answer

(a) Lifetime tax – 2013 CLT

Step 1 There are no chargeable lifetime transfers in the seven years before 10 October 2013 because the 2010 transfer is a PET and therefore exempt during Louise's lifetime. Nil rate band of £325,000 available.

Step 2

		£
Gift		376,000
Less	AE 2013/14	(3,000)
	AE 2012/13 b/f	(3,000)
CLT		370,000

Step 3

	IHT £
£325,000 × 0%	0
£45,000 × 20%	9,000
£370,000	9,000

(b) Death tax – 2010 PET becomes chargeable

Step 1 No lifetime transfers of value in seven years before 1 February 2010 (transfers after 1 February 2003). Nil rate band of £325,000 available.

Step 2

	£
Gift	346,000
Less AE 2009/10	(3,000)
AE 2008/09 b/f	(3,000)
PET now chargeable	340,000

Step 3

	IHT
	£
£325,000 × 0%	0
£15,000 × 40%	6,000
£340,000	6,000

Step 4 Death more than 3 years but less than 4 years after transfer

	£
Death tax	6,000
Taper relief @ 20%	(1,200)
Death tax due	4,800

(c) *Death tax – 2013 CLT additional tax*

Step 1 Lifetime transfer of value of £340,000 in seven years before 10 October 2013 (transfers after 10 October 2006). Note that as the PET becomes chargeable on death, its value is now included in calculating the death tax on the CLT. No nil rate band available.

Step 2 Value of CLT is £370,000 as before

Step 3

	IHT
	£
£370,000 @ 40%	148,000

Step 4 Death within 3 years of transfer so no taper relief.

Step 5 Tax due £(148,000 – 9,000) 139,000

6 Relief for the fall in value of lifetime gifts

FAST FORWARD

If an asset falls in value between a lifetime gift and death, fall in value relief reduces the death tax payable. The relief affects the tax on the transfer concerned. It does not reduce the value of the gross chargeable transfer for the purpose of computing later IHT.

Where a PET or CLT becomes chargeable to IHT on death and the value of the gift has fallen between the date of the gift and the death of the transferor (or the sale of the property if this precedes death) **fall in value relief may be claimed. Relief is available only if the transferee** (or his spouse/civil partner) **still holds the property at the date of death, or it has been sold in an arm's length transaction** to an unconnected person.

Only the tax on the transfer is reduced by the relief. It does not affect the value of the gross chargeable transfer when considering how much of the nil band is used by the gift.

Question — The fall in value of lifetime gifts

H transferred a house worth £335,000 to his son on 1 June 2010. H then gave £205,000 cash to his daughter on 20 August 2012. Shortly before H's death his son sold the house on the open market for £270,000. H died on 14 July 2013. Calculate the IHT liabilities arising.

Answer

1 June 2010

There is no IHT liability when the gift is made because it is a PET.

	£
Gift	335,000
Less AE 2010/11	(3,000)
Less AE 2009/10 b/f	(3,000)
PET	329,000

The PET becomes chargeable as a result of death within seven years. The value of the chargeable transfer is reduced by the fall in value of the house:

Death tax	*Chargeable Transfer* £
PET	329,000
Less relief for fall in value £(335,000 – 270,000)	(65,000)
	264,000

This is within the nil band so the IHT payable by the son is £Nil.

20 August 2012

There is no IHT liability when the gift is made because it is a PET.

	£
Gift	205,000
Less AE 2012/13	(3,000)
Less AE 2011/12 b/f	(3,000)
PET	199,000

Gross chargeable transfers in the seven years prior to the gift total £329,000 (*not £264,000*), so none of the nil band remains available to use when calculating IHT on the PET to the daughter. The IHT payable by her is, therefore, £199,000 × 40% = £79,600. No taper relief applies as gift was within three years of death.

Chapter roundup

- IHT applies to transfers to trusts, transfers on death and to transfers within the seven years before death.
- Exemptions may apply to make transfers or parts of transfers non chargeable. Some exemptions only apply on lifetime transfers (annual, normal expenditure out of income, marriage/civil partnership), whilst some apply on both life and death transfers (eg spouses, charities, political parties).
- If excluded property is given away, there are no IHT consequences.
- Transfers are cumulated for seven years so that the nil rate band is not available in full on each of a series of transfers in rapid succession.
- IHT is charged on what a donor loses. If the donor pays the IHT on a lifetime gift he loses both the asset given away and the money with which he paid the tax due on it. Grossing up is required.
- If an asset falls in value between a lifetime gift and death, fall in value relief reduces the death tax payable. The relief affects the tax on the transfer concerned. It does not reduce the value of the gross chargeable transfer for the purpose of computing later IHT.

Quick quiz

1 What is a transfer of value?
2 Who is chargeable to inheritance tax?
3 What is the effect of property being excluded property?
4 What types of transfer by an individual are potentially exempt transfers?
5 To what extent may unused annual exemption be carried forward?
6 Don gives some money to his daughter on her marriage. What marriage exemption is applicable?
7 Which lifetime transfers may lead to tax being charged on death of the transferor?
8 Why must some lifetime transfers be grossed up?
9 What is taper relief?

Answers to quick quiz

1 A transfer of value is any gratuitous disposition by a person resulting in a diminution of the value of his estate.

2 Individuals and trustees.

3 Excluded property is ignored for IHT purposes.

4 A potentially exempt transfer is a lifetime transfer made by an individual to another individual.

5 An unused annual exemption can be carried forward one tax year.

6 The marriage exemption for a gift to the transferor's child is £5,000.

7 An IHT charge on death arises on PETs and CLTs made within seven years of the transferor's death.

8 Where the donor pays the lifetime tax due it must be grossed up to calculate the total reduction in value of the estate.

9 Taper relief reduces death tax where a transfer is made between three and seven years before death.

Now try the question below from the Exam Question Bank

Number	Level	Marks	Time
Q17	Introductory	16	29 mins

Inheritance tax: valuation, reliefs and the death estate

17

Topic list	Syllabus reference
1 The valuation of assets for IHT purposes	A4(c)(i)
2 Business property relief (BPR)	A4(c)(ii), (f)(i)
3 Agricultural property relief (APR)	A4(c)(ii), (f)(i)
4 The death estate	A4(a)E3, (d)(iii)
5 Quick succession relief (QSR)	A4(d)(v)
6 Grossing up gifts on death	A4(d)(iii)

Introduction

We started our study of IHT in the previous chapter with a look at which transfers are exempt from IHT and the charge to IHT on lifetime transfers which are, or become, chargeable.

This chapter opens with a section on how assets are valued. Pay particular attention to the related property rules, which prevent one way of avoiding IHT.

Two of the reliefs described in this chapter, business property relief and agricultural property relief, are very generous. If the conditions are satisfied, assets can be exempted from IHT without any limit on the value of the assets. These reliefs are meant to ensure that a family business or farm does not have to be sold when an owner dies, but they also extend to non-family businesses and farms.

Finally, we will see how to bring together all of a deceased person's assets at death, and compute the tax on the estate.

In the next chapter we turn our attention to some additional aspects of IHT including the overseas aspects and administration rules.

Study guide

		Intellectual level
4	**Inheritance tax in situations involving further aspects of the scope of the tax and the calculation of the liabilities arising, the principles of valuation and the reliefs available, transfers of property to and from trusts, overseas aspects and further aspects of administration**	
(a)	The contents of the Paper F6 study guide for inheritance tax under headings:	
•	E3 The liabilities arising on chargeable lifetime transfers and on the death of an individual	2
(c)	The basic principles of computing transfers of value:	
(i)	Advise on the principles of valuation	3
(ii)	Advise on the availability of business property relief and agricultural property relief	3
(d)	The liabilities arising on chargeable lifetime transfers and on the death of an individual:	3
(iii)	Advise on the tax liability arising on a death estate	
(v)	Advise on the operation of quick succession relief	
(f)	The use of exemptions and reliefs in deferring and minimising inheritance tax liabilities:	3
(i)	Advise on the use of reliefs and exemptions to minimise inheritance tax liabilities, as mentioned in the sections above	

Exam guide

In the P6 exam, you may be required to deal with advanced aspects of inheritance tax such as valuing overseas property and quick succession relief. These are covered in this Chapter.

Business and agricultural property reliefs are a new topic for P6. They are extremely valuable reliefs as they enable assets to be passed on tax free, and they are therefore likely to feature in IHT planning. You should note the withdrawal of the relief on lifetime transfers if the donee sells the property or ceases to use if for business or agricultural purposes. There is no such limitation for gifts on death. Another new topic is the reduced rate of IHT on the death estate where at least 10% of the net estate passes to charity.

Knowledge brought forward from earlier studies

The basic principles of valuation of assets for inheritance tax and computing inheritance tax on the death estate were covered in the F6 syllabus. The examiner has identified essential underpinning knowledge from the F6 syllabus which is particularly important that you revise as part of your P6 studies. In this chapter, the relevant topic is:

		Intellectual level
E3	**The liabilities arising on chargeable lifetime transfers and on the death of an individual**	
(c)	Compute the tax liability on a death estate.	2

There are no changes in 2013/14 in the topics covered at F6 in 2012/13.

1 The valuation of assets for IHT purposes

FAST FORWARD

There are special rules for valuing particular kinds of assets, such as quoted shares and securities. The related property rules prevent artificial reductions in value.

1.1 The general principle

The value of any property for the purposes of IHT is the price which the property might reasonably be expected to fetch if sold in the open market at the time of the transfer.

Two or more assets can be valued jointly if disposal as one unit is the course that a prudent hypothetical vendor would have adopted in order to obtain the most favourable price: *Gray v IRC 1994.*

1.2 Quoted shares and securities

The valuation of quoted shares and securities is easy: the Stock Exchange daily official list gives the closing bid and offer prices of all quoted securities. **Inheritance tax valuations are done on the same basis as for CGT ie taking the lower of:**

(a) The value on the quarter up basis.

(b) The average of the highest and lowest marked bargains for the day, ignoring those marked at special prices.

The transfer may take place on a day on which the Stock Exchange is closed, in which case the valuation is done on the basis of the prices or bargains marked on the last previous day of business or the first following day of business. The lowest of, in this case, the four alternatives will be taken.

Valuations for transfers on death must be cum dividend or cum interest, including the value of the right to the next dividend or interest payment. However, if the question gives an **ex dividend** or an ex interest price and the transfer is on death then the valuation is done on the basis of **adding the whole of the impending net dividend**, or the whole of the impending interest payment net of 20% tax.

Exam focus point

If a question just gives a closing price you may assume that it is the cum dividend or cum interest price.

For lifetime transfers, the Stock Exchange list prices are used without adjustment, whether they are cum or ex dividend or interest.

1.3 Example: securities quoted ex interest

If someone owned £10,000 12% Government stock (interest payable half yearly) quoted at 94-95 ex interest, the valuation on death would be as follows.

	£	£
£10,000 at 94.25 (quarter up rule)		9,425
Add ½ × 12% × £10,000	600	
Less income tax at 20%	(120)	
		480
		9,905

1.4 Unquoted shares and securities

There is no easily identifiable open market value for shares in an unquoted company. Shares and Assets Valuation at HMRC is the body with which the taxpayer must negotiate. If agreement cannot be reached, an appeal can be made to the Tax Tribunal.

1.5 Unit trusts

Units in authorised unit trusts are valued at the managers' bid price (**the lower of the two published prices**).

1.6 Life assurance policies

Where a person's estate includes a life policy which matures on his death, the proceeds payable to his personal representatives must be included in his estate for IHT purposes. But where a person's estate includes a life policy which matures on the death of someone else, the open market value must be included in his estate.

If an individual writes a policy in trust, or assigns a policy, or makes a subsequent declaration of trust, the policy proceeds will not be paid to his estate but to the assignee or to the trustees for the trust beneficiaries. The proceeds will, therefore, not be included as part of his free estate at death. It is common to write policies in trust for the benefit of dependants to avoid IHT. If the individual continues to pay the premiums on such policies, each premium constitutes a separate transfer of value. However, in many cases these transfers will be exempted as normal expenditure out of income.

1.7 Overseas property

The basis of valuation is the same as for UK property. The value is converted into sterling at the exchange rate (the 'buy' or 'sell' rate) which will give the lower sterling equivalent. Overseas debts are deductible.

If the property passes on death, the costs of administering and realising overseas property are deductible up to a maximum of 5% of the gross value of the property, so far as those expenses are attributable to the property's location overseas. **Capital taxes paid overseas which are the foreign equivalent of IHT may give rise to double taxation relief** (see later in this Text). Such taxes are given as a credit against the IHT payable; they do not reduce the value of the asset.

1.8 Related property

FAST FORWARD

Related property must be valued as a proportion of the value of the whole of the related property if this produces a higher value than the stand alone value.

Key term

Property is related to that in a person's estate (**related property**) if:

(a) It is included in the estate of his spouse/civil partner, or

(b) It has been given to a charity, political party, national public body or housing association as an exempt transfer by either spouse or civil partner and still is, or within the preceding five years has been, the property of the body it was given to.

To reduce the value transferred individuals might fragment an asset into several parts which are collectively worth less than the whole. This way of reducing the value of an asset or set of assets is normally prevented using the diminution in value principle. However, this application of the principle could be thwarted by use of exempt inter-spouse/civil partner transfers. To deter this method of avoiding IHT, there are provisions under which related property is taken into account.

Property which is related to other property must be valued as a proportion of the value of the whole of the related property but only if, by so doing, a higher value is produced. For example, where a husband and wife each hold 40% of the issued shares of a company, the husband's holding will normally be valued as a proportion (one half) of the price which an 80% shareholding would fetch, as an 80% interest would normally be more valuable than two 40% interests.

1.9 Example: related property

Lenny has a leasehold interest in a property. The value of his interest is £25,000. His wife Mandy holds the freehold reversion of the property, which has a market value of £40,000. The value of the freehold not subject to the lease (that is the value of the freehold reversion plus the lease) is £80,000. If Lenny wishes to transfer his interest to their daughter Sarah the value transferred will be the greater of:

(a) The value of the interest by itself, £25,000, and

(b) The value of his part of the total related property, which is

$$\frac{\text{The value of the property transferred at its } \textit{unrelated} \text{ value}}{\text{The value of the property transferred at its } \textit{unrelated} \text{ value} + \text{The value of any related property at its } \textit{unrelated} \text{ value}} \times \text{The value of the whole property}$$

$$\frac{25,000}{25,000 + 40,000} \times £80,000 = £30,769.$$

The higher value is £30,769. This is therefore the value transferred by Lenny.

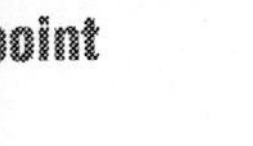

Exam focus point

If the property in question is shares, then in arriving at the fraction set out above, the numbers of shares held are used instead of unrelated values.

Question — Valuation of shares

Shares in an unquoted company are held as follows.

	Number of shares
Husband (H)	4,000
Wife (W)	2,000
Son (S)	750
Shares given by H to a charity by an exempt transfer eight years ago (and still owned by the charity)	3,250
	10,000

Estimated values for different sizes of shareholding are as follows.

Number of shares	*Pence per share*	£
750	60	450
2,000	90	1,800
4,000	130	5,200
7,250	200	14,500
9,250	250	23,125

What is the value of H's holding, taking into account related property?

Answer

There are three related holdings.

	Shares
H	4,000
W	2,000
Charity	3,250
	9,250

The value of H's 4,000 shares is $\frac{4,000}{9,250} \times £23,125 = £10,000$ (ie 250 pence × 4,000 shares).

If in the above exercise H gives away half of his holding to his son, the transfer of value is as follows.

	£
Holding before transfer (as above)	10,000
Less holding after transfer	
$\frac{2,000}{7,250} \times £14,500$	(4,000)
Transfer of value	6,000

If H transferred all his shares the value transferred would be £10,000 (no holding after, so no value in the calculation performed above).

2 Business property relief (BPR)

FAST FORWARD

BPR can reduce the values of assets by 100% or 50%. However, there are strict conditions, which are largely intended to prevent people near death from obtaining the reliefs by investing substantial sums in businesses.

2.1 Business property

One of the competencies you require to fulfil performance objective 20 of the PER is the ability to assist with tax planning. You can apply the knowledge you obtain from this section of the text to help to demonstrate this competence.

BPR is applied to the value of relevant business property transferred, to prevent large tax liabilities arising on transfers of businesses.

Relevant business property is:

(a) Property consisting of a business or an interest (such as a partnership share) in a business

(b) Securities of a company which are unquoted and which (alone or with other securities or unquoted shares) gave the transferor control of the company immediately before the transfer (control may be achieved by taking into account related property)

(c) Any unquoted shares (not securities) in a company

(d) Shares in or securities of a company which are quoted and which (alone or with other such shares or securities) gave the transferor control of the company immediately before the transfer (control may be achieved by taking into account related property)

(e) Any land or building, machinery or plant which, immediately before the transfer, was used wholly or mainly for the purposes of a business carried on by a company of which the transferor then had control, or by a partnership of which he was then a partner

Shares or securities on the AIM count as unquoted.

The reliefs available are percentage reductions in the value transferred: 100% for assets within Paragraph (a), (b) or (c) above, and 50% for assets within Paragraph (d) or (e) above.

2.2 Conditions for BPR

BPR is only available if the relevant business property:

(a) was owned by the transferor for at least the two years preceding the transfer, or

(b) replaced other relevant business property (which includes agricultural property used in a farming business) where the combined period of ownership of both sets of property was at least two out of the last five years. In this situation relief is given on the lower of the values of the two sets of property.

If the property was inherited, it is deemed to have been owned from the date of the death unless it was inherited from the transferor's spouse or civil partner, in which case the transferor is deemed to have owned it for the period the spouse or civil partner owned it.

BPR is still available even if the transferor cannot fulfil either of the two year ownership criteria if when he acquired the property it was eligible for BPR and either the previous or this current transfer was made on death.

2.3 Additional conditions for BPR on lifetime transfers

If, as a result of the donor's death within seven years of a gift, a PET becomes chargeable or additional tax is due on a CLT, two further conditions must be fulfilled for BPR to be available.

(a) The donee must still own the original property at the date of the donor's death, or the donee's death if earlier.

(b) The original property must still qualify as relevant business property at the date of the donor's death, or the donee's death if earlier.

These conditions are fulfilled if the donee disposed of the original property but reinvested **all** of the disposal proceeds in replacement property within three years of the disposal.

2.4 Non-qualifying businesses

BPR is not available if the business consists wholly or mainly of:

(a) Dealing in securities, stocks and shares (except for discount houses and market makers on the Stock Exchange or on LIFFE)

(b) Dealing in land or buildings

(c) Making or holding investments (including land which is let)

Shares in holding companies, where the subsidiaries have activities which would qualify shares in them for BPR, are eligible for relief.

2.5 Excepted assets

Relevant business property excludes assets which were neither used wholly or mainly for the purposes of the business in the two years preceding the transfer nor required at the time of the transfer for future use in the business.

Formula to learn

For shares or securities in a company, the value which we compute BPR on (at 100% or 50%) is:

$$\text{Total value} \times \frac{\text{the company's relevant business property}}{\text{the company's total assets before deducting liabilities}}$$

2.6 Contracts for sale

BPR is not available if at the date of transfer there is a binding contract for the sale of a business or an interest in a business, unless the sale is to a company which will continue the business and the consideration is wholly or mainly shares or securities in the company.

BPR is not available if at the date of the transfer there is a binding contract for the sale of shares or securities of a company unless the sale is for the purpose of reconstruction or amalgamation.

If any other relevant business property is subject to a binding contract for sale, BPR is not available on it at all.

Partnership agreements often contain a buy/sell clause under which surviving partners must buy a deceased partner's share in the partnership. HMRC regard such a clause as a binding contract for sale which disentitles the deceased partner to BPR. However, neither an accruer clause whereby the deceased partner's share accrues to the surviving partners, nor an option for the surviving partners to buy the deceased partner's share is regarded as binding contract for sale. This means that from a tax planning point of view the latter types of arrangement should be used.

Question — BPR

On 31 July 2013 relevant business property valued at £16,800 is transferred to a trust. Assuming that the 2012/13 and 2013/14 annual exemptions have not been used what will the chargeable transfer be if:

(a) The property consists of unquoted shares?
(b) The property consists of land used by a company in which the transferor has a controlling interest?
(c) The property consists of quoted shares which formed part of a 20% interest before the transfer?

Answer

	(a)	*(b)*	*(c)*
	£	£	£
Value transferred	16,800	16,800	16,800
Less BPR	(16,800)	(8,400)	0
	0	8,400	16,800
Less: AE 2013/14		(3,000)	(3,000)
2012/13 b/f		(3,000)	(3,000)
Chargeable transfer	0	2,400	10,800

Question — BPR and related property

J had shares in a quoted trading company, J plc. The shares in the company were held as follows.

	%
J	40
J's wife	30
Other unconnected persons	30
	100

The shareholdings have been unchanged since 2000. On 1 May 2013 J gave a 30% holding to his son. The values of the shares in May 2013 were agreed as follows.

	£
70% holding	1,600,000
40% holding	900,000
30% holding	840,000
10% holding	200,000

J, who had made a previous chargeable lifetime transfer of £350,000 in 2007, died in January 2014.

Calculate the IHT arising on the gift of the shares, if

(a) J's son still holds the shares in January 2014
(b) J's son sells the shares in June 2013 and retains the cash proceeds.

Answer

No IHT arises when the gift was made, because it was a PET. It becomes chargeable as a result of J's death within seven years as follows.

PET – May 2013

(a) If J's son still holds the shares, BPR at 50% is available to reduce the chargeable transfer:

	£
Before: $\frac{40\%}{40\% + 30\%} \times £1{,}600{,}000$	914,286
After: $\frac{10\%}{10\% + 30\%} \times £900{,}000$	(225,000)
	689,286
Less BPR at 50% (control (with related property) of quoted company)	(344,643)
	344,643
Less: AE 2013/14	(3,000)
AE 2012/13 b/f	(3,000)
Chargeable transfer	338,643

Gross chargeable transfers in the seven years before May 2013 amount to £350,000. This means none of the nil band remains and IHT payable on death amounts to:

IHT at 40% = £135,457

(b) If J's son does not hold the shares on J's death, BPR is not available to reduce the value of the chargeable transfer:

	£
Transfer (see above)	689,286
Less: AE 2013/14	(3,000)
AE 2012/13	(3,000)
Chargeable transfer	683,286

IHT @ 40% = £273,314

3 Agricultural property relief (APR)

FAST FORWARD

APR usually reduces a transfer of agricultural property by 100% of agricultural value.

3.1 Agricultural property

One of the competencies you require to fulfil performance objective 20 of the PER is the ability to assist with tax planning. You can apply the knowledge you obtain from this section of the text to help to demonstrate this competence.

APR is available on the agricultural value of agricultural property.

Agricultural property is agricultural land or pasture (including short rotation coppice) situated in the UK, the Channel Islands, the Isle of Man or a country other than the UK which is in the European Economic Area at the time of the transfer. It includes woodland and any building used in connection with the intensive rearing of livestock or fish where the occupation of the woodland or building is ancillary to that of the land or pasture. It also includes cottages, farm buildings and farm houses of a character appropriate to the property.

Exam focus point

The agricultural value will be given to you in the exam.

APR works like BPR in reducing the value being transferred by a certain percentage before any exemptions. APR is given before BPR and double relief cannot be obtained on the agricultural value. If the non-agricultural part of the value of the property meets the relevant business property conditions, however, BPR will be available on that value. **The percentage reduction in agricultural value is, in general, 100%** (it is 50% on some land held under pre-September 1995 tenancies).

3.2 Conditions for relief

For relief to apply the transferor must either:

(a) Own the property and have occupied it themselves for the purpose of agriculture for the two years before the transfer (ie they farm the land themselves), or

(b) Own the property for at least the seven years before the transfer, during which it must have been occupied for the purposes of agriculture by either the transferor or a tenant (ie the property is or has been let out).

If a company controlled by the transferor occupies the property the transferor is treated as occupying it. A farmhouse which is being redecorated, renovated or altered is not treated as though it is occupied for agricultural purposes.

If the property transferred replaces other agricultural property, the condition will be satisfied provided that:

(a) The transferor has occupied the properties for the purposes of agriculture for at least two out of the last five years, or

(b) The transferor has owned the properties (and somebody has occupied them for agricultural purposes) for at least seven out of the last ten years.

If agricultural properties have been replaced the APR will apply only to the lowest of the values of the various properties considered.

If the property transferred was acquired on the death of the transferor's spouse or civil partner then the period of ownership or occupation of the first spouse or civil partner can count towards the seven years or the two years required. If the property transferred was acquired on the death of somebody else the transferor will be deemed to own it from the date of death and if he subsequently occupies it, to have occupied it from the date of death.

APR is still available even if the transferor cannot fulfil any of the two or seven year ownership criteria if when he acquired the property it was eligible for APR and either the previous or this current transfer was made on death.

3.3 Additional conditions for lifetime transfers

If, as a result of the donor's death within seven years of a gift, a PET becomes chargeable or additional tax is due on a CLT, two further conditions must be fulfilled for APR to be available.

(a) The donee must still own the original property at the date of the donor's death, or the donee's death if earlier.

(b) The original property must still qualify as agricultural property immediately prior to the date of the donor's death, or the donee's death if earlier, and must have been occupied as such since the original transfer.

These conditions are fulfilled if the donee disposed of the original property but reinvested **all** of the disposal proceeds in replacement property within three years of the disposal.

3.4 Shares in companies owning agricultural property

If a company owns agricultural property and satisfies the occupation or ownership conditions above then APR is available in respect of the agricultural value that can be attributed to shares or securities transferred by an individual who controls the company. The shares or securities must have been held by the transferor for the relevant period (two years or seven years).

Question

Farming companies

On 13 June 2013 Kevin gives his shares in Farm Ltd to his son. Kevin owns 65% of the shares in issue, with an agreed value of £400,000. Kevin has owned the shares for nine years. The company has owned and occupied farmland (for agricultural purposes) for the last eight years. The agricultural value of this land represents 20% of the total value of the company's net assets.

Calculate the chargeable transfer assuming that Kevin dies on 14 July 2014 and the son still holds the shares at the date of his father's death.

Answer

	£
Unquoted trading company shares	
Value of holding	400,000
Less: APR 100% × 20% × £400,000 (on agricultural value)	(80,000)
BPR 100% × 80% × £400,000 (on balance)	(320,000)
Chargeable transfer	0

3.5 Contracts for sale

No APR is available if, at the time of the transfer, a binding contract for sale of the agricultural property exists unless the sale is to a company (the consideration being wholly or mainly shares or securities which will give the transferor control), or is to enable a reorganisation or reconstruction of a farming company.

4 The death estate

FAST FORWARD

When someone dies, we must bring together all their assets to find the value of their death estate.

4.1 Composition of death estate

An individual's death estate consists of all the property he owned immediately before death, with the exception of excluded property. The estate also includes anything acquired as a result of death, for example the proceeds of a life assurance policy.

The estate at death may include:

(a) Free estate (assets passing by will or intestacy).

(b) Property given subject to a reservation. This is property given away before death, but with strings attached (see next chapter). For example, someone might give away a house but continue to live in it.

The primary responsibility for payment of tax depends on the type of property:

(a) Tax on the free estate is payable by the personal representatives (PRs) (executors or administrators).

(b) Tax on property given subject to a reservation is payable by the person in possession of the property.

The whole of the death estate will be chargeable to tax, subject to reliefs (such as BPR and APR) and any exemptions which may be available on death. In particular, if property passes to the deceased person's spouse this will be an exempt transfer. A transfer to any other person eg children, will be chargeable to IHT, whether this is made outright or to any type of trust.

In order to calculate the tax on the death estate, use the following steps:

Step 1 Look back seven years from the date of death to see if any CLTs or PETs which have become chargeable have been made. If so, these transfers use up the nil rate band available for the death estate. Work out the value of any nil rate band still available.

Step 2 Compute the gross value of the death estate (see further below).

Step 3 Any part of the death estate covered by the nil rate band is taxed at 0%. Any part of the death estate not covered by the nil rate band is charged at 40%. Deduct relevant reliefs from the death tax (eg quick succession relief – see below)

Step 4 Where relevant divide the tax due between PRs and the person in possession of a gift subject to a reservation.

Usually, it will not be necessary to consider grossing up. The situation where it will be needed is dealt with below.

Question

Tax on death estate

Laura dies on 1 August 2013, leaving a free estate valued at £400,000 to a discretionary trust for her children. Laura had made a transfer of value of £163,000 to her sister on 11 September 2012. The amount stated is after all exemptions and reliefs.

Compute the tax payable by Laura's personal representatives.

Answer

Death tax

Note. There is no death tax on the September 2012 PET which becomes chargeable as a result of Laura's death, as it is within the nil rate band at her death. However, it will use up part of the nil rate band, as shown below.

Step 1 Lifetime transfer of value of £163,000 in seven years before 1 August 2013 (transfers after 1 August 2006). Nil rate band of £(325,000 – 163,000) = £162,000 available.

Step 2 Value of death estate is £400,000.

Step 3

		IHT
		£
	£162,000 × 0%	0
	£238,000 × 40%	95,200
	£400,000	95,200
Step 4	Tax payable by personal representatives	£95,200

The computation of an individual's chargeable estate at death should be set out as follows.

	£	£
Death estate		
Personalty		
Stocks and shares		X
Insurance policy proceeds		X
Personal chattels		X
Cash		X
		X
Less debts due by deceased	X	
funeral expenses	X	
		(X)
		X
Realty		
Freehold property (keep UK and foreign property separate)	X	
Less mortgages	(X)	
		X
Net estate		X
Gifts with reservation		X
Chargeable estate		X

4.2 Debts and funeral expenses

The rules on debts are as follows.

(a) Only debts incurred by the deceased *bona fide* and for full consideration may be deducted.

(b) The debts must be such as an executor could pay without making himself personally liable for a misuse of the assets of the estate. So gaming debts are not deductible but statute barred debts are, provided the executor pays them.

(c) **Debts incurred by the deceased but payable after the death may be deducted** but the amount should be discounted because of the future date of payment.

(d) Rent and similar amounts which accrue day by day should be accrued up to the date of death.

(e) **Taxes to the date of death may be deducted** as they are a liability imposed by law.

(f) **Debts incurred by the executor are not allowed.**

(g) **If a debt is charged on a specific property it is deductible primarily from that property**; a mortgage on freehold property is therefore deductible from that freehold.

(h) Debts contracted abroad must first be deducted from non-UK property (whether or not the value of that property is chargeable to inheritance tax). If the foreign debts exceed the value of the foreign property the excess is allowed as a deduction from UK property provided it represents debts recoverable in the UK.

Reasonable funeral expenses may be deducted.

(a) What is reasonable depends on the deceased's condition in life.
(b) Reasonable costs of mourning for the family (and servants) are allowed.
(c) **The cost of a tombstone is deductible.**

Zack died on 19 June 2013. His estate consisted of the following.

10,000 shares in A plc, quoted at 84p – 89p with bargains marked at 85p, 87p and 90p

8,000 shares in B plc, quoted ex div at 111p – 115p. A net dividend of 4p per share was paid on 21 July 2013.

Freehold property valued at £150,000 subject to a mortgage of £45,040

Liabilities and funeral expenses amounted to £2,450.

Zack had made a chargeable lifetime transfer of £340,000 in July 2008. Calculate the IHT liability on the death estate.

Answer

Free estate

	£	£
Personalty		
A plc shares		
10,000 at lower of 85.25p and 87.5p		
10,000 × 85.25p		8,525
B plc		
8,000 × 112p	8,960	
Net dividend 8,000 × 4p	320	
		9,280
		17,805
Less debts and funeral expenses		(2,450)
		15,355
Realty		
Freehold property	150,000	
Less mortgage	(45,040)	
		104,960
Chargeable estate		120,315

Chargeable transfers in the seven years prior to death exceeded the nil band, so IHT on the death estate is £120,315 at 40% = £48,126.

4.3 Transfer of unused nil rate band

One of the competencies you require to fulfil performance objective 20 of the PER is the ability to assist with tax planning. You can apply the knowledge you obtain from this section of the text to help to demonstrate this competence.

4.3.1 How the transfer of unused nil rate band works

If:

- **an individual ("A") dies**; and
- **A had a spouse or civil partner ("B") and A and B were married or in a civil partnership immediately before B's death**; and
- **B had unused nil rate band (wholly or in part) on death;**

then a **claim may be made to increase the nil rate band maximum at the date of A's death by B's unused nil rate band** in order to calculate the IHT on A's death. The revised nil band will apply to the calculation of additional death tax on CLTs made by A, PETs made by A and death tax on A's death estate.

4.3.2 Example

Robert and Claudia were married for many years until the death of Robert on 10 April 2013 leaving an estate of £500,000.

In his will, Robert left £100,000 to his sister and the remainder of his estate to Claudia. He had made no lifetime transfers.

Claudia died on 12 January 2014 leaving an estate (including the assets passed to her by Robert) of £850,000 to her brother. Claudia had made a chargeable lifetime transfer of £50,000 in 2011.

The inheritance tax payable on the death of Claudia, assuming that a claim is made to transfer Robert's unused nil rate band, is calculated as follows:

Step 1 (a) Lifetime transfer of value of £50,000 in seven years before 12 January 2014 (transfers after 12 January 2007).

(b) Nil rate band at death is £325,000. Nil rate band is increased by claim to transfer Robert's unused nil rate band at death £(325,000 – 100,000) = £225,000. The maximum nil rate band at Claudia's death is therefore £(325,000 + 225,000) = £550,000 and the available nil rate band is £(550,000 – 50,000) = £500,000.

Step 2 Value of death estate is £850,000.

Step 3

	IHT
	£
£500,000 × 0%	0
£350,000 × 40%	140,000
£850,000	140,000

Step 4 Tax payable by personal representatives £140,000

Note that the legacy to Robert's sister was a chargeable death transfer but that the gift of the rest of the estate to Claudia was exempt under the spouse exemption.

4.3.3 Changes in nil rate band between deaths of spouses/civil partners

If the nil rate band increases between the death of B and the death of A, the amount of B's unused nil rate band must be scaled up so that it represents the same proportion of the nil rate band at A's death as it did at B's death.

For example, if the nil rate band at B's death was £300,000 and B had an unused nil rate band of £90,000, the unused proportion in percentage terms is therefore 90,000/300,000 × 100 = 30%. If A dies when the nil rate band has increased to £325,000, B's unused nil rate band is £325,000 × 30% = £97,500 and this amount is transferred to increase the nil rate band maximum available on A's death.

The increase in the nil rate band maximum cannot exceed the nil rate band maximum at the date of A's death eg if the nil rate band is £325,000, the increase cannot exceed £325,000, giving a total of £650,000.

Question **Transfer of nil rate band**

Jenna and Rebecca were civil partners until the death of Jenna on 19 August 2007.

Jenna made no lifetime transfers. Her death estate was £440,000 and she left £200,000 to Rebecca and the remainder to her mother.

Rebecca died on 24 February 2014. Her death estate was £550,000 (including the assets passed to her by Jenna) and she left her entire estate to her nephews and nieces. She had made no lifetime transfers.

You are required to calculate the inheritance tax payable on the death of Rebecca, assuming that any beneficial claims are made.

Answer

Step 1 (a) No lifetime transfers of value in seven years before 24 February 2014.

(b) Nil rate band at death is £325,000. Nil rate band is increased by claim to transfer Jenna's unused nil rate band at death. The nil rate band at Jenna's death in August 2007 was £300,000. Unused proportion was £(300,000 – 240,000) = 60,000/300,000 × 100 = 20%. The adjusted unused proportion is therefore £325,000 x 20% = £65,000. The maximum nil rate band at Rebecca's death is therefore £(325,000 + 65,000) = £390,000 and this is also the available nil band.

Step 2 Value of death estate is £550,000.

Step 3

	IHT
	£
£390,000 × 0%	0
£160,000 × 40%	64,000
£550,000	64,000

Step 4 Tax payable by personal representatives £64,000

4.3.4 Claim

The claim to transfer the unused nil rate band is usually made by the personal representatives of A. The time limit for the claim is two years from the end of the month of A's death (or the period of three months after the personal representatives start to act, if later) or such longer period as an officer of HMRC may allow in a particular case.

If the personal representatives do not make a claim, a claim can be made by any other person liable to tax chargeable on A's death within such later period as an officer of HMRC may allow in a particular case.

4.4 Reduced rate on death estate

FAST FORWARD

The rate of inheritance tax on a death estate is reduced to 36% if at least 10% of the estate is left to charity.

We saw earlier in this Text, that gifts to charities are exempt. To encourage more people to leave gifts to charity on their death, there is also **a reduced rate of inheritance tax (36%**, rather than 40%) available **on the remaining death estate** if an individual **leaves at least 10% of his net estate to charity.**

There are therefore two benefits of leaving such a legacy - the donated part of the estate is exempt and the remainder is charged at a lower rate of IHT.

For the purpose of determining whether the 10% condition is met, **the net estate** is calculated as the **assets owned at death as reduced by liabilities, exemptions, reliefs and the available nil rate band, but before the charitable legacy itself is deducted**. However the inheritance tax itself is then charged (at 36%) on the usual death estate (ie after the legacy has been deducted).

Question — Reduced rate of IHT

Margie died on 1 September 2013. The assets in her estate are valued at £380,000, and she had made a gross chargeable transfer of £100,000 in 2008. In her will she left £20,000 to charity and the rest of her estate to a trust for her children. Calculate the inheritance tax payable on her death estate.

Answer

First, work out whether the reduced rate of IHT applies, as follows.

	£
Death estate (before deduction of charitable legacy)	380,000
Less: available nil rate band £(325,000 – 100,000)	(225,000)
Net estate	155,000

10% of £155,000 is £15,500, so the legacy of £20,000 is at least 10% of the net estate and therefore the reduced rate of 36% applies.

	£
Death estate	380,000
Less: charitable legacy	(20,000)
Chargeable estate	360,000
IHT	
£225,000 × 0%	0
£135,000 × 36%	48,600
£360,000	
IHT payable on death estate	48,600

Exam focus point

The calculation can become complicated where there are assets owned jointly with other people or assets held on trust but the examiner has stated that the reduced rate will only be examined where all of the assets are 100% owned by the deceased.

A variation of the will (see later in this Text) may be entered into after the death of an individual in order to increase the amount given to charity, such that the estate then qualifies for the reduced rate. Although the gross value of the remaining estate is then lower for the other beneficiaries of the will, the reduced rate of IHT on this lower amount may outweigh the cost of the increased gift to charity and increase the net assets passing to other beneficiaries.

4.5 Example

Barry died on 1 July 2013 leaving a gross chargeable estate valued at £860,000. In his will, he left a donation of £60,000 to charity and the rest of his estate to his son, Trig. Barry's available nil rate band at his death was £170,000.

Barry's net estate for the purposes of working out whether the reduced rate applies is £(860,000 – 170,000) = £690,000. Therefore at least 10% × £690,000 = £69,000 must be left to charity for the reduced rate of IHT to apply to the death estate.

The reduced rate is not available because Barry's charitable donation is less than £69,000. The inheritance tax on Barry's death estate is therefore £(860,000 – 60,000 – 170,000) = £630,000 × 40% = £252,000. Trig will received net assets of £(860,000 – 60,000 – 252,000) = £548,000.

However, a variation of the will could be used to increase the charitable donation by £9,000 to £69,000. This would reduce the inheritance tax liability to £(860,000 – 69,000 – 170,000) × 36% = £223,560. This is a saving of £252,000 – £223,560 = £28,440 which is greater than the additional charitable donation. Trig will receive net assets of £(860,000 – 69,000 – 223,560) = £567,440.

5 Quick succession relief (QSR)

FAST FORWARD

Quick succession relief applies where there are two charges to IHT within five years.

If a person dies shortly after receiving property by way of a chargeable transfer the same property will be taxed twice within a short space of time: it will be taxed as the original chargeable transfer and it will be taxed again as part of the estate of the deceased transferee. QSR reduces the tax on the estate.

The tax on the estate is calculated normally. A credit is then given as follows.

Formula to learn

$$\text{Tax paid on first transfer} \times \frac{\text{net transfer}}{\text{gross transfer}} \times \text{percentage}$$

The percentage to use is as follows.

Period between the transfer and the death of the transferee	Relief
	%
1 year or less	100
1-2 years	80
2-3 years	60
3-4 years	40
4-5 years	20
Over 5 years	0

If the period is precisely two years, 80% relief is given, and so on.

The relief applies even where the asset has been disposed of before death.

Question

QSR

Oscar died on 29 September 2013 leaving an estate valued at £385,000 to his son. Oscar had received £28,000 gross in July 2009 from his uncle's estate. IHT of £4,200 had been payable by Oscar on this legacy.

Calculate the IHT payable on Oscar's estate, assuming he has made no lifetime transfers.

Answer

	£
IHT on £385,000 (£325,000 @ 0% + £60,000 @ 40%)	24,000
Less QSR: £4,200 × (23,800/28,000) × 20% (4-5 years)	(714)
IHT payable on Oscar's estate	23,286

6 Grossing up gifts on death

FAST FORWARD

Gross up specific gifts on death if the residue of the estate is left to an exempt recipient.

We saw that grossing up applies to CLTs when the donor pays the IHT. **We must also gross up on a death when there is a specific legacy (ie gift on death) of UK property, and the residue of the estate (ie what's left of the estate after specific gifts have been paid out) is exempt. This can happen when the residue is left to a spouse/ civil partner or charity.**

The reason for this is that the recipients of specific gifts of UK property do not pay the tax on the gift. Instead this must be borne by the residue of the estate – which is exempt. Specific gifts of foreign property, on the other hand, do bear their own tax (ie the recipient must pay any IHT) and do not need to be grossed up.

Do not gross up specific gifts if the whole estate is chargeable. In such cases, work out IHT as normal.

Specific gifts of UK property are given to the heirs in full (unless there is not enough residue to pay the IHT), and the IHT on those gifts comes out of the residue. In this case, the formula used to calculate the tax is as follows.

Formula to learn

$$\text{Chargeable amount (in excess of the nil band)} \times \frac{40}{60} \text{ ie } \frac{\text{rate of tax}}{\text{100 minus the rate of tax}}$$

Question — Specific gifts and exempt residue

Rory dies on 29 May 2013 leaving an estate valued at £490,000. Included in this is a house in Manchester valued at £400,000 which he leaves to his son, Ian. He leaves the residue of the estate to his wife, Sonya.

Calculate the IHT liability arising on death assuming Rory has made no lifetime transfers.

Answer

There is an exempt residue and a specific gift of a UK asset. Therefore the specific gift must be grossed up:

	IHT
	£
£325,000 @ 0%	0
£75,000 @ 40/60	50,000
£400,000	50,000

The gross transfer is £(400,000 + 50,000) = £450,000.

Check tax £(450,000 – 325,000) = £125,000 @ 40% = £50,000.

Ian receives £400,000, HMRC receives £50,000.

The residue available to Sonya is £490,000 – £450,000 = £40,000.

This calculation would not have applied if:

(a) The residue of the estate had been chargeable rather than exempt, in which case IHT would have been calculated on a gross chargeable estate of £490,000 in the normal way, or

(b) The will had left a specific gift of £90,000 to Sonya and the residue to Ian. In that case, Ian would have received £400,000 less tax of £(400,000 – 325,000) × 40% = £30,000, giving him a net amount of £370,000 and Sonya would have received £90,000. This would be a tax saving of £20,000.

Chapter roundup

- There are special rules for valuing particular kinds of assets, such as quoted shares and securities. The related property rules prevent artificial reductions in value.
- Related property must be valued as a proportion of the value of the whole of the related property if this produces a higher value than the stand alone value.
- BPR can reduce the values of assets by 100% or 50%. However, there are strict conditions, which are largely intended to prevent people near death from obtaining the reliefs by investing substantial sums in businesses.
- APR usually reduces a transfer of agricultural property by 100% of agricultural value.
- When someone dies, we must bring together all their assets to find the value of their death estate.
- The rate of inheritance tax on a death estate is reduced to 36% if at least 10% of the estate is left to charity.
- Quick succession relief applies where there are two charges to IHT within five years.
- Gross up specific gifts on death if the residue of the estate is left to an exempt recipient.

Quick quiz

1 How are quoted securities valued?

2 What is related property?

3 What rate of BPR is given on a controlling shareholding in

(a) a quoted trading company, and
(b) an unquoted trading company?

4 What periods of ownership or occupation are required to obtain agricultural property relief?

5 How is quick succession relief calculated?

6 Sonia dies leaving the following debts:

(a) Grocery bill
(b) HM Revenue and Customs – income tax to death
(c) Mortgage on house
(d) Gambling debt

Which are deductible against her death estate and why?

7 Mark and Hilary had been married for many years. Mark died on 11 May 2013 leaving his estate to Hilary. He had made a chargeable lifetime transfer of £160,000 in July 2010. If Hilary dies in February 2014, what is the nil rate band maximum on her death?

Answers to quick quiz

1 The value is the lower of:

- the value on the quarter up basis (bid price plus 1/4 of the difference between the bid and offer prices).
- the average of highest and lowest marked bargains for the day (ignoring special price bargains).

2 Related property is property:

- comprised in the estate of the transferor's spouse, or
- which has been given to a charity, political party, national public body or housing association as an exempt transfer by either spouse and still is, or has been within the past five years, been the property of the body it was given to.

3 (a) 50%
(b) 100%

4 For APR the transferor must have either:

- owned and farmed the land themselves for two years before the transfer, or
- owned the property for at least seven years before the transfer during which time it was farmed either by the transferor or a tenant.

5 QSR is calculated as:

$$\text{Tax paid on first transfer} \times \frac{\text{net transfer}}{\text{gross transfer}} \times \%$$

6 (a) grocery bill – deductible as incurred for full consideration
(b) income tax to death – deductible as imposed by law
(c) mortgage – deductible, will be set against value of house primarily
(d) gambling debt – not allowable as executor be liable for misuse of estate assets if paid

7 Hilary's nil rate band is £325,000. Mark's unused nil rate band is £(325,000 – 160,000) = £165,000. The nil rate band maximum on Hilary's death is therefore £490,000.

Now try the question below from the Exam Question Bank

Number	Level	Marks	Time
Q18	Examination	25	45 mins

Inheritance tax: additional aspects

Topic list	Syllabus reference
1 Overseas aspects	A4(b)(i), (b)(iii), (d)(vi)
2 Gifts with reservation	A4(b)(iv)
3 Associated operations	A4(b)(v)
4 Altering dispositions made on death	A4(d)(vii)
5 The administration of IHT	A4(a)E5, (g)(i)–(iii)

Introduction

In the previous two chapters we have studied the charge to IHT both on lifetime transfers and on death, and have looked at some exemptions and reliefs.

In this chapter, we look at overseas aspects, including relief where property is subject both to IHT and to a similar tax abroad.

We also look at two important sets of anti-avoidance provisions. The rules on gifts with reservation prevent people from avoiding IHT by claiming to give property away before death while in fact retaining rights over it. The rules on associated operations allow HMRC to defeat tax avoidance schemes which rely on breaking down one transaction into several artificial steps to avoid IHT.

We also consider how a will can be altered and, finally, we look at the administration and payment of IHT.

In the next chapter we look at trusts and stamp taxes.

Study guide

		Intellectual level
4	**Inheritance tax in situations involving further aspects of the scope of the tax and the calculation of the liabilities arising, the principles of valuation and the reliefs available, transfers of property to and from trusts, overseas aspects and further aspects of administration**	
(a)	The contents of the Paper F6 study guide for inheritance tax under headings:	2
•	E5 Payment of inheritance tax	
(b)	The scope of inheritance tax:	
(i)	Explain the concepts of domicile and deemed domicile and understand the application of these concepts to inheritance tax	2
(iii)	Identify and advise on the tax implications of the location of assets	3
(iv)	Identify and advise on gifts with reservation of benefit	3
(v)	Identify and advise on the tax implications of associated operations	2
(d)	The liabilities arising on chargeable lifetime transfers and on the death of an individual	3
(vi)	Advise on the operation of double tax relief for inheritance tax	
(vii)	Advise on the inheritance tax effects and advantages of the variation of wills	
(g)	The system by which inheritance tax is administered, including the instalment option for the payment of tax:	
(i)	Identify who is responsible for the payment of inheritance tax.	2
(ii)	Identify the occasions on which inheritance tax may be paid by instalments.	2
(iii)	Advise on the due dates, interest and penalties for inheritance tax purposes.	3

Exam guide

The topics covered in this chapter are mainly new at P6 and are important for tax planning questions. The anti-avoidance rules for gifts with reservation and associated operations are designed to ensure that individuals are taxed on what they have effectively given away entirely. The rules for foreign assets are beneficial to non-domiciliaries. Note, however, that you have to take positive action to change your domicile, and that the deemed domicile rules mean that it takes at least three years to escape the UK IHT net.

Knowledge brought forward from earlier studies

The topic of inheritance tax administration was covered in the F6 syllabus and is included in this Chapter. New aspects also covered in this chapter include the payment of tax by instalments, and interest and penalties. There are no changes in 2013/14 from the material studied in F6 for 2012/13.

1 Overseas aspects

1.1 Domicile

1.1.1 UK domicile

FAST FORWARD

A UK domiciled, or deemed UK domiciled, individual is subject to inheritance tax on transfers of all assets, wherever situated.

If an individual is **UK domiciled**, or deemed UK domiciled (see below), **transfers of all assets, wherever situated, are subject to IHT**.

Domicile for IHT has the same meaning as in general law, namely **the country of one's permanent home**.

Also, an individual is **deemed to be domiciled in the UK for IHT purposes**:

(a) If the individual has been **resident in the UK for at least 17 out of the 20 tax years** ending with the year in which any chargeable transfer is made. The term 'residence' has the same meaning as for income tax (see earlier in this Text).

(b) **For 36 months after ceasing to be domiciled in the UK** under general law.

Exam focus point

It is important to remember that this deemed domicile rule only applies to inheritance tax. A common exam mistake is to also apply it to capital gains tax!

FAST FORWARD

An election may be made for a non-UK domiciled individual who is, or was, the spouse or civil partner of a UK domiciled individual, to be treated as UK domiciled for IHT purposes.

An individual who is:

(a) **not UK domiciled, nor deemed UK domiciled, and**
(b) **is the spouse or civil partner of a UK domiciled individual,**

may make an irrevocable election to be treated as UK domiciled for IHT purposes only.

The **effect of the election** is that **transfers by the UK domiciled spouse/civil partner to the non-UK domiciled individual are wholly exempt** and not subject to the restriction for transfers to a non-domiciled spouse/civil partner detailed earlier in this Text. However, the election also has the effect of **bringing the non-UK domiciled individual's assets situated outside the UK within the charge to IHT.** It is therefore important to consider both these aspects before the election is made.

An election is called a **'lifetime election'** if it is **made by the non-UK domiciled spouse/civil partner** in the **lifetime of the UK domiciled spouse/civil partner**.

An election is called a **'death election'** if it is **made after the death of the UK domiciled spouse/civil partner**, where that death was on or after 6 April 2013. That **deceased spouse/civil partner** must have been **UK domiciled within the period of seven years ending with the date of death**. A death election can be made by the non-UK domiciled spouse/civil partner or his personal representatives. A death election must be made within two years of the death of the UK domiciled spouse/civil partner, or such longer period as an officer of HMRC may allow.

UK domicile is treated as taking effect on a date specified in the election. This date **cannot be prior to 6 April 2013**. Subject to this, **the specified date can be within seven years before the date of the election** (for a lifetime election) or **within seven years before the UK domiciled spouse/civil partner's death** (for a death election).

A lifetime or death election cannot be revoked. However, **if the individual who made the election is not resident in the United Kingdom for the purposes of income tax for a period of four successive tax years**, beginning at any time after the election is made, **the election ceases to have effect at the end of that period**.

1.1.2 Non-UK domicile

FAST FORWARD

Non-UK assets of individuals not domiciled in the UK are not subject to IHT.

For individuals **not domiciled in the UK, only transfers of UK assets are within the charge to IHT**, and even some assets within the UK are excluded property.

1.2 The location of assets

For someone not domiciled in the UK, the location of assets is clearly important:

(a) **Land and buildings**, freehold or leasehold, are in the country in which they are **physically situated**.

(b) **A debt** is in the **country of residence of the debtor** unless it is a debt evidenced by a deed, when the debt is where the deed is. Judgement debts are situated wherever the judgement is recorded.

(c) **Life policies** are in the **country where the proceeds are payable**.

(d) **Registered shares and securities** are in the **country where they are registered**, or where they would normally be dealt with in the ordinary course of business.

(e) **Bearer securities** are **where the certificate of title is located** at the time of transfer.

(f) **Bank accounts** are at the **branch** where the account is kept.

(g) **An interest in a partnership** is where the partnership **business is carried on.**

(h) **Goodwill** is where the **business** to which it is attached is **carried on.**

(i) **Tangible property** is at its **physical location.**

(j) Property held in trust follows the above rules regardless of the rules of the trust or residence of the trustees.

1.3 Excluded property

As we saw earlier, foreign property of a non-UK domiciled individual is excluded property so is ignored for IHT purposes. The following are also excluded property.

(a) Foreign assets in a trust established when the settlor was non-UK domiciled for IHT purposes. No IHT is due on the trust assets even if the settlor becomes UK domiciled at a later date.

(b) Certain British Government securities whose terms of issue provide that they shall be exempt from taxation so long as they are owned by non-UK domiciled or not ordinarily resident individuals (the extended IHT definition of deemed domicile above does not apply).

(c) The following savings if held by persons domiciled in the Channel Islands or the Isle of Man (the extended IHT definition of deemed domicile above does not apply):
  - (i) War savings certificates
  - (ii) National Savings & Investments certificates
  - (iii) Premium savings bonds
  - (iv) Deposits in National Savings & Investments accounts or with a trustee savings bank
  - (v) SAYE savings schemes (see earlier in this Text)

(d) Unit trust units or shares in open ended investment companies (OEICs) held by non-UK domiciliaries.

In addition, if someone dies when neither domiciled nor resident in the UK, a foreign currency account held at a UK bank is ignored in computing his death estate.

1.4 Double taxation relief (DTR)

FAST FORWARD

Double taxation relief may reduce the IHT on assets also taxed overseas.

DTR applies to transfers (during lifetime and on death) of assets situated overseas which suffer tax overseas as well as IHT in the UK. Relief may be given under a treaty, but if not then the following rules apply.

DTR is given as a tax credit against the IHT payable on the overseas asset. The amount available as a tax credit is the lower of the foreign tax liability and the IHT (at the average rate) on the asset.

Question

DTR

Peter died on 15 October 2013 leaving a chargeable estate of £282,000. Included in this total is a foreign asset valued at £80,000 in respect of which foreign taxes of £20,000 were paid.

Calculate the IHT payable on the estate assuming that Peter made a gross chargeable lifetime transfer of £187,000 one year before his death.

Answer

	£
IHT on chargeable estate of £282,000	
(available nil rate band £(325,000 – 187,000) = £138,000 @ 0%, £144,000 @ 40%	57,600
(Average rate: 57,600/282,000 = 20.42553%)	
Less DTR: lower of:	
(a) £20,000	
(b) £80,000 × 20.42553% = £16,340	(16,340)
IHT payable on the estate	41,260

2 Gifts with reservation

FAST FORWARD

The rules on gifts with reservation ensure that gifts which are effectively made on death or within the seven years before death, even though apparently made earlier, are taxed.

One of the competencies you require to fulfil performance objective 20 of the PER is the ability to assist with tax planning. You can apply the knowledge you obtain from this section of the text to help to demonstrate this competence.

2.1 Introduction

There are rules to prevent the avoidance of IHT by the making of gifts while reserving some benefit. Without these rules, incomplete lifetime gifts would escape IHT by being PETs but would also reduce the individual's estate at death. The value of the assets could thus escape tax entirely, despite the original owner deriving some benefit from them up to his death.

The obvious example is a gift of a home to the donor's children but with the donor continuing to live in it rent free. Another example is a gift of income-producing assets, for example shares, but with the income continuing to be received by the donor.

Key term

Property given subject to a reservation (**gifts with reservation**) is property where:

(a) Such property is not enjoyed virtually to the entire exclusion of the donor (in the case of land only, also the donor's spouse or civil partner), or

(b) Possession and enjoyment of the property transferred is not *bona fide* assumed by the donee.

'Virtually to the entire exclusion' would, for example, allow a donor occasional brief stays in a house he had given away without creating a reservation, but spending most weekends in the house would create a reservation.

2.2 IHT consequences

Where a gift with reservation is made, it is treated in the same way as any other gift at the time it is made (as a PET or a CLT, as appropriate). **However, special rules apply on the death of the donor.**

(a) **If the reservation still exists at the date of the donor's death, the asset is included in the donor's estate at its value at that time** (not its value at the date the gift was made).

(b) **If the reservation ceases within the seven years before death, then the gift is treated as a PET made at the time the reservation ceased.** The charge is based on its value at that time. The annual exemption cannot be used against such a PET.

If the gift could be taxed as a PET or CLT when made, as well as taxed under (a) or (b) above, it will be taxed either under (a) or (b), or as a PET or CLT when made (but not both), whichever gives the higher total tax.

2.3 Exceptions

There are **exceptions to the gifts with reservation rules** as follows.

(a) A gift will not be treated as being with reservation if **full consideration is given** for any right of occupation or enjoyment retained or assumed by the donor (or his spouse or civil partner, in the case of land), and the property is land or chattels. For example, an individual might give away his house and continue to live in it, but pay a full market rent for doing so.

(b) A gift will not be treated as being with reservation if the circumstances of the donor change in a way that was unforeseen at the time of the original gift and the benefit provided by the donee to the donor only represents reasonable provision for the **care and maintenance of the donor, being an elderly or infirm relative**. This exception only applies to interests in land.

2.4 Pre-owned assets

If the gift with reservation rules do not apply, **an income tax charge may apply if individuals have entered into tax planning to reduce their inheritance tax liability** without completely divesting themselves of the asset. **This was covered in Chapter 3.** The transferor may, however, elect that the asset should be treated as remaining within their estate under the gift with reservation rules so that an income tax charge does not arise.

3 Associated operations

FAST FORWARD

Associated operations (ie transactions affecting the same property) are treated as one disposition for IHT.

Key term

Associated operations are:

(a) Two or more operations which affect the same property or one of which affects the property whilst other operations affect other property directly or indirectly representing the property, or

(b) Any two operations, one of which is effected with reference to the other, or with a view to enabling the other to be effected.

All associated operations are considered as one disposition. If a transfer of value has been made it is treated as made at the time of the last operation in the chain of associated operations. For this purpose, if the earlier operations themselves constituted transfers of value then the value transferred by these is deducted from the value transferred by all associated operations taken together.

The associated operations rule is a powerful weapon against schemes to avoid inheritance tax by using several transactions instead of one. For example, trustees might own some valuable paintings. They could give D, an individual, custody of the paintings for several years, on normal commercial terms (so that there would be no gratuitous intent). The trustees' interest in the paintings would be reduced in value, because someone else had custody of them. The trustees could then give an interest in the paintings to D's son. The value of what was given to D's son would be lower than it would otherwise have been, saving tax. HMRC would, however, retrieve the tax by treating the arrangement with D and the gift to his son as associated operations.

4 Altering dispositions made on death

FAST FORWARD

A variation or disclaimer can be used to vary a will after death. This can have IHT and CGT consequences.

4.1 Introduction

One of the competencies you require to fulfil performance objective 20 of the PER is the ability to assist with tax planning. You can apply the knowledge you obtain from this section of the text to help to demonstrate this competence.

There are **two main ways in which dispositions on death may be altered: by application to the courts, and by means of a voluntary variation or a disclaimer** of a legacy. Application to the courts may be made if the family and dependants of the deceased feel that the will has not made adequate provision for them. Any changes to the will made in this way will be treated for IHT purposes as if made by the deceased when writing his will.

A variation or disclaimer may be of benefit in reducing tax or in securing a fairer distribution of the deceased's estate or both.

4.2 IHT consequences

Within two years of a death the terms of a will can be changed in writing, either by a variation of the terms of the will made by the persons who benefit or would benefit under the dispositions, or by a disclaimer, with the change being effective for IHT purposes. The variation or disclaimer will not be treated as a transfer of value. Inheritance tax will be calculated as if the terms contained in the variation replaced those in the will. If a legacy is disclaimed, it will pass under the terms of the will (or possibly under the intestacy rules) to some other person, usually the residuary legatee, and tax will apply as if the will originally directed the legacy to that new recipient.

There is a similar provision for CGT. **This was covered in Chapter 13.**

If the beneficiaries making the variation wish the relevant terms of the will to be treated as replaced by the terms of the variation, it is necessary to state this in the variation. The statement can apply for inheritance tax or capital gains tax or both. **Where a disclaimer is made, the relevant terms in the will are *automatically* treated as replaced by the terms of the disclaimer for both IHT and CGT purposes,** regardless of whether this is stated in the disclaimer or not.

Question — **Altering disposition made on death**

Monty died on 13 May 2013, leaving his entire estate of £450,000 in his will to his sister, Dora. The inheritance tax payable on his estate was £50,000. It is now November 2013 and Dora wishes to pass the net assets (after payment of inheritance tax) of £400,000 from the estate to her son, Jack. Dora has not made any lifetime transfers of value. She is not in good health and may not survive until November 2020.

Show the inheritance tax consequences if *either*:

(a) Dora makes a potentially exempt transfer to Jack in November 2013, of the net assets of £400,000 from Monty's estate, and Dora dies in May 2019; *or*

(b) Dora makes a variation of her entitlement to Monty's estate in November 2013, such that Monty's will is treated as leaving the entire estate to Jack, and Dora dies in May 2019.

Assume that the nil rate band and the rates of inheritance tax in 2013/14 also apply in 2019/20.

Answer

(a) *Potentially exempt transfer November 2013*

	£
Gift	400,000
Less AE 2013/14	(3,000)
AE 2012/13 b/f	(3,000)
PET now chargeable	394,000

	IHT £
£325,000 × 0%	0
£69,000 × 40%	27,600
£394,000	27,600
Less: taper relief @ 60% (death within 5 - 6 years)	(16,560)
Death tax due	11,040

(b) *Variation November 2013*

The assets from Monty's estate are treated as passing directly to Jack from Monty. Dora does not make a transfer of value of the assets when she makes the variation and so there is no charge to inheritance tax on her death in respect of these assets.

4.3 Other points

These provisions do not apply where the variation or disclaimer is made for consideration.

Property which is deemed to be included in an estate at the date of death because the deceased made a previous gift with reservation cannot be redirected by a deed of variation in a way which is effective for IHT purposes.

Variations or disclaimers can be made in respect of property passing under the intestacy rules in the same way as for property passing under a will, and with the same IHT and CGT consequences.

5 The administration of IHT

FAST FORWARD

IHT is administered by HMRC Inheritance Tax. The due date for payment depends on the type of event giving rise to the charge to tax.

5.1 Accounts

IHT is administrated by HMRC Inheritance Tax.

There is no system of regular returns as for income tax, corporation tax and capital gains tax. **Instead, any person who is liable for IHT on a transfer is required to deliver an account giving details of the relevant assets and their value. An account delivered by the personal representatives (PRs) of a deceased person has to provide full details of the assets in the death estate. The PRs also have to include in their account details of any chargeable transfers made by the deceased person in the seven years before his death.**

PRs must deliver an account within 12 months following the end of the month in which death occurred or, if later, three months following the date when they become PRs. **Where no tax is due, and certain other conditions are satisfied, it is not necessary to submit an account. Estates where no account needs to be submitted are called excepted estates.**

A person responsible for the delivery of an account in relation to a PET that has become chargeable by reason of death, must do so within 12 months following the end of the month in which death occurred unless already reported by the PRs.

Any other account (such as for a chargeable lifetime transfer) must be delivered within 12 months of the end of the month in which the transfer was made or, if later, within three months from the date liability to tax arose.

If a person has delivered an account and then discovers a material defect in it, he must deliver a corrective account within six months.

5.2 Power to call for documents

HMRC may require any person to provide any information, documents, etc needed for the purposes of IHT. There is a right of appeal against such an information notice.

5.3 Determinations and appeals

HMRC issue a written notice of determination where, for example, they do not agree a value of transfer or where payment of tax has not been made. It may be made on the basis of a submitted account or to the best of the inspector's judgement.

An appeal against a notice of determination may be made to the Tax Chamber of the Tribunal within 30 days of its being served. Questions of land valuation are dealt with by the Lands Tribunal.

HMRC cannot take legal proceedings to recover tax charged by a notice of determination while an appeal is pending.

5.4 Liability for IHT

FAST FORWARD

The liability to pay IHT depends on the type of transfer and whether it was made on death.

On death, liability for payment is as follows.

(a) **Tax on the free estate is paid by the PRs** out of estate assets, with the burden generally falling on the residuary legatee (ie the recipient of the assets in the residue).

(b) **Tax on property** not in the possession of the personal representatives, having been transferred by the donor **subject to a reservation, is payable by the person in possession of the property.**

(c) **Tax on PETs that have become chargeable is paid and borne by donees.**

(d) **Additional liabilities on CLTs must be paid and borne by the donees.**

HMRC can look beyond the person primarily responsible. Most significantly a PR may become liable where the tax remains unpaid. This overall liability is limited to the value of estate assets in his possession. HMRC will not pursue the PR for tax if lifetime transfers are later discovered and the PR has made the fullest reasonably practicable enquiries to discover lifetime transfers and has obtained a certificate of discharge before distributing the estate.

If the PRs do not pay IHT due on an estate, HMRC may collect the tax from beneficiaries under the will to the extent they receive assets under the will.

The donor is primarily liable for the tax due on chargeable lifetime transfers.

5.5 Due dates

(a) **For chargeable lifetime transfers the due date is the later of:**

(i) **30 April just after the end of the tax year of the transfer.**

(ii) **Six months after the end of the month of the transfer.**

Interest (not tax deductible) is payable from the due date to the day before the day on which payment is made (inclusive).

(b) **Tax arising on the free estate at death (and on gifts with reservation if the reservation still existed at death) is payable by the PRs on delivery of their account.** The time limit for this is twelve months from the end of the month in which the death occurred. However, most PRs deliver their account before the twelve month deadline as it needs to be submitted to obtain a grant of representation (probate or letters of administration). Interest runs from six months after the end of the month when death occurred.

(c) **Tax arising on death in respect of PETs and CLTs with additional tax is payable within six months from the end of the month of death and interest runs from this due date.**

Interest (not taxable) is paid on repayments of tax from the date of payment to the date of repayment.

Question **Interest on IHT**

Walter died on 10 March 2013. IHT of £375,000 on his estate was paid on 1 November 2013. Calculate the interest payable on the late paid IHT, assuming an interest rate of 3.0%.

Answer

Interest runs from 30 September 2013 until 31 October 2013 (inclusive).

Interest = £375,000 × 3% × 1/12 = £937

5.6 The instalment option

IHT on certain property can be paid by ten equal annual instalments on CLTs where tax is borne by the donee, or on the transfer of a person's death estate.

The instalment option may also be used for IHT payable due to the death of the donor within seven years of making a PET. In this case, the donee must have kept the property (or replacement property qualifying for business or agricultural property relief) until the donor's death (or his own, if earlier), and if the property qualifies under (c) or (d) below the shares must remain unquoted until the earlier of the two deaths.

The first instalment is due for payment:

(a) On transfers on death and liabilities arising as a result of death, six months after the end of the month of death.

(b) On chargeable lifetime transfers, on the normal due date.

The instalment option applies to:

(a) **Land and buildings**

(b) **Shares or securities in a company controlled by the transferor** immediately before the transfer

(c) **Other holdings in unquoted companies** where the tax on them together with that on other instalment property represents **at least 20% of the total liability** on the estate on a death, **or where the tax cannot all be paid at once without undue hardship**

(d) **Shares in an unquoted company (including an AIM listed company) representing at least 10%** of the nominal value of the issued share capital and **valued for IHT purposes at not less than £20,000**

(e) **A business or an interest in a business**

No interest is charged on the instalments if paid on the due dates, unless the property is land not attracting agricultural property relief, or is shares or securities of an investment company or a company whose business is wholly or mainly dealing in securities, stocks or shares or land or buildings. For such property, interest is charged on the balance outstanding, from the normal due date for paying tax in one amount.

If the property is sold, all outstanding tax must then be paid.

Chapter roundup

- A UK domiciled, or deemed UK domiciled, individual is subject to inheritance tax on transfers of all assets, wherever situated.
- An election may be made for a non-UK domiciled individual who is, or was, the spouse or civil partner of a UK domiciled individual, to be treated as UK domiciled for IHT purposes.
- Non-UK assets of individuals not domiciled in the UK are not subject to IHT.
- Double taxation relief may reduce the IHT on assets also taxed overseas.
- The rules on gifts with reservation ensure that gifts which are effectively made on death or within the seven years before death, even though apparently made earlier, are taxed.
- Associated operations (ie transactions affecting the same property) are treated as one disposition for IHT.
- A variation or disclaimer can be used to vary a will after death. This can have IHT and CGT consequences.
- IHT is administered by HMRC Inheritance Tax. The due date for payment depends on the type of event giving rise to the charge to tax.
- The liability to pay IHT depends on the type of transfer and whether it was made on death.

Quick quiz

1 How is domicile defined for IHT purposes?

2 How is double taxation relief given?

3 Within what time limit must a variation of a will be made?

4 When is lifetime inheritance tax on a chargeable lifetime transfer due for payment?

Answers to quick quiz

1 Domicile for IHT is:

- domicile under the general law (permanent home) and
- deemed domicile in the UK if resident for at least 17 out of 20 tax years, and
- deemed domicile in the UK if ceased to be domiciled under general law in last 36 months

2 DTR is given as a tax credit against IHT payable on the overseas asset to the extent of the lower of foreign tax and the IHT (at average rate) on it.

3 A variation of a will must be made within two years of death.

4 The due date for lifetime tax on a chargeable lifetime transfer is the later of:

(a) 30 April just after the end of the tax year of the transfer, and
(b) 6 months after the end of the month of transfer

Now try the question below from the Exam Question Bank

Number	Level	Marks	Time
Q39	Examination	15	27 mins

This question has been analysed to show you how to approach paper P6 exams.

PART E

Trusts and stamp taxes

19

Trusts and stamp taxes

Topic list	Syllabus reference
1 Trusts	A4(e)(i),(ii)
2 IHT and trusts	A4(e)(iii),(iv),(v)
3 Reasons to use trusts	A4(e)(iii),(iv),(v)
4 Stamp duty	A5(a)(i), A5(b)(i)
5 Stamp duty reserve tax (SDRT)	A5(a)(i), A5(b)(i)
6 Stamp duty land tax (SDLT)	A5(a)(i), A5(b)(ii)
7 Exemptions and reliefs relating to stamp taxes	A5(c)(i), (ii)
8 Administration of stamp taxes	A5(d)

Introduction

In the last three chapters we have studied the impact of IHT on transfers by individuals, whether during lifetime or on death.

This chapter reviews the IHT charge on gifts into discretionary trusts and the subsequent impact of IHT on those trusts. Trusts have historically been used in estate planning as they allow the settlor to direct how the assets should be dealt with even after they have been given away. Even though there are periodic and exit charges, discretionary trusts can still be used for tax mitigation. This concludes our study of IHT and trusts.

In the remainder of this chapter we look at stamp taxes. Stamp duty is a charge on transfers of shares and securities by stock transfer form of 0.5% of the consideration for the sale. The same rate of duty applies for stamp duty reserve tax which applies where shares and securities are transferred in a paperless transaction. Stamp duty land tax is charged on transfers of land. In the next chapter we will turn our attention to corporation tax.

Study guide

		Intellectual level
4	**Inheritance tax in situations involving further aspects of the scope of the tax and the calculation of the liabilities arising, the principles of valuation and the reliefs available, transfers of property to and from trusts, overseas aspects and further aspects of administration**	
(e)	The liabilities arising in respect of transfers to and from trusts and on property within trusts:	
(i)	Define a trust	2
(ii)	Distinguish between different types of trust	3
(iii)	Advise on the inheritance tax implications of transfers of property into trust	3
(iv)	Advise on inheritance tax implications of property passing absolutely from a trust to a beneficiary	2
(v)	Identify the occasions on which inheritance tax is payable by trustees	3
5	**Stamp taxes (stamp duty, stamp duty reserve tax and stamp duty land tax)**	
(a)	The scope of stamp taxes:	3
(i)	Identify the property in respect of which stamp taxes are payable.	
(b)	Identify and advise on the liabilities arising on transfers.	3
(i)	Advise on the stamp taxes payable on transfers of shares and securities	
(ii)	Advise on the stamp duty land tax payable on transfers of land	
(c)	The use of exemptions and reliefs in deferring and minimising stamp taxes:	3
(i)	Identify transfers involving no consideration	
(ii)	Advise on group transactions	
(d)	Understand and explain the systems by which stamp taxes are administered.	2

Exam guide

Trusts are useful in tax planning. The trustees retain control over assets until they deem a beneficiary to be sufficiently capable of looking after them. Be aware of the IHT implications for discretionary trusts. Stamp taxes are unlikely to form a major part of a question, but must not be overlooked as they can be a significant cost in many transactions.

Knowledge brought forward from earlier studies

The topics in this chapter are new.

1 Trusts

1.1 What is a trust?

FAST FORWARD

A trust is an arrangement under which a person, the settlor, transfers property to another person, the trustee or trustees, who is required to deal with the trust property on behalf of certain specified persons, the beneficiaries.

A trust may be created during the **lifetime of the settlor**, in which case the terms of the trust will be contained in the trust deed. Alternatively a trust may arise on the **death of the settlor**, in which case the terms of the trust will be laid down in the will, or by the statutory provisions which apply on an intestacy.

The first trustee will normally be specified in the trust deed or will. Trustees may retire and new trustees may be appointed, but for tax purposes they are regarded as a single continuing body of persons. The beneficiaries will also be specified in the trust deed or will. They may be separately named, 'my daughter Ann', or may be members of a particular class of persons, 'my children'. The trust property will comprise the original property settled (or property replacing it), plus any property added to the trust, plus income accumulated as an addition to capital, less any amounts advanced to beneficiaries.

1.2 Example of a discretionary trust

A discretionary trust for a family may have the following provisions:

(a) Settlor: James Brown.
(b) Trustees: John Brown (son) and Jean White (daughter).
(c) Beneficiaries: the children and remoter issue of the settlor, and their spouses/civil partners.
(d) Trust property: £100,000 originally settled and any property deriving therefrom.
(e) Income may be accumulated for up to 21 years from the date of the settlement; subject to which it is to be distributed to the beneficiaries at the trustees' discretion.
(f) Capital may be advanced to beneficiaries at the trustees' discretion. Any capital remaining undistributed on the 80th anniversary of the date of settlement is to be distributed to the settlor's grandchildren then living, failing which to Oxfam.

This gives the trustees complete discretion over income and capital.

1.3 Example of an interest in possession trust

An interest in possession trust may have the following provisions:

(a) Settlor: Alice Rawlings
(b) Trustees: Margaret Ashe and Crispin Armitage (solicitors)
(c) Trust property: 10,000 Tesco plc shares, £5,000 cash
(d) Beneficiaries: Ruth Bishop (daughter), Lawrence Bishop (grandson)
(e) Income: payable to Ruth Bishop during her lifetime
(f) Capital: distributed to Lawrence Bishop on the death of Ruth Bishop

In this trust, the trustees have no discretion over the payment of either income or capital: both must be dealt with in accordance with the terms of the trust. Ruth Bishop has an **interest in possession** in the trust because she is entitled to the income of the trust now. She might also be called the life tenant of the trust because her right to income lasts for her lifetime. Lawrence Bishop has **reversionary interest** in the trust because he is only entitled to the capital after Ruth's interest has come to an end. He may be called the **remainderman**.

2 IHT and Trusts

There is a CLT when a discretionary trust is set up. The trust suffers the IHT principal charge once every ten years and the exit charge when property leaves the trust.

2.1 Discretionary Trusts

2.1.1 IHT on creation of a discretionary trust

As we saw earlier in this Text, **when an individual makes a gift to a discretionary trust it is a CLT for IHT purposes**. If the gift is made on death, IHT is charged on the death estate in the normal way before the assets enter the trust.

2.1.2 IHT charges on a discretionary trust

The property in the trust is known as 'relevant property'. So long as it remains relevant property it is subject to the **principal charge** on every tenth anniversary from the start of the trust.

If property leaves the trust (and so ceases to be relevant property) an **exit charge** arises. An example would be where the trustees advance capital to a beneficiary.

Exit charge before first principal charge

The amount subject to the exit charge is the amount distributed from the trust. The rate of IHT is 30% of the (lifetime) rate that would apply to a notional (ie pretend) transfer of the initial value of the trust, assuming cumulative transfers by the trust equal to those made by the settlor in the seven years prior to the setting up of the trust. Once the rate of IHT has been established, it is then further reduced by multiplying by x/40 where x is the number of complete successive quarters that have elapsed since the trust commenced.

The principal charge

IHT is charged on the value of the property in the trust at each tenth anniversary of the trust. The rate is 30% of the (lifetime) rate that would apply to a transfer of the property in the trust at the tenth anniversary, assuming cumulative transfers equal to the gross amount of any capital paid out of the trust in the previous ten years **plus** the settlor's transfers in the seven years prior to the creation of the trust.

Exit charge after a principal charge

Use the rate that applied at the last tenth anniversary, reduced by multiplying by a fraction that reflects the time elapsed since the tenth anniversary. The fraction is x/40, where x is the number of complete quarters since the last tenth anniversary. If there has been a change in the nil band, the rate applied at the last tenth anniversary is recomputed using the new nil band.

Exam focus point

Although you must have an awareness of these exit and principal charges, you will not be expected to perform a computation in the exam.

2.2 Interest in possession trusts

FAST FORWARD

Inheritance tax on interest in possession trusts generally applies in the same way as for discretionary trusts. The exception is where there is an immediate post death interest in possession. In this case, the trust property is treated as if it was owned outright by the beneficiary with that interest.

2.2.1 IHT on creation of an interest in possession trust

The general rule is that the property in an interest in possession trust is 'relevant property' (ie treated in the same way as property in a discretionary trust).

The exception to this rule is where the trust is created on the death of the settlor giving an immediate interest in possession ('immediate post-death interest'). **The property in such a trust is treated as if it is owned outright by the beneficiary with the interest in possession in the trust**. Therefore, the IHT consequences of transferring property to such an interest in possession trust are the same as if the transfer had been made outright to the beneficiary with the interest in possession.

The IHT implications of the creation of an interest in possession trust can therefore be summarised as follows:

Beneficiary with interest in possession	Created in lifetime of settlor (relevant property trusts)	Created on death of settlor with immediate post death interest in possession
Settlor	Chargeable lifetime transfer	Not applicable
Settlor's spouse/civil partner	Chargeable lifetime transfer	Exempt transfer
Any other individual (eg settlor's son)	Chargeable lifetime transfer	Chargeable death transfer

2.2.2 IHT charges on interest in possession trust

Relevant property trusts

Such trusts are subject to principal charges and exit charges as outlined above in relation to discretionary trusts.

Immediate post death interest trusts

Since the settled property is deemed to be owned by the beneficiary with the interest in possession, when that beneficiary's interest comes to an end the same IHT consequences occur as if that beneficiary had made a transfer of the capital of the trust.

For example, in the trust outlined in 1.3 above, if this had been created as an immediate interest in possession trust on the death of Alice Rawlings, then on the death of Ruth Bishop, Ruth will be treated as making a chargeable death transfer of the trust property to Lawrence Bishop. The settled property will be aggregated with Ruth's own assets (her **free estate**) to compute the IHT and then a proportionate part of that IHT will be payable by the trustees of the interest in possession trust.

If such an interest in possession comes to an end during the lifetime of the beneficiary, for example if the beneficiary attains a specified age, there may be a lifetime transfer depending on who is then entitled to benefit under the trust. Again, remember that the beneficiary with the interest in possession is treated as making a transfer of value of the settled property.

Question — **Ending of interest in possession (immediate post death interest)**

Verity has an interest in possession in a trust created on the death of her mother, Wendy, in August 2010. Verity is married to Simon. Verity has a brother, Mark.

On Verity's 25th birthday on 1 May 2013, her interest in possession comes to an end under the terms of the trust.

State the IHT consequences of the ending of Verity's interest in possession if:

(a) Verity becomes entitled to the trust property;
(b) Simon becomes entitled to the trust property;
(c) Mark becomes entitled to the trust property.

Answer

(a) No transfer of value. Since Verity is already treated as being entitled to the trust property, there is no transfer of value when she actually becomes entitled to the trust property.

(b) Exempt transfer. Verity is treated as making a transfer of the trust property to Simon. Since he is her spouse, the spouse exemption applies.

(c) Potentially exempt transfer. Verity is treated as making a transfer of the trust property to Mark, who is another individual. If Verity dies within seven years of her 25th birthday, the transfer will become a chargeable transfer and Mark may be liable to pay IHT on the transfer.

3 Reasons to use trusts

FAST FORWARD

Trusts help preserve family wealth while maintaining flexibility over who should benefit.

One of the competencies you require to fulfil performance objective 20 of the PER is the ability to assist with tax planning. You can apply the knowledge you obtain from this section of the text to help to demonstrate this competence.

3.1 Introduction

Trusts are useful vehicles for non-tax reasons such as to preserve family wealth, to provide for those who are deemed to be incapable (minors, and the disabled) or unsuitable (due to youth or poor business sense) to hold assets directly.

3.2 Will trusts

A discretionary trust may be set up by will. The rate of inheritance tax on principal charges and exit charges within the trust will then depend on the settlor's cumulative transfers in the seven years before his death and the value of the trust property. The discretionary trust allows the transferee flexibility about who is to benefit from the trust and to what extent. This can be useful if there are beneficiaries of differing ages and whose financial circumstances may differ.

3.3 Lifetime trusts

Although gifts to trusts during lifetime can lead to an IHT charge (a CLT), there can be tax benefits from setting up trusts during the settlor's lifetime. As long as the cumulative total of CLTs in any seven year period does not exceed the nil rate band there will be no lifetime IHT to pay on creation of the trust. The trust will be subject to IHT at 0% on the ten year anniversary and later advances, unless the value of the trust property grows faster than the nil rate band.

If a discretionary trust is used, the settlor can preserve the maximum flexibility in the class of beneficiaries and how income and capital should be dealt with.

If the settlor is included as a beneficiary of the trust the gift will be treated as a gift with reservation.

4 Stamp duty

Stamp duty applies to transfers of shares and securities transferred by a stock transfer form.

One of the competencies you require to fulfil performance objective 19 of the PER is the ability to evaluate and compute taxes payable. You can apply the knowledge you obtain from this section of the text to help to demonstrate this competence.

Stamp duty applies to transfers of shares and securities transferred by a stock transfer form. It is payable by the purchaser.

Transfers of shares are charged to stamp duty at 0.5% of the consideration unless they fall within one of the specific exemptions. The duty is rounded up to the nearest £5.

The tax charge arises on the date the agreement is made or becomes unconditional.

5 Stamp duty reserve tax (SDRT)

FAST FORWARD

Stamp duty reserve tax (SDRT) applies to electronic transfers of shares and securities.

The principal tax in relation to share transactions is now stamp duty reserve tax (SDRT) which is applicable to all sales of chargeable securities effected by electronic paperless transactions. It is payable by the purchaser.

Most of these transactions will be made through an electronic system called CREST. However, some shares are held outside CREST ('Off Market') but may still be transferred electronically, for example if they are held by a nominee such as a bank,

SDRT applies at the rate of 0.5% of the consideration where there is an agreement to transfer chargeable securities for a consideration in money or money's worth unless one of the exemptions applies.

6 Stamp duty land tax (SDLT)

6.1 Land transactions

FAST FORWARD

Stamp duty land tax (SDLT) applies to the sale of land, or of rights over land.

One of the competencies you require to fulfil performance objective 19 of the PER is the ability to evaluate and compute taxes payable. You can apply the knowledge you obtain from this section of the text to help to demonstrate this competence.

Stamp duty land tax applies to land transactions. A land transaction is a transfer of land or an interest in, or right over, land. **SDLT is generally payable as a percentage of the consideration paid for the land. It is payable by the purchaser.**

Exam focus point

The charge to stamp duty land tax on leases is outside the scope of your syllabus.

6.2 Rate of charge

The amount of the charge to SDLT depends on whether the land is residential or non-residential. The following rates apply:

Rate (%)	Residential	Non-residential
0	Up to £125,000	Up to £150,000
1	£125,001 – £250,000	£150,001 – £250,000
3	£250,001 – £500,000	£250,001 – £500,000
4	£500,001 – £1,000,000	£500,001 +
5	£1,000,001 – £2,000,000	n/a
7	£2,000,001 +	n/a

Note that once the relevant rate of SDLT has been ascertained, it applies to the whole of the consideration, not just that above the band threshold.

Exam focus point

Anti-avoidance legislation applies in respect of certain acquisitions of high-value residential property by persons that are not individuals, for example, companies. These rules are not examinable in Paper P6.

6.3 Examples

(a) Beryl buys a flat in January 2014 for £130,000. Her stamp duty land tax is £130,000 × 1% = £1,300.

(b) Raymond buys a shop in November 2013 for £145,000. His stamp duty land tax is nil because this is non-residential property bought for up to £150,000 so the 0% rate applies.

(c) Sandy buys a house in December 2013 for £450,000. His stamp duty land tax is £450,000 × 3% = £13,500.

(d) S Ltd buys a warehouse in February 2014 for £1,500,000. Its stamp duty land tax is £1,500,000 × 4% = £60,000.

7 Exemptions and reliefs relating to stamp taxes

FAST FORWARD

There are exemptions and reliefs for stamp taxes, for example when the transfer does not involve payment of consideration, such as a gift, and on transfers between group companies.

7.1 Transfers with no consideration

Stamp taxes are charged on the consideration passing under the document or transaction. If there is no chargeable consideration, there is no charge to tax. Examples include:

- Gifts (except a gift of land to a connected company)
- A transfer on divorce, annulment of marriage or judicial separation
- Variations of a will or intestacy made within 2 years of death for no consideration
- Transfers to charities if the shares or land is to be used for charitable purposes

If land is transferred to a company, for example on incorporation, SDLT is payable on the market value of land.

If the consideration is not in money, the market value is used.

7.2 Company transactions

Relief from stamp duty and SDLT is given for transfers of assets between associated companies. There is no direct relief for stamp duty reserve tax so the transaction must be made by using a stock transfer form and a claim made for stamp duty relief.

There are two conditions which must be met to attract the relief, namely that:

- the effect must be to transfer the **beneficial interest** in property from one body corporate to another, and
- those bodies corporate must be **associated** at the time of transfer, ie one must be the parent of the other or they must have a common parent.

(The term 'body corporate' includes foreign companies.)

For the 'associated companies' test, one company is regarded as the parent of another if it has:

- beneficial ownership of at least **75% of the ordinary share capital**, ie if all the issued share capital of a company, other than fixed rate preference shares, *and*
- a 75% interest in dividends and assets in a winding up, *and*
- there must not be 'arrangements' for a non-associated person to acquire control of the transferee.

It is necessary for there to be a **parent company**, ie two companies owned by the same *individual* are not 'associated' for stamp duty or SDLT purposes (even though they would be associated for corporation tax purposes). For indirect holdings, it is necessary to reduce the degree of ownership at each level to the appropriate fraction in determining whether the 75% test is met (as for group relief).

Question — **Stamp duty relief**

Allegri Ltd owns 90% of the ordinary share capital of Byrd Ltd, which in turn owns 85% of the ordinary share capital of Corelli Ltd. Shares are transferred from Corelli Ltd to Allegri Ltd under an instrument executed on 1 June 2013. Is stamp duty relief available?

Answer

Relief is available, since Allegri Ltd owns indirectly 76½ % (ie 90% x 85%) of the ordinary share capital of Corelli Ltd.

SDLT relief is withdrawn where land has been transferred from one associated company to another and within three years of the transfer the purchaser company leaves the group whilst still owning the land. Note that the *vendor* company leaving the group does not cause the SDLT relief to be withdrawn as the land is still held within the group.

8 Administration of stamp taxes

8.1 Stamp duty

FAST FORWARD

Stamp duty is collected when the stampable document is sent for stamping to HMRC (Stamp Taxes).

Documents which are chargeable to stamp duty must be sent to HMRC (Stamp Taxes) with the duty payable. The document is then impressed with a duty stamp, usually in red, showing the duty paid and the date of payment.

To be certain that the correct amount of duty has been paid the taxpayer may request that the document be adjudicated, in which case HMRC will examine the underlying facts and determine the duty payable. This is most commonly used where the value of the consideration needs to be ascertained, and must be used in certain cases, such as for intra-group transfers.

Documents must be presented for stamping within 30 days of execution. Interest runs from this date until the document is stamped, and a late filing penalty may be charged. Unstamped documents are not admissible as evidence.

8.2 Stamp duty reserve tax

FAST FORWARD

Stamp duty reserve tax is collected automatically when a transaction is made through CREST.

Stamp duty reserve tax is collected automatically when a transaction is made using CREST.

If an off market transaction is dealt with by a stockbroker, the stockbroker will pay the SDRT direct to HMRC. Otherwise, the purchaser must both report the transaction and pay the tax to HMRC by the seventh of the month following the month in which the transaction is made.

The charge to SDRT is cancelled if, within 6 years after the contract date, a duly stamped transfer is produced to HMRC.

8.3 Stamp duty land tax

FAST FORWARD

Stamp duty land tax is collected under a self assessment system.

If a land transaction takes place which is not exempt, a land transaction return must be filed within 30 days of the transaction. There are late filing penalties of £100 if the return is less than 3 months late, or £200 otherwise. HMRC can apply to the Tax Tribunal or a daily penalty, and the penalty is tax geared if the return is over 12 months late.

SDLT is payable within 30 days of the transaction. Interest is charged on late paid tax.

The taxpayer may amend the return within 12 months of the filing date, and HMRC may amend the return to correct obvious errors within 9 months of the actual filing date.

HMRC may carry out a compliance check into the return within 9 months of the later of the due and actual filing dates. On completion of the compliance check, HMRC must issue a closure notice stating its conclusions and making any necessary amendments to the return. If no return is filed HMRC may issue a determination of the tax due, and they have the power to raise a discovery assessment.

Land transactions cannot be registered with the Land Registry unless accompanied by a certificate from HMRC that duty has been paid or by a self-certificate from the taxpayer that no duty is due.

Chapter roundup

- A trust is an arrangement under which a person, the settlor, transfers property to another person, the trustee or trustees, who is required to deal with the trust property on behalf of certain specified persons, the beneficiaries.
- There is a CLT when a discretionary trust is set up. The trust suffers the IHT principal charge once every ten years and the exit charge when property leaves the trust.
- Inheritance tax on interest in possession trusts generally applies in the same way as for discretionary trusts. The exception is where there is an immediate post death interest in possession. In this case, the trust property is treated as if it was owned outright by the beneficiary with that interest.
- Trusts help preserve family wealth while maintaining flexibility over who should benefit.
- Stamp duty applies to transfers of shares and securities transferred by a stock transfer form.
- Stamp duty reserve tax (SDRT) applies to electronic transfers of shares and securities.
- Stamp duty land tax (SDLT) applies to the sale of land, or of rights over land.
- There are exemptions and reliefs for stamp taxes, for example when the transfer does not involve payment of consideration, such as a gift, and on transfers between group companies.
- Stamp duty is collected when the stampable document is sent for stamping to HMRC (Stamp Taxes).
- Stamp duty reserve tax is collected automatically when a transaction is made through CREST.
- Stamp duty land tax is collected under a self assessment system.

Quick quiz

1 What is the IHT principal charge?

2 What are the IHT consequences of advancing capital from a discretionary trust to a beneficiary 20 months after the tenth anniversary?

3 What is the IHT consequence of creating a trust in a will which gives an immediate post death interest in possession to the spouse of the deceased settlor?

4 What is the stamp duty on a share transfer form if the consideration for sale was £50,000?

5 When is stamp duty reserve tax charged and how is it usually collected?

6 In November 2013, Brianna buys a residential property worth £2,600,000. What is the SDLT payable?

Answers to quick quiz

1. The principal charge is a charge on relevant property held in trust at each ten year anniversary of the trust.
2. If capital is advanced from a discretionary trust there is an exit charge. This is calculated using the rate of tax that applied on the ten year anniversary × 6/40 as between 6 and 7 quarters have elapsed since then.
3. Exempt transfer as the receiving spouse is deemed to own the trust property outright (ie spouse to spouse exempt transfer).
4. £50,000 × 0.5% = £250
5. Stamp duty reserve tax (SDRT) applies to electronic share transactions and is usually collected automatically when a transaction is made.
6. £2,600,000 × 7% = £182,000

Now try the question below from the Exam Question Bank

Number	Level	Marks	Time
Q19	Introductory	11	20 mins

PART F

Corporation tax

Computing taxable total profits

Topic list	Syllabus reference
1 The scope of corporation tax	A2(a)C1
2 Taxable total profits	A2(a)C2,C5
3 Loan relationships	A2(a)C2
4 Intellectual property (intangible fixed assets)	A2(c)(ii),(v)
5 Transfer pricing	A2(c)(vi)
6 Research and development	A2(c)(i)
7 Enhanced capital allowances (ECAs)	A2(c)(iii)

Introduction

At this point in our studies we turn to corporation tax, covering the basic corporation tax rules in this chapter.

We start by looking at accounting periods, which are the periods for which companies pay corporation tax. We then see how to bring together all of a company's profits in a corporation tax computation and discuss the special rules for certain types of income that apply to companies.

In the next chapter we will deal with the rules on chargeable gains for companies.

Study guide

		Intellectual level
2	**Corporation tax liabilities in situations involving further overseas and group aspects and in relation to special types of company, and the application of additional exemptions and reliefs**	
(a)	The contents of the Paper F6 study guide, for corporation tax, under headings:	2
•	C1 The scope of corporation tax	
•	C2 Taxable total profits	
•	C5 The use of exemptions and reliefs in deferring and minimising corporation tax liabilities	
(c)	Taxable total profits:	3
(i)	Identify qualifying research and development expenditure, both capital and revenue, and determine the reliefs available by reference to the size of the individual company/group	
(ii)	Recognise the relevance of a company generating profits attributable to patents	
(iii)	Identify the enhanced capital allowances available in respect of expenditure in respect of expenditure on green technologies, including the tax credit available in the case of a loss making company	
(v)	Recognise the alternative tax treatments of intangible assets and conclude on the best treatment for a given company	
(vi)	Advise on the impact of the transfer pricing and thin capitalisation rules on companies	

Exam guide

Although you are unlikely to get a question requiring a detailed computation of taxable total profits you may be asked to comment on how certain types of income would be included in the computation where there are special rules, such as for loan relationships, intangible fixed assets and research and development expenditure. You may also be asked to discuss how the transfer pricing rules work. It is less likely that you will be examined in detail on the more straightforward adjustments to profits or the rules for capital allowances.

Knowledge brought forward from earlier studies

This chapter revises the scope of corporation tax and the basic computation of taxable total profits. The examiner has identified essential underpinning knowledge from the F6 syllabus which is particularly important that you revise as part of your P6 studies. In this chapter, the relevant topic is:

C2	**Taxable total profits**	
(e)	Explain the treatment of interest paid and received under the loan relationship rules.	1

There are no changes in the material covered in F6 in Financial Year 2013 from Financial Year 2012.

There are two new topics: intangible fixed assets (including the patent box) and research and development.

1 The scope of corporation tax

1.1 Introduction

FAST FORWARD

Companies pay corporation tax on their taxable total profits of each accounting period.

Corporation tax is paid by companies. It is charged on the taxable total profits of each accounting period. Corporation tax is not charged on dividends received from UK resident or non-resident companies.

Key term

A '**company**' is any corporate body (limited or unlimited) or unincorporated association eg sports clubs.

1.2 The residence of companies

A company incorporated in the UK is resident in the UK. A company incorporated abroad is resident in the UK if its central management and control are exercised here.

1.3 Accounting periods

FAST FORWARD

An accounting period cannot exceed twelve months in length. A long period of account must be split into two accounting periods, the first of which is twelve months long.

Corporation tax is chargeable in respect of accounting periods. It is important to understand the difference between an accounting period and a period of account. A period of account is any period for which a company prepares accounts; usually this will be 12 months in length but it may be longer or shorter than this. An accounting period starts when a company starts to trade, or otherwise becomes liable to corporation tax, or immediately after the previous accounting period finishes. An accounting period finishes on the earliest of:

- 12 months after its start
- The end of the company's period of account
- The company starting or ceasing to trade
- The company entering/ceasing to be in administration (see later in this Text)
- The commencement of a company's winding up (see later in this Text)
- The company ceasing to be resident in the UK
- The company ceasing to be liable to corporation tax

In many cases the company will have a period of account of 12 months and an accounting period of 12 months. We will deal with long periods of account (exceeding 12 months) later in this chapter.

2 Taxable total profits

FAST FORWARD

Taxable total profits are the total profits (income and gains) less some losses and qualifying charitable donations.

One of the competencies you require to fulfil performance objective 19 of the PER is the ability to evaluate and compute taxes payable. You can apply the knowledge you obtain from this section of the text to help to demonstrate this competence.

2.1 Introduction

The corporation tax computation draws together all of the company's income and gains from various sources. The income from each different type of source must be computed separately because different computational rules apply. These rules are set out in the Corporation Tax Act 2009.

The taxable total profits for an accounting period are derived as follows.

	£
Trading income	X
Property business income	X
Interest income from non-trading loan relationships	X
Miscellaneous income	X
Chargeable gains	X
Total profits	X
Less losses relieved by deduction from total profits	(X)
Less qualifying charitable donations	(X)
Taxable total profits for an accounting period	X

Each of the above items is dealt with in further detail later in this Text.

Exam focus point

It would be of great help if you could learn this proforma. The calculation of taxable total profits may be required in an exam, so you must understand how different types of income and gains are dealt with. You will then be able to advise on the marginal tax effects of suggested courses of action.

Dividends received from both UK and non-UK resident companies are usually exempt and so not included in taxable total profits.

Exam focus point

The examiner has stated that dividends which are taxable in the hands of the recipient company are not examinable.

2.2 Trading income

The trading income of companies is derived from the profit before taxation shown in the accounts. The adjustments that need to be made to the accounts are broadly the same for companies as they are for income tax purposes (companies cannot use the cash basis) (see Chapter 6). Companies may also claim relief for the expenses of managing their investments (see Chapter 25). Where shares in UK companies are held as trading assets, and not as investments, any dividends on those shares will be treated for tax purposes as trading profits.

Qualifying charitable donations are added back into calculation of adjusted profit. They are instead deducted from total profits (see below).

Interest received on a trading loan relationship (see later in this chapter) is included within trading profits on an accruals basis. Similarly, interest paid on a trading loan relationship is deducted at arriving at trading profits.

Exam focus point

When adjusting profits as supplied in an income statement confusion can arise as regards to whether the figures are net or gross. Properly drawn up company accounts should normally include all income gross. However, some examination questions include items 'net'. Read the question carefully.

Pre-trading expenditure incurred by the company within the 7 years before trade commences is treated as an allowable expense incurred on the first day of trading provided it would have been allowable had the company been trading when the expense was actually incurred.

Trading income also includes post cessation receipts arising from a trade which would not otherwise be chargeable to tax.

The calculation of capital allowances follows income tax principles. However, for companies, there is never any restriction of allowances to take account of any private use of an asset. The director or employee suffers a taxable benefit instead.

2.3 Property business income

The taxation of UK property business income follows similar rules to those for income tax (see earlier in this Text). In summary:

(a) All UK rental activities are treated as a single source of income calculated in the same way as trading profits.

(b) Capital allowances on plant and machinery (but not furniture) are taken into account when computing property income or losses.

However **interest paid by a company on a loan to buy or improve property is not a property income expense. The loan relationship rules apply instead** (see later in this chapter).

2.4 Interest income

UK companies normally receive interest gross. Interest relating to non-trading loan relationships is taxed separately as interest income on an accruals basis (see later in this chapter for the loan relationship rules).

2.5 Miscellaneous income

Income and expenditure relating to intellectual property, which is not used in the trade nor in a property business, are dealt with as miscellaneous income. We consider intellectual property in more detail later in this chapter.

2.6 Chargeable gains

Companies do not pay capital gains tax. Instead their chargeable gains are included in the taxable total profits. We look at companies' chargeable gains in the next chapter.

2.7 Qualifying charitable donations

Qualifying charitable donations are deductible from total profits when computing taxable total profits.

Almost all donations of money to charity by a company can be qualifying charitable donations whether they are single donations or regular donations. There is no need for a claim to be made in order for a payment to be treated as a qualifying charitable donation (compare with gift aid donations where a declaration is required).

Donations to local charities which are incurred wholly and exclusively for the purposes of a trade are deducted in the calculation of the tax adjusted trading profits.

Question — **The calculation of taxable total profits**

The following is a summary of the income statement of A Ltd for the year to 31 March 2014.

	£	£
Gross profit		180,000
Other income		
Treasury stock interest (non-trading investment)		700
Dividends from UK companies (net)		3,600
Loan interest from UK company (non-trading investment)		4,000
Building society interest received (non-trading investment)		292
Expenses		
Trade expenses (all allowable)	62,000	
Qualifying charitable donation paid	1,100	
		(63,100)
Profit before taxation		125,492

The capital allowances for the period total £5,500. There was also a chargeable gain of £13,867. Compute the taxable total profits.

Answer

	£	£
Profit before taxation		125,492
Less Treasury stock interest	700	
dividends received	3,600	
building society interest	292	
loan interest received	4,000	
		(8,592)
		116,900
Add qualifying charitable donation		1,100
		118,000
Less capital allowances		(5,500)
Trading income		112,500
Interest income £(700 + 292 + 4,000)		4,992
Chargeable gain		13,867
Total profits		131,359
Less: qualifying charitable donation		(1,100)
Taxable total profits		130,259

2.8 Long periods of account

If a company has a long period of account, exceeding 12 months, it is split into two accounting periods: the first 12 months and the remainder.

Where the period of account differs from the corporation tax accounting periods, profits are **allocated to the relevant periods** as follows:

- **Trading income** before capital allowances and property income are apportioned on a **time basis.**
- **Capital allowances** and balancing charges are **calculated for each accounting period.**
- **Other income is allocated to the period to which it relates** (eg interest to the period when accrued). Miscellaneous income, however, is apportioned on a time basis.
- **Chargeable gains and losses** are allocated to the **period in which they are realised.**
- **Qualifying charitable donations** are deducted in the accounting **period in which they are paid.**

Question

Long period of account

Xenon Ltd makes up an 18 month set of accounts to 30 June 2014 with the following results.

	£
Trading profits	180,000
Interest income	
18 months @ £500 accruing per month	9,000
Capital gain (1 May 2014 disposal)	250,000
Less qualifying charitable donation (paid 31 December 2013)	(50,000)
	389,000

What are the taxable total profits for each of the accounting periods?

Answer

The 18 month period of account is divided into:

Year ending 31 December 2013
6 months to 30 June 2014

Results are allocated:

	Y/e 31.12.13	*6m to 30.6.14*
	£	£
Trading profits 12:6	120,000	60,000
Interest income		
12 × £500	6,000	
6 × £500		3,000
Capital gain (1.5.13)		250,000
Total profits	126,000	313,000
Less qualifying charitable donation (31.12.13)	(50,000)	
Taxable total profits	76,000	313,000

3 Loan relationships

FAST FORWARD

A loan relationship arises when a company lends or borrows money. Trading loan relationships are dealt with as trading income. Non-trading loan relationships are dealt with as interest income.

3.1 Introduction

If a company borrows or lends money, including issuing or investing in loan stock or buying gilts, it has a loan relationship. This can be a creditor relationship (where the company lends or invests money) or a debtor relationship (where the company borrows money or issues securities). The loan relationship rules apply to both revenue and capital items.

3.2 Trading loan relationships

If the company is a party to a **loan relationship for trade purposes, any debits, ie interest payable or other debt costs, charged through its accounts are allowed as a trading expense** and are therefore deductible in computing trading profits. For example, a company paying interest on a loan taken out to purchase plant and machinery, or a factory or office premises for use in the trade will be able to deduct the interest payable for tax purposes.

Similarly **if any credits, ie interest income or other debt returns, arise on a trading loan these are treated as a trading receipt and are taxable as part of trading profit**. This is not likely to arise unless the trade is one of money lending so will usually fall within the rules for non-trading loan relationships (below).

3.3 Non-trading loan relationships

If the company is a party to a **loan relationship for non-trade purposes, any debits and credits must be pooled.** For example, a company paying interest on a loan taken out to purchase an investment property will not be able to deduct the interest from trading profits for tax purposes. Instead this 'non-trade debit' must be netted off against 'non trade credits' such as bank interest.

A net credit (ie income) on the pool is chargeable as interest income. Relief is available if there is a net 'deficit' (ie loss) (see later in this Text).

3.4 Example: loan relationships

During its year ended 31 December 2013 Jello Ltd received bank interest of £13,500 and loan stock interest from Wobble Ltd of £45,400. It also paid loan stock interest of £40,000 to Shaker Ltd on a loan of £1,000,000. The loan stock was issued to Shaker Ltd in May 2012 to raise £700,000 for the purchase of a factory to use in the trade and £250,000 for the purchase of an investment property. The balance was used as working capital. All figures are stated gross and are the amounts shown in the accounts.

The loan stock interest payable to Shaker Ltd was used partly for trade purposes, and partly for non trade purposes and must be apportioned:

	£
Non-trade purposes 250,000 × £40,000/1,000,000	10,000
Trade purposes (700,000 + 50,000 (bal)) = 750,000 × 40,000/1,000,000	30,000
Total interest payable	40,000

The £30,000 of interest paid for trade purposes is deducted in the computation of trading profits.

The £10,000 of interest paid for non-trade purposes is deducted from non-trading interest received. The amount taxable as a non-trading loan relationship credit is:

	£
Bank interest (received gross)	13,500
Debenture interest receivable from Wobble Ltd	45,400
	58,900
Non-trade loan stock interest paid to Shaker Ltd	(10,000)
Non-trading loan relationship credit	48,900

3.5 Incidental costs of loan finance

Under the loan relationship rules expenses ('debits') are allowed if incurred directly:

(a) Bringing a loan relationship into existence
(b) Entering into or giving effect to any related transactions
(c) Making payment under a loan relationship or related transactions, or
(d) Taking steps to ensure the receipt of payments under the loan relationship or related transaction.

A related transaction means 'any disposal or acquisition (in whole or in part) of rights or liabilities under the relationship, including any arising from a security issue in relation to the money debt in question'.

The above categories of incidental costs are also allowable even if the company does not enter into the loan relationship (ie abortive costs). Cost directly incurred in varying the terms of a loan relationship are also allowed.

3.6 Other matters

It is not only the interest costs of borrowing that are allowable or taxable. The capital costs are treated similarly. Thus if a company issues a loan at a discount and repays it eventually at par, the capital cost is allowed over the life of the loan.

Relief for pre-trading expenditure extends to expenses incurred on trading loan relationships in accounting periods ending within seven years of the company starting to trade. An expense that would have been a trading debit if it was incurred after the trade had commenced, is treated as a trading debit of the first trading period. An election has to be made within two years of the end of the first trading period.

Interest charged on underpaid tax is deductible and interest received on overpaid tax is assessable under the loan relationship rules as interest income.

4 Intellectual property (intangible fixed assets)

Gains/losses arising on intangible assets are recognised for tax purposes on the same basis as they are recognised in the accounts.

4.1 Definition and general treatment

Any income or expenditure (including depreciation or amortisation) associated with:

(a) **intellectual property** (including patents and copyrights)
(b) **goodwill**
(c) **other intangible assets** (including agricultural quotas and brands)

is, in general, **taxable/deductible as trading income**. Provided the accounts have been prepared using generally accepted accounting practice, no adjustment will be needed to profit before taxation for tax purposes.

There is one exception to this. **Instead of deducting the depreciation or amortisation as shown in the accounts the company may claim a writing down allowance of 4%.** Such a claim might be made if, for example, the company did not charge depreciation on a particular intangible fixed asset.

Exam focus point

Exam questions in this area will normally cover goodwill and/or patents.

Question — **Disposal of intellectual property**

Moon Ltd prepares accounts to 31 December each year. It sold some patent rights to an unrelated company on 1 December 2013 for £28,000. Moon Ltd had acquired these patent rights for use in its trade on 1 December 2011 for £25,000. The patent rights are being written off in Moon Ltd's accounts on a straight-line basis over a ten-year period. What are the corporation tax implications of the sale of the patent rights?

Answer

The patent rights are an intangible fixed asset. On a disposal of the rights, the sales proceeds will be compared with the amortised cost.

	£	£
Proceeds		28,000
Cost	25,000	
Less amortisation £25,000 × 10% × 2	(5,000)	
		(20,000)
Profit on sale		8,000

The profit on sale will be included as part of Moon Ltd's trading income because the patent rights were purchased for the purposes of the trade.

All debits/credits relating to intellectual property are brought in/deducted either as:

(a) **trading income**, if the asset is used for trade purposes, or
(b) as **income from property** if the asset is used for a property letting business, or
(c) as **miscellaneous income**.

As for loan relationships, **the rules apply to capital debits and credits as well as revenue items**. Thus amounts relating to disposals are also dealt with in the income statement.

When an intangible asset is disposed of, a claim for replacement of business assets relief may be made similar to that for chargeable gains. Details are covered when we look at rollover relief for chargeable gains in companies.

4.2 Patent box

FAST FORWARD

A company that makes a patent box election is taxed at a reduced rate of corporation tax on its patent box profits.

4.2.1 Introduction

From 1 April 2013, companies that own patents can elect for the profits relating to those patents to arise within a 'patent box'.

The scheme applies to all profits attributable to qualifying patents. Such profits include royalty income received directly from the patents, but may also include a proportion of the profits from the sale of products where the patent has been used in their production. In order to qualify, the company must carry on 'qualifying development' in relation to the patent, which includes development of the patent itself or of products incorporating the patent.

The rules are being phased in over time but **broadly** the aim is **that a company that makes a patent box election will only be taxed at an effective rate of 10% on its patent box profits.** The relief is given by granting a tax deduction in the calculation of taxable total profits such that the effective rate of tax on the patent box profit is 10%. We look at the usual calculation of corporation tax, and the rates involved, later in this Text and you might want to revisit this section then.

4.2.2 Operation of the patent box

The first task is to determine the patent profit. This figure is then subject to a number of deductions in order to arrive at the net patent profit.

Exam focus point

You will not be required to calculate the patent profit or to apply the necessary deductions: the net patent profit will be provided in the exam question.

The reduced rate of tax is arrived at by deducting an amount from the company's taxable profits such that when the corporation tax rate is applied to the reduced figure, the effective rate is 10% on the patent profits.

In FY 2013 only 60% of the profit within the patent box is taxed at the 10% rate, so the deduction is calculated as follows:

$$\text{Net patent profit} \times 60\% \times \frac{(\text{MR} - 10\%)}{\text{MR}}$$

where MR is the main rate of corporation tax. The main rate of corporation tax in financial year 2013 is 23%.

Exam focus point

This formula will be provided in the exam paper.

Question — **Patent box**

Blue plc prepares accounts to 31 March each year. In the year ending 31 March 2014, it had taxable total profits (before the patent box adjustment) of £1,800,000, of which the net patent profit was £220,000. Calculate the corporation tax liability of Blue plc for the year ending 31 March 2014 assuming that it makes a patent box election.

Answer

	£	£
Profit other than net patent profit £(1,800,000 – 220,000)		1,580,000
Net patent profit	220,000	
Less Deduction in respect of patent profit $£220{,}000 \times 60\% \times \dfrac{(23\% - 10\%)}{23\%}$	(74,609)	
		145,391
Taxable total profits		1,725,391
Corporation tax liability £1,725,391 × 23%		396,840

Note: The corporation liability can be analysed as follows.

	£
Net patent profit @ 10% £(220,000 × 60%) = £132,000 × 10%	13,200
Balance of taxable profits £(1,800,000 – 132,000) = £1,668,000 × 23%	383,640
Corporation tax liability	396,840

5 Transfer pricing

FAST FORWARD

The transfer pricing legislation prevents manipulation of profits between members of a group which can occur when a company chooses to buy and sell goods at a price which is not a market price.

5.1 General rules

Companies under common control can structure their transactions in such a way that they can shift profit (or losses) from one company to another. For example consider a company which wishes to sell goods valued at £20,000 to an independent third party.

Selling company —— Goods invoice value: £20,000 ——→ Buying company

In this case all the profit on the sale arises to the selling company. Alternatively the sale could be rearranged:

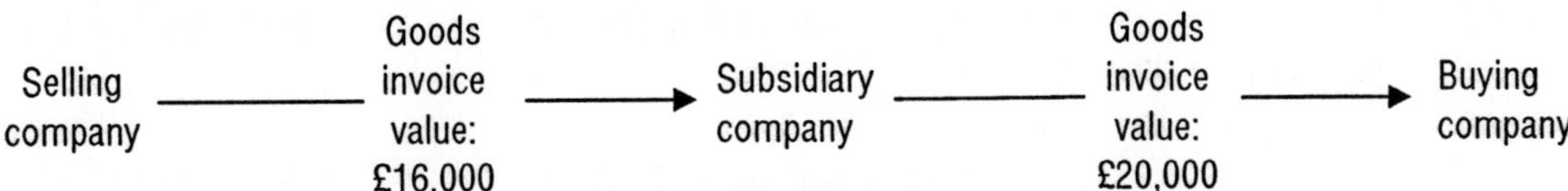

In this case £4,000 of the profit has been diverted to the subsidiary.

This technique could be used to direct profits to a company with a lower tax rate, or where they can be sheltered by losses brought forward, or even to an overseas company paying tax at a lower rate. This is a 'tax advantage' and there is **anti avoidance legislation** which **requires the profit to be computed as if the transactions had been carried out at arm's length and not at the prices actually used.** This is called a **transfer pricing adjustment**.

The transfer pricing rules apply to transactions between two persons if either:

(a) one person directly or indirectly participates in the management, control or capital of the other, or
(b) a third party directly or indirectly participates in the management, control or capital of both.

Where a **transfer pricing adjustment is required to the tax computation of a company subject to UK corporation tax** and **the other person to the transaction (who is disadvantaged) is within the charge to UK tax, a claim can be made to amend the tax computation of the disadvantaged person to arm's**

length basis, in place of the actual price used. The claim must be made within two years from the date of the return which includes the transfer adjustment.

5.2 Exemption for small and medium sized enterprises

Small and medium-sized enterprises (SMEs) are normally exempt from the transfer pricing requirements.

The definition of SMEs for the purposes of the transfer pricing rules are that the number of staff must be less than, and either the turnover or the balance sheet total not more than, the limits in the table below:

	Staff	Turnover	Balance Sheet
Small	50	€10M (about £8.5m)	€10M (about £8.5m)
Medium	250	€50M (about £42.5m)	€43M (about £36.5m)

The exemption does not apply to transactions with parties which are resident in a non-qualifying territory. This includes most foreign countries which do not have a double tax treaty with the UK, and certain other designated countries.

HMRC may direct that a medium sized enterprise should be brought within the scope of the legislation.

5.3 Transactions affected

The rules apply to all types of transactions. This includes not only the simple cases of sales of goods or provision of services, but also **loans**. A transfer pricing adjustment may be required if the loan would not have been made between the companies had there not been a relationship between them, or if a different amount would have been lent, or if the interest rate would have been different. Thus an adjustment to the interest charged in the accounts would be needed if the loan was sufficiently large that in an arm's length situation the lending company would have required equity, ie shares, instead of the loan. This situation is referred to as '**thin capitalisation**'.

5.4 Tax implications

Companies must self-assess their liability to tax under the transfer pricing rules and pay any corporation tax due. A statutory procedure exists for advance pricing arrangements (APAs) whereby a company can agree in advance that its transfer pricing policy is acceptable to HMRC ie not requiring a self-assessment adjustment. The APA facility is voluntary but companies may feel the need to use the facility as it provides necessary advance confirmation that their approach to transfer pricing in their self-assessment is acceptable.

6 Research and development

FAST FORWARD

Companies can claim a deduction for the actual amount of revenue and capital expenditure on research and development. SMEs can obtain 225% relief for qualifying research and development expenditure and large companies may obtain 130% relief. There is an alternative 'above the line' tax credit for large companies.

6.1 General rules

Research and development expenditure of a revenue nature may be deducted as allowable expenditure if it is related to the company's trade and the activity is undertaken by the company or on its behalf.

'Research and development' covers any activities that would be described as such under generally accepted accounting practice. It is related to the trade if it will lead to an extension of the trade or is directed towards the medical welfare of workers employed in the trade. The definition does not cover expenditure incurred on acquiring rights arising from research and development.

Expenditure of a capital nature on research and development related to the company's trade is also wholly allowable as a deduction ie 100% allowances are available. This covers capital expenditure on the provision of laboratories and research equipment. Note, however, that no allowance is available for expenditure on land. If any proceeds are received from the disposal of the capital assets, that receipt is taxable as trading income.

6.2 R&D relief: SMEs

A **small or medium sized enterprise** which incurs research and development expenditure of a specific nature may claim R&D tax relief.

The general definition of an SME for R&D purposes is the same as for the transfer pricing rules (see above). The definition of SME has also been extended to companies ('larger SMEs') with fewer than 500 employees, an annual turnover not exceeding €100 million and/or an annual balance sheet not exceeding €86 million. An SME must not be owned as to 25% or more by a non-SME.

Exam focus point

The examiner has said that he will state whether or not a company is a SME for R&D purposes in examination questions.

Research and development expenditure which **qualifies for the relief** is revenue expenditure on:

(a) **staff costs**, ie salaries (but not benefits), pension contributions and employer's Class 1 NICs
(b) **software and consumable items**, including fuel, power and water
(c) subcontracted expenditure of the same nature, and
(d) expenditure on externally related workers. Unless the workers are provided by a connected company this is limited to 65% of the amounts paid in respect of these workers.

R&D relief for SMEs is given by allowing the company to claim 225% of the expenditure as a deduction instead of the actual cost.

6.3 R&D tax credits

If a company that qualifies for SME R&D relief makes a trading loss it may claim a tax credit which will entitle it to an immediate repayment. The credit is 11% of the lower of the trading loss or 225% of qualifying R&D expenditure. The trading loss eligible for relief under the normal rules (see later in this Text) is reduced accordingly.

Question — R&D expenditure

Saturn Ltd is a small enterprise for the purposes of research and development. It was incorporated and started trading on 1 April 2013. During the year to 31 March 2014, it made a tax adjusted trading loss of £(100,000) before taking into account research and development expenditure of £30,000. It has no other income or gains.

Explain the tax deductions and/or credits available in the year ending 31 March 2014 in respect of the R&D expenditure and comment on any choices available to Saturn Ltd.

Answer

Since Saturn Ltd is a small enterprise for the purposes of research and development, the expenditure of £30,000 will result in a tax deduction of £30,000 × 225% = £67,500. This will result in an increase in the loss of £67,500 which it must carry forward against future profits of the same trade since it has no other

income or gains in the current period (and has no previous accounting periods since this is its first accounting period).

Saturn Ltd can choose to claim tax credit of 11% of the lower of its trading loss (£167,500) and £67,500 as an alternative to carrying the loss forward. This is therefore 11% x £67,500 = £7,425.

Saturn Ltd should consider claiming the 11% tax credit if cash flow is its main priority. Alternatively, if the company wishes to maximise the tax saved in respect of the expenditure, it should carry the loss forward. It will then save tax at a minimum rate of 20% (provided it succeeds in becoming profitable).

6.4 R&D relief: large companies

6.4.1 Deduction relief

A large company, ie one which is not an SME, that incurs research and development expenditure of a specific nature may claim a less generous R&D tax relief.

Research and development expenditure which **qualifies for the relief** is revenue expenditure on:

(a) **staff costs, software and consumable items, and** expenditure on externally related workers in connection with its own research or with research subcontracted to the company by a large company or non-trading organisation

(b) expenditure of the same nature **subcontracted** by the company to a research organisation, an individual or a partnership of individuals.

R&D relief for large companies is given by allowing the company to claim 130% of the expenditure as a deduction instead of the actual cost.

6.4.2 Above the line (ATL) tax credit

An alternative 'above the line' (ATL) credit for large company research and development (R&D) investment can be claimed from 1 April 2013.

The company must elect for the ATL tax credit within two years of the end of the accounting period. Once the company has claimed the ATL tax credit method it cannot claim deduction relief for future accounting periods.

The credit is 10% of R&D expenditure. It is a taxable receipt but is also a credit against the company's corporation tax liability.

For **companies with no corporation tax liability**:

(a) The tax credit is **paid net of main rate corporation tax** (23% in FY 2013),

(b) The amount of **tax credit it can receive is limited to the PAYE/NIC liabilities of the company's R&D staff.**

Any amount above this PAYE/NIC cap is carried forward and treated as a tax credit of the following accounting period. Alternatively the company can claim to offset the excess against the corporation tax liabilities of other accounting periods or of other group companies.

Question — **R&D expenditure for large companies**

Innovative plc, a large company, spends £100,000 on qualifying R&D expenditure during the year to 31 March 2014. The company has taxable total profits of £2,135,000 before any deduction is taken for the R&D expenditure.

Calculate the company's corporation tax liability for the year to 31 March 2014 if:

(a) The company claims the 30% additional R&D deduction, or
(b) The company claims the ATL tax credit.

Answer

(a) *If 30% additional R&D deduction claimed*

	£
Taxable total profit before R&D expenditure	2,135,000
Less R&D expenditure	(100,000)
R&D additional deduction £100,000 × 30%	(30,000)
Taxable total profit	2,005,000
Corporation tax payable £2,005,000 × 23%	461,150

Note: The tax saving on R&D expenditure is £100,000 × 30% × 23% = £6,900 or 6.9% of the expenditure.

(b) *If ATL tax credit claimed*

	£
Taxable total profit before R&D expenditure	2,135,000
Add ATL credit £100,000 × 10%	10,000
Less R&D expenditure	(100,000)
Taxable total profit	2,045,000
Corporation tax £2,045,000 × 23%	470,350
Less ATL credit £100,000 × 10%	(10,000)
Corporation tax payable	460,350

Note: The tax saving using the ATL credit is as follows:

	£
Corporation tax on additional income £10,000 × 23%	2,300
Less ATL credit deduced from CT liability £100,000 × 10%	(10,000)
Corporation tax saving (7.7% of R&D expenditure)	7,700

The additional tax saving by using the ATL credit is therefore £(461,150 – 460,350) = £800 which is (7.7% - 6.9% × £100,000).

7 Enhanced capital allowances (ECAs)

FAST FORWARD

ECAs are available on energy-saving and water-saving plant and machinery. A company may surrender tax losses attributable to ECAs for a first year tax credit of 19% of the loss surrendered.

7.1 Availability of ECAs

As was described earlier in this Text, expenditure on energy saving or water saving plant and machinery qualifies for enhanced capital allowances of 100%.

7.2 Surrender of ECAs

Companies are able to surrender tax losses attributable to ECAs for a cash payment called a first-year tax credit.

The first-year tax credit is 19% of the loss surrendered, subject to an upper limit which is the greater of:

- **the total of the company's PAYE and NICs liabilities for the period for which the loss is surrendered; or**
- **£250,000.**

Where the loss could be used by the company against its taxable profits in the same period or surrendered as group relief, then it cannot be surrendered for a first-year tax credit. Any losses available to carry forward are reduced by the amount of the loss that has been surrendered.

The company must claim first-year tax credits in its corporation tax return for the relevant accounting period.

There will be a claw-back of the relief if the ECA qualifying plant and machinery is sold within four years after the end of the period for which the tax credit was paid. If this happens, the surrendered loss will become available for relief again.

Chapter roundup

- Companies pay corporation tax on their taxable total profits of each accounting period.
- An accounting period cannot exceed twelve months in length. A long period of account must be split into two accounting periods, the first of which is twelve months long.
- Taxable total profits are the total profits (income and gains) less some losses and qualifying charitable donations.
- A loan relationship arises when a company lends or borrows money. Trading loan relationships are dealt with as trading income. Non-trading loan relationships are dealt with as interest income.
- Gains/losses arising on intangible assets are recognised for tax purposes on the same basis as they are recognised in the accounts.
- A company that makes a patent box election is taxed at a reduced rate of corporation tax on its patent box profits.
- The transfer pricing legislation prevents manipulation of profits between members of a group which can occur when a company chooses to buy and sell goods at a price which is not a market price.
- Companies can claim a deduction for the actual amount of revenue and capital expenditure on research and development. SMEs can obtain 225% relief for qualifying research and development expenditure and large companies may obtain 130% relief. There is an alternative 'above the line' tax credit for large companies.
- ECAs are available on energy-saving and water-saving plant and machinery. A company may surrender tax losses attributable to ECAs for a first year tax credit of 19% of the loss surrendered.

Quick quiz

1. When does an accounting period end?
2. How are trading profits (before capital allowances) of a long period of account divided between accounting periods?
3. Does a company pay loan stock interest to another UK company gross or net of tax?
4. How is interest arising on a non-trading loan relationship taxed?
5. What steps can be taken against the use of artificial transfer prices?
6. A small or medium sized company can claim ....% relief for qualifying research and development expenditure. Fill in the blank.
7. X plc spends £100,000 on energy saving plant and machinery in the year to 31 March 2014. X plc has a trading loss of £500,000 for the year including the enhanced capital allowance, the energy saving plant and machinery. What first year tax credit can it claim?

Answers to quick quiz

1 An accounting period ends on the earliest of:

(a) 12 months after its start
(b) the end of the company's period of account
(c) the company starting or ceasing to trade
(d) the company entering/ceasing to be in administration
(e) the commencement of the company's winding up
(f) the company ceasing to be resident in the UK
(g) the company ceasing to be liable to corporation tax

2 Trading income (before capital allowances) is apportioned on a time basis.

3 Gross.

4 Interest on a non-trading loan relationship is aggregated with all other income and gains from non-trading loans. From this is deducted interest paid on and losses on non-trading loans. The resulting net amount is taxed as interest income.

5 Although a company may buy and sell goods at any price it wishes, the transfer pricing anti-avoidance legislation requires profit to be computed as if the transactions had been carried out at arm's length, in certain circumstances.

6 A small or medium sized company can claim **225%** relief for qualifying research and development expenditure.

7 £100,000 × 100% × 19% = £19,000 (less than upper limit of £250,000).

Now try the question below from the Exam Question Bank

Number	Level	Marks	Time
Q20	Introductory	15	27 mins

Chargeable gains for companies

Topic list	Syllabus reference
1 Corporation tax on chargeable gains	A2(a)C1
2 Indexation allowance	A2(a)C2
3 Disposal of shares by companies	A3(a)D4
4 Disposal of substantial shareholdings	A3(f)(ii)
5 Relief for replacement of business assets (rollover relief)	A2(a)C5
6 Disincorporation relief	A2(f)(i)

Introduction

We studied chargeable gains for individuals earlier in this Text. In this chapter, we will consider the treatment of chargeable gains for companies.

Companies pay corporation tax on their chargeable gains, rather than capital gains tax. The computation of gains for companies is slightly more complicated than for individuals because companies are entitled to indexation allowance.

We also consider the matching rules for companies which dispose of shares in other companies. Again, these rules are slightly more complicated than for individuals. We also consider the relief for substantial shareholdings.

Next, we look at how the relief for replacement of business assets applies to companies.

Finally, we consider the relief which is available to some small companies which disincorporate and transfer the company's business to its shareholders.

In the next chapter we look at the computation of corporation tax.

Study guide

		Intellectual level
2	**Corporation tax liabilities in situations involving further overseas and group aspects and in relation to special types of company, and the application of additional exemptions and reliefs**	
(a)	The contents of the Paper F6 study guide, for corporation tax, under headings:	2
•	C1 The scope of corporation tax	
•	C2 Taxable total profits	
•	C5 The use of exemptions and reliefs in deferring and minimising corporation tax liabilities	
(f)	The use of exemptions and reliefs in deferring and minimising corporation tax liabilities	3
(i)	Advise on the availability and the application of disincorporation relief	
3	**Chargeable gains and capital gains tax liabilities in situations involving further overseas aspects and in relation to closely related persons and trusts together with the application of additional exemptions and reliefs**	
(a)	The contents of the Paper F6 study guide for chargeable gains under headings:	2
•	D4 Gains and losses on the disposal of shares and securities	
(f)	Gains and losses on the disposal of shares and securities:	3
(ii)	Determine the application of the substantial shareholdings exemption	

Exam guide

You may well be asked to compute chargeable gains or losses for a company as part of a tax planning question so you must know the rules in this chapter very well.

Knowledge brought forward from earlier studies

This chapter mainly revises topics you should be familiar with from F6. There have been no substantial changes in Financial Year 2013 from Financial Year 2012 in the material you have studied previously. The two new topics are disincorporation relief and the substantial shareholdings exemption.

1 Corporation tax on chargeable gains

FAST FORWARD

Chargeable gains for companies are computed in broadly the same way as for individuals, but indexation allowance applies and there is no annual exempt amount.

One of the competencies you require to fulfil performance objective 19 of the PER is the ability to evaluate and compute taxes payable. You can apply the knowledge you obtain from this section of the text to help to demonstrate this competence.

Companies do not pay capital gains tax. Instead their chargeable gains are included in taxable total profits.

A company's capital gains or allowable losses are computed in a similar way to individuals but with a few major differences:

- There is relief for inflation called the **indexation allowance**
- **No annual exempt amount** is available
- **Different matching rules for shares** apply if the shareholder is a company.

2 Indexation allowance

FAST FORWARD

The indexation allowance gives relief for the inflation element of a gain.

The purpose of having an indexation allowance is to remove the inflation element of a gain from taxation.

Companies are entitled to indexation allowance from the date of acquisition until the date of disposal of an asset. It is based on the movement in the Retail Price Index (RPI) between those two dates.

For example, if J Ltd bought a painting on 2 January 2003 and sold it on 19 November 2013, the indexation allowance is available from January 2003 until November 2013.

Exam formula

The indexation factor is:

$$\frac{\text{RPI for month of disposal} - \text{RPI for month of acquisition}}{\text{RPI for month of acquisition}}$$

The calculation is expressed as a decimal and is rounded to three decimal places.

Indexation allowance is available on the allowable cost of the asset from the date of acquisition (including incidental costs of acquisition). It is also available on enhancement expenditure from the month in which such expenditure becomes due and payable. Indexation allowance is not available on the costs of disposal.

Question — The indexation allowance

An asset is acquired by a company on 15 February 2003 (RPI = 179.3) at a cost of £5,000. Enhancement expenditure of £2,000 is incurred on 10 April 2004 (RPI = 185.7). The asset is sold for £25,500 on 20 December 2013 (RPI =254.4). Incidental costs of sale are £500. Calculate the chargeable gain arising.

Answer

The indexation allowance is available until December 2013 and is computed as follows.

	£
$\frac{254.4-179.3}{179.3} = 0.419 \times £5,000$	2,095
$\frac{254.4-185.7}{185.7} = 0.370 \times £2,000$	740
Indexation allowance	2,835

The computation of the chargeable gain is as follows.

	£
Proceeds	25,500
Less incidental costs of sale	(500)
Net proceeds	25,000
Less allowable costs £(5,000 + 2,000)	(7,000)
Unindexed gain	18,000
Less indexation allowance (see above)	(2,835)
Indexed gain	15,165

Indexation allowance cannot create or increase an allowable loss. If there is a gain before the indexation allowance, the allowance can reduce that gain to zero but no further. If there is a loss before the indexation allowance, there is no indexation allowance.

If the indexation allowance calculation gives a negative figure, treat the indexation as nil: do not add to the indexed gain.

3 Disposal of shares by companies

FAST FORWARD

There are special rules for matching shares sold by a company with shares purchased. Disposals are matched with acquisitions on the same day, the previous nine days and the FA 1985 share pool.

3.1 The matching rules

We have discussed the share matching rules for individuals earlier in this Text. We also need special rules for companies.

For companies the matching of shares sold is in the following order.

(a) Shares acquired on the **same day**

(b) Shares acquired in the **previous nine days**, if more than one acquisition on a "first in, first out" (FIFO) basis

(c) Shares from the **FA 1985 pool**

The composition of the FA 1985 pool in relation to companies which are shareholders is explained below.

Exam focus point

Learn the 'matching rules' because a crucial first step to getting a shares question right is to correctly match the shares sold to the original shares purchased.

3.2 Example: share matching rules for companies

Nor Ltd acquired the following shares in Last plc:

Date of acquisition	*No of shares*
9.11.02	15,000
15.12.04	15,000
11.7.13	5,000
15.7.13	5,000

Nor Ltd disposed of 20,000 of the shares on 15 July 2013.

We match the shares as follows:

(a) Acquisition on same day: 5,000 shares acquired 15 July 2013.

(b) Acquisitions in previous 9 days: 5,000 shares acquired 11 July 2013.

(c) FA 1985 share pool: 10,000 shares out of 30,000 shares in FA 1985 share pool (9.11.02 and 15.12.04).

3.3 The FA 1985 share pool

Exam focus point

The examiner has stated that a detailed question will not be set on the pooling provisions. However, work through the examples below as you are expected to understand how the pool works.

The FA 1985 pool comprises the following shares of the same class in the same company.

- **Shares held by a company on 1 April 1985 and acquired by that company on or after 1 April 1982.**
- **Shares acquired by that company on or after 1 April 1985.**

We must keep track of:

(a) the **number** of shares
(b) the **cost** of the shares ignoring indexation
(c) the **indexed cost** of the shares

The first step in constructing the FA 1985 share pool is to calculate the value of the pool at 1 April 1985 by indexing the cost of each acquisition before that date up to April 1985.

3.4 Example: the FA 1985 share pool

Oliver Ltd bought 1,000 shares in Judith plc for £2,750 in August 1984 and another 1,000 for £3,250 in December 1984. RPIs are August 1984 = 89.9, December 1984 = 90.9 and April 1985 = 94.8. The FA 1985 pool at 1 April 1985 is as follows.

	No of shares	*Cost*	*Indexed Cost*
		£	£
August 1984 (a)	1,000	2,750	2,750
December 1984 (b)	1,000	3,250	3,250
	2,000	6,000	6,000
Indexation allowance			
$\frac{94.8-89.9}{89.9} = 0.055 \times £2,750$			151
$\frac{94.8-90.9}{90.9} = 0.043 \times £3,250$			140
Indexed cost of the pool at 1 April 1985			6,291

Disposals and acquisitions of shares which affect the indexed value of the FA 1985 pool are termed **'operative events'. Prior to reflecting each such operative event within the FA 1985 share pool, a further indexation allowance (an 'indexed rise') must be computed up to the date of the operative event concerned from the date of the last such operative event** (or from the later of the first acquisition and April 1985 if the operative event in question is the first one).

Indexation calculations within the FA 1985 pool (after its April 1985 value has been calculated) **are not rounded to three decimal places**. This is because rounding errors would accumulate and have a serious effect after several operative events. If there are several operative events between 1 April 1985 and the date of a disposal, the indexation procedure described above will have to be performed several times over.

Question — **Value of FA 1985 pool**

Following on from the above example, assume that Oliver Ltd acquired 2,000 more shares on 10 July 1986 at a cost of £4,000. Recalculate the value of the FA 1985 pool on 10 July 1986 following the acquisition. RPI July 1986 = 97.5.

Answer

	No of shares	Cost £	Indexed cost £
Value at 1.4.85 b/f	2,000	6,000	6,291
Indexed rise $\frac{97.5-94.8}{94.8} \times £6,291$			179
	2,000	6,000	6,470
Acquisition	2,000	4,000	4,000
Value at 10.7.86	4,000	10,000	10,470

In the case of a disposal, following the calculation of the indexed rise to the date of disposal, the cost and the indexed cost attributable to the shares disposed of are deducted from the amounts within the FA 1985 pool. The proportions of the cost and indexed cost to take out of the pool should be computed by using the proportion of cost that the shares disposed of bear to the total number of shares held.

The indexation allowance is the indexed cost taken out of the pool minus the cost taken out. As usual, the indexation allowance cannot create or increase a loss.

Question — Disposals from the FA 1985 pool

Continuing the above exercise, suppose that Oliver Ltd sold 3,000 shares on 10 July 2013 for £23,000. Compute the gain, and the value of the FA 1985 pool following the disposal. Assume RPI July 2013 = 249.6.

Answer

	No of shares	Cost £	Indexed cost £
Value at 10.7.86	4,000	10,000	10,470
Indexed rise			
$\frac{249.6-97.5}{97.5} \times £10,470$			16,333
	4,000	10,000	26,803
Disposal	(3,000)		
Cost and indexed cost $\frac{3,000}{4,000} \times £10,000$ and £26,803		(7,500)	(20,102)
Value at 10.7.13	1,000	2,500	6,701

The gain is computed as follows:

	£
Proceeds	23,000
Less cost	(7,500)
Unindexed gain	15,500
Less indexation allowance £(20,102 – 7,500)	(12,602)
Indexed gain	2,898

3.5 Bonus and rights issues

When **bonus issue shares are issued**, all that happens is that **the size of the original holding is increased.** Since **bonus issue shares are issued at no cost** there is **no need to adjust the original cost** and there is **no operative event for the FA 1985 pool** (so no indexation allowance needs to be calculated).

When **rights issue shares are issued**, the **size of the original holding is increased** in the same way as for a bonus issue. So if the original shareholding was part of the FA 1985 pool, the rights issue shares are added to that pool. This might be important for the matching rules if a shareholding containing the rights issue shares is sold shortly after the rights issue.

However, in the case of a rights issue, the **new shares are paid for and this results in an adjustment to the original cost**. For the purpose of **calculating the indexation allowance, expenditure on a rights issue is taken as being incurred on the date of the issue** and not the date of the original holding.

3.6 Example: bonus and rights issue

S Ltd bought 10,000 shares in T plc in May 2000 (RPI = 170.7) at a cost of £45,000. There was a 2 for 1 bonus issue in October 2002. There was a 1 for 3 rights issue in June 2006 (RPI = 198.5) at a cost of £4 per share. S Ltd took up all of its rights entitlement. S Ltd sold 20,000 shares in T plc for £120,000 in January 2014 (RPI = 253.4).

FA 1985 share pool

		No of shares	*Cost*	*Indexed cost*
			£	£
5.00	Acquisition	10,000	45,000	45,000
10.02	Bonus 2:1	20,000		
		30,000		
6.06	Indexed rise			
	$\frac{198.5-170.7}{170.7} \times £45,000$			7,329
	Rights 1:3	10,000	40,000	40,000
		40,000	85,000	92,329
1.14	Index rise			
	$\frac{253.4-198.5}{198.5} \times £92,329$			25,536
				117,865
	Disposal	(20,000)	(42,500)	(58,933)
c/f		20,000	42,500	58,932

The gain is:

	£
Proceeds	120,000
Less: cost	(42,500)
Unindexed gain	77,500
Less: indexation allowance (£58,933 – 42,500)	(16,433)
Indexed gain	61,067

3.7 Reorganisations and takeovers

The rules on reorganisation and takeovers apply in a similar way for company shareholders as they do for individuals.

In the case of a **reorganisation, the new shares or securities take the place of the original shares. The original cost and the indexed cost of the original shares is apportioned between the different types of capital issued on the reorganisation.**

Where there is a takeover of shares which qualifies for the 'paper for paper' treatment, the cost and indexed cost of the original holding is passed onto the new holding which take the place of the original holding.

J Ltd acquired 20,000 shares in G Ltd in August 1990 (RPI = 128.1) at a cost of £40,000. It acquired a further 5,000 shares in December 2006 (RPI = 202.7) at a cost of £30,000.

In March 2014, G Ltd was taken over by K plc and J Ltd received one ordinary share and two preference shares in K plc for each one share held in G Ltd. Immediately following the takeover, the ordinary shares in K plc were worth £4 per share and the preference shares in K plc were worth £1 per share.

Show the cost and indexed cost of the ordinary shares and the preference shares.

Answer

G Ltd FA 1985 share pool

		No. of shares	*Cost*	*Indexed cost*
			£	£
8.90	Acquisition	20,000	40,000	40,000
12.06	Indexed rise			
	$\frac{202.7 - 128.1}{128.1} \times £40,000$			23,294
	Acquisition	5,000	30,000	30,000
Pool at takeover		25,000	70,000	93,294

Note that the takeover is not an operative event because the pool of cost is not increased or decreased and so it is not necessary to calculate an indexed rise.

Apportionment of cost/indexed cost to K plc shares

	No. of shares	*MV*	*Cost*	*Indexed cost*
		£	£	£
Ords × 1	25,000	100,000	46,667	62,196
Prefs × 2	50,000	50,000	23,333	31,098
Totals		150,000	70,000	93,294

On a disposal of shares in K plc, indexation allowance will be calculated from December 2006.

4 Disposal of substantial shareholdings

4.1 Principles

FAST FORWARD

Where a trading company owns shares in another trading company, there is an exemption on disposal if 10% or more of the shares are held.

One of the competencies you require to fulfil performance objective 19 of the PER is the ability to evaluate and compute taxes payable. You can apply the knowledge you obtain from this section of the text to help to demonstrate this competence.

There is an exemption from corporation tax for any gain arising when a **trading company (or member of a trading group) disposes of the whole or any part of a substantial shareholding in another trading company** (or in the holding company of a trading group or sub-group).

Key term

> A **substantial shareholding** is one where the investing company holds 10% of ordinary share capital and is beneficially entitled to at least 10% of the
>
> (a) profits available for distribution to equity holders, and
> (b) assets of the company available for distribution to equity holders on a winding up.

To meet the 10% test shares owned by members of a chargeable gains group (see later in this Text) may be amalgamated. **The 10% test must have been met for a continuous twelve month period during the two years preceding the disposal.**

The twelve month period condition can also be satisfied by including a period during which assets, which are being used in its trade by the company whose shares are being disposed of (Company A), were being used in the trade of another group company (Company B) and then transferred to Company A before the sale of the Company A shares. This enables the exemption to apply in the situation where an existing trade carried on by one group company is transferred to a new group company before that new company is sold outside the group. This may be preferred to selling the original company carrying on the trade, for example if it also has contingent liabilities.

The exemption is given automatically and cannot be disclaimed. This means that as well as exempting gains, it denies relief for losses.

The exemption applies to the disposal of part of a substantial holding. This means that if A Ltd owns 10% of the ordinary share capital in B Ltd, and disposes of 1% of that share capital, any gain will be exempt. In addition, the disposal of the remaining 9% may result in an exempt gain.

4.2 Example: disposal of substantial shareholding

On 1 December 2006 SD Ltd bought 20% of the shares in AM Ltd. The shareholding qualifies for the substantial shareholding exemption. During its accounting period to 31 March 2014, SD Ltd made the following disposals:

(a) On 30 June 2013 it disposed of a 15% holding in AM Ltd.
(b) On 30 December 2013 it disposed of the remaining 5% holding in AM Ltd.

Both of these shareholdings qualify for the substantial shareholdings exemption. Clearly the first disposal is of at least a 10% holding which was held for twelve months prior to disposal. The second disposal also qualifies despite being only a 5% holding, because SD Ltd owned a 10% holding throughout a twelve month period beginning in the two years prior to this second disposal.

5 Relief for replacement of business assets (rollover relief)

FAST FORWARD

> Relief for replacement of business assets is available to companies to defer gains arising on the disposal of business assets.

5.1 Conditions for relief

As for individuals, a gain may be rolled over by a company where the proceeds on the disposal of a business asset are spent on a replacement business asset under rollover relief.

A claim for the relief must be made by the later of four years of the end of the accounting period in which the disposal of the old asset takes place and four years of the end of the accounting period in which the new assets is acquired. For example, if a disposal is made by a company in its accounting period to 30 June 2014 and a claim to roll-over relief is made in respect of a new asset acquired in the accounting period to 30 June 2013 the time limit for a claim is 30 June 2018 (four years after the end of the accounting period in which the disposal of the old asset was made).

The conditions for the relief to apply to company disposals are:

(a) The old assets sold and the new asset bought are both used only in the trade of the company (apportionment into business and non-business parts available for buildings).

(b) The old asset and the new asset both fall within one (but not necessarily the same one) of the following classes.

  (i) **Land and buildings** (including parts of buildings) occupied as well as used only for the purposes of the trade

  (ii) **Fixed plant and machinery**

(c) Reinvestment of the proceeds received on the disposal of the old asset takes place in a period beginning one year before and ending three years after the date of the disposal.

(d) The new asset is brought into use in the trade on its acquisition.

Note that goodwill is not a qualifying asset for the purposes of corporation tax.

5.2 Operation of relief

Deferral is obtained by deducting the indexed gain from the cost of the new asset. For full relief, the whole of the proceeds must be reinvested. If only part is reinvested, a gain equal to the amount not invested, or the full gain, if lower, will be chargeable to tax immediately.

The new asset will have a base cost for chargeable gains purposes of its purchase price less the gain rollover over.

Question — Rollover relief

D Ltd acquired a factory in April 2000 (RPI = 170.1) at a cost of £120,000. It used the factory in its trade throughout the period of its ownership.

In August 2013 (RPI = 250.5), D Ltd sold the factory for £220,000. In November 2012, it acquired another factory at a cost of £190,000.

Calculate the gain chargeable on the sale of the first factory and the base cost of the second factory.

Answer

Chargeable gain on sale of first factory

	£
Proceeds	220,000
Less: cost	(120,000)
Unindexed gain	100,000
$\frac{250.5-170.1}{170.1}$ = 0.473 × £120,000	(56,760)
Indexed gain	43,240
Less: rollover relief (balancing figure)	(13,240)
Chargeable gain: amount not reinvested £(220,000 – 190,000)	30,000

Base cost of second factory

	£
Cost of second factory	190,000
Less: rolled over gain	(13,240)
Base cost	176,760

5.3 Depreciating assets

The relief for investment into depreciating assets works in the same way for companies as it does for individuals.

The indexed gain is calculated on the old asset and is deferred until the gain crystallises on the earliest of:

(a) The disposal of the replacement asset
(b) The date the replacement asset ceases to be used in the trade
(c) Ten years after the acquisition of the replacement asset.

5.4 Intangible fixed assets

FAST FORWARD

There is a similar replacement of business assets relief for replacement of intangible fixed assets. However, relief is restricted to the gain based on original cost, not on the written down cost.

As we have seen earlier in this Text, gains on the disposal of intangible fixed assets are taxable as trading income rather than as chargeable gains. However, there is a form of **relief for replacement of intangible business assets for companies which is very similar to that for chargeable gains** and so it is convenient to consider it in this section.

A profit on the disposal of an intangible fixed asset can be rolled over by the acquisition of a replacement asset within the period beginning one year before and ending three years after the date of the disposal. Relief is given by rolling over the gain into the base cost of the replacement asset.

The maximum profit which can be rolled over is the profit comparing proceeds with original cost, not with the written down cost. Therefore, if the intangible fixed asset has been written down, the gain relating to the amount written down will be chargeable as trading income.

If the expenditure on the new intangible fixed asset equals or exceeds the proceeds of the old intangible fixed asset, then relief is available to roll over the whole of the gain based on the original cost.

If expenditure on the new intangible fixed asset is less than the proceeds of the old intangible fixed asset, the relief is restricted to the excess of the amount invested in the new intangible fixed asset over the original cost of the old asset.

Question — Intangible fixed assets

In August 2016, Turnbull Ltd disposed of patent rights acquired in 2013 for use in its trade. The rights had cost £150,000 but had been written down to £110,000 by the date of sale. The sale realised £200,000 and the company acquired the goodwill of a trade from a competitor two months later. Calculate how much of the profit could be rolled over, any amount remaining taxable as trading income and the base cost of the new asset, if the goodwill was acquired for (a) £280,000, or (b) £180,000.

Answer

(a) **New investment £280,000 (ie all proceeds invested in new asset)**

Accounting profit on patent rights £200,000 – £110,000	£90,000
Profit for potential rollover £200,000 – £150,000	£50,000
Profit which cannot be rolled over taxable as trading income £90,000 – £50,000	£40,000
Base cost of replacement asset (new goodwill) £280,000 – £50,000	£230,000

(b) **New investment £180,000 (ie partial investment in new asset)**

Accounting profit (as above)	£90,000
Profit for potential rollover £180,000 – £150,000	£30,000
Profit which cannot be rolled over taxable as trading income £90,000 – £30,000	£60,000
Base cost of replacement new asset £180,000 – £30,000	£150,000

6 Disincorporation relief

FAST FORWARD

Disincorporation relief allows a company to transfer its business to its shareholders without giving rise to taxable gains/profits on land and buildings and goodwill.

6.1 Introduction

A business may be run as either an incorporated business (ie a company) or an unincorporated business (ie a sole trader or partnership).

Where the shareholders (owners) of a company decide that they would prefer to operate the business as an unincorporated business (ie they want to disincorporate), the company will transfer the business to the shareholders and thus **dispose of its capital assets.** This is likely to result in a **corporation tax charge on any gain/profit arising on the assets transferred**. This may be a disincentive to disincorporation.

Disincorporation relief allows certain small companies to transfer the company's business to its shareholders without a corporation tax charge arising on the transfer of particular assets, provided certain conditions are satisfied.

6.2 Operation of the relief

When a company transfers its business to its shareholders, it is deemed to dispose of its assets at market value. Any **chargeable gains on chargeable assets** such as land and buildings, and **trading profits on intangible assets** such as goodwill, will give rise to a **corporation tax charge.**

Where disincorporation relief is claimed, any **land and buildings are deemed to be transferred at the lower of their market value and their allowable acquisition cost, and goodwill is deemed to be transferred at the lower of its market value and its tax written down value. The result is that no gain/profit arises on the disposal of these assets. The shareholders are deemed to acquire the assets at that same value.**

Note that **disincorporation relief does not provide relief for other tax charges which may arise** on the transfer of the business such as capital allowance balancing charges or a profit on the deemed transfer of stock (inventory) at market value. Other reliefs may, however, be available for these tax charges where the company and the shareholders are connected persons (see earlier in this Text).

6.3 Conditions for relief

Disincorporation relief applies where:

(a) **A company transfers its business to some or all of its shareholders**, and
(b) The transfer is a **qualifying business transfer,** and
(c) The business transfer occurs in the **period 1 April 2013 to 31 March 2018.**

A **qualifying business transfer** is one where:

(a) The business is transferred as a **going concern**, and

(b) **All of the assets of the business are transferred** (except cash), and

(c) The **total market value of goodwill and land and buildings transferred does not exceed £100,000**, and

(d) **All of the shareholders** to whom the business is transferred are **individuals** and have **held their shares for 12 months prior to the date of transfer.**

6.4 Claim for relief

A claim for disincorporation relief must be made **within 2 years of the date of the transfer.** The claim must be made **jointly by the company and all of the shareholders** to whom the business is transferred. It is irrevocable.

Question — **Disincorporation relief**

Mr Small is a director of Little Ltd and owns all of the shares of the company. The company was incorporated on 1 January 2006 and has traded since that date, preparing accounts to 31 December each year.

Mr Small has now decided that he would prefer to operate the trade of Little Ltd as a sole trader. The company therefore transferred all of the assets of the business to Mr Small on 1 June 2013. The assets of Little Ltd on 1 June 2013 are as follows.

	Market value at 1.6.13	*Cost*
	£	£
Business premises	68,000	25,000
Goodwill	27,000	–
Plant and machinery (capital allowances claimed)	10,000	15,000
Motor car	4,000	–
Net current assets	22,000	–
	131,000	

Explain:

(a) Why an election for disincorporation relief can be made.
(b) The tax implications of the election being made.
(c) The date by which the election must be made.

Answer

(a) The transfer qualifies for disincorporation relief because:

(i) The company is transferring its business as a going concern to a shareholder.

(ii) All of the assets of the business are being transferred

(iii) The market value of the goodwill and land and buildings (£95,000) does not exceed £100,000

(iv) The transfer is to an individual who has held shares in the company for at least 12 months prior to the transfer and

(v) The transfer occurred after 1 April 2013 but before 31 March 2018.

(b) Without disincorporation relief there would be gains arising on the business premises of £43,000 (£68,000 – £25,000) and the goodwill of £(27,000 – nil) = £27,000.

With disincorporation relief, the business premises are deemed to have been disposed of at the lower of market value (£68,000) and cost (£25,000). The deemed proceeds are therefore £25,000, so producing a nil gain. The goodwill is deemed to have been disposed of at the lower of market value (£27,000) and tax written down value (£nil). The deemed proceeds are therefore £nil, so producing no profit.

Mr Small acquires the land and buildings at a base cost of £25,000 and he goodwill at a base cost of £nil.

(c) The company and Mr Small must make a joint claim by 31 May 2015 (within two years of the date of the transfer of the business).

Chapter roundup

- Chargeable gains for companies are computed in broadly the same way as for individuals, but indexation allowance applies and there is no annual exempt amount.
- The indexation allowance gives relief for the inflation element of a gain.
- There are special rules for matching shares sold by a company with shares purchased. Disposals are matched with acquisitions on the same day, the previous nine days and the FA 1985 share pool.
- Where a trading company owns shares in another trading company, there is an exemption on disposal if 10% or more of the shares are held.
- Relief for replacement of business assets is available to companies to defer gains arising on the disposal of business assets.
- There is a similar replacement of business assets relief for intangible fixed assets. However, relief is restricted to the gain based on original cost, not on the written down cost.
- Disincorporation relief allows a company to transfer its business to its shareholders without giving rise to taxable gains/profits on land and buildings and goodwill.

Quick quiz

1. A company is entitled to an annual exempt amount against its chargeable gains. TRUE/FALSE?
2. Indexation allowance runs from the date of __ to date of __. Fill in the blanks.
3. What are the share matching rules for company shareholders?
4. A Ltd has a long standing 15% shareholding in B Ltd, an investment company. Does the substantial shareholding exemption apply on a disposal of an 8% holding by A Ltd?
5. H Ltd sells a warehouse for £400,000. The warehouse cost £220,000 and the indexation allowance available is £40,000. The company acquires another warehouse ten months later for £375,000. What is the amount of rollover relief?
6. If a disincorporation relief claim is made no tax charge will arise on the transfer of a business to its shareholders. TRUE/FALSE?

Answers to quick quiz

1 FALSE. A company is not entitled to an annual exempt amount against its chargeable gains.

2 Indexation allowance runs from the date of acquisition to date of disposal.

3 The matching rules for shares disposed of by a company shareholder are:

   (a) Shares acquired on the same day
   (b) Shares acquired in the previous nine days
   (c) Shares from the FA 1985 pool

4 No. B Ltd is an investment company, not a trading company.

5 The gain on the sale of first warehouse is:

	£
Proceeds	400,000
Less: cost	(220,000)
Unindexed gain	180,000
Less: indexation allowance	(40,000)
Indexed gain	140,000
Less: rollover relief (balancing figure)	(115,000)
Chargeable gain: amount not reinvested £(400,000 – 375,000)	25,000

6 FALSE. Disincorporation relief allows goodwill and land and buildings to be transferred at no tax cost to the company. However, it will not prevent tax charges arising on any other chargeable assets, capital allowance balancing charges or the transfer of stock (inventory) at market value (although other tax reliefs may be available).

Now try the question below from the Exam Question Bank

Number	Level	Marks	Time
Q21	Introductory	10	18 mins

Computing corporation tax payable

Topic list	Syllabus reference
1 Charge to corporation tax	A2(a)C3
2 Returns, records, compliance checks, assessments and claims	A6(c)H1-4
3 Payment of corporation tax and interest	A6(c)H2

Introduction

In this chapter we look at how to calculate the corporation tax payable on taxable total profits. We look at the effect of short accounting periods and associated companies on the rate of corporation tax payable.

Finally, we look at the administration of corporation tax.

In the next chapter we will consider the rules for winding up companies and for companies purchasing their own shares.

Study guide

		Intellectual level
2	**Corporation tax liabilities in situations involving further overseas and group aspects and in relation to special types of company, and the application of additional exemptions and reliefs**	
(a)	The contents of the Paper F6 study guide, for corporation tax, under headings:	2
•	C3 The comprehensive computation of corporation tax liability	
6	**National insurance, value added tax, tax administration and the UK tax system:**	
(c)	The contents of the Paper F6 study guide for the obligations of taxpayers and/or their agents under headings:	
•	H1 The systems for self assessment and the making of returns	
•	H2 The time limits for the submission of information, claims and payment of tax, including payments on account	
•	H3 The procedures relating to compliance checks, appeals and disputes	
•	H4 Penalties for non-compliance	

Exam guide

Although you are unlikely simply to be asked to calculate the corporation tax payable for an accounting period you are very likely to have to be able to work out marginal tax rates when giving advice about using losses, new projects, etc. It is therefore very important to know the rules for small profits rate and marginal relief, and how the limits are affected by the length of the accounting period and the number of associated companies. You must know the rules regarding administration as the company's obligations could form a part of any question.

Knowledge brought forward from earlier studies

This chapter revises the computation of corporation tax payable that you will have studied previously. The rules for administration are also revision. The examiner has identified essential underpinning knowledge from the F6 syllabus which is particularly important that you revise as part of your P6 studies. In this chapter, the relevant topic is:

		Intellectual level
C3	**The comprehensive computation of corporation tax liability**	
(a)	Compute the corporation tax liability and apply marginal relief.	2

The major changes in Financial Year 2013 from Finance Act 2012 concern the new main rate of corporation tax and the consequential change in the standard fraction used to compute marginal relief.

1 Charge to corporation tax

1.1 Augmented profits

FAST FORWARD

Augmented profits are taxable total profits plus franked investment income (FII).

Although we tax taxable total profits another figure needs to be calculated (augmented profits) to determine the rate of corporation tax to use to tax taxable total profits.

Augmented profits means taxable total profits plus the grossed-up amount of dividends received from UK and non-UK companies. There is an exception for dividends which are received from a 51% subsidiary of the recipient company or from a company where both the paying company and the recipient company are 51% subsidiaries of a third company (sometimes referred to as 'group dividends' or 'group income') – such dividends are ignored.

The grossed-up amount of both UK and non-UK dividends is the dividend received multiplied by 100/90. This is because dividends are treated as paid net of a 10% tax credit (see earlier in this Text). You may see the grossed up amount of dividend received referred to as **franked investment income (FII)**.

Exam focus point

Be careful to charge corporation tax on taxable total profits, not on augmented profits.

1.2 Financial years

FAST FORWARD

Tax rates are set for financial years.

The rates of corporation tax are fixed for financial years.

A financial year runs from 1 April to the following 31 March and is identified by the calendar year in which it begins. For example, the year ended 31 March 2014 is the Financial Year 2013 (FY 2013). This should not be confused with a tax year, which runs from 6 April to the following 5 April.

1.3 The main rate

FAST FORWARD

Companies are taxed at either the main rate, the small profits rate or receive marginal relief, depending on their augmented profits.

The main rate of corporation tax is 23% for FY 2013 (24% for FY 2012, 26% for FY 2011) and applies to companies with augmented profits of £1,500,000 or more. A company with total taxable profits of, say, £2 million, will pay £460,000 corporation tax.

1.4 The small profits rate

The small profits rate of corporation tax of 20% for FY 2013, FY 2012, and FY 2011 applies to the taxable total profits of UK resident companies whose augmented profits are not more than £300,000.

Question — The small profits rate

B Ltd had the following results for the year ended 31 March 2014.

	£
Trading profits	42,000
Dividend received 1 May 2013 from 10% subsidiary	9,000

Compute the corporation tax payable.

Answer

	£
Trading profits/taxable total profits	42,000
Dividend plus tax credit £9,000 × 100/90	10,000
Augmented profits (below the £300,000 limit)	52,000
Corporation tax payable	
£42,000 × 20%	£8,400

1.5 Marginal relief

Marginal relief applies where the augmented profits of an accounting period of a UK resident company are over £300,000 but under £1,500,000. We first calculate the corporation tax at the main rate and then deduct:

(U – A) × N/A × standard fraction

where U = upper limit (currently £1,500,000)
A = augmented profits (see above Paragraph)
N = taxable total profits

The standard fraction is 3/400 for FY 2013 (1/100 for FY 2012 and 3/200 for FY 2011).

You will be given this formula in the rates and allowances section of the exam paper.

Question **Marginal relief**

Lenox Ltd has the following results for the year ended 31 March 2014.

	£
Taxable total profits	296,000
Dividend received 1 December 2013 from 25% subsidiary	12,600

Calculate the corporation tax liability.

Answer

	£
Taxable total profits	296,000
Dividend plus tax credit £12,600 × 100/90	14,000
Augmented profits	310,000

Augmented profits are above £300,000 but below £1,500,000, so marginal relief applies.

	£
Corporation tax on taxable total profits £296,000 × 23%	68,080
Less marginal relief	
£(1,500,000 – 310,000) × 296,000/310,000 × 3/400	(8,522)
	59,558

FAST FORWARD

The marginal rate of corporation tax between the upper and lower limits is 23.75%. The marginal tax rate is an effective rate; it is never actually used in working out corporation tax.

In exam questions you often need to be aware that there is a **marginal rate of 23.75%** which applies to any taxable total profits that lies in between the upper and lower limits.

This is calculated as follows:

	£			£
Upper limit	1,500,000	@	23%	345,000
Lower limit	(300,000)	@	20%	(60,000)
Difference	1,200,000			285,000

$$\frac{285,000}{1,200,000} = 23.75\%$$

Effectively the band of profits (here £1,200,000) falling between the upper and lower limits are taxed at a rate of 23.75%.

1.6 Example: effective marginal rate of tax

A Ltd has taxable total profits of £350,000 for the year ended 31 March 2014. Its corporation tax liability is

	£
£350,000 × 23%	80,500
Less marginal relief	
3/400 (1,500,000 – 350,000)	(8,625)
	71,875

This is the same as calculating tax at 20% × £300,000 + 23.75% × £50,000 = £60,000 + £11,875 = £71,875.

Consequently tax is charged at an effective rate of 23.75% on taxable total profits between the lower limit and the upper limit.

Note that although there is an effective corporation tax charge of 23.75%, this rate of tax is never used in actually calculating corporation tax. The rate is just an effective marginal rate that you must be aware of. It is particularly important when considering loss relief and group relief (see later in this Text).

The effective marginal rate of tax in FY 2012 was 25% and in FY 2011 was 27.5%.

1.7 Accounting period in more than one Financial Year

An accounting period **may fall within more than one Financial Year. If the rates and limits for corporation tax are the same in both Financial Years, tax can be computed for the accounting period as if it fell within one Financial Year.**

However, **if the rates and/or limits for corporation tax are different in the Financial Years, taxable total profits and augmented profits are time apportioned between the Financial Years**. This will be the case where a company has an accounting period partly in FY 2012 and partly in FY 2013, unless the company pays tax at the small profits rate.

1.8 Example: accounting period in more than one Financial Year

Wentworth Ltd makes up its accounts to 31 December each year. For the year to 31 December 2013, it has taxable total profits of £1,460,000. It receives a dividend of £54,000 on 1 December 2013.

The corporation tax payable by Wentworth Ltd is calculated as follows.

	£
Taxable total profits	1,460,000
Dividend plus tax credit £54,000 × 100/90	60,000
Augmented profits	1,520,000

	FY 2012 3 months to 31.3.13 £	FY 2013 9 months to 31.12.13 £
Taxable total profits (3:9)	365,000	1,095,000
Augmented profits (3:9)	380,000	1,140,000
Upper limit:		
£1,500,000 × 3/12	375,000	
£1,500,000 × 9/12		1,125,000
Main rate applies in both FYs		
FY 2012 £ 365,000 × 24%	87,600	
FY 2013 £1,095,000 × 23%		251,850
Total corporation tax payable		
£(87,600 + 251,850)		£339,450

Question — Accounting period in more than one financial year

In the year to 30 September 2013, Elliot Ltd has taxable total profits of £360,000. It receives a dividend of £8,100 on 15 July 2013. Calculate the corporation tax payable by Elliot Ltd.

Answer

	£
Taxable total profits	360,000
Add: FII £8,100 × 100/90	9,000
Augmented profits	369,000

	FY 2012 6 months to 31.3.13 £	FY 2013 6 months 30.9.13 £
Taxable total profits (6:6)	180,000	180,000
Augmented profits (6:6)	184,500	184,500
Lower limit:		
£300,000 × 6/12	150,000	150,000
Upper limit:		
£1,500,000 × 6/12	750,000	750,000
Marginal relief applies in both FYs		
FY 2012		
£180,000 × 24%	43,200	
Less: marginal relief $£(750,000 - 184,500) \times \frac{180,000}{184,500} \times 1/100$	(5,517)	
	37,683	
FY 2013		
£180,000 × 23%		41,400
Less: marginal relief $£(750,000 - 184,500) \times \frac{180,000}{184,500} \times 3/400$		(4,138)
		37,262
Total corporation tax payable		
£(37,683 + 37,262)		£74,945

1.9 Associated companies and short accounting periods

FAST FORWARD

The upper and lower limits which are used to determine tax rates are divided by the number of associated companies and may also need to be pro-rated on a time basis if an accounting period lasts for less than 12 months.

Key term

The expression **'associated companies'** in tax has no connection with financial accounting. For tax purposes a company is associated with another company if either controls the other or if both are under the control of the same person or persons (individuals, partnerships or companies). Whether such a company is UK resident or not is irrelevant (even though non-UK resident companies cannot benefit from the small profits rate or from marginal relief). Control is given by holding over 50% of the share capital or the voting power or being entitled to over 50% of the distributable income or of the net assets in a winding up.

If a company has one or more 'associated companies', then the profit limits for small profits rate purposes are divided by the number of associated companies + 1 (for the company itself).

Companies which have only been associated for part of an accounting period are deemed to have been associated for the whole period for the purpose of determining the profit limits.

An associated company is ignored for these purposes if it is dormant ie has not carried on any trade or business at any time in the accounting period (or the part of the period during which it was associated). A holding company counts as not carrying on any trade or business so long as:

- Its only assets are shares in subsidiaries
- It is not entitled to deduct any outgoings as charges or management expenses, and
- Its only profits are dividends from subsidiaries, which are distributed in full to its shareholders.

The profit limits are reduced proportionately if an accounting period lasts for less than 12 months.

Question — Associated companies and short accounting periods

For the nine months to 31 January 2014 a company with two other associated companies had taxable total profits of £78,000 and no dividends paid for or received. Compute the corporation tax payable.

Answer

(a) Reduction in the upper limit

Multiply by 1/(number of associated companies + 1) = $^1/_3$

Then multiply by number of months in AP/12 = $^9/_{12}$

£1,500,000 × $^1/_3$ × $^9/_{12}$ = £375,000

(b) Reduction in the lower limit

£300,000 × $^1/_3$ × $^9/_{12}$ = £75,000

(c) Augmented profits = £78,000. As augmented profits fall between the lower and upper limits, the main rate less marginal relief applies:

(d) Corporation tax

	£
£78,000 × 23%	17,940
Less marginal relief £(375,000 – 78,000) × 3/400	(2,228)
Corporation tax	15,712

2 Returns, records, compliance checks, assessments and claims

2.1 Notification to HMRC

FAST FORWARD

A company must notify HMRC within three months of starting to trade.

A company must notify HMRC of the beginning of its first accounting period (ie usually when it starts to trade) and the beginning of any subsequent period that does not immediately follow the end of a previous accounting period. The notice must be in the prescribed form and submitted within three months of the relevant date.

A company which is chargeable to tax for an accounting period and has not received a notice to file a tax return must give notice of chargeability within 12 months of the end of the accounting period. The common penalty regime for failing to notify applies (see earlier in this Text)**.**

2.2 Returns

FAST FORWARD

Corporation tax returns must usually be filed within twelve months of the end of an accounting period.

A company's tax return must be filed electronically and must include a self assessment of any tax payable. Limited companies are also required to file electronically a copy of their accounts. The filing of accounts must be done in inLine eXtensible Business Reporting Language (iXBRL).

iXBRL is a standard for reporting business information in an electronic form which uses tags which can be read by computers. HMRC supplies software which can be used by small companies with simple accounts. This software automatically produces accounts and tax computations in the correct format. Other companies can use:

(a) other software that automatically produces iXBRL accounts and computations; or
(b) a tagging service which will apply the appropriate tags to accounts and computations; or
(c) software that enables the appropriate tags to be added to accounts and computations.

The tags used are contained in dictionaries known as taxonomies, with different taxonomies for different purposes. The tagging of tax computations is based on the corporation tax computational taxonomy, which includes over 1,200 relevant tags.

An obligation to file a return arises only when the company receives a notice requiring a return. A return is required for each accounting period ending during or at the end of the period specified in the notice requiring a return. A company also has to file a return for certain other periods which are not accounting periods (eg for a period when the company is dormant).

A company that does not receive a notice requiring a return must, if it is chargeable to tax, **notify HMRC within twelve months of the end of the accounting period**. Failure to do so results in a maximum penalty equal to the tax unpaid twelve months after the end of the accounting period. Tax for this purpose includes corporation tax and notional tax on loans to participators of close companies (see later in this Text).

A notice to file a return may also require other information, accounts and reports. For a UK resident company the requirement to deliver accounts normally extends only to the accounts required under the Companies Act.

A return is due on or before the filing date. This is the later of:

(a) **12 months after the end of the period to which the return relates**
(b) **if the relevant period of account is not more than 18 months long, 12 months from the end of the period of account**
(c) **if the relevant period of account is more than 18 months long, 30 months from the start of the period of account**, and
(d) **three months from the date on which the notice requiring the return was made.**

The relevant period of account is that in which the accounting period to which the return relates ends.

Question

Filing date

A Ltd prepares accounts for the eighteen months to 30 June 2013. A notice requiring a return for the period ended 30 June 2013 was issued to A Ltd on 1 September 2013. State the periods for which A Ltd must file a tax return and the filing dates.

Answer

The company must file a return for the two accounting periods ending in the period specified in the notice requiring a return. The first accounting period is the twelve months to 31 December 2012 and the second is the six months to 30 June 2013. The filing date is twelve months after the end of the relevant period of account, 30 June 2014.

There is a £100 penalty for a failure to submit a return on time, rising to £200 if the delay exceeds three months. These penalties become £500 and £1,000 respectively when a return was late (or never submitted) for each of the preceding two accounting periods.

An additional tax geared penalty is applied if a return is more than six months late. The penalty is 10% of the tax unpaid six months after the return was due if the total delay is up to 12 months, and 20% of that tax if the return is over 12 months late.

The common penalty regime for making errors in tax returns discussed earlier in this Text in relation to individuals also applies to companies.

HMRC may amend a return to correct obvious errors, or anything else that an officer has reason to believe is incorrect in the light of information available, within nine months of the day the return was filed, or if the correction is to an amended return, within nine months of the filing of an amendment. The company may amend its return so as to reject the correction. If the time limit for amendments has expired, the company may reject the correction by giving notice within three months.

2.3 Records

Companies must keep records until the latest of:

(a) six years from the end of the accounting period
(b) the date any compliance checks are completed
(c) the date after which compliance checks may not be commenced.

All business records and accounts, including contracts and receipts, must be kept, or information showing that the company has prepared a complete and correct tax return.

If a return is demanded more than six years after the end of the accounting period, any records which the company still has must be kept until the later of the end of any compliance check and the expiry of the right to start a compliance check.

Failure to keep records can lead to a penalty of up to £3,000 for each accounting period affected. However, this penalty does not apply when the only records which have not been kept are ones which could only have been needed for the purposes of claims, elections or notices not included in the return.

2.4 Compliance checks

A compliance check enquiry into a return, claim or election can be started by an officer of HMRC within a limited period.

2.4.1 Starting a compliance check enquiry

HM Revenue and Customs may decide to conduct a compliance check enquiry on a return, claim or election that has been submitted by a company, in the same way as for individuals.

The officer of HM Revenue and Customs must give written notice of his intention to conduct a compliance check enquiry. The notice must be given by the later of:

(a) **The first anniversary of the due filing date** (most group companies) or **the actual filing date** (other companies), **if the return was delivered on or before the due filing date,** or

(b) **The quarter day following the first anniversary of the actual filing date, if the return is filed after the due filing date. The quarter days are 31 January, 30 April, 31 July and 31 October.**

If the company amends the return after the due filing date, the compliance check enquiry 'window' extends to the quarter day following the first anniversary of the date the amendment was filed. Where the compliance check enquiry was not started within the limit which would have applied had no amendment been filed, the enquiry is restricted to matters contained in the amendment.

2.4.2 Conduct of compliance check enquiry

The procedure for the conduct of compliance check enquiries relating to individuals, discussed earlier in this Text, also applies to companies.

2.5 Determinations

The rules about determinations relating to individuals, discussed earlier in this Text, also applies to companies.

2.6 Discovery assessments

The rules about discovery assessments relating to individuals, discussed earlier in this Text, also applies to companies.

2.7 Appeals

The procedure for HMRC internal reviews and appeals relating to individuals, discussed earlier in this Text, also applies to companies.

2.8 Personal accountability of senior accounting officer of large company

FAST FORWARD

The senior accounting officer of a large company has personal accountability for ensuring that it has appropriate financial systems in place to ensure that the company accurately reports taxable profits and gains.

The senior accounting officer of a qualifying company has personal accountability for ensuring that financial systems are maintained by the company to enable it to accurately report taxable profits and gains. A qualifying company is one which, in the previous financial year, had a relevant turnover of £200 million and/or a balance sheet total of more than £2 billion.

The senior accounting officer (probably the finance director of the company) must take reasonable steps to establish and monitor accounting systems within the company that are adequate for the purposes of accurate tax reporting. The senior accounting officer must also certify annually that the accounting systems are in operation or specify any inadequacies.

The company must notify HMRC of the identity of the senior accounting officer of the company. The company and/or the senior accounting officer personally may be liable to a financial penalty for a careless or deliberate failure to comply with these requirements. The penalty applicable to the senior accounting officer is likely to be £5,000.

3 Payment of corporation tax and interest

FAST FORWARD

Large companies pay their corporation tax in four quarterly instalments. Other companies pay their tax nine months after the end of an accounting period.

3.1 Due dates

Corporation tax is due for payment by companies which do not pay tax at the main rate **nine months and one day after the end of the accounting period**. So if an accounting period ends on 31 December 2013, the corporation tax for that period is due on 1 October 2014.

Large companies, however, must pay their corporation tax in instalments. **Broadly, a large company is any company that pays corporation tax at the main rate** (augmented profits exceed £1,500,000 in a 12 month period where there are no associated companies).

Instalments are due on the 14th day of the month, starting in the seventh month. Provided that the accounting period is twelve months long subsequent instalments are due in the tenth month during the accounting period and in the first and fourth months after the end of the accounting period.

If an accounting period is less than twelve months long subsequent instalments are due at three monthly intervals but with the final payment being due in the fourth month of the next accounting period.

3.2 Example: quarterly instalments

X Ltd is a large company with a 31 December accounting year end. Instalments of corporation tax will be due to be paid by X Ltd on:

- 14 July and 14 October in the accounting period
- 14 January and 14 April after the accounting period ends

So for the year ended 31 December 2013 instalment payments are due on 14 July 2013, 14 October 2013, 14 January 2014 and 14 April 2014.

Instalments are based on the estimated corporation tax liability for the current period (not the previous period). It will be extremely important for companies to forecast their tax liabilities accurately. Large companies whose directors are poor at estimating may find their company's incurring significant interest charges. The amount of each instalment is computed by:

(a) working out $3 \times CT/n$ where CT is the amount of the estimated corporation tax liability payable in instalments for the period and n is the number of months in the period

(b) allocating the smaller of that amount and the total estimated corporation tax liability to the first instalment

(c) repeating the process for later instalments until the amount allocated is equal to the corporation tax liability. This gives four equal instalments for 12 month accounting periods and also caters for periods which end earlier than expected.

The company is therefore required to estimate its corporation tax liability before the end of the accounting period, and must revise its estimate each quarter.

Question — **Short accounting period**

A large company has a CT liability of £880,000 for the eight month period to 30 September 2013. Accounts had previously always been prepared to 31 January. Show when the CT liability is due for payment.

Answer

£880,000 must be paid in instalments.

The amount of each instalment is $3 \times \frac{£880,000}{8} = £330,000$

The due dates are:

	£
14 August 2013	330,000
14 November 2013	330,000
14 January 2014	220,000 (balance)

3.3 Exceptions

A company is not required to pay instalments in the first year that it is 'large', unless its augmented profits exceed £10 million. The £10 million limit is reduced proportionately if there are associated companies. For this purpose only, a company will be regarded as an associated company where it was an associated company at the **start** of an accounting period. (This differs from the normal approach where being an associated company for any part of the AP affects the CT thresholds of both companies for the whole of the AP.)

Any company whose liability does not exceed £10,000 need not pay by instalments.

3.4 Interest on late or overpaid tax

Interest runs from the due date on over/underpaid instalments. The position is looked at cumulatively after the due date for each instalment. HMRC calculate the interest position after the company submits its corporation tax return.

Companies which do not pay by instalments are charged interest if they pay their corporation tax after the due date, and will receive interest if they overpay their tax or pay it early.

Interest paid/received on late payments or over payments of corporation tax is dealt with as investment income as interest paid/received on a non-trading loan relationship. For the purpose of the 2014 exam papers, the assumed rate of interest on underpaid tax is 3.0% and the assumed rate of interest on overpaid tax is 0.5%.

3.5 Group payment arrangements

Where more than one company in a group is liable to pay their tax by instalments, arrangements may be made for the instalments to be paid by one company (the nominated company), and allocated amongst the group. These provisions were introduced because groups often have uncertainties over the tax liabilities of individual group members until all relevant group reliefs and claims are decided upon following the end of the accounting period.

Chapter roundup

- Augmented profits are taxable total profits plus franked investment income (FII)
- Tax rates are set for financial years.
- Companies are taxed at either the main rate, the small profits rate or receive marginal relief, depending on their augmented profits
- The marginal rate of corporation tax between the upper and lower limits is 23.75%. The marginal tax rate is an effective rate; it is never actually used in working out corporation tax
- The upper and lower limits which are used to determine tax rates are divided by the number of associated companies and may also need to be pro-rated on a time basis if an accounting period lasts for less than 12 months
- A company must notify HMRC within three months of starting to trade.
- Corporation tax returns must usually be filed within twelve months of the end of an accounting period.
- A compliance check enquiry into a return, claim or election can be started by an officer of HMRC within a limited period.
- The senior accounting officer of a large company has personal accountability for ensuring that it has appropriate financial systems in place to ensure that the company accurately reports taxable profits and gains.
- Large companies pay their corporation tax in four quarterly instalments. Other companies pay their tax nine months after the end of an accounting period.

Quick quiz

1. Which companies are entitled to the small profits rate of corporation tax in FY 2013?
2. What is the marginal relief formula?
3. What is an associated company?
4. Youngs Ltd makes up a 12 month set of accounts to 31 December 2013. When must the company file its CT return based on these accounts?
5. When must HMRC give notice that they are going to start a compliance check enquiry if a return was filed on time by a company not in a group?
6. Which companies must pay quarterly instalments of their corporation tax liability?
7. State the due dates for the payment of quarterly instalments of corporation tax for a 12 month accounting period.
8. Freeman Ltd changes its accounting date and makes up accounts for the 8 months to 31 December 2013. The company is large and is due to pay tax by instalments. Outline when the tax is due.
9. In question 8 if the CT liability is £1,000,000 for the 8 month period what amount is due at each date?

Answers to quick quiz

1 Companies with augmented profits of up to £300,000.

2 (U – A) × N/A × standard fraction

where:

U = upper limit
A = augmented profits
N = taxable total profits

3 A company is associated with another company if either controls the other or if both are under the control of the same person or persons (Individual, partnership or companies).

4 By 31 December 2014.

5 Notice must be given by one year after the actual filing date.

6 'Large' companies ie: companies that pay corporation tax at the main rate.

7 14th day of:

(a) 7th month in AP
(b) 10th month in AP
(c) 1st month after AP ends
(d) 4th month after AP ends

8 Due dates are:

14 November 2013
14 February 2014
14 April 2014

9 £375,000, £375,000 and finally £250,000.

Now try the questions below from the Exam Question Bank

Number	Level	Marks	Time
Q22	Introductory	16	29 mins
Q23	Introductory	5	9 mins
Q24	Introductory	10	18 mins

Administration, winding up, purchase of own shares

Topic list	Syllabus reference
1 Winding up	A2(b)(iii),(iv)
2 The purchase by a company of its own shares	A2(b)(v)

Introduction

In the last two chapters we have studied the computation of taxable total profits and the corporation tax payable.

In this chapter we look at some of the consequences of placing a company into administration or liquidation.

We also consider the tax consequences which accrue when a company purchases its own shares.

In the next chapters we will consider further aspects of corporation tax, starting with losses.

Study guide

		Intellectual level
2	**Corporation tax liabilities in situations involving further overseas and group aspects and in relation to special types of company, and the application of additional exemptions and reliefs**	
(b)	The scope of corporation tax:	3
(iii)	Identify and evaluate the significance of accounting periods on administration or winding up	
(iv)	Conclude on the tax treatment of returns to shareholders after winding up has commenced	
(v)	Advise on the tax implications of a purchase by a company of its own shares	

Exam guide

If the exam includes a question which includes the purchase by a company of its own shares you must be careful to consider whether the capital treatment will apply, and if so, whether it is beneficial. You must be prepared to advise whether any variation to a suggested purchase would be beneficial.

Knowledge brought forward from earlier studies

The topics in this chapter are new.

1 Winding up

FAST FORWARD

A new accounting period (AP) begins when a winding up commences. Thereafter APs are for 12 months until the winding up is complete. Distributions made during a winding up are capital. There are special rules in respect of accounting periods when companies go into administration.

1.1 Liquidation

A company **in liquidation is chargeable to corporation tax on the profits arising during the winding up.**

An accounting period ends and a new one begins when a winding up commences. Thereafter, accounting periods end *only* on each anniversary of the commencement of winding up, until the final period which ends when the winding up is completed. A cessation of trade after a winding up has commenced will not bring an accounting period to an end.

1.2 Example: accounting periods on a winding up

Totterdown Ltd, a company with a 31 December year end, ceased trading on 10 June 2012. The members passed a resolution to wind up the company on 12 September 2012 and the winding up was completed on 15 January 2014. From 1 January 2012 the accounting periods will be:

1.1.12 – 10.6.12	To the date trade ceased.
11.6.12 – 11.9.12	The commencement of a winding up brings an AP to an end.
12.9.12 – 11.9.13	Anniversary of commencement of winding up.
12.9.13 – 15.1.14	Final AP ends when winding up complete.

1.3 Administration

The Enterprise Act 2002 provides for companies to go from liquidation to administration and for assets to be distributed without a formal liquidation. In such cases, the following rules apply relating to when an accounting period will be deemed to end.

A new accounting period begins when a company goes into administration. An accounting period ends when a company ceases to be in administration and a new accounting period begins when a company moves out of liquidation into administration.

In contrast to the position in liquidation, where the corporation tax accounting periods are then annual from the date of appointment of the liquidator, there is no requirement to change the accounting reference date of the company. Therefore, future accounting periods in administration follow the original accounting dates.

1.4 Example: accounting periods in administration

Company A has a normal accounting date of 31 December annually. An administrator is appointed on 17 August 2013. As a result, for corporation tax purposes the company's accounting periods will be 1 January to 16 August 2013 before administration and 17 August to 31 December 2013 after the appointment of the administrator. Accounting periods will then be 31 December annually while the company remains in administration.

When an administration ceases, a new accounting period must start for tax purposes, whether the company comes out of administration and recommences to trade normally or goes from administration into winding up.

1.5 Example: administration to liquidation

Company A remains in administration for 14 months and a liquidator is appointed on 10 October 2014.

The accounting period in administration will therefore be 1 January 2014 to 9 October 2014. The next accounting period will be the first liquidation accounting period, 10 October 2014 to 9 October 2015. Accounting periods will then be annually to 9 October until the company ceases to be in liquidation (either by striking off or returning to administration).

When a company comes out of liquidation into administration, a new accounting period must start. Again, this permits proper computation of the tax due as an expense of liquidation or administration.

1.6 Example: liquidation to administration

Following the above example, company A remains in liquidation for only three months, and a court order appointing a new administrator is granted on 14 January 2015.

The accounting periods are therefore 10 October 2014 to 13 January 2015 in liquidation, then 14 January to (presumably) 31 December 2015 in administration.

If the company had been in liquidation for some time, so that liquidation accounts had been prepared to 9 October for a number of years, the post-liquidation accounting periods would end on 9 October annually unless the administrator changed the accounting reference date.

1.7 Significance of accounting periods

The date on which an accounting period ends will affect the accounting periods into which income and capital profits and losses fall. This may prevent relief being obtained in the most beneficial way. For example trading losses of the current year or carried back can be set against other income or gains, whilst trading losses carried forward can only be set against trading profits. Capital gains may therefore be taxable if made after trade ceases even though there may be unrelieved trading losses.

1.8 Distributions

One of the competencies you require to fulfil performance objective 20 of the PER is the ability to assist with tax planning. You can apply the knowledge you obtain from this section of the text to help to demonstrate this competence.

1.8.1 Distributions during a liquidation

Distributions made after the liquidation has started are capital and treated as a part disposal of shares in the hands of the shareholder. This is the position even if the distributions include accumulated net profits of the company out of which dividends could be paid.

Where a company has distributable profits, it may be preferable to pay these out as a dividend before the liquidation starts. Any such distribution will be chargeable to income tax on a shareholder who is an individual.

Assets distributed in specie (ie in their existing form rather than sold and distributed as cash) by the liquidator are deemed to be disposed of at market value. Where the assets are chargeable assets, any chargeable gain arising is charged to corporation tax in accordance with the normal rules. Consequently there is double taxation on assets distributed to shareholders in the liquidation since the asset distribution will also be treated as a capital distribution in the hands of the shareholders. However, disincorporation relief may be available to avoid this double taxation (see earlier in this Text).

1.8.2 Distributions outside a formal winding up

Ordinarily, assets distributed outside a formal winding up represent an income distribution. This might occur prior to an application to strike the company off the Companies Register which is a cheaper way of ending a company's existence than a formal liquidation.

However, under limited circumstances, distributions made in anticipation of such an application to strike off a company, are treated as capital receipts of the shareholders for the purpose of calculating any chargeable gains arising to them on the disposal of their shares. This may or may not be advantageous to the shareholders.

The conditions that have to be met for this treatment to apply are:

- at the time of the distribution, the company intends to secure (or has secured) **payment of any sums due to it**, and intends to satisfy (or has satisfied) any **debts or liabilities of the company**, and
- the amount of the distribution (or total amount of distributions if there is more than one) **does not exceed £25,000**.

If the company has not been dissolved **two years** after making the distribution, or has failed to secure payment of all sums due to it, or to satisfy all its debts and liabilities, then the capital treatment does not apply.

An alternative method for distributing assets outside a formal winding up is to use the provisions of Companies Act 2006 to reduce the capital of the company prior to striking off. A distribution made as a result of such a capital reduction will automatically be a capital distribution and so the above conditions for the capital treatment do not have to be met.

1.9 Other points

The appointment of a receiver, a manager or administrator has no tax consequences, apart from determining accounting periods as discussed above.

When a company is put into liquidation, it loses beneficial ownership of its assets. If the company to be liquidated is a parent company, it will therefore lose its group relationship with its former subsidiaries. No group relief (see later in this Text) will be available to any of the companies in the former group. By contrast, a group continues to exist for chargeable gains purposes (see later in this Text), notwithstanding the commencement of liquidation.

2 The purchase by a company of its own shares

A purchase of a company's own shares may be taxable on the vendor shareholder as the receipt of an income distribution or (if certain conditions are satisfied) as capital proceeds.

One of the competencies you require to fulfil performance objective 20 of the PER is the ability to assist with tax planning. You can apply the knowledge you obtain from this section of the text to help to demonstrate this competence.

2.1 Tax treatment for vendor shareholder

2.1.1 Income treatment

If a company buys its own shares for more than the amount originally subscribed, general tax rules state that there is an income distribution of the excess of the amount received over the subscription. This is called the **income treatment.**

Recipients of such distributions are treated in the same way as recipients of ordinary dividends. This means that basic rate taxpayers have no further tax to pay and higher rate and additional rate taxpayers must pay further tax.

The remainder of the proceeds (ie those not treated as income) will be a capital receipt. Thus there will also be a disposal of the shares by the vendor shareholder for capital gains tax. If the vendor shareholder originally subscribed for the shares, there will be no gain or loss, since the shareholder is merely getting back the subscription cost as the disposal proceeds. If, however, the vendor shareholder acquired the shares other than by subscription (for example by purchase), a gain or, more usually, a loss may arise. The proceeds for the disposal is equal to the original subscription cost, since this is the capital amount received by the shareholder on the purchase of the shares by the company.

2.1.2 Example

Jess bought 5,000 shares in Pink Ltd in July 2011 for £3 per share. The original subscription cost for these shares was £1 per share. Pink Ltd has agreed to repurchase these shares from Jess for £10 each in December 2013.

If the income treatment applies, Jess will receive a distribution from Pink Ltd as follows:

	£
Cash received £10 × 5,000	50,000
Less: subscription price (capital) £1 × 5,000	(5,000)
Net distribution subject to income tax	45,000

Jess will also have a capital gains tax allowable loss on his disposal of Pink Ltd shares as follows:

	£
Proceeds: return of subscription £1 × 5,000	5,000
Less: cost of shares for Jess £3 × 5,000	(15,000)
Allowable loss	(10,000)

2.1.3 Capital treatment

When an unquoted trading company (or the unquoted parent of a trading group) **buys back its own shares in order to benefit its trade, and certain other conditions are satisfied (see section 2.2), the capital treatment *automatically* applies. This means that the distribution is treated as a capital receipt for the disposal of the shares by the shareholder rather than as an income distribution.**

Under the current CGT rules, the capital treatment may result in less tax being payable, particularly if the disposal qualifies for entrepreneurs' relief, than if the income treatment applies.

Question — **Income treatment or capital treament**

Walter subscribed for 1,000 shares in BB Ltd, an unquoted trading company, at £1 per share. BB Ltd has agreed to repurchase Walter's shares for £15 each in March 2014.

Walter has taxable income of £40,000 in 2013/14. He has made no other gains in 2013/14.

Show the tax payable by Walter if:

(a) The income treatment applies.

(b) The capital treatment applies and *either*:
  (i) a claim is made for entrepreneurs' relief; *or*
  (ii) a claim is not made for entrepreneurs' relief.

Answer

(a) If the income treatment applies, Walter will have a net distribution as follows:

	£
Cash received £15 × 1,000	15,000
Less: subscription price (return of capital) £1 × 1,000	(1,000)
Distribution	14,000
Income tax	
£14,000 × 25% (note)	£3,500

Note: remember from earlier in the Text, only the extra tax needs to be calculated, not Walter's full income tax liability.

For capital gains tax, there will be no gain or loss:

	£
Proceeds: return of subscription £1 × 1,000	1,000
Less: cost £1 × 1,000	(1,000)
	0

(b) If the capital treatment applies, the gain will be as follows:

	£
Cash received £15 × 1,000	15,000
Less: cost £1 × 1,000	(1,000)
Gain	14,000
Less: annual exempt amount	(10,900)
Taxable gain	3,100
Capital gains tax	
(i) If claim made for entrepreneurs' relief £3,100 × 10%	310
(ii) If claim not made for entrepreneurs' relief £3,100 × 28%	868

2.2 Conditions for capital treatment to apply

The company purchasing its own shares must be an unquoted trading company (or the unquoted parent of a trading group). The trade must not consist of dealing in shares, securities, land or futures.

The **'benefit to the trade' test** will be satisfied where:

- a **dissident and disruptive shareholder** is bought out
- the **proprietor wishes to retire** to make way for new management
- an **outside investor** who provided equity wishes to **withdraw his investment**
- a **shareholder dies** and his personal representatives do not wish to retain his shares.

The **conditions to be satisfied by the vendor shareholder** are as follows.

(a) **The shareholder must be resident in the UK** when the purchase is made

(b) **The shares must have been owned by the vendor or his spouse/civil partner throughout the five years preceding the purchase**. This is reduced to three years if the vendor is the personal representative or the heir of a deceased member and previous ownership by the deceased will count towards the qualifying period.

Exam focus point

> The period of ownership will often be an essential point in an exam question. For example, you may be given a scenario where the purchase can be timed either before the five year deadline, or after it, and asked to show the taxation consequences in each case.

(c) **The vendor and his associates must as a result of the purchase have their interest in the company's share capital reduced to 75% or less of their interest before the disposal**. Associates include spouses/civil partners, minor children, controlled companies, trustees and beneficiaries. Where a company is a member of a group the whole group is effectively considered as one for this test.

(d) **The vendor must not be connected with the company or any company in the same 51% group after the transaction.** A person is connected with a company if he can control more than 30% of the ordinary share capital, the issued share capital and loan capital or the voting rights in the company.

Question — **The reduction of a shareholding**

Henry holds 300 of H Ltd's 1,000 issued ordinary shares.

Will the capital treatment apply if the company buys 80 shares back from him?

Answer

	Total shares	*Held by Henry*
Initially	1,000	300
Less repurchased (and cancelled)	(80)	(80)
	920	220

Henry originally had a 30% interest. This is reduced to 220/920 = 23.9%, a reduction to 23.9/30 = 79.7% of his original interest. For a capital gain to arise, he must sell at least 97 shares back to H Ltd, thus reducing his percentage holding below 30% × 75% = 22.5%.

2.3 Other points

The capital gains treatment is not given if a main objective is tax avoidance.

As seen in the above example, any shares repurchased by the company must usually be cancelled. They cannot be re-issued.

The capital treatment is also available where a company purchases shares to enable the vendor to pay any inheritance tax arising on a death (the 'benefit to the trade' test and the other conditions in section 2.2 do not then apply).

Companies considering the purchase of their own shares may seek HMRC clearance to ensure that the capital treatment applies.

Chapter roundup

- A new accounting period (AP) begins when a winding up commences. Thereafter APs are for 12 months until the winding up is complete. Distributions made during a winding up are capital. There are special rules in respect of accounting periods when companies go into administration.
- A purchase of a company's own shares may be taxable on the vendor shareholder as the receipt of an income distribution or (if certain conditions are satisfied) as capital proceeds.

Quick quiz

1 Inca Ltd makes up accounts to 31 March. The company goes into liquidation on 1 November 2013 and cease to trade on 31 December 2013. The company is finally wound up on 31 July 2014. What are the accounting periods from 1 April 2012?

2 Does the appointment of an administrator affect a company's accounting periods?

3 What is the impact (if any) on a company accounting period when a company moves out of liquidation into administration?

4 Are distributions made during a liquidation treated as capital or income distributions?

5 A company is about to make an application to be struck off the Companies Register. It has secured payments of sums due to it and satisfied its debts and liabilities. The company has surplus cash of £20,000 to distribute to its shareholders. How will the distribution be treated for tax purposes in relation to the shareholders?

6 When a company buys its own shares, what potential tax consequences may occur for the shareholder whose shares are being bought?

Answers to quick quiz

1. 1 April 2012 – 31 March 2013
   1 April 2013 – 31 October 2013
   1 November 2013 – 31 July 2014
2. Yes. A new accounting period begins when a company goes into administration. An accounting period ends when a company ceases to be in administration.
3. A new accounting period begins when a company moves status from liquidation into administration.
4. Distributions are capital distributions and are treated as a part disposal of the shares in the hands of the shareholder.
5. The distribution will be treated as a capital receipt for the shareholders as the conditions for payments and debts have been satisfied and the amount of the distribution does not exceed £25,000.
6. If a company buys its own shares from a shareholder and pays more than the amount originally subscribed, the general tax rules treat the excess amount paid as a distribution (taxed in the same way as an ordinary dividend) made by the company to the shareholder. Income tax applies to the shareholder recipient of the distribution. There will also be a disposal of the shares for capital gains tax purposes: the proceeds will be the original subscription for the shares.

   If certain conditions are met, however, the full amount paid by the company for a purchase of own shares will be treated as capital proceeds for the shareholder and capital gains tax will be due on the gain. A claim may be made for entrepreneurs' relief on the disposal.

Now try the question below from the Exam Question Bank

Number	Level	Marks	Time
Q25	Introductory	10	18 mins

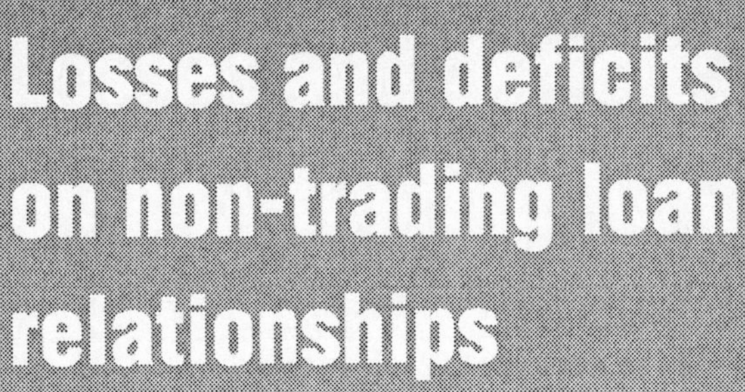

Losses and deficits on non-trading loan relationships

24

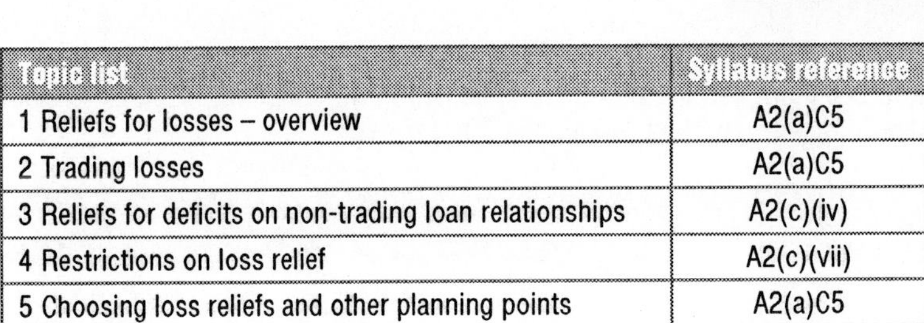

Topic list	Syllabus reference
1 Reliefs for losses – overview	A2(a)C5
2 Trading losses	A2(a)C5
3 Reliefs for deficits on non-trading loan relationships	A2(c)(iv)
4 Restrictions on loss relief	A2(c)(vii)
5 Choosing loss reliefs and other planning points	A2(a)C5

Introduction

We have studied the computation of taxable total profits and the corporation tax payable.

We now see how a company may obtain relief for trading losses and also for deficits on non trading loan relationships. We look at the factors to take into account when deciding which loss relief to choose.

In the next chapter we will look at close companies and investment companies, and then we will turn to groups and consortia.

Study guide

		Intellectual level
2	**Corporation tax liabilities in situations involving further overseas and group aspects and in relation to special types of company, and the application of additional exemptions and reliefs**	
(a)	The contents of the Paper F6 study guide for corporation tax, under headings:	
•	C5 The use of exemptions and reliefs in deferring and minimising corporation tax liabilities.	2
(c)	Taxable total profits:	3
(iv)	Determine the tax treatment of non trading deficits on loan relationships	
(vii)	Advise on the restriction on the use of losses on a change in ownership of a company	

Exam guide

You are likely to come across company losses at some point in the exam, although the question may include group relief. Always look to see if any requirements are specified in the question, such as to claim relief as early as possible, and then consider how to optimise the relief.

Knowledge brought forward from earlier studies

This chapter revises the treatment of trading losses which should be familiar from your F6 studies. The examiner has identified essential underpinning knowledge from the F6 syllabus which is particularly important that you revise as part of your P6 studies. In this chapter, the relevant topics are:

		Intellectual level
C2	**Taxable total profits**	
(g)	Understand how trading losses can be carried forward.	2
(h)	Understand how trading losses can be claimed against income of the current or previous accounting periods.	2
(i)	Recognise the factors that will influence the choice of loss relief claim.	2
(j)	Explain how relief for a property business loss is given.	1

There are no changes for Financial Year 2013 in the material studied for F6 in Financial Year 2012.

The relief for deficits on non-trading loan relationships and the restriction on the use of losses are new to you.

1 Reliefs for losses – overview

1.1 Trading losses

FAST FORWARD

Trading losses may be relieved by deduction from current total profits, total profits of earlier periods or future trading income.

In summary, the following reliefs are available for trading losses incurred by a company.

(a) Claim to deduct from current profits
(b) Claim to carry back and deduct from earlier profits
(c) Make no claim and automatically carry forward to be deducted from future trading profits

These reliefs may be used in combination. The options open to the company are:

(a) Do nothing, so that the loss is automatically carried forward and deducted from future trading profits

(b) Claim to deduct from current profits, and carry any remaining unrelieved loss forward

(c) Claim to deduct from current profits, then claim to carry any unused loss back and deduct from earlier profits, and then carry any remaining unrelieved loss forward.

The reliefs are explained in further detail below.

1.2 Non-trading deficits

Non-trading deficits on loan relationships can be relieved in similar ways to trading losses, but against different profits (see below).

1.3 Capital losses

Capital losses can only be deducted from capital gains in the same or future accounting periods, never from income (except losses suffered by an investment company on shares in a qualifying trading company). Capital losses must be deducted from the first available gains.

1.4 Foreign income losses

In the case of a trade which is controlled outside the UK, **any loss made in an accounting period can only be deducted from trading income from the same trade in later accounting periods.** The same rule applies to losses on overseas property businesses.

1.5 Miscellaneous income losses

Where in an accounting period a company makes a loss in a transaction where income would be taxable as miscellaneous income (such as one involving intangible fixed assets used for non trade purposes), **the company can deduct the loss from any income on other transactions taxable as miscellaneous income in the same or later accounting periods.** The loss must be deducted from the earliest such income available.

1.6 Property income losses

FAST FORWARD

Property business losses are deducted first from total profits of the current period and then carried forward to be deducted from future total profits.

Property business losses are first deducted from the company's total profits of the current accounting period. Any excess is then:

(a) **carried forward to the next accounting period** and treated as a loss made by the company in that period, or

(b) available for surrender as **group relief** (see later in this Text).

2 Trading losses

2.1 Carry forward trade loss relief

FAST FORWARD

Trading losses carried forward can only be deducted from future trading profits of the same trade.

If a company makes no claim for relief for its trading losses they will be automatically carried forward and deducted from income of the same trade in future accounting periods. Relief is by deduction from the first available trading profits.

Question — **Carrying forward losses**

A Ltd has the following results for the three years to 31 March 2014.

		Year ended	
	31.3.12	*31.3.13*	*31.3.14*
	£	£	£
Trading profit/(loss)	(8,550)	3,000	6,000
Property income	0	1,000	1,000
Qualifying charitable donation	300	1,400	1,700

Calculate the taxable total profits for all three years showing any losses available to carry forward at 1 April 2014.

Answer

		Year ended	
	31.3.12	*31.3.13*	*31.3.14*
	£	£	£
Trading income	0	3,000	6,000
Less carry forward trade loss relief		(3,000)	(5,550)
	0	0	450
Property income	0	1,000	1,000
Total profits			
Less qualifying charitable donation	0	(1,000)	(1,450)
Taxable total profits	0	0	0
Unrelieved qualifying charitable donation	300	400	250

Note that the trading loss carried forward is deducted from the trading profit in future years. It cannot be deducted from the property income.

The qualifying charitable donations that become unrelieved are wasted as they cannot be carried forward.

Loss memorandum

	£
Loss for y/e 31.3.12	8,550
Less used y/e 31.3.13	(3,000)
Loss carried forward at 1.4.13	5,550
Less used 31.3.14	(5,550)
Loss carried forward at 1.4.14	0

2.2 Trade loss relief by deduction from total profits

FAST FORWARD

Loss relief against total profits may be given by deduction from current period profits and by deduction from profits of the previous 12 months. A claim for current period loss relief can be made without a claim for carry back. However, if a loss is to be carried back a claim for current period relief must have been made first.

2.2.1 Current year claim

A company may claim to deduct a trading loss (arising in a UK trade) **incurred in an accounting period from total profits of the same accounting period before deducting qualifying charitable donations.**

Any loss remaining unrelieved is automatically carried forward to be deducted from future profits of the same trade unless a carry back claim is made.

2.2.2 Carry back claim

Such a loss may then be carried back and deducted from total profits before deducting qualifying charitable donations of an accounting period falling wholly or partly within the 12 months of the start of the period in which the loss was incurred.

Any possible loss relief claim for the period of the loss must be made before any excess loss can be carried back to a previous period.

Any carry back is to more recent periods before earlier periods. Relief for earlier losses is given before relief for later losses.

Any loss remaining unrelieved after any loss relief claims against total profits is carried forward to be deducted from future profits of the same trade.

2.2.3 The claim

A claim for relief against current or prior period profits must be made within two years of the end of the accounting period in which the loss arose.

Any claim must be for the *whole* loss (to the extent that profits are available to relieve it). The loss can however be reduced by not claiming full capital allowances, so that higher capital allowances are given (on higher tax written down values) in future years.

Question — **Loss relief by deduction from total profits**

Helix Ltd has the following results.

	Y/e 30.11.12	*y/e 30.11.13*
		£
Trading profit/(loss)	22,500	(19,500)
Bank interest	500	500
Chargeable gains	0	4,000
Qualifying charitable donation	250	250

Show the taxable total profits for both years affected assuming that loss relief by deduction from total profits is claimed.

Answer

The loss of the year to 30 November 2013 is relieved by deduction from current year total profits and from total profits of the previous 12 months.

	y/e 30.11.12	*y/e 30.11.13*
	£	£
Trading profit	22,500	0
Investment income	500	500
Chargeable gains	0	4,000
Total profits	23,000	4,500
Less current period loss relief	0	(4,500)
	23,000	0
Less carry back loss relief	(15,000)	(0)
	8,000	0
Less qualifying charitable donation	(250)	0
Taxable total profits	7,750	0
Unrelieved qualifying charitable donation		250

Loss memorandum

		£
Loss incurred in y/e 30.11.13		19,500
Less used:	y/e 30.11.13	(4,500)
	y/e 30.11.12	(15,000)
Loss available to carry forward		0

2.2.4 Periods of account which are not 12 months in length

If a period falls partly outside the 12 months, loss relief is limited to the proportion of the period's profits (before qualifying charitable donations) equal to the proportion of the period which falls within the 12 months.

Question

Short accounting period and loss relief

Tallis Ltd had the following results for the three accounting periods to 31 December 2013.

	Y/e 30.9.12	*3 months to 31.12.12*	*Y/e 31.12.13*
	£	£	£
Trading profit (loss)	20,000	12,000	(39,000)
Building society interest	1,000	400	1,800
Qualifying charitable donations	600	500	0

Show the taxable total profits for all years. Assume loss relief is claimed by deduction from total profits where possible.

Answer

	Y/e 30.9.12	3 months to 31.12.12	Y/e 31.12.13
	£	£	£
Trading profit	20,000	12,000	0
Interest income	1,000	400	1,800
Total profits	21,000	12,400	1,800
Less current period loss relief			(1,800)
	21,000	12,400	0
Less carry back loss relief	(15,750)	(12,400)	
	5,250	0	0
Less qualifying charitable donations	(600)		0
Taxable total profits	4,650	0	0
Unrelieved qualifying charitable donations	0	500	0

Loss memorandum	£
Loss incurred in y/e 31.12.13	39,000
Less used y/e 31.12.13	(1,800)
Less used p/e 31.12.12	(12,400)
Less used y/e 30.9.12 £21,000 × 9/12 (max)	(15,750)
C/f	9,050

Notes

1 The loss can be carried back to be deducted from profits of the previous 12 months. This means profits in the y/e 30.9.12 must be time apportioned by multiplying by 9/12.

2 Losses remaining after the loss relief claims by deduction from total profits are carried forward to be deducted from future trading profits.

2.2.5 Terminal loss relief

FAST FORWARD

Trading losses in the last 12 months of trading can be carried back and deducted from profits of the previous 36 months.

For trading losses incurred in the twelve months up to the cessation of trade the carry back period is extended from twelve months to three years, later years first.

Question

Terminal losses

Brazil Ltd had the following results for the accounting periods up to the cessation of trade on 30 September 2013.

	Y/e 30.9.10	Y/e 30.9.11	Y/e 30.9.12	Y/e 30.9.13
	£	£	£	£
Trading profits	60,000	40,000	15,000	(180,000)
Gains	0	10,000	0	6,000
Property income	12,000	12,000	12,000	12,000

You are required to show how the losses are relieved assuming the maximum use is made of loss relief by deduction from total profits.

Answer

	Y/e 30.9.10	Y/e 30.9.11	Y/e 30.9.12	Y/e 30.9.13
	£	£	£	£
Trading profits	60,000	40,000	15,000	0
Property income	12,000	12,000	12,000	12,000
Gains	0	10,000	0	6,000
Total profits	72,000	62,000	27,000	18,000
Less current period loss relief				(18,000)
Less carry back loss relief	(72,000)	(62,000)	(27,000)	
Taxable total profits	0	0	0	0

Loss memorandum

	£
Loss in y/e 30.9.13	180,000
Less used y/e 30.9.13	(18,000)
Loss of y/e 30.9.13 available for 36 months carry back	162,000
Less used y/e 30.9.12	(27,000)
	135,000
Less used y/e 30.9.11	(62,000)
	73,000
Less used y/e 30.9.10	(72,000)
Loss remaining unrelieved	1,000

3 Reliefs for deficits on non-trading loan relationships

FAST FORWARD

Deficits on non-trading loan relationships can be used in a similar way to trading losses.

A deficit on a non-trading loan relationship may be deducted, in whole or part, from any profit of the same accounting period. Relief is given after relief for any trading loss brought forward but before relief is given for a trading loss of the same or future period.

Question

Relief for deficit on non-trading loan relationship

Witherspoon Ltd has the following results for the two years ended 31 December 2013:

	2012	2013
	£	£
Trading profit/(loss)	70,000	(42,000)
Trading losses brought forward	(20,000)	–
Bank interest receivable	2,000	
Interest payable on a loan for non-trading purposes	(11,000)	

Show how relief may be given for the deficit on the non-trading loan relationship in the year ended 31 December 2012.

Answer

Y/e 31.12.12	£
Trading income	70,000
Losses brought forward	(20,000)
	50,000
Less: non-trading deficit £(11,000 – 2,000)	(9,000)
	41,000
Losses carried back	(41,000)
Total taxable profits	Nil

Loss memorandum		£
Incurred in y/e 31.12.13		42,000
Less used:	y/e 31.12.12	(41,000)
Available to carry forward		1,000

A deficit is eligible for group relief (see later in this Text).

A deficit may be deducted from non-trading income arising from loan relationships in the previous twelve months. In this case, relief is given after any trading loss of the same or future period. A claim must be made within two years of the deficit period.

Any deficits unrelieved after claiming the above reliefs are automatically carried forward and deducted from non trading profits of the company for succeeding accounting periods.

A company can choose how much deficit to relieve in the current period, how much to carry back and how much to carry forward; unlike trading loss relief, these are not all or nothing claims, and the company can choose to carry back a deficit even if it does not claim current period relief.

4 Restrictions on loss relief

FAST FORWARD

If there is a change in ownership of a company, the carry forward of losses is restricted if there is also a major change in the nature of the trade within three years of the change in ownership.

4.1 The continuity of trades

Carry forward loss relief is only available against future profits arising from the same trade as that in which the loss arose.

The continuity of trade for this purpose was considered in a case involving a company trading as brewers: *Gordon & Blair Ltd v CIR 1962.* It ceased brewing but continued to bottle and sell beer. The company claimed that it carried on the same trade throughout so that its losses from brewing could be set off against profits from the bottling trade. The company lost their case and were prevented from obtaining any further relief for losses in the brewing trade.

4.2 The disallowance of loss relief following a change in ownership

Trading losses may be restricted where there is a change in ownership of a company and there is either:

(1) A major change in the nature or conduct of the trade within three years before or three years after the change in ownership, or

(2) After the change in ownership there is a considerable revival of the company's trading activities which at the time of the change had become small or negligible.

If the restriction applies:

- **Any losses incurred before the change in ownership cannot be carried forward against post-acquisition profits.**
- **Any losses incurred after the change in ownership cannot be carried back against profits arising before the date of the change of ownership.**

For example, if a company changes its ownership on 1 July 2013 and there is a major change in the nature or conduct of its trade between 1 July 2010 and 30 June 2016 the carry back and carry forward of losses is restricted.

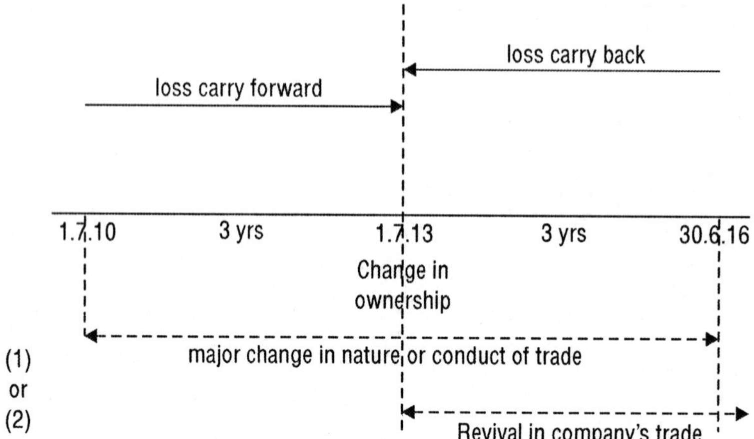

Examples of a major change in the nature or conduct of a trade include changes in:

- The type of property dealt in (for example a company operating a dealership in saloon cars switching to a dealership in tractors)
- The services or facilities provided (for example a company operating a public house changing to operating a discotheque)
- Customers
- Outlets or markets

However, changes to keep up to date with technology or to rationalise existing ranges of products are unlikely to be regarded as major. HMRC consider both qualitative and quantitative issues in deciding if a change is major.

If the change in ownership occurs in (rather than at the end of) an accounting period, the period is divided into two, one up to and one after the change, for the purposes of this rule, with profits and losses being time-apportioned.

A change in ownership is disregarded for this purpose if both immediately before and immediately after the change the company is an effective 75% subsidiary of the same company.

4.3 Uncommercial trades

A loss made in a trade which is not conducted on a commercial basis and with a reasonable expectation of gain cannot be set off against the company's profits in the same or previous accounting periods. Such losses are only available to carry forward against future profits of the same trade.

4.4 Farming and market gardening

A company carrying on the trade of farming or market gardening is treated in the same way as one that trades on an uncommercial basis in any accounting period if, in the five successive years immediately before that accounting period, the trade made a loss (before capital allowances).

5 Choosing loss reliefs and other planning points

When selecting a loss relief, firstly consider the rate at which relief is obtained and, secondly, the timing of the relief.

One of the competencies you require to fulfil performance objective 20 of the PER is the ability to assist with tax planning. You can apply the knowledge you obtain from this section of the text to help to demonstrate this competence.

5.1 Choosing loss reliefs

Several alternative loss reliefs may be available. In making a choice consider:

- **The rate at which relief will be obtained:**
  - 23% at the main rate (FY 2013) (24% in FY 2012, 26% in FY 2011)
  - 20% at the small profits rate (FY 2013) (20% in FY 2012 and FY 2011)
  - 23.75% if marginal relief applies (FY 2013) (25% in FY 2012, 27.5% in FY 2011)

  We previously outlined how the 23.75% marginal rate is calculated. Remember this is just a marginal rate of tax; it is never actually used in computing a company's corporation tax.
- **How quickly relief will be obtained**: loss relief against total profits is quicker than carry forward loss relief.
- **The extent to which relief for qualifying charitable donations might be lost.**

Exam focus point

When choosing between loss relief claims **always** consider the rate of tax 'saved' by the loss first.

If in the current period the loss 'saves' 20% tax but if carried forward saves 23% tax then a carry forward is the better choice (even though the timing of loss relief is later).

If the tax saved now is 20% and in the future is the same (20%) **then** consider timing (in this example a current claim is better timing wise).

So, first – rate of tax saved, second – timing.

Question — The choice between loss reliefs

M Ltd has had the following results.

	Year ended 31 March			
	2011	*2012*	*2013*	*2014*
	£	£	£	£
Trading profit/(loss)	2,000	(1,000,000)	200,000	138,000
Chargeable gains	35,000	750,000	0	0
Qualifying charitable donations paid	30,000	20,000	20,000	20,000

Recommend appropriate loss relief claims, and compute the corporation tax for all years based on your recommendations. Assume that future years' profits will be similar to those of the year ended 31 March 2014 and the rates of corporation tax in FY 2013 apply in later years. The small profits rate in FY 2010 was 21%.

Answer

A loss relief against total profits claim for the year ended 31 March 2012 will save tax partly in the marginal relief band and partly at the small profits rate. It will waste the qualifying charitable donation of £20,000.

Taxable total profits in the previous year is £7,000 (£35,000 + £2,000 – £30,000) and falls in the small profits band and so taxable at 21%. Carry back would waste qualifying charitable donations of £30,000 and would use £37,000 of loss to save tax on £7,000.

If no current period loss relief claim is made, £200,000 of the loss will save tax at the small profits rate of 20% in the year ended 31 March 2013, with £20,000 of qualifying charitable donations being wasted. The remaining £800,000 of the loss, would be carried forward to the year ended 31 March 2014 and later years to save tax at the small profits rate of 20%.

To conclude, a loss relief claim by deduction from total income should be made for the year of the loss but not in the previous year. £20,000 of qualifying charitable donations would be wasted in the current year, but much of the loss would save tax at the marginal rate and relief would be obtained quickly.

The final computations are as follows.

	Year ended 31 March			
	2011	*2012*	*2013*	*2014*
	£	£	£	£
Trading income	2,000	0	200,000	138,000
Less carry forward loss relief	0	0	(200,000)	(50,000)
	2,000	0	0	88,000
Chargeable gains	35,000	750,000	0	0
Total profits	37,000	750,000	0	88,000
Less current period loss relief	0	(750,000)	0	0
	37,000	0	0	88,000
Less qualifying charitable donations	(30,000)	0	0	(20,000)
Taxable total profits	7,000	0	0	68,000

	Year ended 31 March			
	2011	*2012*	*2013*	*2014*
	£	£	£	£
CT at 21/20%	1,470	0	0	13,600
Unrelieved qualifying charitable donations	0	20,000	20,000	0

5.2 Other tax planning points

A company must normally claim capital allowances on its tax return. A company with losses could consider claiming less than the maximum amount of capital allowances available. This will result in a higher tax written down value to carry forward and therefore higher capital allowances in future years.

Reducing capital allowances in the current period reduces the loss available for relief against total profits. As this relief, if claimed, must be claimed for all of a loss available, a reduced capital allowance claim could be advantageous where all of a loss would be relieved at a lower tax rate in the current (or previous) period than the effective rate of relief for capital allowances will be in future periods.

Chapter roundup

- Trading losses may be relieved by deduction from current total profits, total profits of earlier periods or future trading income.
- Property business losses are deducted first from total profits of the current period and then carried forward to be deducted from future total profits.
- Trading losses carried forward can only be deducted from future profits of the same trade.
- Loss relief by deduction from total profits may be given by deduction from current period profits and from profits of the previous 12 months. A claim for current period loss relief can be made without a claim for carry back. However, if a loss is to be carried back a claim for current period relief must have been made first.
- Trading losses in the last 12 months of trading can be carried back and deducted from profits of the previous 36 months.
- Deficits on non-trading loan relationships can be used in a similar way to trading losses.
- If there is a change in ownership of a company, the carry forward of losses is restricted if there is also a major change in the nature of the trade within three years of the change in ownership.
- When selecting a loss relief, firstly consider the rate at which relief is obtained and, secondly, the timing of the relief.

Quick quiz

1 From what profits may trading losses carried forward be deducted?

2 To what extent may losses in a continuing trade be carried back?

3 What relief is available in the current accounting period for a non-trading deficit?

4 Why might a company make a reduced capital allowances claim?

Answers to quick quiz

1 Profits from the same trade.

2 A loss may be carried back and deducted from total profits (before deducting qualifying charitable donations) of the prior 12 months. The loss carried back is the trading loss left unrelieved after a claim against total profits (before deducting qualifying charitable donations) of the loss making accounting period has been made.

3 A deficit on a non-trading loan relationship may be deducted from profits of the same accounting period. Relief is given after relief for any trading loss brought forward but before relief is given for a current or future trading loss.

The deficit is also eligible for group relief.

4 Reducing capital allowances in the current accounting period reduces the loss available for relief against total profits. This relief demands that all of the available loss is utilised. Reducing capital allowances reduces the size of the available loss.

Now try the question below from the Exam Question Bank

Number	Level	Marks	Time
Q26	Introductory	15	27 mins

Close companies and investment companies

Introduction

Having looked at the general rules for companies we now look at the specific rules for investment companies and close companies.

Companies with investment business are any companies that make investments, for example in shares, and collect the income from them. Expenses of managing those investments are generally deductible for corporation tax purposes.

A close company may have any type of business, but it needs special tax treatment because it is under the control of a few people who might try to take profits out of it in non-taxable forms.

In the next chapter we will go on to look at groups and consortia.

Study guide

		Intellectual level
2	**Corporation tax liabilities in situations involving further overseas and group aspects and in relation to special types of company, and the application of additional exemptions and reliefs**	
(b)	The scope of corporation tax:	3
(i)	Identify and calculate corporation tax for companies with investment business.	
(ii)	Close companies: • Apply the definition of a close company to given situations • Conclude on the tax implications of a company being a close company or a close investment holding company	

Exam guide

Questions involving planning for families may include a consideration of close companies. The rules for treating benefits as distributions are fairly straightforward, but you must be careful not to overlook the disallowance of the expenses in the corporation tax computation. The tax charge for loans to participators is a significant cost of making any such loan, even though it is recovered when the loan is repaid or written off.

Knowledge brought forward from earlier studies

The topics in this chapter are new.

1 Companies with investment business

FAST FORWARD

A company that generates income from investments can usually deduct the expenses of managing their investments for corporation tax purposes.

1.1 Companies with investment business

A company with investment business is any company whose **business consists wholly or partly in making investments.**

The principal overhead of the investment business will be the costs of running the business which are called management expenses. These are generally deductible in computing taxable profits. An unrelieved excess of such expenses in one accounting period may be carried forward as management expenses of the following accounting period and, if still unrelieved, to future accounting periods.

Excessive directors' remuneration is not deductible for tax purposes. Capital expenditure is excluded from deduction as a management expense and HMRC may also refuse a deduction for any amounts which are not in fact expenses of management. Capital allowances on plant and machinery used for the investment business are allowed as a management expense if they cannot be relieved in any other way.

Non-trading loan relationships expenses and losses are dealt with under the loan relationship rules, not as a management expense. A company with investment business may or may not also fall within the definition of a close investment-holding company (see below).

1.2 Corporation tax

Corporation tax is applied to companies with investment business in the normal way (there is an exception for *close* investment holding companies outlined below). Thus companies with investment business can benefit from the small profits rate or marginal relief.

Question — **Investment companies**

TC Ltd, a non-close company with wholly investment business, has the following results for the year ended 31 March 2014.

	£
Rental income	150,000
Building society interest	8,000
Chargeable gains	100,000
Management expenses	
Property management	40,000
General	50,000
Capital allowances	
On property	800
General	1,000
Qualifying charitable donations	47,000

Unrelieved management expenses carried forward at 1 April 2013 amounted to £60,500.

Compute the corporation tax payable.

Answer

	£	£
Rents		150,000
Less: capital allowances	800	
property management expenses	40,000	
		(40,800)
Property income		109,200
Interest income		8,000
Chargeable gains		100,000
		217,200
Less: general management expenses	50,000	
general capital allowances	1,000	
management expenses brought forward	60,500	
		(111,500)
Total profits		105,700
Less qualifying charitable donations		(47,000)
Taxable total profits		58,700
Corporation tax payable £58,700 × 20%		£11,740

2 Close companies

Owner-managed and family-owned companies could easily be used for tax avoidance. **Special rules apply to these 'close' companies** to counteract this. Broadly, a close company is one that is under the control of either five or fewer shareholders or any number of its shareholding directors. Shareholders and shareholding directors are known as 'participators'.

Direct relatives, business partners and certain trusts set up by the participator (or their direct relatives or business partners) are known as 'associates'. The rights and powers of associates are attributed to participators when determining control.

Thus if the five largest shareholders of X Ltd own 9% of the shares each, and they have no associates, the company will not be close. If, however, the wife and son of Mr A, one of the five largest shareholders, each hold 3% the company will be close as Mr A is deemed to hold (9 + 3 + 3) = 15%, so that the holdings of the five largest shareholders is (4 × 9 + 15) = 51%.

A company which is controlled by a close company will also itself be a close company.

2.1 Loans to participators

FAST FORWARD

The rules on loans and benefits from close companies are intended to deter shareholders from using the obvious ways of extracting value from their company without paying tax.

When a close company makes a loan to one of its participators or an associate it must make a tax payment to HMRC equal to 25% of the loan. If the loan is repaid, HMRC will repay this tax charge.

For companies which are not large, the tax charge is due for payment nine months after the end of the accounting period. The tax charge is subject to the quarterly payments on account regime if the company is large. If the loan is repaid before the tax charge is due to be paid then the requirement to pay the penalty tax charge is cancelled. Interest runs from the due date until the earlier of payment of the tax and repayment of the loan. The loan must be notified on the company's tax return.

A loan for these purposes includes:

- A debt owed to the company
- A debt incurred by a participator or his associate and assigned to the company
- An advance of money
- A director's overdrawn current account

Certain loans are excluded from these provisions. These are:

- Money owed for goods or services supplied in the ordinary course of the company's trade unless the credit period exceeds:
  - Six months, or, if less
  - The normal credit period given to the company's other customers.
- Loans to directors and employees providing they do not exceed £15,000 in total per borrower and:
  - The borrower works full-time for the close company, and
  - He does not have a material interest (entitlement to over 5% of the assets available for distribution on a winding up) in the close company.

If at the time a loan was made the borrower did not have a material interest but he later acquires one, the company is regarded as making a loan to him at that date.

When all or part of the loan is repaid by the participator to the company, or the company writes off all or part of the loan, then the company can reclaim all or a corresponding part of the tax charge paid over to HMRC. If the loan is repaid or written of after the due date for paying the tax charge, the tax is not repayable until nine months after the end of the accounting period of repayment or write off of the loan.

HMRC pay interest up to the time they repay the tax. If the loan is repaid/written off before nine months from the end of the accounting period in which the loan is made, interest runs from the end of those nine months. Otherwise, it runs from the date when the tax is repayable.

Exam focus point

If a loan made during an accounting period is to be repaid during the next accounting period, repayment before the due date for payment of the corporation tax will avoid the need for the penalty tax charge to be paid. Later repayment will defer the refund date for a year.

Although tax is charged on the company when a loan is made to a participator, the loan is not at that stage treated as the participator's income. If the loan is later written off:

(a) **The amount written off is treated as the participator's income** and is included within his total income grossed up accordingly. It is taxed **as if it were a dividend** received by him (the net dividend equalling the loan written off), so a basic rate taxpayer has no more tax to pay, but a higher or additional rate taxpayer must pay more tax

(b) If the participator is a director or employee, there is no taxable benefit because the above tax charge applies instead

Question — **Close company loan**

C Ltd, a close company which prepares accounts to 31 July each year, lends £50,000 to a shareholder in July 2012. C Ltd is required to account for a tax charge of £12,500 to HMRC. In July 2013 the shareholder repays £20,000. In January 2014 C Ltd writes off the remaining £30,000. Compute the amount of penalty tax recovered by C Ltd following the repayment in July 2013 and the write off in January 2014.

Answer

(a) The penalty tax recovered after the repayment is $\frac{20,000}{50,000} \times £12,500 = £5,000$.

(b) The penalty tax recovered after the write off is £7,500.

2.2 Benefits treated as distributions

Benefits given by a close company to participators and their associates and which are not taxable earnings, for example where the participator does not work for the company, **are treated as distributions.** The amount of the deemed distribution is the amount that would otherwise be taxed as earnings. The actual cost is a disallowable expense for corporation tax purposes.

Question — **Benefits**

A close company provides a new car for a participator who is not a director or employee in May 2013. The taxable benefit in 2013/14 under the income tax legislation would be valued at £3,500. No fuel is provided. What are the tax consequences?

Answer

The participator is taxed as if he had received a net dividend of £3,500 in 2013/14. The company cannot deduct capital allowances on the car or any running costs in computing its taxable profits.

2.3 Close investment-holding companies

FAST FORWARD

Close investment-holding companies are singled out for special treatment so as to deter people with substantial investments from putting their investments into a company and using the company status to reduce or defer tax liabilities.

Key term

A **close investment-holding company** (CIC) is a close company which is not a trading company and is not a member of a trading group.

A company is a trading company for an accounting period if it exists wholly or mainly for the purpose of trading. A company will not necessarily have to trade in an accounting period in order to satisfy this test but the trade must, when it is carried on, be carried on a commercial basis.

A member of a trading group is a company which co-ordinates the administration of trading companies which it controls.

Companies which deal in land, shares or securities are treated as trading companies for this purpose. Similarly, a company which invests in property let or to be let on a commercial basis will not be treated as a CIC.

A CIC always pays corporation tax at the main rate, whatever its level of profits. However, a CIC associated with another company still counts as an associated company for the purposes of reducing the limits for the small profits rate and marginal relief.

Chapter roundup

- A company that generates income from investments can usually deduct the expenses of managing their investments for corporation tax purposes.
- The rules on loans and benefits from close companies are intended to deter shareholders from using the obvious ways of extracting value from their company without paying tax.
- Close investment-holding companies are singled out for special treatment so as to deter people with substantial investments from putting their investments into a company and using the company status to defer tax liabilities.

Quick quiz

1 How may an investment company obtain relief for management expenses?

2 What is a close company?

3 What are the immediate consequences of a loan by a close company to a participator?

4 What items are treated as distributions by close companies?

5 What rate(s) of corporation tax may apply to close investment-holding companies?

Answers to quick quiz

1 Management expenses are deductible when computing taxable profits. Any unrelieved management expenses may be carried forward to be relieved in a similar fashion in the following accounting period.

2 A close company is one that is under the control of either five or fewer shareholders or any number of shareholding directors.

3 When a close company makes a loan to one of its participators it must make a payment to HMRC equal to 25% of the loan.

4 Benefits given to participators or their associates which are not taxed under the benefits legislation.

5 CICs always pay the main rate of corporation tax irrespective of the level of their profits.

Now try the questions below from the Exam Question Bank

Number	Level	Marks	Time
Q27	Introductory	15	27 mins
Q38	Examination	25	45 mins

Q38 has been analysed to show you how to approach paper P6 exams.

Groups and consortia

26

Topic list	Syllabus reference
1 Types of group	A2(a)C4
2 Annual investment allowance	A2(e)(i)
3 Group relief	A2(e)(iv),(v),(viii)
4 Capital gains group	A2(e)(ii),(vi),(vii)
5 Succession to trade	A2(e)(iii)

Introduction

So far we have studied the corporation tax rules for single companies. In this chapter we consider the extent to which tax law recognises group relationships between companies.

Companies in a group are still separate entities with their own tax liabilities but tax law recognises the close relationship between group companies. They can, if they meet certain conditions, share their losses and pass assets between each other without chargeable gains.

Consortium companies are companies which are controlled by several companies. They can also share their losses, but the rules are restricted to recognise the ownership shares of the controlling companies.

In the next chapter we will complete our study of corporation tax by looking at overseas aspects.

Study guide

		Intellectual level
2	**Corporation tax liabilities in situations involving further overseas and group aspects and in relation to special types of company, and the application of additional exemptions and reliefs**	
(a)	The contents of the Paper F6 study guide, for corporation tax, under heading:	2
•	C4 The effect of a group structure for corporation tax purposes	
(e)	The effect of a group structure for corporation tax purposes:	3
(i)	Advise on the allocation of the annual investment allowance between group or related companies	
(ii)	Advise on the tax consequences of a transfer of intangible assets	
(iii)	Advise on the tax consequences of a transfer of a trade and assets where there is common control	
(iv)	Understand the meaning of consortium owned company and consortium member	2
(v)	Advise on the operation of consortium relief	
(vi)	Determine pre-entry losses and understand their tax treatment	
(vii)	Determine the degrouping charge where a company leaves a group within six years of receiving an asset by way of a no gain/no loss transfer	
(viii)	Determine the effects of the anti-avoidance provisions, where arrangements exist for a company to leave a group	

Exam guide

Groups and consortia are likely to be examined at most sittings. You must understand the difference between the definitions between a 75% group for group relief and a capital gains group, and understand the definition of a consortium. The question is likely to require a consideration of the various reliefs specifically available in group situations, with a view to minimising the group's tax liability.

Knowledge brought forward from earlier studies

This chapter revises the rules for group relief and for the transfer of capital assets between group companies and extends these to cover intangible fixed assets. It introduces the rules on allocation of the annual investment allowance between companies, consortium relief, and examines the anti-avoidance rules specifically applicable to groups.

There are no major changes in Financial Year 2013 from Financial Year 2012 in the material you have studied at F6.

1 Types of group

1.1 Groups

A group exists for taxation purposes where one company is a subsidiary of another. The percentage shareholding involved determines the taxation consequences of the fact that there is a group.

The five types of relationship for tax purposes are:

- **Associated companies**
- **Parent and subsidiary undertakings**
- **75% subsidiaries**
- **Consortia**
- **Groups for chargeable gains purposes (capital gains groups)**

1.2 Associated companies

Two companies are associated with each other for taxation purposes if one is under the control of the other, or both are under the control of a third party. Control for these purposes means entitlement to more than 50% of any one of:

- The share capital
- The income
- The votes
- The net assets on a winding up

The number of associated companies determines the limits for the small profits rate of corporation tax and marginal relief.

2 Annual investment allowance

FAST FORWARD

A group of companies is only entitled to a single annual investment allowance (AIA) which can be allocated between the companies as they think fit. A similar rule applies to companies under common control.

One of the competencies you require to fulfil performance objective 20 of the PER is the ability to assist with tax planning. You can apply the knowledge you obtain from this section of the text to help to demonstrate this competence.

2.1 Allocation of AIA between group companies

A group of companies is entitled to a single annual investment allowance between the group companies. The companies may allocate the allowance between them as they think fit.

A group for these purposes is defined in relation to a "parent undertaking". A company is a parent undertaking of another company ("the subsidiary undertaking") if:

- **it holds a majority of the voting rights in the undertaking; or**
- **it is a member of the undertaking and has the right to appoint or remove a majority of its board of directors**, or
- **it has the right to exercise a dominant influence over the undertaking** by virtue of a provision in the articles or under a control contract; or
- **it is a member of the undertaking and controls alone,** pursuant to an agreement with other shareholders or members, **a majority of the voting rights in the undertaking.**

The parent undertaking company must satisfy one of these conditions at the end of the subsidiary company's chargeable period of account ending in the Financial Year being considered.

The following factors may be relevant when considering how to allocate the annual investment allowance:

- **nature of expenditure**, for example main pool or special rate pool (more tax efficient to set against special rate pool because of lower subsequent WDA).
- **if the company is making a profit, the rate of corporation tax payable by the company** (best use to the extent that company is paying corporation tax at the marginal rate of 23.75%, then against companies paying at the main rate of 23% and then against companies paying at the small profits rate of 20%).
- **if the company is making a loss, how that loss can be relieved** (the AIA will create or increase a loss).

2.2 Allocation of AIA between companies under common control

Companies under common control are entitled to a single annual investment allowance between them and the companies may allocate the allowance between them as they think fit.

Companies are under common control if:

- **they are controlled by the same person, and**
- **they are related to one another.**

"Control" means that a person has power to secure that the affairs of a company are conducted in accordance with the wishes of that person. This could be by the holding of shares or voting rights or as the result of any powers in the company's constitution or that of another body.

Companies are related to one another if either they share premises or carry on similar activities.

Similar considerations apply to the consideration of how to allocate the annual investment allowance between companies under common control as to companies within a group.

3 Group relief

One of the competencies you require to fulfil performance objective 20 of the PER is the ability to assist with tax planning. You can apply the knowledge you obtain from this section of the text to help to demonstrate this competence.

3.1 Definitions

FAST FORWARD

Group relief is available where the existence of a group or consortium is established through companies resident anywhere in the world.

The group relief provisions enable companies within a 75% group to transfer trading losses to other profit making companies within the group, in order to reduce the group's overall corporation tax liability. **Group relief is given by the company receiving the loss deducting it from total profits.**

Key term

For one company to be a **75% subsidiary** of another, the holding company must have:

- At least 75% of the ordinary share capital of the subsidiary
- A right to at least 75% of the distributable income of the subsidiary, and
- A right to at least 75% of the net assets of the subsidiary were it to be wound up.

Two companies are members of a group for group relief purposes where one is a 75% subsidiary of the other, or both are 75% subsidiaries of a third company. Ordinary share capital is any share capital other than most preference shares.

Two companies are in a group only if there is a 75% effective interest. Thus an 80% subsidiary (T) of an 80% subsidiary (S) is not in a group with the holding company (H), because the effective interest is only

80% × 80% = 64%. However, S and T are in a group and can claim group relief from each other. S **cannot** claim group relief from T and pass it on to H; it can only claim group relief for its own use.

A group relief group may include non-UK resident companies. However, losses may generally only be surrendered between companies within the charge to corporation tax (UK resident companies and overseas resident companies with a UK permanent establishment). We look in detail at overseas aspects of groups in the next chapter.

3.2 Example

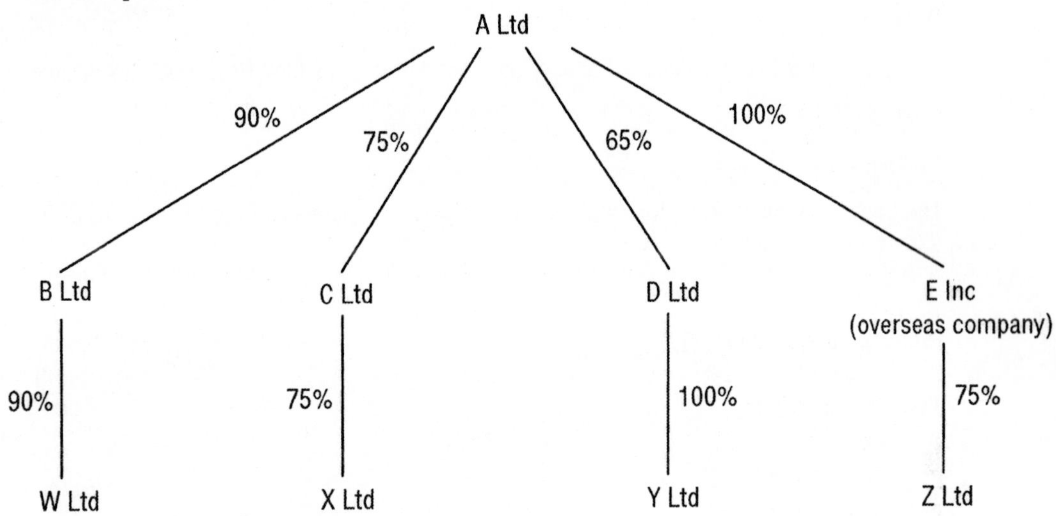

The companies in the group for group relief purposes are:

A Ltd
B Ltd
W Ltd (81% effective holding by A)
C Ltd
E Inc
Z Ltd (75% effective holding by A)

In addition C Ltd and X Ltd and also D Ltd and Y Ltd form their own separate mini-groups.

3.3 The relief

FAST FORWARD

Within a 75% group trading losses can be surrendered between UK companies.

A **claimant company** is assumed to use its own current year losses or losses brought forward in working out the profits against which it may claim group relief, even if it does not in fact claim loss relief against total income for current losses. Furthermore, **group relief is against profits after all other reliefs for the current period or brought forward from earlier periods**, including non-trading deficits on loan relationships and qualifying charitable donations. Group relief is given before relief for any amounts brought back from later periods.

A surrendering company may group relieve a loss before setting it against its own profits for the period of the loss, and may specify any amount to be surrendered. This is **important for tax planning as it enables the surrendering company to leave profits in its own computation to be charged to corporation tax at the small profits rate, while surrendering its losses to other companies to cover profits which would otherwise fall into the marginal relief band or be taxed at the main rate**. Note that profits in the marginal relief band are taxed at the marginal rate of 23.75%.

Question

Group relief of losses

In a group of four companies, the results for the year ended 31 March 2014 are as follows.

	Profit/(loss)
	£
A Ltd	52,000
B Ltd	212,500
C Ltd	1,000,000
D Ltd	(400,000)

How should the loss be allocated to save as much tax as possible? How much tax is saved?

Answer

The upper and lower limits for small profits marginal relief are £1,500,000/4 = £375,000 and £300,000/4 = £75,000 respectively.

	A Ltd	*B Ltd*	*C Ltd*
	£	£	£
Profits before group relief	52,000	212,500	1,000,000
Less group relief (note)	0	(137,500)	(262,500)
Taxable total profits	52,000	75,000	737,500
Tax saved			
£137,500 × 23.75%		32,656	
£262,500 × 23%			60,375
Total £(32,656 + 60,375) = £93,031			

Note. We wish to save the most tax possible for the group.

Since A Ltd is in the small profits band any loss given to it will save tax at the small profits rate of 20%.

B Ltd is in the marginal relief band. Therefore, any loss given to B saves the effective marginal rate of 23.75% until the profits fall to £75,000 (the lower limit). After this only 20% is saved.

C Ltd is in the main rate band of 23% until profits fall to £375,000 (the upper limit).

So to conclude it is best to give B Ltd £137,500 of loss and save 23.75% tax on the profits in the marginal relief band. The balance of the loss is then given to C Ltd to save 23% tax.

Any amount of trading losses, non-trading loan relationships deficits and excess capital allowances may be surrendered: they need not first be used by the loss-making company.

Excess qualifying charitable donations, property business losses, management expenses and non-trading losses on intangible fixed assets can be surrendered as group relief only to the extent that they exceed the surrendering company's other profits of the accounting period, ignoring any losses of the current period or any other period. Other profits include any amounts apportioned from controlled foreign companies.

Where a surrendering company has more than one of these types of loss available for surrender, the order of surrender is:

- Qualifying charitable donations
- Property business losses
- Management expenses
- Non-trading losses on intangible fixed assets.

The legislation does not specify the order of surrender of trade losses, excess capital allowances or non-trading loan relationship deficits. The surrendering company is free to choose which of these it surrenders in what order.

Capital losses cannot be group relieved. However, see later in this chapter for details of how a group may net off its gains and losses.

Only current period losses are available for group relief. Furthermore, they must be set against profits of a corresponding accounting period. If the accounting periods of a surrendering company and a claimant company are not the same this means that both the profits and losses must be apportioned so that only the results of the period of overlap may be set off. Apportionment is on a time basis.

However, in the period when a company joins or leaves a group, an alternative method may be used if the result given by time-apportionment would be unjust or unreasonable.

Question — Corresponding accounting periods

	£
S Ltd incurs a trading loss for the year to 30 September 2013	(150,000)
H Ltd makes taxable profits:	
for the year to 31 December 2012	200,000
for the year to 31 December 2013	100,000

What group relief can H Ltd claim from S Ltd?

Answer

H Ltd can claim group relief as follows.

	£
For the year ended 31 December 2012 profits of the corresponding accounting period (1.10.12 – 31.12.12) are £200,000 × 3/12	50,000
Losses of the corresponding accounting period are £150,000 × 3/12	37,500
A claim for £37,500 of group relief may be made against H Ltd's profits	
For the year ended 31 December 2013 profits of the corresponding accounting period (1.1.13 – 30.9.13) are £100,000 × 9/12	75,000
Losses of the corresponding accounting period are £150,000 × 9/12	112,500
A claim for £75,000 of group relief may be made against H Ltd's profits	

If a claimant company claims relief for losses surrendered by more than one company, the total relief that may be claimed for a period of overlap is limited to the proportion of the claimant's profits attributable to that period. Similarly, if a company surrenders losses to more than one claimant, the total losses that may be surrendered in a period of overlap is limited to the proportion of the surrendering company's losses attributable to that period.

A claim for group relief is normally made on the claimant company's tax return. It is ineffective unless a notice of consent is also given by the surrendering company. Where the surrendering company is also claiming loss relief against its own profits the group relief surrender must be made first.

Any payment by the claimant company for group relief, up to the amount of the loss surrendered, is ignored for all corporation tax purposes.

3.4 Arrangements to leave a group

Group relief is not available for any period during which there are arrangements in force for either the surrendering company or the claimant company to leave the group. If necessary, profits and losses are apportioned on a time basis.

The term 'arrangements' is not defined, but HMRC normally accept that negotiations to sell a company are not arrangements until an offer is accepted, even if it is then subject to contract or is conditional. If shareholder approval is required for the sale, arrangements do not exist until approval has been given.

3.5 Consortium relief

Within a consortium there is some scope for loss relief.

The definition of a consortium is given below.

Key term

A company is owned by a consortium (and is known as a **consortium-owned company**) if:

- 75% or more of its ordinary share capital is owned by companies (the members of the consortium), none of which has a holding of less than 5%, and
- Each member of the consortium is entitled to at least 5% of any profits available for distribution to equity holders of the company and at least 5% of any assets so available on a winding up.

Illustration of a consortium

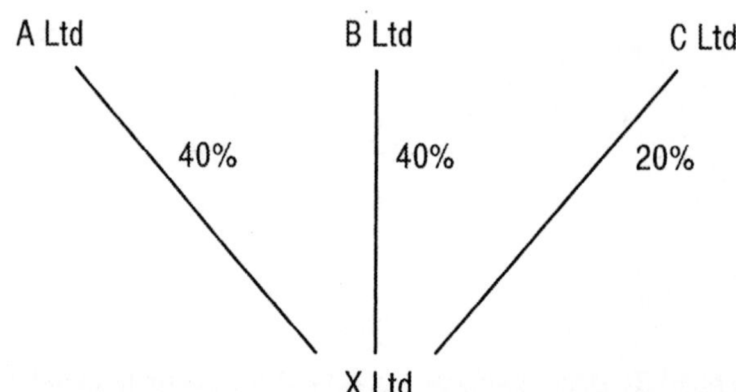

X Ltd is the consortium-owned company A Ltd, B Ltd and C Ltd are the consortium members.

Consortium relief is a loss relief which is available:

(a) Where the surrendering company is a trading company owned by a consortium and is not a 75% subsidiary of any one company and the claimant company belongs to the consortium

(b) Where the surrendering company is a trading company which is a 90% subsidiary of a holding company which is owned by a consortium and is not a 75% subsidiary of any one company and the claimant company is a member of the consortium

(c) Where the surrendering company is a holding company owned by a consortium and is not a 75% subsidiary of any one company and the claimant company is a member of the consortium.

A **trading company** is one whose business consists wholly or mainly in carrying on a trade. A holding company is one whose business consists wholly or mainly in holding shares in companies which are trading companies.

A consortium-owned company can surrender losses in proportion to the stakes of the members of the consortium. Thus if a member holds 20% of the shares in the company, up to 20% of the company's losses can be surrendered to that member. **Consortium relief is given by the company receiving the loss deducting it from total profits.**

Consortium relief can also flow downwards. **A consortium member may surrender its losses to set against its share of the consortium-owned company's profits.** So, a member with a 25% stake in the consortium-owned company can surrender losses to cover up to 25% of the company's profits.

Whereas normally a surrendering company can surrender group relief without having to consider any possible current period loss relief claim, **a loss made by a consortium-owned company must be reduced by any potential loss relief claims against current period profits** (not profits of previous periods) **before it may be surrendered as consortium relief.**

Although a consortium can be established with non-UK resident companies, losses cannot, in general, be surrendered to/from a non-UK resident.

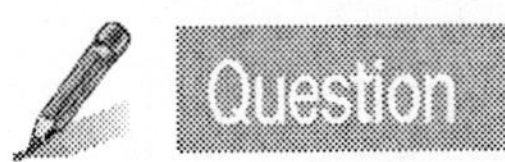

C Ltd is owned 60% by A Ltd, 30% by B Ltd and 10% by an overseas company X Inc. Results for the year ended 31 March 2014 are as follows.

	A Ltd	*B Ltd*	*C Ltd*
	£	£	£
Trading profit/(loss)	200,000	75,000	(50,000)
Property income	0	0	12,000

No dividends are paid or received by C Ltd. Each company has no other associates.

Compute the corporation tax liabilities of all three companies, assuming that all possible consortium relief claims are made but that C Ltd does not claim current period loss relief.

Answer

A Ltd may claim £(50,000 – 12,000) × 60% = £22,800.
B Ltd may claim £(50,000 – 12,000) × 30% = £11,400.
A Ltd has one associated company (C Ltd).

A Ltd's corporation tax liability is as follows.

	£
Total profits	200,000
Less consortium relief	(22,800)
Taxable total profits	177,200

Corporation tax	£
£177,200 × 23%	40,756
Less marginal relief £(750,000 – 177,200) × 3/400	(4,296)
	36,460

B Ltd's corporation tax liability is £(75,000 – 11,400) = £63,600 × 20% = £12,720.

C Ltd's corporation tax liability is:

	£
£12,000 × 20%	2,400

Note. The limits for marginal relief are divided by 2 since there are two associated companies (A Ltd and C Ltd).

C Ltd has a loss to carry forward of £(50,000 – 22,800 – 11,400) = £15,800.

3.6 Tax planning for group relief

This section outlines some tax planning points to bear in mind when dealing with a group.

Group relief should first be given in this order:

1st To companies in the marginal relief band paying 23.75% tax (but only sufficient loss to bring augmented profits down to the lower limit)

2nd To companies paying the main rate of tax at 23%

3rd To companies paying small profits rate at 20%

Similarly, a company should make a current period loss relief claim to use a loss itself rather than surrender the loss to other group companies if the current period claim would lead to a tax saving at a higher rate.

Companies with profits may benefit by reducing their claims for capital allowances in a particular year. This may leave sufficient profits to take advantage of group relief which may only be available for the current year. The amount on which writing-down allowances can be claimed in later years is increased accordingly.

4 Capital gains group

4.1 Definition

Companies are in a capital gains group if:

(a) At each level, there is a 75% holding, and
(b) The top company has an effective interest of over 50% in the group companies.

If A holds 75% of B, B holds 75% of C and C holds 75% of D, then A, B and C are in such a group, but D is outside the group because A's interest in D is only 75% × 75% × 75% = 42.1875%. Furthermore, D is not in a group with C, because the group must include the top company (A). This is illustrated in the diagram below.

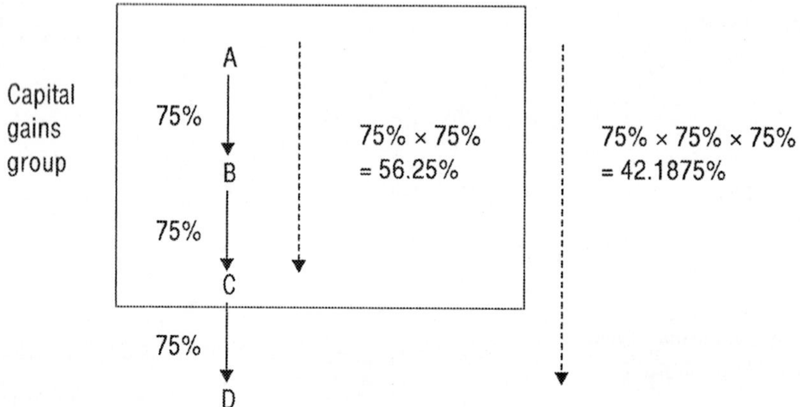

4.2 Example

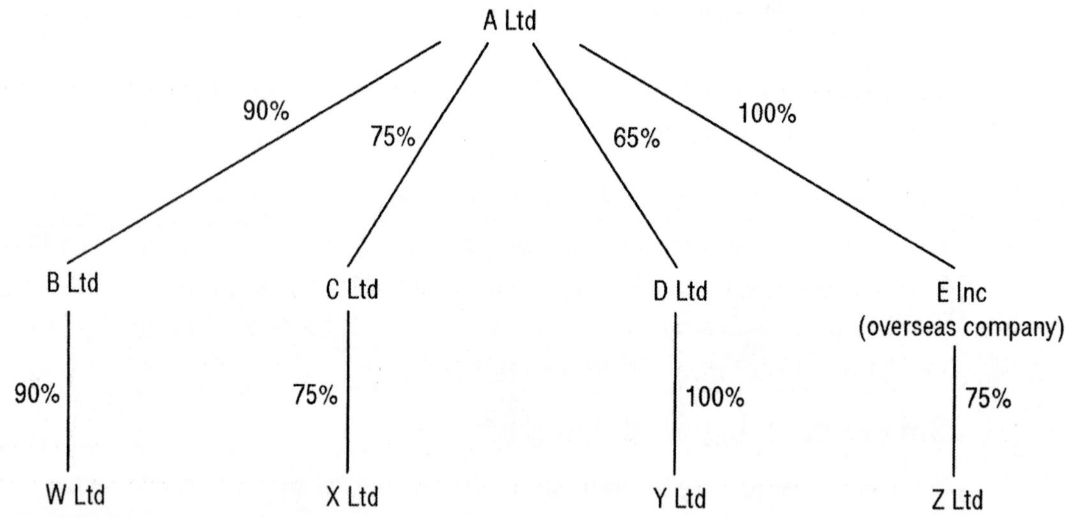

The companies in a group for chargeable gains purposes are:

A Ltd
B Ltd
W Ltd
C Ltd
X Ltd (75% subsidiary of 75% subsidiary, effective interest over 50%)
E Inc
Z Ltd

There is a separate capital gains group of D Ltd and Y Ltd.

4.3 Intra-group transfers

FAST FORWARD

Within a capital gains group, assets are automatically transferred at no gain/no loss.

Companies in a capital gains group make intra-group transfers of chargeable assets without a chargeable gain or an allowable loss arising. No election is needed, as this relief is compulsory. The assets are deemed to be transferred at such a price as will give the transferor no gain and no loss. Similarly, intangible assets can be transferred between members of a capital gains group without a trading profit or loss arising (see earlier in this Text).

Non-UK resident companies are included as members of a capital gains group. Provided the assets transferred do not result in a potential leakage of UK corporation tax, no gain/no loss transfers are possible within a worldwide (global) group of companies. This means that it may be possible to make no gain/no loss transfers to non-UK resident companies with a branch or agency in the UK.

4.4 Degrouping charge on company leaving the group

FAST FORWARD

A degrouping charge arises if a company leaves a group within six years of acquiring an asset from another group member.

A charge arises if a company leaves a group while it owns one or more assets transferred to it by another group member within the previous six years under the provisions described above. The departing company is treated as though it had, at the time of its acquisition of such assets, sold and immediately re-acquired them at their then market values. The consequent gain or loss (computed using indexation allowance up to the date of the no gain/no loss transfer) is sometimes referred to as a degrouping charge. This gain is added to (or if a loss, deducted from) the consideration received by the selling company when calculating the gain or loss on the disposal of shares of the departing company.

Any exemption or relief that may apply to the share disposal, such as the substantial shareholding exemption (dealt with earlier in this Text), also applies to the element of a gain on the share disposal relating to the degrouping charge.

Question — Company leaves an 'assets group'

In May 2013, Top Ltd, a trading company, sold the whole of the share capital of Bottom Ltd, a 100% subsidiary, to Take plc for £600,000. Bottom Ltd is an investment company and had been owned by Top Ltd since July 2001 when Top Ltd acquired the entire share capital for £50,000. The indexation allowance on the sale is £22,100.

Included in Bottom Ltd's assets is a warehouse acquired by Side Ltd in January 2003 for £96,000. Side Ltd is also a 100% subsidiary of Top Ltd. The warehouse was transferred by Side Ltd to Bottom Ltd in August 2007 for £100,000. Its market value at the date of transfer was £310,000. The indexation allowance on a sale in August 2007 would have been £15,552.

What is the effect of Bottom Ltd leaving the group? Compute Top Ltd's corporation tax for the year ended 31 March 2014 if it has trading income of £2,000,000. How would your answer be different if Bottom Ltd was a trading company?

Answer

Bottom Ltd leaves the group within six years of acquiring the warehouse from Side Ltd. Bottom Ltd will be treated as if it had sold the warehouse at its market value in August 2007 and then immediately reacquired it.

	£	£
Proceeds (ie MV in August 2007)		310,000
Less cost: cost to Side Ltd	96,000	
indexation allowance to August 2007	15,552	
		(111,552)
Chargeable gain		198,448

Top Ltd's gain on the sale of the shares in Bottom Ltd is as follows.

	£	£
Proceeds received from Take plc		600,000
Degrouping charge gain		198,448
		798,448
Less cost: cost	50,000	
indexation allowance	22,100	
		(72,100)
Chargeable gain		726,348

Top Ltd's corporation tax for the year to 31.3.14 is as follows.

	£
Trading profits	2,000,000
Chargeable gain on sale of Bottom Ltd shares	726,348
Taxable total profits	2,726,348
Corporation tax £2,726,348 × 23%	£627,060

If Bottom Ltd was a trading company, Top Ltd will not have a chargeable gain on the sale of its shares in Bottom Ltd, due to the substantial shareholdings relief applying to the sale of the subsidiary. This will include the element relating to the de grouping charge. The corporation tax liability of Top Ltd for the year to 31.3.14 will therefore be £2,000,000 × 23% = £460,000.

4.5 Transfer of gains and losses within group

FAST FORWARD

Gains and losses can be transferred between group companies.

One of the competencies you require to fulfil performance objective 20 of the PER is the ability to assist with tax planning. You can apply the knowledge you obtain from this section of the text to help to demonstrate this competence.

Two members of a capital gains group can elect to transfer a chargeable gain or allowable loss, or any part of a gain or loss, between them. This election must be made within two years of the end of the accounting period in which the gain or loss accrues in the company which is making the transfer.

From a tax planning point of view, elections(s) should be made to match gains and losses and ensure that net taxable gains arise in the company subject to the lowest rate of corporation tax.

4.6 Rollover relief

FAST FORWARD

Rollover relief is available in a capital gains group.

If a member of a capital gains group disposes of an asset eligible for capital gains rollover relief it may treat all of the group companies as a single unit for the purpose of claiming such relief.

Acquisitions by other group members within the qualifying period of one year before the disposal to three years afterwards may **be matched with the disposal**. However, both the disposing company and the acquiring company must make the claim. If an asset is transferred at no gain and no loss between group members, that transfer does not count as the acquisition of an asset for rollover relief purpose. Claims may also be made by non-trading group members which hold assets used for other group members' trades.

Exam focus point

Try to remember the following summary – it will be of great help in the exam.

Parent Co controls > 50% of subsidiary

- Associated companies for upper and lower limits

Parent Co owns ≥ 75% of subsidiary and has indirect holding of ≥ 75% of sub-subsidiaries

- Surrender trading losses, excess property income losses, excess qualifying charitable donations, loan deficits, excess management expenses to companies with some taxable total profits for same time period

Parent Co owns ≥ 75% of subsidiary and has indirect holding of > 50% of sub-subsidiaries (but must be ≥ 75% at each level)

- Transfer assets between companies automatically at no gain/no loss
- Chargeable gains and losses can be matched between group member companies
- All companies treated as one for rollover relief purposes.

4.7 Intangible fixed assets

Similar rules apply to intangible fixed assets held within a capital gains group. The rules are:

(a) **Rollover relief** can be claimed where an intangible fixed asset used for trade purposes is sold where the reinvestment is made by another member of the capital gains group, and also where the reinvestment is in the shares of another company which becomes a member as a result

(b) **Transfers of intangible assets between members of a capital gains group are on a 'no gain/loss basis'**

(c) Where a company leaves a capital gains group holding an intangible asset transferred to it in the previous six years the gain or loss that would have arisen on the date of the transfer is realised and included in trading profits (if the asset is used for the trade), the profits of a UK property letting business (if the asset is used for letting), or miscellaneous income (if the asset is an investment)

(d) The degrouping charge may be transferred from the company leaving the group to another group company

(e) Either the company leaving the capital gains group or a continuing member can claim to rollover any profit arising. The departing company can claim relief if it retains the profit and acquires a new asset. The continuing company can claim relief if the profit has been switched to it and it acquires a new intangible asset.

4.8 Pre-entry capital losses

FAST FORWARD

Restrictions apply to the use of pre-entry losses within capital gains groups.

A group might acquire a company that has capital losses brought forward. The use of such 'pre-entry' losses is restricted.

If a company (X) joins a group (G), X's pre-entry (capital) losses are losses made on disposals before X joined G.

X's pre-entry losses may (subject to the usual rule against carrying back capital losses) **be set against gains on assets which:**

- X disposed of before joining G
- X already owned when it joined G, or
- X acquired after joining G from someone outside G and which have, since acquisition, not been used except for the purposes of any trade or business which X was carrying on immediately before joining G and either continued to carry on or was carried on by another group member until the disposals giving rise to the gains.

In any one accounting period, pre-entry losses (whether of the current period or brought forward) are used (so far as possible) before other losses.

5 Succession to trade

FAST FORWARD

A succession occurs when a trade carried on by one company is transferred to another company in substantially the same ownership. In this case losses may be carried forward and balancing adjustments do not arise for capital allowances purposes.

Generally, if a trade is transferred from one company to another, that is treated as a cessation of the trade by the transferor and a commencement of the trade by the transferee. Any trading losses brought forward by the transferor are extinguished and cannot be utilised by the transferee. In addition, balancing adjustments may arise on assets qualifying for capital allowances. If however the transfer of the trade amounts to a '**succession**', it is treated as continuing for certain specific purposes.

Key term

A **'succession to trade'** occurs if a trade carried on by one company (the 'predecessor') is transferred to another company (the 'successor') in **substantially the same ownership**.

The above test is met if the same persons hold an interest of at least 75% in the trade **both:**

(a) at some time during the 12 months prior to transfer, and
(b) at some time during the 24 months following the transfer

and throughout those periods the trade is carried on by a company chargeable to tax in respect of it.

The transfer of a trade from a company to its 75% subsidiary will generally qualify as a succession. Such a transfer is often referred to as a 'hive down'.

Other circumstances where a succession takes place include a transfer from a 75% subsidiary to its parent and a transfer of trade between two companies with a common 75% parent (or indeed owned to the extent of at least 75% by the same individual). There is no stipulation that the companies have to be UK resident, so the provisions can apply to UK branches of non-resident companies.

When a trade is transferred in this way:

(a) an **accounting period ends** on the date of transfer

(b) the predecessor may claim **capital allowances** in the final accounting period as if no transfer had taken place. The successor takes over the unrelieved expenditure and is entitled to capital allowances thereon in the period in which the transfer takes place

(c) the successor is entitled to relief for **carried forward trading losses** not utilised by the predecessor, against future profits from the trade in which the losses were incurred.

The following are **not** transferred and remain with the transferor company:

(a) capital losses
(b) deficits on non-trading loan relationships.

These provisions do **not** enable a trading loss incurred by the successor company to be carried back against profits realised by the predecessor. Also, the predecessor's cessation of trade does not qualify it for a three year carry back of losses.

Chapter roundup

- A group of companies is only entitled to a single annual investment allowance (AIA) which can be allocated between the companies as they think fit. A similar rule applies to companies under common control.
- Group relief is available where the existence of a group or consortium is established through companies resident anywhere in the world.
- Within a 75% group trading losses can be surrendered between UK companies.
- Within a consortium there is some scope for loss relief.
- Within a capital gains group, assets are automatically transferred at no gain/no loss.
- A degrouping charge arises if a company leaves a group within six years of acquiring an asset from another group member.
- Gains and losses can be transferred between group companies.
- Rollover relief is available in a capital gains group.
- Restrictions apply to the use of pre-entry losses within capital gains groups.
- A succession occurs when a trade carried on by one company is transferred to another company in substantially the same ownership. In this case losses may be carried forward and balancing adjustments do not arise for capital allowances purposes.

Quick quiz

1. Under what circumstance may companies be entitled to a single annual investment allowance between them?
2. List the losses which may be group relieved.
3. What is the definition of a consortium?
4. When may assets be transferred intra-group at no gain and no loss?
5. How can capital gains and losses within a group be matched with each other?

Answers to quick quiz

1. Companies are entitled to a single annual investment allowance between them either if they are in a group with a parent undertaking and a subsidiary undertaking or if the companies are under common control (controlled by a person and either sharing premises or carrying on similar activities).
2. Trading losses, excess UK property business losses, non-trading deficits on loan relationships, excess qualifying charitable donations and excess management expenses of investment companies.
3. A company is owned by a consortium if 75% or more of its ordinary share capital is owned by companies none of which have a holding of less than 5%.

   Each consortium member (ie company shareholders) must have at least a 5% stake in profits and assets on a winding up in the consortium company.
4. No gain no loss asset transfers are automatic between companies in a capital gains group.
5. Two member of a capital gains tax group can elect to transfer gains and losses between them.

Now try the question below from the Exam Question Bank

Number	Level	Marks	Time
Q28	Introductory	20	36 mins

Overseas aspects of corporate tax

27

Topic list	Syllabus reference
1 Company residence	A2(d)
2 Double taxation relief (DTR)	A2(d)(i),(v)
3 Groups of companies	A2(e)(ix)
4 Controlled foreign companies	A2(d)(iii)
5 Permanent establishment (PE) or subsidiary abroad	A2(d)(ii),(e)(ix),(x)
6 Non-UK resident companies	A2(d)(iv)

Introduction

We have nearly completed our study of corporation tax, except for the consideration of overseas aspects.

This chapter starts by considering which country a company 'lives' in. We then see how relief may be given for overseas taxes suffered, how overseas companies may impact a group and how UK companies are taxed on the profits of certain overseas subsidiaries.

Finally, we look at UK companies trading abroad, and some miscellaneous points on overseas companies trading in the UK.

In the next chapter we will turn our attention to VAT.

Study guide

		Intellectual level
2	**Corporation tax liabilities in situations involving further overseas and group aspects and in relation to special types of company, and the application of additional exemptions and reliefs**	
(d)	The comprehensive calculation of corporation tax liability:	3
(i)	Assess the impact of the OECD model double tax treaty on corporation tax	
(ii)	Evaluate the meaning and implications of a permanent establishment	
(iii)	Identify and advise on the tax implications of controlled foreign companies	
(iv)	Advise on the tax position of overseas companies trading in the UK	
(v)	Calculate double taxation relief	
(e)	The effect of a group structure for corporation tax purposes:	3
(ix)	Advise on the tax treatment of an overseas branch	
(x)	Advise on the relief for trading losses incurred by an overseas subsidiary	

Exam guide

A question on the overseas aspects of corporation tax could require you to advise on the tax consequences of relationships with overseas companies. This could involve a discussion of the merits of trading through a permanent establishment (eg a branch) or subsidiary, and could extend to the anti-avoidance controlled foreign company rules where the subsidiary is resident overseas but controlled by UK shareholders. Double tax relief is an important consideration; the relief is the lower of the UK corporation tax and the foreign tax paid.

Knowledge brought forward from earlier studies

You will be familiar with the basics of double tax relief and the advantages of trading through a branch or subsidiary as these were in the F6 syllabus in previous years.

Controlled foreign companies are new.

1 Company residence

FAST FORWARD

Company residence is important in determining whether its profits are subject to UK tax.

1.1 Introduction

A company is resident in the UK if it is incorporated in the UK or if its central management and control are exercised in the UK. Central management and control are usually treated as exercised where the board of directors meets.

A UK resident company is subject to corporation tax on its worldwide profits. It can be taxable at the small profits rate and can obtain marginal relief.

1.2 Non-UK resident companies trading in the UK

A non-UK resident company will be chargeable to corporation tax if it carries on a trade in the UK through a permanent establishment (PE).

The profits of such a company which are chargeable to corporation tax, whether or not they arise in the UK, are:

- any trading income arising directly or indirectly from the PE
- any income from property or rights used by, or held by or for, the PE (other than dividends from UK companies)
- any chargeable gains arising from the disposal of assets situated in the UK.

Key term

A **permanent establishment** is a fixed place of business through which the business of the enterprise is wholly or partly carried on. It includes a branch, office, factory, workshop, mine, oil or gas well, quarry and construction project lasting more than twelve months. It does not include use of storage facilities, maintenance of a stock of goods and delivery of them or a fixed place of business used solely for purchasing goods or any ancillary activity.

The profits of the permanent establishment are taxable at the main rate of corporation tax only. The small profits rate and marginal relief do not apply.

1.3 UK resident companies with overseas income

If a UK resident company makes investments overseas it will be liable to corporation tax on the profits made, the taxable amount being before the deduction of any foreign taxes. The profits may be any of the following.

(a) Trading income: profits of an overseas permanent establishment controlled from the UK (unless an election for the exemption of profits and losses from overseas permanent establishments is made – see later in this chapter)

(b) Interest income: income from overseas securities, for example loan stock in overseas companies

(c) Overseas income: income from other overseas possessions including:

  (i) dividends from overseas subsidiaries
  (ii) profits of an overseas branch or agency controlled abroad

(d) Chargeable gains on disposals of overseas assets

A UK resident company may receive dividends from an overseas subsidiary. Most dividends received by a UK resident company from a non-UK resident company are exempt from corporation tax.

Exam focus point

Taxable overseas dividends will not be examined in Paper P6.

A company may be subject to overseas tax as well as to UK corporation tax on the same profits usually if it has a PE in that overseas country. Double taxation relief (see below) is available in respect of the overseas tax suffered.

2 Double taxation relief (DTR)

FAST FORWARD

A company may obtain DTR for overseas withholding tax. The allocation of qualifying charitable donations and losses can affect the relief.

2.1 General principles

In the UK relief for overseas tax suffered by a company may be currently available in one of three ways.

(a) **Treaty relief**
Under a treaty entered into between the UK and the overseas country, a treaty may exempt certain profits from taxation in one of the countries involved, thus completely avoiding double taxation. More usually treaties provide for credit to be given for tax suffered in one of the countries against the tax liability in the other.

(b) **Unilateral credit relief**
Where no treaty relief is available, unilateral relief may be available in the UK giving credit for the overseas tax against the UK tax.

(c) **Unilateral expense relief**
Not examined in your syllabus.

2.2 Treaty relief

A tax treaty based on the OECD Model Agreement may use either the exemption method or the credit method to give relief for tax suffered on income from a business in country B by a resident of country R.

(a) Under the **exemption method**, the income is not taxed at all in country R, or if it is dividends or interest (which the treaty allows to be taxed in country R) credit is given for any country B tax against the country R tax

(b) Under the **credit method**, the income is taxed in country R, but credit is given for any country B tax against the country R tax.

Under either method, any credit given is limited to the country B tax attributable to the income.

2.3 Unilateral credit relief

FAST FORWARD

Double tax relief (DTR) is the lower of the UK tax on overseas profits and the overseas tax on overseas profits.

Relief is available for overseas tax suffered on PE profits, interest and royalties, up to the amount of the UK corporation tax (at the company's average rate) attributable to that income. The tax that is deducted overseas is usually called withholding tax. The gross income including the withholding tax is included within the taxable total profits. It is not relevant whether those profits are remitted back to the UK or not.

The amount of double tax relief (DTR) is the lower of:

(a) **the UK tax on overseas profits;**

(b) **the overseas tax on overseas profits.**

Question — **Unilateral credit relief (1)**

AS plc has UK trading income of £2,000,000 in the year to 31 March 2014. In that year, AS plc also operated an overseas branch. The profits of the branch were £80,000, after deduction of 20% withholding tax. Compute the corporation tax payable, assuming that no election has been made to exempt the branch profits.

Answer

	Total	UK	Overseas
	£	£	£
Trading income	2,000,000	2,000,000	
Overseas trading profit (W1)	100,000		100,000
Taxable total profits	2,100,000	2,000,000	100,000
Corporation tax at 23%	483,000	460,000	23,000
Less DTR (W2)	(20,000)		(20,000)
	463,000	460,000	3,000

Working:

1 £80,000 × 100/(100 – 20) = £100,000.

2 DTR is lower of

(i) UK tax on overseas profit £100,000 × 23% = £23,000

(i) Overseas tax on overseas profit £100,000 × 20% = £20,000

Question

Unilateral credit relief (2)

T Ltd is a UK company with an overseas branch. The results of T Ltd for the year ended 31 March 2014 are as follows:

	Total	UK	Branch
	£	£	£
Trading profits (before tax)	1,000,000	800,000	200,000

The overseas branch is subject to tax overseas at the rate of 24%. Compute the UK corporation tax payable, assuming that no election has been made to exempt the branch profits.

Answer

The corporation tax liability of T Ltd for the year ended 31 March 2014 is as follows.

	£
UK trading profit	800,000
Overseas trading profit	200,000
Taxable total profits	1,000,000
Corporation tax at 23%	230,000
Less marginal relief 3/400 (1,500,000 – 1,000,000)	(3,750)
	226,250
Less double taxation relief (W)	(45,250)
UK corporation tax payable	181,000

Working

DTR is lower of

(i) UK tax on overseas profit £(200,000/1,000,000) × £226,250 = £45,250

(ii) Overseas tax on overseas profit £200,000 × 24% = £48,000

A company may allocate its qualifying charitable donations and losses relieved against total profits in whatever manner it likes for the purpose of computing double taxation relief. It should set the maximum amount against any UK profits, thereby maximising the corporation tax attributable to the overseas profits and hence maximising the double taxation relief available.

If a company has several sources of overseas profits, then deficits, qualifying charitable donations and losses should be allocated first to UK profits, and then to overseas sources which have suffered the **lowest** rates of overseas taxation.

Losses relieved by carry forward must in any case be set against the first available profits of the trade which gave rise to the loss.

A company with a choice of loss reliefs should consider the effect of its choice on double taxation relief. For example, a loss relief claim might lead to there being no UK tax liability, or a very small liability, so that overseas tax would go unrelieved. Carry forward loss relief might avoid this problem and still leave very little UK tax to pay for the period of the loss.

Companies that have claimed DTR must notify HMRC if the amount of overseas tax they have paid is adjusted and this has resulted in the DTR claim becoming excessive. The notification must be in writing within one year of any adjustment to the overseas tax.

Question — Allocation of qualifying charitable donations

Kairo plc is a UK resident company with five UK resident subsidiaries and two overseas branches, one in Atlantis and one in Utopia. The company produced the following results for the year to 31 March 2014.

	£
UK trading profits	10,000
Profits from overseas branch in Atlantis (before overseas tax of £8,000)	40,000
Profits from overseas branch in Utopia (before overseas tax of £110,000)	250,000
Qualifying charitable donations	(15,000)

Compute the UK corporation tax liability, assuming an election has not been made to exempt the profits of overseas PEs.

Answer

Kairo plc - corporation tax year to 31 March 2014

	Total	*UK*	*Atlantis*	*Utopia*
	£	£	£	£
Total profits	300,000	10,000	40,000	250,000
Less qualifying charitable donations (W)	(15,000)	(10,000)	(5,000)	–
Taxable total profits	285,000	Nil	35,000	250,000
Corporation tax @ 23% (N)	65,550	–	8,050	57,500
Less DTR (W)	(65,500)	–	(8,000)	(57,500)
Corporation tax	50	–	50	–

Note

The main rate of corporation tax applies, since the upper limit for marginal relief (£1,500,000 ÷ 6 = £250,000) is exceeded.

Working

The DTR is the lower of:

Atlantis: UK tax £8,050;
Overseas tax £8,000 (Rate of overseas tax = 20%), ie £8,000

Utopia: UK tax £57,500;
Overseas tax £110,000 (Rate of overseas tax = 44%), ie £57,500

Note. The Atlantis branch profits suffer the lower rate of overseas tax so the qualifying charitable donations remaining after offset against the UK income are allocated against the Atlantis branch income in preference to the Utopia branch income.

Exam focus point

If there are several sources of overseas income it is important to keep them separate and to calculate double tax relief on each source of income separately. Get into the habit of setting out a working with a separate column for UK income and for each source of overseas income. You should then find arriving at the right answer straightforward.

3 Groups of companies

FAST FORWARD

The group relief rules allow groups and consortia to be established through companies resident anywhere in the world.

3.1 Introduction

Groups and consortia can be established through companies resident anywhere in the world.

However, group relief is normally only available to, and may only be claimed from, companies which are within the charge to corporation tax. Group relief therefore applies to companies which are:

(a) **resident in the UK**, or
(b) **resident overseas but operating through a permanent establishment in the UK.**

If the company is operating through a permanent establishment in the UK, it can only usually surrender losses made by that permanent establishment. There is a **very limited exception** for group **companies resident in another country in the European Economic Area** (EEA). Such companies may **surrender non-UK losses to UK group members**, but only **where all current and future loss relief options have been exhausted overseas.** In practice, this means it may be difficult to make a claim unless the company is in liquidation.

Similarly, a consortium may exist for relief purposes where one or more of the members is not resident in the UK but relief cannot be passed to or from a company which is not within the charge to corporation tax.

3.2 Example

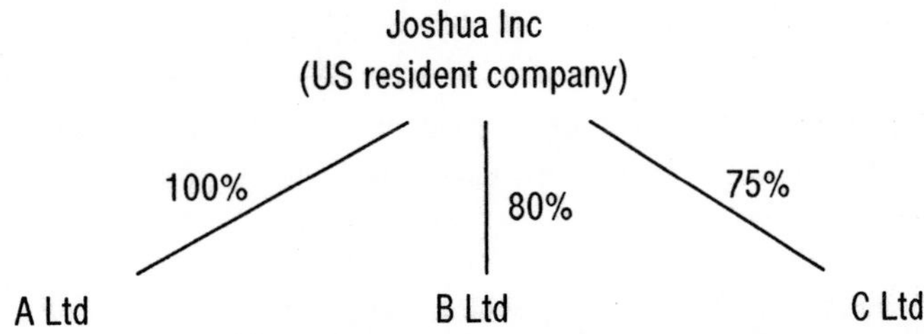

A Ltd, B Ltd and C Ltd are all UK resident companies. As the three UK companies share a common parent they will be treated as part of a group relief group despite the fact that the parent company is not UK resident. The UK companies may surrender losses to each other (but not normally to or from the overseas parent company).

3.3 Permanent establishments (PEs) of companies

UK PEs of EEA resident companies can **surrender UK losses** under group relief to **UK group members**, if **those losses have not been relieved against profits in the overseas country.**

UK PEs of companies resident in non-EEA countries can also surrender UK losses to UK group members, but only if **those losses are not available for against profits in the overseas country** (regardless of whether the losses have actually been relieved overseas).

Losses incurred by overseas PEs of UK companies can be surrendered as group relief only if they not available for relief against profits in the overseas country.

The following table summarises how losses may be surrendered for group relief:

Where surrendering company resident	Where loss made	Can surrender losses under group relief?
UK	In UK	Yes
UK	Outside UK by permanent establishment	Yes – unless **available for relief** outside UK
Elsewhere in EEA	In UK by permanent establishment	Yes – unless **actually relieved** outside UK
Elsewhere in EEA	Outside UK	Yes – unless **no possibility that could be relieved** outside UK
Not in EEA	In UK by permanent establishment	Yes – unless **available for relief** outside UK
Not in EEA	Outside UK	No

3.4 The global group concept

The 'global group concept' means that instead of looking at the residence of a company one needs to look at whether the company is subject to UK corporation tax on any of its chargeable gains. Provided the assets transferred do not result in a potential leakage of UK corporation tax, no gain/no loss transfers will be possible within a worldwide (global) group of companies.

The global group concept applies to the transfer of the whole or part of a trade and extends to certain intra-group transfers of assets and to transfers of assets where one company disposes of the whole or part of its business to another company as part of a scheme of reconstruction or amalgamation.

3.5 Interest restriction

The tax deduction for interest payable by UK members of a group of companies are restricted to the consolidated gross finance expense of the group. This is known as the 'worldwide debt cap'. The rules apply to groups other than those consisting entirely of companies that are small or medium sized.

Exam focus point

The examiner has stated that students are only required to be aware of the worldwide debt cap to the extent that it might result in an interest expense being disallowed.

4 Controlled foreign companies

FAST FORWARD

Chargeable profits of a controlled foreign company (CFC) are apportioned to UK resident companies entitled to at least 25% of those profits, and are subject to a CFC charge at the main rate of corporation tax.

4.1 Introduction

The controlled foreign company (CFC) rules focus on the artificial diversion of income profits (ie not chargeable gains) from the UK.

Where a **CFC has 'chargeable profits'** and the **CFC is not covered by one of the exemptions**, those **chargeable profits are apportioned to the CFC's UK corporate shareholders.**

Any **UK resident company with at least a 25% holding in the CFC** will be required to **self-assess a CFC charge, in respect of the apportioned profits, at the main rate of corporation tax.** Any **overseas tax** attributable to the apportioned profits can be **credited against the CFC charge.**

4.2 What is a CFC?

Key term

A controlled foreign company is a company which is not resident in the UK but is controlled by persons resident in the UK.

A **company is controlled by persons resident in the UK** if:

(a) A **UK person, or persons, controls the company** (ie more than 50%, or control as a matter of fact), or

(b) It is **at least 40% held by a UK resident** and **at least 40% but no more than 55% by a non-UK resident.**

Question

Controlled foreign company

Alpha AG is resident in Germany and is owned as follows:

Orange Ltd } UK resident companies	35%
Lemon Ltd } UK resident companies	15%
Lime Ltd } UK resident companies	25%
Pomegranate Ltd (Resident in the Bahamas)	25%
	100%

Beta Ltd is resident in Ireland and is owned as follows:

Apple GmbH (resident in Switzerland, 80% owned by Orchard plc which is UK resident)	60%
Pear SpA (resident in Italy)	40%
	100%

Gamma Ltd is resident in Jersey and is owned as follows:

Tiny SA (also resident in Jersey)	56%
Big plc (UK resident)	42%
Mr Average (resident in Guernsey)	2%
	100%

Explain which of the companies are CFCs.

Answer

Alpha AG is a CFC because it is 75% owned by UK resident persons.

Beta Ltd is a CFC because, although Orchard plc only has a 48% 'effective' interest, Orchard plc can control it as a matter of fact. This is because it controls Apple GmbH, which in turn controls Beta Ltd.

Gamma Ltd is not a CFC. This is because although there is a UK shareholder (Big plc) with a shareholding of at least 40%, and also a non-UK shareholder with a shareholding of at least 40% (Tiny SA), the non-UK shareholder has a holding of more than 55%.

Note that if Tiny SA's shareholding had been 55% or less, Gamma Ltd would be a CFC under the 40% test.

4.3 Chargeable profits

Chargeable profits are those income profits (not chargeable gains) of the CFC, calculated using UK tax rules, **which have been artificially diverted from the UK.**

Profits are chargeable profits unless a company meets at least one of the following conditions:

(a) The **company has not been a party to arrangements**, one of the main purposes of which is to **reduce or eliminate a charge to UK or overseas tax** at any time in the accounting period.

(b) **None of the company's assets or risks are managed or controlled from the UK to any significant extent** at any time in the accounting period.

(c) If the company does have assets or risks that are managed or controlled from the UK, it has the **commercial capability to ensure that the company's business could continue if the UK managed assets and risks were no longer being managed from the UK**. This is intended as a test of how reliant the CFC is on UK management.

Exam focus point

There are further rules in relation to, among other things, finance companies, and companies in the financial services industry. These rules are not examinable in P6(UK).

4.4 Exemptions

Even if a CFC has chargeable profits, there is **no CFC charge if one of the following exemptions applies**.

4.4.1 Exempt period

This is intended to **give companies coming within the UK CFC rules time to restructure** so that they are not subject to a charge.

An exempt period ends 12 months after a company comes under the control of UK residents. An accounting period ending within the exempt period is exempt (with periods falling partly within the exempt period being partly exempt). To qualify for exemption, the company must be within the scope of the CFC rules in its first accounting period after the end of the exempt period, but with none of its profits in that subsequent accounting period subject to an apportionment (ie subject to a CFC charge).

4.4.2 Excluded territories

HMRC issues regulations **setting out a list of 'good' territories, where a company's profits are not generally subject to a low rate of tax.**

A company which is resident and fully taxable in a listed territory will not generally be subject to a CFC charge.

4.4.3 Low profits

A company is exempt from an apportionment (and so a CFC charge) **where its profits are**:

(a) **No more than £50,000**, or
(b) **No more than £500,000, of which no more than £50,000 is non-trading profits**

Profits can be determined on either a tax or accounts basis, and the limits are scaled down for accounting periods of less than 12 months.

4.4.4 Low profit margin

A company is exempt from an apportionment if its **accounting profits are no more than 10% of its relevant operating expenditure.**

4.4.5 Tax exemption

A company is exempt from an apportionment if **its tax paid in its territory of residence is at least 75% of the UK corporation tax which would have been payable if it had been resident in the UK.**

The local tax must be adjusted for items which are taxed locally but not in the UK, and expenditure which is allowed locally but is not allowed in the UK computation.

4.5 The CFC charge

4.5.1 Apportionment of profits

UK companies which own at least 25% of a CFC will be **taxed on their share of the CFC's profits which represent its chargeable profits.**

The UK company is responsible for **self-assessing** the corporation tax due on the CFC's chargeable profits.

The chargeable profits of the CFC are **taxed at the main rate of UK corporation tax.**

4.5.2 Creditable tax

Where CFC profits are apportioned **the UK tax payable may be reduced by 'creditable tax' which is the aggregate of:**

(a) **Any DTR which would be available if the CFC's chargeable profits were chargeable to UK corporation tax under normal rules**, ie the lower of the UK corporation tax payable and actual foreign corporation tax paid,

(b) **Any income tax deducted at source on income received by the CFC,**

(c) **Corporation tax payable in the UK on any CFC income taxable in this country.**

Question — **CFC charge**

R Inc is owned 75% by J Ltd and 25% by Mr J. Both J Ltd and Mr J are UK resident. R Inc is a non UK resident company such that it is a controlled foreign company. None of the CFC exemptions apply to R Inc.

In the year to 31 March 2014, R Inc had chargeable profits of £650,000. It paid income tax in its own country at the rate of 8%.

Show how the profits of R Inc will be apportioned to J Ltd and the CFC charge on J Ltd.

Answer

	£
Chargeable profits of R inc	650,000
Apportioned to J Ltd (75%)	487,500
J Ltd's CFC charge	
Tax on apportioned profits	
£487,500 × 23%	112,125
Less creditable tax (8% × £650,000) × 75%	(39,000)
CFC charge	73,125

4.6 Clearance procedure

There is a **clearance procedure** whereby HMRC will confirm how the rules will apply in a company's particular circumstances.

5 Permanent establishment (PE) or subsidiary abroad

FAST FORWARD

A UK resident company intending to do business abroad must choose between a permanent establishment and a subsidiary.

One of the competencies you require to fulfil performance objective 20 of the PER is the ability to assist with tax planning. You can apply the knowledge you obtain from this section of the text to help to demonstrate this competence.

5.1 General principles

Where a overseas country has a lower rate of company taxation than the UK, it can be beneficial for the UK company to conduct its overseas activities through a **non-UK resident subsidiary** if profits are anticipated (assuming that the CFC rules (see above) do not apply), or through a **PE, if losses are likely to arise**.

The general rule is that the **profits of a overseas PE** are treated as part of the profits of the UK company and are normally included in its computation of trading profits. If, however, the operations of the overseas PE amount to a separate trade which is wholly carried on overseas, the profits are assessed as overseas income.

The losses of a overseas PE are normally netted off against the UK company's trading income and the usual loss reliefs are available. Losses can be surrendered as group relief to the extent they cannot be relieved against profits in the overseas country. Alternatively an overseas income trading loss can be carried forward to set against future profits of the same trade.

The profits of a non-resident **overseas subsidiary** are not liable to UK tax when remitted to the UK, for example in the form of dividends. However, no relief can be obtained against the UK parent's profits for any overseas losses of a non-resident subsidiary except in very limited circumstances.

5.2 Election to exempt overseas PE profits and losses

FAST FORWARD

An irrevocable election can be made to exempt profits and losses of all overseas PEs from UK corporation tax.

A UK company may make an **election to exempt the profits and losses of all its overseas PEs from UK corporation tax**. Note that the election will **disallow loss relief** for overseas PEs against UK profits and that the **election must apply to all of the UK company's PEs** – it is not possible to exclude, for example, a loss making PE from the election. The election also means that **no capital allowances** can be claimed by the UK parent company in respect of past or current future capital expenditure by exempt overseas PEs.

The election **takes effect from the start of the accounting period after the one in which the election is made**. The election is **irrevocable** and so it is important to consider the effect of making the election for all future accounting periods, in particular whether any of the PEs is likely to make a loss.

Double taxation relief should also be taken into account when deciding whether or not to make the election. If the **operation of DTR means that there is little or no UK corporation tax payable** on overseas profits, it may be **better not to make the election**. This means that **loss relief will be available** in future accounting periods.

Election to exempt PE profits

Brown Ltd is a UK resident company with two overseas PEs. It prepares accounts to 31 March each year. In the year to 31 March 2014, Brown Ltd made a UK trading profit of £210,000, the first overseas PE made a trading profit of £40,000 (overseas tax payable £6,000), and the second overseas PE made a trading loss of £25,000. Compute the UK corporation tax payable for the year to 31 March 2014 by Brown Ltd if:

(i) no election has been made to exempt the profits and losses of the overseas PEs; or
(ii) an election was made prior to 1 April 2013 to exempt the profits and losses of the overseas PEs.

Answer

(i) **No election made**

	£
UK trading profit	210,000
First overseas PE trading profit	40,000
Second overseas PE trading loss	(25,000)
Taxable total profits	225,000
Corporation tax at 20%	45,000
Less double taxation relief (W)	(6,000)
UK corporation tax payable by Brown Ltd	39,000

Working

DTR is lower of

(i) UK tax on overseas profit £40,000 × 20% = £8,000
(ii) Overseas tax on overseas profit £6,000

(ii) **Election made**

	£
UK trading profit/Taxable total profits	210,000
UK corporation tax at 20% payable by Brown Ltd	42,000

The election was therefore not beneficial.

Exam focus point

The rules regarding the exemption of overseas PE profits are complex, especially where small companies are concerned. The examiner has stated that these more complex aspects are not examinable. In any examination question, **it should therefore be assumed that the exemption option is available for all overseas PEs.**

5.3 Incorporating an overseas PE

5.3.1 The decision to incorporate

Where a overseas operation is likely to show a loss in the early years, it may be worthwhile to trade through an overseas PE whilst losses arise (these are usually then automatically netted off against the company's UK profits).

If the **PE then becomes profitable**, consideration should be given to either **making the election to exempt all branch profits and losses** or **converting the PE into a non-UK resident subsidiary company (so that profits can be accumulated at potentially lower rates of overseas tax).**

Both of these methods mean that the overseas profits will not be subject to UK corporation tax (provided the subsidiary does not become a controlled foreign company). However, they also both mean that any future overseas losses cannot be relieved against UK profits and capital allowances are not available.

It is important to remember that the **election to exempt PE profits and losses is irrevocable** and **applies to all the PEs** operated by the UK company. It may therefore be better to incorporate profitable PEs and maintain a **mixture of PEs and subsidiaries** which may give more flexibility.

If it is decided to convert a overseas PE into a non-UK resident subsidiary, there are important tax implications both in the UK and the overseas country.

5.3.2 Issue of shares/loan stock by non-UK company

It is illegal for a UK resident company to cause or permit a non-UK resident company over which it has control to create or issue any shares or loan stock. It is also illegal for a UK resident company to transfer to any person, or cause or permit to be transferred to any person, any shares or loan stock of a non-UK resident company over which it has control.

However, there are a number of situations which are excluded from these rules, for example where the transaction is intra-group or full consideration is given.

Where the transaction has a value of more than £100m, the transaction must be reported to HMRC within six months, subject to certain exclusions, for example where the transaction is carried out in the ordinary course of a trade.

5.3.3 Postponement of gains

The conversion will constitute a disposal of the assets of the PE giving rise to a chargeable gain or loss in the hands of the UK company. A chargeable gain can be postponed where:

(a) the trade of the overseas PE is transferred to the non-UK resident company with all the assets used for that trade except cash, and

(b) the consideration for the transfer is wholly or partly securities (shares or shares and loan stock), and

(c) the transferring company owns at least 25% of the ordinary share capital of the non-resident company, and

(d) a claim for relief is made.

There is full postponement of the net gains arising on the transfer where the consideration is wholly securities. Where part of the consideration is in a form other than securities, eg cash, that proportion of the net gains is chargeable immediately.

The postponement is indefinite. The gain becomes chargeable only when:

(a) the transferor company at any time disposes of any of the securities received on the transfer, or

(b) the non-UK resident company within six years of the transfer disposes of any of the assets on which a gain arose at the time of the transfer.

The 'global group' concept applies to certain intra-group transfers of assets and also where one company disposes of the whole of part of its business to another company as part of a reconstruction or amalgamation scheme. Such asset transfers are on a no gain/no loss basis provided the assets transferred do not result in a potential leakage of UK corporation tax.

5.4 European Union companies

If all or part of a trade carried on in the UK by a company resident in one EU state is transferred to a company resident in another EU state, then the transfer is deemed to be at a price giving no gain and no loss, if all the following conditions are fulfilled.

(a) The transfer is wholly in exchange for shares or securities

(b) The company receiving the trade would be subject to UK corporation tax on any gains arising on later disposals of the assets transferred

(c) Both parties claim this special treatment

(d) The transfer is for bona fide commercial reasons. Advance clearance that this condition is satisfied may be obtained.

6 Non-UK resident companies

FAST FORWARD

A non resident company is liable to UK corporation tax if it carries on trade in the UK through a permanent establishment.

6.1 Corporation tax charge

A non resident company is liable to tax in the UK if it carries on a trade in the UK through a permanent establishment (defined as above).

The PE has **the profits it would have made if it were a distinct and separate establishment engaged in the same or similar activities in the same or similar conditions, dealing wholly independently with the non resident company attributed to it.** Deductions are available for allowable expenses incurred for the purposes of the PE including executive and general administrative expenses whether in the UK or elsewhere. The term 'allowable expenses' has the same meaning as for a UK resident company. Relief is available for the expenses of managing investments for all companies whether or not they qualify as 'investment companies'.

Transactions between the PE and the non resident company are treated as taking place at **arm's length prices.**

For the purposes of collection of tax a PE will be treated as the UK representative through which the non resident company carries on a trade in the UK.

These rules align with the normal provision in tax treaties (based on the OECD Model Agreement) **that a overseas trader is taxable on his trading profits in the UK if he has a permanent establishment in the UK.**

6.2 Tax charge on income

Income charged to corporation tax comprises:

(a) Trading income arising directly or indirectly through or from the permanent establishment, and

(b) Any income, wherever arising, from property or rights used by, held by or held for the permanent establishment.

Annual interest and other annual payments are received under deduction of income tax. Provided that the income is charged to corporation tax, the company can offset the income tax suffered against its corporation tax liability and, in appropriate circumstances, obtain repayment in the same manner as a resident company.

Income from sources within the UK which is not subject to corporation tax is subject to income tax. This could arise, for example, if a non-resident company carries on a trade in the UK without having a permanent establishment, or receives letting income from a UK property.

6.3 Tax charge on capital gains

Capital gains are charged to corporation tax where the company carries on a trade in the UK through a permanent establishment if they arise on:

(a) Assets situated in the UK used in or for the purposes of the trade at or before the time when the gain accrued

(b) Assets situated in the UK held or used for the purposes of the permanent establishment at or before the time when the gain accrued.

As it would be possible to avoid gains being chargeable by, for example, ceasing to trade in the UK through a permanent establishment prior to selling the asset or exporting the asset, there are two further charging provisions:

(a) Where a non-UK resident company ceases to trade through a permanent establishment in the UK, a charge will arise. Any chargeable asset which would otherwise become non-chargeable shall be deemed to be disposed of and reacquired at market value immediately before it ceases to trade.

(b) Where a non-UK resident company trading through a UK permanent establishment exports a chargeable asset, so that it becomes non-chargeable, the gain will crystallise immediately before it is exported.

6.4 Tax planning

An overseas resident company may have to decide **whether to trade in the UK through a PE or via a UK subsidiary**. The advantage of a subsidiary if profits are low is that it will be able to take advantage of the small profits rate of tax. However, if the subsidiary makes losses the overseas company may be restricted in the relief it can claim. The overseas company would also need to consider the repatriation of profits and the provision of finance.

Chapter roundup

- Company residence is important in determining whether its profits are subject to UK tax.
- A company may obtain DTR for overseas withholding tax. The allocation of qualifying charitable donations and losses can affect the relief.
- Double tax relief (DTR) is the lower of the UK tax on overseas profits and the overseas tax on overseas profits.
- The group relief rules allow groups and consortia to be established through companies resident anywhere in the world.
- Chargeable profits of a controlled foreign company (CFC) are apportioned to UK resident companies entitled to at least 25% of those profits, and are subject to a CFC charge at the main rate of corporation tax.
- A UK resident company intending to do business abroad must choose between a permanent establishment and a subsidiary.
- An irrevocable election can be made to exempt profits and losses of all overseas branches from UK corporation tax.
- A non resident company is liable to UK corporation tax if it carries on trade in the UK through a permanent establishment.

Quick quiz

1 When is a company UK resident?

2 How best should qualifying charitable donations be allocated in computing credit relief for overseas tax?

3 What is the definition of a CFC?

4 A UK company is planning to set up a new operation in Australia that will initially be loss making. Should it set up as a permanent establishment or a subsidiary of the UK company?

Answers to quick quiz

1 A company is resident in the UK if it is incorporated in the UK or if its central management and control are exercised in the UK.

3 Qualifying charitable donations should be set-off firstly from any UK profits, then from overseas income sources suffering the lowest rates of overseas taxation before those suffering at the higher rates.

3 A CFC is a non-UK resident company that is controlled by UK resident companies and/or individuals.

4 If losses are expected then a PE is best since losses of a overseas PE can be used by the UK company whereas losses of an Australian subsidiary cannot be group relieved.

Now try the question below from the Exam Question Bank

Number	Level	Marks	Time
Q29	Introductory	15	27 mins

PART G

Value added tax

Value added tax 1

Topic list	Syllabus reference
1 Basic principles	A6(b)G1
2 The scope of VAT	A6(b)G1
3 Registration	A6(b)G2, (i),(ii)
4 Accounting for VAT	A6(b)G3
5 The valuation of supplies	A6(b)G3
6 Administration	A6(b)G3
7 Penalties	A6(b)G3

Introduction

In this and the next chapter, we study value added tax (VAT). VAT is a tax on turnover rather than on profits.

As the name of the tax suggests, it is charged on the value added. If someone in a chain of manufacture or distribution buys goods for £1,000 and sells them for £1,200 he has increased their value by £200. (He may have painted them, packed them or distributed them to shops to justify his mark-up, or he may simply be good at making deals to buy cheaply and sell dearly.) Because he has added value of £200, he collects VAT of £200 × 20% = £40 (assuming a standard rate of 20%) and pays this over to the government. The VAT is collected bit by bit along the chain and finally hits the consumer who does not add value, but uses up the goods.

VAT is a tax with simple computations but many detailed rules to ensure its enforcement. You may find it easier to absorb the detail if you ask yourself, in relation to each rule, exactly how it helps to enforce the tax.

In the next chapter we will look at the rules for zero-rated and exempt supplies, the rules for imports and exports and some of the special schemes.

Study guide

		Intellectual level
6	**National insurance, value added tax and tax administration:**	
(b)	The contents of the Paper F6 study guide for value added tax (VAT) under headings:	2
•	G1 The scope of value added tax (VAT)	
•	G2 The VAT registration requirements	
•	G3 The computation of VAT liabilities	
	The following additional material is also examinable:	
(i)	Advise on the impact of the disaggregation of business activities for VAT purposes	3
(ii)	Advise on the impact of divisional registration	3

Exam guide

VAT is a very important tax for businesses as there are few small enough not to be registerable. You may be required to advise on almost any aspect, such as registration, including group and divisional registration.

Knowledge brought forward from earlier studies

This chapter revises your knowledge of the scope of VAT, the requirement to register and the computation of the VAT liability in straightforward cases. The examiner has identified essential underpinning knowledge from the F6 syllabus which is particularly important that you revise as part of your P6 studies. In this chapter, the relevant topics are:

		Intellectual level
G2	**The VAT registration requirements**	
(a)	Recognise the circumstances in which a person must register for VAT.	2
(b)	Explain the advantages of voluntary VAT registration.	2
(d)	Explain how and when a person can deregister for VAT.	1
(e)	Explain the conditions that must be met for two or more companies to be treated as a group for VAT purposes, and the consequences of being so treated.	1

The main change in 2013/14 from 2012/13 in the material you have previously studied at F6 level is to the limits for registering and deregistering for VAT.

Disaggregation and divisional registration are new topics.

1 Basic principles

FAST FORWARD

VAT is charged on turnover at each stage in a production process, but in such a way that the burden is borne by the final consumer.

One of the competencies you require to fulfil performance objective 19 of the PER is the ability to evaluate and compute taxes payable. You can apply the knowledge you obtain from this section of the text to help to demonstrate this competence.

1.1 Introduction

The legal basis of value added tax (VAT) is to be found in the Value Added Tax Act 1994 (VATA 1994), supplemented by regulations made by statutory instrument and amended by subsequent Finance Acts. VAT is administered by HM Revenue and Customs (HMRC).

VAT is a tax on turnover, not on profits. The basic principle is that the VAT should be borne by the final consumer. Registered traders may deduct the tax which they suffer on supplies to them (input tax) from the tax which they charge to their customers (output tax) at the time this is paid to HMRC. So, at each stage of the manufacturing or service process, the net VAT paid is on the value added at that stage.

1.2 Example: the VAT charge

During 2013 a forester sells wood to a furniture maker for £100 plus VAT. The furniture maker uses this wood to make a table and sells the table to a shop for £150 plus VAT of 20%. The shop then sells the table to the final consumer for £300 plus VAT. VAT will be accounted for to HMRC as follows.

	Cost	*Input tax 20%*	*Net sale price*	*Output tax 20%*	*Payable to HMRC*
	£	£	£	£	£
Forester	0	0	100	20.00	20.00
Furniture maker	100	20.00	150	30.00	10.00
Shop	150	30.00	300	60.00	30.00
					60.00

Because the traders involved account to HMRC for VAT charged less VAT suffered, their profits for income tax or corporation tax purposes are based on sales and purchases net of VAT.

2 The scope of VAT

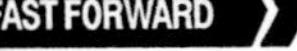

VAT is charged on taxable supplies of goods and services made by a taxable person in his business.

2.1 General principles

VAT is charged on taxable supplies of goods and services made in the UK by a taxable person in the course or furtherance of any business carried on by him. It is also chargeable on the import of goods into the UK (whether they are imported for business purposes or not, and whether the importer is a taxable person or not), and on certain services received from abroad if a taxable person receives them for business purposes.

Special rules for trade with the European Union (the EU) are covered later.

Key term

A **taxable supply** is a supply of goods or services made in the UK, other than an exempt supply.

A taxable supply is either standard-rated or zero-rated. The standard rate is usually 20%.

Certain supplies, which fall within the classification of standard rate supplies, are charged at a reduced rate of 5%. An example is the supply of domestic fuel.

2.2 Supplies of goods

Goods are supplied if exclusive ownership of the goods passes to another person.

The following are treated as supplies of goods.

- The supply of any form of power, heat, refrigeration or ventilation, or of water
- The grant, assignment or surrender of a major interest (the freehold or a lease for over 21 years) in land
- Taking goods permanently out of the business for the non-business use of a taxable person or for other private purposes including the supply of goods by an employer to an employee for his private use
- Transfers under an agreement contemplating a transfer of ownership, such as a hire purchase agreement

Gifts of goods are normally treated as sales at cost (so VAT is due). **However, business gifts are not supplies of goods if:**

(a) **The total cost of gifts made to the same person does not exceed £50 in any 12 month period.** If the £50 limit is exceeded, output tax will be due in full on the total of gifts made. Once the limit has been exceeded a new £50 limit and new 12 month period begins

(b) **The gift is a sample** (unlimited number of samples allowed)

2.3 Supplies of services

Apart from a few specific exceptions, **any supply which is not a supply of goods and which is done for a consideration is a supply of services.** Consideration is any form of payment in money or in kind, including anything which is itself a supply.

A supply of services also takes place if:

- Goods are lent to someone for use outside the business
- Goods are hired to someone
- Services bought for business purposes are used for private purposes

The European Court of Justice has ruled that restaurants supply services rather than goods.

2.4 Taxable persons

The term 'person' includes individuals, partnerships (which are treated as single entities, ignoring the individual partners), **companies, clubs, associations and charities. If a person is in business making taxable supplies, then the value of these supplies is called the taxable turnover. If a person's taxable turnover exceeds certain limits then he is a taxable person and should be registered for VAT.**

3 Registration

FAST FORWARD

A trader becomes liable to register for VAT if the value of taxable supplies in any period up to 12 months exceeds £79,000 or if there are reasonable grounds for believing that the value of the taxable supplies will exceed £79,000 in the next 30 days. A trader may also register voluntarily.

3.1 Compulsory registration

At the end of every month a trader must calculate his cumulative turnover of taxable supplies to date. However this cumulative period does not extend beyond the previous 12 months. **The trader becomes liable to register for VAT if the value of his cumulative taxable supplies** (excluding VAT) **exceeds £79,000.** The person is required to notify HMRC within 30 days of the end of the month in which the £79,000 limit is exceeded. HMRC will then register the person with effect from the end of the month following the month in which the £79,000 was exceeded, or from an earlier date if they and the trader agree.

Registration under this rule is not required if HMRC are satisfied that the value of the trader's taxable supplies (excluding VAT) in the year then starting will not exceed £77,000.

A person is also liable to register at any time if there are reasonable grounds for believing that his taxable supplies (excluding VAT) in the following 30 days will exceed £79,000. Only taxable turnover of that 30 day period is considered **not** cumulative turnover. HMRC must be notified by the end of the 30 day period and registration will be with effect from the beginning of that period.

When determining the value of a person's taxable supplies for the purposes of registration, supplies of goods and services that are *capital assets* of the business are to be disregarded, except for non zero-rated taxable supplies of interests in land.

If a business makes taxable supplies in the UK but has no establishment here, it has to register for VAT, whatever the value of its taxable supplies ie even if this is below the VAT registration threshold.

Exam focus point

Unless factors in the question indicate otherwise, assume the business does have an establishment in the UK when determining whether to register for VAT.

Question

VAT registration

Fred started to trade in cutlery on 1 January 2013. Sales (excluding VAT) were £7,500 a month for the first nine months and £7,900 a month thereafter. From what date should Fred be registered for VAT?

Answer

	£	
Sales to 31 October 2013	75,400	
Sales to 30 November 2013	83,300	(exceeds £79,000)

Fred must notify his liability to register by 30 December 2013 (not 31 December) and will be registered from 1 January 2014 or from an agreed earlier date.

When a person is liable to register in respect of a past period, it is his responsibility to pay VAT. If he is unable to collect it from those to whom he made taxable supplies, the VAT burden will fall on him. A person must start keeping VAT records and charging VAT to customers as soon as it is known that he is required to register. However, VAT should not be shown separately on any invoices until the registration number is known. The invoice should show the VAT inclusive price and customers should be informed that VAT invoices will be forwarded once the registration number is known. Formal VAT invoices should then be sent to such customers within 30 days of receiving the registration number.

Notification of liability to register must be made on form VAT 1. This can be downloaded from the HMRC website, can be requested by telephone, or an application to register can be made online through the website. Simply writing to, or telephoning, a local VAT office is not enough. On registration the VAT office will provide the trader with a certificate of registration. This shows the VAT registration number, the date of registration, the end of the first VAT period and the length of later VAT periods.

If a trader makes a supply before becoming liable to register, but gets paid after registration, VAT is not due on that supply.

3.2 Voluntary registration

A person may decide to become registered even though his taxable turnover falls below the registration limit. Unless a person is registered he cannot recover the input tax he pays on purchases.

Voluntary registration is advantageous where a person wishes to recover input tax on purchases. For example, consider a trader who has one input during the year which cost £1,000 plus £200 VAT; he works on the input which becomes his sole output for the year and he decides to make a profit of £1,000.

(a) If he is not registered he will charge £2,200 and his customer will obtain no relief for any VAT.

(b) If he is registered he will charge £2,000 plus VAT of £400. His customer will have input tax of £400 which he will be able to recover if he, too, is registered.

If the customer is a non-taxable person he will prefer (a) as the cost to him is £2,200. If he is taxable he will prefer (b) as the net cost is £2,000. Thus, a decision whether or not to register voluntarily may depend upon the status of customers. It may also depend on the status of the outputs and the image of his business the trader wishes to project (registration may give the impression of a substantial business). The administrative burden of registration should also be considered.

3.3 Intending trader registration

Providing that a trader satisfies HMRC that he is carrying on a business, and intends to make taxable supplies, he is entitled to be registered if he chooses. But, once registered, he is obliged to notify HMRC within 30 days if he no longer intends to make taxable supplies.

3.4 Exemption from registration

If a person makes only zero-rated supplies, he may request exemption from registration. The trader is obliged to notify HMRC of any material change in the nature of his supplies.

HMRC may also allow exemption from registration if only a small proportion of supplies are standard-rated, provided that the trader would normally receive repayments of VAT if registered.

3.5 Group registration

Companies under common control may apply for group registration. The effects and advantages of group registration are as follows.

- Each VAT group must appoint a representative member which must **account for the group's output tax and input tax, thus simplifying VAT accounting** and allowing payments and repayments of VAT to be netted off. However, all members of the group are jointly and severally liable for any VAT due from the representative member.
- **Any supply of goods or services by a member of the group to another member of the group is, in general, disregarded for VAT purposes,** reducing the VAT accounting required.
- Any other supply of goods or services by or to a group member is in general treated as a supply by or to the representative member.
- Any VAT payable on the import of goods by a group member is payable by the representative member.

Two or more companies are eligible to be treated as members of a group provided each of them is either established in the UK or has a fixed establishment in the UK, and:

- **One of them controls each of the others**, or
- **One person** (which could be an individual or a holding company) **controls all of them**, or
- **Two or more persons carrying on a business in partnership control all of them.**

Anti-avoidance rules prevent a company from belonging to a VAT group where it would otherwise be eligible but it is in fact run for the benefit of an external third party.

An application to create, terminate, add to or remove a company from a VAT group may be made at any time. Applications may be refused when it appears to HMRC to be necessary to do so for the protection of the revenue. However, if a company is no longer eligible to belong to a VAT group because the common control test is failed, the company must leave the VAT group even if revenue might not be lost.

A group registration, or any change to it, will take effect from the date the application is received by HMRC although applications may have an earlier or later effect. Therefore it is possible to apply in advance for group changes and it is also possible to apply for changes having a retrospective effect. However, HMRC have 90 days to refuse an application.

Individual companies which are within a group for company law purposes may still register separately and stay outside the VAT group. This may be done to ensure that a company making exempt supplies does not restrict the input tax recovery of the group as a whole (see the partial exemption rules in the next chapter).

It is not possible for a company to be in two VAT groups at the same time.

3.6 Divisional registration

A company which is divided into several units which each prepare accounts can apply for divisional registration. The only advantage of divisional registration is administrative convenience; the separate divisions do not become separate taxable persons and the company is itself still liable for the VAT. However, if divisions account for VAT separately it may make it more likely that VAT returns will be made on time, because data for the divisions do not have to be consolidated before returns are completed.

Broadly, the conditions for divisional registration are as follows.

(a) HMRC must be satisfied that there would be real difficulties in submitting a single VAT return by the due date.

(b) Each division must be registered even where that division's turnover is beneath the registration limits.

(c) The divisions must be independent, self-accounting units, carrying on different activities or operating in separate locations.

(d) Input tax attributable or apportioned to exempt supplies (see the partial exemption rules in the next chapter) for the company as a whole must be so low that it can all be recovered (apart from VAT which can never be recovered because of the type of expenditure).

(e) Each division must make VAT returns for the same tax periods.

(f) Tax invoices must not be issued for supplies between the divisions of the same company as they are not supplies for VAT purposes.

3.7 Deregistration

3.7.1 Voluntary deregistration

A person is eligible for voluntary deregistration if HMRC are satisfied that the value of his taxable supplies (net of VAT and excluding supplies of capital assets) **in the following one year period will not exceed £77,000.** However, voluntary deregistration will not be allowed if the reason for the expected fall in value of taxable supplies is the cessation of taxable supplies or the suspension of taxable supplies for a period of 30 days or more in that following year.

HMRC will cancel a person's registration from the date the request is made or from an agreed later date.

3.7.2 Compulsory deregistration

Traders may be compulsorily deregistered. Failure to notify a requirement to deregister within 30 days may lead to a penalty. Compulsory deregistration may also lead to HMRC reclaiming input tax which has been wrongly recovered by the trader since the date on which he should have deregistered.

Other points to note are:

- If HMRC are misled into granting registration then the registration is treated as void from the start.
- A person may be compulsorily deregistered if HMRC are satisfied that he is no longer making nor intending to make taxable supplies.
- Changes in legal status also require cancellation of registration. For example:
  - A sole trader becoming a partnership
  - A partnership reverting to a sole trader
  - A business being incorporated
  - A company being replaced by an unincorporated business

3.7.3 The consequences of deregistration

On deregistration, VAT is chargeable on all stocks and capital assets in a business on which input tax was claimed, since the registered trader is in effect making a taxable supply to himself as a newly unregistered trader. If the VAT chargeable does not exceed £1,000, it need not be paid.

This special VAT charge does not apply if the business (or a separately viable part of it) **is sold as a going concern to another taxable person** (or a person who immediately becomes a taxable person as a result of the transfer). **Such transfers are outside the scope of VAT** (except for certain buildings being transferred which are 'new' or opted buildings and the transferee does not make an election to waive exemption – refer to the section on land in the next chapter).

If the original owner ceases to be taxable, the new owner of the business may also take over the existing VAT number. If he does so, he takes over the rights and liabilities of the transferor as at the date of transfer.

3.8 Pre-registration input tax

VAT incurred before registration can be treated as input tax and recovered from HMRC subject to certain conditions.

If the claim is for input tax suffered on goods purchased prior to registration then the following conditions must be satisfied.

(a) The goods were acquired for the purpose of the business which either was carried on or was to be carried on by him at the time of supply.

(b) The goods have not been supplied onwards or consumed before the date of registration (although they may have been used to make other goods which are still held).

(c) The VAT must have been incurred in the four years prior to the effective date of registration.

If the claim is for input tax suffered on the supply of services prior to registration then the following conditions must be satisfied.

(a) The services were supplied for the purposes of a business which either was carried on or was to be carried on by him at the time of supply.

(b) The services were supplied within the six months prior to the date of registration.

Input tax attributable to supplies made before registration is not deductible even if the input tax concerned is treated as having been incurred after registration.

3.9 Disaggregation

A person's registration covers all his business activities together. **The turnover of all business activities carried on by a 'person' must be aggregated to find taxable turnover.** However, if the same individual both carries on trade A alone and is a member of a partnership carrying on trade B, the turnover of the two trades will not normally be aggregated: the individual will have his taxable turnover in respect of trade A only, and the partnership will have its taxable turnover in respect of trade B only.

For example, a brother and sister might operate a pub with catering and bed and breakfast facilities. The catering could be operated by the brother, the pub could be operated by a partnership of the two people and the bed and breakfast business could be operated by the sister. This could avoid the need to register and account for output tax, if the turnover of each business was below the threshold for registration.

There are anti-avoidance provisions to prevent VAT benefits from the operation of one business through two or more entities. These provisions enable HMRC to direct that any connected businesses which have avoided VAT by artificially separating should be treated as one, whatever the reason for the separation. When deciding whether businesses are artificially separated, HMRC consider the extent to which those persons are bound by financial, economic or organisational links.

In the case of an individual carrying on trade A alone and trade B in partnership, to determine if the individual is essentially carrying on trade B alone, HMRC may consider whether there is:

- A proper written partnership agreement
- Evidence of the parties' intentions
- Actual sharing of profits (not just income or expenses)
- Notification of customers, suppliers and other authorities (eg on stationery)
- Authority of partners to bind the firm
- Ownership of common assets

They may also consider how the business is treated for direct tax purposes.

If they consider the partnership to be artificial, the activities of the partnership will be treated as carried on in conjunction with the sole trade.

4 Accounting for VAT

4.1 VAT periods

FAST FORWARD

VAT is accounted for on regular returns. Extensive records must be kept.

The VAT period (also known as the tax period) is the period covered by a VAT return. It is usually three calendar months. The return shows the total input and output tax for the tax period.

HMRC allocate VAT periods according to the class of trade carried on (ending in June, September, December and March; July, October, January and April; or August, November, February and May), to spread the flow of VAT returns evenly over the year. When applying for registration a trader can ask for VAT periods which fit in with his own accounting year. It is also possible to have VAT periods to cover accounting systems not based on calendar months.

A registered person whose input tax will regularly exceed his output tax can elect for a one month VAT period, but will have to balance the inconvenience of making 12 returns a year against the advantage of obtaining more rapid repayments of VAT.

Certain small businesses may submit an annual VAT return (see later in this Text).

4.2 The VAT return

The regular VAT return to HMRC is made on form VAT 100. The boxes on a VAT return which a trader must fill in are as follows.

(a) Box 1: the VAT due on sales and other outputs

(b) Box 2: the VAT due on acquisitions from other EU member states

(c) Box 3: the total of boxes 1 and 2

(d) Box 4: the VAT reclaimed on purchases and other inputs

(e) Box 5: the net VAT to be paid or reclaimed: the difference between boxes 3 and 4

(f) Box 6: the total value (before cash discounts) of sales and all other outputs, excluding VAT but including the total in box 8

(g) Box 7: the total value (before cash discounts) of purchases and all other inputs, excluding VAT but including the total in box 9

(h) Box 8: the total value of all sales and related services to other EU member states

(i) Box 9: the total value of all purchases and related services from other EU member states

Input and output tax figures must be supported by the original or copy tax invoices, and records must be maintained for six years.

4.3 Electronic filing

Nearly all VAT registered businesses must file their VAT returns online and make payments electronically.

The time limit for submission and payment is one month plus seven days after the end of the VAT period. For example, a business which has a VAT quarter ending 31 March 2014 must file its VAT return and pay the VAT due by 7 May 2014.

4.4 Substantial traders

If the total VAT liability over 12 months to the end of a VAT period exceeds £2,300,000, the trader must make payments on account of each quarter's VAT liability during the quarter.

Payments are due one month before the end of the quarter, at the end of the month which is the final month of the quarter, and one month after the end of the quarter. Payments must be made electronically. There is no additional seven days, after the end of the month, for payment.

The amount of each payment on account is 1/24 of the total annual VAT liability. The obligation to pay on account starts with the first VAT period starting *after* 31 March.

The default surcharge (see below) applies to late payments.

A trader may elect to pay their actual VAT liability monthly. For example, the actual liability for January would be due at the end of February. The trader can continue to submit quarterly returns so long as HMRC is satisfied the trader is paying sufficient monthly amounts.

Question — **Payments on account**

Large Ltd is liable to make payments on account calculated at £250,000 each for the quarter ended 31 December 2013.

What payments/repayment are due if Large Ltd's VAT liability for the quarter is calculated as:

(a) £680,000?
(b) £480,000?

Answer

(a)	30 November 2013	– payment of £250,000
	31 December 2013	– payment of £250,000
	31 January 2014	– payment of £180,000 with submission of VAT return for quarter
(b)	30 November 2013	– payment of £250,000
	31 December 2013	– payment of £250,000
	31 January 2014	– on submission of return HMRC will repay £20,000

If a trader's total annual liability increases to 120% or more of the amount used to calculate the payments on account, then the new higher annual liability is used to calculate new payments on account. The increase applies from the end of the 12 months with the new higher annual liability.

Once a trader is in the scheme, the payments on account are also recomputed annually. If the trader's annual liability falls below £1,800,000, the trader can apply to stop making payments on account.

For the purposes of calculating the payments on account (but not for the purposes of the £2,300,000 limit for entry into the scheme), a trader's VAT due on imports from outside the EU is ignored.

4.5 Refunds of VAT

There is a four year time limit on the right to reclaim overpaid VAT. This time limit does not apply to input tax which a business could not have reclaimed earlier because the supplier only recently invoiced the VAT, even though it related to a purchase made some time ago. Nor does it apply to overpaid VAT penalties.

If a taxpayer has overpaid VAT and has overclaimed input tax by reason of the same mistake, HMRC can set off any tax, penalty, interest or surcharge due to them against any repayment due to the taxpayer and repay only the net amount. In such cases the normal four year time limit for recovering VAT, penalties, interest, etc by assessment does not apply.

HMRC can refuse to make any repayment which would unjustly enrich the claimant. They can also refuse a repayment of VAT where all or part of the tax has, for practical purposes, been borne by a person other than the taxpayer (eg by a customer of the taxpayer) except to the extent that the taxpayer can show loss or damage to any of his businesses as a result of mistaken assumptions about VAT.

4.6 Records

Every VAT registered trader must keep records for six years, although HMRC may sometimes grant permission for their earlier destruction. They may be kept on paper, on microfilm or microfiche or on computer. However, there must be adequate facilities for HMRC to inspect records.

All records must be kept up to date and in a way which allows:

- The calculation of VAT due
- Officers of HMRC to check the figures on VAT returns

The following records are needed.

- Copies of VAT invoices, credit notes and debit notes issued
- A summary of supplies made
- VAT invoices, credit notes and debit notes received
- A summary of supplies received
- Records of goods received from and sent to other EU member states
- Documents relating to imports from and exports to countries outside the EU
- A VAT account
- Order and delivery notes, correspondence, appointment books, job books, purchases and sales books, cash books, account books, records of takings (such as till rolls), bank paying-in slips, bank statements and annual accounts
- Records of zero-rated and exempt supplies, gifts or loans of goods, taxable self-supplies and any goods taken for non-business use

5 The valuation of supplies

FAST FORWARD

VAT is charged on the VAT-exclusive price. Where a discount is offered for prompt payment, VAT is chargeable on the net amount even if the discount is not taken up.

One of the competencies you require to fulfil performance objective 19 of the PER is the ability to evaluate and compute taxes payable. You can apply the knowledge you obtain from this section of the text to help to demonstrate this competence.

5.1 General principles

The value of a supply is the VAT-exclusive price on which VAT is charged. The consideration for a supply is the amount paid in money or money's worth. Thus with a standard rate of 20%:

Value + VAT = consideration
£100 + £20 = £120

and the VAT fraction is

$$\frac{\text{rate of tax}}{100+\text{rate of tax}} = \frac{20}{100+20} = \frac{1}{6}$$

Provided the consideration for a bargain made at arm's length is paid in money, the value for VAT purposes is the VAT-exclusive price charged by the trader. If it is paid in something other than money, as in a barter of some goods or services for others, it must be valued and VAT will be due on the value.

If the price of goods is effectively reduced with money off coupons, the value of the supply is the amount actually received by the taxpayer.

5.2 Mixed supplies and composite supplies

Different goods and services are sometimes invoiced together at an inclusive price (a *mixed supply*). Some items may be chargeable at the standard rate and some at the zero-rate. **The supplier must account for VAT separately on the standard rated and zero rated elements by splitting the total amount payable in a fair proportion between the different elements and charging VAT on each at the appropriate rate.** There is no single way of doing this: one method is to split the amount according to the cost to the supplier of each element, and another is to use the open market value of each element. Mixed supplies are also known as 'multiple supplies'.

If a supply cannot be split into components, there is a *composite supply*, to which one VAT rate must be applied. The rate depends on the nature of the supply as a whole. Composite supplies are also known as 'compound supplies'.

A supply of air transport including an in-flight meal has been held to be a single, composite supply of transport (zero-rated) rather than a supply of transport (zero-rated) and a supply of a meal (standard-rated). Contrast this with catering included in the price of leisure travel – there are two separate supplies: standard-rated catering and zero-rated passenger transport.

Broadly, a composite supply occurs when one element of the supply is merely incidental to the main element. A mixed supply occurs where different elements of the supply are the subject of separate negotiation and customer choice giving rise to identifiable obligations on the supplier.

5.3 Discounts

Where a discount is offered for prompt payment, VAT is chargeable on the net amount, regardless of whether the discount is taken up (except that for imports from outside the EU, the discount is ignored unless it is taken up). Supplies of retailer vouchers made on contingent discount terms (for example depending on the level of purchases) must be invoiced with VAT based on the full amount, an adjustment being made when the discount is earned. When goods are sold to staff at a discount, VAT is only due on the discounted price.

5.4 Miscellaneous

For goods supplied under a hire purchase agreement VAT is chargeable on the cash selling price at the start of the contract.

If a trader charges different prices to customers paying with credit cards and those paying by other means, the VAT due in respect of each standard-rated sale is the full amount paid by the customer × the VAT fraction.

When goods are permanently taken from a business for non-business purposes VAT must be accounted for on their market value. Where business goods are put to a private or non-business use, the value of the resulting supply of services is the cost to the taxable person of providing the services. If services bought for business purposes are used for non-business purposes (without charge), then VAT must be accounted for on their cost, but the VAT to be accounted for is not allowed to exceed the input tax deductible on the purchase of the services.

6 Administration

FAST FORWARD

VAT is administered by HMRC and the Tax Tribunal hears appeals.

6.1 Introduction

The administration of VAT is dealt with by HM Revenue and Customs (HMRC).

6.2 Local offices

Local offices are responsible for the local administration of VAT and for providing advice to registered persons whose principal place of business is in their area. They are controlled by regional collectors.

From time to time a registered person will be visited by HMRC staff from a local office to ensure that the law is understood and is being applied properly. If a trader disagrees with any decision as to the application of VAT given by HMRC he can ask his local office to reconsider the decision. It is not necessary to appeal formally while a case is being reviewed in this way. Where an appeal can be settled by agreement, a written settlement has the same force as a decision decided through the normal appeals process (see below). A trader can ask for a reconsideration even if he has already appealed to a VAT Tribunal.

HMRC may issue assessments of VAT due to the best of their judgement if they believe that a trader has failed to make returns or if they believe those returns to be incorrect or incomplete. The time limit for making assessments is normally four years after the end of a VAT period, but this is extended to 20 years in the case of fraud, dishonest conduct, certain registration irregularities and the unauthorised issue of VAT invoices.

HMRC sometimes write to traders, setting out their calculations, before issuing assessments. The traders can then query the calculations.

6.3 Appeals

A trader may appeal to the Tax Tribunal in the same way as an appeal may be made for income tax and corporation tax (see earlier in this Text). VAT returns and payments shown thereon must have been made before an appeal can be heard.

The Tribunal can waive the requirement to pay all VAT shown on returns before an appeal is heard in cases of hardship. It cannot allow an appeal against a purely administrative matter such as HMRC's refusal to apply an extra statutory concession.

There may be a dispute over the deductibility of input tax which hinges on the purposes for which goods or services were used, or on whether they were used to make taxable supplies. The trader must show that HMRC acted unreasonably in refusing a deduction, if the goods or services are luxuries, amusements or entertainment.

6.4 Tax avoidance and evasion

Significant resources are deployed to tackle fraud, tax evasion and avoidance.

Avoidance is also countered by the requirement for traders to disclose to HMRC any use of a notifiable VAT avoidance scheme (see later in this Text).

7 Penalties

FAST FORWARD

A default occurs when a trader either submits his VAT return late, or submits the return on time but pays the VAT late. A default surcharge is applied if there is a default involving late payment during a default surcharge period.

7.1 The default surcharge

A default occurs when a trader either submits his VAT return late, or submits the return on time but pays the VAT late. It also occurs when a payment on account from a substantial trader is late. **If a trader defaults, HMRC will serve a surcharge liability notice on the trader. The notice specifies a surcharge period running from the date of the notice to the anniversary of the end of the period for which the trader is in default.**

If a further default occurs in respect of a return period ending during the specified surcharge period, the original surcharge period will be extended to the anniversary of the end of the period to which the new default relates. In addition, if the default involves the late payment of VAT (as opposed to simply a late return) **a surcharge is levied.**

The surcharge depends on the number of defaults involving late payment of VAT which have occurred in respect of periods ending in the surcharge period, as follows.

Default involving late payment of VAT in the surcharge period	Surcharge as a percentage of the VAT outstanding at the due date
First	2%
Second	5%
Third	10%
Fourth or more	15%

Surcharges at the 2% and 5% rates are not normally demanded unless the amount due would be at least £400 but for surcharges calculated using the 10% or 15% rates there is a minimum amount of £30 payable.

If a substantial trader is late with more than one payment (on account or final) for a return period, this only counts as one default. The total VAT paid late is the total of late payments on account plus the late final payment.

Question — **Default surcharge**

Peter Popper has an annual turnover of around £300,000. His VAT return for the quarter to 31.12.13 is late. He then submits returns for the quarters to 30.9.14 and 31.3.15 late as well as making late payment of the tax due of £12,000 and £500 respectively.

Peter's VAT return to 31.3.16 is also late and the VAT due of £1,100 is also paid late. All other VAT returns and VAT payments are made on time. Outline Peter Popper's exposure to default surcharge.

Answer

A surcharge liability notice will be issued after the late filing on the 31.12.13 return outlining a surcharge period extending to 31.12.14.

The late 30.9.14 return is in the surcharge period so the period is extended to 30.9.15. The late VAT payment triggers a 2% penalty. 2% × £12,000 = £240. Since £240 is less than the £400 de minimis limit it is not collected by HMRC.

The late 31.3.15 return is in the surcharge period so the period is now extended to 31.3.16. The late payment triggers a 5% penalty. 5% × £500 = £25. Since £25 is less than the £400 de minimis limit it is not collected by HMRC.

The late 31.03.16 return is in the surcharge period. The period is extended to 31.03.17. The late payment triggers a 10% penalty. 10% × £1,100 = £110. This is collected by HMRC since the £400 de minimis does not apply to penalties calculated at the 10% (and 15%) rate.

Peter will have to submit all four quarterly VAT returns to 31.3.17 on time and pay the VAT on time to 'escape' the default surcharge regime.

A trader must submit one year's returns on time and pay the VAT shown on them on time in order to break out of the surcharge liability period and the escalation of surcharge percentages.

A default will be ignored for all default surcharge purposes if the trader can show that the return or payment was sent at such a time, and in such a manner, that it was reasonable to expect that HMRC would receive it by the due date. Posting the return and payment first class the day before the due date is generally accepted as meeting this requirement. A default will also be ignored if the trader can demonstrate a reasonable excuse for the late submission or payment.

The application of the default surcharge regime to small businesses is modified. A small business is one with a turnover below £150,000. When a small business is late submitting a VAT return or paying VAT **it will first receive a letter from HMRC offering help**. No penalty will be charged. If **a further default occurs within 12 months of the letter** then a surcharge liability notice is issued, and the surcharge system formally begins as described above. Subsequent defaults then lead to surcharges of 2%, 5%, 10% and 15% if the VAT payment is late as described above, with the surcharge period extended each time. Effectively a small business is allowed an extra chance to default (and receive a help letter first) before the usual default surcharge system begins.

7.2 Penalties for errors

FAST FORWARD

There is a common penalty regime for errors in tax returns, including VAT. Errors in a VAT return up to certain amounts may be corrected in the next return.

7.2.1 Common penalty regime

The common penalty regime for making errors in tax returns discussed earlier in this Text applies for value added tax.

7.2.2 Errors corrected in next return

Errors on previous VAT returns not exceeding the greater of:

- **£10,000** (net under-declaration minus over-declaration); or
- **1% × net VAT turnover for return period** (maximum £50,000);

may be **corrected in the next return**.

Other errors should be notified to HMRC on form VAT652 or by letter.

In both cases, a penalty for error may be imposed. Correction of an error on a later return is not, of itself, an unprompted disclosure of the error and fuller disclosure is required for the penalty to be reduced. Default interest (see below) on the unpaid VAT as a result of the error is only charged where the limit is exceeded for the error to be corrected on the next VAT return.

7.3 Interest on unpaid VAT

FAST FORWARD

> Default interest is charged on unpaid VAT if HMRC raise an assessment of VAT or the trader makes a voluntary payment before the assessment is raised. It runs from the date the VAT should have been paid to the actual date of payment but cannot run for more than three years before the assessment or voluntary payment.

Interest (not deductible in computing taxable profits) **is charged on VAT which is the subject of an assessment** (where returns were not made or were incorrect), **or which could have been the subject of an assessment but was paid before the assessment was raised. It runs from the reckonable date until the date of payment.** This interest is sometimes called 'default interest'.

The reckonable date is when the VAT should have been paid (one month from the end of the return period), or in the case of VAT repayments, seven days from the issue of the repayment order. However, where VAT is charged by an assessment, interest does not run from more than three years before the date of the assessment. Where the VAT was paid before an assessment was raised, interest does not run for more than three years before the date of payment.

In practice, interest is only charged when there would otherwise be a loss to the Exchequer. It is not, for example, charged when a company failed to charge VAT but if it had done so another company would have been able to recover the VAT.

7.4 Reasonable excuse

A penalty may not be due if the trader can show that there is reasonable excuse for the failure, or the penalty may be mitigated by HMRC or by the Tribunal. There is no definition of 'reasonable excuse'. However the legislation states that the following are not reasonable excuses:

- An insufficiency of funds to pay any VAT due
- Reliance upon a third party (such as an accountant) to perform the task in question

Many cases have considered **what constitutes a reasonable excuse** but decisions often conflict with one another. Each case depends on its own facts. Here are some examples:

(a) Whilst **'ignorance of basic VAT law'** is not an excuse, ignorance of more complex matters can constitute a reasonable excuse.

(b) There have been a number of cases where it has been accepted that **misunderstandings as to the facts** give rise to a reasonable excuse.

(c) Although the law expressly excludes an insufficiency of funds from providing a reasonable excuse, the Tribunal will, in exceptional circumstances, look behind the shortage of funds itself and examine the case of it – this is generally restricted to cases where an unexpected event (eg bank error) has led to the shortage of funds.

Exam focus point

> You are not required to know any of the other VAT penalties for your exam.

Chapter roundup

- VAT is charged on turnover at each stage in a production process, but in such a way that the burden is borne by the final consumer.
- VAT is charged on taxable supplies of goods and services made by a taxable person in his business.
- A trader becomes liable to register for VAT if the value of taxable supplies in any period up to 12 months exceeds £79,000 or if there are reasonable grounds for believing that the value of the taxable supplies will exceed £79,000 in the next 30 days. A trader may also register voluntarily.
- VAT is accounted for on regular returns. Extensive records must be kept.
- VAT is charged on the VAT-exclusive price. Where a discount is offered for prompt payment, VAT is chargeable on the net amount even if the discount is not taken up.
- VAT is administered by HMRC and the Tax Tribunal hears appeals.
- A default occurs when a trader either submits his VAT return late, or submits the return on time but pays the VAT late. A default surcharge is applied if there is a default involving late payment during a default surcharge period.
- There is a common penalty regime for errors in tax returns, including VAT. Errors in a VAT return up to certain amounts may be corrected in the next return.
- Default interest is charged on unpaid VAT if HMRC raise an assessment of VAT or the trader makes a voluntary payment before the assessment is raised. It runs from the date the VAT should have been paid to the actual date of payment but cannot run for more than three years before the assessment or voluntary payment.

Quick quiz

1. On what transactions will VAT be charged?
2. What is a taxable person?
3. When may a taxable person be exempt from registration?
4. How are transfers between group companies treated under a VAT registration?
5. When may a person choose to be deregistered?
6. What is the time limit in respect of claiming pre-registration input tax on goods?
7. What is a default?

Answers to quick quiz

1 VAT is charged on taxable supplies of goods and services made in the UK by a taxable person in the course or furtherance of any business carried on by him.

2 Any 'person' whose taxable turnover exceeds the registration limit, or a person with no UK establishment, making taxable supplies in the UK. The term 'person' includes individuals, partnerships, companies, clubs, associations and charities.

3 If a taxable person makes only zero-rated supplies he may request exemption from registration.

4 Any supplies between VAT group members are ignored for VAT purposes.

5 A person is eligible for voluntary deregistration if HMRC are satisfied that the value of his taxable supplies in the following year will not exceed £77,000.

6 The VAT must have been incurred in the four years prior to the effective date of registration.

7 A default occurs when a trader either submits his VAT return late or submits the return on time but pays the VAT late.

Now try the questions below from the Exam Question Bank

Number	Level	Marks	Time
Q30	Introductory	10	18 mins
Q31	Introductory	10	18 mins

Value added tax 2

Topic list	Syllabus reference
1 Zero-rated and exempt supplies	A6(b)G1
2 Land and buildings	A6(b)(iii)
3 The deduction of input tax	A6(b)G3
4 Partial exemption	A6(b)(iv)
5 Capital goods scheme	A6(b)(v)
6 Imports, exports, acquisitions and dispatches	A6(b)G3
7 Special schemes	A6(b)G4

Introduction

In this chapter we continue our VAT studies by looking at zero-rated and exempt supplies and we see how making exempt supplies can affect the deduction of input tax.

VAT needs to be applied to imports, so that people do not have a tax incentive to buy abroad, and VAT is taken off many exports in order to encourage sales abroad. We see how this is achieved for transactions both within and outside the European Community.

Finally, we look at special VAT schemes designed for particular types of smaller trader.

In the next chapter we will draw together all of our studies by looking at the impact of taxes and tax planning.

Study guide

		Intellectual level
6	**National insurance, value added tax and tax administration:**	
(b)	The contents of the Paper F6 study guide for value added tax (VAT) under headings:	2
•	G1 The scope of value added tax (VAT)	
•	G3 The computation of VAT liabilities	
•	G4 The effect of special schemes	
	The following additional material is also examinable:	
(iii)	Advise on the VAT implications of the supply of land and buildings in the UK	3
(iv)	Advise on the VAT implications of partial exemption	3
(v)	Advise on the application of the capital goods scheme	3

Exam guide

In the exam you may be required to advise on almost any aspect of VAT, such as imports and exports or the special schemes. A question may require you to consider the effect of following a particular course of action, for example commencing to make exempt supplies may lead to a greater than expected VAT cost as the partial exemption rules result in the disallowance of a proportion of input tax.

Knowledge brought forward from earlier studies

This chapter continues to revise your knowledge of the basic principles of VAT, including zero rated and exempt supplies, the deduction of input tax, overseas aspects and the special schemes for smaller traders. The examiner has identified essential underpinning knowledge from the F6 syllabus which is particularly important that you revise as part of your P6 studies. In this chapter, the relevant topics are:

		Intellectual level
G3	**The computation of VAT liabilities**	
(h)	Explain the treatment of imports, exports and trade within the European Union	1
G4	**The effect of special schemes**	
(a)	Describe the cash accounting scheme, and recognise when it will be advantageous to use the scheme.	2
(b)	Describe the annual accounting scheme, and recognise when it will be advantageous to use the scheme.	2
(c)	Describe the flat rate scheme, and recognise when it will be advantageous to use the scheme.	2

Land and buildings, partial exemption and the capital goods scheme are all new topics.

The main change in 2013/14 from 2012/13 in the material you have previously studied at F6 level is that, in some circumstances, the actual cost of private fuel may be used instead of the fuel scale charge.

1 Zero-rated and exempt supplies

Some supplies are taxable (either standard-rated, reduced-rated or zero-rated). Others are exempt.

One of the competencies you require to fulfil performance objective 19 of the PER is the ability to evaluate and compute taxes payable. You can apply the knowledge you obtain from this section of the text to help to demonstrate this competence.

1.1 Types of supply

Zero-rated supplies are taxable at 0%. A taxable supplier whose outputs are zero-rated but whose inputs are standard-rated will obtain repayments of the VAT paid on purchases.

A **person making exempt supplies is unable to recover VAT on inputs** (in exactly the same way as for a non-registered person). An exempt supplier has to shoulder the burden of VAT. He may increase his prices to pass on the charge, but he cannot issue a VAT invoice which would enable a taxable customer to obtain a credit for VAT, since no VAT is chargeable on his supplies.

1.2 Example: standard-rated, zero-rated and exempt supplies

Here are figures for three traders, the first with standard-rated outputs, the second with zero-rated outputs and the third with exempt outputs. All their inputs are standard-rated at 20%.

	Standard-rated	*Zero-rated*	*Exempt*
	£	£	£
Inputs	20,000	20,000	20,000
VAT	4,000	4,000	4,000
	24,000	24,000	24,000
Outputs	30,000	30,000	30,000
VAT	6,000	0	0
	36,000	30,000	30,000
Pay/(reclaim)	2,000	(4,000)	0
Net profit	10,000	10,000	6,000

VAT legislation lists zero-rated, reduced-rate and exempt supplies. There is no list of standard-rated supplies.

If a trader makes a supply you need to categorise that supply for VAT as follows:

Step 1 Consider if it is a zero-rated supply. If not:

Step 2 Consider if it is exempt. If not:

Step 3 Consider if it is reduced-rated supply. If not:

Step 4 The supply is standard-rated.

1.3 Zero-rated supplies

The following are some common items on the **zero-rated list**.

(a) Human and animal food

(b) Printed matter used for reading (eg books, newspapers)

(c) Construction work on new homes or the sale of the freehold, or a lease over 21 years (at least 20 years in Scotland), of new homes by builders

(d) Exports of goods to outside the EU

(e) Clothing and footwear for young children and certain protective clothing eg motor cyclists' crash helmets

1.4 Exempt supplies

The following are some common items on the **exempt** list.

(a) Sales of freeholds of buildings (other than commercial buildings within three years from completion) and leaseholds of land and buildings of any age including a surrender of a lease
(b) Financial services
(c) Insurance

1.5 Reduced rate of VAT

Certain supplies are charged at **5%. The supplies are still taxable supplies.**

The main supplies are:

(a) Supplies of fuel for domestic use, and
(b) Supplies of the services of installing energy saving materials to homes

1.6 Exceptions to the general rule

There are many exceptions to the general rule.

For example the zero-rated list states human food is zero-rated. However, the legislation then states that food supplied in the course of catering (eg restaurant meals, hot takeaways) is not zero-rated. Luxury items of food (eg crisps, peanuts, chocolate covered biscuits) are also not zero-rated.

In the exempt list we are told that financial services are exempt. However the legislation then goes on to state that credit management and processing services are not exempt. Investment advice is also not exempt.

Great care must be taken when categorising goods or services as zero-rated, exempt or standard-rated. It is not as straightforward as it may first appear.

1.7 Standard-rated supplies

There is no list of standard-rated supplies. If a supply is not zero-rated and is not exempt then it is treated as standard-rated. The standard rate of VAT is 20%.

2 Land and buildings

FAST FORWARD

Transactions in land may be zero rated, standard rated or exempt.

2.1 Transactions in land

Transactions in land may be zero rated, standard rated or exempt.

(a) **The construction of new dwellings or buildings to be used for residential or charitable purposes is zero-rated.**
(b) **The sale of the freehold of a 'new' commercial building is standard-rated. The definition of 'new' is less than three years old.** The construction of commercial buildings is also standard-rated.
(c) Other sales and most leases of land and buildings are exempt.

2.2 Option to tax

Owners may elect to treat sales and leases of land and *commercial* buildings as taxable instead of exempt. This is known as 'waiving the exemption' or the option to tax.

The owner must become registered for VAT (if he is not already so registered) in order to make the election. The election replaces an exempt supply with a standard rated one, usually to enable the recovery of input VAT.

A taxpayer may make a 'real estate election' (REE) instead of making separate elections for each property he owns. **If a taxpayer makes a REE, he will be treated as having made the election for each property he acquires after making the REE**, although he may revoke the option on a particular property under the 'cooling-off' provisions described below.

The election may be revoked:

(a) **During the 'cooling off' period**: within six months of the election taking effect, provided that no use (including own use) has been made of the land, no tax has been charged on a supply of the land as a result of the option, no TOGC has occurred and HMRC has been notified of the revocation on the appropriate form

(b) **Where no interest has been held in the property for over six years**

(c) **Where more than twenty years have elapsed since the election first had effect**, provided certain conditions are met or with the prior consent of HMRC

3 The deduction of input tax

FAST FORWARD

Not all input VAT is deductible, eg VAT on most motor cars.

3.1 Introduction

Input tax is deductible for supplies to a taxable person in the course of his business.

3.2 Capital items

There is no distinction between capital and revenue expenditure for VAT. So a manufacturer paying VAT on the purchase of plant to make taxable supplies will be able to obtain a credit for all the VAT immediately (see below for the capital goods scheme).

3.3 Non-deductible input tax

The following input tax is not deductible.

(a) **VAT on motor cars** not used wholly for business purposes. VAT on cars is never reclaimable unless the car is acquired new for resale or is acquired for use in or leasing to a taxi business, a self-drive car hire business or a driving school (see below for treatment of motor expenses). **If VAT is not recoverable on a car because it is not used wholly for business purposes, then VAT is not charged if the car is subsequently sold.**

(b) **VAT on business entertaining** where the cost of the entertaining is not a tax deductible trading expense unless the entertainment is of overseas customers in which case the input tax is deductible.

(c) **VAT on expenses incurred on domestic accommodation for directors or proprietors of a business.**

(d) **VAT on non-business items passed through the business accounts.** If goods are bought partly for business use the purchaser may:

    (i) Deduct all the input tax, and account for output tax in respect of the private use, or
    (ii) Deduct only the business proportion of the input tax.

3.4 Irrecoverable VAT

Where input tax on a purchase is not deductible that input **VAT is included in the cost for income tax, corporation tax, capital allowance or capital gains purposes.**

Deductible VAT is omitted from costs, so that only net amounts are included in accounts. Similarly, sales (and proceeds in chargeable gains computations) **are shown net of VAT**, because the VAT is paid over to HMRC.

3.5 Motoring expenses

3.5.1 Accessories and maintenance costs

Input VAT can be reclaimed if accessories for business use are fitted after the original purchase of a car and a separate invoice is raised. If a car is used for business purposes then any VAT charged on repair and maintenance costs can be treated as input tax.

3.5.2 Fuel

FAST FORWARD

If fuel is supplied for private purposes all input VAT incurred on the fuel is allowed and the business will normally account for output VAT using a set of scale charges.

If a business pays for fuel which is only used for business purposes, it can claim all the input tax paid on that fuel. However, many businesses will pay for fuel which is used for private motoring by employees.

If a business does provide fuel for private and business use to an employee but the employee reimburses the business the full cost of the private fuel, there is an actual taxable supply by the business valued at the amount received from that employee. The business can claim its input tax on all fuel, but then must account for output tax on the amount paid by the employee. HM Revenue and Customs will accept that the full cost of all private fuel has been reimbursed where a log is kept recording private miles and the employee pays a fuel-only mileage rate that covers the average fuel cost (on its website, HM Revenue and Customs publish a set of such rates for different sizes of engine).

If a business provides fuel to its employees for private use without charge or at a charge below the full cost, there is a deemed taxable supply. The business then has the following options for how to account for VAT on fuel:

(i) **Not to claim any input tax in respect of fuel** purchased by the business. **No output tax is charged.** In effect, the fuel is not brought into the VAT system at all.

(ii) **Claim input VAT only on the fuel purchased for business journeys.** This requires the business to keep detailed mileage records of business and private use. **No output tax is charged in respect of private use.** In effect, the private fuel is not brought into the VAT system.

(iii) **Claim input tax on all fuel purchased and charge output tax based either on the full cost of the private fuel supplied** (again, this requires detailed mileage records to be kept) **or the fuel scale charge which reflects the deemed output in respect of private use. The fuel scale charge is based on the CO_2 emissions of the car.**

Exam focus point

In the P6(UK) exam, questions on the treatment of private use fuel will normally involve the use of the fuel scale charge.

The above rules apply **even where employees pay for the fuel themselves and the business reimburses them**: as long as the business obtains VAT invoices for the fuel, it can treat the fuel as its own purchase/input.

Question — **Fuel scale charge**

Iain is an employee of ABC Ltd. He has the use of a car with CO_2 emissions of 176 g/km for one month and a car with CO_2 emissions of 208 g/km for two months during the quarter ended 31 August 2013.

ABC Ltd pays all the petrol costs in respect of both cars without requiring Iain to make any reimbursement in respect of private fuel. Total petrol costs for the quarter amount to £300 (including VAT). ABC Ltd wishes to use the fuel scale charge as detailed records of private mileage have not been kept.

What is the VAT effect of the above on ABC Ltd?

VAT scale rates (VAT inclusive) for 3 month periods

CO_2 emissions	£
175	421
205	523

Answer

Value added tax for the quarter:

	£
Car 1	
£421 × 1/3 =	140
Car 2	
£523 × 2/3 =	349
	489
Output tax:	
1/6 × £489	£81
Input tax	
1/6 × £300	£50

3.6 Relief for impairment losses (bad debts)

FAST FORWARD

Relief for VAT on impairment losses (bad debts) is available if the VAT has been accounted for, the debt is over six months old (measured from when the payment is due) and has been written off in the trader's accounts.

A trader may claim a refund of VAT on amounts unpaid by debtors if:

(a) He has accounted for VAT, and
(b) The debt is over six months old, and
(c) Has been written off in the creditor's accounts.

If the debtor later pays all (or part) of the amount owed, the corresponding amount of VAT repaid must be paid back to HMRC.

Impairment loss relief claims must be made within four years of the time the impairment loss became eligible for relief (in other words, within four years and six months from when the payment was due).

4 Partial exemption

FAST FORWARD

A trader making both taxable and exempt supplies may be unable to recover all of his input tax.

4.1 Introduction

A trader may only recover the VAT on supplies made to him if it is attributable to his taxable supplies. **Where a person makes a mixture of taxable and exempt supplies, he is partially exempt. In this case, not all his input tax may be recoverable because some of it is attributable to his exempt supplies.**

4.2 The standard method of attributing input tax

For a trader who is partially exempt, input tax must be apportioned between that relating to **taxable supplies** (and recoverable) **and** that relating to **exempt supplies** (exempt input tax). The standard method of attributing input tax is to:

Step 1 **Calculate how much of the input tax relates to making taxable supplies**: this input tax is deductible in full.

Step 2 **Calculate how much of the input tax relates to making exempt supplies**: this is exempt input tax.

Step 3 **Calculate how much of any residual (ie remaining) input tax is deductible using the percentage:**

Formula to learn

$$\frac{\text{Taxable turnover excluding VAT}}{\text{Total turnover excluding VAT}} \times 100\%, \text{ rounded up}$$

Where the residual input tax does not exceed £400,000, the figure is rounded up to the nearest whole percentage. Otherwise, the figure is rounded to two decimal places.

For each VAT return period, the trader usually works out the amount of input tax he can recover (subject to the de minimis tests – see further below). The trader can either use the previous year's recovery percentage or the percentage for the return period. However, the trader must use only one of these methods in a year ie either the previous year's recovery percentage for all return periods in the year or the actual percentages for each return period. Note that the same amount of input VAT will be recoverable for the year overall because the difference between the percentages used will be adjusted at the end of the year (see further below).

Question

Calculation of recoverable input tax (part 1)

In the three month VAT period to 30 June 2013, Mr A makes £105,000 of exempt supplies and £300,000 of taxable supplies. Most of the goods purchased are used for both types of supply which means that much of the input tax cannot be directly attributed to either type of supply. After directly attributing as much input tax as possible the following position arises.

	£
Attributed to taxable supplies	1,200
Attributed to exempt supplies	600
Unattributed VAT	8,200
	10,000

How much input tax can Mr A recover, assuming that Mr A uses the percentage for the return period?

Answer

The amount of unattributed VAT which is apportioned to the making of taxable supplies is

$$\frac{300{,}000}{405{,}000} = 74.07\% \text{ rounded up to } 75\% \times £8{,}200 = £6{,}150$$

Note. The percentage is rounded up since residual (unattributed) input tax does not exceed £400,000 per month.

Mr A can therefore recover £1,200 + £6,150 = £7,350 of his input tax.

The balance of input tax of £2,650 (£600 + £(8,200 – 6,150)) is exempt input tax.

An alternative method of attributing input tax ('special' method) may be agreed in writing with HMRC.

4.3 De minimis tests

All the input VAT is recoverable if one the amount of input VAT relating to exempt supplies is small ('de minimis') under one of the following tests:

Test 1

The **total input VAT incurred is no more than £625 per month on average** and the **value of exempt supplies is no more than 50% of all supplies.**

Test 2

The **total input VAT incurred less input VAT directly attributed to taxable supplies is no more than £625 per month on average** and the **value of exempt supplies is no more than 50% of the value of all supplies.**

Test 3

The **input VAT wholly attributable to exempt supplies plus the residual VAT attributed to exempt supplies (ie the total of exempt input tax) is no more than £625 per month on average** and **no more than 50% of its input tax.**

4.4 Annual test

The annual test gives a trader the option of applying the de minimis test once a year instead of every VAT return period.

To use the annual test, **the trader must satisfy the following conditions:**

(a) have been **de minimis in the previous partial exemption year**;

(b) **consistently apply the annual test throughout any given partial exemption year** (ie does not switch between the quarterly tests and the annual test in the year);

(c) have reasonable grounds for **not expecting to incur more than £1m input tax in its current partial exemption year.**

If these conditions are satisfied, the trader can opt to treat himself as de minimis in the current partial exemption year. The trader can therefore recover input tax in full in each VAT return period without needing to see if one of the de minimis tests are satisfied for each VAT return period meaning that there is provisional recovery of all input tax in the year.

At the end of the year, the trader must review his de minimis status using the de minimis tests applied to the year as a whole. If **one of the tests is failed**, the trader must carry out an **annual adjustment** as described below and which will result in a repayment of part of the input VAT previously recovered in full.

4.5 Test for each return period

If the trader does not use the annual test, he must apply the de minimis tests for every VAT return period.

Tests 1 and 2 are simple to apply because they do not require the trader to make a calculation of residual VAT.

Test 3 is more complicated as it requires the calculation of residual VAT, usually using the standard method explained in Section 4.2.

Question — **De minimis tests**

Sue makes the following supplies in the quarter ended 31 October 2013.

	£
Taxable supplies (excl. VAT)	28,000
Exempt supplies	6,000
	34,000

Sue analyses her input tax for the period as follows.

		£
Wholly attributable to:	taxable supplies	1,500
	exempt supplies	900
Non-attributable (overheads)		1,200
		3,600

How much input tax is available for credit on Sue's VAT return assuming that she uses the percentage for the return period, where relevant?

Answer

Test 1

Total input VAT is $\frac{3,600}{3}$ = £1,200 per calendar month, more than £625 per calendar month.

Proportion of exempt supplies $\frac{6,000}{34,000}$ = 17.6%

Test 1 failed as only one part of test satisfied.

Test 2

	£
Total input VAT for period	3,600
Less wholly attributable to taxable supplies	(1,500)
	2,100

Monthly average $\frac{2,100}{3}$ = £700 per calendar month, more than £625 per calendar month.

Proportion of exempt supplies $\frac{6,000}{34,000}$ = 17.6%

Test 2 failed as only one part of test satisfied.

Test 3

	£
Wholly attributable to taxable supplies	1,500
Partly attributable to taxable supplies	
$\frac{28,000}{28,000+6,000}$	
ie 82.35% rounded up to 83% × £1,200	996
	2,496
£(900 + (1,200 – 996)) = 1,104	
Exempt input tax is de minimis (W)	1,104
Input tax recoverable	3,600
ie all input tax is recoverable	

Working

Monthly average $\frac{1,104}{3}$ = £368 ie not more than £625

Proportion of total $\frac{1,104}{3,600}$ = 30.7% ie not more than 50%.

Both parts of Test 3 satisfied so Test 3 passed.

4.6 Annual adjustment

An annual adjustment is made with the de minimis tests applied to the year as a whole.

If **Tests 1 or 2 passed** for the year, **the trader can recover all of his input tax for the year and does not need to carry out a partial exemption calculation.**

If Tests 1 or 2 are failed, the trader will need to carry out a **full partial exemption calculation for the year to determine whether Test 3 is passed.** If it is, **the trader can recover all of his input tax for the year.**

The result for the year is compared with the total of results for the individual VAT periods and any difference is added to or deducted from the input tax either on the return for the last period in the year or on the return for the first period after the end of the year, at the option of the trader.

Question — **Calculation of recoverable input tax (part 2)**

Following on from the example in Section 4.2 Mr A has the following results in the remaining VAT quarters of his VAT year ended 31 March 2014.

	Input tax attributed to		
Quarter to	*Taxable supplies*	*Exempt supplies*	*Unattributed*
	£	£	£
30.9.13	1,500	1,000	5,000
31.12.13	2,000	500	1,800
31.3.14	1,900	850	7,000
	5,400	2,350	13,800

	Turnover	
Quarter to	*Taxable*	*Exempt*
	£	£
30.9.13	400,000	100,000
31.12.13	500,000	150,000
31.3.14	450,000	120,000
	1,350,000	370,000

It has already been ascertained that neither Test 1 nor Test 2 is satisfied for any of the four quarters nor for the year as a whole.

Calculate the annual adjustment required assuming that Mr A uses the percentage for the return period in each of the quarters and state the latest return it will be made on.

Answer

First we calculate the recoverable input tax in each VAT return.

	£	*Recovered* £
Return to 30.6.13		
See above Taxable	7,350	7,350
Exempt (more than £625 per month)	2,650	
	10,000	
Return to 30.9.13		
$\frac{400,000}{500,000}$ = 80% × £5,000 = Non-attributable	4,000	
Wholly taxable	1,500	
Taxable total	5,500	5,500
Exempt £(1,000 + 1,000) (more than £625 per month)	2,000	
	7,500	
c/f		12,850

	£	Recovered £
b/f		12,850
Return to 31.12.13		
$\frac{500,000}{650,000}$ = 76.92% rounded up to 77% × £1,800	1,386	
Non-attributable		
Wholly taxable	2,000	
Taxable total	3,386	
Exempt £(500 + 414)	914	
	4,300	4,300

The exempt input tax at £914 is less than £1,875 (£625 × 3 months) and 50% of total input tax (50% × £4,300 = £2,150) so is de minimis and recoverable under Test 3.

	£	Recovered £
Return to 31.3.14		
$\frac{450,000}{570,000}$ = 78.94% rounded up to 79% × £7,000	5,530	
Non-attributable		
Wholly taxable	1,900	
Taxable total	7,430	7,430
Exempt £(850 + 1,470) (more than £625 per month)	2,320	
	9,750	
Recovered over the VAT year		24,580

Now we do the same calculation again but using the results for the whole VAT year to 31.3.14.

	£	Recovered £
Annual adjustment		
$\frac{1,350,000+300,000}{1,720,000+405,000}$ = 77.64% rounded up to 78% × £(13,800 + 8,200) (note)	17,160	
Wholly taxable £(5,400 + 1,200)	6,600	
Taxable total	23,760	(23,760)
Exempt £(31,550 – 23,760) (more than £625 per month)	7,790	
	31,550	
VAT to repay to HMRC on VAT return (latest) to 30 June 2014 as annual adjustment		820

Note. We must include the quarter to June 2013's results.

5 Capital goods scheme

FAST FORWARD

The capital goods scheme (CGS) allows HMRC to ensure the VAT claimed on the purchase of certain capital items accurately reflects the taxable use to which they are put over a period of time.

The scheme mainly affects partially exempt businesses and enables the amount of VAT recovered to be adjusted for each year's use.

The CGS applies to:

(a) Computers, boats and aircraft costing £50,000 or more, which are dealt with over 5 VAT years, and
(b) Land and building costing £250,000 or more, which are dealt with over 10 VAT years.

In the VAT year the asset is acquired the input recovery is initially based on use for the quarter of purchase, and is then subject to the annual adjustment as described above.

For each subsequent VAT year over the recovery period of 5 or 10 years an adjustment is made to the VAT recovery.

ormula to earn

The adjustment is equal to the difference in percentage use between the first VAT year and the VAT year under review × 1/5 (for computers, boats and aircraft) or 1/10 (for land and buildings) × the original input tax on them

The adjustment is made in the second VAT return following the end of the VAT year.

If the asset is sold before the end of the recovery period, two adjustments are needed:

(a) The normal adjustment for the VAT year of sale as if the proportion of use for the period from the start of the year until the date of sale had applied for the whole VAT year, and

(b) An additional adjustment for each remaining VAT year of recovery calculated assuming 100% use for taxable supplies.

Question

Capital goods scheme

Z Ltd purchased a computer for £100,000 + 20% VAT on 1 July 2013. It used it 58% for taxable use in the quarter of purchase and 60% for taxable purposes in the year to 31 December 2013.

The taxable use in the year to 31 December 2014 was 50%. The computer was sold on 10 May 2015. The taxable use in the period 1 January 2015 to 10 May 2015 was 50%.

Calculate the initial input recovery and adjustments required for all other years. Assume that the standard rate of VAT is 20% throughout.

Answer

For the first VAT year to 31 December 2013 the recovery (after the annual partial exemption adjustment) is £100,000 × 20% = £20,000 × 60% = £12,000.

For the second VAT year to 31 December 2014 the adjustment is £20,000 × 10% (ie 60%-50%) × 1/5 = £400, payable to HMRC.

For the third VAT year to 31 December 2015 there are two adjustments:

(a) £20,000 × 10% × 1/5 = £400, payable to HMRC

(b) £20,000 × 40% (ie 100%-60%) × 2/5 = £3,200

The net adjustment for the third VAT year to 31 December 2015 is £400 - £3,200 = £2,800 recoverable from HMRC.

6 Imports, exports, acquisitions and dispatches

Imports from outside the EU are subject to VAT and exports to outside the EU are zero-rated. Taxable acquisitions from other EU states are also subject to VAT and sales to registered traders in other EU states are zero-rated.

6.1 Introduction

The terms **import and export** refer to purchases and sales of goods with countries **outside the EU**.

The terms **acquisition and dispatch** refer to purchases and sales of goods with countries **in the EU**.

The EU comprises Austria, Belgium, Bulgaria, the Czech Republic, Cyprus, Denmark, Estonia, Finland, France, Germany, Greece, Hungary, the Republic of Ireland, Italy, Latvia, Lithuania, Luxembourg, Malta, the Netherlands, Poland, Portugal, Romania, Slovakia, Slovenia, Spain, Sweden and the UK.

Exam focus point

There are different rules for transactions between EU member states and for transactions with non-EU countries.

6.2 Place of supply

The place of supply of goods and services is important because it determines how the supply is treated for VAT. For example, if a supply is made in the UK, it is subject to the rules and rates of UK VAT.

If the supply is a **supply of goods**, it will be treated as **made in the UK if the goods are in the UK at the time they are supplied**. Similarly, a supply of goods which are not in the UK when they are supplied will not be treated as made in the UK and so will not be subject to UK output tax.

If the supply is a **supply of services**, the basic rule for services made to a **business** (B2B supplies) is that the **supply is made where the customer has established his business**.

The basic rule for **supplies of services to other consumers** (B2C supplies) **is that the supply is made where the supplier has established his business**. There are some exceptions to this rule. For example, certain services relating to land are treated as made where the land is located.

6.3 Trade in goods outside the European Union

6.3.1 Imports

An importer of goods from outside the EU:

(a) Must account for the output VAT at the point of entry into the UK
(b) Can claim the input VAT payable on his next VAT return

6.3.2 Exports

The export of goods outside the EU is zero rated.

The trader must provide evidence of the export such as copy invoices and consignment notes.

6.4 Trade in goods within the European Union

6.4.1 Purchases (acquisitions)

Goods acquired by a VAT registered person in the UK from another EU member state are liable to VAT in this country. Consequently, output tax has to be accounted for on the relevant VAT return.

The 'tax point' for such acquisitions is the earlier of:

- **The fifteenth day of the month following the month of acquisition, and**
- **The date of issue of an invoice.**

The transaction is entered on the relevant VAT return as an output *and* an input so, subject to the partial exemption provisions, the effect is neutral. Thus the trader is in the same position as he would have been if he had acquired the goods from a UK supplier.

If the goods acquired are zero-rated or exempt under UK VAT legislation there is no requirement to account for VAT at the standard rate.

6.4.2 Sales (dispatches)

Where goods are sold to a customer in another EU member state, the supply is zero-rated if the following conditions are satisfied:

- **The supply is made to a registered trader**
- **The supplier quotes his customer's VAT number on the invoice**
- **The supplier holds evidence that the goods were delivered to another member state**

If these conditions are not satisfied, the trader must charge VAT in the same way as for a supply to a customer within the same member state as the trader.

6.5 International services

FAST FORWARD

International services between VAT-registered businesses require the customer to account for both output and input tax under the reverse charge rules. Output tax on other international services is usually accounted for by the supplier in the usual way.

As we have seen, B2B services are treated as supplied in the place where the customer has established his business. Where the supply is treated as made in the UK under these rules, the UK business customer must apply the 'reverse charge'. This means that the UK business charges itself output tax which it recovers as input tax in the normal way. This means that the foreign supplier has no obligation to register for VAT in the UK or to charge UK VAT on such supplies. Instead, the customer is required to account for VAT.

If the customer is not registered for VAT, the purchase of the services counts as a deemed supply in measuring the registerable turnover for the customer. This might lead to the customer becoming liable to register for VAT.

If the business customer only makes taxable supplies, the overall effect of the reverse charge will normally be tax-neutral as the output tax and input tax will cancel each other out. However, if the business customer is partially exempt, not all of the input tax may be recoverable and so the reverse charge will lead to a net payment of output tax.

The tax point for a single supply to which the reverse charge applies is the earlier of:

- **The time the service is completed, and**
- **The time the service is paid for.**

If the supply is continuous, the tax point will be the end of each billing or payment period, Where the service is not subject to billing or payment periods, the tax point will be 31 December each year unless a payment has already been made, in which case the tax point will be the date of the payment.

For B2C services, the supply will be made by the supplier where he has established his business and the supplier will charge output tax in the normal way. No input tax is recoverable on B2C supplies since, by definition, the consumer is not a VAT-registered business.

7 Special schemes

FAST FORWARD

Special schemes include the cash accounting scheme, the annual accounting scheme and the flat rate scheme. These schemes make VAT accounting easier for certain types of trader usually with relatively low turnover.

One of the competencies you require to fulfil performance objective 20 of the PER is the ability to assist with tax planning. You can apply the knowledge you obtain from this section of the text to help to demonstrate this competence.

7.1 The cash accounting scheme

The cash accounting scheme enables businesses to account for VAT on the basis of cash paid and received. The date of payment or receipt determines the return in which the transaction is dealt with. This means that the cash accounting scheme gives automatic impairment loss relief (bad debt relief) because VAT is not due on a supply until payment has been received.

The scheme can only be used by a trader whose annual taxable turnover (exclusive of VAT) is not expected to exceed £1,350,000 over the following 12 months and whose returns and VAT payments are up to date.

If the value of taxable supplies exceeds £1,600,000 in the 12 months to the end of a VAT period a trader must leave the cash accounting scheme immediately.

Advantages of the scheme are:

- Automatic relief for impairment losses
- Cash flow

7.2 The annual accounting scheme

The annual accounting scheme is only available to traders who regularly pay VAT to HMRC, not to traders who normally receive repayments. It is available for traders **whose VAT exclusive taxable turnover is not expected to exceed £1,350,000 over the following 12 months.**

Traders file annual VAT returns and must make nine monthly payments on account equal to 90% of their previous year's VAT liability, with the first payment due at the end of the fourth month of the year. An annual VAT return must be submitted to HMRC along with any balancing payment due within two months of the end of the year. There is an option to pay three larger interim instalments. Late payment of instalments is not a default for the purposes of the surcharge liability notice system.

To use the scheme all returns must have been made up to date. Annual accounting is not available where VAT registration is in the name of a VAT group or a division.

If the expected value of a trader's taxable supplies exceeds £1,600,000 notice must be given to HMRC within 30 days and he may then be required to leave the scheme. If the £1,600,000 limit is actually exceeded, the trader must leave the scheme.

Advantages of annual accounting:

- Only one VAT return each year so fewer occasions to trigger a default surcharge
- Ability to manage cash flow more accurately
- Avoids need for quarterly calculations for partial exemption purposes and input tax recovery

Disadvantages of annual accounting:

- Need to monitor future taxable supplies to ensure turnover limit not exceeded
- Timing of payments have less correlation to turnover (and hence cash received) by business
- Payments based on previous year's turnover may not reflect current year turnover which may be a problem if the scale of activities has reduced

7.3 Flat rate scheme

The flat rate scheme enables businesses to calculate VAT due to HMRC by simply applying a flat rate percentage to their VAT inclusive turnover, including all zero-rated and exempt income. The percentage depends upon the trade sector into which a business falls. The percentage depends upon the trade sector into which a business falls. It ranges from 4% for retailing food, confectionery or newspapers) to 14.5% for accountancy and book-keeping. A 1% reduction off the flat rate % can be made by businesses in their first year of VAT registration.

Exam focus point

The flat rate percentage will be given to you in your examination.

Businesses using the scheme must issue VAT invoices to their VAT registered customers but they do not have to record all the details of the invoices issued or purchase invoices received to calculate the VAT due. Invoices issued will show VAT at the normal rate rather than the flat rate.

To join the flat rate scheme businesses must have a tax exclusive annual taxable turnover of up to £150,000. A business must leave the flat rat scheme if the total value of its tax inclusive supplies in the year (excluding sales of capital assets) is more than £230,000.

7.4 Example: flat rate scheme

An accountant undertakes work for individuals and for business clients. In a VAT year, the business client work amounts to £35,000 and the accountant will issue VAT invoices totalling £42,000 (£35,000 plus VAT at 20%). Turnover from work for individuals totals £18,000, including VAT. Total gross sales are therefore £60,000. The flat rate percentage for an accountancy businesses is 14.5%.

VAT due to HMRC will be 14.5% × £60,000 = £8,700. Under the normal VAT rules the output tax due would be:

	£
£35,000 × 20%	7,000
£18,000 × 1/6	3,000
	10,000

Whether the accountant is better off under the scheme depends on the amount of input tax incurred as this would be offset, under normal rules, from output tax due.

Chapter roundup

- Some supplies are taxable (either standard-rated, reduced-rated or zero-rated). Others are exempt.
- Transactions in land may be zero rated, standard rated or exempt.
- Not all input VAT is deductible, eg VAT on most motor cars.
- If fuel is supplied for private purposes all input VAT incurred on the fuel is allowed and the business will normally account for output VAT using a set of scale charges.
- Relief for VAT on impairment losses (bad debts) is available if the VAT has been accounted for, the debt is over six months old (measured from when the payment is due) and has been written off in the trader's accounts.
- A trader making both taxable and exempt supplies may be unable to recover all of his input tax.
- The capital goods scheme (CGS) allows HMRC to ensure the VAT claimed on the purchase of certain capital items accurately reflects the taxable use to which they are put over a period of time.
- Imports from outside the EU are subject to VAT and exports to outside the EU are zero-rated. Taxable acquisitions from other EU states are also subject to VAT and sales to registered traders in other EU states are zero-rated.
- International services between VAT-registered businesses require the customer to account for both output and input tax under the reverse charge rules. Output tax on other international services is usually accounted for by the supplier in the usual way.
- Special schemes include the cash accounting scheme, the annual accounting scheme and the flat rate scheme. These schemes make VAT accounting easier for certain types of trader usually with relatively low turnover.

Quick quiz

1 What input tax is never deductible?

2 What relief is available for bad debts?

3 What is partial exemption?

4 Are goods exported from the EU standard-rated or zero-rated?

5 Mr Higgins is registered for VAT in the UK. He only makes taxable supplies. Mr Higgins is supplied with services by a French business on 1 December 2013. The value of the supply is £50,000. What are the VAT consequences of the supply?

6 What are the turnover limits for the annual accounting scheme?

7 What is the optional flat rate scheme?

Answers to quick quiz

1 VAT on:

- Motor cars (where there is an element of private use)
- Business entertaining (UK customers)
- Expenses incurred on domestic accommodation for directors
- Non-business items passed through the accounts

2 Where a supplier has accounted for VAT on a supply and the customer fails to pay, then the supplier may, after 6 months, write it off in the accounts and claim a refund of the VAT.

3 Where a 'person' makes a mixture of taxable and exempt supplies he is partially exempt and cannot recover input tax incurred by the business in full.

4 In general, exports from the EU are zero-rated.

5 Mr Higgins will have to account for output tax of £50,000 × 20% = £10,000 on the supply and also £10,000 of input tax. The reverse charge is therefore tax neutral for him.

6 Turnover not exceeding £1,350,000 to join the scheme. Once turnover exceeds £1,600,000 must leave the scheme.

7 The optional flat rate scheme enables businesses to calculate VAT simply by applying a percentage to their tax-inclusive turnover ie the total turnover generated, including all zero-rated and exempt income. The percentage depends upon the trade sector into which a business falls.

Now try the question below from the Exam Question Bank

Number	Level	Marks	Time
Q32	Introductory	10	18 mins

PART H

Impact of taxes and tax planning

Impact of taxes and tax planning

Topic list	Syllabus reference
1 Impact of taxes	B1, B2(a), B4, B5, D1-6
2 Personal finance	B3(a)
3 Business finance	B3(b),(c),(d)
4 Tax planning	C1-4, C6
5 Ethics	B5, C5

Introduction

You have now completed your studies of the individual taxes covered in the syllabus so we will turn our attention to how to use your knowledge. First we consider how to answer questions about the impact of taxes on a given scenario.

Next, we look at the tax treatment of sources of finance and investment products for individuals. We also compare the tax implications of businesses raising equity and loan finance, and leasing an asset rather than buying it.

We then turn to tax planning, which is an integral part of any tax advice you give. We have dealt with various tax planning aspects as they have arisen earlier in this Text. In this chapter, we bring together topics by considering nine specific scenarios in personal and business tax.

Finally, we consider the ethical rules which should be applied to every situation that you are required to consider. Up to five marks on every paper will be given for your comments on ethical matters. It is therefore important that you identify ethical issues and comment as appropriate.

Study guide

		Intellectual level
B	**THE IMPACT OF RELEVANT TAXES ON VARIOUS SITUATIONS AND COURSES OF ACTION, INCLUDING THE INTERACTION OF TAXES**	
1	**Identify and advise on the taxes applicable to a given course of action and their impact.**	3
2	**Identify and understand that the alternative ways of achieving personal or business outcomes may lead to different tax consequences.**	3
(a)	Calculate the receipts from a transaction, net of tax and compare the results of alternative scenarios and advise on the most tax efficient course of action.	3
3	**Advise how taxation can affect the financial decisions made by businesses (corporate and unincorporated) and by individuals.**	
(a)	Understand and compare and contrast the tax treatment of the sources of finance and investment products available to individuals.	3
(b)	Understand and explain the tax implications of the effect of the raising of equity and loan finance.	3
(c)	Explain the tax differences between decisions to lease, use hire purchase or purchase outright.	3
(d)	Understand and explain the impact of taxation on the cash flows of a business.	3
4	**Assess the tax advantages and disadvantages of alternative courses of action.**	3
5	**Understand the statutory obligations imposed in a given situation, including any time limits for action and advise on the implications of non-compliance.**	3
C	**MINIMISE AND/OR DEFER TAX LIABILITIES BY THE USE OF STANDARD TAX PLANNING MEASURES**	
1	**Identify and advise on the types of investment and other expenditure that will result in a reduction in tax liabilities for an individual and/or a business.**	3
2	**Advise on legitimate tax planning measures, by which the tax liabilities arising from a particular situation or course of action can be mitigated.**	3
3	**Advise on the appropriateness of such investment, expenditure or measures given a particular taxpayer's circumstances or stated objectives.**	3
4	**Advise on the mitigation of tax in the manner recommended by reference to numerical analysis and/or reasoned argument.**	3
5	**Be aware of the ethical and professional issues arising from the giving of tax planning advice.**	3
6	**Be aware of and give advice on current issues in taxation.**	3

		Intellectual level
D	**COMMUNICATE WITH CLIENTS, HM REVENUE AND CUSTOMS AND OTHER PROFESSIONALS IN AN APPROPRIATE MANNER**	
1	**Communicate advice, recommendations and information in the required format:**	3
	For example the use of Reports, Letters, Memoranda and Meeting notes	
2	**Present written information, in language appropriate to the purpose of the communication and the intended recipient.**	3
3	**Communicate conclusions reached, together, where necessary with relevant supporting computations.**	3
4	**State and explain assumptions made or limitations in the analysis provided; together with any inadequacies in the information available and/or additional information required to provide a fuller analysis.**	3
5	**Identify and explain other, non-tax, factors that should be considered.**	3

Exam guide

A significant number of marks in the exam will be available for evaluation and advice. Before you start to write your answer, assess what is required. You may simply be asked to advise on the tax consequences of one course of action, or you may have to compare the tax consequences of two or more options. The options may be specified in the question, or you may be required to identify possible options. You may have to cover all taxes, or to restrict your answer to a single tax. Present your answer in the required format; if you are asked for notes do not write an essay and if you are asked to write a letter, do so.

There may be up to five marks awarded for your comments on ethical matters. You need to know the fundamental principles of the ACCA's code of conduct, and when presented with a scenario you should quickly review these to make sure that they are not compromised. If there is a threat then consider how serious it is and how you should respond.

One of the competencies you require to fulfil performance objective 20 of the PER is the ability to assist with tax planning. You can apply the knowledge you obtain from this chapter of the text to help to demonstrate this competence.

1 Impact of taxes

FAST FORWARD

Questions on impact of taxes require you to use your technical knowledge of taxation in relation to particular scenarios. Avoid writing about technical areas in general terms as opposed to in relation to the question's requirements.

1.1 Answering questions involving impact of taxes

In the P6 examination, most of the questions will require you to identify and advise on the taxes applicable to a given course of action and their impact. Here are some tips which will help you prepare for answering such exam questions.

1.1.1 Practise questions from past exams

Practise questions from past exams with the aim of adopting the style of the model answers. Questions 36 and 37 in the Questions Bank are examples of past exam questions which you should attempt when you have finished studying this chapter. **BPP's Practice and Revision Kit contains over 50 such questions** and should be the core of your revision.

Avoid looking at the model answers whilst attempting questions – the biggest problem most students face is knowing how to approach answering questions. You do not want to be attempting this for the first time in the exam! Remember that you are not required to make all the points shown in the model answer, so don't be discouraged if there are some that you miss when attempting a question. However, there will be a core of marks in each question which you should be aiming to obtain.

1.1.2 Address the requirement

Make sure you understand what you are required to do. In Section B questions, this means reading the requirement of the question. In Section A questions, you will usually need to look also at the more detailed instructions in one of the documents your are given (for example, an email or notes of a meeting) to find out exactly what is required. Look for key phrases in the question such as 'I need the following ....' or 'Please prepare the following for me...'.

Apply your knowledge to the facts by reference to the requirement. Marks are awarded for satisfying the requirements and not for other information even if it is technically correct. Avoid writing about technical areas in general terms as opposed to in relation to the requirements of the question.

The requirements of each question are carefully worded in order to provide you with guidance as regards the style and content of your answers. You should note the command words (calculate, explain etc), any matters which are *not* to be covered, and the precise issues you have been asked to address.

You should also note **any guidance given in the question or in any notes following the requirement** regarding the approach you should take when answering the question. For example, you may be asked to provide explanations 'briefly' or, on the other hand, 'in detail'. A brief explanation requires a succinct statement of the main points, a detailed explanation requires a wider consideration of the issues.

Pay attention to the number of marks available – this provides you with a clear indication of the amount of time you should spend on each question part. There is no point writing a page of explanation for a part which is allocated two or three marks.

Only provide explanations when you are asked to. For example, if you are asked to calculate, there is no need to explain what you are going to do before you do it; just get on with it.

1.1.3 Think before you start

Before you start writing, think about the issues and identify all of the points you intend to address and/or any strategy you intend to adopt to solve the problem set.

You should be methodical in your approach. Unless you are asked to consider only one or more specific taxes, you should get into the habit of **running through all the taxes**, even if to eliminate them from consideration. For P6, the taxes in the syllabus are:

(a) Income tax
(b) Capital gains tax
(c) Inheritance tax
(d) National insurance contributions
(e) Stamp duties
(f) Corporation tax
(g) Value added tax

If you are asked to compare the tax consequences of two or more options, you must consider the impact of *each* tax on *each* option in order to produce a complete picture.

1.1.4 Consider future consequences

Make sure that you consider the future consequences of your proposals, not just the immediate tax impact. In particular, remember that deferred gains crystallise on certain events; it may not be a good idea to claim gift relief if the donee will not be entitled to entrepreneurs' relief to reduce the tax on a subsequent sale, and paying tax now at a lower rate is usually better than delaying paying tax at a higher rate. Sometimes it is better to make a gift of a business asset as part of a will where a CGT uplift will be given – BPR will extinguish any IHT charge.

1.1.5 Present your answer appropriately

Read the question carefully to ascertain the type of answer that may be required. You may have to prepare a formal report, letter or memorandum, or you may have to write notes for a colleague. In other cases you may just be required to prepare explanations or calculations.

Where the answer is formal, **marks will be specifically awarded for the presentation of the material and the effectiveness with which the information is presented**. There will be four such professional marks available in question one of the exam. You should get used to setting out the points in your answer in a logical order, giving full explanations and yet still being concise. You may find using headings will help you organise your answer. It is often better to present any calculations as an appendix, unless they are extremely short. Look back to the question; if you are asked to draw conclusions or make recommendations have you done so?

It is important to know who the report, letter etc is being prepared for. If you are writing to a client they are unlikely to understand technical terms, and certainly will not know, for example, what 'early trade losses relief' is. If, on the other hand, you are writing a memorandum to a partner you can assume a certain degree of familiarity with the underlying concepts.

1.1.6 Consider non-tax factors

Sometimes **the information not given in the question is just as important as the information which is. You may have to make assumptions** about what the taxpayer has done, or intends to do, or about his personal circumstances. If so, state them in your answer, so that if your assumptions are wrong the reader's attention will be drawn to them. Otherwise the course of action that you are recommending may be totally unsuitable. You may be able to give some indication of how your answer would differ, but do not go wildly off on a tangent.

Remember also that **tax should never be the only factor** in a decision. For example, if you are advising someone to invest under the enterprise investment scheme to obtain a tax reducer and also to defer a gain, stop and think about the nature of the investment. Small unquoted companies often fail, and your client may prefer to pay the tax rather than lose his investment. There may be hints and clues in the question; a 74-year old is not likely to want to invest in a personal pension.

1.2 Alternative ways of achieving outcomes and different tax consequences

In the exam, you will often be asked to compare alternative ways of achieving personal or business outcomes and advise on the most tax efficient course of action.

For example, an individual may which to raise funds, to buy a house. Conversely, he may have funds which he can invest to generate an income or for capital growth. The tax treatment of the different sources of finance or investment products available (as detailed in this chapter), may affect the individual's decision regarding which source or product to use.

1.3 Example: tax efficient deposit investment

Tony, aged 29, is employed on a remuneration package of £30,000 a year. This is his only source of income. He is saving towards buying a house and can save approximately £2,500 each year. He wants to have the money in a bank or building society so that he can withdraw it to pay the deposit when he finds a house, although this may not be for a year or two.

The options are:

(a) To select a suitable instant access or short notice account paying a competitive rate of interest
(b) To select a cash ISA

The annual after tax receipts, assuming that Tony could achieve a rate of interest of 5% on either sort of account, are calculated as follows:

(a) £2,500 × 5% = £125 less tax of £125 × 20% = £25, net receipt £100
(b) £2,500 × 5% = £125, no tax, net receipt £125

The most tax efficient option is to invest in a cash ISA. This achieves the same objectives and increases the after tax receipt by £25.

2 Personal finance

2.1 Sources of finance for individuals

FAST FORWARD

There are many sources of finance available for individuals, long or short term, secured or unsecured.

2.1.1 Introduction

Investments can only be made if funds are available. The private investor will generally have his own funds to invest, accumulated from salary or from business profits, but he may even decide to borrow money in order to make an investment which is expected to be particularly profitable. And of course, many private individuals borrow money to invest in land and buildings, buying their homes with mortgage loans.

2.1.2 Sources of finance for private purposes

The following **sources of finance** are available to individuals for private purposes.

- Bank overdrafts
- Unsecured bank and building society loans
- Mortgage loans from banks and building societies, secured on the borrower's home
- Credit cards
- Hire purchase facilities
- Credit facilities provided by retailers

If the individual wishes to **buy or improve a house**, a **mortgage loan** is likely to be the most suitable source of finance. The fact that it is secured reduces the risk to the lender, and therefore the interest charged. For other large purchases, hire purchase facilities or the credit facilities provided by retailers may be the most suitable: the cost may be reduced as an incentive to make the purchase concerned, and using a specific facility avoids tying up a large proportion of a more general facility such as an overdraft or a credit card. An alternative to such specific facilities is an unsecured bank or building society loan, which must be repaid by agreed instalments over a fixed period.

Small and varied purchases may be made using a credit card, although if credit is taken the interest rate is very high, to reflect the risk of non-payment accepted by the credit card company. A bank overdraft facility can be useful to allow the individual to cope with times when expenditure temporarily exceeds income, perhaps because of fluctuating business profits or because of occasional worthwhile new investment opportunities such as new share issues.

2.1.3 Mortgage products

FAST FORWARD

A mortgage may be a repayment or interest only mortgage. Pensions or ISAs may be used to accumulate the capital required to repay an interest only mortgage.

Most people who buy a house need to **borrow** to finance the purchase. Mortgage loans are normally repayable not later than the end of a fixed term agreed at the start of the loan.

Key term

A **mortgage** is a loan given on the **security** of a property. The purchaser pays a proportion of the purchase price of a property – a **mortgage deposit** – and the balance is lent by the mortgage lender.

The borrower gives the lender **legal rights over the property** for the duration of the loan. While the loan is outstanding the property is the lender's security that the loan will be repaid. If the borrower does not keep up repayments on the loan – defaults – **the lender has the right to take possession of the property**, sell it, recover the amount of the loan (assuming the sale price is higher than the loan) and pay the balance to the borrower. If the loan is repaid according to the terms of the mortgage, the legal rights of the lender over the property cease **at the end of the term**.

During the term of the mortgage the borrower must pay **interest**. The **interest rate** charged by a lender may be variable (**variable rate mortgage**). Some variable rates of interest are limited to a specified maximum but may rise or fall subject to that maximum. These are **'capped' mortgages. Fixed rate mortgages** are available at a rate of interest which is fixed for a specific period of time.

There are two methods of **repaying the capital**: during the term or at the end of it. It is possible to **combine the two types of mortgage**. For example, a borrower might borrow £70,000 on a repayment basis and £30,000 on an interest only basis.

With a **repayment mortgage** each time interest is paid to a lender, part of the capital is repaid at the same time. Payments are often of a fixed regular amount. However, flexible mortgages may allow underpayments (ie less than the regular monthly amount), overpayments or payment holidays. There may also be additional borrowing facilities.

With an interest only mortgage **the entire capital sum is repaid on the last day of the mortgage**. Most lenders will want the borrower to take some action over the term of the mortgage to accumulate sufficient money to repay the loan, for example by investing in a pension or individual savings account.

2.1.4 Tax treatment of borrowings

Tax relief is only available for interest paid in limited circumstances.

Apart from business borrowings or in connection with a property letting business, where the interest paid is a deduction from profits, interest relief is only available if the interest is charged on a qualifying **loan** such as for loans to invest in close companies or partnerships. This precludes relief for interest on overdrafts or credit card borrowings.

Note that **interest relief is not available** on a loan to buy shares in a close company **if EIS relief is claimed** for the investment.

Unless tax relief is available for interest, it may be advisable to repay loans if surplus funds are available. In evaluating the situation, however, as well as comparing the interest charge on the borrowing with the income generated by the surplus funds you need to take into account any capital return which may be generated if the surplus funds are invested.

2.2 Investment products for individuals

2.2.1 Introduction

There is a **very wide range of investment products available to individuals**, ranging from an almost risk free bank deposit to a high risk investment in shares in a small unquoted trading company under the seed enterprise investment scheme.

It may be preferable to **invest for capital growth**, rather than income, since capital gains are taxed at 28% for an individual who is a higher or additional rate taxpayer compared with the higher and additional rates of income tax of 40% and 45% (or 32.5% and 37.5% for dividends).

2.2.2 Deposit based investments

FAST FORWARD

Most deposit based investments are fairly low risk investments in which an investor receives a low rate of interest in return for depositing his capital with the institution.

Some of the products available and their tax treatment are:

Provider	Type of account	Tax treatment
Banks and building societies	Instant access accounts, notice accounts, fixed term deposits, money market accounts	Interest taxable as savings income. Normally paid net of 20% tax, except on money market deposits over £50,000 or if investor certifies that he is a non-taxpayer.
Banks and building societies, National Savings and Investments (NS&I)	Cash ISAs	Tax free
National Savings and Investments (NS&I)	Direct Saver accounts, Investment accounts	Interest taxable as savings income. Paid gross.
National Savings and Investments (NS&I)	Savings certificate, fixed interest or index linked	Tax free

2.2.3 Fixed interest securities

FAST FORWARD

A fixed interest security pays a fixed rate of interest and has a known maturity value so long as it is held until its redemption date.

Key term

A **fixed interest security** is a loan to a government, a local authority, a company, or a building society. **The security pays a fixed rate of interest and has a known maturity value so long as the stock is held until its redemption date**.

Government securities and corporate bonds are negotiable and can therefore be traded in the market.

The securities available and their tax treatment are:

Investment	Income tax	Capital gains tax
Government securities, Local authority bonds	Interest is taxed as savings income. Paid gross. Accrued income scheme applies.	Exempt gains, losses not allowable
Company loan stock which is qualifying corporate bond	Interest is taxed as savings income. Paid net of 20% tax unless loan stock is listed on a recognised stock exchange, when paid gross. Accrued income scheme applies.	Exempt gains, losses not allowable
Company loan stock which is not a qualifying corporate bond	Interest is taxed as savings income. Paid net of 20% tax unless loan stock is listed on a recognised stock exchange, when paid gross. Accrued income scheme applies.	Taxable gains, losses allowable

2.2.4 Individual savings accounts (ISAs)

FAST FORWARD

Individual savings accounts (ISAs) provide a tax-free wrapper for investments in cash, and stocks and shares.

Key term

ISAs are tax efficient savings accounts. They can be made up of two components.

- Cash
- Stocks and shares

The investor must be resident and ordinarily resident in the UK in the year the investment is made. The investor must normally be 18 years or over. However, a cash only ISA can be held by individuals aged 16 or 17.

The annual subscription limits are:

(a) Cash component: £5,760
(b) Stocks and shares component: balance to £11,520

The stock and shares element may contain medium term stakeholder products (unit trust, OEIC and unit linked insurance). **All non-stakeholder life insurance may also be held in the stocks and shares component. Investments producing a 'cash like' return** (capital not at risk or at minimum risk) **are restricted to the cash component.**

Investments within an ISA are exempt from both income and capital gains tax. If, however, cash is held in a stocks and shares ISA a 20% deduction is made from interest received. This is not recoverable. There is no deduction from interest in a cash ISA.

2.2.5 Equities

FAST FORWARD

Equities are high risk investments as neither the income nor the capital is secure.

When an investor buys a share in Marks and Spencer plc that is exactly what he has done; he has bought a share in the ownership of the company.

Dividends are received with a non-refundable tax credit of 10%. The gross amount of dividends received are subject to income tax as described earlier in this Text.

A capital gain arising on shares, calculated using the matching rules, is subject to CGT. Losses are allowable losses.

Equities are **high risk investments** as neither the income nor the capital is secure. Equities in companies listed on a recognised stock exchange are generally less risky than those in unlisted companies.

2.2.6 The enterprise investment scheme (EIS)

FAST FORWARD

The enterprise investment scheme (EIS) is a scheme designed to promote enterprise and investment by helping high-risk, unlisted trading companies raise finance by the issue of ordinary shares to individual investors who are unconnected with that company.

Individuals who subscribe for EIS shares are entitled to income tax relief. This has already been discussed earlier in this Text, but as a summary the rules are that individuals can claim a **tax reducer of the lower of 30% of the amount subscribed for qualifying investments** (maximum qualifying investment is £1,000,000 and the individual's tax liability for the year after deducting VCT relief).

The investor may claim to have all or part of the shares treated as issued in the previous tax year. This is subject to the total actual and deemed investment not exceeding the limit for the previous year.

The relief may be withdrawn if certain events, such as the sale of the shares, occur within three years.

Where EIS income tax relief is available there are also **capital gains tax reliefs**:

(a) Where EIS shares are **disposed of after the three year period** any gain is **exempt** from CGT. If the shares are disposed of within three years any gain is computed in the normal way.

(b) If EIS shares are **disposed of at a loss at any time**, the loss is **allowable** but the acquisition cost of the shares is reduced by the amount of EIS relief attributable to the shares. The loss is eligible for share loss relief against general income (see earlier in this Text).

EIS reinvestment, or deferral, relief may be available to defer chargeable gains if an individual invests in EIS shares in the period commencing one year before and ending three years after the disposal of the asset (see earlier in this Text). Note that this relief is not conditional on income tax relief being available.

2.2.7 Seed enterprise investment scheme (SEIS))

FAST FORWARD

The seed enterprise investment scheme (SEIS) is similar to the EIS scheme but rewards investment in small, start up unquoted trading companies with a greater tax reducer.

Individuals can also invest in SEIS shares and obtain income tax relief and capital gains tax reliefs as detailed earlier in this Text.

The **qualifying companies are smaller, start up companies** and the **greater tax reducer of 50%** (available on up to £100,000 of investment) reflects the **greater risk of investing in these companies**. In the exam, you may advise investing in an EIS or SEIS company: remember to **point out the risks as well as the tax reliefs**.

2.2.8 Venture capital trusts (VCTs)

FAST FORWARD

Venture capital trusts (VCTs) are listed companies which invest in unquoted trading companies, so enabling investors to spread their risk over a number of higher-risk, unquoted companies whilst obtaining income tax and capital gains tax reliefs.

Venture capital trusts (VCTs) are listed companies which invest in unquoted trading companies and meet certain conditions. **The VCT scheme differs from EIS in that the individual investor may spread his risk over a number of higher-risk, unquoted companies.**

An individual investing in a VCT obtains the following tax benefits on a maximum qualifying investment of £200,000:

- A tax reduction of 30% of the amount invested. There is a withdrawal of relief if the shares are disposed of within five years or if the VCT ceases to qualify.
- Dividends received are tax-free income.
- Capital gains on the sale of shares in the VCT are exempt from CGT (and losses are not allowable).

In addition, capital gains which the VCT itself makes on its investments are not chargeable gains, and so are not subject to corporation tax.

Note that there is no minimum holding period requirement for the benefits of tax-free dividends and CGT exemption.

3 Business finance

3.1 Sources of finance for business

FAST FORWARD

Businesses may require short or long term finance to start up, carry on or expand.

Businesses need funds in order to start up and expand, and their requirements are often far beyond the means of the entrepreneurs concerned. Outside capital may be sought from banks, from other lenders or from new shareholders or partners.

The following sources of finance are available for businesses.

- The entrepreneur's own capital
- Bank overdrafts
- Bank loans (which may be short term, medium term or long term)
- Loans secured by mortgages of land
- Leasing and hire purchase arrangements
- Sale and leaseback arrangements
- Loans from private individuals
- Capital invested by partners
- Share issues (for incorporated businesses)
- Loan stock issues (for incorporated businesses)
- Venture capital institutions

The tax treatments of equity and loan finance differ, as do the tax implications of leasing equipment compared with buying it outright.

3.2 The tax implications of equity finance and of loan finance

FAST FORWARD

A business may obtain finance through loans and obtain tax relief for interest paid. A company can raise finance by issuing shares to shareholders.

3.2.1 Loan finance

You saw earlier in this Text that if a company is a party to a loan relationship for the purposes of its trade, any debits are deductible in computing its trading profits. If, however a loan relationship is not one for the purposes of a trade any debits or credits are pooled. A net credit on the pool is chargeable as interest income. A net deficit may be relieved in the various ways described earlier in this Text.

It is not only the interest costs of borrowing that are allowable or taxable. The **capital costs are treated similarly**. Thus if a company issues a loan at a discount and repays it eventually at par, the capital cost is allowed.

A sole trader or partnership will not obtain a deduction in respect of capital repayments of loan finance. A trading deduction will only be available in respect of interest incurred wholly and exclusively for trade purposes.

3.2.2 Equity finance

Companies can raise finance by issuing shares to shareholders. Capital can be raised in this way for trading and non-trading purposes. Companies can distribute profits to shareholders in a variety of ways, of which the payment of dividends is the most common. **The cost of making distributions to shareholders is not allowable in computing taxable profits.**

The **main types of share** are:

Type of share	Features
Ordinary shares	The shareholder is entitled: (a) To a share of profit distributed as a dividend (b) To the right to vote on matters affecting the company (c) In the event of a winding up, to a share of assets, but note that shareholders do not take precedence over the creditors
Preference shares	(a) These shareholders are placed ahead of the ordinary shareholders for dividend payments and in the event of a liquidation (b) The dividend is usually a guaranteed amount but if the distribution to the ordinary shareholders is higher, the preference shareholders do not receive the increase
Convertible preference shares	The dividend paid on these is usually less than the non-convertible preference share but there is the option to convert to ordinary shares in the future at pre-set dates and at pre-set prices

3.2.3 Legal and professional expenses

Legal and professional expenses relating to capital or non-trading items are disallowable. This includes fees incurred, for example, in issuing share capital. However, a deduction is allowed to companies under the loan relationship rules for the incidental costs of obtaining medium or long term business loans and for issuing loan stock.

3.2.4 Investors

Interest income received from a company on loan stock etc is taxable income for the recipient (and will have suffered 20% tax at source if paid on unlisted loan stock).

Dividend income received from a shareholding in a company is taxable on an individual investor only to the extent he is a higher or additional rate tax payer. The tax credit on dividend income can never be repaid to non-taxpayers but the tax suffered on interest income is repayable.

UK dividend income is not taxable in the hands of a company shareholder.

No gain or loss can arise to the original creditor when he disposes of his debt. A purchaser of a debt may have a chargeable gain and (unless he is connected with the original creditor) **an allowable loss.**

A debt on a security can give rise to a gain or loss to the original creditor.

3.3 The lease or buy decision

FAST FORWARD

A business may lease or buy assets. Short term leasing costs may be deductible expenses. Longer term costs may attract capital allowances in a similar way to buying an asset outright.

If assets are leased and the term of the lease is less than 5 years, then the lease payments are in general deductible in computing taxable profits. If they are bought on hire purchase or leased under a long term lease, then the cash price of the assets may qualify for capital allowances and the finance charges are deductible in computing taxable profits, making the tax effects very similar to those of taking out a loan and then buying the asset.

If assets are bought outright then capital allowances may be available on the purchase cost. These will be given on a reducing balance basis each year. The ultimate lease or buy decision is likely to depend on the availability of funds and whether leasing the asset allows the company to keep funds free to finance other activities.

4 Tax planning

4.1 Introduction

It would be impossible to write a definitive section on tax planning and mitigation, as no two scenarios are ever the same. This section covers nine scenarios, highlighting the points which need to be considered, both tax and non-tax. You may well think of other situations where taxpayers may seek advice.

4.2 Employment and self-employment

FAST FORWARD

As a general rule, self-employment leads to lower overall tax and NIC burdens than employment.

A taxpayer who has a choice between being employed and being self-employed, on similar gross incomes, should consider the following points.

(a) An employee must pay **income tax and NICs as salary is received, under the PAYE system** and on a current year basis. A self-employed person pays **income tax and NICs which are at least partly payable after all of the profits concerned have been earned**. There is thus a cash flow advantage in self-employment.

(b) **An employee is likely to suffer significantly higher NICs in total than a self employed person,** although the employee's entitlement to state benefits will also be higher. In particular, note that the self-employed earn no entitlement to the State Second Pension.

(c) An **employee may receive benefits as well as salary**. Taxable values of benefits may be less than their actual value to the employee and benefits do not attract employee NICs. Most benefits attract employer's Class 1A NIC.

(d) The **rules on the deductibility of expenses are much stricter for employees** (incurred wholly, exclusively and necessarily in the performance of duties) than for the self-employed (normally incurred wholly and exclusively for the purposes of the trade).

4.3 Remuneration packages

FAST FORWARD

If someone is to be an employee, the tax effects of the remuneration package should be taken into account.

4.3.1 Income tax planning for employment situations

An employee will usually be rewarded largely by salary, but several other elements can be included in a remuneration package. Some of them bring tax benefits to the employee only, and some will also benefit the employer.

Bonuses are treated like salary, except that if a bonus is accrued in the employer's accounts but is paid more than nine months after the end of the period of account, its deductibility for tax purposes will be delayed.

The general position for **benefits** is that they are subject to **income tax and employer Class 1A NICs**. The cost of providing benefits is generally deductible in computing trading profit for the employer (but if a car with carbon dioxide emissions over 130 g/km is provided, the employer's capital allowances (or deductions for lease payments) are reduced). However, there are a large number of **tax and NI free benefits** and there is a great deal of planning that can be done to ensure a tax and NIC efficient benefits package for directors and employees. The optimum is to ensure that the company receives a tax deduction for the expenditure while creating tax and NI free remuneration for employees.

Comparison of two remuneration packages

Employee A receives a salary of £31,500.

Employee B receives a salary of £26,500, the use of a new digital camera which cost £800 on 6 April 2013 and the use of a car purchased by the employer on 6 April 2013 which has a list price of £15,000 and has CO_2 emissions of 115g/km, so the taxable percentage is 15%. No fuel is supplied.

Employee B is also in a pension scheme (not contracted out) to which he contributes 5% of his gross salary (excluding benefits) and his employer company contributes 10% of his gross salary (excluding benefits).

Show the tax and the NIC effects of the two remuneration packages on both the employees and their employers. Use 2013/14 tax rates and allowances and assume that the employer prepares accounts to 31 March each year and that the employer will only claim writing down allowances for capital allowance purposes. A and B both have no other income.

Answer

A's income tax and NIC computations are as follows.

	£
Earnings	31,500
Less personal allowance	(9,440)
Taxable income	22,060
Income tax	
£22,060 × 20%	£4,412
NICs	
£(31,500 – 7,755) × 12%	£2,849

A's employer must pay NICs of (£31,500 – £7,696) × 13.8% = £3,285, and can deduct £(31,500 + 3,285) = £34,785 in computing trading profits.

B's income tax and NIC computations are as follows.

	£
Salary	26,500
Use of digital camera £800 × 20%	160
Car £15,000 × 15%	2,250
	28,910
Less pension contribution £26,500 × 5%	(1,325)
Earnings	27,585
Less personal allowance	(9,440)
Taxable income	18,145
Income tax	
£18,145 × 20%	£3,629
NICs	
£(26,500 – 7,755) × 12%	£2,249

B's employer must pay NICs as follows.

	£
Class 1 NICs	
£(26,500 – 7,696) × 13.8%	2,595
Class 1A NICs	
£(2,250 + 160) × 13.8%	333
	2,928

B's employer will have the following deductions in computing profits.

	£	£
Salary		26,500
Pension contribution £26,500 × 10%		2,650
NICs		2,928
Capital allowances		
Car £15,000 x 18%	2,700	
Digital camera £800 × 18%	144	
		2,844
		34,922

4.3.2 NIC planning for employment situations

NIC is payable on 'earnings' which is defined as 'any remuneration or profit derived from employment'. Remuneration packages structured to include the following items which are not 'earnings' would reduce the NIC burden.

(a) **Dividends** – director/shareholders could take remuneration in the form of dividends. Dividend waivers and adjustments to bonuses would probably be required. There are CT implications as salary and NIC costs are allowable business expenses whereas dividends are not.

Dividends are an efficient way of avoiding NIC. However dividend income is not earnings for pension purposes. There is also a cash flow impact since PAYE does not apply to dividends.

(b) **Rents** – a director owning a property used by a company could be paid rent instead of remuneration. However, this will impact entrepreneurs' relief for associated disposals (if available) on the subsequent sale of the property. The rental expense is a deductible business expense for the company but the income is not earnings for pension contribution purposes for the individual.

4.4 The choice of a business medium

FAST FORWARD

An individual can choose between trading as a sole trader or trading through a company. That choice, and if a company is chosen, the choice between dividends and remuneration, can significantly affect the overall tax and NIC burden. Cashflow is also an important consideration.

4.4.1 General considerations

When starting in business the first decision must be whether to trade as a company (with the individual as a director taxable on earnings) or as an unincorporated business, either as a sole trader or a partnership. Certain professions may not be practised through a limited company (although unlimited companies and limited liability partnerships may be allowed).

The attraction of incorporation lies in the fact that a sole trader or a partner is liable for business debts to the full extent of his personal assets. A limited company's shareholder's liability is limited to the amount, if any, unpaid on his shares. However, limited liability is often reduced by the demands of bankers or landlords for personal guarantees from company directors. In addition, compliance with the statutory obligations (eg annual returns, audits etc) that apply to a company can be costly.

A company often finds raising finance easier than an unincorporated business. This is partly because of the misguided view that a company has greater reliability and permanence. A company can obtain equity finance through venture capital institutions and can borrow by giving a floating charge over its assets as security whereas a sole trader or partnership cannot do this.

A business may be seen as **more reputable or creditworthy if conducted through the medium of a company.** Companies, however, have to comply with disclosure requirements and this may be unattractive to proprietors who wish to keep information from employees, potential competitors etc. This could be avoided by using an unlimited company but in that case any advantage of limited status is lost. The disclosure requirements could be reduced by filing abbreviated accounts.

4.4.2 The effect of marginal tax rates and national insurance

A trader's profits whether retained or withdrawn are taxed at a marginal rate of 40% on taxable income between £32,010 and £100,000, at a marginal rate of 60% between £100,000 and £118,880 (due to the withdrawal of the personal allowance), at a marginal rate of 40% between £118,880 and £150,000 and at a marginal rate of 45% on taxable income above £150,000. In addition Class 2 and Class 4 National Insurance contributions are payable.

A controlling director/shareholder can decide whether profits are to be paid out as remuneration or dividends, or retained in the company.

If profits are retained, the consequent growth in asset values will increase the potential capital gain when shares are sold. Where remuneration is paid the total national insurance liability is greater than for the proprietor of an unincorporated business.

Where a spouse is employed his or her salary must be justifiable as 'wholly and exclusively for the purposes of the trade'; HMRC may seek to disallow excessive salary cost. On the other hand, a spouse as active partner can take any share in profits, provided that he or she is personally active in the business and there is evidence of a bona fide partnership. Thus the spouse's personal allowance, basic rate and higher rate bands can be used.

In choosing a business medium, we should also remember that a sole trader will be denied the enhanced state benefits that are available to an employee who pays Class 1 national insurance contributions. In particular, note that the self-employed do not build an entitlement to the State Second Pension.

Question — **Net income from a business**

Alan was born in 1975. He is starting a new business and expects to make annual profits of £36,000 before tax and national insurance. Consider the fiscal effects of his choosing to trade as a sole trader or, alternatively, through a company, paying him a salary of £20,000 and then the largest possible dividend not giving rise to a loss of capital. Assume that accounting profits equal taxable trade profits. Use 2013/14 tax rates.

Answer

As a sole trader

	£
Profits	36,000
Less personal allowance	(9,440)
Taxable income	26,560
Tax thereon at 20%	5,312
National Insurance Classes 2 (52 × £2.70) and 4 (£(36,000 – 7,755) × 9%)	2,682
	7,994
Net income £(36,000 – 7,994)	28,006

Through a company

	£
Profits	36,000
Less: salary	(20,000)
employer's NI (20,000 – 7,696) × 13.8%	(1,698)
Taxable profits	14,302
Less: corporation tax 20% × £14,302	(2,860)
Net profits	11,442

A dividend of £11,442 can be paid without loss of capital.

	Non-savings income	Dividend income	Total
	£	£	£
Earnings	20,000		
Dividends £11,442 × 100/90		12,713	
Net income	20,000	12,713	32,713
Less personal allowance	(9,440)		
Taxable income	10,560	12,713	23,273
Non-savings income			
£10,560 × 20%			2,112
Dividend income			
£12,713 × 10%			1,271
			3,383
Less tax suffered £12,713 × 10%			(1,271)
Income tax payable			2,112

Net income		£
Salary		20,000
Dividends		11,442
	£	31,442
Less: income tax	2,112	
employee's NIC £ (20,000 – 7,755) × 12%	1,469	
		(3,581)
		27,861

Trading as a sole trader would give annual net income of £(28,006 – 27,861) = £145 more than trading through a company.

Question — Small business as sole trader versus company

Let's say we have a business earning profits of £17,696.

Compare the retained profit for the business owner if he operates the business as a sole trader with a year ended 31 March 2014 to that of a company with the same year end but paying out £7,696 as a salary and the remaining post-tax profits as a dividend.

Answer

Sole Trader

Trading profits of £17,696 in 2013/14

Year ended 31 March 2014

Income tax	
£(17,696 – 9,440) = £8,256	£
£8,256 @ 20%	1,651
National Insurance	
Class 2	140
Class 4	
£(17,696 – 7,755) × 9%	895
Total Income Tax and NIC	2,686
Net income	
£(17,696 – 2,686)	£15,010

Company	£
Year ended 31 March 2014	
Taxable total profits = £(17,696 – 7,696)	10,000
Corporation tax	
£10,000 @ 20% before distribution	(2,000)
Maximum distribution is	8,000

Income tax
Salary covered by PA
Gross dividend income = £8,889

	£
£8,889 @ 10%	889
Less tax credit	(889)
	Nil
Class 1 NIC	Nil
Net income £(7,696 + 8,000)	£15,696

As a sole-tradership the business would typically pay £2,686 in the 2013/14 tax year as income tax and National Insurance contributions. The same business operating as a limited company for the same year would have a tax bill of £2,000.

4.4.3 Benefits and expenses

The restrictions on deducting expenses against earnings may make self-employment rather more attractive than employment as a company director. Although the same expense deduction rules apply to a company and a sole trader, the company's deductible business expenses may give rise to taxable benefits as earnings for directors.

On the other hand, the provision of fringe benefits can be an advantage of incorporation. Tax exempt benefits can be used to maximise directors' net spendable income, although care is required because not all benefits are tax-efficient.

4.4.4 Opening years

Companies have no equivalent of the opening year rules that apply for income tax purposes. For a sole trader or partnership, profits earned when basis periods overlap are taxed twice. Relief is available for such overlap profits but that may not take place for many years, by which time inflation may have reduced the value of the relief for overlap profits.

If a partnership is envisaged it may be worthwhile to commence trading with the prospective partner as a salaried employee for a year or so, thereby obtaining tax relief twice on his salary during the overlap period.

4.4.5 Losses

Losses in the first four years of an unincorporated business can be used to obtain tax repayments (using early trade losses relief). In these and later years a loss relief claim against general income permits **relief for trading losses against other income** (and capital gains) of either or both of two tax years.

With corporation tax, although there is considerable flexibility for the company itself, **a company's losses are not available to reduce shareholders' taxable income.**

4.4.6 Capital gains tax

One difference between companies and individuals is that **companies do not benefit from an exempt amount of the first £10,900 of total gains** (for 2013/14).

Chargeable gains of an individual are charged to capital gains tax at 10%, 18% or 28%. By contrast, companies' gains are charged at normal corporation tax rates (23% main rate, 20% small profits rate or 23.75% effective marginal rate).

The principal disadvantage of incorporation is the double charge to tax which arises when a company sells a chargeable asset. Firstly, the company may pay corporation tax on the chargeable gain. Secondly, the shareholders may be taxed when they attempt to realise those proceeds, either in the form of dividends or, when the shares are sold, incurring a further charge on capital gains.

If there are no tax advantages in the company owning an asset, the asset should be held outside the company, perhaps being leased to the company. The lessor may receive rent without restricting IHT business asset relief. However, rent received will restrict entrepreneurs' relief for CGT.

4.4.7 Tax cash flows

A sole trader/partner is assessable to income tax and NICs on a current year basis but will use a prior year basis to calculate two payments on account due on 31 January in and 31 July directly following the tax year. The balance of tax is due on 31 January following the tax year. Thus tax on profits earned in the year to 30 April 2013 (assessable 2013/14) will not be payable in full until 31 January 2015 and will be used to calculate payments on account due 31 January 2015 and 31 July 2015. **Where profits are rising this lag gives a considerable benefit**. A sole trader's/partner's drawings do not of themselves attract or accelerate a tax charge.

A company usually pays corporation tax nine months after the end of its accounts period. Companies paying tax at the main rate are required to make **quarterly payments on account** based on the current year's estimated liability. As an employer it will have to account for **PAYE and NICs 14 days after the end of each tax month** in which the pay date falls.

Generally therefore a business held by a company will pay tax earlier than a business held by a sole trader or partnership.

4.4.8 What if things go wrong?

Sound tax planning should always take account of possible changes in circumstances. A successful business may fail or a struggling concern may eventually become profitable.

Running down an unincorporated business does not normally give rise to serious problems. The proprietor may be able to cover any balancing charges with loss relief.

Taking a business out of a company (disincorporation), or winding up a corporate trade altogether is more complex and involves both tax and legal issues. Consider the following:

- No subsequent relief is available for a company's unused losses once the trade ceases
- Liquidation costs may be considerable
- A double charge on capital gains may arise, although certain small companies may be able to take advantage of relief if they disincorporate (see earlier in this Text).

4.4.9 Personal service companies (PSCs)

The 'IR 35 provisions' (see earlier in this Text) are anti-avoidance rules which attack the provision of personal services by personal service companies (PSCs). If an individual would have been an employee if he had been working directly for a client, he will generally be subject to tax and NIC on income from the PSC as if he was in fact an employee of the client.

4.5 The incorporation of a business

FAST FORWARD

The incorporation of a business should be carefully planned, taking account of consequent tax liabilities. There are both advantages and disadvantages to incorporating a business. A disposal of shares can also have several tax consequences.

4.5.1 Advantages of incorporating a business

(a) Retained profits subject only to corporation tax not income tax or NIC.

(b) Easier to dispose of shares in a company than interest in a business – thus advantage for raising equity and selling to outside investors.

(c) Pension provision can be made by employer (the company) for employees (eg directors) with no national insurance liability.

(d) Benefits for employees can be more tax efficient.

(e) Loan finance easier to arrange as lender can take out charge on company assets.

(f) Limited liability for shareholders if the company is a limited company.

(g) A company arguably has a more respectable image than a sole trader or partnership.

(h) Incorporation is a means of converting the value of a business into shares which could eventually become listed on a recognised stock exchange. This provides for succession of ownership and can make the original proprietors very wealthy.

4.5.2 Disadvantages of incorporating a business

(a) Potential double capital gains charge on assets (see above).

(b) Trading losses restricted to set-off against corporate profits.

(c) No carry back of trading losses in opening years (ie no early trade losses relief equivalent).

(d) Partner's share of profit not openly challenged by HMRC provided the recipient is a genuine partner. Conversely excessive remuneration to employee/director can be challenged.

(e) NIC for employer company and employee will generally exceed the contributions required of a self-employed person.

(f) Tax payment dates for tax for a company and its employees (CT, PAYE and NIC) are generally well in advance of those for self-employed.

(g) Assets used in a business but held outside the business entity can qualify for 50% BPR for IHT. In the case of a partnership the owner merely has to be a partner but in the case of a company using an asset the owner must be a controlling shareholder.

(h) There may be statutory requirements of audit, keeping books, filing accounts etc.

(i) Disclosure requirements of published accounts may give information to employees/ competitors that business owners would not have willingly disclosed.

4.5.3 Income tax

When an unincorporated trade is transferred to a company the **trade is treated as discontinued for tax purposes and the cessation rules apply**. Careful consideration of the level of profit, available overlap profits and date of transfer is required **to avoid large taxable profits in one year and to utilise the personal allowance and basic rate tax band as effectively as possible.**

For example, if a trader with a 31 December year end incorporates his business on 31 March 2014, the year of cessation will be 2013/14. If he makes profits of £3,000 per month, he will be taxed on profits in 2013/14 between 1 January 2013 to 31 March 2014 (15 months) which will be £45,000 (less any overlap relief). If, however, he delayed incorporation until 30 April 2014, the year of cessation will be 2014/15. He will be taxed on profits of £12,000 in 2014/15 (again less any overlap relief) and on 12 months of profit in 2013/14 (£36,000). This may be more advantageous if he does not have other income to use up his personal allowance and/or his basic rate band in 2014/15.

On the transfer of a trade to a company **a balancing charge will usually arise as plant and machinery are treated as being sold at market value**. However, where the company is controlled by the transferor, **the two are connected and an election may be made** so as not to treat the transfer as a permanent discontinuance for capital allowances purposes. **Plant is then transferred at its tax written down value.**

Unrelieved trading losses cannot be carried forward to a company as such, but **may be set against any income derived from the company** by way of dividends, remuneration and so on, provided the business is exchanged for shares and those shares are still held at the time the loss is set off. Terminal loss relief may also be available for the loss of the last twelve months of trading.

4.5.4 Capital gains tax

When the transfer takes place the **chargeable assets are deemed to be disposed of to the company at their open market values**. Capital gains tax liabilities are likely to arise, particularly on land and buildings and on goodwill.

If the whole business (or the whole business other than cash) **is transferred to the company as a going concern in exchange for shares in the company, any chargeable gains are automatically rolled over through incorporation relief**, reducing the base cost of the shares on a subsequent disposal. If the shares are held until death the tax liability may never arise as no capital gains tax arises on death.

Individuals who incorporate a business can elect that incorporation relief should not apply. This election must usually be made within two years of 31 January following the end of the tax year in which the business was incorporated. Making the election could be advantageous if the gains are quite small and entrepreneurs' relief would apply.

It may not be desirable for all the assets comprised in the business to be transferred to the company. **As an alternative**, an individual can **use gift relief** to transfer chargeable business assets to a company and **defer any gains by deducting them from the base costs of the assets** for the company.

4.5.5 Value added tax

The transfer of assets will not be treated as a supply for VAT purposes (a transfer of a going concern (TOGC)) if all of the following conditions are satisfied.

(a) The assets are to be used by the company in the same kind of business (whether or not as part of an existing business) as that carried on by the transferor, the business being transferred as a going concern

(b) If only part of the business is transferred, that part is capable of separate operation

(c) If the transferor is a taxable person, the company is a taxable person when the transfer takes place or immediately becomes one as a result of the transfer

(d) There must be no significant break in the normal trading pattern before or immediately after the transfer

(e) In the case of land and buildings, the company makes an election to tax if the transferor has done so

(f) In the case of 'new' buildings the company makes an election to tax.

Note. For the last two points if the election to tax is not made by the company the supply of land or buildings is standard rated. All the other business assets can be transferred outside the scope of VAT under the TOGC rules.

An application may be made for the company to take over the existing VAT registration number. In this case the company will take over all the debts and liabilities of the business but it will be able to claim VAT impairment loss relief in respect of supplies made before the transfer.

If the above conditions cannot be satisfied VAT will be charged on the transfer, but this will only represent a cash flow problem in most cases.

HMRC should be notified of the incorporation within 30 days.

4.5.6 Stamp duty land tax

The transfer of land will be subject to Stamp Duty Land Tax as a transfer at market value. The use of the gift relief route should be considered so that land can be retained outside the company.

4.6 Disincorporation of a company

FAST FORWARD

If disincorporation relief applies, there will be no corporation tax charge on the transfer of land and buildings and goodwill by a company to its shareholders. Other reliefs may apply to transfers of inventory and plant and machinery. A tax charge may arise for the shareholders on the distribution of assets, either income tax or capital gains tax.

4.6.1 Introduction

Disincorporation is the process of a business changing its legal form from a limited company to one run by a self employed individual or partnership. It is achieved by the transfer of the business as a going concern, with its assets and liabilities, from the company to one or all of the shareholders. The business is then continued by them in their capacity as a sole trader or a partnership.

A **key reason for wanting to disincorporate** may be **to avoid the additional administrative and regulatory requirements of being a limited company**. This includes sending a **corporation tax return** to HMRC. The **directors and shareholders** of the company may also need to complete **individual tax returns**. Operating as a company is also likely to entail **operating PAYE**, which would not otherwise be necessary if the business has no other employees.

Some individuals find it difficult to understand the notion of the company as a legal entity separate from the shareholders/directors, and consequently **fail to keep personal cash separate from the business**: this may result in **errors or underpayment in their tax returns**. In these circumstances, it may be **better for the business to be carried on in an unincorporated form.**

On the other hand, where **a business is operated properly through a limited company**, the **company's finances are kept separate from the personal finances of the shareholders/directors** who are not directly liable for company's debts. The **loss of limited liability for the business** as a result of disincorporation must be **balanced against the simpler administration required** for an unincorporated business.

4.6.2 Tax implications for company on disincorporation

(a) **Land and buildings** – disposal by company on transfer to shareholders. If **disincorporation relief applies, deemed to be transferred at the lower of market value and allowable acquisition cost so that no gain arises for the company.** Acquired by shareholders at the deemed disposal value.

(b) **Goodwill** – disposal by company on transfer to shareholders. If **disincorporation relief applies, deemed to be transferred at the lower of its market value and its tax written down value so that no profit arises for the company.** Acquired by shareholders at the deemed disposal value.

(c) **Inventory** – disposal by company on transfer to shareholders. **If the company and the shareholders are connected persons** and **an election is made, the transfer is made at the greater of the original cost of the stock and the transfer price** (see Chapter 6 Section 2.12.2).

(d) **Plant and machinery** – disposal by company on transfer to shareholders. **Balancing adjustments can be avoided** if the **company and the shareholders are connected persons** and **an election is made for assets to be transferred at tax written down value** (see Chapter 7 Section 9).

(e) **Losses** – any **unused losses will not be transferable to the unincorporated business** and will therefore be lost.

4.6.3 Tax implications for shareholders on disincorporation

(a) **Distribution** - generally, **distributions of assets to the shareholders are treated as income** and taxed like a dividend (see Chapter 23 Section 1.8.2) However, if the shareholder is a basic rate taxpayer, the tax credit relating to the dividend will cover the income tax liability.

(b) **Capital receipt** - if **assets are distributed to the shareholders as part of a liquidation**, this will be **as a part disposal of shares in the hands of the shareholder** (see Chapter 23 Section 1.8.1). A similar situation arises in relation to certain distributions made in anticipation of an application to strike off a company (see Chapter 23 Section 1.8.2). Any chargeable gain may be covered by the annual exempt amount. Entrepreneurs' relief may be applicable.

4.7 Tax efficient profit extraction

There are several methods by which profit can be extracted from a company.

4.7.1 Methods of extracting profits

When trading activities are carried on through a limited company, careful thought needs to be given to the level and method of extraction of the profits generated. This decision should take into account both the needs of the individual shareholders and directors as well as the needs of the company itself. For instance, the company may need to retain a certain level of profit in order to reduce its bank overdraft or fund an expansion project.

The table below compares the various methods of extracting profits in outline. They are looked at in more detail below.

Method of extraction	Company	Individual
Remuneration Salary Benefits Tax free benefits	 Deductible/Class 1 NICs Deductible/Class 1A NICs Deductible/No NICs	 Taxable/Class 1 NICs Taxable Tax/NI free
Dividends	Not deductible	No tax for basic rate taxpayer Higher rate tax at 32.5% or additional rate at 37.5%, reduced by 10% tax credit No NICs
Loan interest	Deductible on accruals basis as interest on a loan relationship	Taxable as savings income
Rental income	Deductible	Taxable non-savings income
Pension contributions to registered pension schemes	Deductible	Tax free

4.7.2 Dividends or remuneration

Director/shareholders may wish to consider either extracting profits as dividend or remuneration. Payments of dividends or remuneration will reduce a company's retained profits which means a reduction in net asset value and hence the value of the shares, ultimately reducing any chargeable gain on the disposal of those shares. However, the immediate tax cost of paying dividends or remuneration must be weighed against this advantage.

Remuneration and the cost of benefits will be allowed as deductions in computing the company's total profits. The decision whether or not to make such payments could affect the rate of corporation tax by reducing the level of profits. However, **the national insurance cost must also be borne in mind**. A combination of dividends and remuneration may give the best result.

Question — **Dividends and remuneration**

A Ltd makes a profit before remuneration of £38,000 in the year to 31 March 2014. The shareholder/director is entitled to only the standard personal allowance. Consider the director's disposable income available by paying out the profit entirely as salary (of £34,325, allowing for employer's national insurance contributions) or by paying it out as a mixture of salary (at £7,696, so that no national insurance contributions are payable but preserving the director's entitlement to state benefits) and the remaining profits as a dividend.

Answer

		Salary only £	Salary and dividend £
(a)	**The company's tax position**		
	Profits	38,000	38,000
	Less: salary	(34,325)	(7,696)
	employer's national insurance	(3,675)	
	Taxable profits	0	30,304
	Corporation tax at 20%	£Nil	£6,061
	Cash dividend (30,304 – 6,061)		£24,243

(b) **The director's tax position**

	Non-savings income £	Dividend Income £	Total £
Salary only			
Earnings	34,325		
Less personal allowance	(9,440)		
Taxable income	24,885		24,885
Salary and dividends			
Earnings	7,696		
Dividends (× 100/90)		26,937	
Less personal allowance	(7,696)	(1,744)	
Taxable income	–	25,193	25,193

	Salary only £	Salary and dividend £
Non-savings income		
£24,885 × 20%	4,977	–
Dividend income		
£25,193 × 10%		2,519
Less tax credit on dividend (restricted)		(2,519)
Tax payable	4,977	–
Disposable income		
Salary	34,325	7,696
Less employee's national insurance		
£(34,325 – 7,755) × 12%	(3,188)	
Dividend		24,243
Less tax payable	(4,977)	
	26,160	31,939

The overall saving through paying a dividend is £(31,939 – 26,160) = £5,779.

4.7.3 Dividend payments

If dividends are paid, timing can be important. The tax year in which a dividend is paid affects the due date for any additional tax, and if a shareholder's other income fluctuates it may determine whether or not there is any additional tax to pay. Higher rate taxpayers must pay tax at 32.5% on dividend income and additional rate taxpayers tax at 37.5%, subject to a 10% tax credit.

Dividends carry a 10% tax credit and are taxed only at 10% in the hands of basic rate taxpayers which means that dividends are attractive to such individuals. However, the 10% tax credit is not repayable to non-taxpayers.

The payment of dividends does allow flexibility, ie family members need not work for a company in order to receive a dividend. However, this must be weighted against the fact that the company must generate sufficient profit to pay a dividend. Furthermore, HMRC may seek to invoke anti-avoidance legislation if dividends are paid to non-working family members if those who do work for the company do not draw a commercial salary. Most banks and building societies will recognise regular dividends from an owner managed company as income for mortgage or other loan purposes. This takes away a potential drawback of extraction of funds in the form of investment income.

Dividends are not subject to NICs. They do not give rise to an entitlement to pay pension contributions whereas remuneration and benefits do. They are not an allowable trading expense for the company.

4.7.4 Liquidation

An alternative to both dividends and remuneration is to retain profits in a company and then liquidate it. The company itself may have capital gains on the sale of its assets, and the shareholders will have capital gains on the liquidation, which will be treated as a disposal of their shares for the amounts paid to them. The CGT charges on the shareholders may be mitigated by spreading the capital distributions over two tax years, so as to use both years' annual exempt amounts. Entrepreneurs' relief may be available, in which case the rate of CGT will be 10%.

This route may be worth considering when a company is set up to undertake a single project which will be completed within a few years.

4.7.5 Loans

A director/shareholder may choose to lend money to the company and extract profits as interest income in return.

Interest income is taxed on the director/shareholder as savings income but it is not subject to NIC. It does not count as relevant earnings for pension purposes.

From the company's point of view, tax relief for the interest will be available under the loan relationship rules (ie either as a trading expense or as a deficit on a non-trading loan relationship).

4.7.6 Loans by close companies

Although loans by close companies to participators are not treated as distributions, on making such a loan the company suffers a tax charge: a payment equal to the amount of the loan × 25% is made to HMRC. This tax charge cannot be recovered until the loan is repaid or written off.

4.7.7 Rental income

On incorporation the owner(s) may decide to retain business premises outside the company and charge rent for its use. **The advantages of this method of profit extraction are that the company will obtain a trading income deduction for rent charged up to a commercial rate. Also, no NIC is payable.**

The disadvantage is that income from a property business does not qualify as relevant income for pension purposes. The payment of rental income will also restrict entrepreneurs' relief on a subsequent disposal of the premises.

For many small companies, the directors' own homes are often used for company business. It is possible to claim a deduction in the company for reasonable rent paid by the company. Care should be taken so as not to deny principal private residence relief on a proportion of the home. To do this, it must be shown that the room(s) are not used exclusively for company business, ie the occasional guest stays in the 'study'.

4.7.8 Pension provision

It is becoming increasingly important to save for one's own retirement. Fortunately, it is also something the government recognises as important and, as a result, pension provision has become the most efficient way of extracting funds from a family company.

Employers may set up an **occupational pension plan** for their employees. Employees may contribute to the occupational pension plan and all individuals may contribute to a **personal pension plan**. Employers may also contribute to an employee's personal pension plan.

The tax breaks for registered pension schemes are listed below.

(a) No taxable benefit for employer contributions
(b) No NIC is due on employer contributions
(c) The individual receives tax relief on his contributions
(d) The employer obtains tax relief for normal contributions actually paid during its accounting period.
(e) Pension fund grows tax free (tax credits on dividends not repayable)
(f) Tax free lump sum available up to 25% of the fund

4.7.9 Conclusion

The most tax efficient method of profit withdrawal hinges upon the marginal rate of corporation tax the company pays. For a small company dividends are the cheapest form of profit withdrawal. For a medium-sized or large company a bonus would seem the preferable option on the assumption that the director/shareholder is already paying maximum Class 1 primary NICs.

If the succession of the company is likely to be achieved by passing the shares down the family, profit retention will only increase the gain to be rolled over by way of a gift relief claim.

4.8 Tax efficient exit routes

FAST FORWARD

Capital gains and inheritance tax planning are important when disposing of a family business.

4.8.1 Introduction

Advice on tax efficient exit routes is probably the biggest area that a professional adviser is asked to deal with in tax planning for an owner managed business. This section will explore the key tax implications of passing on and selling the family business or company and suggest useful planning tips to help structure the business in the most efficient manner from the outset.

4.8.2 Capital gains tax planning

Regardless as to whether the business or company is to be sold or passed down to the next generation, a capital gain is likely to arise. It is therefore **essential to maximise the reliefs available**. Entrepreneurs' relief may be particularly valuable especially since the lifetime limit for gains is £10 million.

4.8.3 Inheritance tax planning

IHT is only a consideration where the family business or company is to be passed on to the next generation. An outright sale of the business to a third party does not constitute a transfer of value for IHT.

When a taxpayer wants to pass on his family business a major question exists as to whether to gift the assets now or wait until death.

If the assets are given during lifetime there may never be an IHT liability, either because the PET does not become chargeable or because the gift is covered by BPR provided the transferee still owns it (or other relevant business property) at the time of the transferor's death.

A lifetime gift will be subject to CGT at some point, either on transfer or on sale of the assets by the transferee assuming a gift relief claim is made.

However, a **transfer of assets on death receives a free uplift in the CGT base cost to current market value and any business property is passed on with the benefit of 100% BPR.**

There are strong arguments in favour of the approach to hold business property until death but other points are worthy of serious consideration:

(a) If a business is hit by recession the gain itself may be fairly low in any case.

(b) The gain may be deferred through EIS reinvestment relief.

(c) BPR at 100% may not be around forever.

(d) Free CGT uplift on business assets may be abolished in the future on the basis that such assets should either be taxed under capital gains tax or under inheritance tax.

Some other tax pitfalls exist which can be avoided provided they are identified and acted upon. The main areas as to consider include:

(a) Holding assets, such as business premises, outside the company or partnership restricts BPR to a rate of only 50%. This reduces to nil if the shares or partnership interest are disposed of before the business premises.

(b) Where a lifetime gift is made it is important that the property remains 'business property' for the next seven years and that the transferee retains ownership of it (or owns alternative business property) to prevent a charge to IHT on a sudden death.

(c) Beware of buy and sell arrangements included in the Articles of Association or partnership or shareholder agreements as BPR may be denied.

(d) It will be important to ensure that a gift does not fall foul of the 'reservation of benefit' rules.

4.8.4 Repurchases of own shares

It may be advantageous for individuals to sell shares back to the issuing company as a repurchase of own shares (see earlier in this Text). This will be treated as a capital gain (if the conditions are satisfied) or, if not, as a distribution. If distribution treatment is preferable it may be necessary to alter the proposal to ensure the conditions are *not* satisfied.

4.9 Planning for corporate growth

FAST FORWARD

At each stage of a 'company's life' from its beginning, through growth and future expansion overseas, tax planning strategies should be adopted.

Exam focus point

This section looks at a company as it begins trading, acquires additional business, and eventually expands abroad. It looks at the commercial decisions taken by the company and its shareholders at the different stages in the company's development, and summarises the tax implications of those decisions. It focuses, in particular, on those elements of corporation tax that are likely to be examined.

4.9.1 New company

Companies often start small. **One or two individuals will set up a company using their own funds (or borrowed funds) to do so.** Some shareholders may be active in running the company on a daily basis whilst others will be passive investors looking for a return on their investment.

Points to consider:

- *Is the company a close company?*
  This will impact the rate of tax paid if the company does not trade (ie main rate of corporation tax on a close investment company). Also are any benefits provided to participators (treated as dividends) or loans made to participators (trigger a charge at 25% on the company).

- *Can the shareholders receive tax relief for their investment?*
  If the company is a close company interest paid on a loan to invest in the company is deductible from total income.

  EIS income tax relief may be available to small investors.

- *Level of tax paid on company profits*
  Small profits rate will apply to profits below £300,000 with marginal relief for profits below £1,500,000.

  Salaries paid to employees reduce total profits, dividends paid to shareholders do not.
- *Losses* made can be relieved by carry back up to 12 months (if there are any profits to carry back against) or carry forward against future trading profits.
- Don't forget to consider registration for VAT.

4.9.2 Expansion in UK

A company can grow bigger by increasing its own activities or purchasing the activities of another business and either assuming those activities within itself or setting up a subsidiary company.

Points to consider:

(a) Single company (no associates) or group of companies. Number of associates affects CT profit limits

(b) If a group is formed: group relief for losses; asset transfers and tax planning regarding asset groups in respect of capital gains and losses; VAT group registration

(c) As taxable total profits grow, may need to consider payment of CT and VAT in instalments (large company)

(d) When a company acquires the trade of another company, capital losses remain within the vendor company. Trading losses will also remain with the vendor company unless the two companies are under common ownership.

4.9.3 Expansion overseas

As a company grows it may consider expanding overseas.

The tax implications of the overseas business depend on the legal structure used. From a tax point of view, there are two distinct ways of establishing the business:

- **It could be owned by the UK company**. Under this option, it would be an overseas PE of a UK resident company
- The UK company could **incorporate a new subsidiary in the overseas country** to acquire the business. Under this option, it would be an overseas subsidiary of a UK resident company.

Points to consider:

(a) *Overseas permanent establishment (PE)*

A PE is not a separate legal entity but is an extension of the company that owns it. **The profits or losses of the PE belong directly to the company.**

Provided the PE is controlled from the UK, **any trading loss made could be offset by the UK company (or group) against its income and gains of that year**, reducing the company's UK corporation tax liability. Once the PE is profitable, the company owning the PE will be subject to overseas corporation tax on the PE profits, because it is trading within the boundaries of the overseas country from a PE.

The profits will also be subject to UK corporation tax because a UK resident company is subject to tax on its worldwide income and gains. However the **UK corporation tax liability, in respect of the PE profits, will be relieved by double tax relief.**

A UK company may make an election to exempt the profits and losses of all its overseas PEs from UK corporation tax. The election means that the profits of a PE are only taxed overseas, but the election will disallow loss relief or overseas PEs against UK profits. Once made, the election must apply to all of the UK company's PEs and is irrevocable, so it is important to consider whether PEs in the future are likely to make a loss.

Double tax relief should also be taken into account when deciding whether to make the election. If the operation of DTR means that there is little or no UK corporation tax payable on overseas profits, it may be better not to make the election, and keep loss relief available in future accounting periods.

(b) *Overseas subsidiary*

A subsidiary is a separate legal entity. **A company incorporated in an overseas country will be resident in that country for tax purposes**, provided it is not managed and controlled from the UK. Its profits or losses will then be subject to the tax regime of the overseas country.

Any trading loss of the year would be carried forward and deducted from the company's future trading profits arising out of the same trade.

Once the company is profitable, it will be subject to tax in the overseas country. Any dividends paid to the UK parent company will normally be exempt from corporation tax.

(c) It is usually suggested that a **PE should be used where an overseas enterprise is expected to make initial losses**. This strategy enables the losses to be offset against any other profits of the company (as long as the exemption election is not made). The PE can be incorporated once it is profitable. However, the particular facts of the situation must be considered carefully.

(d) A subsidiary is an associate for the purpose of determining the rate of tax paid by group companies, whereas a PE is not. Accordingly, the use of a subsidiary (rather than a PE) could increase the rate of corporation tax paid by the UK companies.

4.10 Group tax minimisation strategies

FAST FORWARD

There are several tax planning opportunities available to groups of companies.

There are many **tax planning opportunities for groups of companies**. The following points should be considered, in addition to the points made earlier in this Text.

(a) **Minority interests should be restricted so as to ensure that the holding company has a 75% effective interest in every company. This will enable losses to be group relieved** to whichever company can make the best use of them (particularly companies in the marginal relief band).

(b) **The group can be regarded as one unit for the purposes of rollover relief** on the replacement of business assets.

(c) **The small profits rate limits will be shared equally among group members; profits may be shared to take advantage of them by fixing transfer prices for intra-group trading (transfer pricing rules generally do not apply to small and medium sized enterprises).** However, minority shareholders might then be unfairly advantaged or disadvantaged.

Careful consideration will need to be given to the number of associated companies in the group as setting up an additional subsidiary may affect the tax rate of all group companies.

(d) **VAT will arise on intra-group trading unless a VAT group is formed. It may be best to concentrate all exempt supplies in one or two companies which can be left outside the VAT group, and zero rated supplies in one or two other companies which can also be left outside the VAT group (or can form their own separate VAT group) and can make monthly repayment claims.**

(e) **Capital losses cannot be group relieved. However, an election can be made to transfer gains and losses between group members. It will be advantageous for net gains to be in the company paying the lowest marginal rate of corporation tax.** However, there are restrictions on the use of pre-entry losses and gains.

4.11 Divisionalised v group company structure

FAST FORWARD

Careful consideration needs to be given as to whether a group structure or a divisionalised company would be better.

4.11.1 General principles

In certain circumstances a business can be operated through a group company structure or through a single divisionalised company.

The setting up of a **trading group has a number of implications**, namely:

(a) It is **easier to give status to a key employee** by appointing him director of a subsidiary company.
(b) **Group relief of losses** is available.
(c) **Assets may be transferred between the group without giving rise to a charge to tax**.
(d) **Group wide rollover relief** may be claimed.

There are a number of disadvantages to a group structure that must be considered, particularly where the parent company or subsidiaries are to be sold.

Where the parent company is sold then the group would either:

(a) **Sell the group and then buy back the required subsidiaries**
(b) **Reconstruct the group which would need tax clearances and cause delays**, or
(c) **Sell assets**

Where a subsidiary is sold this could give rise to a capital gain although the relief for substantial shareholdings may be available.

The main advantage of a divisional structure is the fact that the **full amount of the small profits tax band will be available rather than being divided among all companies under common control.**

The other advantages are:

(a) **Automatic set-off losses** in respect of the various divisions
(b) **Automatic set-off of capital gains and losses**
(c) **Administration is simplified**

On the other hand, the disadvantages include:

(a) **Lack of incentive for divisional directors**
(b) **Difficulty in giving equity interest in a venture** (but may consider profit-related bonuses)
(c) It may be **difficult to find a prospective purchaser for the whole company**
(d) **Group profits can decrease the possibility of making optimum use of the small profits rate.**

4.11.2 Example: group v divisionalised structure

Sumner Limited carries on two trades through two separate divisions. The furniture production division makes profits of £1.35m in the year to 31 March 2014. The antique furniture restoration division makes profits of £150,000 in the same year.

Sumner Limited will pay tax of £345,000 (ie £1,500,000 × 23%).

If the company were to operate the trades through two separate companies the CT limits would be divided and the tax payable would be:

	£
£1,350,000 × 23%	310,500
£150,000 × 20%	30,000
Total	340,500

This creates a tax saving of £4,500 (ie £150,000 × 3%) as part of the profit utilises the small profits rate. However for this small saving, it may not be worth setting up a subsidiary company and channelling £150,000 profit into it.

5 Ethics

5.1 Introduction

In common with most professional organisations, the ACCA require members and students to observe the highest professional standards in all aspects of their work. This section discusses how these standards can be maintained, with particular reference to giving tax planning advice. The requirements apply equally to members and students, and in this section the term 'members' should be taken to include students.

In addition to the ACCA's own requirements, there are many instances where **members are required to comply with statutory and regulatory requirements**. If a member is in doubt as to the course of action he should take, he should approach the ACCA for guidance. **Failure to observe the ACCA's standards may result in disciplinary action.**

The ACCA publish a **Code of Ethics and Conduct** covering the standards and ethical requirements which they expect. It details the **fundamental principles and sets out a framework for applying those principles.** Members must apply this framework to particular situations to identify instances where compliance with the ethical standards may be compromised so that safeguards may be put in place to avoid threats, or to reduce them to below the minimum level that can be regarded as acceptable.

Normally a member's responsibility will be to a client, or to an employer, but there may be instances where a member may need to act in the public interest.

5.2 The fundamental principles

FAST FORWARD The fundamental principles of ethics should underlie all of a member's professional behaviour.

The fundamental principles are:

(a) **Integrity**: Requires all members to be straightforward and honest in professional and business relationships.

A member should not be associated with information if he believes that the information contains a materially false or misleading statement, statements or information furnished recklessly, or omits or obscures information required to be included where such omission or obscurity would be misleading.

(b) **Objectivity**: Imposes an obligation on members not to compromise their professional or business judgement because of bias, conflict of interest or the undue influence of others.

Relationships that bias or unduly influence the professional judgement of the member should be avoided.

(c) **Professional competence and due care**: Requires members to:

(i) Maintain professional knowledge and skill at the level required to ensure that clients or employers receive competent professional service based on current developments in practice, legislation and techniques; and

(ii) Act diligently in accordance with applicable technical and professional standards when providing professional services.

Any limitations relating to the service being provided must be made clear to clients and other users to ensure that misinterpretation of facts or opinions does not take place.

(d) **Confidentiality**: Imposes an obligation on members to refrain from:

(i) Disclosing outside the firm confidential information acquired as a result of professional and business relationships without proper and specific authority or unless there is a legal or professional right or duty to disclose; and

(ii) Using confidential information acquired as a result of professional and business relationships to their personal advantage or the advantage of third parties

A member should consider the need to maintain confidentiality of information within the firm. A member should also maintain confidentiality of information disclosed by a prospective client or employer.

The need to maintain confidentiality continues even after the end of relationships between a member and a client or employer. When a member changes employment or acquires a new client, the member is entitled to use prior experience, but not confidential information obtained from the previous relationship.

(e) **Professional behaviour**. Imposes an obligation on a member to comply with relevant laws and regulations and avoid any action that may bring discredit to the profession.

This includes actions which a reasonable and informed third party, having knowledge of all relevant information, would conclude negatively affects the good reputation of the profession.

Members should be honest and truthful and should not:

(i) Make exaggerated claims for the services they are able to offer, the qualifications they possess, or experience they have gained

(ii) Make disparaging references or unsubstantiated comparisons to the work of others

5.3 The conceptual framework

5.3.1 Introduction

A member may find himself in a situation where there is a **specific threat to compliance with the fundamental principles**. There are many possible scenarios, and rather than trying to specify how each situation should be dealt with, the ACCA provide a conceptual framework that requires members to identify, evaluate and address such threats. Unless an identified threat is clearly insignificant, members should apply safeguards to eliminate the threat or reduce it to an acceptable level so that compliance with the fundamental principles is not compromised.

5.3.2 Threats

The member is obliged to evaluate any threat as soon as he knows, or should be expected to know, of its existence. Both qualitative and quantitative factors should be taken into account.
Most threats to compliance with the fundamental principles fall into the following categories:

(a) **Self-interest threat**, which may occur as a result of the financial or other interests of a member or of an immediate or close family member

(b) **Self-review threat**, which may occur when a previous judgment needs to be re-evaluated by the member responsible for that judgement

(c) **Advocacy threat**, which may occur when a member promotes a position or opinion to the point that subsequent objectivity may be compromised

(d) **Familiarity threats**, which may occur when, because of a close relationship, a member becomes too sympathetic to the interests of others

(e) **Intimidation threats**, which may occur when a member may be deterred from acting objectively by threats, actual or perceived

5.3.3 Safeguards to offset the threats

If a member cannot implement appropriate safeguards, he should decline or discontinue the specific professional service involved, or where necessary resign from the client.

Safeguards that may eliminate or reduce threats to an acceptable level fall into two broad categories:

(a) **Safeguards created by the profession, legislation or regulation**, such as education and training, continuing professional development, professional or regulatory monitoring and disciplinary procedures

(b) **Safeguards in the work environment**, such as effective, well publicised complaints systems operated by the employing organisation

The nature of the safeguards to be applied will vary depending on the circumstances. In exercising professional judgement, a member should consider what a reasonable and informed third party, having knowledge of all relevant information, including the significance of the threat and the safeguards applied, would conclude to be unacceptable.

5.4 Ethical conflict resolution

There may be instances where a particular situation leads to a **conflict in the application of the fundamental principles.**

When initiating either a formal or informal conflict resolution process, a member should consider five factors:

(a) **Relevant facts**
(b) **Ethical issues**
(c) **Fundamental principles related to the matter**
(d) **Established internal procedures**
(e) **Alternative courses of action**

Having considered these issues, the appropriate course of action can be determined which resolves the conflict with all or some of the five fundamental principles. If the matter remains unresolved, the member should consult with other appropriate persons within the firm for help in obtaining resolution.

Where a matter involves a conflict with, or within, an organisation, a member should also consider consulting with those charged with governance of the organisation.

It is advisable for the member to **document the issue and details of any discussions held or decisions taken, concerning that issue.**

If a significant conflict cannot be resolved, a member may wish to obtain **professional advice from the ACCA or legal advisors**, to obtain guidance on ethical and legal issues without breaching confidentiality.

If, after exhausting all relevant possibilities, **the ethical conflict remains unresolved, a member should, where possible, refuse to remain associated with the matter creating the conflict.**

The member may determine that, in the circumstances, it is appropriate to withdraw from the engagement team or specific assignment, or to resign altogether from the engagement or the firm.

5.5 Disclosure of information

5.5.1 When to disclose

A member may disclose confidential information if:

(a) Disclosure is permitted by law and is authorised by the client or the employer

(b) Disclosure is required by law, such as under anti-money laundering legislation

(c) There is a professional duty or right to disclose, when not prohibited by law, such as under a quality review

5.5.2 Factors to consider regarding disclosure

In deciding whether to disclose confidential information, members should consider:

(a) Whether the interests of all parties, including third parties, could be harmed if the client or employer consents to the disclosure of information

(b) Whether all the relevant information is known and substantiated, to the extent it is practicable to do so. When the situation involves unsubstantiated facts, incomplete information or unsubstantiated conclusions, professional judgement should be used in determining the type of disclosure to be made, if any

(c) The type of communication that is expected and to whom it is addressed; in particular, members should be satisfied that the parties to whom the communication is addressed are appropriate recipients

5.6 Conflicts of interest

FAST FORWARD

A conflict of interest is a commonly met threat to compliance with the fundamental principles.

5.6.1 The threat of a conflict of interest

A member should take reasonable steps to identify circumstances that could pose a conflict of interest. These may give rise to threats to compliance with the fundamental principles.

A conflict may arise between the firm and the client or between two conflicting clients being managed by the same firm. For example, where a firm acts for both a husband and wife in a divorce settlement or acts for a company and for its directors in their personal capacity.

Evaluation of threats includes consideration as to whether the member has any business interests or relationships with the client or a third party that could give rise to threats. Safeguards should be considered and applied as necessary.

5.6.2 Safeguards

Depending upon the circumstances giving rise to the conflict, safeguards should ordinarily include the member in public practice:

(a) **Notifying the client** of the firm's business interest or activities that may represent a conflict of interest

(b) **Notifying all known relevant parties** that the member is acting for two or more parties in respect of a matter where their respective interests are in conflict

(c) **Notifying the client that the member does not act exclusively for any one client** in the provision of proposed services (for example, in a particular market sector or with respect to a specific service)

In each case the member should obtain the consent of the relevant parties to act.
Where a member has requested consent from a client to act for another party (which may or may not be an existing client) and that consent has been refused, then he must not continue to act for one of the parties in the matter giving rise to the conflict of interest.

The following additional safeguards should also be considered:

(a) The use of separate engagement teams

(b) Procedures to prevent access to information (eg strict physical separation of such teams, confidential and secure data filing)

(c) Clear guidelines for members of the engagement team on issues of security and confidentiality

(d) The use of confidentiality agreements signed by employees and partners of the firm

(e) Regular review of the application of safeguards by a senior individual not involved with relevant client engagements

Where a conflict of interest poses a threat to one or more of the fundamental principles that cannot be eliminated or reduced to an acceptable level through the application of safeguards, the member should conclude that it is not appropriate to accept a specific engagement or that resignation from one or more conflicting engagements is required.

5.6.3 Example

You have acted for Robenick Ltd for several years, and also for the three director shareholders, Rob, Ben and Nick. During 2013 Rob has a disagreement with Ben and Nick over the direction of the company. What should you do?

When you commenced acting for both the company and Rob, Ben and Nick you should have advised each that you were acting for the others, and asked their permission to act. Providing there were no areas where the interests of the clients conflicted, there is no reason why you should not have acted for all the clients, although it may be advisable to have ensured that, for example, a different tax manager was responsible for each client.

However, now that there has been a disagreement between Rob and the other clients the situation has changed and there is a conflict of interest. It is most likely that it would be inappropriate to continue to act for all the clients, and you will need to cease to act, either for Rob, or for Ben, Nick and the company.

5.7 Prospective clients

Members invited to act as tax advisers by clients must **contact the existing tax advisers** to ascertain if there are any matters they should be aware of when deciding whether to accept the appointment.

5.7.1 Acceptance

Before accepting a new client, members should consider whether acceptance of the client or the particular engagement would create any threats to compliance with the fundamental principles.

Potential threats to integrity or professional behaviour may be created from, for example, questionable issues associated with the client, or a threat to professional competence and due care may be created if the engagement team does not possess the necessary skills to carry out the engagement. Where it is not possible to implement safeguards to reduce the threats to an acceptable level, members should decline to enter into the relationship.

There are also client identification procedures to be followed (see later in this chapter).

5.7.2 Changes in professional appointment

Members who are asked to replace another accountant should ascertain whether there are any professional or other reasons for not accepting the engagement. This may require direct communication with the existing accountant to establish the facts and circumstances behind the proposed change so that members can decide whether it is appropriate to accept the engagement.

Communication with the existing accountant is not just a matter of professional courtesy. Its main purpose is to enable members to ensure that there has been no action by the client which would on ethical grounds, preclude members from accepting the appointment and that, after considering all the facts, the client is someone for whom members would wish to act. Thus, members must always communicate with the existing accountant on being asked to accept appointment for any recurring work.

The existing accountant is bound by confidentiality. This means the extent to which a client's affairs may be discussed with a prospective accountant will depend on the nature of the engagement and on whether the client's permission has been obtained. **If the client refuses permission, the existing accountant should inform the prospective accountant, who should then inform the client that he is unable to accept the appointment.**

If the existing accountant fails to communicate with the prospective accountant despite the client's permission, the prospective accountant will need to make other enquiries to ensure there are no reasons not to accept the appointment. This could be through communications with third parties, such as banks.

Where the member is the existing accountant then, subject to obtaining the client's permission, he should disclose all information requested without delay.

5.7.3 Example

You have acted for Mr X but have discovered a serious tax irregularity which Mr X has refused to correct and you have advised Mr X that you can no longer act for him. You receive a letter from another ACCA member advising you that he has been asked to act for Mr X. Mr X has forbidden you to divulge any information about him. What should you do?

You should advise the new accountant that Mr X has not given you permission to divulge any information. The new accountant should then refuse to act for Mr X.

5.7.4 Acting as agent or principal

Where you are performing tax compliance work eg preparing and submitting tax returns, you will be acting as agent to the client. This means that the client remains responsible for all of the information provided in the return.

When you are **providing tax planning advice, however, you will be acting as 'principal'** which means that you are fully responsible for the advice you give.

5.7.5 Tax planning concerns

At the very least, **anything you recommend must be legal**. Most people understand the basic distinction between tax avoidance (tax mitigation through legal means) and tax evasion (illegal, such as fraud). Apart from the specific rules regarding disclosure of avoidance schemes (see below), you must understand that the taxpayer has the responsibility of preparing a tax return that is complete and correct (see above), and this will include an accurate disclosure of the facts.

That is not to say that you may not suggest a course of action where HMRC might disagree with your conclusion as to the tax consequences. You need to explain to the client that full details must be given to enable HMRC to consider the matter, and you should warn him that any negotiations with HMRC will take time and incur expense.

Make sure that you **know the time limits for any claims** that need to be made. If you miss the limit, the relief will be denied. Late returns incur penalties, and late payment of tax leads to an interest charge.

5.8 Tax irregularities

FAST FORWARD

If a member discovers that a client has misled him in order to obtain a tax advantage, the member has to consider his position in relation to both the client and the tax authorities.

5.8.1 Discovery of errors

A member may discover that a client has committed a taxation offence. Tax legislation prescribes monetary penalties for a number of offences. There is also the possibility of criminal proceedings being brought against the client.

The evasion or attempted evasion of tax may be the subject of criminal charges under both tax law and money laundering legislation. This applies not only to direct taxes such as income tax or corporation tax, but also to indirect taxes such as VAT.

The member has the following responsibilities:

(a) If the information obtained concerns computations or returns that the member is currently preparing, the member must ensure that the information is accurately reflected therein. **If the client fails to provide any information requested by the member, or objects to way in which the member has presented the information, the member needs to consider whether he can continue to act for that client.**

(b) If the information obtained concerns computations or returns that the member has already prepared and submitted to HMRC, the member cannot allow HMRC to continue to rely on them. **He should advise his client to make full disclosure to HMRC, or to authorise him to do so, without delay. If the client refuses, then the member can no longer act for the client.** The client should be advised of this, and also that the member must inform HMRC that they have ceased to act for the client. If the documents submitted to HMRC contain any accountant's report, the member must also advise HMRC that the report should no longer be relied on. The member should not, however, advise HMRC in what way the accounts are defective unless the client has consented to such disclosure.

(c) If the information relates to a new client and concerns computations or returns that have been prepared by the client or a third party and submitted to HMRC, the member should advise the client to make full and prompt disclosure. If the error affects the current computations or returns then the member must inform the client that an appropriate adjustment must be made in the current accounts, and **if the client refuses the member should consider whether he should act for that client**. Indeed, even if the error does not affect current returns and computations the member should consider whether he should act for the client if the client refuses to disclose the error to HMRC.

Whether or not the member feels able to act for a client, he is still under a **professional duty to ensure that the client understands the seriousness of offences against HMRC**. He should also warn the client that notification that he is no longer acting for a client may alert HMRC, and urge the desirability of making a full disclosure, subject to any legal advice obtained. Any accounts, returns, computations or reports submitted on behalf of taxpayers are deemed to be submitted by the taxpayer and/or with their consent unless they prove otherwise.

This emphasises the need for members to ensure that clients have approved computations and returns, and signified their approval by signing them. There should always be a letter of engagement in place setting out the precise responsibilities of both the member and the client.

5.8.2 Example

You are preparing the tax return for Mrs Y and amongst her papers you find a bank statement for a new account which was opened with the transfer of a significant amount from her own account. Mrs Y says that this new account belongs to her young son, and that the interest should not be put on her tax return. What should you do?

First, you should explain that income from funds provided by a parent are taxed as the parent's income, unless the income is less that £100, so that the interest must be shown. If Mrs Y still refuses to enter the interest on her return you should advise her that you can no longer act for her, and you must also advise HMRC that you no longer act. You are not obliged to disclose the reason to HMRC.

At this stage you have a suspicion that a tax offence may be committed, and you should discuss this with your firm's money laundering officer.

5.8.3 HMRC powers

HMRC have certain statutory powers to compel disclosure in particular instances. Where information is sought under such powers, members must check that the statutory power being invoked actually covers the information sought and, if in any doubt, should take legal advice.

In some cases HMRC will ask for information to be provided voluntarily, rather than resorting to the use of their statutory powers. In this case the member must consider carefully whether it is in the client's interest to make voluntary disclosure, rather than await a statutory demand, and again may wish to take legal advice.

5.8.4 Errors by HMRC in the taxpayers' favour

Problems may arise if HMRC erroneously makes an excessive repayment of tax to taxpayers, even though they have received full disclosure of the facts.

If the repayment is made directly to the client, the member should urge them to refund the excess sum to HMRC as soon as possible. Failure to correct the error may be a civil and/or criminal offence by the client. **If the client refuses the member must consider whether he should continue to act for the client.** If he ceases to act, he must notify HMRC that he no longer acts for the client, but is under no duty to give

HMRC any further details, although it may be necessary to consider whether a report should be made under the money laundering rules.

If the repayment is made to the member on the client's behalf, the member must notify the tax authorities. Failure to do so could involve both the member and client in a civil and/or criminal offence.

It should be noted that if HMRC make the repayment because they have adopted a different treatment of a transaction to that taken by the member and client, this is not an excessive repayment, it merely arises from a different interpretation of the legislation. This is subject to the proviso that full details of the transaction has been returned, so that HMRC have reached their decision on an informed basis.

5.9 Money laundering

Money laundering is the process by which criminals attempt to conceal the true origin and ownership of the proceeds of their criminal activity, often with the unwitting assistance of professionals such as accountants and lawyers.

Members are bound by legislation to implement preventative measures and to report suspicions to the appropriate authority. Failure to follow these legislative requirements will often be a criminal offence, leading to a fine and/or imprisonment. The legal position and its application to any given set of facts may not be straightforward and members are advised to take legal advice whenever they are uncertain as to their conduct.

Members should have appropriate procedures to ensure that client identification procedures are carried out correctly and that knowledge and suspicions of money laundering are reported to the firm's money laundering officer.

5.9.1 Client identification procedures

Where a new client is taken on a member should verify his identity by reliable and independent means. This could comprise the following:

(a) Where the client is an individual: by obtaining independent evidence, such as a passport, driving licence, HMRC document such as a notice of coding, and proof of address;

(b) Where the client is a company: by obtaining proof of incorporation; by establishing the primary business address; by identifying the members and directors of the company; and by establishing the identities of those persons instructing the member on behalf of the company and verifying that those persons are authorised to do so.

If satisfactory evidence cannot be obtained, no work should be undertaken.

Members should **retain all client identification records for at least five years after the end of the client relationship**, together with records of all work carried out for the client.

5.9.2 Suspicions of money laundering

During the course of the engagement, members should regularly review the client's actions to satisfy themselves that they are consistent with the client's usual activities. Anything which appears to be out of the ordinary should be closely examined and a written record made of the member's conclusions. **If members' suspicions are aroused, a money laundering report should be made.**

Suspicion is more than mere speculation, but which falls short of proof based on firm evidence. What is suspicious in relation to one client may not be suspicious in relation to another client. Therefore, the key to recognising a suspicious transaction or situation is for members to have a full understanding of the client and his activities.

Transactions which appear to have no apparent economic or visible lawful purpose should be looked at carefully to establish their purpose and any findings recorded in writing. If no purpose for the transaction can be established, this may be a ground for suspicion.

Where members know or suspect that funds are directly or indirectly the proceeds of crime, they should report their suspicions promptly to the Serious Organised Crime Agency (SOCA). Where tax evasion is involved members will also need to examine their responsibilities to the tax authorities.

Where the work done by members for their clients is covered by legal professional privilege, members are not required to report their suspicions. Whether or not legal professional privilege applies to members and in what circumstances will depend on local law and members are strongly advised to seek legal advice as and when the issue arises.

5.9.3 Tipping off

Members should not 'tip off' a client that a report has been made. This may cause a member difficulties if a client refuses to disclose tax irregularities to HMRC as ceasing to act for the client might tip off the client that a report has been made. Any attempts to persuade a client not to proceed with an intended crime will not constitute tipping off.

Members faced with money laundering issues may call upon the Advisory Services Section of the ACCA for confidential advice.

5.10 Disclosure of tax avoidance schemes

FAST FORWARD

There are disclosure requirements for promoters of direct tax avoidance schemes. Businesses may be required to disclose use of VAT avoidance schemes.

5.10.1 Direct tax avoidance schemes

Promoters of tax avoidance schemes have disclosure obligations. There is also an obligation on taxpayers to disclose details of schemes in certain cases.

Notification is required from a promoter of arrangements or proposed arrangements, the main benefit of which is to enable any person to obtain an advantage in relation to tax. A 'promoter' is defined as a person who, in the course of a trade, profession or business involving the provision of tax services to other persons, is to any extent responsible for the design of the arrangements, or who makes a proposal available for implementation by other persons.

The information to be given by a promoter must be provided within a prescribed period of five days after being made available. The information to be provided and the manner in which it is to be provided is set out in the regulations.

A taxpayer is required to provide details of arrangements where the arrangements have been purchased from an offshore promoter, and that promoter has made no disclosure. Disclosure must also be made by large businesses which have **entered into arrangements not involving a promoter.**

HMRC may allocate a reference number to arrangements notified under the disclosure rules. Promoters are required to notify clients of that reference number so that they can enter that number on their tax return.

Any person that fails to comply with any of the disclosure provisions is liable to a penalty not exceeding £5,000. If the failure continues after that penalty has been imposed, that person is liable to a further penalty or penalties not exceeding £600 for each day on which the failure continues.

A tax advantage is defined as relief or increased relief from tax, repayment or increased repayment of tax, avoidance or reduction of a charge to a tax. It also includes the deferral of any payment of tax or advancement of any repayment of tax or the avoidance of any obligation to deduct or account for tax. Hallmarks are laid down by regulations specifying types of notifiable schemes.

The taxes covered by these provisions are IT, CGT, CT, IHT, SDLT and stamp duty. NIC is also included.

5.10.2 VAT avoidance schemes

Businesses using VAT avoidance schemes must disclose their use. Certain VAT avoidance schemes ('notifiable' schemes) are put on a statutory register.

Businesses with an annual turnover of £600,000 or more that use designated schemes must inform HMRC. A designated scheme is one which has been designated by the Treasury.

Businesses with an annual turnover of £10 million or more must also inform HMRC if they use notifiable schemes, that are not designated schemes, for the purpose of securing a tax advantage.

Detailed regulations deal with the notification procedure to be used.

The **penalty for failure to notify HMRC of the use of a designated scheme is 15% of the VAT saving** as a result of the use of the scheme. The **penalty for using other arrangements is £5,000.**

5.11 General anti-abuse rule (GAAR)

FAST FORWARD

There is a general anti-abuse rule to enable HMRC to counteract tax advantages gained from abusive tax arrangements.

5.11.1 Introduction

The GAAR provides **additional means for HMRC to 'counteract' tax advantages arising from abusive 'tax arrangements'**.

5.11.2 Tax arrangements

Tax arrangements are arrangements with a main purpose of obtaining a tax advantage.

Arrangements are **abusive** if they **cannot be regarded as a reasonable course of action**, for example, where they **lead to unintended results involving one or more contrived or abnormal steps and exploit any shortcomings in the tax provisions**.

Examples of **abusive arrangements** include those that result in:

(a) Significantly less income, profits or gains

(b) Significantly greater deductions or losses, or

(c) A claim for the repayment or crediting of tax (including foreign tax) that has not been, and is unlikely to be, paid

5.11.3 Tax advantage

A **'tax advantage'** includes:

(a) Relief or increased relief from tax
(b) Repayment or increased repayment of tax
(c) Avoidance or reduction of a charge to tax
(d) Avoidance of a possible assessment to tax
(e) Deferral of a payment of tax or advancement of a repayment of tax
(f) Avoidance of an obligation to deduct or account for tax

5.11.4 Counteracting tax advantages

HMRC may counteract tax advantages arising by, for example, increasing the taxpayer's tax liability.

HMRC must follow certain procedural requirements and, if it makes any adjustments, these must be on a 'just and reasonable' basis.

Chapter roundup

- Questions on impact of taxes require you to use your technical knowledge of taxation in relation to particular scenarios. Avoid writing about technical areas in general terms as opposed to in relation to the question's requirements.
- There are many sources of finance available for individuals, long or short term, secured or unsecured.
- A mortgage may be a repayment or interest only mortgage. Pensions or ISAs may be used to accumulate the capital required to repay an interest only mortgage.
- Most deposit based investments are fairly low risk investments in which an investor receives a low rate of interest in return for depositing his capital with the institution.
- A fixed interest security pays a fixed rate of interest and has a known maturity value so long as it is held until its redemption date.
- Individual savings accounts (ISAs) provide a tax-free wrapper for investments in cash, and stocks and shares.
- Equities are high risk investments as neither the income nor the capital is secure.
- The enterprise investment scheme (EIS) is a scheme designed to promote enterprise and investment by helping high-risk, unlisted trading companies raise finance.
- The seed enterprise investment scheme (SEIS) is similar to the EIS scheme but rewards investment in small, start up unquoted trading companies, with a greater tax reducer.
- Venture capital trusts (VCTs) are listed companies which invest in unquoted trading companies, so enabling investors to spread their risk over a number of higher-risk, unquoted companies whilst obtaining income tax and capital gains tax reliefs.
- Businesses may require short or long term finance to start up, carry on or expand.
- A business may raise finance through loans and may be able to obtain tax relief for interest paid. A company can raise finance by issuing shares to shareholders.
- A business may lease or buy assets. Short term leasing costs may be deductible expenses. Longer term costs may attract capital allowances in a similar way to buying an asset outright.
- As a general rule, self-employment leads to lower overall tax and NIC burdens than employment.
- If someone is to be an employee, the tax effects of the remuneration package should be taken into account.
- An individual can choose between trading as a sole trader or trading through a company. That choice, and if a company is chosen, the choice between dividends and remuneration, can significantly affect the overall tax and NIC burden. Cash flow is also an important consideration.
- The incorporation of a business should be carefully planned, taking account of consequent tax liabilities. There are both advantages and disadvantages to incorporating a business. A disposal of shares can also have several tax consequences.
- If disincorporation relief applies, there will be no corporation tax charge on the transfer of land and buildings and goodwill by a company to its shareholders. Other reliefs may apply to transfers of inventory and plant and machinery. A tax charge may arise for the shareholders on the distribution of assets, either income tax or capital gains tax.
- There are several methods by which profit can be extracted from a company.
- Capital gains and inheritance tax planning are important when disposing of a family business.
- At each stage of a 'company's life' from its beginning, through growth and future expansion overseas, tax planning strategies should be adopted.
- There are several tax planning opportunities available to groups of companies.

- Careful consideration needs to be given as to whether a group structure or a divisionalised company would be better.
- The fundamental principles of ethics should underlie all of a member's professional behaviour.
- A conflict of interest is a commonly met threat to compliance with the fundamental principles.
- If a member discovers that a client has misled him in order to obtain a tax advantage, the member has to consider his position in relation to both the client and the tax authorities.
- There are disclosure requirements for promoters of direct tax avoidance schemes. Businesses may be required to disclose use of VAT avoidance schemes.
- There is a general anti-abuse rule to enable HMRC to counteract tax advantages gained from abusive tax arrangements.

Quick quiz

1. What are the main sources of finance for private purposes?
2. What are the two main methods of repaying the capital of a mortgage?
3. How are the returns on NS&I savings certificates taxed?
4. What are the two components in an individual savings account?
5. What are the features of a preference share?
6. What are the main NIC differences between the tax positions of employees and the self employed?
7. What is a major attraction of incorporation?
8. Why might a newly commencing trader employ a prospective partner at first, before forming a partnership?
9. What is the major disadvantage for an individual shareholder of an incorporated business where losses are anticipated?
10. List the methods by which profit may be extracted from a company.
11. What are the advantages of a divisionalised company structure?
12. Can an ACCA member act for both parties in a marriage/civil partnership?
13. What should you do if you suspect that a client may have taken a bribe from a customer?
14. What is the maximum initial penalty for failure to notify a tax avoidance scheme relating to income tax?
15. When may HMRC use the general anti-abuse rule?

Answers to quick quiz

1 (a) Bank overdrafts
(b) Unsecured bank and building society loans
(c) Mortgage loans
(d) Credit cards and credit facilities provided by retailers
(e) Hire purchase facilities

2 Capital of a mortgage may be paid back during the term or at the end of the term.

3 Returns on NS&I savings certificates are tax free.

4 (a) Cash
(b) Stocks and shares

5 Preference shares:

(a) Ahead of ordinary shares for dividends/liquidation
(b) Guaranteed dividend amount (but no increase if surplus)

6 Employees suffer Class 1 NIC. Their employers suffer Class 1 and Class 1A NIC too.

The self employed pay Class 2 and Class 4 NIC. The rates of NIC due under these classes are smaller than Class 1 and Class 1A NIC.

7 The attraction of incorporation is limited liability. A sole trader or partner is liable for business debts to the full extent of his personal wealth. A limited company's shareholder is liable to the amount, if any, unpaid on his shares.

8 Commencing trade with a prospective partner as a salaried employee for a year or two obtains tax relief twice on his salary during any overlap period.

9 A company's losses are not available to reduce shareholders' taxable incomes (unlike losses of an unincorporated business which can reduce the sole trade/partners incomes).

10 (a) Remuneration
(b) Dividends
(c) Loan interest
(d) Rental income
(e) Pension contributions

11 (a) Full amount of small profit tax bands available rather than being divided among all companies under common control
(b) Automatic set off of trading losses in respect of various divisions
(c) Automatic set off of capital gains and losses
(d) Administration is simplified

12 It depends on whether there are any relationships between the two that could give rise to a conflict of interest. For example, they may be business partners, or one may employ the other. Even so, it may be sufficient to ensure that each is aware that you act for both, provided you keep the position under review. In other cases the conflict of interest might be such that you should not; for example if there has been a breakdown in their relationship.

13 This is likely to be a criminal offence and you should report your suspicions to the firm's money laundering officer.

14 £5,000

15 The general anti-abuse rule may be used by HMRC where a taxpayer has used abusive tax arrangements to obtain a tax advantage.

Now try the questions below from the Exam Question Bank

Number	Level	Marks	Time
Q33	Introductory	25	45 mins
Q34	Introductory	21	38 mins
Q35	Introductory	15	27 mins
Q36	Examination	29	52 mins
Q37	Examination	26	47 mins

Exam question and answer bank

1 The Wrights **36 mins**

Eric Wright (born 31 January 1939) is a partner in a firm of architects. His taxable trade profits for 2013/14 are £26,560. In 2012, he took out a loan to buy some plant and machinery used in the partnership business. The amount of loan interest in 2013/14 was £1,000.

Eric has a bank account with the Halifax Bank. His account was credited with interest of £1,600 on 31 March 2014. In October 2013 Eric invested £11,000 in a venture capital trust.

Eric is married to Melanie. Melanie (born 1 April 1958) is employed as a head teacher in a local primary school. In 2013/14 she had earnings of £50,000. PAYE of £10,000 was deducted from these earnings.

Melanie received dividends of £4,500 during 2013/14. She also cashed in National Savings & Investments Certificates and received £250 interest in addition to the repayment of the capital invested.

Eric and Melanie are considering buying a cottage together in May 2014 and renting it out. The cottage will cost £120,000. The net rental income will be about £12,000 per year. Eric and Melanie have not decided exactly in what proportions they will contribute to the cost of buying the cottage.

Required

(a) Compute the net income tax payable by Eric and Melanie for 2013/14. **(10 marks)**

(b) Explain how the rental income from the cottage will be taxed on Eric and Melanie. What advice would you give them to reduce their total tax liability? Assume Eric and Melanie have the same other income and expenditure in 2014/15 as in 2013/14 and that the rates of tax and allowances also remain the same in both tax years. **(5 marks)**

(c) A friend of Melanie has offered her the opportunity to subscribe £12,000 for shares in an EIS company. If Melanie does so she will borrow the money from the bank at an interest rate of 8%. Melanie's friend assures her that the company will start to pay dividends in five years' time. Alternatively Melanie could invest £12,000 to buy a 10% stake in another friend's company, and in this case dividends are likely to be paid at the rate of £1,000 in the first year, increasing by £100 a year. Melanie would like to know how much her cash outlay will be over five years for each investment. **(5 marks)**

(Total = 20 marks)

2 Pensions **29 mins**

(a) You have received the following e-mail from a client, Mr Lee:

'I have just started a new job and thought that I ought to start making some pension provision now that I am in my mid-30s. My initial salary is £40,000 a year, but I am hoping that, with bonuses, it may increase in the next few years.

My employer operates a pension scheme and I have been given a booklet about it. The booklet says that the scheme is a 'money purchase' scheme. If I join the scheme, my employer will make contributions to the scheme in addition to the amount that I pay into it.

Could you answer the following questions:

(1) Do I have to join my employer's pension scheme or can I make other pension arrangements? What is a 'money purchase' scheme?

(2) If I join my employer's pension scheme, how much can I contribute to the scheme and how much can my employer contribute? The booklet refers to an annual limit and a lifetime limit. How do these work?

(3) I have heard that there is tax relief on my contributions to a pension scheme. How does that work if I join my employer's pension scheme?

Required

Draft an e-mail in response. **(11 marks)**

(b) It is March 2014. Another of your clients, Mr Holloway, who was born in 1980, will have employment income of £118,880 for 2013/14. Mr Holloway has no other income in 2013/14.

Required

(i) Compute Mr Holloway's tax liability for 2013/14 based on this information.

(ii) Advise Mr Holloway how he can make a personal pension contribution which would be most tax efficient. **(5 marks)**

(Total = 16 marks)

3 Hamburg **45 mins**

(a) Hamburg (born in 1950) retired in January 2013 and used income from his investments to live on.

On 31 December 2013, he received the following interest payments on his National Savings & Investments accounts:

Direct Saver account	£90
Investment account	£460

Hamburg received an income payment of £6,875 from a discretionary trust set up by his aunt on 1 February 2014. The whole of the trust fund was invested in quoted shares.

Hamburg also received dividends of £19,125 during 2013/14 from his own investments.

Hamburg owned £20,000 6% Treasury loan stock which he bought in 1996. Interest is payable gross on 1 June and 1 December each year. On 21 May 2013, Hamburg sold £10,000 of the loan stock ex interest. The accrued interest due to the purchaser was £35. Hamburg sold a further £7,500 of loan stock including interest of £150 on 1 October 2013.

On 1 May 2013 Hamburg started to invest in rented properties. He bought three houses in the first three months, as follows.

House 1

Hamburg bought house 1 for £62,000 on 1 May 2013. It needed a new roof before it was fit to be let out, and Hamburg paid £5,000 for the work to be done in May. He then let it unfurnished for £600 a month from 1 June to 30 November 2013. The first tenant then left, and the house was empty throughout December 2013. On 1 January 2014, a new tenant moved in. The house was again let unfurnished. The rent was £6,000 a year, payable annually in advance.

Hamburg paid water rates of £320 for the period from 1 May 2013 to 5 April 2014 and a buildings insurance premium of £480 for the period from 1 June 2013 to 31 May 2014.

House 2

Hamburg bought house 2 for £84,000 on 1 June 2013. He immediately bought furniture for £4,300, and let the house fully furnished for £8,000 a year from 1 August 2013. The rent was payable quarterly in arrears. Hamburg paid water rates of £240 for the period from 1 June 2013 to 5 April 2014. He claimed the wear and tear allowance for furniture.

House 3

Hamburg bought house 3 for £45,000 on 1 July 2013. He spent £1,000 on routine redecoration and £2,300 on furniture in July, and let the house fully furnished from 1 August 2013 for £7,800 a year, payable annually in advance. Hamburg paid water rates of £360 for the period from 1 July 2013 to 5 April 2014, a buildings insurance premium of £440 for the period from 1 July 2013 to 30 June 2014 and a contents insurance premium of £180 for the period from 1 August 2013 to 31 July 2014. He also paid £850 for a new sofa. He claimed the wear and tear allowance for furniture.

During 2013/14 Hamburg also rented out one furnished room of his main residence. He received £4,600 and incurred allowable expenses of £875.

Required

Compute Hamburg's income tax payable or repayable for 2013/14. **(14 marks)**

(b) Hamburg is thinking about investing in two holiday cottages in Cornwall.

Required

Outline the requirements for the cottages to be furnished holiday lettings and the income tax treatment of such lettings. **(6 marks)**

(c) Hamburg is thinking about selling a one half share in his main residence to his son to raise the funds to buy the holiday cottages instead of raising a bank loan. He will continue to live in the property.

Required

Advise Hamburg of any income tax consequences of this plan. **(5 marks)**

(Total = 25 marks)

4 Taker 27 mins

(a) Taker is employed at an annual salary of £50,000. He is not in a pension scheme, but receives the following benefits in 2013/14.

(i) He has the use of a motor car with a petrol engine, which cost £20,000. Its CO_2 emissions are 152g/km. Fuel is provided for both business and private motoring, and Taker contributes £500 a year (half the cost of fuel for private motoring) for fuel.

(ii) He makes occasional private calls on the mobile phone provided by his employer.

(iii) He usually borrows his employer's digital camera (which cost £600) at weekends.

(iv) He has an interest free loan of £3,000 from his employer.

(v) His employer pays £4,000 a year to a registered childminder with whom the employer has a contract. The childminder looks after Taker's three year old son for 48 weeks during the year.

In 2013/14, Taker pays expenses out of his earnings as follows.

(i) He pays subscriptions to professional bodies (relevant to his employment) of £180.

(ii) He makes business telephone calls from home. The cost of business calls is £45. The cost of renting the line for the year is £100, and 40% of all Taker's calls are business calls.

(iii) He pays a golf club subscription of £150. He does not play golf at all, but goes to the club to discuss business with potential clients. These discussions frequently lead to valuable contracts.

Required

Compute Taker's taxable earnings for 2013/14. **(8 marks)**

(b) Taker is considering changing his employment and has received two offers. One is from a nearby company which is offering a salary of £50,000 a year and a choice of the provision of a company car with a taxable benefit of £3,250 (no private use fuel would be provided) or an increase in salary of £3,000 and a mileage allowance of 40p per business mile. If he does not accept the company car Taker would need to buy a new car costing £15,000 with annual running expenses of £2,200, including private use fuel of £500. Taker would sell the car after 3 years for £5,000, and estimates that extra interest charges over the period would amount to £1,800. Taker would drive 6,000 business miles a year.

The other offer is from a company 100 miles away, and it offers a salary of £55,000. Taker would be required to relocate, and the company would pay allowable relocation expenses of £12,000.

Taker does not wish to sell his old house and would let it out unfurnished for £6,000 a year renting a property at the new location for £4,000 a year. Alternatively the company would pay only £6,000 of relocation expenses but would provide Taker with a company flat which cost the company £120,000 four years ago and which has an annual value of £2,500. Taker could obtain an additional £1,000 rent for letting out his old house furnished. Taker estimates that he would spend three years in this job before moving back to his old house. He thinks his actual relocation costs will be £2,000 lower if he chooses the company flat.

Required

For each offer, compute the effect on Taker's net income of the available options. (You may ignore NICs). **(7 marks)**

(Total = 15 marks)

5 National insurance contributions 18 mins

(a) Albert works for Poster plc. He receives a salary of £48,500. He is entitled to company car (benefit £4,500). No private fuel is provided. Albert is also provided with private medical insurance at a cost to the company of £750.

Required

Show all NICs payable for 2013/14 in respect of Albert. **(3 marks)**

(b) Poster plc has had a good year and wants to reward its employees. Instead of paying bonuses it has decided that the employees should all have an additional holiday and it is offering the following options:

(i) A week on a health farm. The place will be booked by Poster plc, and will cost £2,000.

(ii) A week's sailing on a yacht chartered directly by the employees. The charter costs £5,000 per week, and a professional skipper a further £1,000 per week. Three members of staff must charter together, and each will take a partner.

(iii) A voucher which may be exchanged for a holiday at a high street travel agent. The face value is £2,200, but the voucher cost the company £2,000.

(iv) For employees with commitments that mean they cannot leave home, a payment of £1,500 cash.

Required

Explain the NICs payable under each of these options. **(7 marks)**

(Total = 10 marks)

6 Colin Jessop 36 mins

ENVIROTECH plc
Conservation House
Valley Park
Guildford

1 April 2014

Brian Andrews
Andrews, Simmons & Finch
25 High Street
Dorking

Dear Brian,

Share Option Schemes

I wonder if you could help me with a couple of issues we are having with our share option schemes.

Bonus schemes

For the last 10 years we have been paying relatively modest cash bonuses to our workforce. It has been suggested that if we pay the bonuses in the form of shares, our employees would be committed to our company, and could see their hard work reflected in the value of their shares. Is there a tax efficient way of dealing with this?

Derek Forrest

You will be aware that Derek (assistant Chief Executive on a salary of £200,000 a year) is due to retire on 30 June 2014 after 20 years with the company.

Executive options

In 2010 Envirotech granted him the right to buy 100,000 shares for £1.50 each. These options were in addition to the 20,000 'approved' options you told us about at the time. Derek could exercise at any time until 2016 but actually did so last week as he is keen to get the shares before he leaves the company. The share price is currently up around £3.60. Derek wants to know what the position is for income tax and CGT.

Retirement bonus

We are considering awarding Derek a 'thank you' bonus of £30,000 in cash as a retirement gift. Derek doesn't know yet. The company has no obligation to do this, but Derek who was born in 1956 and has been with us since the beginning. He has been talking about retreating to the Algarve to play a bit of golf and the rest of the Board thought that this would be a nice gesture.

I hope you are well.

Colin Jessop

Managing Director.

You are required to write a letter to Colin dealing with his queries. **(20 marks)**

7 Helen Strube and Gemma Hoyle 31 mins

(a) Helen started trading as a physiotherapist on 1 July 2008. Her accounts were initially made up to 30 June each year but in 2011 she changed her accounting date to 30 September by preparing accounts for the fifteen months to 30 September 2011. She ceased trading on 31 December 2013 and accounts were prepared for the three months to 31 December 2013.

Helen's trade profits were as follows.

	£
Year to 30 June 2009	36,000
Year to 30 June 2010	48,000
Fifteen months to 30 September 2011	60,000
Year to 30 September 2012	30,000
Year to 30 September 2013	24,000
Three months to 31 December 2013	10,000

Required

Show the taxable trade profits for each tax year. Show clearly when overlap profits arise and how these are relieved. **(10 marks)**

(b) Gemma Hoyle (born in 1955) has traded for some years preparing accounts to 30 April each year. Her business has been making profits at the rate of £2,300 per month for the last three years, but when she commenced trading on 1 May 2006 profits were only earned at the rate of £100 per month for the first 12 months of trading. She has decided to sell her business and is unsure whether to sell on 31 March 2014 or 30 April 2014. Gemma has no other income in 2013/14 and expects to have other income of £27,000 in 2014/15 onwards.

Required

Advise Gemma of the income tax and Class 4 national insurance advantages or disadvantages of selling on 31 March as opposed to 30 April. **(5 marks)**

(c) Daniel is a self-employed designer. In 2013/14, he has taxable profits of (i) £35,000 or (ii) £47,000.

Required

Show the NICs payable by Daniel for 2013/14. **(2 marks)**

(Total = 17 marks)

8 Sheila — 18 mins

Sheila began trading as a dress designer on 1 January 2014, made up her first accounts to 31 March 2014 and thereafter made up accounts to 31 March each year.

Sheila incurred the following expenditure on plant and machinery.

Date	*Item*	£
4.1.14	General plant	10,000
1.3.14	Integral feature in building (air conditioning system)	63,600
25.9.14	Delivery van	11,800
15.10.14	General plant	241,000
15.11.14	Car for Sheila CO_2 emissions 150 g/km	18,600
30.11.15	General plant	10,000
30.3.16	Car for salesperson CO_2 emissions 110 g/km	9,000

The private use of Sheila's car is 35%.

Required

Calculate the maximum capital allowances for all periods of account. Assume that the rates and rules applying to capital allowances in 2013/14 apply in later years. **(10 marks)**

9 Arrol and Louisa — 45 mins

Arrol, a dentist who was born in 1975, has been employed for several years as a representative by Bean Ltd, dental equipment manufacturers. His salary was £22,000 in the year ended 5 April 2013 and £25,000 in the year ended 5 April 2014. His employer provides him with a petrol engined motor car (cost £19,370) with CO2 emissions of 213g/km. All petrol is purchased on Bean Ltd's account at a garage. Arrol makes a nominal £25 a month reimbursement to Bean Ltd for part of the petrol used by him in private usage of the motor car.

On 1 May 2013 Arrol and his wife Louisa (born in 1978) received substantial gifts in cash and shares from a relative. On that day Arrol exchanged contracts and completed purchase of a private dental practice. Since then he has continued his employment and has worked part time in his practice. The result of the practice for the first year of trading to 30 April 2014 as adjusted for income tax but before capital allowances was a loss of £27,652. Indications are that the practice will be profitable in the year ending 30 April 2015, and after that will become very profitable.

Dental furniture (chairs, lamps etc) was purchased with the practice for £12,800. Additions to this equipment in the year ended 30 April 2014 cost £11,960 on 26 January 2014. Arrol wishes to claim the maximum capital allowances as soon as possible.

In 2013/14 Arrol and Louisa, who were both born in the 1960s, had other income as follows.

	Arrol	*Louisa*
	£	£
Bank interest received	235	
Building society interest received	3,005	5,012
Interest on National Savings & Investments investment account		1,742
Salary as part-time receptionist in Arrol's practice		5,135

Required

(a) Calculate Arrol's income tax liability in 2013/14 on the assumption that he claims to have the loss incurred in 2013/14 set against his general income of that year.

(b) Calculate Louisa's income tax liability in 2013/14.

(c) Calculate the loss remaining unrelieved in the year 2013/14, state the alternative ways in which this loss may be used and give Arrol any advice you consider beneficial to maximise the tax relief.

(25 marks)

10 Partnerships 45 mins

(a) Adam, Bert and Charlie started in partnership as secondhand car dealers on 6 April 2010, sharing profits in the ratio 2:2:1, after charging annual salaries of £15,000, £12,000 and £10,000 respectively.

On 5 July 2011 Adam retires and Bert and Charlie continue, taking the same salaries as before, but dividing the balance of the profits in the ratio 3:2.

On 6 May 2013 Donald is admitted as a partner on the terms that he received a salary of £18,000 a year, that the salaries of Bert and Charlie should be increased to £18,000 a year each and that of the balance of the profits, Donald should take one tenth, Bert six tenths and Charlie three tenths.

The trade profits of the partnership as adjusted for tax purposes are as follows.

Year ending 5 April	*Profits*
	£
2011	102,000
2012	208,000
2013	126,000
2014	180,000

Required

Show the taxable trade profits for each partner for 2010/11 to 2013/14 inclusive. **(15 marks)**

(b) Eric (born in 1970) has been running a hardware store for several years. His shop assistant is retiring and Eric would like to take his wife Freda (born in 1973) into the business. He is unsure whether to take her on as a part time salaried assistant, or to take her into partnership. Eric's profits are in the order of £70,000 a year before deducting his assistant's wages. If Eric took on a new assistant on the same terms as he would employ Freda he would expect to pay wages of £14,000 a year. Freda has no other income.

Required

Advise Eric of the advantages or disadvantages of employing Freda as an employee or of taking her into partnership with him

(i) assuming Freda would receive £14,000 of gross income in both scenarios.
(ii) assuming a profit share for Freda that would maximise the couple's tax saving. **(10 marks)**

(Total = 25 marks)

11 Overseas aspects of income tax 36 mins

(a) Susan (born in 1972) received the following income in 2013/14.

UK dividends	£9,000
Overseas property business income	£10,000
UK earnings income (gross)	£21,535

The overseas property business income suffered £4,705 of overseas tax before being paid to Susan.

Required

(i) Calculate the tax payable by Susan if she has suffered £2,300 of tax under PAYE for the year. **(7 marks)**

(ii) To correct an error made on the behalf of the overseas country in 2013/14 on 1 November 2015 Susan receives from the overseas authorities a refund of £2,600 of the overseas tax suffered. What should Susan do in respect of this receipt? **(3 marks)**

(b) Maria was born in Brazil and had lived there all her life until she married Henry, a UK resident, in June 2013. Maria owns a house in Brazil. She does not work.

Maria and Henry bought a flat in London in July 2013. Maria spent 150 days in the UK during the tax year 2013/14 living in the flat. She spent the remaining 215 days living in her house in Brazil.

Required

Explain, giving reasons, whether Maria is UK resident in the tax year 2013/14. **(5 marks)**

(c) James, who is domiciled in Utopia, and has always lived there, is to be seconded to the UK for one year from 1 April 2014, although he will be required to carry out some duties in Utopia for which he will be paid £20,000.

Required

Explain how James will be taxed on his earnings and whether he will have any UK tax liability on his interest of £1,000 from a Utopian bank account. **(5 marks)**

(Total = 20 marks)

12 Sophie Shaw **34 mins**

Sophie Shaw made the following disposals in 2013/14:

(a) A painting for proceeds of £50,000 at auction on 12 October 2013. The auctioneer's costs of sale were 1% of the gross proceeds. Sophie had bought the painting for £2,500.

(b) A freehold shop on 1 February 2014 for £85,000. The shop was acquired by Sophie's husband for £45,000. He had transferred the shop to Sophie in 2008 when it was worth £60,000.

(c) 2 acres of land on 10 July 2013 for £18,000. This was part of a 10 acre plot of land acquired by Sophie for £11,000. Immediately before the sale, the 10 acre plot as a whole was valued at £92,000. At the date of the sale, the remaining 8 acres was valued at £70,000.

(d) 4,000 shares in JKL plc to her son Jason for £20,000 (their market value) on 23 December 2013. Sophie bought the shares on 1 February 2007 for £52,000. Jason sold the shares in January 2014 for £18,000.

Sophie has taxable income of £50,000 in 2013/14.

Sophie's husband Terry has made no capital disposals during the year. He has taxable income of £30,000 in 2013/14.

Jason is a student with no capital assets and no taxable income in 2013/14.

Required

(a) Calculate the capital gains tax liability for Sophie for 2013/14, giving details of your treatment of the disposals.

(b) Advise Sophie of any steps that could have been taken to reduce the capital gains tax liability for 2013/14.

(19 marks)

13 The Green family **27 mins**

(a) John Green acquired 20,000 shares in Miller plc on 1 May 2007 for £40,000. On 10 July 2013, Miller plc was taken over by Wall plc. Clearance was obtained from HMRC that this was a bona fide commercial arrangement. John received 1 ordinary share (worth £4.90) in Wall plc and cash of £1.60 for each Miller plc share.

(b) John's wife, Matilda, made the following purchases of ordinary shares in Read plc, a quoted company.

Date	*Number*	*Cost*
		£
15 May 2007	1,800	1,900
1 October 2013	2,000	25,750

On 12 July 2013, there was a 1 for 1 bonus issue.

On 30 September 2013 she sold 3,200 of the shares for £42,000.

Entrepreneurs' relief does not apply to any of the disposals. John and Matilda each have taxable income of £20,000 in 2013/14.

Required

(a) Compute the capital gain on the takeover of Miller plc for John Green. Show the base cost of his shares in Wall plc. **(4 marks)**

(b) Explain whether there would have been any advantages for John Green if instead of receiving cash on the take over of Wall plc shares he had received loan stock. **(4 marks)**

(c) Compute the capital gain or allowable loss on the sale of Matilda Green's shares. **(4 marks)**

(d) State how much capital gains tax John and Matilda will have to pay for 2013/14 if they have no other chargeable gains or allowable losses, but John had £16,760 of allowable losses brought forward at 6 April 2013. Show any amounts carried forward. **(3 marks)**

(Total = 15 marks)

14 Hazel **22 mins**

Hazel has been running a retail business as a sole trader for the past three years. She wishes to incorporate the business and will hold 100% of the shares issued. She also wishes to receive some of the consideration for incorporation other than in shares provided that this does not trigger a tax charge.

Hazel estimates that her business is worth £155,000, comprising the following assets which would result in the following gains on disposal:

Asset	*Market value*	*Gain*
	£	£
Cash	25,000	n/a
Goodwill	30,000	30,000
Freehold shop	90,000	50,500
Inventory	20,000	n/a
Creditors	(10,000)	n/a

Hazel has no other chargeable assets.

Required

Prepare a report for Hazel addressing the following issues set out below, and where appropriate, include supporting calculations.

(a) State the conditions that must be satisfied if Hazel's business is to be sold to a company without incurring an immediate CGT charge. **(2 marks)**

(b) Assuming the relief **is** available, advise Hazel on the maximum amount of non-share consideration she could receive on incorporation without triggering a CGT liability. **(5 marks)**

(c) State any disadvantages in using the relief that Hazel should be aware of. **(3 marks)**

(d) Identify and describe another relief that Hazel might use without incurring an immediate CGT charge. **(2 marks)**

You may assume that the rates and allowances for the tax year 2013/14 continue to apply for the foreseeable future.

(Total = 12 marks)

15 Miss Wolf, Mr Hen and Mr Fox — 45 mins

(a) On 30 June 2013 Miss Wolf assigned the lease of a building originally acquired as an investment for £30,750; the lease expires on 30 June 2029. She had acquired the lease for £8,000 on 1 January 2005 and the building had never been her principal private residence.

You may assume that the relevant percentages from the lease percentage table are as follows:

16 years	64.116
24 years	79.622
25 years	81.100

Required

Calculate the gain or loss on the assignment. **(5 marks)**

(b) Mr Hen is a sole trader. He bought a factory for use in his trade on 10 July 2012 for £150,000.

On 9 November 2013, the factory was damaged in a flood. Mr Hen received compensation from the water company of £20,000 on 1 September 2014. He had incurred costs of £15,000 in July 2014 on renovations. The value of the factory after the renovations is £250,000.

On 1 December 2015, Mr Hen sold the factory for £260,000.

Required

Show the chargeable gains (if any) for Mr Hen for 2013/14, 2014/15 and 2015/16 assuming that any claims to defer gains are made. Mr Hen made no other disposals except to utilise his annual exempt amount each year. **(8 marks)**

(c) Mr Fox bought a house on 1 August 1992 for £50,000. He lived in the house until 31 July 1995. He then went abroad to work as a self-employed engineer until 31 July 2000.

Mr Fox went back to live in the house until 31 January 2006. He then moved in with his sister.

Mr Fox sold the house on 31 July 2013 for £180,000.

Required

(i) Calculate the gain on sale after all reliefs.

(ii) Advise Mr Fox whether he could have taken any action to reduce the gain on sale.

(iii) Assuming Mr Fox's sister had died in July 2012 leaving her house to Mr Fox and that Mr Fox intends to sell this house also, reinvesting the proceeds of both sales in a larger house, what steps could Mr Fox have taken to reduce any capital gains? Mr Fox is likely to make a gain on the sale of his sister's house. **(12 marks)**

(Total = 25 marks)

16 Mr & Mrs Brown **31 mins**

Mr Brown's income tax liability for 2012/13 was £16,000. He had suffered tax by deduction at source of £4,000 and paid two payments on account of £6,000 each on the due dates.

He submitted his 2012/13 return on 31 January 2014 and made a claim to reduce his payments on account for 2013/14 on the basis that his total liability for 2013/14 would be £14,000 with tax suffered of £5,000.

He made the payments on account of £4,500 on 28 February and 31 August 2014.

Finally, on 31 March 2015 he submitted his return for 2013/14 which showed total tax due of £17,000 and tax deducted at source of £4,000. He therefore paid a further £4,000 on the same date.

Mrs Brown's tax return for 2013/14 included a transaction which it was commonly understood gave rise to a tax liability of £10,000. The return was filed in December 2014. In February 2015 another taxpayer who had undertaken a similar transaction challenged HMRC's interpretation of the legislation, succeeding before the Tax Tribunal and the case is expected to proceed to the Court of Appeal during early 2016. If the alternative interpretation was correct it would have saved Mrs Brown tax of £8,000.

Required

(a) Outline the time limits for submission of returns and payments of tax under self assessment for 2013/14 and detail the provisions for failure to comply. **(9 marks)**

(b) Calculate the interest on overdue tax chargeable in respect of Mr Brown's tax payments for 2013/14.
(3 marks)

(c) Advise Mrs Brown of any action she should take to enable her to take advantage of the alternative interpretation should the other taxpayer be successful before the Courts. **(5 marks)**

(Total = 17 marks)

17 Rodin **29 mins**

Rodin dies unexpectedly on 20 December 2013. His record of gifts is as follows.

Date	£	*Recipient*
25.12.05	60,000	Son
21.1.08	321,000	Discretionary trust (Rodin paid the IHT)
20.8.10	31,000	Daughter
19.6.11	88,000	Discretionary trust (Trustees paid the IHT)
1.8.13	73,000	Cousin
1.9.13	400,000	Wife

Both Rodin and his wife have always been UK domiciled.

Required

(a) Compute all amounts of inheritance tax due on these gifts. **(10 marks)**

(b) Comment on whether your answer would have been the same had Rodin's wife not been domiciled in the UK at the time of the transfer to her. Assume that no election has been made in respect of her domicile. **(2 marks)**

(c) Rodin's cousin wishes to give £50,000 to each of his son and daughter and to transfer £350,000 to a discretionary trust for his grandchildren. His daughter is widowed, and he thinks it likely that in the next few months she will remarry. Rodin's cousin has not made any gifts recently. What advice would you give Rodin's cousin? **(4 marks)**

(Total = 16 marks)

18 Mr Bright **45 mins**

Hubert Bright, for whom you act as tax adviser, had over the years acquired 3,000 £1 ordinary shares in Bod Ltd, an unquoted trading company with an issued share capital of 5,000 ordinary shares. None of the shares were acquired under the Enterprise Management Incentive scheme. All the assets of Bod Ltd are in use for the purpose of its trade. Mr Bright has been a director of the company since 1982. His wife, Rose, also owns 1,000 ordinary shares in the company.

Hubert had acquired his shares as follows.

	Shares	*Cost*
		£
1.11.85	2,200	3,300
15.6.04	200	1,366
18.8.10	600	3,000

The current market values attributable to various percentage shareholdings in Bod Ltd are estimated as follows.

% *Shareholding*	*Value of £1 ordinary share*
100	40.50
80	36.67
60	25.00
40 or below	18.00

On 1 April 2014 Mr Bright sold 2,000 of his shares in Bod Ltd for £10,000 to his daughter Maxine, who sold them to an unconnected buyer ten days later. Mr Bright has taxable income of £100,000 in 2013/14.

He has made no previous transfer of assets other than a gift of £349,000 cash to a discretionary trust (which did not include Mr Bright as a beneficiary) on 1 May 2013. Mr Bright had agreed to bear any costs or taxes in respect of the gift. Apart from his shares in Bod Ltd, Mr Bright currently has no other assets apart from cash of £40,000. He has left everything in his will to his son Roger. You should assume that today's date is 14 April 2014.

Required

(a) Advise Mr Bright of his potential inheritance tax and capital gains tax liabilities.

(b) Advise Mr Bright on the inheritance tax implications which would arise if he were to die on 20 April 2014. (Assume that any CGT on lifetime gifts is unpaid at the date of death but that any IHT has been paid.)

(c) Roger has suggested to Mr Bright that he should gift his shares in Bod Ltd now rather than retaining them until his death. Prepare brief notes of matters which will have a bearing on a decision in preparation for a meeting with Mr Bright.

Assume that the IHT nil rate band is £325,000 and the CGT annual exempt amount is £10,900 throughout and that the rules and rates of CGT and IHT are the same in 2014/15 as in 2013/14.

(25 marks)

19 Trusts **20 mins**

On 17 July 2006 Rhys Jones settled his portfolio of quoted shares on the RJ discretionary trust. Rhys died on 3 September 2013.

Under his will Rhys left his estate on discretionary will trusts for his sister Blodwen and her children, with the trust to be wound up and the capital to be distributed to Blodwen's children on her death.

Blodwen died on 28 February 2018.

Half of the assets of the RJ discretionary trust were distributed to beneficiaries on 5 March 2015 and the remainder was finally distributed on 18 April 2019.

Rhys made no other gifts other than to use his annual exemptions each year.

Required

(a) Explain the occasions of charge to IHT in respect of the above transactions. Calculations are not required. **(9 marks)**

(b) Comment on how your answer would have been affected had Rhys died on 3 July 2013. **(2 marks)**

(Total = 11 marks)

20 Fraser Ltd **27 mins**

Fraser Ltd is a trading company. It has no associated companies and it makes up accounts to 31 March in each year.

The income statement for the year ended 31 March 2014 showed a profit before taxation of £413,278.

The following items were included in the accounts.

	£
Income	
Dividend from an unconnected UK company (including tax credit)	1,655
Interest on bank deposits	6,834
Interest from gilts (gross)	2,208
Surplus on the disposal of an office building and a lease	61,806
Expenditure	
Directors' remuneration	62,075
Miscellaneous	3,837
Depreciation	13,876

The company's bank deposits and gilts are held for non-trading purposes.

The company sold an office building for £120,633 on 15 August 2013. It had cost the company £79,000 in May 2004.

A lease of one of the company's retail outlets was sold on 30 April 2013 for £40,161. The term of the lease was 30 years from 1 November 2000 and the company acquired it on 1 November 2005 at a cost of £17,500. The lease percentage for 17 years is 66.470, for 18 years is 68.697 and for 25 years is 81.100.

There are no other unused losses or reliefs brought forward at 31 March 2013.

Miscellaneous expenses comprise the following.

	£
Hire purchase interest on two new fork lift trucks	783
Christmas gifts to customers: 40 executive desk diaries bearing the company's name	2,085
Entertaining customers	969
	3,837

The main pool value of plant at 1 April 2013 was £nil. With the exception of the acquisition of the two new fork lift trucks under the hire purchase agreements at a cash price of £9,800 each on 1 December 2013 there were no purchases or sales of plant in the year ended 31 March 2014.

Fraser Ltd has build up a cash surplus and is considering several schemes.

Fraser Ltd is considering acquiring a new office building. There are two possible options.

(i) Office building A could be acquired at a cost of £150,000.

(ii) Office building B could be acquired at a cost of £400,000. Fraser Ltd would need to raise additional finance of £250,000, partly through a bank loan and partly through the issue of loan stock. Initially the office building would be too large, and Fraser Ltd would let out approximately half of the building to another company.

Alternatively, Fraser Ltd would purchase all of the issued share capital of Simmonds Ltd. The cost of the investment would be £250,000, and Fraser Ltd would need to raise £100,000 through bank loans.

To do well in the new area in which Simmonds Ltd operates, Fraser Ltd is likely to have to buy patents and similar rights, which it expects would cost £50,000. These will be written off over their useful lives in the accounts.

Instead of raising loan finance, Fraser Ltd is contemplating issuing new shares.

Required

(a) Compute Fraser Ltd's taxable total profits for the year ended 31 March 2014. **(10 marks)**

(b) Advise Fraser Ltd of the corporation tax consequences of its proposals. **(5 marks)**

Assume indexation	May 2004 – August 2013	0.343
	November 2005 – April 2013	0.291

(Total = 15 marks)

21 Melson Ltd **18 mins**

Melson Ltd, a trading company, made the following disposals in the year ended 31 December 2013.

(a) On 31 May 2013 it sold a warehouse for £125,000. The company had bought the warehouse for £65,000 on 1 July 2005. It has always been rented out to another company. Melson Ltd had invested £100,000 in another warehouse for use in its own trade on 1 May 2013.

(b) On 18 June 2013 Melson Ltd sold a house for £75,000. It had bought it for £20,000 on 1 April 2000 and had spent £4,000 extending the house in July 2002.

(c) On 25 June 2013 Melson Ltd sold an office building for £180,000. It had bought the office building for £65,000 on 16 October 2000 and it has always been rented out to another company.

(d) On 30 July 2013 Melson Ltd sold 12,000 ordinary shares in Leigh Ltd, a trading company, for £180,000. This was a 12% holding which Melson Ltd had acquired in July 2002 for £12,000.

Required

Compute Melson Ltd's chargeable gains for the year ended 31 December 2013. **(10 marks)**

Assume retail prices index

May 2013 = 249.9
June 2013 = 249.3
July 2013 = 249.6

July 2005 = 192.2
July 2002 = 175.9
October 2000 = 171.6
April 2000 = 170.1

22 Major Ltd **29 mins**

Major Ltd is a trading company resident in the United Kingdom. It has one associated company. Until 2013 Major Ltd made up accounts each year to 31 July, but decided to change its accounting date to 31 March. The information below relates to the eight month period to 31 March 2014:

	£
Income	
Adjusted trading profit	165,000
Rents received *less* expenses	30,000
Loan interest received – (see Note 1)	24,000
Capital gains	40,000
Franked investment income (FII) (received September 2013)	20,000
Payments	
Qualifying charitable donation (paid September 2013)	3,000
Loan interest paid (see Note 2)	30,000

Notes

1. The loan interest was received in respect of a loan of £100,000 made by the company to Z Ltd, a main supplier of materials to Major Ltd. The directors of Major Ltd are concerned about the financial position of Z Ltd, but have decided to take no action at present.
2. The loan interest paid was to a UK bank in respect of funds raised to acquire the company's 80% interest in its associated company.

Major Ltd is considering investing in another supplier and has identified two possibilities. 20% of the shares of S Ltd are being offered for sale by one of the retiring directors at a cost of £40,000. Alternatively Major Ltd could subscribe for new shares in T Ltd, taking either an 8% holding at a cost of £15,000. Whichever acquisition is made Major Ltd would hope to sell the shares after a few years at twice its original cost, although it is possible that either of the two target companies could collapse. Major Ltd would have to borrow to fund the purchase.

Required

(a) Compute the corporation tax payable by Major Ltd in respect of the above accounting period.

(b) Advise the directors of Major Ltd in a brief memo of the taxation implications of the loan to Z Ltd proving irrecoverable.

(c) Advise Major Ltd of the tax consequences of its alternative share acquisitions.

(16 marks)

23 Hogg Ltd — 9 mins

(a) Hogg Ltd prepares accounts for the year to 31 March 2014. In September 2013 it estimates that its corporation tax liability for the year will be £500,000. In April 2014 it revises its estimate to £520,000. In January 2015 it submits its corporation tax return, showing a total liability of £525,000. The company has always paid corporation tax at the main rate.

Required

State the amounts that would have been paid and due dates for the payment of corporation tax by Hogg Ltd in respect of the year to 31 March 2014. **(3 marks)**

(b) Explain the maximum late-filing penalty that would arise if Hogg Ltd did not submit its corporation tax return for the year to 31 March 2014 in January 2015 but instead submits the return on 10 October 2015. **(2 marks)**

(Total = 5 marks)

24 Norma — 18 mins

Norma (born in 1985) is intending to start a new business on 1 April 2014, and anticipates a profit of £60,000 in the first year of trading. She is undecided whether to:

(a) Operate as a sole trader,

(b) Operate as a limited company and draw out all the profits as a dividend, or

(c) Operate as a limited company, draw a salary of £15,000 a year and draw out all the remaining profits as a dividend.

Required

Compare the tax and national insurance resulting from each alternative. You should assume that the tax rates and allowances for the tax year 2013/14 and for the financial year to 31 March 2014 will continue to apply for the foreseeable future. **(10 marks)**

25 Clarke Ltd **18 mins**

Alex, one of the directors of Clarke Ltd, has had a serious disagreement with the other directors over the direction in which the business should be moving, and as a consequence wishes to resign as a director and dispose of his shares. It has been agreed that Clarke Ltd will repurchase Alex's shares for £5 per share, either in March 2014 or in June 2014.

In January 1997 Alex subscribed for 5,000 shares at par. In May 2009 he purchased a further 2,000 from another director, Benny, at a cost of £3 per share. Benny had also subscribed for these share at par in January 1997. Clarke Ltd is an unquoted trading company and has 150,000 ordinary shares in issue. Alex has utilised his capital gains tax annual exempt amount on the disposal of other assets in both 2013/14 and 2014/15. He has taxable income of £160,000 in 2013/14 and 2014/15.

Required

Explain how the repurchase will be dealt with for tax purposes for Alex and indicate whether it would be preferable for the repurchase to take place in March or June 2014, assume the tax rules and rates in 2013/14 continue to apply. **(10 marks)**

26 Daley plc **27 mins**

Assume that it is December 2014.

Daley plc has recently become a client, having previously prepared its own accounts and corporation tax computations on the basis that reliefs should always be claimed as soon as possible. The return for the year to 30 June 2014 has been prepared but not yet filed.

The company has had the following results since it started to trade.

	Year ended 31.12.11	*Year ended 31.12.12*	*Six months ended 30.6.13*	*Year ended 30.6.14*
	£	£	£	£
Trading profit/(loss)	(29,000)	110,000	85,000	(202,000)
Interest income	10,000	11,000	12,000	14,000
Chargeable gains/(losses)	18,000	(5,000)	2,000	(1,000)
Qualifying charitable donation	Nil	2,000	3,000	1,000

There are no associated companies, although Daley plc intends to acquire Terry Ltd in April 2015. Terry Ltd has one subsidiary company. It is expected that Daley plc's profits in the year to 30 June 2015 will be in the region of £150,000, and that this level will be maintained in the future.

Required

(a) Compute the corporation tax liability for all four periods on the basis that relief is claimed as soon as possible, and show all amounts to be carried forward at 30 June 2014.

(b) Write a letter to the directors of Daley plc explaining how losses can be relieved and advise whether best use has been obtained for the losses.

Assume that tax rates and allowances for FY 2013 apply to all years. **(15 marks)**

27 Huis Ltd **27 mins**

(a) Huis Ltd is a close company which pays corporation tax at the small profits rate. On 31 May 2013, six months before the company's year end, it lent £45,000 to Sartre, a shareholder. Sartre is not an employee of the company. The loan carried a market rate of interest.

The company advised Sartre on 31 March 2015 that he would not be required to repay the loan. It has also agreed to include Sartre in its medical insurance scheme at an annual cost of £1,000, and to allow him to use the company yacht (annual value £24,000) for a month each summer.

Required

Set out the tax consequences of the transactions with Sartre, giving the dates on which any amounts are payable to HMRC.

(b) Beauvoir Ltd is a close investment-holding company. It has had the following results for the last two years.

	Year ended 31.3.13	*Year ended 31.3.14*
	£	£
Property income	14,000	25,000
Interest income	20,000	100,000
Management expenses	36,000	45,000
Dividends received in August from non-group companies	16,000	27,000

Required

Compute the company's corporation tax liability for both years. **(15 marks)**

28 H, S and N **36 mins**

H Ltd has owned 60% of the issued ordinary share capital of S Ltd since its incorporation, the remaining 40% being held by individuals. Both UK companies have always prepared accounts to 30 June, their most recent accounts showing the following.

	H Ltd		*S Ltd*	
	Year ended 30.6.13	*Year ended 30.6.14*	*Year ended 30.6.13*	*Year ended 30.6.14*
	£	£	£	£
Adjusted trading profit	2,000		30,000	100,000
Adjusted trading loss		(48,000)		
Qualifying charitable donation paid			12,000	12,000

On 1 January 2013, H Ltd acquired 100% of the issued ordinary share capital of N Ltd, a company which had always previously prepared accounts to 31 December.

N Ltd's accounts for the period of 1 January 2013 to 30 June 2014 show the following.

	£
Adjusted trading profit, before capital allowances	65,250
Investment interest, amount accrued	20,000

N Ltd had capital allowances of £4,250 in the year to 31 December 2013 and £17,569 in the 6 months to 30 June 2014.

The group are planning several property transactions for 1 January 2015:

(i) N Ltd will sell a factory for £200,000 realising a loss of £13,333. N Ltd also has an unused capital loss of £26,667 which arose on a disposal of a warehouse in November 2012.

(ii) H Ltd will sell an office block for £250,000 realising a chargeable gain of £80,000.

(iii) S Ltd will sell a warehouse for £300,000 realising a gain of £70,000.

(iv) S Ltd will acquire a new warehouse at a cost of £290,000.

It is anticipated that for the year to 30 June 2015 H Ltd will have trading profits of £10,000, S Ltd of £150,000 and N Ltd of £75,000.

Required

(a) Compute the corporation tax payable by H Ltd, S Ltd and N Ltd for the above periods of account, assuming all available claims and surrenders are made to minimise the corporation tax payable by the group. Assume the limits and rates for FY13 apply throughout.

(b) Draft a memorandum to the directors of H Ltd suggesting the extent to which H Ltd, S Ltd and N Ltd can minimise the corporation tax on chargeable gains for the year to 30 June 2015.

(20 marks)

29 Exotica Inc and W Ltd — 27 mins

(a) Exotica Inc (for which you act as United Kingdom tax adviser) is a company resident and incorporated in Ruritania, a country which is outside the European Union and does not have a double tax agreement with the UK. The company manufactures items of advanced industrial equipment and now wishes to increase its sales within the UK. The company has no subsidiaries and currently makes worldwide profits equivalent to £300,000 sterling a year.

It intends to acquire an office in London and to staff it with full-time salesmen assigned from its head office in Ruritania. Exotica Inc is still considering whether the salesmen will be given the authority to conclude contracts with UK customers or whether such authority will be reserved for the head office only. It is also considering whether customers' orders should be met from stocks held in Ruritania or whether stocks should be maintained in the UK. While tax considerations will be taken into account, other commercial factors are likely to influence these decisions strongly. Projected additional profits from the UK operation are £75,000 a year.

Required

Advise Exotica Inc on the corporation tax implications of the various alternative courses of action still under consideration.

(b) The directors of W Ltd have decided to set up an operation in a country where the rate of corporation tax is 22%.

They are considering two alternative approaches:

(i) to run the overseas operation as a permanent establishment of the UK company; or
(ii) to run it as a foreign-registered subsidiary of the UK company.

Required

Draft a report to the board on the taxation implications of each of the alternative proposals.

(15 marks)

30 Paul — 18 mins

Paul Sand is in business as a general builder but he is also in partnership with John Rowe as 'A1 Repairs', Peter Dene as 'Kwik Repairs' and in partnership with his wife as 'Speedy Builders'.

Required

Discuss how many VAT 'persons' exist here. **(10 marks)**

31 VAT groups **18 mins**

It is February 2014. Barry Franklin, the Finance Director of Banner plc, has written to you, asking for your advice on certain VAT matters. Banner plc has two wholly owned subsidiaries, Flag Ltd and Ensign Ltd. All three companies are fully taxable and are included in a group registration for VAT. Two months ago, in December 2013, Banner plc acquired 75% of the ordinary share capital of Union Ltd, a partly exempt company. Union Ltd generally recovers around 60% of its input tax. To date, no action has been taken to include Union Ltd in the group registration.

As Union Ltd is not wholly owned, other group companies will be required to pay for any losses surrendered to them as group relief.

Mr Franklin has specifically asked whether Union Ltd should be included in the group registration and, if so, what action he should take in this regard.

All four companies are UK resident with an established place of business in the UK.

Required

Write a letter in reply to Mr Franklin. **(10 marks)**

32 Stewart Ltd **18 mins**

Stewart Ltd, a partially exempt trader, has the following information for the year ended 31 March 2014:

Supplies

Quarter ended	*Taxable (excl VAT)*	*Exempt*	*Total (excl VAT)*
	£	£	£
30.6.13	403,920	52,072	455,992
30.9.13	*384,177	23,194	*407,371
31.12.13	467,159	18,791	485,950
31.3.14	520,321	37,439	557,760
	*1,775,577	131,496	*1,907,073

* This includes £25,000 in respect of a computer used in the business and subsequently sold. The computer was originally purchased for £45,000 in 2012.

Input tax

Quarter ended	*Re taxable supplies*	*Re exempt supplies*	*Non-attributable*	*Total*
	£	£	£	£
30.6.13	44,404	3,120	14,719	62,243
30.9.13	39,098	2,775	12,613	54,486
31.12.13	24,926	1,374	10,412	36,712
31.3.14	36,020	1,876	11,919	49,815
	144,448	9,145	49,663	203,256

Stewart Ltd has decided to use the actual recovery rate percentage to account for VAT in each quarter in the year ended 31 March 2014 rather than the recovery rate for the year ended 31 March 2013. You may assume that neither of the de minimis Tests 1 nor 2 apply and the conditions for the annual test are not satisfied.

Required

Calculate the amount of recoverable input tax for each quarter and the annual adjustment, if any.

(10 marks)

33 Tax planning **45 mins**

You are a partner in a firm of certified accountants with particular responsibility for tax planning.

Required

Draft an answer to each of the following queries which have been passed on to you by your fellow partners. You should assume that today's date is 1 April 2013.

(a) Client A is about to commence business as a management consultant on 1 May 2013. She was previously employed as a school headteacher for several years at a salary in excess of £55,000 a year. The business involves virtually no expenditure on capital assets. She expects to make operating losses in her first two years of trading, after which she expects the business slowly to become profitable. She will have no other taxable sources of income. For reasons of prestige she is proposing to trade through a specially formed company, A Ltd. However, she could delay forming the company for a short while and she asks what the best course of action would be from a tax viewpoint.

(b) Client B currently manufactures fitted bedroom furniture for the general public from a small workshop. The market is highly competitive. He has a turnover of £60,000 a year which yields a current gross profit percentage of 40% and he incurs minimal overheads. He has been offered a contract to manufacture bookcases for a VAT registered trader at a price of £20,000 a year from 1 March 2014 (exclusive of any VAT). B estimates that this project would involve a similar cost structure to his existing operations. B is concerned that, since he will become liable to register for VAT if he takes on the new contract, it may not be worthwhile to accept it.

He has asked for calculations showing the net annual gain to him from taking on the contract. He has also enquired whether it would be possible to avoid the requirement to register by setting up a new company, B Ltd, to carry out the new contract. (*Note.* You are required to consider VAT issues *only*.)

(c) Client C is about to acquire shares in a publicly quoted company for £350,000 out of his own funds. The shares currently yield a dividend of £28,000 a year paid in September and March each year. The prospects for significant capital appreciation in the future are excellent. At the end of ten years C may decide to sell some or all of the shares. It has been suggested to C by a friend, D, that instead of buying the shares himself he should form a new investment company, C Ltd. C would subscribe for 350,000 £1 shares in C Ltd, which would then use the cash to buy the shares. D has told C that he could draw out director's remuneration of up to £10,000 a year and that C Ltd could deduct this against the dividend income and that the balance of £18,000 would only be liable to the small profits corporation tax rate of 20%. D has also said that C could obtain tax relief by paying premiums into a personal pension scheme. C has asked whether the advice which he has received from D is correct.

(d) Client D is setting up in business as an aromatherapist. She is considering structuring her business either as a sole trader or through a limited company. If she operates as a sole trader she will be starting in business on 6 April 2013, making up her first accounts to 5 April 2014 with an expected trading profit of £30,000. If she uses a limited company, it will start in business on 1 April 2013, make up accounts to 31 March 2014, with expected taxable trading profits of £30,000. Client D would extract all available profits by way of dividends on 31 March 2014.

Client D has investment income which exactly covers her personal allowance for 2013/14. Client D wants to know how much net spendable income she would have from the business in each of these cases.

(25 marks)

34 Hulse Finds Ltd **38 mins**

Paul Hulse and his friend Nick Royle set up the company Hulse Finds Ltd with Paul and Nick holding 40% of the shares each. The remaining 20% of the company is held by five of their friends. Hulse Finds Ltd runs a shop in Didsbury selling unusual objects which are sourced from around the world. Paul and Nick work full time in the management of the company but their five friends are passive investors in the business.

Paul took out a bank loan of £150,000 secured on his apartment in central Manchester to purchase his shares whereas Nick used his redundancy payout from his old employer (a large bank).

Hulse Finds Ltd incurred significant start-up costs in its first 18 months of trade. Taxable total profits were £60,000 and £160,000 in the years to 31 March 2013 and 2014 respectively.

During June in the second year the company made a loan to Chris Newn (one of the investor friends) of £10,000.

Nick has identified a company Sweet Nothings Ltd (SNL) as a possible acquisition. The company sells French furniture and fixtures which it imports into the UK. After negotiations with the board of directors of SNL it has been agreed that Hulse Finds Ltd can purchase the trade and assets of SNL on 1 April 2015.

SNL has trading losses which are being carried forward of £50,000 and capital losses being carried forward of £25,000. Hulse Finds Ltd will set up a wholly owned subsidiary SN2 Ltd to acquire the trade and assets of SNL.

Predicted taxable total profits for the two companies for year ended 31 March 2016 are:

Hulse Finds Ltd		£250,000
SN2 Ltd	Trading profits	40,000
	Capital gains	10,000

By 2017 Paul and Nick expect the existing business to have grown considerably and they expect to have taxable profits of £1 million in the year ended 31 March 2017. SN2 Ltd is expected to have taxable profits of £100,000 in the same period.

Paul and Nick have been looking to expand overseas in order to take advantage of new emerging markets. They intend to start a new business in Newland on 1 April 2016.

It is anticipated that the overseas business will make a trading loss of £60,000 in the year ended 31 March 2017, a profit of £80,000 in the year ended 31 March 2018 and a profit of £100,000 per year in future years.

The system of corporation tax in Newland is broadly the same as that in the UK, although loss relief is only available to companies resident in Newland. In addition, the rate of corporation tax is 45% regardless of the level of profits and there is no withholding tax when dividends are paid to overseas shareholders. There is no double tax treaty between the UK and Newland.

You are meeting with Paul and Chris next week. Assume that the rates of corporation tax in FY13 also apply in later years.

Required

Make brief notes on the following for discussion at that meeting:

(a) Any relief for Pauls' investment in the company? **(2 marks)**

(b) What is the impact to the company, if any, of the loan to Chris and would this be different if Chris was an employee of the company? **(4 marks)**

(c) What are the tax implications of the acquisition of SNL? In particular suggest any way to maximise the tax advantages for Hulse Finds Ltd. **(7 marks)**

(d) Discuss the tax implications of the proposed expansion overseas. **(8 marks)**

(Total = 21 marks)

35 Financial planning **27 mins**

The directors of M Ltd, a medium-sized unquoted company engaged in manufacturing, have decided to embark on a major expansion of the business.

The company has a significant amount of unissued share capital and, to finance the expansion, the directors have been considering issuing further shares. They have also considered raising loan capital, using as security identified pieces of valuable property owned by the company.

Required

Draft a report to the board, dated 19 May 2013, setting out the taxation implications for the company under each of the alternative methods of raising finance.

Your report should also identify any taxation implications for the providers of this finance. **(15 marks)**

36 Daniel Dare **52 mins**

An extract from an email from your manager is set out below.

I had a telephone conversation with Daniel Dare (DD), the managing director of Saturn Ltd, first thing this morning. We discussed the anticipated results of the Saturn Ltd group of companies and the proposed acquisition of a majority holding in Tethys Ltd. All the relevant details are included in the attached memorandum.

I need the following:

(i) A memorandum that I can use to prepare for my telephone call to DD. I realise that DD did not give me all of the information we need so please identify any additional information that you think could have an effect on our advice.

(ii) A summary of the information we need and any action we should take before agreeing to become tax advisers to the Saturn Ltd group.

Tax manager

The memorandum attached to the email is set out below.

To: Internal filing
From: Tax manager
Date: 2 June 2014
Subject: Saturn Ltd group of companies

This memorandum sets out the matters discussed with Daniel Dare (DD), the managing director of Saturn Ltd, earlier today.

Group structure

Saturn Ltd has three wholly-owned subsidiaries: Dione Ltd, Rhea Ltd and Titan Inc. Titan Inc trades in and is resident in the country of Galactica. The other three group companies are resident in the UK. Saturn Ltd has owned all three subsidiary companies for many years.

Budgeted results for the year ending 30 June 2014

It is estimated that Dione Ltd will make a tax adjusted trading loss of £187,000 in the year ending 30 June 2014; it will have no other income or capital gains in the period. The budgeted taxable total profits of the other companies in the group are set out below.

	£
Saturn Ltd	385,000
Rhea Ltd	590,000
Titan Inc	265,000

Rhea Ltd paid a dividend of £240,000 to Saturn Ltd on 1 May 2014.

Proposed acquisition of 65% of Tethys Ltd

On 1 August 2014, Saturn Ltd will purchase 65% of the ordinary share capital of Tethys Ltd for £235,000 from the personal representatives of George Jetson. The whole of the balance of the company's share capital is owned either by Edith Clanger or by her family company, Clangers Ltd; DD cannot remember which.

It is anticipated that Tethys Ltd will make a tax adjusted trading loss of approximately £80,000 in the year ending 31 December 2014.

In early 2015, Tethys Ltd will sell its manufacturing premises for £240,000 and move to a rented factory. The premises were acquired new for £112,000 and immediately brought into trade use. We agreed that the indexation factor on the disposal can be assumed to be 27%.

Information requested by DD

(i) The maximum amount of tax that can be saved via the use of the loss of Dione Ltd assuming it is not carried forward and the day by which the necessary claims must be submitted.

(ii) The amount of the trading loss of Tethys Ltd for the year ending 31 December 2014 that can be used by Saturn Ltd and the ability of Tethys Ltd to use this loss in the future.

(iii) In respect of the sale of the manufacturing premises:

- Whether or not Tethys Ltd should charge value added tax (VAT) on the sale of the property
- The taxable profit arising in respect of the sale
- The amount of the gain that could be rolled over if Tethys Ltd or any of the other Saturn Ltd group companies acquired assets costing £200,000, the types of asset that would have to be purchased and the period during which the assets would need to be acquired

(iv) Any stamp duty and/or stamp duty land tax payable by the Saturn Ltd group in respect of the proposed transactions.

Tax manager

Required

(a) Prepare the memorandum requested by your manager. The memorandum should include explanations together with supporting calculations and should identify any further information that you think is required. The following marks are available for the four components of the memorandum:

(i) The amount of tax that can be saved via the use of the loss of Dione Ltd; **(7 marks)**

(ii) The use of the trading loss of Tethys Ltd for the year ending 31 December 2014; **(6 marks)**

(iii) Advice in connection with the sale of the manufacturing premises by Tethys Ltd; **(7 marks)**

(iv) The stamp duty and/or stamp duty land tax payable by the Saturn Ltd group. **(2 marks)**

Additional marks will be awarded for the appropriateness of the format and presentation of the memorandum and the effectiveness with which the information is communicated. **(2 marks)**

(b) Prepare a summary of the information needed to satisfy our obligations under the money laundering legislation and any action that should be taken before agreeing to become tax advisers to the Saturn Ltd group. **(5 marks)**

(Total = 29 marks)

37 Stuart and Rebecca **47 mins**

Your manager has had a meeting with Stuart and Rebecca Lundy and has sent you a copy of the following memorandum.

To	The files
From	Tax manager
Date	1 December 2014
Subject	Stuart and Rebecca Lundy – Estate planning

Stuart has recently been diagnosed with a serious illness. He is expected to live for another two or three years only. He is concerned about the possible inheritance tax that will arise on his death. Rebecca is in good health.

In November 2014 Stuart sold a house in Plymouth for £422,100. Stuart had inherited the house on the death of his mother on 1 May 2002 when it had a probate value of £185,000. The subsequent pattern of occupation was as follows:

1 May 2002 to 28 February 2003	Occupied by Stuart and Rebecca as main residence
1 March 2003 to 31 December 2006	Unoccupied
1 January 2007 to 31 March 2009	Let out (unfurnished)
1 April 2009 to 30 November 2009	Occupied by Stuart and Rebecca
1 December 2009 to 30 November 2014	Used occasionally as second home

Both Stuart and Rebecca had lived in London from March 2003 onwards. On 1 March 2009 Stuart and Rebecca bought a house in London in their joint names. No other capital disposals were made by Stuart in the tax year 2014/15. He has £29,350 of capital losses brought forward from previous years.

Stuart intends to invest the gross sale proceeds from the sale of the Plymouth house, and is considering two investment options, both of which he believes will provide equal risk and returns. These are as follows:

(1) Acquiring shares in Omikron plc, a listed UK trading company, with 50,250,000 shares in issue. Its shares currently trade at 42p per share, or

(2) Acquiring further shares in Omega plc. The issued share capital of Omega plc is currently 10,000,000 shares. The share price is quoted at 208p – 216p with marked bargains at 207p, 211p, and 215p

Stuart and Rebecca's assets (following the sale of the Plymouth house but before any investment of the proceeds) are as follows:

Assets	*Stuart*	*Rebecca*
	£	£
Family house in London	450,000	450,000
Cash from property sale	422,100	–
Cash deposits	165,000	165,000
Portfolio of quoted investments	–	250,000
Shares in Omega plc	see files	see files
Life insurance policy	note	note

Note. The life insurance policy will pay out a sum of £200,000 on the death of the first spouse to die.

Tax manager

An extract from an email from your manager is set out below.

> Please prepare a letter from me to Stuart incorporating the following:
>
> 1 State the taxable capital gain on the sale of the Plymouth house in November 2014, setting out the amounts of any reliefs claimed.
>
> 2 Given his recent diagnosis, advice for Stuart on which of the two proposed investments (Omikron plc/Omega plc) would be the more tax efficient alternative.
>
> Give reasons for your choice.
>
> 3 Assuming that Stuart:
>
> (i) uses proceeds from the house sale to purchase 201,000 shares in Omega plc on 3 December 2014; and
>
> (ii) dies on 20 December 2016,
>
> calculations of the potential IHT liability which would arise if Rebecca were to die on 1 March 2017, and no further tax planning measures were taken.
>
> Assume that all asset values remain unchanged.
>
> 4 Advice on any lifetime IHT planning that could be undertaken to help reduce the potential liability calculated above.
>
> Tax manager

You have extracted the following further information from client files.

- Stuart is a self-employed business consultant born in 1956. He is married to Rebecca, who was born in 1959.
- They have one child, Sam, who was born in 1990 and is single.
- Both Stuart and Rebecca have wills whose terms transfer all assets to the surviving spouse.
- On 1 January 2010 Stuart and Rebecca elected for their London house to be their principal private residence with effect from that date, up until that point the Plymouth property had been their principal private residence.
- Omega plc was formerly Omega Ltd and Stuart and Rebecca helped start up the company. The company was formed on 1 June 1995, when they each bought 24,000 shares for £1 per share. The company became listed on 1 May 2004. On this date their holding was subdivided, with each of them receiving 100 shares in Omega plc for each share held in Omega Ltd.
- Neither Stuart nor Rebecca has made any previous chargeable lifetime transfers for IHT purposes.

Required

Prepare the letter requested by your manager. Marks are available for the four components of the letter as follows:

1 Relevant calculations of the taxable capital gain on the sale of the Plymouth house in November 2014. **(8 marks)**

2 Advice on which of the two proposed investments would be more tax efficient alternative. **(3 marks)**

3 Calculations of the potential IHT liability which would arise if no further tax planning measures are taken and Rebecca dies in March 2017. **(6 marks)**

4 Advice on any lifetime IHT planning that could be undertaken for both Stuart and Rebecca to help reduce their potential IHT liability (in three above). **(7 marks)**

Appropriateness of the format and presentation of the report and the effectiveness with which its advice is communicated. **(2 marks)**

You may assume that the rates and allowances for the tax year 2013/14 continue to apply for the foreseeable future.

(Total = 26 marks)

38 Landscape Ltd **45 mins**

Landscape Ltd is an unquoted trading company that operates a nationwide chain of retail shops.

(a) Landscape Ltd employed Peter Plain as a computer programmer until 31 December 2013. On that date he resigned from the company, and set up as a self-employed computer programmer. Peter has continued to work for Landscape Ltd, and during the period 1 January to 5 April 2014 has invoiced them for work done based on an hourly rate of pay. Peter works five days each week at the offices of Landscape Ltd, uses their computer equipment, and does not have any other clients. The computer function is an integral part of Landscape Ltd's business operations. Peter considers himself to be self-employed but Landscape Ltd's accountant is not sure if this is correct.

(b) On 15 March 2014 Landscape Ltd dismissed Simon Savannah, the manager of their shop in Manchester, and gave him a lump sum redundancy payment of £55,000. This amount include statutory redundancy pay of £2,400, holiday pay of £1,500, and £5,000 for agreeing not to work for a rival company. The balance of the payment was compensation for loss of office, and £10,000 of this was not paid until 31 May 2014.

(c) Trevor Tundra is one of the Landscape Ltd's shareholders, and is not a director or employee of the company. On 6 April 2013 Landscape Ltd provided Trevor with a new motor car that had a CO_2 emissions figure of 215g/km and that had an original list price of £14,000. No private petrol was provided. On 1 July 2013 Landscape Ltd made an interest free loan of £40,000 to Trevor. He repaid £25,000 of the loan on 31 August 2013, and the balance of the loan was written off on 31 March 2014.

(d) On 1 October 2013 Landscape Ltd opened a new shop in Cambridge, and assigned three employees from the London shop to work there on a temporary basis.

   (1) Ursula Upland is to work in Cambridge for a period of 18 months. Her ordinary commuting is a daily total of 90 miles, and her daily total from home to Cambridge to home again is 40 miles. She uses her private motor car for business mileage.

   (2) Violet Veld was initially due to work in Cambridge for a period of 30 months, but this was reduced to a period of 20 months on 1 January 2014. Violet walks to work whereas the cost of her train fare from home to Cambridge is £30 per day. This is paid by Landscape Ltd.

   (3) Wilma Wood is to work in Cambridge for a period of six months. Her ordinary commuting is a daily total of 30 miles, and her daily total from home to Cambridge is 150 miles. Wilma passes the London shop on her daily journey to Cambridge. She uses her private motor car for business mileage.

   All three employees worked at Cambridge for 120 days during 2013/14. Landscape Ltd pays a mileage allowance of 41p per mile for business use.

(e) Landscape Ltd is considering setting up a share incentive plan to reward its key employees. The company would like to know how many tax and NIC free shares it can give to each employee and how long the employees concerned must hold the shares for in order to obtain this advantage.

Required

Explain the income tax implications arising from the payments and benefits that have been made or provided by Landscape Ltd to Peter, Richard, Simon, Trevor, Ursula, Violet and Wilma. Your answer should be confined to the implications for 2013/14 and should assume that Landscape Ltd meets the definition of a close company. **(25 marks)**

Marks for this question will be allocated on the basis of:

6 marks to (a)
4 marks to (b)
4 marks to (c)
7 marks to (d)
4 marks to (e)

Approaching the answer

You should read through the requirement before working through and annotating the question as we have done so that you are aware of what things you are looking for.

Landscape Ltd is an unquoted trading company that operates a nationwide chain of retail shops.

ployment v self ployment

(a) Landscape Ltd employed Peter Plain as a computer programmer until 31 December 2013. On that date he resigned from the company, and set up as a self-employed computer programmer. Peter has continued to work for Landscape Ltd, and during the period 1 January to 5 April 2014 has invoiced them for work done based on an hourly rate of pay. Peter works five days each week at the offices of Landscape Ltd, uses their computer equipment, and does not have any other clients. The computer function is an integral part of Landscape Ltd's business operations. Peter now considers himself to be self-employed but Landscape Ltd's accountant is not sure if this is the correct interpretation.

Suggest self-employed

Suggest employee

Suggest employee

Suggest employee

Suggest employee

(b) On 15 March 2014 Landscape Ltd dismissed Simon Savannah, the manager of their shop in Manchester, and gave him a lump sum redundancy payment of £55,000. This amount includes statutory redundancy pay of £2,400, holiday pay of £1,500, and £5,000 for agreeing not to work for a rival company. The balance of the payment was compensation for loss of office, and £10,000 of this was not paid until 31 May 2014.

30,000 exempt if *x gratia*

Exempt

Taxable

Taxable

Taxed 14/15

(c) Trevor Tundra is one of the Landscape Ltd's shareholders, and is not a director or an employee of the company. On 6 April 2013 Landscape Ltd provided Trevor with a new motor car that had a CO_2 emissions figure of 215g/km and that had an original list price of £14,000. No private petrol was provided. On 1 July 2013 Landscape Ltd made an interest free loan of £40,000 to Trevor. He repaid £25,000 of the loan on 31 August 2013, and the balance of the loan was written off on 31 March 2014.

Participator taxed on distribution

Calculate benefit

Calculate benefit

Taxable

(d) On 1 October 2013 Landscape Ltd opened a new shop in Cambridge, and assigned three employees from the London shop to work there on a temporary basis.

Travel deductible

(1) Ursula Upland is to work in Cambridge for a period of 18 months. Her ordinary commuting is a daily total of 90 miles, and her daily total from home to Cambridge to home again is 40 miles. She uses her private motor car for business mileage.

Temporary

Authorised mileage rates

Temporary

(2) Violet Veld was initially due to work in Cambridge for a period of 30 months, but this was reduced to a period of 20 months on 1 January 2014. Violet walks to work whereas the cost of her train fare from home to Cambridge is £30 per day. This is paid by Landscape Ltd.

Not temporar

Temporary

(3) Wilma Wood is to work in Cambridge for a period of six months. Her ordinary commuting is a daily total of 30 miles, and her daily total from home to Cambridge is 150 miles. Wilma passes the London shop on her daily journey to Cambridge. She uses her private motor car for business mileage.

Authorised mileage rates

All three employees worked at Cambridge for 120 days using 2013/14. Landscape Ltd pays a mileage allowance of 41 pence per mile for business use.

'Free' shares plus matching & partnership

(e) Landscape Ltd is considering setting up a share incentive plan in order to reward its key employees. The company would like to know how many tax and NIC free shares it can give to each employee and how long the employees concerned must hold the shares for in order to obtain this advantage.

Required

Explain the income tax implications arising from the payments and benefits that have been made or provided by Landscape Ltd to Peter, Richard, Simon, Trevor, Ursula, Violet and Wilma. Your answer should be confined to the implications for 2013/14 and should assume that Landscape Ltd meets the definition of a close company.

Marks for this question will be allocated on the basis of:

6 marks to (a)
4 marks to (b)
4 marks to (c)
7 marks to (d)
4 marks to (e)

39 Marilyn Corniche **27 mins**

Marilyn Corniche was widowed on 20 May 2012. Under the terms of the will of her late husband Max she benefited absolutely from his share of the family home which they had held jointly as tenants in common. The mortgage on the family home was repaid out of the proceeds of a joint first death life assurance policy. In addition Marilyn inherited the holiday home in Cornwall, bank balances and a portfolio of quoted investments, all of which had previously been owned by Max personally. Marilyn's will leaves her estate equally to their twin sons, Douglas and Archie, aged 24, absolutely. Under Max's will the chattels passed to his brother Mark. Max, who had died suddenly, had made no lifetime gifts. The base cost, probate value and current market value of the items contained in Max's estate are as follows:

	Base cost	*Probate value May 2012*	*Market value February 2014*
	£	£	£
Family home (½ share)	61,500	90,000	110,000
Holiday home	42,000	63,000	73,000
Quoted investments			
Spiro plc 10,000 ordinary shares	50,000		
quoted at		685-677	635-647
with bargains marked at		690, 670, 675	630, 642, 641
Unit trusts	50,000	60,300	81,000
Unit trusts contained in ISAs	40,000	48,800	67,600
Bank deposits contained in ISAs	9,000	11,000	11,300
Bank deposit account	20,000	20,000	20,000
Chattels			
Chirico painting – Creation	4,000	5,000	7,000
Rene writing desk	8,000	7,000	4,000
Beckman's Diary – first edition	3,500	3,000	4,500

Marilyn also has £33,400 on deposit at Berkley's Bank, unit trust units invested in stocks and shares ISAs valued at £72,000 and a cash ISA of £10,600.

Marilyn is concerned about the exposure to inheritance tax in the event of her death.

Required

(a) Calculate the inheritance tax liability that arose on Max's estate as a result of his death on 20 May 2012 and that which would arise on Marilyn's estate if she were to die today (ie February 2014). Assume that no claims are made which might reduce the inheritance tax liability on either estate.

(8 marks)

(b) Advise Marilyn about any beneficial claims that may be made to reduce the inheritance tax liability on her death. **(7 marks)**

(Total = 15 marks)

Approaching the answer

You should read through the requirement before working through and annotating the question as we have done so that you are aware of what things you are looking for.

Marilyn Corniche was widowed on 20 May 2012. Under the terms of the will of her

Spouse exemption

late husband Max she benefited absolutely from his share of the family home which they had held jointly as tenants in common. The mortgage on the family home was repaid out of the proceeds of a joint first death life assurance policy. In addition Marilyn inherited the holiday home in Cornwall, bank balances and a portfolio of quoted investments, all of which had previously been owned by Max personally. Marilyn's will leaves her estate equally to their twin sons, Douglas and Archie, aged 24, absolutely. Under Max's will, the chattels passed to his brother Mark. Max, who had died suddenly, had made no lifetime gifts. The base cost, probate value and current market value of the items contained in Max's estate are as follows:

Taxable?

ONLY death estate

	Base cost	*Probate value May 2012*	*Market value February 2014*
	£	£	£
Family home (½ share)	61,500	90,000	110,000
Holiday home	42,000	63,000	73,000
Quoted investments			
Spiro plc 10,000 ordinary shares	50,000		
quoted at		685-677	635-647
with bargains marked at		690, 670, 675	630, 642, 641
Unit trusts	50,000	60,300	81,000
Unit trusts contained in ISAs	40,000	48,800	67,600
Bank deposits contained in ISAs	9,000	11,000	11,300
Bank deposit account	20,000	20,000	20,000
Chirico painting – Creation	4,000	5,000	7,000
Rene writing desk	8,000	7,000	4,000
Beckman's Diary – first edition	3,500	3,000	4,500

Lowest of
(i) ¼ up
(ii) Average highest and lowest marked bargain

Marilyn also has £33,400 on deposit at Berkley's Bank, unit trust with units invested in stocks and shares ISAs valued at £72,000 and a cash ISA of £10,600.

All subject to IHT

Marilyn is concerned about her exposure to inheritance tax in the event of her death.

Required

(a) Calculate the inheritance tax liability that arose on Max's estate as a result of his death on 20 May 2012 and that which would arise on Marilyn's estate if she were to die today (ie February 2014). Assume that no claims are made which might reduce the inheritance tax liability on either estate

(8 marks)

(b) Advise Marilyn about any beneficial claims that may be made to reduce the inheritance tax liability on her death. **(7 marks)**

Transfer of unused nil rate band

(Total = 15 marks)

1 The Wrights

Tutorial note. By this stage you should be proficient at setting up an income tax computation in three columns, grossing up income etc. This question also tests a new area at Paper P6 – tax reducers – and introduces an element of tax planning which will usually be found in questions at this level.

(a) (i) *Eric*

	Non-savings income	*Savings income*	*Dividend income*	*Total*
	£	£	£	£
Taxable trade profits	26,560			
BI £1,600 × 100/80		2,000		
Total income	26,560	2,000		28,560
Less deductible interest	(1,000)			
Net income	25,560	2,000	Nil	27,560
Less: higher personal allowance(W1)	(9,770)			
Taxable income	15,790	2,000	Nil	17,790

Tax

	£
£15,790 × 20%	3,158
£2,000 × 20%	400
	3,558
Less: tax reducer VCT £11,000 × 30%	(3,300)
	258
Less tax deducted at source	(400)
Tax repayable	(142)

(ii) *Melanie*

	Non-savings income	*Savings income*	*Dividend Income*	*Total*
	£	£	£	£
Earnings	50,000			
Dividends £4,500 × 100/90			5,000	
Net income	50,000	Nil	5,000	55,000
Less: personal allowance	(9,440)			
Taxable income	40,560	Nil	5,000	45,560

Tax

	£
£32,010 × 20%	6,402
£8,550 × 40%	3,420
£5,000 × 32.5%	1,625
	11,447
Less: PAYE	(10,000)
dividend tax credit	(500)
Tax due	947

Note. Interest on the National Savings & Investments Certificate is exempt from income tax.

(b) The total income will be split 50:50 between Eric and Melanie if no declaration of underlying interests is made.

The tax liability would be:

	£
Eric £6,000 × 20%	1,200
Add tax on reduction in higher personal allowance (W2)	66
Melanie £6,000 × 40%	2,400
Total extra tax	3,666

It would be better for the cottage to be bought by Eric as the additional income would fall within his basic rate band. If Melanie wished to have some interest in the cottage she could be given a notional 5% (say) as this would only have a marginal tax cost. A declaration for this treatment would need to be made.

Workings

1 Higher personal allowance (born between 6 April 1938 and 5 April 1948)

	£
Net income as above	27,560
Reduction £(27,560 – 26,100) × 0.5	730
Higher personal allowance £(10,500 – 730)	9,770

2

	£	
Net income including rent	33,560	
Reduction £(33,560 – 26,100) × 0.5	3,730	
Higher personal allowance £(10,500 – 3,730)	9,440	(minimum)

So there is a tax increase resulting from the loss of personal allowance of £9,770 - £9,440 = £330 × 20% = £66.

(c) *EIS investment*

Assuming the shares are subscribed for the initial investment will qualify for EIS relief at the rate of 30%. In this case the interest paid on the bank loan will not qualify for tax relief. Her outlay over five years will be £12,000 – £(12,000 × 30%) + £(12,000 × 8% × 5) = £13,200.

Purchase of 10% stake

In this case the bank interest paid will be allowed as deductible interest, but the dividends received will be liable to higher rate tax. Her outlay will be £12,000 + £[(12,000 × 8% × 5) × (100 – 40)%] – £(1,000 + 1,100 + 1,200 + 1,300 + 1,400) × (100 - 32.5)/90 = £10,380.

2 Pensions

> **Tutorial note.** Although you are asked to reply by e-mail, you must remember that you are writing to a client and present a structured reply.

(a) To: Mr Lee@red.co.uk
From: An Advisor@taxadvice.co.uk
Date: [ ]
Re: Pension advice

Thank you for your e-mail about pension advice. My answers to your questions are as follows:

(1) You do not have to join your new employer's pension scheme. Instead you could start a pension with a financial institution such as a bank or insurance company. However, your employer may not want to contribute to private pension arrangements so you need to bear this in mind when considering whether or not to join your employer's scheme.

A money purchase scheme is one where the value of your pension benefits depends on the value of the investments in the pension scheme at the date that you set aside ('vest') funds to produce those benefits. This is distinct from a defined benefits scheme where the benefits are defined from the outset. If you decide to use private pension arrangements, these are also likely to be money purchase arrangements.

(2) You can contribute an amount up to your earnings into the pension scheme and obtain tax-relief on those contributions (although the annual allowance which I explain below, effectively limits relief). You can also make any amount of further contributions, for example out of capital, but these will not obtain initial tax relief. However, since there is no income tax or capital gains tax payable by a pension fund, it may still be beneficial for such extra contributions to be made into this tax-exempt fund.

In addition, your employer can make any amount of contributions provided that the tax authorities are happy that such contributions are not excessive and so not for the purposes of the employer's trade.

The annual allowance limits the inputs that can be put into the pension fund and still receive tax relief. For 2013/14, this limit is £50,000. If you are a member of a pension scheme but do not use your full allowance for a tax year, you can carry forward the excess amount to be used against pension contributions for up to 3 tax years. The amounts that you contribute **and** obtain tax relief on, plus any contributions made by your employer, will count towards the annual allowance. If those contributions exceed the annual allowance, there will be a tax charge on the excess which is payable by you. This might be relevant in later years when your earnings may be above the annual allowance limit.

The lifetime allowance limit is the maximum value of the pension fund that you are allowed to build up to provide pension benefits without incurring adverse tax consequences. The lifetime allowance is £1,500,000 in 2013/14. This limit is tested against the value of your pension fund when you vest pension benefits. If your fund exceeds the lifetime allowance at that time, there will be a tax charge of 55% on funds vested to provide a lump sum and 25% on funds vested to provide a pension income. Although there are no adverse tax consequences if your pension fund exceeds the lifetime allowance other than at the time that pension benefits are vested, it would be wise to keep an eye on how your fund is growing so that you can adjust your contributions accordingly so as to keep within the lifetime allowance.

(3) Your employer will deduct your pension contributions gross from your pay before applying PAYE. This means that tax relief is given automatically at your highest rate of tax and no adjustment is needed in your tax return. As an example, if you contribute £1,000 to your pension and that amount of income would have been taxed at 40%, your pay will be reduced by £1,000 but the amount of tax that would be deducted from your pay would be reduced by £400, so that the net amount of the contribution payable by you would be £600.

The above is only an outline of the basics of pension provision as this is very complex area, so I suggest that we meet once you have decided how you wish to proceed.

AN Advisor

(b) (i) *Mr Holloway Tax liability 2013/14*

	Non-savings income
	£
Employment income/Net income/Taxable income (no PA available)	118,880
Tax	
	£
£32,010 × 20%	6,402
£(118,880 – 32,010) = 86,870 × 40%	34,748
Tax liability	41,150

(ii) *Pension contribution*

If Mr Holloway made a gross pension contribution of £18,880 in 2013/14, his adjusted net income would be reduced by this amount which would bring it down to £100,000. This would mean that there is no excess over the income limit and his personal allowance would be available in full.

Mr Holloway's tax liability would then be:

	Non-savings income
	£
Employment income/Net income	118,880
Less: personal allowance	(9,440)
Taxable income	109,440

Tax

	£
£32,010 × 20%	6,402
£18,880 × 20% (increased limit)	3,776
£(109,440 – 32,010 – 18,880) = 58,550 × 40%	23,420
Tax liability	33,598

This is a tax saving of (£41,150 – 33,598) = £7,552.

3 Hamburg

Tutorial note. It is important to realise that for individuals income from a property business is computed for tax years on an accruals basis. Don't forget to look out for rent a room relief in questions. You should have spotted the possibility of a pre-owned assets charge in part (c)

(a)

	Non-Savings Income	*Savings income*	*Dividend income*	*Total*
	£	£	£	£
Income from UK property business (W1)	12,220			
Trust income £6,875 × 100/55	12,500			
Interest – Direct Saver a/c		90		
– investment a/c		460		
– gilt interest (W2)		640		
Accrued income on sale		150		
Dividends £19,125 × 100/90			21,250	
Net income	24,720	1,340	21,250	47,310
Less: personal allowance	(9,440)			
Taxable income	15,280	1,340	21,250	37,870

Tax

	£
£15,280 × 20%	3,056
£1,340 × 20%	268
£15,390 × 10%	1,539
£32,010	
£5,860 × 32.5%	1,904
Tax liability	6,767
Less: tax deducted on dividends	(2,125)
tax deducted on trust income	(5,625)
Tax repayable	(983)

Workings

1

	£	£
Rent		
House 1: first letting £600 × 6		3,600
House 1: second letting £6,000 × 3/12		1,500
House 2 £8,000 × 8/12		5,333
House 3 £7,800 × 8/12		5,200
		15,633
Expenses		
House 1: new roof, disallowable because capital	0	
House 1: water rates	320	
House 1: buildings insurance £480 × 10/12	400	
House 2: water rates	240	
House 2: furniture £(5,333 – 240) × 10%	509	
House 3: redecoration	1,000	
House 3: water rates	360	
House 3: buildings insurance £440 × 9/12	330	
House 3: contents insurance £180 × 8/12	120	
House 3: furniture £(5,200 – 360) × 10%	484	
		(3,763)
UK property business income from 3 houses		11,870

Hamburg should claim rent a room relief in respect of the letting of the furnished room in his main residence, since this is more beneficial than the normal basis of assessment (£4,600 – £875 = £3,725). This means that Hamburg will be taxed on additional income of £350 (£4,600 – £4,250) from the UK property business.

Total property income £(11,870 + 350)	£12,220

2

	£
Interest June 2013 £20,000 × 6% × 6/12	600
Less: due to purchaser	(35)
	565
Interest December 2013 £2,500 × 6% × 6/12	75
	640

(b) If the cottages are to be treated as furnished holiday lettings, the first condition is that the lettings must be made on a commercial basis with a view to the realisation of profit.

Each property must be available for letting to the public for not less than 210 days in a tax year. Between them, the properties must be let for at least 105 days each in the 210 day period. For example, if the first cottage is let for 135 days in the year, the second cottage must be let for at least 75 days in the year to give an average of 105 days. If one of the cottages satisfies the 105 day test but the aggregation of the other cottage would pull the average down to below 105 days, the landlord can choose to treat the cottage which satisfies the 105 days test as furnished holiday accommodation.

In addition, each property must not normally be in longer term occupation (ie for more than 31 days) for more than 155 days in the year.

If the cottages satisfies these conditions, the income from the lettings is taxed as income from a UK property business but as if the landlord was carrying on a trade (except for the basis period rules). This means that capital allowance are available on furniture (instead of the 10% wear and tear allowance) and the income qualifies as relevant earnings for pension contribution purposes. However, loss relief is restricted to carry forward loss relief against future income from this accommodation.

(c) There are two income tax consequences resulting from Hamburg's proposal.

If Hamburg raises a bank loan the interest payable will be an allowable expense of the property letting, and will therefore save tax at Hamburg's marginal tax rate. Assuming Hamburg's income continues at a comparable level the rate of tax saving will be 42.5% since tax is saved at the basic rate (20%) on the property income covered by the interest and at 22.5% (32.5% - 10%) on gross dividends no longer falling in the higher rate band.

If Hamburg raises funds by selling a one half share in his house to his son but continues to live there, he will fall within the pre-owned assets rules. Unless he pays a full rental for his occupation out of after tax income he will be liable to an income tax charge on the rental value of this half of the property unless this is below the de minimis limit of £5,000. The charge will be at his marginal rate, ie effectively at 42.5% as shown above.

4 Taker

Tutorial note. The CO_2 emissions of the car are rounded down to 150g/km. The baseline figure for CO_2 emissions given in the tax rates and allowances tables is 95g/km at which the % is 11%. The % increases by 1% for each 5g/km that this figure is exceeded, ie here to 22%.

The exemption for childcare is only available for the weeks in which the childminder looks after Taker's son. Since Taker is a higher rate employee, the weekly exempt amount is £28.

Part (b) requires you to compare the after tax effects of different options based on your knowledge of the benefits rules.

(a)

	£	£
Salary		50,000
Car £20,000 × 22%		4,400
Fuel £21,100 × 22% (partial contribution gives no reduction)		4,642
Mobile telephone – exempt		0
Use of digital camera £600 × 20%		120
Loan: does not exceed £5,000		0
Childminder (4,000 – [48 × £28])		2,656
		61,818
Less: professional subscriptions	180	
cost of business telephone calls (no deduction for line rental)	45	
golf club: fails wholly, exclusively, and necessarily test	0	
		(225)
Earnings		61,593

(b) *Company car*

If Taker chooses the company car he will be charged 40% income tax on a car benefit of £3,250, ie a cost of £1,300 per tax year.

If Taker accepts the higher salary the position will be:

	£
Extra salary	3,000
Less tax @ 40%	(1,200)
	1,800
Add mileage allowance 6,000 × 40p	2,400
Add tax relief on expenses claim 6,000 × (45p – 40p) × 40%	120
Net additional income from company	4,320
Less running costs (excluding private use fuel) (2,200 – 500)	(1,700)
Less depreciation (15,000 – 5,000) × 1/3	(3,333)
Less extra interest paid £1,800 × 1/3	(600)
Net cost per tax year	(1,313)

Taking the additional salary would only cost Taker an extra £13, so the decision should be made on non-cash flow grounds.

Note. The cost of private use fuel is excluded from running costs as it would also be a cost of accepting the company car.

Company flat

If Taker moves to rented accommodation for three years the position is as follows:

	£
Relocation cost paid	12,000
Less tax on excess (12,000 – 8,000) @ 40%	(1,600)
	10,400
Net rent on old house £6,000 × 3 × (100 – 40)%	10,800
Less rent paid £4,000 × 3	(12,000)
Net inflow (before actual relocation costs)	9,200

If Taker moves to the company flat for three years the position is as follows:

	£
Relocation cost paid (not taxable)	6,000
Less tax on benefit of company flat £(2,500 + (120,000 – 75,000) × 4%) × 3 × 40%	(5,160)
	840
Net rent on old house £(6,000 + 1,000) × 3 × (100 – 40)%	12,600
Net inflow (before actual relocation costs)	13,440

If Taker chooses to rent accommodation he will be £(13,440 – 9,200) = £4,240 worse off over three years and will also have to pay an extra £2,000 in relocation costs. The relative merits of the different accommodation must also be taken into account.

5 National insurance contributions

Tutorial note. Part (a) is revision of the basic rules of NICs for an employee which should be familiar from F6.

Part (b) illustrates how different payments and benefits can have different NIC implications.

(a) *Albert*

	£
Primary contributions	
Total earnings exceed UEL	
£(41,450 – 7,755) = £33,695 × 12% (main)	4,043
£(48,500 – 41,450) = £7,050 × 2% (additional)	141
Total primary contributions	4,184
Secondary contributions	
£(48,500 – 7,696) = £40,804 × 13.8%	5,631
Class 1A contributions	
£(4,500 + 750) = £5,250 × 13.8%	724

(b) (i) A week on a health farm. This is a payment in kind and Poster plc will be liable to Class 1A NICs on each place, at a cost of £2,000 × 13.8% = £276. There will be no NICs for the employee.

(ii) A week's sailing on a yacht chartered by the employee. This is the payment of the employee's personal liability and so is liable to Class 1 NICs. Each employee's share of the bill is £(5,000 + 1,000)/3 = £2,000 and Class 1 NICs for each employee will be £2,000 × 12% = £240, or £2,000 × 2% = £40 if the upper earnings limit is exceeded. Poster plc will be liable to secondary Class 1 NICs, at a cost of £2,000 × 13.8% = £276 per employee.

(iii) A voucher which may be exchanged for a holiday at a high street travel agent. Vouchers are liable to Class 1 NICs even if they cannot be exchanged for cash. The cost to the employee will be £2,000 × 12% = £240, or £2,000 × 2% = £40 if the upper earnings limit is exceeded. Poster plc will be liable to secondary Class 1 NICs, at a cost of £2,000 × 13.8% = £276 per employee.

(iv) Payment of £1,500 cash. This is liable to primary Class 1 NICs of £1,500 × 12% = £180 per employee, or £1,500 × 2% = £30 if the upper earnings limit is exceeded. Poster plc will be liable to secondary Class 1 NICs, at a cost of £1,500 × 13.8% = £207 per employee.

6 Colin Jessop

Tutorial note. You need to identify which type of share scheme is appropriate for the particular needs of the employer. In this case, the Share Incentive Plan would best fit the requirements of the employer.

Our address

Your address

Date

Dear Colin,

Share option schemes

Thank you for your letter, I shall reply to your queries in turn.

Bonus scheme

There is indeed an approved scheme, the Share Incentive Plan (SIP) which can be used to reward employees with shares in a tax-efficient way. I set out the main features of the scheme below.

The company establishes a UK trust which acquires shares and appropriates them to employees in accordance with the plan. These shares are free of charge ('free shares'). The value of these free shares cannot exceed £3,000 to any employee in any tax year (although the award can be less). These free shares must stay in the trust for a period of five years if the award is to be completely free of income tax in the hands of the employee. If the employee removes the shares between three and five years after appropriation, there is an income tax charge on the value of the shares at award (or at withdrawal if lower). If the employee removes the shares from the trust before three years have elapsed, there will be an income tax charge on the value of the shares at the date of withdrawal.

The 'free shares' could replace your existing cash bonus scheme. The SIP provisions provide further incentives to your employees to invest in the company as outlined below.

'Partnership shares'

Employees who are awarded free shares can purchase up to £1,500 worth of 'partnership shares' from their pre-tax salary. Thus, for example, an employee can authorise Envirotech plc to deduct up to £125 per month from gross salary. This money is passed to the trustees who then acquire shares on behalf of the employee.

The income tax rules on the withdrawal of partnership shares from the trust are the same as the rules for the free shares.

'Matching shares'

Where an employee buys partnership shares, the company can award free 'matching shares'. The ratio of matching shares to partnership shares must be specified and cannot exceed 1:2 (ie the maximum value of 'matching shares' award to an employee in any tax year will not exceed £3,000).

The income tax rules on withdrawal of these shares from the trust are the same as for free and partnership shares.

'Dividend shares'

Employees can opt to reinvest the dividends on their SIP shares to acquire further shares. Any such dividends reinvested are not treated as taxable income for the participant.

The company may specify what percentage of dividends can be used to acquire dividend shares.

General Conditions

All employees (full or part-time) must be invited to participate in the scheme. Employees with less than 18 months service can be excluded.

The shares must be ordinary shares of a class listed or a recognised stock exchange, fully paid up and not redeemable.

An employee can only participate in one SIP in any given tax year.

Derek Forrest

Executive share options

As these options were granted under an 'unapproved' scheme, Derek will have an income tax charge at the date he exercised his options. You will see from the Appendix attached that his income tax liability will be £94,500 since Derek is a 45% taxpayer.

Assuming Derek sells his shares in the very near future, he will have no CGT to pay as his allowable cost is effectively equal to the market value of the shares at the date of exercise. If he retains the shares, any growth will be subject to CGT.

Retirement bonus

It is likely that the £30,000 'thank you' bonus will be taxable in full and will not be eligible for the exemption given to ex-gratia payments.

HMRC are likely to argue that the payment is made in return for services thereby making the bonus taxable under normal principles. It is therefore important that any documentation stresses that the payment is ex-gratia.

Failing this, HMRC could contend that as a payment is made to an employee 'at or near the age of retirement' the payment should be taxable in full in the same way as a benefit under a non-registered pension scheme.

I hope this deals with your queries but do please let me know if I can be of further help.

Yours sincerely

Brian Andrews.

Appendix

Derek Forrest

Tax on exercise of share options	£
100,000 × £(3.60 – 1.50)	210,000
Income tax @ 45%	94,500

7 Helen Strube and Gemma Hoyle

Tutorial note. Part (a) of this question is a very basic revision of material examinable in Paper F6. You **must** be fully competent with these basic computations at Paper P6. Part (b) is an example of how the rules on cessation of a sole trade can be used in a tax-efficient manner. Part (c) is also revision of a basic F6 computation of national insurance contributions for a sole trader.

(a)

	£
2008/09 (1.7.08 to 5.4.09)	
9/12 × £36,000	27,000
2009/10 (1.7.08 to 30.6.09)	36,000
2010/11 (1.7.09 to 30.6.10)	48,000

Overlap profits of £27,000 arise as a result of the trade profits accruing in the nine months to 5.4.09 being taxed in both 2008/09 and in 2009/10.

There is a change of accounting date which results in one long period of account ending during 2011/12. As a result the basis period is the fifteen months to 30 September 2011 and three months' worth of the overlap profits can be relieved:

2011/12	£
Basis period (1.7.10 – 30.9.11)	60,000
Less overlap profits 27,000 × 3/9	(9,000)
	51,000
2012/13 (year to 30.9.12)	£30,000
2013/14 (1.10.12 to 31.12.13)	
Year to 30.9.13	24,000
Three months to 31.12.13	10,000
Less overlap profits (27,000 – 9,000)	(18,000)
	16,000

The trade ceases during 2013/14 so the basis period for this year runs from the end of the last basis period to the date of cessation. Overlap profits which were not relieved on the change of accounting date are relieved against this final year's taxable profits.

(b) Gemma will have overlap profits from the period 1 May 2006 – 5 April 2007 of 11 × £100 = £1,100. These will be relieved on cessation.

If Gemma sells her business on 31 March 2014 the basis period for 2013/14 will be 1 May 2012 – 31 March 2014, and her taxable profits will be 23 × £2,300 – £1,100 = £51,800. This will all be taxed in 2013/14, so Gemma will pay higher rate tax on £(51,800 – 32,010 – 9,440) = £10,350. The top £(51,800 – 41,450) = £10,350 of profits will only be liable to Class 4 NICs at the additional 2% rate. In 2014/15, Gemma will pay no income tax at the higher rate as her taxable income will be £(27,000 – 9,440) = £17,560.

If Gemma sells her business on 30 April 2014 the basis period for 2013/14 will be 1 May 2012 – 30 April 2013, and her taxable profits will be 12 × £2,300 = £27,600. Her basis period for 2014/15 will be 1 May 2013 – 30 April 2014, and her taxable profits will be 12 × £2,300 – £1,100 = £26,500. Gemma will not be liable to higher rate tax in 2013/14 but will be liable to higher rate tax in 2014/15 on £(27,000 + 26,500 – 32,010 – 9,440) = £12,050. The first £7,755 of profits in 2014/15 will not be liable to Class 4 NICs (ie an additional £7,755 is not charged to NIC compared with the sale on 31 March 2014).

Thus if a 31 March 2014 date is selected, £(12,050 – 10,350) × (40 – 20)% = £340 tax will be saved, and £(10,350 × (9 – 2)% - 7,755 × 9%) = £27 less Class 4 NICs will be payable, but one month's less profits (£2,300) will be earned.

There may be other considerations to take into account, such as sale proceeds and capital gains tax.

(c) *Class 2 contributions (for both)*

	£
52 × £2.70	140
Class 4 contributions	
(i) £(35,000 – 7,755) = £27,245 × 9% (main only)	2,452
(ii) £(41,450 – 7,755) = £33,695 × 9% (main)	3,033
£(47,000 – 41,450) = £5,550 × 2% (additional)	111
Total Class 4 contributions	3,144

8 Sheila

Tutorial note. Watch out for special rate pool assets such as integral features. Use the annual investment allowance first against special rate pool assets for maximum tax efficiency.

	AIA	*Main pool*	*Special rate pool*	*Private use car*	*Allowances*
	£	£	£	£	£
p/e 31 March 2014					
Additions qualifying for AIA only					
1.3.14 Integral feature	63,600				
AIA 3/12 × £250,000	(62,500)				62,500
Transfer balance to special rate pool	1,100		1,100		
Additions not given AIA					
4.1.14 Plant		10,000			
WDA @ 18% × 3/12		(450)			450
WDA @ 8% × 3/12			(22)		22
TWDV c/f		9,550	1,078		
Allowances					62,972
y/e 31 March 2015					
Additions qualifying for AIA					
25.9.14 Van	11,800				
15.10.14 Plant	241,000				
	252,800				
AIA	(250,000)				250,000
Transfer balance to main pool	2,800	2,800			
		12,350			
Additions not qualifying for AIA					
15.11.14 Car				18,600	
WDA @ 18%		(2,223)			2,223
WDA @ 8%			(86)		86
WDA @ 8%				(1,488) × 65%	967
TWDV c/f		10,127	992	17,112	
Allowances					253,276

	AIA	Main pool	Special rate pool	Private use car		Allowances
	£	£	£	£		£
y/e 31 March 2016						
TWDV b/f		10,127	992	17,112		
Additions qualifying for AIA						
30.11.15 Plant	10,000					
AIA	(10,000)					10,000
Addition not qualifying for AIA						
30.3.16 Car		9,000				
		19,127				
WDA @ 18%		(3,443)				3,443
WDA small pool			(992)			992
WDA @ 8%				(1,369)	× 65%	890
TWDV c/f		15,684	0	15,743		
Allowances						15,325

9 Arrol and Louisa

Tutorial note. The disadvantage of a loss relief claim against general income can be that it wastes the personal allowance, demonstrated here in the current year. Note how restricting the capital allowances claimed can avoid the wastage of personal allowances.

(a) **Income tax computation for Arrol**

	Non-savings income	Savings income	Total
	£	£	£
Earnings: salary	25,000		
car benefit £19,370 × 34% (W1)	6,586		
fuel benefit £21,100 × 34%	7,174		
Bank interest £235 × 100/80		294	
Building society interest £3,005 × 100/80		3,756	
Total income	38,760	4,050	42,810
Less loss relief against general income (W2)	(38,760)	(4,050)	(42,810)
Net income	0	0	0
Income tax liability: nil			

Workings

1 **Car and fuel benefit**

213 g/km is rounded down to 210 g/km. Excess over base figure 210 – 95 = 115 g/km.

115 ÷ 5 = 23. Taxable % = 11 + 23 = 34%.

Partial contributions towards the cost of petrol do not reduce the fuel benefit.

2 **The loss available for relief**

			£
Loss			27,652
Capital allowances:	AIA	£(12,800 + 11,960)	24,760
			52,412
Loss in 2013/14: £52,412 × 11/12 (1.5.13 – 5.4.14)			£48,044

(b) **Income tax computation for Louisa**

	Non-savings income	*Savings income*	*Total*
	£	£	£
Earnings	5,135		
Building society interest £5,012 × 100/80		6,265	
NS&I interest		1,742	
Net income	5,135	8,007	13,142
Less personal allowance	(5,135)	(4,305)	(9,440)
Taxable income	0	3,702	3,702

Income tax	£		£
Savings starting rate band	2,790	× 10%	279
Basic rate band: savings income	912	× 20%	182
	3,702		461

(c) **The loss remaining unrelieved**

	£
Loss available for relief	48,044
Less used	(42,810)
Unrelieved balance	5,234

Relief for the remaining loss may be obtained:

(i) In 2012/13 against Arrol's general income

(i) under early trade losses relief against Arrol's general income for 2010/11, 2011/12 and 2012/13 in that order, or

(ii) by carry forward loss relief against future profits of the practice.

A claim against general income for 2012/13 or early years trade losses relief will obtain tax relief probably at the basic rate and might lead to a wastage of personal allowances.

Carry forward loss relief will obtain tax relief in 2015/16 against the profits of the year to 30 April 2015 at the basic rate and may lead to a wastage of personal allowances, unless these are covered by investment income. If any loss remains to carried forward to 2016/17 it is likely to obtain tax relief at the higher rate, or even the additional rate, as the business is expected to become very profitable.

£24,760 of the loss derives from Arrol making the maximum claim to capital allowances. A proportion of this loss is wasted by being set against income covered by the personal allowance in the current year. Arrol should consider restricting his claim for capital allowances to avoid wastage of personal allowance. Capital allowances not claimed are effectively carried forward in the pool of expenditure, and although they can then only be relieved on a reducing balance basis, relief will be obtained at a higher rate.

10 Partnerships

Tutorial note. Always divide the profits of a period of account between the partners before you begin allocating them to tax years. In part (b) do not forget to consider national insurance as well as tax, and also non-tax advantages/disadvantages.

(a)

	Total	*A*	*B*	*C*	*D*
	£	£	£	£	£
Year ending 5 April 2011					
Salaries	37,000	15,000	12,000	10,000	
PSR (balance)	65,000	26,000	26,000	13,000	
Total	102,000	41,000	38,000	23,000	
Year ending 5 April 2012					
6 April to 5 July					
Salaries	9,250	3,750	3,000	2,500	
PSR (balance)	42,750	17,100	17,100	8,550	
Total	52,000	20,850	20,100	11,050	
6 July to 5 April					
Salaries	16,500		9,000	7,500	
PSR (balance)	139,500		83,700	55,800	
Total	156,000		92,700	63,300	
Totals for the year	208,000	20,850	112,800	74,350	
Year ending 5 April 2013					
Salaries	22,000		12,000	10,000	
PSR (balance)	104,000		62,400	41,600	
Total	126,000		74,400	51,600	
Year ending 5 April 2014					
6 April to 5 May					
Salaries	1,833		1,000	833	
Balance	13,167		7,900	5,267	
Total	15,000		8,900	6,100	
6 May to 5 April					
Salaries	49,500		16,500	16,500	16,500
Balance	115,500		69,300	34,650	11,550
Total	165,000		85,800	51,150	28,050
Totals for the year	180,000		94,700	57,250	28,050

Taxable trade profits are as follows.

	A	*B*	*C*	*D*
	£	£	£	£
Year				
2010/11	41,000	38,000	23,000	
2011/12	20,850	112,800	74,350	
2012/13		74,400	51,600	
2013/14		94,700	57,250	28,050

(b) (i) If Freda is employed on a salary of £14,000 a year the tax and NI costs and savings will be:

	£
Employer's NI £(14,000 – 7,696) × 13.8%	870
Employee's NI £(14,000 – 7,755) × 12%	749
Income tax payable by Freda £(14,000 – 9,440) × 20%	912
Income tax saved by Eric £(14,000 + 870) × 40%	(5,948)
Class 4 NI saved by Eric £(14,000 + 870) × 2%	(297)
Total saving	(3,714)

If Freda is taken on as a partner with a 20% profit share, ie £14,000, the tax and NI costs and savings will be:

	£
Class 4 NI payable by Freda £(14,000 – 7,755) × 9%	562
Class 2 NI payable by Freda £2.70 × 52	140
Income tax payable by Freda £(14,000 – 9,440) × 20%	912
Income tax saved by Eric £14,000 × 40%	(5,600)
Class 4 NI saved by Eric £14,000 × 2%	(280)
Total saving	(4,266)

In this case the savings are £552 (£4,266 – £3,714) greater because of the reduction in NI contributions due.

(ii) If Eric increased Freda's share of partnership profits so that Eric did not pay higher rate tax, the savings would be maximised. Freda's share of profits would be £(70,000 – 32,010 – 9,440) = £28,550. The savings would be:

	£
Class 4 NI payable by Freda £(28,550 – 7,755) × 9%	1,872
Class 2 NI payable by Freda £2.70 × 52	140
Income tax payable by Freda £(28,550 – 9,440) × 20%	3,822
Income tax saved by Eric £28,550 × 40%	(11,420)
Class 4 NI saved by Eric £28,550 × 2%	(571)
Total saving	(6,157)

Note that unless Eric's share of profits is reduced below £41,450 there is no Class 4 NI advantage in increasing Freda's share of profits because she would pay Class 4 NI at 9% whilst Eric would only save Class 4 NI at 2%.

In addition to the tax and NI advantages/disadvantages of taking Freda into partnership as opposed to employing her there are other considerations. These include the unlimited liability of partners, employment law, PAYE obligations and entitlement to state benefits.

11 Overseas aspect of income tax

Tutorial note. Double tax relief is an important topic which could be examined in the Section A compulsory questions. Take great care when calculating the amount of UK tax on overseas income. The statutory residence test is very topical. Remember that the tax tables contain useful information to help you determine whether an individual is UK resident or not in a tax year.

(a) (i) **Susan – income tax computation 2013/14**

	Non-savings income	*Dividend income*	*Total*
	£	£	£
Earnings	21,535		
UK dividends (× 100/90)		10,000	
Overseas property business income (10,000 + 4,705)	14,705		
Net income	36,240	10,000	46,240
Less personal allowance	(9,440)		
Taxable income	26,800	10,000	36,800

	£
Income tax on non-savings income:	
£26,800 × 20%	5,360
Income tax on dividend income:	
£5,210 × 10%	521
£4,790 × 32.5%	1,557
	7,438
Less DTR (W)	(4,019)
	3,419
Less tax credit and PAYE £(2,300 + 1,000)	(3,300)
Tax payable	119

Working

UK tax on overseas income:	*Non-savings income*	*Dividend income*
	£	£
Taxable income	26,800	10,000
Less overseas property business income	(14,705)	
	12,095	10,000

Income tax	£
12,095 × 20%	2,419
10,000 × 10%	1,000
22,095	
Tax on UK income	3,419
Tax on taxable income (above)	(7,438)
UK tax on overseas income	4,019

DTR is lower of:

1 UK tax on overseas income £4,019
2 overseas tax £4,705

(ii) A UK taxpayer can claim relief from UK tax in respect of overseas tax paid by that person. There is a clear requirement in the legislation that the taxpayer should advise HMRC if subsequently the overseas tax is adjusted by the overseas tax authority so that if a DTR claim is rendered excessive an alteration can be made.

The taxpayer must notify HMRC within one year of any adjustment to the amount of overseas tax. So Susan must notify HMRC before 1 November 2016.

Her DTR claim for 2013/14 becomes the lower of:

1	UK tax suffered on overseas income	£4,019
2	overseas tax suffered (£4,705 – 2,600)	£2,105

ie £2,105 not £4,019 as before.

(b) Maria is arriving in the UK. She is not automatically non-UK resident during 2013/14 as she is in the UK for 46 days or more.

Maria is not automatically UK resident during 2013/14 as she is not in the UK for 183 days or more, she has a home outside the UK, and she does not work in the UK.

Maria's residence status will therefore be determined by 'sufficient ties'. Since she is in the UK for between 121 and 182 days, she will be UK resident if she has 2 UK ties. She does have 2 UK ties since she has close family (her spouse) in the UK and a house in the UK which is available to her for at least 91 days in the tax year and is made use of during the tax year.

Maria is therefore UK resident in the tax year 2013/14.

(c) James will be in the UK for 183 days or more during 2014/15 and so will be automatically resident in the UK.

James will be taxed in the UK on his earnings for working in the UK.

If James claims the remittance basis, he will only be taxed in the UK on his earnings for duties carried out in Utopia (because he has been non-UK resident for three consecutive years out of the previous five tax years) and on his Utopian bank interest, to the extent that the income is remitted to the UK. James should therefore try to avoid remitting such income to the UK. He will also lose his personal allowance if he claims the remittance basis.

If James does not claim the remittance basis, he will be taxed on his world-wide income on an arising basis.

12 Sophie Shaw

Tutorial note. This question covers the basics of CGT with which you must be completely familiar by the time you sit Paper P6. You are also required to consider how the CGT liability could have been reduced; there are several basic strategies.

(a) *Summary*

	£
Total gains £(47,000 + 40,000 + 15,750)	102,750
Less annual exempt amount	(10,900)
Taxable gains	91,850
CGT @ 28% on £91,850	25,718

Workings

(1) *Painting*

The costs of sale (auctioneer's costs) can be deducted from the sale proceeds.

	£
Proceeds	50,000
Less costs of sale	(500)
Net proceeds of sale	49,500
Less cost	(2,500)
Gain	47,000

(2) *Freehold shop*

The transfer of the shop between the spouses is on a no gain/no loss basis. The base cost for Sophie is therefore £45,000. The value of the shop at the transfer is not relevant.

The gain is:

	£
Proceeds	85,000
Less cost	(45,000)
Gain	40,000

(3) *2 acres of land*

This is a part disposal of the land. The fraction of cost used is:

$$\frac{\text{Proceeds of sale}}{\text{Proceeds of sale + value of part remaining}} \times \text{cost}$$

that is: $\frac{18,000}{18,000+70,000} \times £11,000 = £2,250$

The gain is:

	£
Proceeds	18,000
Less cost	(2,250)
Gain	15,750

(4) *JKL plc shares*

	£
Proceeds	20,000
Less cost	(52,000)
Loss	(32,000)

This is a loss on a disposal to a connected person. The loss is only allowable against a gain on a disposal to the same connected person.

(b) There are several ways in which Sophie's CGT liability could have been reduced.

(i) Sophie should have sold the JKL plc shares and gifted the proceeds to her son. She would then have generated an allowable loss of £52,000 – £18,000 = £34,000 (assuming she had achieved the same proceeds as did Jason), instead of realising a restricted loss of £32,000 and Jason generating the loss of £2,000 which can only be used if Jason makes capital gains, which is likely to be some time in the future. Sophie would save CGT of £34,000 × 28% = £9,520.

(ii) Terry has made no capital gains in 2013/14 so his annual exempt amount of £10,900 is unused and not all of his basic rate band is utilised. Sophie should have transferred one of the assets to Terry so that the gain would be realised in his hands thereby saving CGT of £10,900 × 28% = £3,052 plus £(32,010 – 30,000) = £2,010 × (28 – 18)% = £201, a total saving of £3,253.

(iii) Sophie has made a part disposal of 2 acres of land. This does not qualify for the small part disposal relief in Sophie's hands as the proceeds of this disposal plus the proceeds of the disposal of the shop exceed £20,000.

It might, however, have been possible to have transferred the land to Terry so that he could make a disposal which would fall within the limits. Sophie would transfer the land to Terry (at nil gain nil loss). The disposal by Terry would then fall within the small part disposal rules because the proceeds are less than £20,000 and do not exceed 20% of the market value of the entire holding of land prior to the part disposal. Terry may then deduct the proceeds of the land sold from the base cost of the land retained. Sophie would therefore save CGT of £15,750 × 28% = £4,410.

13 The Green family

Tutorial note. The key to a question in parts like this is to ensure that you make an attempt at each individual requirement.

(a) *Total value due to John Green on takeover*

	£
Shares 20,000 × £4.90	98,000
Cash 20,000 × £1.60	32,000
	130,000

Cash element exceeds both £3,000 and 5% of £130,000, so there is a part disposal

	£
Disposal proceeds (cash)	32,000
Less cost $\frac{32,000}{32,000+98,000} \times$ £40,000	(9,846)
Gain	22,154
Base cost of Wall plc shares £(40,000 – 9,846)	£30,154

(b) If John Green had received loan stock instead of cash there would not be an immediately chargeable gain. If the corporate bonds were qualifying corporate bonds the gain of £22,154 would be deferred until the QCBs were sold. This would enable John to sell the QCBs in tranches realising sufficient gains to utilise the annual exempt amount over several years, and preserve brought forward losses.

If the bonds are not QCBs the base cost of the original shares would simply be apportioned between the new shares and bonds, and no gain would arise until the bonds were disposed of. Again, this allows for phased disposals.

(c) *Match acquisitions in next 30 days first*

1 October 2013

	£
Disposal proceeds (£42,000 × $\frac{2,000}{3,200}$)	26,250
Less cost	(25,750)
Gain	500

Then match with share pool

15 May 2007

Shares held after bonus issue 1,800 + 1,800 = 3,600

No change to base cost

	£
Disposal proceeds (£42,000 × $\frac{1,200}{3,200}$)	15,750
Less cost (£1,900 × $\frac{1,200}{3,600}$)	(633)
Gain	15,117

The total chargeable gain on the sale of Matilda Green's shares in Read plc is £15,617 (£500 + £15,117).

(d) *Summary: John Green*

	£
Gain	22,154
Less loss brought forward	(11,254)
	10,900
Less annual exempt amount	(10,900)
Taxable gains	0
CGT payable	£nil

The losses brought forward are only set against gains to bring the gains down to the annual exempt amount.

Loss carried forward £(16,760 – 11,254)	£5,506

Summary: Matilda Green

	£
Gain	15,617
Less annual exempt amount	(10,900)
Taxable gains	4,717
CGT payable	
£4,717 × 18% (within unused basic rate band of £32,010 - £20,000 = £12,010)	£849

14 Hazel

Tutorial note. This question requires you to write a report so it is important that you did so. Marks may be specifically allocated for report writing or letter writing skills.

Report

To: Hazel
From: An Advisor
Date: [date]
Subject: Incorporation of your business

(a) If you sell your business to a company you will make a disposal of all the business's assets. You can avoid an immediate charge to capital gains tax through incorporation relief.

This relief applies automatically where:

- There is a transfer of a going concern
- All assets (or all the assets except cash) are transferred
- The consideration is wholly or partly for shares

An election can be made to disapply the relief, for example if you wished to use another relief (see further below).

(b) The gains on disposal are wholly deferred against the cost of shares received on incorporation where all of the consideration is received as shares.

If any of the consideration is received in cash (or loan notes or left on a loan account) a proportion of the gain will remain chargeable.

The maximum amount of cash that you could receive without triggering a charge to capital gains tax is £20,988 (see Appendix).

(c) The disadvantages to incorporation relief are as follows:

- The cost of the shares that you will be able to use when you eventually dispose of the shares will be reduced by the relief given to £64,412 (£134,012 – £69,600).
- You have to transfer all the assets (with the exception of cash) even if you wanted to retain, for example, the freehold shop outside the company
- The transfer of assets (such as the shop) may lead to a double tax charge in the future as corporation tax would be due from the company on the disposal of the asset and then when the proceeds are paid out to you as the shareholder there may be a further tax charge (either income tax or capital gains tax depending on how the proceeds are extracted from the company).

(d) As an alternative, you could consider gift relief. In this case you would need to gift the business's assets to the company. You would therefore be able to choose which assets to transfer and which to retain, eg the shop.

Gift relief defers your gain by reducing the base cost of the asset for company. The company then has a lower cost when it comes to sell the assets and therefore a higher gain.

Appendix – Maximum non-share consideration to take on incorporation

	£
Total consideration	155,000
Less: share consideration (W1)	(134,012)
Cash consideration	20,988

Workings

(1) *Share consideration*

	£
We want relief of (W2) :	69,600
Gain before reliefs is:	80,500
Total consideration is:	155,000

Therefore share consideration must be:

$$\frac{69,600}{80,500} \times £155,000 \qquad £134,012$$

(2) *Relief to bring gain to nil*

	£
Total gain:	
Goodwill	30,000
Property	50,500
	80,500
Less: incorporation relief (balance)	(69,600)
Gain	10,900
Less: annual exempt amount	(10,900)
Taxable gain	Nil

15 Miss Wolf, Mr Hen and Mr Fox

> **Tutorial note.** In part (c), no further absence can be counted as deemed occupation because Mr Fox did not go back to live in the house (compare absence followed by occupation between 1.8.95 and 31.1.06). Note also how the election as to which house is used as the PPR can be advantageous.

(a) Miss Wolf

The lease

	£
Proceeds	30,750
Less $\frac{64.116\,(16\text{ years})}{80.361\,(24\frac{1}{2}\text{ years})} \times £8,000$	(6,383)
Gain	24,367

The percentage for 24½ years is 79.622 + (81.100 – 79.622) × 6/12 = 80.361.

(b) Mr Hen

2013/14

No CGT event on the damage to the factory.

2014/15

Receipt of compensation is treated as part disposal. The amount not used in restoration is not 'small'. The restoration must also be taken into account.

	£
Amount not used in restoration £(20,000 – 15,000)	5,000
Less cost plus restoration	
$\frac{5,000}{5,000 + 250,000} \times £(150,000 + 15,000)$	(3,235)
Gain	1,765

2015/16

Sale of factory

	£
Sale proceeds	260,000
Less cost £(150,000 + 15,000 – 3,235 – 15,000)	(146,765)
Gain	113,235

(c) Mr Fox

(i) *Gain on sale*

	£
Proceeds	180,000
Less cost	(50,000)
Gain before PPR exemption	130,000
Exempt gain (W): $\frac{16\frac{1}{2}}{21} \times £130,000$	(102,143)
Gain	27,857

Working

Principal private residence relief	*Exempt years*	*Chargeable years*
1.8.92 – 31.7.95 (actual occupation)	3	
1.8.95 – 31.7.99 (up to 4 yrs due to place of work – *not* employed abroad)	4	
1.8.99 – 31.7.00 (up to 3 years any other reason)	1	
1.8.00 – 31.1.06 (actual occupation)	5½	
1.2.06 – 31.7.10 (not followed by actual occupation)		4½
1.8.10 – 31.7.13 (last 3 years)	3	
Totals	16½	4½

(ii) If Mr Fox had moved back into his house before it was sold, then the two years from 1.2.06 to 31.1.08 would have been treated as a period of occupation (balance of up to three years for any other reason) since Mr Fox had re-occupied the property after the period of absence. The exempt portion of the gain would have increased to 18½/21 × £130,000 = £114,524, leaving a chargeable gain of £15,476.

(iii) When Mr Fox inherited the house from his sister he had two residences available. He should have moved back to his own house for a few months. He should then have returned to his sister's house, electing for that to be treated as his PPR. Any remaining months before his old house was sold would be covered by the exemption for the last 36 months.

Provided the sister's house was sold within three years of her death any gain would also be covered by the exemption for the last 36 months.

16 Mr & Mrs Brown

Tutorial note. Administration should be a very familiar topic from F6. It can be examined in the compulsory Section A questions so you should ensure that you have a thorough knowledge of it.

(a) *Returns*

For the tax year 2013/14, a tax return must usually be submitted by 31 January 2015 (electronically) or 31 October 2014 (paper).

However, if the notice to file the tax return is issued by HMRC to the taxpayer after 31 July 2014 but on or before 31 October 2014, the latest filing date is the end of 3 months following the notice if a paper return filed. The latest date for filing electronically remains 31 January 2015. If the notice to file the tax return is issued by HMRC after 31 October 2014, the latest filing date is the end of 3 months following the notice. This applies whether the return is filed electronically or on paper.

An individual is liable to a penalty where a tax return is filed after the due filing date. The penalty date is the date on which the return will be overdue (ie the date after the due filing date). The initial penalty for late filing of the return is £100.

If the failure continues after the end of the period of three months starting with the penalty date, HMRC may give the individual notice specifying that a daily penalty of £10 is payable for a maximum of 90 days.

If the failure continues after the end of the period of six months starting with the penalty date, a further penalty is payable. This penalty is the greater of 5% of the tax liability which would have been shown in the return and £300.

If the failure continues after the end of the period of 12 months starting with the penalty date, a further penalty is payable. This penalty is determined in accordance with the taxpayer's conduct in withholding information which would enable or assist HMRC in assessing the taxpayer's liability to tax. The penalty is between 5% and 100% of the tax liability which would have been shown on the return depends on the taxpayer's conduct in withholding information which would enable or assist HMRC in assessing the taxpayer's liability to tax. The penalty is computed as follows:

Type of conduct	Penalty
Deliberate and concealed	Greater of: • 100% of tax liability which would have been shown on return; and • £300
Deliberate not concealed	Greater of: • 70% of tax liability which would have been shown on return; and • £300
Any other case (eg careless)	Greater of: • 5% of tax liability which would have been shown on return; and • £300

Self assessment of tax

If the taxpayer files his return electronically, the calculation of the tax liability is made automatically when the return is made online.

If the taxpayer files his return non-electronically on or before 31 October 2014 (or within two months of the notice if the notice is issued after 31 August 2014), the taxpayer may ask HMRC to make the tax calculation. Otherwise, the taxpayer must make the calculation.

Payments of tax

An individual may be required to make payments on account of his income tax and Class 4 NICs liability for 2013/14 on 31 January 2014 and 31 July 2014. Class 2 NICs will also be due on 31 January 2014 and 31 July 2014 (unless paid monthly by direct debit). A balancing payment of income tax and Class 4 NICs, and the whole of the individual's capital gains tax liability, is due on 31 January 2015.

Payments on account for 2013/14 are required where the individual's income tax and Class 4 NICs due in 2012/13 exceed the amount deducted at source: the excess is called the 'relevant amount'. The payments on account are 50% of the relevant amount for 2012/13. Payments on account are not required if the relevant amount is less than £1,000 nor if the tax deducted at source in 2012/13 was 80% or more of the total tax liability of that year.

The taxpayer may make a claim to reduce his payments on account if he expects his 2013/14 tax liability to be lower than his 2012/13 liability. The payments may be reduced to a stated amount or to nil. The claim must state why the taxpayer believes his liability will be lower. If the eventual liability is more than estimated, interest will be charged on the over-reduction. If the claim was made fraudulently or negligently, a penalty up to the amount of the over-reduction may be imposed.

Interest on overdue tax is charged on all unpaid tax from the due date. Where the balance of the tax due on 31 January 2015 is not paid within 30 days (the penalty date), a penalty for later payment is charged. Where payment is made within five months of the penalty date, the penalty will be 5% of the unpaid tax, rising to 10% where the payment is made more than five months but less than 11 months after the penalty date and 15% thereafter.

(b) *Mr Brown*

Due dates of tax – 2013/14

Payments made	*Paid*	*No claim to reduce payments on account*	*Due date*
£		£	
4,500	28 February 2014	6,000	31 January 2014
4,500	31 August 2014	6,000	31 July 2014
4,000	31 March 2015	1,000	31 January 2015
13,000		13,000	

Interest due

Payments on account:

	£
£4,500 × 1/12 × 3%	11
£4,500 × 1/12 × 3%	11
£1,500 × 14/12 × 3%	52
£1,500 × 8/12 × 3%	30
Final payment:	
£1,000 × 2/12 × 3%	5
	109

(c) Mrs Brown's tax return was prepared in accordance with the practice prevailing at that time. She will therefore be precluded from making a claim for the revised treatment if the court case should go in the taxpayer's favour.

Mrs Brown is, however, able to amend her tax return at any time up until 31 January 2016. She should therefore file an amendment to her return, using the more favourable treatment.

It is likely that HMRC will open a compliance check enquiry into her tax return, thereby enabling them to amend the return should the taxpayer fail in the Courts. Even at that stage Mrs Brown could appeal against any amendment HMRC made on closing a compliance check enquiry if it was likely that the matter would progress to higher courts.

17 Rodin

Tutorial note. This answer follows the 'steps' set out within the text but in a streamlined format which is equally acceptable in the exam.

(a) **IHT paid during Rodin's lifetime was as follows.**

25.12.05

	£
Gift	60,000
Less: A/E (2005/06)	(3,000)
A/E (2004/05) b/f	(3,000)
PET	54,000

This gift was a PET so no lifetime tax was due.

21.1.08

No gross chargeable transfers were made in the seven years prior to 21.1.08 so all of the nil band remained available for use.

This means the IHT paid by Rodin was:

		£
Gift		321,000
Less:	A/E (2007/08)	(3,000)
	A/E (2006/07) b/f	(3,000)
		315,000

			£
IHT	£300,000	× 0% =	Nil
	£15,000	× 20/80 =	3,750
	£315,000		3,750

The gross chargeable transfer was: £315,000 + £3,750 = £318,750.

Check: tax £(318,750 – 300,000) = £18,750 × 20% = £3,750.

20.8.10

		£
Gift		31,000
Less:	A/E (2010/11)	(3,000)
	A/E (2009/10) b/f	(3,000)
PET		25,000

This was a PET so no lifetime tax was due.

19.6.11

Gross chargeable transfers of £318,750 had been made in the seven years prior to 19.6.11 so £(325,000 – 318,750) = £6,250 of the nil band remains and the lifetime IHT due was:

		£
Gift		88,000
Less:	A/E (2011/12)	(3,000)
		85,000

			£
IHT	£6,250	× 0% =	Nil
	£78,750	× 20% =	15,750
	£85,000		15,750

1.8.13

		£
Gift		73,000
Less:	A/E (2013/14)	(3,000)
	A/E (2012/13) b/f	(3,000)
PET		67,000

This was a PET so no lifetime tax was due.

1.9.13

This was an exempt transfer to Rodin's UK domiciled spouse so no lifetime tax was due.

IHT due as a result of death.

As a result of death, IHT will be due on transfers made in the seven years before the death.

Lifetime transfers

25.12.05

This PET was made more than seven years before death, so no IHT arises as a result of death.

21.1.08

Gross transfer	£318,750

None of the nil band had been used in calculating death tax in the seven years before 21.1.08 so the IHT due on death is nil because the transfer is completely covered by the nil band at death of £325,000. There is no repayment of lifetime tax.

20.8.10

Gross chargeable transfers of £318,750 had been made in the seven years prior to 20.8.10 so £(325,000 – 318,750) = £6,250 of the nil band remains and the death IHT due is

			£
PET			25,000
			£
IHT	£6,250	× 0% =	Nil
	£18,750	× 40% =	7,500
	£25,000		7,500
Less taper relief @ 20% (3-4 years)			(1,500)
IHT payable by daughter (80%)			6,000

19.6.11

All of the nil band has been used in calculating death tax on the gifts made in the seven years prior to 19.6.11, so the death tax due on this gift is:

Gross chargeable transfer	£85,000
	£
£85,000 × 40% =	34,000
Less lifetime tax	(15,750)
Tax due on death (no taper relief as death within 3 years of gift)	18,250

1.8.13

No nil band remains so IHT due on this now chargeable PET is:

PET (valued at 1.8.13)	£67,000
£67,000 × 40%	£26,800

No taper relief as death occurs within 3 years of the gift.

1.9.13

No IHT arises on an exempt transfer to a spouse.

(b) If Rodin's wife had not been domiciled in the UK at the time of the transfer to her, only the first £325,000 of the transfer would have been exempt. The balance of the transfer would still be a PET, so there would be no IHT to pay unless Rodin died within seven years. The IHT that would be due following Rodin's death would be £(400,000 – 325,000) × 40% = £30,000.

(c) The gift by Rodin's cousin into the discretionary trust is a CLT which is in excess of the nil rate threshold of £325,000. He should therefore make this gift first to ensure that the annual exemption for the current year and the previous year are set against this transfer, so reducing the amount of lifetime IHT payable. If Rodin's cousin pays the tax the gift would need to be grossed up, so the immediate IHT saving would be £3,000 × 2 × 20/80 = £1,500, whereas if the trustees paid the tax the saving would be £3,000 × 2 × 20% = £1,200.

The gifts to the two children are PETs and no tax will be payable unless Rodin's cousin dies within seven years of the gifts.

Rodin's cousin could delay his gift to his daughter until her marriage so that he can utilise the marriage exemption. For a parent the exemption is £5,000. Should Rodin's cousin die within three years of the gift this will save IHT of £5,000 × 40% = £2,000, with reduced savings (because of taper relief) if death is between three and seven years from the gift. There is a small element of risk should Rodin's cousin die more than seven years after the gift to the son, but within seven years of the gift to the daughter.

18 Mr Bright

Tutorial note. Note the different valuation rules for CGT and IHT. The shares are valued at market value for CGT purposes. For IHT purposes the diminution in value principle is used to value the shares.

(a) *Capital gains tax liability*

	£
Gain on shares (W)	30,889
Less annual exempt amount	(10,900)
Taxable gain	19,989

The CGT is £19,989 × 10% = £1,999.

Inheritance tax liability

The gift to the discretionary trust is a chargeable lifetime transfer. As he pays the tax, grossing up is necessary. Two annual exemptions of £3,000 each (for 2013/14 and 2012/13) are available to reduce the net transfer.

	£
Transfer	349,000
Less: A/E (2013/14)	(3,000)
A/E (2012/13) b/f	(3,000)
Net transfer	343,000

There have been no previous transfers so all of the nil band remains available for use in calculating the IHT on this transfer.

		£
£325,000	× 0%	Nil
£18,000	× 20/80	4,500
£343,000		4,500

Gross transfer is thus £347,500 (£343,000 + 4,500). The IHT payable by Mr Bright is £4,500.

Check: tax £(347,500 – 325,000) = £22,500 × 20% = £4,500.

The gift to Maxine on 1 April 2014 is a potentially exempt transfer so no tax is due during Mr Bright's lifetime.

Working

Share Pool

	No. of shares	*Cost*
		£
1.11.85 Acquisition	2,200	3,300
15.6.04 Acquisition	200	1,366
18.8.10 Acquisition	600	3,000
	3,000	7,666
1.4.14 Disposal	(2,000)	(5,111)
c/f	1,000	2,555

	£
Disposal proceeds (2,000 × £18) (market value)	36,000
Less cost	(5,111)
Gain qualifying for entrepreneurs' relief	30,889

Entrepreneurs' relief applies because

- there is a disposal of shares in a company which is the individual's personal company (owns at least 5% of ordinary share capital); and
- the individual is an officer of the company; and
- these conditions were met throughout the period of one year ending with the date of disposal.

(b) If Mr Bright were to die on 20 April 2014, the potentially exempt transfer to Maxine on 1 April 2014 would become chargeable. The amount of this transfer, applying both the diminution in value principle and the related property rules (since Mrs Bright owns 1,000 shares) is as follows.

	£
Before the transfer, Mr Bright had 3,000 shares in a holding of 3,000 + 1,000 = 4,000 shares (80%), worth £36.67 a share	110,010
After the transfer, Mr Bright had 1,000 shares in a holding of 1,000 + 1,000 = 2,000 shares (40%), worth £18 a share	(18,000)
	92,010
Less actual proceeds	(10,000)
	82,010
Less business property relief: unavailable because shares sold by date of Mr Bright's death	(0)
Transfer of value (no annual exemptions available)	82,010

On Mr Bright's death, his remaining shares would also be valued using the related property rules, as follows.

	£
1,000 shares in a holding of 2,000 shares, worth £18 a share	18,000
Less business property relief at 100% (unquoted shares)	(18,000)
	0

The inheritance tax liabilities which would arise on Mr Bright's death on 20 April 2014 are as follows.

1 May 2013 transfer

Gross transfer (valued on 1 May 2013)	£347,500

IHT at death (no taper relief – death within 3 years)

		£
£325,000	× 0%	Nil
£ 22,500	× 40%	9,000
£347,500		9,000
Less: Lifetime tax paid		(4,500)
Tax payable at death		4,500

1 April 2014 transfer

	£
Transfer of value 2014	82,010
Less: A/E (2013/14 – already used)	–
A/E (2012/13 – already used)	–
	82,010

All nil band used in previous seven years so IHT due on death is:

£82,010 × 40% = £32,804

Death estate

	£
Shares	Nil
Cash	40,000
Less CGT liability	(1,999)
	38,001

IHT at 40% = £15,200

The trustees of the settlement must pay IHT of £4,500.

Maxine must pay IHT of £32,804.

Mr Bright's personal representatives must pay IHT of £15,200.

(c) Notes for meeting

Immediate gift of shares in Bod Ltd:

(i) PET for IHT purposes, only chargeable if Mr Bright dies within seven years.

(ii) BPR only available on Mr Bright's death within seven years if Roger retains the shares and they are still eligible for BPR.

(iii) Disposal for CGT purposes. Entrepreneurs' relief will reduce tax rate. Gift relief will also apply.

(iv) Loss of influence over running of Bod Ltd; Mrs Bright has a 20% holding.

Retention of shares in Bod Ltd until death:

(i) BPR likely to be available on Mr Bright's death, so no IHT.

(ii) Tax free uplift to market value at date of death for CGT purposes.

(iii) Retention of influence over running of Bod Ltd; Mr & Mrs Bright each have a 20% holding.

(iv) If Roger is involved in the business he may be unhappy not to have received shares whilst his sister purchased shares at an undervalue.

19 Trusts

Tutorial note. Work through the transactions methodically to identify when an IHT charge will arise.

(a) Death 3 September 2013

RJ discretionary trust

The occasions of charge are:

17 July 2006: CLT by Rhys. If Rhys pays the tax this will be grossed up. The full nil rate band at 17 July 2006 is available. There is no additional tax on Rhys Jones' death as he survived 7 years from the gift.

5 March 2015: exit charge on the assets distributed. This is calculated using 30% of an assumed rate of tax scaled down by 34/40 to reflect the number of complete quarters that have elapsed since the settlement was created. The assumed rate is calculated using a transfer equal to the initial value of the settlement with prior transfers equal to the chargeable transfers made by Rhys in the seven years prior to the settlement (£nil).

17 July 2016: principal charge calculated using 30% of an assumed rate. The assumed rate is calculated using a transfer equal to the value of the settlement at the date of the anniversary with prior transfers equal to the chargeable transfers made by Rhys in the seven years prior to the settlement (£nil) plus the transfers made on 5 March 2015.

18 April 2019: exit charge on the assets distributed. This is calculated using 30% of the assumed rate of tax calculated at the last principal charge scaled down by 11/40 to reflect the number of complete quarters that have elapsed since the anniversary.

Rhys Jones discretionary will trust

3 September 2013: charge on death estate. The full nil rate band is available as the Rhys Jones discretionary trust was set up more than seven years earlier.

28 February 2018: exit charge on death of Blodwen causing capital to pass to her children (the actual date of distribution is not relevant). This is calculated using 30% of an assumed rate of tax scaled down by 17/40 to reflect the number of complete quarters that have elapsed since Rhys Jones' death. The assumed rate is calculated using a transfer equal to the initial value of the settlement with prior transfers equal to the chargeable transfers made by Rhys in the seven years prior to the death (£nil).

(b) Death 3 July 2013

RJ discretionary trust

If Rhys dies on 3 July 2013 this will be within seven years of the settlement and there may be additional IHT to pay by the trustees. Taper relief will be available to reduce the death tax and any lifetime tax paid will be deducted.

Rhys Jones discretionary will trust

As death occurred within seven years of the transfer to the RJ discretionary trust, the available nil rate band at death will be reduced by the transfer of value and this will increase the IHT due on the death estate.

When computing the exit charge due on death of Blodwen on 28 February 2018 the chargeable lifetime transfer by Rhys to the RJ discretionary trust will be an assumed prior transfer, so increasing the rate of IHT payable on the exit charge.

20 Fraser Ltd

Tutorial note. The first part of this question is revision of material that you should know well from Paper F6. The second part requires you to apply your knowledge to several different proposals.

(a) **Corporation tax computation**

	£
Trading income (W1)	338,105
Interest income £(6,834 + 2,208)	9,042
Chargeable gains (W3)	35,870
Taxable total profits	383,017

Workings

(1) *Adjusted profit computation*

	£	£
Profit before taxation		413,278
Add: depreciation	13,876	
gifts (over £50 each)	2,085	
entertaining	969	
		16,930
		430,208
Less: dividend including tax credit	1,655	
bank interest	6,834	
interest from gilts	2,208	
surplus on disposal of office building and lease	61,806	
capital allowances (W2)	19,600	
		(92,103)
Taxable trading profit		338,105

(2) *Capital allowances*

AIA £9,800 × 2	£19,600

(3) *Chargeable gains*

(a) *The lease*

	£
Proceeds	40,161
Less cost	
$£17,500 \times \frac{66.470 + ½(68.697 - 66.470)}{81.100} = \frac{17.5 \text{ years}}{25 \text{ years}}$	(14,583)
Unindexed gain	25,578
Less indexation allowance to April 2013	
0.291 × £14,583	(4,244)
Chargeable gain	21,334

(b) *The office building*

	£
Proceeds	120,633
Less cost	(79,000)
Unindexed gain	41,633
Less indexation allowance to August 2013	
0.343 × £79,000	(27,097)
Indexed gain	14,536

Total gains are £(21,334 + 14,536) = £35,870.

(b) *Purchase of office building A*

The building will cost £150,000. The two disposals by Fraser Ltd during the year to 31 March 2014 realised proceeds of £160,794, so Fraser Ltd can make a claim to roll over all but £10,794 of the gains realised in the year ended 31 March 2014.

Purchase of office building B

If Fraser is to use half of the office building itself, the cost of that half will be £200,000, so that full rollover relief will be available. Rollover relief is not available against let property.

Rent received, less property expenses, will be taxed as property income.

Any interest paid on bank borrowings or loan stock would be allowable, either as a trading deduction or as a deduction from interest income, but not as a deduction from property income. It would be necessary to identify how the borrowings had been applied, and to apportion the interest payable between trading and non-trading.

Purchase of subsidiary

If a subsidiary is purchased Fraser Ltd will not be able to roll over any of the gains from the disposals in the year ended 31 March 2014 as shares are not qualifying assets.

No tax relief will be available for the cost of the shares until Fraser Ltd disposes of them, and the disposal may then be exempt as the disposal of a substantial shareholding.

Any interest paid on borrowings for the share purchase will be allowed as a deduction from non-trading interest.

As there will now be an additional company in the group, this will affect the small profits limits, and since Fraser Ltd is a marginal company this may increase the corporation tax payable.

Purchase of patents etc

The tax treatment of patents etc follows the accounting treatment. Fraser Ltd will therefore obtain a deduction for the cost of these intangible fixed assets over their useful lives. Any royalties payable will be allowed as an expense. As the patents are to be used in the trade the costs will be trading expenses; if Fraser Ltd acquires the subsidiary the patents should therefore also be acquired by the subsidiary.

Equity capital

If Fraser Ltd realises funds through the issue of shares rather than by raising loans, then there will be no interest payments to deduct in the accounts. Investors may require the payment of dividends; these are not tax deductible.

21 Melson Ltd

> **Tutorial note**. Rollover relief is not available to defer the gain arising on the sale of the warehouse because it was not used in the trade of Melson Ltd. Watch out for substantial shareholding exemption on a sale of trading company shares.

CHARGEABLE GAINS COMPUTATION

	£
Warehouse (W1)	40,500
House (W2)	40,012
Office building (W3)	85,555
Shares (W4)	0
Chargeable gains	166,067

Workings

1 *Warehouse*

	£
Proceeds	125,000
Less cost	(65,000)
	60,000
Less indexation allowance $\frac{249.9-192.2}{192.2}$ (0.300) × £65,000	(19,500)
	40,500

Rollover relief is not available as the old asset was not used by Melson Ltd in its trade.

2 *House*

	£
Proceeds	75,000
Less cost	(20,000)
extension	(4,000)
	51,000
Less indexation allowance	
$\frac{249.3-170.1}{170.1}$ (0.466) × £20,000	(9,320)
$\frac{249.3-175.9}{175.9}$ (0.417) × £4,000	(1,668)
	40,012

3 *Office building*

	£
Proceeds	180,000
Less cost	(65,000)
	115,000
Less indexation allowance $\frac{249.3-171.6}{171.6}$ (0.453) × £65,000	(29,445)
	85,555

4 *Shares*

The gain on the disposal of the shares in Leigh Ltd is exempt under the substantial shareholding exemption because:

- Melson Ltd is a trading company
- Leigh Ltd is also a trading company
- Melson Ltd held 10% of the ordinary share capital of Leigh Ltd for a continuous period of twelve months in the two years preceding the disposal

22 Major Ltd

Tutorial note. It is important to distinguish between trading and non-trading loan relationships. Interest on the former is dealt with as trading income whilst interest on the latter is dealt with as interest income.

(a) *Corporation tax*

	£
Taxable trading income	165,000
Property income	30,000
Capital gains	40,000
Total profits	235,000
Less qualifying charitable donation	(3,000)
Less non-trade deficit (£24,000 – £30,000)	(6,000)
Taxable total profits	226,000
Add Franked investment income	20,000
Augmented profits	246,000

The eight month accounting period all falls within Financial Year 2013.

Lower limit	£300,000 × 8/12 × ½	£100,000
Upper limit	£1,500,000 × 8/12 × ½	£500,000

Marginal relief applies

Corporation tax

	£
£226,000 × 23%	51,980
Less marginal relief	
(3/400 × (£500,000 – £246,000) × 226,000/246,000)	(1,750)
Corporation tax	50,230

(b) To: The Directors of Major Ltd
From: Certified Accountant
Date: 31 March 2014
Re: Tax implications of the loan to Z Ltd becoming irrecoverable

It will not be possible for any amount of the loan written off to be deducted in computing Major Ltd's trading profits. This means that if the loan is written off in the company's income statement, the amount written off must be added back to compute trading profits. Instead any amount written off will be treated as a deficit on a non-trading loan relationship. This means that it will initially be deducted from income arising on non-trading loan relationships in the same accounting period. Any overall net deficit can be:

(i) Set against the company's total profits in the same accounting period, or

(ii) Set against income from non trading loan relationships arising in the previous twelve months, or

(iii) Set off against non-trading profits in the following period, or

(iv) Surrendered as group relief.

Signed: Certified Accountant

(c) *General considerations*

Any dividends received on the shares acquired are not subject to corporation tax, but will be taken into account in determining the rate of corporation tax applicable to Major Ltd's taxable trading profits. Any interest paid on borrowings to fund the purchase would be allowed as a deduction from non-trading interest, and if there is a deficit it can be relieved as described above.

Purchase of 20% holding from a retiring director

If Major Ltd purchases a 20% holding from a retiring director no tax relief will be obtained for the cost of the shares until they are sold. Provided the shares are held for at least twelve months and the target company is a trading company, the conditions for the substantial shareholding exemption to apply are likely to be satisfied so that any gain on disposal would be exempt. Conversely, if the target company collapses the loss would not be allowable. If it appears that the target company is declining it may be worthwhile attempting to sell the shares within twelve months of acquisition to ensure the loss is allowable.

Subscription for 8% holding

As the shareholding will be less than 10%, it will not qualify for the substantial shareholding exemption. If a gain is made on the disposal it will be fully taxable. If there is a loss it will be allowable.

23 Hogg Ltd

Tutorial note. The information required in this question should be very familiar knowledge to you from Paper F6.

(a) The due dates for the payment of corporation tax by Hogg Ltd in respect of the year to 31.3.14 are:

	£	£
14 October 2013 (1/4 × £500,000)		125,000
14 January 2014 (1/4 × £500,000)		125,000
14 April 2014 (1/4 × £520,000)	130,000	
plus underpaid 2 × £(130,000 – 125,000)	10,000	
		140,000
14 July 2014 (1/4 × £520,000)		130,000
1 January 2015 100% × £525,000		
– £125,000 – £125,000 – £140,000 – £130,000		5,000
Total		525,000

(b) There is a £100 penalty for a failure to submit a return on time, rising to £200 if the delay exceeds three months. These penalties become £500 and £1,000 respectively when a return was late (or never submitted) for each of the preceding two accounting periods.

An additional tax geared penalty is applied if a return is more than six months late. The penalty is 10% of the tax unpaid six months after the return was due if the total delay is up to 12 months, and 20% of that tax if the return is over 12 months late.

24 Norma

Tutorial note. This question takes a situation of an individual commencing a new trade and contrasts the tax treatment of trading as a company or as an unincorporated business. It is simply a question of applying your knowledge of the tax rules to the given scenario.

	(a) *Sole trader* £	*(b)* *Dividend* £	*(c)* *Dividend + salary* £
Company			
Profits	N/A	60,000	60,000
Less salary			(15,000)
Less employers' NI (15,000 – 7,696) × 13.8%			(1,008)
			43,992
Less corporation tax @ 20%		(12,000)	(8,798)
Profits available for dividend		48,000	35,194
Individual			
Profits/salary	60,000		15,000
Dividend 48,000/35,194 × 100/90		53,333	39,104
Less PA	(9,440)	(9,440)	(9,440)
Taxable income	50,560	43,893	44,664
Income tax payable			
32,010/nil/5,560 @ 20%	6,402		1,112
nil/32,010/26,450 @ 10%		3,201	2,645
18,550/nil/nil @ 40%	7,420		
nil/11,883/12,654 @ 32.5%		3,862	4,113
	13,822	7,063	7,870
Less tax credits nil/43,893/39,104 @ 10%		(4,389)	(3,910)
	13,822	2,674	3,960
National insurance			
Class 2 52 × £2.70	140		
Class 4 (60,000 – 41,450) × 2% + (41,450 – 7,755) × 9%	3,404		
	3,544		
Class 1 employees (15,000 – 7,755) × 12%			869
Net cash received			
Profit/Salary	60,000		15,000
Net dividend		48,000	35,194
Less income tax	(13,822)	(2,674)	(3,960)
Less national insurance	(3,544)		(869)
	42,634	45,326	45,365

From this it can be seen that Norma's net receipt is greatest if she operates as a company and draws a £15,000 salary and the balance as dividend. The net inflow is only marginally lower if she draws all the profits as a dividend. Drawing a salary also ensures that her national insurance record is up to date and would enable her to pay pension contributions in excess of the £3,600 limit available to all individuals.

It should also be noted that corporation tax is payable 9 months after the year end, PAYE and class 1 NI are payable monthly during the tax year, and any income tax not collected through PAYE and Classes 2 and 4 NI is payable by instalments on 31 January in and 31 July following the tax year, and any balance on the following 31 January.

25 Clarke Ltd

> **Tutorial note.** This question concerns the purchase of a company's own shares. The choice of dates should have alerted you to the likelihood of the conditions not being satisfied on one of the disposals.

Since Clarke Ltd is an unquoted trading company the capital treatment will automatically apply if the conditions are satisfied. Alex is selling all of his shares, so the reduction to 75% or less of his interest is clearly satisfied. The buying out of a dissident shareholder/director is generally accepted by HMRC as being for the benefit of the company's trade. The shares subscribed for in 1997 have been held for more than the requisite five years, whereas the shares purchased in May 2009 will only qualify if the repurchase is delayed until June 2014. Entrepreneurs' relief does not apply because Alex holds less than 5% of the ordinary shares in the company.

Disposal March 2014

May 2009 acquisition – distribution treatment.

	£
Distribution – excess of proceeds over subscription 2,000 × £(5 – 1)	8,000
Additional rate tax £8,000 × 100/90 × (37.5 – 10)%	2,444
Capital gain	
Proceeds not treated as distribution 2,000 × £1	2,000
Less cost 2,000 × £3	(6,000)
Capital loss	(4,000)

January 1997 acquisition – capital treatment.

	£
Capital gain	
Proceeds 5,000 × £5	25,000
Less cost 5,000 × £1	(5,000)
	20,000
Less capital loss on May 2009 shares (above)	(4,000)
Gain	16,000
CGT payable @ 28%	4,480

Total tax liability £2,444 + £4,480 = £6,924.

Disposal June 2014

May 2009 acquisition – capital treatment.

	£
Capital gain	
Proceeds 2,000 × £5	10,000
Less cost 2,000 × £3	(6,000)
Gain	4,000

January 1997 acquisition – capital treatment.

	£
Capital gain	
Proceeds 5,000 × £5	25,000
Less cost 5,000 × £1	(5,000)
Gain	20,000

Total gains £(4,000 + 20,000) = £24,000.

CGT liability £24,000 × 28% = £6,720.

Delaying the disposal until June 2014 enables the capital treatment to apply to the total shareholding and saves tax of £6,924 – £6,720 = £204. More significantly, it also delays the due date for payment of the tax by one year.

26 Daley plc

Tutorial note. Your discussion of loss relief is required to take the form of a letter to the directors, and you should ensure that you give a full and clear explanation.

(a) *Taxable total profits*

	Year ended	*Year ended*	*6 months ended*	*Year ended*
	31.12.11	*31.12.12*	*30.6.13*	*30.6.14*
	£	£	£	£
Trading profits	–	110,000	85,000	–
Less carry forward loss relief	–	(1,000)	–	–
	–	109,000	85,000	–
Interest income	10,000	11,000	12,000	14,000
Chargeable gains	18,000	–	–	–
(losses are carried forward)	–			
Total profits	28,000	120,000	97,000	14,000
Less current period loss relief	(28,000)	–	–	(14,000)
	–	120,000	97,000	–
Less carryback loss relief	–	(60,000)	(97,000)	–
	–	60,000	–	–
Less qualifying charitable donation	–	(2,000)	–	–
Taxable total profits	–	58,000	–	–
CT @ 20%	–	11,600	–	–
Unrelieved qualifying charitable donation	–	–	3,000	1,000

Loss memorandum

Loss	29,000	202,000
Less current period loss relief	(28,000)	(14,000)
Less carry back loss relief (6 months)		(97,000)
Less carry back loss relief 6/12 × £120,000 (restricted)		(60,000)
Loss carried forward	1,000	31,000

A trading loss of £31,000 is available at 30 June 2014 to carry forward against future profits of the same trade, and there is also a capital loss of £4,000 to carry forward against future chargeable gains at 30 June 2014.

(b) My address

The directors of Daley plc

Their address

Date

Dear Directors

Relief for losses

I am writing to set out for you how Daley plc can obtain relief for losses that it has incurred during its first few years of trading. The company has incurred two different types of losses, capital losses and trading losses.

Capital losses

Capital losses incurred must first be set against any capital gains made in the same accounting period. Any capital losses which cannot be so offset are carried forward and set against capital gains in future accounting periods, as soon as they arise. The offset is automatic, and cannot be disapplied. Capital losses cannot be carried back.

Daley plc incurred a net capital loss of £5,000 in the year ended 31 December 2012. This cannot be carried back against the chargeable gains of £18,000 arising in the year to 31 December 2011 but is carried forward. £2,000 must be offset against the chargeable gains arising in the 6 months to 30 June 2013, leaving £3,000 of unrelieved capital losses to carry forward. Further capital losses of £1,000 arise in the year to 30 June 2014, and these are added to the £3,000 brought forward, so that capital losses of £4,000 are carried forward at 30 June 2014.

Trading losses

Trading losses can be relieved in several different ways, and there are strict rules about how the reliefs interact.

(i) A claim can be made for trading losses to be relieved by set off against other profits of the same accounting period. Other profits includes interest income, property income, miscellaneous income and chargeable gains. The trading loss is, however, set off against total profits which is calculated before qualifying charitable donations are deducted, so that if the trading loss exceeds the other income, the qualifying charitable donation is unrelieved.

If the claim is made, the amount of trading loss that is set off is the lower of the company's other income or the trading loss. It is not possible to restrict the claim, for example to prevent qualifying charitable donations from being unrelieved.

(ii) If a claim has been made under (i) but not all of the trading loss has been relieved, then a claim may be made for the unrelieved amount to be carried back against the company's other income of the previous twelve months. Other income is as above, before the deduction of qualifying charitable donations.

Again, the amount of trading loss that is set off is the lower of the company's other income or the trading loss, and the claim cannot be restricted.

As Daley plc's previous accounting periods are not all twelve months long, the loss will be carried back against the other profits of the previous accounting period, then against the relevant proportion of the other income of the accounting period before that. Thus because there is an accounting period which is six months long immediately before the loss making period, any loss carried back is set against the profits of the six month accounting period, then against 6/12ths of the profits of the twelve month accounting period before that. When apportioning the profits it is acceptable to apportion the profits before deducting qualifying charitable donations and then to deduct the qualifying charitable donations from the profits which fall outside the twelve month carry back period.

(iii) Any trading loss which has not been relieved by a claim under (i) or (ii) is carried forward and set off against future profits from the same trade. The set off is automatic, is made against the first available profits, and is equal to the lower of the available loss and the available profits. It is not possible to restrict the amount of loss offset.

Best use of loss

Whilst making a claim under (i) or (ii) for offset against other income achieves relief at the earliest possible time, it may not achieve the best use of the loss. The rate at which a company pays corporation tax for an accounting period depends upon the level of its profits for that accounting period, so that a company may pay corporation tax at a higher rate in some accounting periods than in others. It may, therefore, be preferable to carry a loss forward if it will obtain a higher rate of relief, although this must be weighed against the disadvantage of receiving relief later.

The rates of corporation tax are as follows:

- the small profits rate of 20% applies to profits of up to £300,000.
- the marginal rate of 23.75% applies to the next £1,200,000 of profits
- the main rate of 23% applies to profits in excess of £1,500,000.

These limits are reduced where companies are associated, so that if Daley plc acquires Terry Ltd in April 2015 the small profits limits will be reduced from £300,000 to £100,000 and from £1,500,000 to £500,000 for the year to 30 June 2015.

Loss of year ended 31 December 2011

A claim was made for this loss to be set against other income of the same accounting period and the balance was carried forward against the loss of the year to 31 December 2012. This meant that £29,000 was relieved at the small profits rate of 20%.

Loss of the year to 30 June 2014

It is proposed that a claim should be made for the loss of the year to 30 June 2014 to be relieved against current and prior year profits. This will result in relief of £41,563 being obtained as follows:

Y/e 30.6.14	£14,000 × 20% = £2,800, and qualifying charitable donation of £1,000 is wasted
6m/e 30.6.13	£97,000 × 20% = £19,400, and qualifying charitable donation of £3,000 is wasted
y/e 31.12.12	£60,000 × 20% = £12,000
y/e 30.6.15	£31,000 × 23.75% = £7,363

If the whole loss of £202,000 is carried forward the relief obtained will be £44,150:

y/e 30.6.15	£50,000 × 23.75% + £100,000 × 20% = £31,875
y/e 30.6.16	£50,000 × 23.75% + £2,000 × 20% = £12,275

In addition relief will be obtained of qualifying charitable donations of £4,000 that would otherwise have been wasted, ie a further £800 (£4,000 @ 20%).

It must be borne in mind that the relief will be delayed compared to a current year and carry back claim.

If I can provide any further information please do not hesitate to contact me.

Yours sincerely

Certified Accountant

27 Huis Ltd

> **Tutorial note**. The tax consequences of close company status are designed to ensure that people do not use this type of company as a means of avoiding tax.

(a) The loan to Sartre will lead to Huis Ltd being required to make a payment of £45,000 × 25% = £11,250 to HMRC. This amount is payable at the same time as the corporation tax for the accounting period, so it is payable by 1 September 2014. (Note that if Huis Ltd was a 'large' company the tax on the loan is subject to the quarterly instalment regime.)

When the loan is written off on 31 March 2015 the company will be entitled to a refund of 25% of the amount waived (ie £45,000 × 25% = £11,250 refund). This refund will be due nine months after the end of the accounting period of the write off, ie it will be due on 1 September 2016.

Sartre will be deemed to receive income of £45,000 × 100/90 = £50,000 in the year in which the loan is written off, 2014/15. There will be no further basic rate liability, but for the income falling above the higher rate or additional rate thresholds, tax at 32.5% or 37.5% (but subject to the deduction of the 10% tax credit) will be payable by 31 January 2016. That is, Sartre will be taxed just as if he had received a net dividend of £45,000.

The provision of private medical cover and the use of the yacht are provisions of benefits to a shareholder who is not an employee. Each year they will be treated as net distributions of £(1,000 + 24,000 × 1/12) = £3,000. This is equivalent to gross income of £3,000 × 100/90 = £3,333. No further tax will be payable if Sartre is a basic rate tax payer (which will probably not be the case in 2014/15 due to the loan write off). If he is a higher rate taxpayer he will have a higher rate tax liability of £3,333 × (32.5 – 10)% = £750 and if he is an additional rate taxpayer an additional rate tax liability of £3,333 × (37.5 – 10)% = £917, payable by 31 January following the end of the tax year through self-assessment.

Huis Ltd will not be able to deduct the medical insurance premium nor the running costs of the yacht for that month in its corporation tax computation.

(b) Because Beauvoir Ltd is a close investment-holding company, the main rate of corporation tax applies. Excess management expenses are carried forward.

	Year ended 31.3.13	*Year ended 31.3.14*
	£	£
Property income	14,000	25,000
Interest income	20,000	100,000
	34,000	125,000
Less management expenses – current	(34,000)	(45,000)
– brought forward (note)		(2,000)
Taxable total profits	–	78,000

Note. £2,000 carried forward from ye 31.3.13

Corporation tax at 23% £17,940

28 H, S and N

Tutorial note. It is important to realise that N Ltd counts as associated for the whole period to 30.6.13 despite the fact that it was only acquired on 1.1.13.

(a) *H Ltd: corporation tax computations for the accounting periods of 12 months to*

	30.6.13	*30.6.14*
	£	£
Trading profit	2,000	–
Less loss carried back	(2,000)	–
Taxable trading profits	–	–
Corporation tax payable	£–	£–

S Ltd: corporation tax computations for the accounting periods of 12 months to

	30.6.13	*30.6.14*
	£	£
Trading profits	30,000	100,000
Less qualifying charitable donations	(12,000)	(12,000)
Taxable trading profits	18,000	88,000

S Ltd: corporation tax computations for the accounting periods of 12 months to

	30.6.13	*30.6.14*
	£	£
Corporation tax		
£18,000 × 20%	3,600	
£88,000 × 20%		17,600
Corporation tax payable	3,600	17,600

Note. small profits rate applies in both periods (W2).

N Ltd: corporation tax computations for the accounting periods of 12 months and 6 months to

	31.12.13	*30.6.14*
	£	£
Adjusted profit split 12:6	43,500	21,750
Less capital allowances	(4,250)	(17,569)
Trading profits	39,250	4,181
Interest income	–	20,000
Total profits	39,250	24,181
Less group relief surrendered by H Ltd (W1)	(19,625)	(24,000)
Taxable total profits	19,625	181

Corporation tax

	£	£
£19,625 × 20%	3,925	
£181 × 20%		36

Workings

(1) *Group relief / loss relief*

	£
Loss of H Ltd y/e 30.6.14 available for group relief	48,000
Surrendered to N Ltd	
6 months to 31.12.13 lower of ($^6/_{12}$ × £48,000) or ($^6/_{12}$ × £39,250)	(19,625)
6 months to 30.6.14 lower of ($^6/_{12}$ × £48,000) or £24,181	(24,000)
	4,375
Loss of H Ltd carried back	(2,000)
Loss of H Ltd carried forward	2,375

Group relief is not available for S Ltd because it is only a 60% subsidiary.

(2) *Upper and lower limits*

Y/e 30.6.13 and 30.6.14 there are three companies associated. Even though N Ltd only became associated with H and S on 1 January 2013 it is counted as associated for the whole period to 30.6.13. Thus the limits are:

UL £1,500,000 ÷ 3 = £500,000
LL £300,000 ÷ 3 = £100,000

For N Ltd's six months to 30.6.14 these limits must be halved.

(b) To: The Directors of H Ltd
From: Certified Accountant
Date: 31 December 2014
Re: Minimisation of corporation tax on property transactions

H Ltd and N Ltd are in a capital gains group because H Ltd holds 100% of the shares in N Ltd. S Ltd is not part of a group with H Ltd because H Ltd only has a 60% shareholding (75% required for a capital gains group)

There are several factors which will affect the corporation tax liability on the proposed disposals.

(i) The loss of £26,667 made by N Ltd in November 2012 is a pre-entry loss and so cannot be offset against gains on the disposals by H Ltd.

(ii) Rollover relief is available against the purchase of the new warehouse. As the cost is only £290,000, only £60,000 of the gain on the old warehouse can be rolled over into the purchase of the new warehouse acquired by S Ltd. The balance of £10,000 cannot be rolled over, as there are surplus proceeds of £10,000 and S Ltd is not in a group with H Ltd and N Ltd so cannot benefit from group rollover relief.

(iii) H Ltd pays corporation tax at the small profits rate, N Ltd will pay corporation tax at the small profits rate on the first £25,000 of any chargeable gains and at the marginal rate on any excess. It is therefore preferable for the gains to be taxable in H Ltd so as to bear corporation tax at the lowest rate. An election should be made for N Ltd to transfer its post-entry loss on the factory to H Ltd.

The net position for H Ltd is then:

	£
Sale of factory	(13,333)
Sale of office block	80,000
Total gains	66,667
Corporation tax £66,667 × 20%	13,333

S Ltd will have a gains of £10,000 on which corporation tax will be £10,000 × 23.75% = £2,375 because S Ltd pays tax at the marginal rate for y/e 30 June 2015 on profit in excess of £100,000.

N Ltd will have a pre-entry loss of £26,667 carried forward.

Signed: Certified Accountant

29 Exotica Inc and W Ltd

> **Tutorial note**. In part (b) you were asked to produce a report so it is important that you did so. Marks may be specifically allocated for report writing or letter writing skills.

(a) If the salesmen have authority to conclude contracts, there will almost certainly be a permanent establishment in the United Kingdom, and its profits would therefore be liable to UK corporation tax. The holding of stocks would not, however, by itself show that there was a permanent establishment.

Taxable profits would be determined as if the permanent establishment had an arm's length relationship with the company, so that tax liabilities could not be manipulated by transfer pricing. Profits would be liable to tax at 23%, because the small profits rate and marginal relief are not available to non-resident companies.

(b) REPORT

To: The Board of Directors
From: Certified Accountant Date: 1 November 2013
Subject: Taxation implications of the overseas operation

(i) UK taxation arises on the profits of an overseas permanent establishment (PE), and any losses of such a PE will, provided that the PE is controlled in the UK, be aggregated with the profits or losses of the UK division. It is possible to make an election so that the profits of the overseas PE are exempt from UK corporation tax. However, this means that no relief would be available if the PE were to make a loss. The election is irrevocable and applies to all permanent establishments, so may not be appropriate if you anticipate that you may set up further PEs in the future that may initially be loss-making.

There will normally be no UK taxation on dividends paid by an overseas subsidiary to a UK company and they will not form part of the UK company's franked investment income if the payment is from a 51% subsidiary. Losses of an overseas subsidiary cannot be relieved against the UK company's profits, as group relief is only available between UK resident companies and between UK and EU resident companies in certain restricted circumstances.

(ii) Foreign tax will arise on the profits of both PEs and subsidiaries. To the extent that the profits of the PE suffer both foreign and UK taxation, double taxation relief will be available, either under a treaty or under the UK's unilateral relief provisions. The usual effect is that the overall tax rate is the higher of the average UK rate on the UK company's profits and the foreign rate subject to an overall 23% ceiling. Since any dividends paid by a subsidiary will not normally be subject to UK tax, double taxation relief will not be relevant.

(iii) Assets cannot be transferred outside the scope of UK taxation to a foreign subsidiary on a no gain/no loss basis, so capital gains may arise. However, any such gains may be deferred until shares in the subsidiary are sold. If assets are transferred to a PE, there is no change of ownership so CGT is not triggered.

(iv) A subsidiary will only be treated as not UK resident if it is not incorporated in the UK and its central management and control are abroad.

Signed: Certified Accountant

30 Paul

Tutorial note. These rules are really designed to stop people avoiding VAT by establishing several different businesses with a turnover below the registration threshold.

VAT law recognises a 'taxable person' rather than a business. All business activities of the same person are regarded as a single VATable activity, and are brought within the same registration if the person is, or is required to be, registered. The same individual is a single 'person' for all activities carried on in his own capacity; and two partnership activities are also a single person, if exactly the same people are partners in both firms.

Conversely, related business activities may be regarded separately under VAT law if they are carried out by different 'persons'. Examples of different persons would be:

- Individuals
- Partnerships with different partners
- Different limited companies

HMRC may question whether there really is a separation of activities between different persons. If the activities are in reality carried on by someone else, they will form part of that person's taxable turnover, even if that person argues that the supplies are made by another.

In this situation, there are four possible taxable persons:

- Paul Sand trading alone (as a sole trader)
- Paul Sand and John Rowe
- Paul Sand and Peter Dene
- Paul Sand and Mrs Sand

HMRC may question the reality of any of the partnerships. They will consider whether the parties involved are closely bound by financial, economic and organisational links.

For example HMRC may consider whether there is:

- A proper written partnership agreement
- Evidence of the parties' intentions
- Actual sharing of profits (not just income or expenses)
- Notification of customers, suppliers and other authorities (eg on stationery)
- Authority of partners to bind the firm
- Ownership of common assets

They may also consider how the business is treated for direct tax purposes.

If they consider any of the partnerships to be artificial, the activities of that partnership will be treated as carried on in conjunction with the sole trade.

Conversely HMRC may also issue a business splitting direction.

31 VAT groups

> **Tutorial note**. Marks may be specifically allocated for letter writing skills. Would you have gained them here?

Our address

Your address

Date

Dear Mr Franklin

Group registration

I am writing in reply to your recent enquiry regarding Union Ltd, specifically the question of whether that company should be included in the group VAT registration and the procedure for so doing.

First, I confirm that group registration is possible, since all the companies are either established or have a fixed establishment in the UK and they are all under common control.

It would be advisable for Union Ltd to be included in the group registration, for two reasons:

(1) To avoid the need to account for VAT on intra group transactions and hence minimise the risk of VAT being underdeclared in error. For example, the group relief payments to which you refer in your letter would not normally constitute consideration for taxable supplies and so would not give rise to the need to account for VAT, even between companies which are not in a group registration. However, in certain circumstances HMRC might argue that the 'group relief payments' in fact amount to consideration for a taxable supply, giving rise to an output tax liability; for example, if the payments were linked to services provided by Union Ltd to other group companies.

By including Union Ltd in the group registration, such potential problems are avoided.

(2) As Union Ltd is partly exempt, around 40% of any input tax it incurs is irrecoverable. If Union Ltd is not included in the group registration, any standard-rated supplies which it receives from other group companies would generate additional irrecoverable VAT.

It is also necessary to consider, however, the effect of including a partly exempt company in the group registration. This will depend in part on the partial exemption method used by Union Ltd at present and the method to be used by the group if Union Ltd is included. Under the standard method, more of Union Ltd's overhead input tax would become recoverable but some of the group's would be lost.

It should however be borne in mind that the partial exemption de minimis limit will apply to the group as a whole and is not multiplied by the number of companies in the group registration.

So far as the procedure is concerned, an application needs to be made to HMRC for Union Ltd to be added to the group registration. All applications to join an existing VAT group will automatically be approved by HMRC and will take effect from the date they are received by HMRC (or such earlier or later time as HMRC may allow). HMRC will not normally permit retrospective grouping, so Union Ltd will have to be accounted for separately until you make the application.

HMRC do have the power to refuse an application within 90 days of its receipt if the application does not meet all of the eligibility criteria (which should not be a problem in your case) or presents a risk to the revenue. It is not thought that a slight improvement in the partial exemption position would be sufficient to warrant a refusal on the grounds of risk to the revenue; the improvement would have to go beyond the simple effects of grouping, so something 'artificial' would have to be involved.

Please do not hesitate to contact me if I can be of further assistance.

Yours sincerely

Certified Accountant

32 Stewart Ltd

Tutorial note. Remember to round up the percentage recovery to the nearest whole number.

(a) Residual input tax

	6/13	*9/13*	*12/13*	*3/14*	*Total*
	£	£	£	£	£
'T' (note 1)	403,920	359,177	467,159	520,321	1,750,577
'T + E'	455,992	382,371	485,950	557,760	1,882,073
T/T + E (note 2)	89%	94%	97%	94%	94%
Residual tax	14,719	12,613	10,412	11,919	49,663

Notes

(1) Excludes sale of capital asset used in the business.
(2) Rounded up to nearest whole percentage point.

(b) Exempt input tax

	6/13	*9/13*	*12/13*	*3/14*	*Total*
	£	£	£	£	£
Direct	3,120	2,775	1,374	1,876	9,145
Share of residual	1,619	757	312	715	2,980
	4,739	3,532	1,686	2,591	12,125
De minimis test 3? (note)	N	N	Y	N	N

Note. Less than £625 pm and less than 50% of the total

(c) Recoverable input tax

	6/13	*9/13*	*12/13*	*3/14*	*Total*
	£	£	£	£	£
Direct	44,404	39,098	24,926	36,020	144,448
Exempt de min.			1,686		
Share of residual	13,100	11,856	10,100	11,204	46,683
	57,504	50,954	36,712	47,224	191,131
Total recovered in the four quarterly returns:					192,394
Annual adjustment – due to HMRC					(1,263)

The annual adjustment will be made by reducing the input tax for the return period to June 2014.

33 Tax planning

Tutorial note. In this question it was important to allocate your time carefully between each of the queries raised.

(a) Incorporation should take place when the business starts to make profits, on 1 May 2015.

Advantage can then be taken of early trade loss relief, which is only available to unincorporated businesses. This relief is against income of the three tax years preceding the year of loss, taking earlier years first. Relief will be obtained against the salary of the last few years before Client A became self-employed, leading to repayments of tax.

(b) B's current annual profit is £60,000 × 40% = £24,000.

With the contract, B's turnover will be over the registration limit so he will have to register for VAT. He will be able to charge VAT on top of the contract price, as the customer is registered and will be able to reclaim the VAT. However, as the business is highly competitive he will have to absorb the VAT which he will have to charge to other customers, and not increase his prices. This will be offset to some extent by the fact that he will be able to reclaim VAT suffered on his purchases.

Thus his overall profit margin on normal sales will be reduced to 40% × 100/120. The new annual profit will be as follows.

	£	£
Normal sales		60,000
Less VAT on normal sales × $^1/_6$		(10,000)
		50,000
Less normal purchases £60,000 × 60%	36,000	
Less VAT on normal purchases × $^1/_6$	(6,000)	
		(30,000)
Profit on normal sales		20,000
Contract sales	20,000	
Less cost of contract sales £20,000 × 60%	(12,000)	
		8,000
Revised annual profit		28,000

Therefore annual profit will only increase by £4,000, despite the new contract of value being £20,000.

If B attempted to avoid VAT registration by having a separate company handle the contract, HMRC could aggregate the turnovers of B's own business and the company's business, making both B and the company liable to register. The consequence would be that no saving would be achieved.

(c) It is in general bad planning to hold an asset likely to rise in value in a company. When the asset is sold, the company will have to pay corporation tax on the gain (at 23% in this case, since close investment-holding companies are not entitled to the small profits rate nor to marginal relief). If the proceeds are paid out as a dividend, further tax will be suffered by higher rate taxpayers. If they are paid out in the course of winding up the company, the shareholders will have chargeable gains on their shares.

The scheme has several other flaws. Dividend income is not taxable in the hands of a UK company so there is no question of a deduction for the director's fees from the company's taxable income, as it will not have any taxable income. Also, the payment of the fees will have adverse consequences as both primary (employee's) and secondary (employer's) Class 1 NICs will arise. Finally, tax relief is only available on pension premiums up to the level of his earnings, not on any dividends he draws out from the company.

(d) *Sole trader*

	£
Profits	30,000
IT £30,000 × 20%	(6,000)
NIC Class 2 £2.70 × 52	(140)
Class 4 £(30,000 – 7,755) × 9%	(2,002)
Net spendable income	21,858

Company

	£
CT £30,000 × 20%	6,000
Net profits before distribution (£30,000 – £6,000)	24,000
Dividend × 100/90	26,667
Tax @ 10%	2,667
Less tax credit	(2,667)
Income tax	nil
Net spendable income = net dividend	24,000

34 Hulse Finds Ltd

> **Tutorial note**. Although the question may appear long on first reading note how it breaks down into a series of points.

(a) The interest paid by Paul on the loan to acquire the shares in the company is qualifying annual interest. This is because Hulse Finds Ltd is a close company (it is controlled by Paul and Nick) and Paul works full-time for the company. Qualifying annual interest is a deductible payment that is deducted from Paul's total income, and consequently reduces his net income.

(b) Hulse Finds Ltd is a close company and has made a loan to a participator, Chris. Accordingly, the company should have paid HM Revenue & Customs (HMRC) £2,500 (25% of the loan) by 1 January 2015 (ie nine months after the end of the accounting period). HMRC will repay the £2,500 when the loan is repaid by Chris or waived by Hulse Finds Ltd. The company would not have had to make any payment if Chris had worked full-time for the company, as the loan is for less than £15,000 and Chris does not own more than 5% of Hulse Finds Ltd.

(c) The tax implications arising out of the acquisition are:

(i) The capital losses of SNL will remain with SNL. SNL will sell its trade and assets to Hulse Finds Ltd and capital losses remain with a company when it sells its trade. SNL can use its capital losses to relieve any gains arising on the assets sold to SN2 Ltd.

(ii) The trading losses of SNL will also remain with SNL and will not to be transferred with the trade. Where a company sells its trade to an unconnected company, any trading losses remain with the vendor company. SNL may be able to offset the losses against any capital allowance balancing charges arising on the sale.

It is possible for trading losses to be transferred to the purchaser when a company sells its trade to another company, but only when certain conditions are satisfied. Broadly, the same persons must beneficially own at least 75% of the business both before and after the sale. These conditions would have been satisfied if SNL had formed a subsidiary, Newco, sold its trade to Newco, and then sold Newco to SN2 Ltd.

SNL is the legal and beneficial owner of its trade prior to the sale. If the trade had been sold to Newco, SNL would no longer be the legal owner of the trade but would still be the beneficial owner as it owns Newco.

In such circumstances, Newco could have used the trading losses against future trading profits arising from the same trade, provided there was no major change in the nature or conduct of its trade within three years of the purchase by Hulse Finds Ltd.

(iii) There are now two companies in the Hulse Finds Ltd group. Accordingly, the limits used to determine the rate of corporation tax payable must be divided by two. The corporation tax liability of the group is continued as follows:

	£
Hulse Finds Ltd	
£250,000 × 23%	57,500
Less marginal relief (£750,000 – £250,000) × 3/400	(3,750)
	53,750
SN2 Ltd	
£50,000 (£40,000 + £10,000) × 20%	10,000
Group tax liability	63,750

(iv) Consideration should have been given to Hulse Finds Ltd acquiring the trade of SNL without the use of a separate subsidiary. This would have resulted in a single company with taxable total profits of £300,000 (£250,000 + £50,000) and a lower tax liability as asset out below:

Hulse Finds Ltd (owning the trade of SN2 Ltd)

	£
£300,000 × 20%	60,000
Reduction in tax liability (£63,750 – £60,000)	3,750

(d) The tax implications of the Newland business depend on the legal structure used. From a tax point of view, there are two distinct ways of establishing the business:

(i) It could be owned directly by Hulse Finds Ltd (or SN2 Ltd). Under this option, it would be an overseas permanent establishment of a UK resident company.

(ii) Hulse Finds Ltd (or SN2 Ltd) could incorporate a new subsidiary in Newland to acquire the business. Under this option, it would be an overseas subsidiary of a UK resident company.

Overseas permanent establishment

A permanent establishment is not a separate legal entity but is an extension of the company that owns it. The profits or losses of the permanent establishment belong directly to the company.

Provided the permanent establishment is controlled from the UK, the trading loss made in the year ended 31 March 2017 could be offset by Hulse Finds Ltd (or SN2 Ltd) against its income and gains of that year, reducing the company's UK corporation tax liability. Once the permanent establishment is profitable, the company owning the permanent establishment will be subject to 45% Newland corporation tax on the permanent establishment profits, because it is trading within the boundaries of Newland from permanent establishment.

The profits will also be subject to UK corporation tax because a UK resident company is subject to tax on its worldwide income and gains. However, the UK corporation tax liability, in respect of the permanent establishment profits, will be fully relieved by double tax relief as the rate of corporation tax in Newland is higher than that in the UK. Accordingly, there will be no UK corporation tax to pay on the permanent establishment's profits.

It is possible to make an election to exempt the profits and losses of an overseas permanent establishment from UK corporation tax. However, this election would not be appropriate here. The losses in the first year would not be available for relief against Hulse Finds Ltd's (or SN2 Ltd's) profits as described above, and it is not necessary to exempt the profits in future years, because, as explained above, double tax relief means there will be no UK corporation tax on these profits anyway.

Overseas subsidiary

A subsidiary is a separate legal entity. A company incorporated in Newland will be resident in Newland for tax purposes, provided it is not managed and controlled from the UK. Its profits or losses will then be subject to the tax regime of Newland.

The trading loss of the year ended 31 March 2017 would be carried forward and deducted from the company's future trading profits arising out of the same trade.

Once the company is profitable, it will be subject to tax in Newland at the rate of 45%. No UK tax will be due on the overseas dividends.

It is usually suggested that a permanent establishment should be used where an overseas enterprise is expected to make initial losses. This strategy enables the losses to be offset against any other profits of the company. However, the particular facts of the situation must be considered carefully.

The use of a permanent establishment in Newland will enable Hulse Finds Ltd (or SN2 Ltd) to offset the losses against its profits for the year ended 31 March 2017. This will save UK corporation tax at a maximum rate of 23%.

The use of a subsidiary would mean that the losses could not be offset in the year ended 31 March 2017, as the subsidiary will not have any other income. However, in the following year the losses will reduce that year's profits and save tax in Newland at 45%.

Accordingly, provided the group is willing to wait for a year (from a cash flow point of view) a greater tax saving can be achieved by using a subsidiary in Newland rather than a permanent establishment. This assumes, of course, that the anticipated profits materialise in the year ended 31 March 2018.

It must also be recognised that a subsidiary is an associate for the purpose of determining the rate of tax paid by group companies, whereas a permanent establishment is not. Accordingly, the use of a subsidiary (rather than a permanent establishment) could increase the rate of corporation tax paid in the

UK companies. However, on the facts given, whether a permanent establishment or a subsidiary is used makes no difference to the liabilities of the UK companies in the year ended 31 March 2017.

35 Financial planning

Tutorial note. The choice between equity and debt finance is a very important consideration when raising additional funds. An individual subscribing for shares in a seed enterprise investment company (SEIS) can receive 50% income tax relief on investment up to £100,000 in 2013/14, but M Ltd is unlikely to be a qualifying company, as it is not a small start up.

Report

To: The Board of M Ltd

From: Certified Accountant

Date: 19 May 2013

Re: Taxation consequences of alternative methods of raising finance

The choice of raising additional funds to finance a major expansion of the business can be summarised as being between loan capital or equity. A major distinction between the two forms of financing is that interest payable on borrowings is deductible for corporation tax purposes whereas dividends payable to shareholders are not.

Loan capital

Interest is tax deductible on an accruals basis under either from trading profit (if put to a trading use) or from interest income.

If the loan interest being paid represents an annual payment other than to a UK bank or a UK resident company, income tax should be deducted at source and accounted for to HMRC.

Costs of obtaining loan finance will be treated as tax-deductible in the same manner as interest payable on the loan. In contrast, costs in respect of issuing share capital are not deductible for CT purposes.

Interest income received by the providers of loan finance is taxable. It will be interest income of a company and subject to tax at normal corporation tax rates. Individuals in receipt of interest income will be subject to tax on the gross amount at 20%, 40% or 45%.

Equity finance

Dividends represent appropriations of profit after tax. They are not tax deductible and any costs associated with the raising of share capital are not tax deductible.

With regard to providers of equity finance, there are tax benefits available to investors who invest in Enterprise Investment Scheme (EIS) shares:

(1) An individual subscribing for new ordinary shares in an unquoted trading company can claim income tax relief at 30% for an investment of up to £1,000,000 in a tax year. The individual can also make a claim to carry back an investment to the previous tax year, subject to the maximum for that year. For example, if an individual has not previously made any EIS investment, he can invest £2,000,000 in EIS shares in 2013/14 and treat £1,000,000 as invested in 2012/13 and £1,000,000 in 2013/14.

    If the EIS shares are held for three years, there is exemption from capital gains tax on a disposal of the shares. A capital loss may arise on a disposal before or after expiry of the three year period but it is restricted by reducing the issue price by the amount of relief obtained.

(2) Chargeable gains realised by individuals may be deferred provided that those gains are reinvested in the ordinary shares of a qualifying EIS unquoted trading company. The reinvestment of gains must be made in the period twelve months before to three years after the relevant disposal. The gain is deferred and does not therefore crystallise before a subsequent disposal of the new EIS shares.

If you wish to discuss further any of the above points do not hesitate to contact me.

Signed: Certified Accountant

36 Daniel Dare

Tutorial note. There are only a very few calculations needed here. You need to write a memo and include the figures at the relevant points. Take care to plan your answer well ensuring you know what headings are needed so you cover all the points. Draw out your group structure and calculate the CT limits so that you can quickly see what you should do with the loss before you start writing.

MEMORANDUM

To: Tax manager
From: Tax assistant
Date: 2 June 2014
Subject: Saturn Ltd group of companies

This memorandum considers a number of issues raised by Daniel Dare (DD), the managing director of Saturn Ltd.

(a) (i) **Dione Ltd – Value of tax loss**

Any amount of the loss can be surrendered to the UK resident members of the 75% loss group, ie Saturn Ltd and Rhea Ltd.

The maximum tax saving will be obtained by offsetting the loss against profits between the limits for the small profits rate of corporation tax. The limits are divided by four as there are four associated companies (Titan Inc is included as overseas companies are associated for the purposes of determining the rate of corporation tax). Accordingly, for the year ending 30 June 2014 the limits are £75,000 and £375,000.

The maximum tax saving will be achieved by surrendering the loss to Saturn Ltd. The first £10,000 of loss will relieve profits at the main rate of tax and the balance of the loss will save tax at 23.75%. Surrendering the loss to Rhea Ltd would only save tax at 23%.

The dividend received by Saturn Ltd does not affect its corporation tax liability. Dividends are not subject to corporation tax and dividends received from a 51% subsidiary are not franked investment income.

The corporation tax saved via the offset of the loss will be £44,338 ((£10,000 × 23%) + (£177,000 × 23.75%)).

The claim must be submitted by 30 June 2016 (one year after the filing date of the corporation tax return).

Further information required

Income and gains of Dione Ltd for the year ended 30 June 2013.

The loss could be carried back for offset against the total profits of Dione Ltd for the year ended 30 June 2013. Whether or not this would be advantageous would depend on the company's total profits for that year. Although the maximum additional tax saving would be very small, there would be a cashflow benefit.

(ii) **Tethys Ltd – Use of trading loss**

The two companies will not be in a group relief group as Saturn Ltd will not own 75% of Tethys Ltd.

For a consortium to exist, 75% of the ordinary share capital of Tethys Ltd must be held by companies which each hold at least 5%. Accordingly, Tethys Ltd will be a consortium company if the balance of its share capital is owned by Clangers Ltd but not if it is owned by Edith Clanger.

If Tethys Ltd qualifies as a consortium company: 65% of its trading losses in the period from 1 August 2014 to 31 December 2014 can be surrendered to Saturn Ltd, ie £21,667

(£80,000 × 5/12 × 65%). Saturn Ltd must have taxable profits in excess of this in the period 1 August 2014 to 31 December 2014.

If Tethys Ltd does not qualify as a consortium company, none of its loss can be surrendered to Saturn Ltd.

The acquisition of 65% of Tethys Ltd is a change in ownership of the company. If there is a major change in the nature or conduct of the trade of Tethys Ltd within three years of 1 August 2014, the loss arising prior to that date cannot be carried forward for relief in the future.

Further information required

Ownership of the balance of the share capital of Tethys Ltd.
Estimate of taxable profits of Saturn Ltd for the year ended 30 June 2015.

(iii) **Tethys Ltd – Sale of the manufacturing premises**

Value added tax (VAT)

The building is not a new building (ie it is more than three years old). Accordingly, the sale of the building is an exempt supply and VAT should not be charged unless Tethys Ltd has opted to tax the building in the past.

Taxable profits on sale

The capital gain arising on the sale of the building will be £97,760 (£240,000 – (£112,000 × 1.27)).

Rollover relief

Tethys Ltd is not in a capital gains group with Saturn Ltd. Accordingly, rollover relief will only be available if Tethys Ltd, rather than any of the other Saturn Ltd group companies, acquires sufficient qualifying business assets.

The amount of sales proceeds not spent in the qualifying period is chargeable, ie £40,000 (£240,000 – £200,000). The balance of the gain, £57,760 (£97,760 – £40,000), can be rolled over.

Qualifying business assets include land and buildings and fixed plant and machinery. The assets must be brought into immediate use in the company's trade.

The assets must be acquired in the four-year period beginning one year prior to the sale of the manufacturing premises.

Further information required

Whether or not Tethys has opted to tax the building in the past for the purposes of VAT.

(iv) **Stamp duty and stamp duty land tax**

The purchase of Tethys Ltd will give rise to a liability to *ad valorem* stamp duty of £1,175 (£235,000 × 0.5%). The stamp duty must be paid by Saturn Ltd within 30 days of the share transfer in order to avoid interest being charged. It is not an allowable revenue expense for the purposes of corporation tax.

There are no stamp duty land tax implications for the Saturn Ltd group.

(b) **Before agreeing to become tax advisers to the Saturn Ltd group**

Information needed

Proof of incorporation and primary business address and registered office.

The structure, directors and shareholders of the company.

The identities of those persons instructing the firm on behalf of the company and those persons that are authorised to do so.

Action to take

Consider whether becoming tax advisers to the Saturn Ltd group would create any threats to compliance with the fundamental principles of professional ethics, for example integrity and professional competence. Where such threats exist, we should not accept the appointment unless the threats can be reduced to an acceptable level via the implementation of safeguards

Contact the existing tax adviser in order to ensure that there has been no action by the Saturn Ltd group that would, on ethical grounds, preclude us from accepting appointment.

37 Stuart and Rebecca

Tutorial note. Read the question requirements carefully. Part 2, for example, asks you to consider two alternatives. There are no marks available for doing anything else.

PRIVATE AND CONFIDENTIAL

[Our address]

[Your address]

[Date]

Dear Stuart

TAX POSITION AND ESTATE PLANNING

This letter deals with the capital gains implications of your recent property sale and your current and potential inheritance tax liabilities.

1 **Capital gains on property disposal 2014/15**

The capital gain arising on the disposal of the Plymouth house is £15,532.

This is after taking account of principal private residence relief of £141,318, based on an exempt period of 90 months out of a total ownership period of 151 months, and letting relief of £40,000.

The calculation of the above figures can be found in Appendix 1.

2 **Proposed investment**

As you are considering making an investment in a quoted company you will only be able to obtain business property relief for inheritance tax purposes if you, together with Rebecca, control the company, ie over 50% of the shares.

You could buy approximately 1 million shares in Omikron plc. This would be in the region of a 2% holding, so no business property relief would be available.

Alternatively you could buy approximately 195,000 shares in Omega plc with the proceeds, at a cost of 216p. Currently you and Rebecca jointly hold 4.8 million shares. Provided you achieve a slightly lower price or invest slightly more so that you purchase 200,001 shares, you and Rebecca will have a controlling holding. Provided you then survive for at least two years you will achieve 50% business property relief on your Omega plc shares. Therefore, it would be preferable to invest in future Omega plc shares.

3 **Inheritance tax on Rebecca's estate 1 March 2017**

Upon your death, the transfer of your assets to Rebecca would be exempt from IHT. If, following your death, Rebecca were to die on 1 March 2017, and no IHT planning is implemented, the IHT liability would be £2,512,420 (Appendix 2).

4 **Lifetime IHT planning**

As your will leaves all of your estate to Rebecca you have not taken advantage of your nil rate band. However on Rebecca's death her nil rate band will be increased by the proportion of nil rate band unused at your death. She will therefore have an additional 100% of your nil rate band available on her death. This will be based on the value of the nil rate band at that time.

The Omega plc shares should be left to Rebecca so that the 50% BPR would be available on her death or earlier gift of the whole shareholding.

Rebecca should consider making lifetime gifts, perhaps to Sam, in the hope that she will survive for seven years, so that they become completely exempt. If she survived more than three but less than seven years, and IHT was payable on the lifetime gifts, then the IHT payable would be tapered.

Both of you should make lifetime gifts utilising your annual exemptions. Each of you would have a current year and a prior year annual exemption available, as you have made no earlier gifts. You may also be able to establish a regular pattern of giving to use the exemption for normal expenditure out of income. Your wealth would appear to be such that it would be simple to demonstrate that capital was not being eroded by this strategy, and that you can maintain your usual standard of living.

It could be possible to give away the life policy before death at a lower value than the death benefit. It would then be excluded from the death estate and escape any IHT liability.

If you wish to discuss further any of the above points do not hesitate to contact me.

Yours sincerely

Certified Accountant

Appendix 1 – disposal of Plymouth property

	£
Sale proceeds	422,100
Less cost May 2002	(185,000)
	237,100
Less PPR exemption $\frac{90}{90+61} \times £237,100$ (W)	(141,318)
	95,782
Less letting exemption, lowest of:	
(i) PPR relief given: £141,318	
(ii) Gain in let period: $\frac{27}{90+61} \times £237,100 = £42,395$	
(iii) Maximum: £40,000	(40,000)
Gain	55,782
Less capital losses brought forward	(29,350)
	26,432
Less annual exempt amount	(10,900)
Taxable gain	15,532

Working

Periods of occupation		*Exempt Months*	*Non-exempt Months*
1 May 2002 – 28 Feb 2003	Occupied	10	
1 March 2003 – 31 Dec 2006	Unoccupied – absence for any reason	36	
	Unoccupied		10
1 Jan 2007 – 31 Mar 2009	Let		27
1 Apr 2009 – 30 Nov 2009	Occupied	8	
1 Dec 2009 – 30 Nov 2011	Unoccupied		24
1 Dec 2011 – 30 Nov 2014	Last 36 months	36	
		90	61

Appendix 2 – Rebecca's IHT liability with no IHT planning

	£	£
London property		900,000
Cash deposits (including £200,000 from life policy)		530,000
Quoted investments		250,000
Shares in Omega plc 5,001,000 × 210p (1/4 up is lower)	10,502,100	
Less BPR @ 50%	(5,251,050)	
		5,251,050
		6,931,050
Less nil rate band (£325,000 + 100% × £325,000)		(650,000)
Taxable at 40%		6,281,050
IHT liability		2,512,420

38 Landscape Ltd

Tutorial note. Make sure you make an attempt at each part of the question and do not spend too long on any one part.

(a) *Peter Plain*

The distinction between employment and self employment is a fine one. Employment involves a contract of service, whereas self employment involves a contract for services. Taxpayers tend to prefer self employment because the rules for the deductibility of expenses are more generous but the following factors suggest that HMRC will regard Peter as an employee rather than self employed:

(i) Peter works five days each week: If Peter cannot work when he chooses it suggests the **company has control** over him and he is an employee

(ii) Peter **uses the company's equipment**

(iii) Peter **does not have any other clients**

(iv) The **computer function (and hence Peter) is an integral part of the company's business.**

Other factors HMRC may consider are:

- **whether Peter must accept further work**
- **whether the company must provide further work**
- **whether Peter hires his own helpers**
- **what degree of financial risk Peter takes**
- **what degree of responsibility for investment and management Peter has**
- **whether Peter can profit from sound management**
- **the wording used in any agreement between Peter and the company.**

(b) *Simon Savannah*

The **statutory redundancy pay of £2,400 is exempt from income tax**. However, **both the holiday pay of £1,500 and the £5,000** in respect of the agreement not to work for a rival company are taxable in 2013/14.

The balance of the lump sum redundancy payment is £46,100 (£55,000 – £2,400 – £1,500 – £5,000). If the payment is a genuine *ex gratia* redundancy payment, £27,600 (£30,000 – £2,400) is exempt. £8,500 is taxable in 2013/14. The balance of £10,000 is taxable when received in 2014/15.

(c) *Trevor Tundra*

Landscape Ltd is a close company and Trevor Tundra is a participator. This means that Trevor will be treated as though he has received dividends equal to the earnings that would have arisen in 2013/14 if he had been a director or an employee of Landscape Ltd.

	£
Car (£14,000 × 35%) (W)	4,900
Loan (£40,000 × 2/12 × 4%) + (£15,000 × 7/12 × 4%)	617
Loan written off	15,000
‘'Taxable benefits' = net dividend	20,517

Working

CO_2 emissions = 215 g/km
Above baseline figure 215 – 95 = 120g/km
Divide by 5 = 24
% = 11 + 24 = 35%

(d) *Ursula, Violet and Wilma*

Ursula, Violet and Wilma are all working in Cambridge in the performance of their duties. **Tax relief is available for the cost of travel between home and Cambridge, if Cambridge is a 'temporary' place of work. A place of work is classed as a temporary workplace if the employee does not work there continuously for a period which lasts (or is expected to last) more than 24 months.**

Therefore, the cost of all of Ursula's travel to Cambridge qualifies for tax relief. The mileage allowance that Ursula receives from the company falls within the authorised mileage rates and so is tax free and she can make an expense claim as follows:

Authorised mileage rates	£
(120 × 40) = 4,800 × 45p	2,160
Less mileage allowance received (4,800 × 41p)	(1,968)
Expense claim	192

As Violet was initially expected to work in Cambridge for more than 24 months the train fare initially paid by Landscape Ltd is a taxable benefit. However, from 1 January 2014 no taxable benefit arises in respect of the train fare because Violet's period of secondment to Cambridge is no longer expected to exceed 24 months.

Wilma should be entitled to full tax relief for the cost of her journey's to Cambridge. Wilma will be assessed on a benefit as follows:

	£
Mileage allowance received (120 × 150) = 18,000 × 41p	7,380
Less authorised mileage rates 10,000 × 45p	(4,500)
8,000 × 25p	(2,000)
Taxable benefit	880

(e) Landscape Ltd can give an employee up to **£3,000 worth of 'free' shares a year**. Employees can buy **'partnership'** shares with their pre-tax salary up to a maximum of 10% of gross earnings, subject to an upper limit of £1,500 per year.

In addition, employers can give employees up to two free matching shares for each partnership share purchased. Provided the shares are held for **five years before disposal**, employees will not be subject to income tax or NIC on them. If the shares are held for more than three years but less than five years, tax and NIC is due on the lower of the market value of the shares on the date they were given to the employee and the market value at the date of withdrawal.

39 Marilyn Corniche

Tutorial note. In part (a) it was essential to recognise that the spouse exemption applied to the result bulk of Max's estate. Part (b) concerned the rules on transfer of unused nil band between spouses on the death of the survivor. Make sure you learn this topic.

(a) *Inheritance tax liability on the death of Max Corniche 20 May 2012*

All of Max's estate (except the chattels) passes to Marilyn for IHT purposes. Therefore the **spouse exemption** applies to these assets.

The chattels passing to Max's brother total £15,000 (£5,000 + £7,000 + £3,000) and are covered by the nil rate band.

Therefore, there is no IHT payable on the death of Max.

Inheritance tax liability on death of Marilyn Corniche February 2014

Free estate		
Personalty	£	£
Berkley's Bank a/c	33,400	
Unit trust units in ISAs	72,000	
Cash ISA	10,600	
Ex-cash ISA from Max	11,300	
Bank deposit a/c from Max	20,000	
Spiro plc (W)	63,600	
Unit trusts	81,000	
Unit trusts – ISAs	67,600	
	359,500	
Realty		
Family home (whole)	220,000	
Holiday home	73,000	293,000
Gross estate		652,500

Tax is:	£
£325,000 × 0%	Nil
£327,500 × 40%	131,000
	131,000

Working

Valuation of Spiro plc shares at February 2014 is lower of:

¼ up

$$\frac{(647-635)}{4}+635=638$$

Mid-bargain

$$\frac{642+630}{2}=636$$

ie 636 × 10,000 = £63,600

(b) A claim can be made to transfer Max's unused nil rate band to increase the maximum nil rate band available on the death of Marilyn. The claim will usually be made by the personal representatives of Marilyn's estate within two years following the end of the month of Marilyn's death (ie by 28 February 2016).

Max's unused nil rate band is £(325,000 – 15,000) = £310,000. Since the nil rate bands are the same in 2012/13 and 2013/14, this is also the amount available to transfer to Marilyn.

The nil rate band available to set against Marilyn's estate is therefore £(325,000 + 310,000) = £635,000.

The IHT on her estate is therefore:

	£
£635,000 × 0%	0
£17,500 × 40%	7,000
	7,000
The inheritance tax saving is £(131,000 – 7,000)	124,000
(which is 40% of £310,000)	

Tax tables

SUPPLEMENTARY INSTRUCTIONS

1. You should assume that the tax rates and allowances for the tax year 2013/14 and for the financial year to 31 March 2014 will continue to apply for the foreseeable future unless you are instructed otherwise.
2. Calculations and workings need only be made to the nearest £.
3. All apportionments may be made to the nearest month.
4. All workings should be shown.

TAX RATES AND ALLOWANCES

The following tax rates and allowances are to be used in answering the questions.

Income tax

		Normal rates	Dividend rates
		%	%
Basic rate	£1 – £32,010	20	10
Higher rate	£32,011 – £150,000	40	32.5
Additional rate	£150,001 and over	45	37.5

A starting rate of 10% applies to savings income where it falls within the first £2,790 of taxable income.

Personal allowances

	£
Personal allowance	
Born on or after 6 April 1948	9,440
Born between 6 April 1938 and 5 April 1948	10,500
Born before 6 April 1938	10,660
Income limit	
Personal allowance	100,000
Personal allowance (born before 6 April 1948)	26,100

Residence status

Days in UK	Previously resident	Not previously resident
Less than 16	Automatically not resident	Automatically not resident
16 to 45	Resident if 4 UK ties (or more)	Automatically not resident
46 to 90	Resident if 3 UK ties (or more)	Resident if 4 UK ties
91 to 120	Resident if 2 UK ties (or more)	Resident if 3 UK ties (or more)
121 to 182	Resident if 1 UK ties (or more)	Resident if 2 UK ties (or more)
183 or more	Automatically resident	Automatically resident

Child benefit income tax charge

Where income is between £50,000 and £60,000, the charge is 1% of the amount of child benefit received for every £100 of income over £50,000.

Car benefit percentage

The base level of CO_2 emissions is 95 grams per kilometre.

The percentage rates applying to petrol cars with CO_2 emissions up to this level are:

	%
75 grams per kilometre or less	5
76 grams to 94 grams per kilometre	10
95 grams per kilometre	11

Car fuel benefit

The base figure for calculating the car fuel benefit is £21,100.

Individual savings accounts (ISAs)

The overall investment limit is £11,520, of which £5,760 can be invested in a cash ISA.

Pension scheme limits

Annual allowance	£50,000
Lifetime allowance	£1,500,000

The maximum contribution that can qualify for tax relief without any earnings is £3,600.

Authorised mileage allowances: cars

Up to 10,000 miles	45p
Over 10,000 miles	25p

Capital allowances: rates of allowance

Plant and machinery	%
Main pool	18
Special rate pool	8
Motor cars	
New cars with CO_2 emissions up to 95 grams per kilometre	100
CO_2 emissions between 96 and 130 grams per kilometre	18
CO_2 emissions over 130 grams per kilometre	8

Annual investment allowance

First £250,000 of expenditure (since 1 January 2013)	100

Enhanced capital allowances

Energy saving and water saving plant and machinery	100

Cap on income tax reliefs

Unless otherwise restricted, reliefs are capped at the higher of £50,000 or 25% of income.

Corporation tax

Financial year	**2011**	**2012**	**2013**
Small profits rate	20%	20%	20%
Main rate	26%	24%	23%
Lower limit	£300,000	£300,000	£300,000
Upper limit	£1,500,000	£1,500,000	£1,500,000
Standard fraction	3/200	1/100	3/400

Marginal relief

Standard fraction × (U – A) × N/A

Value Added Tax (VAT)

Standard rate	20%
Registration limit	£79,000
Deregistration limit	£77,000

Inheritance tax

	£
Nil rate band	
6 April 2013 to 5 April 2014	325,000
6 April 2012 to 5 April 2013	325,000
6 April 2011 to 5 April 2012	325,000
6 April 2010 to 5 April 2011	325,000
6 April 2009 to 5 April 2010	325,000
6 April 2008 to 5 April 2009	312,000
6 April 2007 to 5 April 2008	300,000
6 April 2006 to 5 April 2007	285,000
6 April 2005 to 5 April 2006	275,000
6 April 2004 to 5 April 2005	263,000
6 April 2003 to 5 April 2004	255,000
6 April 2002 to 5 April 2003	250,000
6 April 2001 to 5 April 2002	242,000
6 April 2000 to 5 April 2001	234,000
6 April 1999 to 5 April 2000	231,000

Excess	Death rate	40%
	Lifetime rate	20%

Inheritance tax: taper relief

Years before death	**% reduction**
Over 3 but less than 4 years	20
Over 4 but less than 5 years	40
Over 5 but less than 6 years	60
Over 6 but less than 7 years	80

Capital gains tax

Rates of tax	Lower rate	18%
	Higher rate	28%
Annual exempt amount		£10,900
Entrepreneurs' relief	Lifetime limit	£10,000,000
	Rate of tax	10%

National insurance (not contracted out rates)

		%
Class 1 employee	£1 – £7,755 per year	Nil
	£7,756 – £41,450 per year	12.0
	£41,451 and above per year	2.0
Class 1 employer	£1 – £7,696 per year	Nil
	£7,697 and above per year	13.8
Class 1A		13.8
Class 2	£2.70 per week	
	Small earnings exception limit - £5,725	
Class 4	£1 – £7,755 per year	Nil
	£7,756 – £41,450 per year	9.0
	£41,451 and above per year	2.0

Rates of Interest (assumed)

Official rate of interest	4.0%
Rate of interest on underpaid tax	3.0%
Rate of interest on overpaid tax	0.5%

Stamp Duty Land Tax

Ad valorem duty	Rate
£150,000 or less [1]	Nil
£150,001 to £250,000	1%
£250,001 to £500,000	3%
£500,001 to £1,000,000	4%
£1,000,001 to £2,000,000[2]	5%
£2,000,001 or above[2]	7%

[1] for residential property, the nil rate is restricted to £125,000

[2] the 5% and 7% rates do not apply to non-residential property

Stamp Duty and Stamp Duty Reserve Tax

Ad valorem duty	Rate
Shares	0.5%

Index

Note: Key Terms and their page references are given in **bold**

BPP
LEARNING MEDIA

BPP
LEARNING MEDIA

Review Form – Paper P6(Advanced Taxation) Finance Act 2013 (11/13)

Please help us to ensure that the ACCA learning materials we produce remain as accurate and user-friendly as possible. We cannot promise to answer every submission we receive, but we do promise that it will be read and taken into account when we update this Study Text.

Name: ______________________ **Address:** ______________________

____

____

How have you used this Study Text?
(Tick one box only)

- ☐ Home study (book only)
- ☐ On a course: college ______________
- ☐ With 'correspondence' package
- ☐ Other ______________

Why did you decide to purchase this Study Text? *(Tick one box only)*

- ☐ Have used BPP Texts in the past
- ☐ Recommendation by friend/colleague
- ☐ Recommendation by a lecturer at college
- ☐ Saw information on BPP website
- ☐ Saw advertising
- ☐ Other ______________

During the past six months do you recall seeing/receiving any of the following?
(Tick as many boxes as are relevant)

- ☐ Our advertisement in *ACCA Student Accountant*
- ☐ Our advertisement in *Pass*
- ☐ Our advertisement in *PQ*
- ☐ Our brochure with a letter through the post
- ☐ Our website www.bpp.com

Which (if any) aspects of our advertising do you find useful?
(Tick as many boxes as are relevant)

- ☐ Prices and publication dates of new editions
- ☐ Information on Text content
- ☐ Facility to order books off-the-page
- ☐ None of the above

Which BPP products have you used?

Text	☑	*Success CD*	☐
Kit	☐	*i-Pass*	☐
Passcard	☐	*i-Learn*	☐

Your ratings, comments and suggestions would be appreciated on the following areas.

	Very useful	*Useful*	*Not useful*
Introductory section	☐	☐	☐
Chapter introductions	☐	☐	☐
Key terms	☐	☐	☐
Quality of explanations	☐	☐	☐
Case studies and other examples	☐	☐	☐
Exam focus points	☐	☐	☐
Questions and answers in each chapter	☐	☐	☐
Fast forwards and chapter roundups	☐	☐	☐
Quick quizzes	☐	☐	☐
Question Bank	☐	☐	☐
Answer Bank	☐	☐	☐
Index	☐	☐	☐

Overall opinion of this Study Text. *Excellent* ☐ *Good* ☐ *Adequate* ☐ *Poor* ☐

Do you intend to continue using BPP products? *Yes* ☐ *No* ☐

On the reverse of this page is space for you to write your comments about our Study Text. We welcome your feedback.

The BPP Learning Media author of this edition can be e-mailed at: AlisonPriest@bpp.com

Please return this form to: Barry Walsh, ACCA Publishing Manager, BPP Learning Media Ltd, FREEPOST, London, W12 8BR

TELL US WHAT YOU THINK

Please note any further comments and suggestions/errors below. For example, was the text accurate, readable, concise, user-friendly and comprehensive?